WITHDRAWN

THE
ENCYCLOPEDIA OF
LAWMEN, OUTLAWS, and GUNFIGHTERS

THE
ENCYCLOPEDIA OF
LAWMEN, OUTLAWS, and GUNFIGHTERS

Leon Claire Metz

Facts On File, Inc.

The Encyclopedia of Lawmen, Outlaws, and Gunfighters

Facts On File, Inc.
132 West 31st Street
New York NY 10001

Library of Congress Cataloging-in-Publication Data

Metz, Leon Claire.
The encyclopedia of lawmen, outlaws, and gunfighters / Leon Claire Metz.
p. cm.
Includes bibliographical references and index.
ISBN 0-8160-4543-7
1. Outlaws—West (U.S.)—Biography—Dictionaries. 2. Peace officers—West
(U.S.)—Biography—Dictionaries. 3. West (U.S.)—Biography—Dictionaries. I. Title.

F596 .M48 2002
978′.02′0922—dc21

[B]   2002070853

Facts On File books are available at special discounts when purchased in bulk quantities for businesses, associations, institutions, or sales promotions. Please call our Special Sales Department in New York at (212) 967-8800 or (800) 322-8755.

You can find Facts On File on the World Wide Web at http://www.factsonfile.com

Text design by Erika K. Arroyo
Cover design by Cathy Rincon

Printed in the United States of America

VB Hermitage 10   9   8   7   6   5   4   3   2   1

This book is printed on acid-free paper.

This encyclopedia is affectionately dedicated
to my grandchildren:

Brandt Baars
Little Brandy
and to my daughter-in-law, Misty Metz.

Contents

The Way of a Gunfighter: An
Introduction   ix

Acknowledgments   xv

Entries   1

Bibliography   273

Index   281

The Way of the Gunfighter
An Introduction

As a boy growing up in Parkersburg, West Virginia, during the late 1940s, I remember reading my first western gunfighter biography. I do not recall the publisher, but the book was entitled *The Saga of Billy the Kid,* by Walter Noble Burns.

That book had a profound effect upon my life, although I would not realize it until much later. In those simple, beguiling days, it never occurred to this gullible youngster that not everything in print was necessarily true. I thought it was illegal to lie in print, that one went to jail for things like that. Another 20 years would pass before it finally dawned on me that Billy the Kid had never killed the fabled 21 men, that he had not likely slain over six. During later years I almost cried when I learned that he was probably born in New York City, that his real name wasn't William Bonney but Henry McCarty, and that he could have been as old as 24 or 25 when Sheriff Pat Garrett shot him dead at around midnight at Fort Sumner, New Mexico.

I carried many of my false western impressions and beliefs with me when I moved to El Paso, Texas, during the early 1950s. Roughly 10 years later I began researching and writing about the Wild West, initially skipping over Billy the Kid and John Wesley Hardin, believing them to have already been too well covered by other authors. Hardin in particular had written his autobiography in 1895, finishing it per-

haps only hours before his death. Who could quarrel with the authenticity of that?

So my research began with the gathering of information regarding lesser-known individuals, gunfighters, and outlaws, significant personalities who had not yet become household words regarding the Wild West. Thus my first book was a biography of John Selman, the lawman/outlaw gunman who killed John Wesley Hardin. In the process of researching Selman, even though his and Hardin's lives did not come together until the mid-1890s, shortly before their deaths, I nevertheless accumulated considerable information regarding Hardin, information I retained but rarely utilized for 20 years until the early 1990s, when it occurred to me that the 100th anniversary of Hardin's violent death in El Paso, Texas, was coming up. "This might be a good time to write his biography," I said to myself.

My next book after Selman was a biography of Dallas Stoudenmire, a gunman whose name was hardly a household word anywhere in the world. He both built his reputation and met his death in El Paso.

After that, with two gunfighter biographies behind me, I ached to write about Billy the Kid, even though at the time I suspected that I could add little that was new to what Walter Noble Burns, and many other writers as well, had already recorded. Therefore, I changed my mind and instead wrote a biography of the tall sheriff who killed Billy the Kid—Pat Garrett. Surprisingly, although Billy the Kid had by now become the subject of uncounted articles and biographies, since Burns no author had turned his or her attention to Garrett. Sheriff Pat Garrett in these Billy the Kid stories had been reduced to little more than a footnote. But Garrett was much more than that. During my research, Garrett turned out to be quite a revelation; in fact, Pat Garrett changed my life. He is in many respects responsible for this encyclopedia. He made me realize that in terms of the American gunfighting West, there truly were no minor or irrelevant figures. There are merely lives that have never been properly investigated.

Pat Garrett, who even I anticipated would be peripheral to Billy the Kid, if still a figure worth writing about, turned out to be one of southwestern America's most dynamic and tragic images. In the Pat Garrett biography, it surprisingly wasn't he who was marginal but Henry McCarty—or Henry Antrim, or William Bonney, or Billy the Kid, or whatever else one prefers to call him.

From this writer's perspective, Garrett was a fascinating and towering, if deeply flawed, individual. Billy the Kid was just flawed. Nevertheless, old heroes die hard in our mental and emotional pantheons. In spite of my efforts, it remains Billy the Kid and not Pat Garrett whom folks remember. The reason, I believe, lies in the name. The name "Billy the Kid" somehow grabs the imagination, implying perpetual youth, a young man full of promise cruelly cut down in his prime. If his real name, Henry McCarty, had been used, I am convinced most folks would never have heard of him. "Pat Garrett," on the other hand, would be a nice name for a bottle of Ketchup; it is small wonder that Garrett has never grabbed intense public attention.

Still, this encyclopedia is about outlaw/lawman violence and associate themes in the American West, the West understood to lie between Canada and the Mexican border, between the Mississippi River and the Pacific Ocean. The time period starts immediately after the Civil War and closes shortly after 1900, when the last remnants of outlaw/lawmen/gunfighters rode across the western horizon and into legend.

It is fair to say that the Civil War set the stage for the gunfighter era. The war left not only chaos but hopelessness, lawlessness, and an uprooted population, especially in the South. The South also had the added burden of military occupation by a federal army unequipped for stabilization and rehabilitation.

Hundreds of ex-Confederate soldiers wandered the dusty roads and village towns, communities where most civilian jobs had been swept away. Markets had vanished. Schools had closed. Families had scattered. Many aimless southerners subsequently turned westward.

Oklahoma was still mostly Indian. Kansas and Missouri had hardly entered the war in the accepted sense of the word, and yet guerrilla forces had bitterly mangled each other there, leaving Kansas with an apt nickname it never deserved but certainly earned—Bleeding Kansas. Although California took the side of the Union, it had no real presence in the war and was remote from everywhere. Arkansas contributed manpower primarily to the South but became little more than a footnote to the war. As for Texas, it was big and wide, empty and yet settled when the war started, perhaps the only state still struggling with Indian problems. It was a land harboring its own sense of destiny, a people still wondering if they had done the right thing by joining the American union in the first place.

It wasn't long before two widely separated states, Kansas and Texas, far apart in distance and time, recognized that each had something the other needed. By the late 1860s, Kansas had railroads and grass but little in the way of manufactured or grown products. On the other hand, Texas had thousands of wandering longhorn cattle but no transportation and no markets.

So trails 1,000 miles long arose between Texas and Kansas, main trails and feeder trails with colorful names like Chisholm, Western, National, Potter-Bacon, Sedalia, and Goodnight-Loving. Within months of the end of the Civil War, the great cattle drives from Texas began in earnest, and from these drives grew violent, wide-open Kansas communities with names like Wichita, Dodge City, Newton, Ellsworth, Kansas City, Abilene, and Ogollala (in Nebraska).

Young Texas cowboys, many having just returned from the war but many away from home for the first time, spent lonesome months on the trails north. At their termini the cattle were sold, the cowhands were paid, and everybody went to town. In town it wasn't the churches that greeted them but saloons, plus firewater, wild women, and gambling. These boisterous and disorderly communities, known as "cow towns," catered to young, wild cowboys used to carrying firearms. Out of this, with many twists and turns and shades of opinion, arose the American gunfighter, without question the most colorful individual ever to grace the old Wild West.

A wide-open gunfighting era spread from Texas to Montana, and into New Mexico, Arizona, Wyoming, Nevada, California, Idaho, Missouri, and Oklahoma.

This does not mean that every cowboy was a gunfighter, for in fact, very few cowboys drew guns in anger. All would have argued that they carried guns only for self-defense, when in reality they shot snakes, lame horses, livestock that couldn't keep up, or whatever object stirred the cowboy's fancy in terms of rocks, trees, posts, and signs. Most disputes, however, were resolved by fistfights.

Of course, it can be legitimately asked, "Did not these states and territories have laws against carrying firearms, both concealed and exposed?" The answer is yes! Practically all of them did, as did their respective communities. The useful question is, "Why were the laws and ordinances not enforced?"

One reason was that many laws lacked specifics. On occasion, a law would forbid someone from carrying concealed weapons but say nothing about packing them openly. Other laws specified or implied "intent to harm." That "intent to harm" became a difficult motivation to prove in court.

Other laws implied that a person might openly bear firearms if he feared assault or other injury or violence to himself, his family, or his property. In this case the word "feared" became difficult to *dis*prove in court. Furthermore, fines were typically set somewhere between three and 10 dollars, which in those days might have been a lot of money, but not sufficiently large to discourage most desperados.

To keep a relative peace, the towns retained gunmen—Wild Bill Hickok, the Earps, and the Masterson brothers. They became known as city marshals, lawmen, shooters, and finally gunfighters, although the term "gunfighter" is far better known and more widely used in modern times than it ever was during the wildest periods of the Old West.

It could be said, and likely with enough patience could be proved, that hundreds, perhaps thousands of gunfighters drifted around the American West, at one time or another participating in perhaps thousands of gunfights. Richard Maxwell Brown, in his *No Duty to Retreat: Violence and Values in American History and Society,* has argued that these gunmen fell into two different categories, glorified gunfighters and grassroots gunfighters. The glorified gunfighters have names that still echo down the halls of history: Wild Bill Hickok, Billy the Kid, Wyatt Earp, John Wesley Hardin, and the like. Few people ever heard of grassroots gunfighters, examples being John Behan, Elzy Lay, John Hays, Clay Allison, and David Kemp. The former were well known during their own time and were originals. The latter were known primarily in their own localities.

The exceptions to this rule would have been Billy the Kid and Pat Garrett. Garrett should have been the glorified gunfighter and Billy the Kid the grassroots man. Instead it is the Kid whom folks remember, not Garrett.

Oddly, the best of the glorified top guns rarely "shot it out." There was none of this "fastest gun around" business, no great feuds among the best. Hardin and Hickok never shot it out, in this writer's judgement, because they respected each other, although Hardin tried Hickok's patience on several occasions. Look at Holliday and the Earps, the Earps and the Mastersons, all well known, perhaps more from modern day movies and books than because of any other factor. One might argue about where that left John Ringo, a glorified name even though Ringo was a loner whom few associates particularly liked.

The same could be said for John Wesley Hardin. He has a rather prominent name, particularly in Texas, but Hardin was never a "company man" in the sense of Hickok and the Earps. Gallons of liquor, a murderous disposition, bad luck at the gambling table, his family dead and children scattered, plus 16 justifiable years in the Texas State Prison produced a man who shot a lot of people, most of them society rejects like himself. Later, in September 1895, when Hardin stood at an El Paso bar with his back to the door, one could build a case that he was simply looking for a way to die without pulling the trigger himself. It is no surprise that he was murdered.

Perhaps the "purest" gunfight, in the technical sense of the word, stemmed from the eastern and European practice of dueling, where two men stepped off 10 paces, turned, and fired. In the western sense, this was epitomized during a showdown on July 21, 1865, between Wild Bill Hickok—a Unionist who won the sobriquet "Wild Bill" during the Civil War—in Springfield, Missouri, when he killed Dave Tutt. The men, who had quarreled over a gambling debt, approached each other from across the city square. They drew their sidearms at about the same time, roughly 100 yards apart, stood still, aimed, and fired. Hickok scored a direct hit, sending a bullet squarely into Tutt's heart. But truth be known, Hickok was only a so-so shot. On this particular day, he had phenomenal luck.

Nevertheless, from this gunfight arose the modern-day gunfighter tradition. In literature and the movies, both men draw, and the faster draw wins. In reality, few people were stupid enough to stand in the middle of the street and risk being shot down, and those who did were usually intoxicated. Sensible and sober individuals took cover behind a barrel or telephone pole. After all, even losers win sometimes. Like Hickok in his killing of Tutt, someone could just be lucky.

Most gunfights were brawls that got out of hand, shootouts occurring after too much drink and not enough luck at the gambling table. Speed and fair play had nothing to do with it. Likely as not, more bystanders died or were wounded than gunfight participants, most of the slain onlookers being hit as they frantically scrambled to clear the room or the street.

Who was considered the best shot in the desperado/outlaw/lawman category is impossible to say. Probably it would be an unrecognizable name among gunfighter buffs and those who write about such things. None likely could match today's shooters, but today's shooters have advantages of finer weapons, more reliable (and smokeless) ammunition, and better training. An even more important advantage would be that today's expert marksmen do not have someone shooting back at them.

As an example of someone shooting back, take the case of James Butler (Wild Bill) Hickok again. He is usually cited as one of the most deadly—if not the deadliest—of the shootists. However, when he and gambler Phil Coe commenced banging away at one another in Abilene, Kansas, from a distance of less than six feet, Hickok emptied two six-shooters, putting only one bullet in Coe but killing his (own) deputy with another. Even under the best, or

worst, of situations, that would not be considered good shooting.

As for who killed the most people, that too is controversial. Almost all numbers are inaccurate or misleading, and one gets the feeling that over time numbers became inflated. As mentioned, Billy the Kid is reputed to have killed 21 men, but the real figure seems to be somewhere between four and six.

The numbers are all over the place. Biographers sometimes fill in the gaps, giving their subjects credit for every shooting in the countryside. Sometimes a desperado himself claimed numerous killings but cited little to back it up. John Wesley Hardin, wrote his autobiography, in which he described page after page of killings. Altogether he claimed to have killed approximately 50 men, although only about half have been documented through independent investigations. Yet, until all the evidence is in, Hardin stands alone in terms of deaths.

Readers might also note that most "gunfighters" who come to mind were actually lawmen, like Hickok and the Earps. Stage, train, and bank robbers rarely had the gunfighter/shooter/gunman reputation. They were usually called desperadoes, and desperadoes killed people. Jesse James, for instance, always carried a gun, and he murdered people with it, his gun being primarily a tool of coercion. Unlike Hickok, we never think of Jesse as meeting anyone in the middle of a dusty street. Desperadoes like Butch Cassidy and Sam Bass weren't ordinarily trying to kill folks; they were simply trying to take all their money. To get a reputation for killing people during a robbery was to ensure a fight every time a holdup took place—and fights, in addition to turning public opinion against you, were too risky insofar as one's own safety was concerned. Furthermore, killing people took the Robin Hood romanticism out of theft; sooner or later, the passengers or guards would win one.

While this encyclopedia has striven for gunfighter/gunman completeness, it has failed. Readers will find here the names of all the well-known outlaws and lawmen—the Billy the Kids, the John Wesley Hardins, the Wild Bill Hickoks, the Earps, the Ringos, the Wild Bunch, the Texas Rangers, the Pinkertons, and so forth—but many of the names in this encyclopedia are little known to the average reader. Furthermore, there are perhaps dozens, even hundreds, of obscure names still awaiting biographers. There is no such thing—and never will be any such thing—as a "complete" outlaw/lawman/gunfighter book. Itemizing all of them would not be like counting stars in the sky, but it might be roughly similar to counting books in a large public library.

Finally, in addition to these major and minor characters, I have also included definitions where appropriate, as well as explanations of geographical locations. Furthermore, the scope has occasionally been broadened—with certain distinctions—by descriptions of some of the differences between city marshals, federal marshals, deputy marshals, sheriffs, and so forth.

Leon Claire Metz

Acknowledgments

I would like to thank a multitude of librarians and archivists from all over the United States, and especially the American Southwest. I need to thank Robert G. McCubbin, owner of Western Publications, for his friendship and always good advice, as well as his generous contribution of photographs. My thanks also go out to Bob Alexander, who put me on to many gunmen I would never have otherwise considered, to my Tombstone friend Ben Traywick, who read portions of the manuscript and gave me much-needed advice and encouragement; to Bob DeArment, Bill O'Neal, Chuck Parsons, and Lee Silva, great gunfighter buffs and biographers, all of whom know more about gunfighters than I ever will; and finally to a longtime friend and breakfast companion Dale L. Walker, to my mind the dean of western historians.

Entries A–Z

ABILENE, Kansas

Kansas did not become a state until January 29, 1861, and it sided with the Union during the Civil War. Strong Confederate guerrilla activity ripped the state asunder, actions that helped set the stage for confrontations between Texas cowboys—many of them Confederate veterans—and Kansas officials with Union sympathies and their own brand of bitterness. Abilene itself was founded in 1861, and after the war it quickly evolved into the first of the notorious cattle-trading centers and shipping points. In 1870 alone, nearly 200,000 head went through Abilene for shipment east. With the completion of the Union Pacific Railroad through Kansas around 1870, and the need for meat in the eastern United States, more than 5 million head of livestock prior to 1885 followed the Chisholm Trail up from Texas.

John Wesley Hardin, a notorious gunfighter as well as a drover, in his memoirs described Abilene as filled with sporting men and women, gamblers, cowboys, and desperadoes. "I have seen many fast towns," he wrote, "but I think Abilene beat them all."

A Kansas newspaper, the *Junction City Union* of October 29, 1871, agreed:

> *For two or three things Abilene is noted. It is the principal rendezvous for the Texas cattle trade: drovers, buyers, sellers and shippers. It handles more money than any town its size in the West, and has a class of transient men decidedly rough and reckless. Cut loose from all the refining influences and enjoyment of life, these herdsmen toil for tedious months behind their slow herds, seeing scarcely a house, garden, woman, or child for nearly 1,000 miles, like a cargo of sea-worn sailors coming into port, they must have—when released—some kind of entertainment. In the absence of something better, they at once fall into the liquor and gambling saloons at hand.*

The Alamo and Bull's Head saloons were what passed for elegance in the community, although the Drovers Cottage Hotel and Stables could house over 150 guests with accommodations, meaning horses or carriages.

Abilene established a city government in 1870, retaining officials who hired James Butler "Wild Bill" Hickok as a captain of police. A monthly tax on the 11 saloons, plus gambling halls and numerous summer prostitutes financed the municipal venture. By 1871, with the railroads moving closer to (and even within) Texas, the career of Abilene, Kansas, as a wild cattle town had substantially run its course.

See also: HARDIN, JOHN WESLEY; HICKOK, JAMES BUTLER; LANE, JAMES HENRY; SALOONS; THOMPSON, BEN

ABRAHAM, David (a.k.a. Dobrzinsky) (1824–1894)

Originally from Poland, then London, and finally New Mexico, David Abraham applied for and was granted the first patented mining claim in New Mexico, the Peabody Mine. Abraham was a respected businessman in early Silver City, other merchants crediting him with erecting the first brick building in town. David was not of the outlaw or frontier lawman ilk, but he was also not to be trifled with.

A Mexican burglar attempted to rob Abraham's store during a crisp September night in 1872. He shouldn't have. Abraham, assisted by C. Bennett, shot the miscreant, wounding him in both legs.

A year later, on November 7, 1873, David Abraham emptied his shotgun, a Parker breech-loader, into Robert Everett, who, intoxicated, had trespassed into and refused to vacate Abraham's corral. Everett forfeited his life for the transgression. Not long afterward, Abraham not only killed a "crazy man" but fired his trusty shotgun at an unidentified Silver City citizen, who "stood him off" with an old "knuckle pistol."

David Abraham, 70 years old and a true southwestern "tough as nails" pioneer, died in bed under the care of a physician on March 7, 1894.

ALCALDE

In New Mexico and Arizona in particular, along with some parts of southern California and West Texas in general, the legal system for the Hispanic population usually operated through *alcaldes,* these individuals being defined as mayors or justices of the peace, lawyers, or leaders, to whom a mayor could delegate authority in various areas around a community. They were usually considered spokesmen or arbitrators. Since most Hispanics were desperately poor and yet had occasional need for legal guidance and remedies, the decision of the alcalde generally passed for law among Spanish-speaking citizens. Ordinarily the alcalde did not insist upon fines, since few residents had money, but he could and did make arrests, and he had the authority to call upon others for assistance.

Alcaldes made their own decisions, ignoring jury systems, but they seldom inflicted jail sentences. They dealt out punishment through the whip or banishment, or through subtle "threats of persuasion." Spanish-speaking people gave deference to the alcalde system, most alcaldes being held in great respect. After these Spanish territories passed into American hands, U.S. legal justice gradually supplanted these systems and customs, although the alcalde approach was the last to go.

ALLEN, James (1860–1880)

James Allen, while he lived, was three things—young, an apparent member of the scandalous Dodge City Gang, and a murderer. Originally from Lawrence, Kansas, James Allen ended up by a circuitous route in East Las Vegas, New Mexico, in 1879 where he freely associated with disreputable and sometimes desperate frontier scallywags. By the time Allen reached Las Vegas, an end-of-the-line railroad town, Hyman G. Neill, better known as "Hoodoo Brown," was a justice of the peace and maintained his own informal, private police force.

On March 2, 1880, Allen hired out as a waiter at the St. Nicholas Hotel, where he met James Morehead, a St. Louis–based salesman representing Derby & Day wholesale liquor dealers, who frequented the establishment nearly each morning. When Morehead called for eggs following a late arrival for breakfast, Allen grumbled that the cook was too busy to prepare them; it was too late in the morning. Morehead grabbed Allen, and a scuffle commenced. Finally breaking free, Allen dashed to the kitchen, snatched a six-shooter, and returned to the dining room, where he called Morehead a "son of a bitch" and shot him through the liver. Morehead died that night.

Following his arrest, Allen described what happened as "a rather rough transaction for one his age." Indeed the transaction was rough for East Las Vegas; a coroner's jury determined that his act had been "willful, malicious and felonious murder, without justification or provocation whatsoever."

On that very same day, at 4 A.M., another notorious figure, John Joshua Webb, acting as a police officer, shot and killed Michael Kelliher at Goodlet & Robert's Saloon. On March 5, a grand jury returned murder indictments against both J. J. Webb and James Allen.

Upon a change of venue, Allen was tried at Santa Fe, found guilty, and returned under a sentence of death to the San Miguel County Jail at Las Vegas. On November 10, 1880, James Allen, along with J. J. Webb and four fellow prisoners, aided by associates on the outside, broke jail and departed. Sheriff Desiderio Romero tracked the escapees to Chaperito, on the Gallinas River, where a one-sided gun battle left James Allen and George Davidson dead. William Mullen and John Murray were returned to custody. J. J. Webb and George Davis escaped. Meanwhile, back at the St. Nicholas Hotel, the patrons started arriving on time for breakfast.

See also: WEBB, JOHN JOSHUA

ALLISON, Robert A. (a.k.a. Clay Allison)
(1840–1887)

Clay Allison was born in Waynesboro, Wayne County, Tennessee. For the first half of his life, until the Civil War interrupted, he did little but farm. The six-foot-two-inch youth with wavy black hair and blue eyes joined the Confederacy on October 15, 1861; a "mental condition" led to his discharge at Bowling Green, Kentucky, in January 1862. He also had a physical condition, what many would call a clubfoot, but neither element prevented him from reenlisting in the Ninth Regiment of Tennessee cavalry and serving as a scout for Lt. Gen. Nathan B. Forrest. War's end found him drinking heavily and incarcerated by the Union near Gainsville, Alabama. Upon being released, Allison went home, gathered up some of his brothers, sisters, and their families and migrated to Texas.

In Brazos County, Texas, Allison hired out to cattlemen Oliver Loving and Charles Goodnight, although that never slowed his drinking. During one of his binges, Clay rode into Mobeetie, Texas, wearing only his sombrero, boots, and gunbelt. Most folks looked the other way. In 1886, a photographer took his picture at Las Vegas, New Mexico, the locality suggesting that he probably participated in opening the Goodnight-Loving Trail from Texas to New Mexico and on to the South Platte north of Denver.

In 1870, Allison moved to Colfax County, New Mexico, and ranched near Cimarron. The story is told that in September, at the nearby community of Elizabethtown, a weeping Mrs. Kennedy stunned a saloon gathering with the story that her rancher husband had been murdering travelers pausing for the night at their cabin and had now killed their infant daughter. Allison and a group of cowboys therefore rode out to the home, seized Kennedy, and dug up the area. They found numerous bones, but no one could agree on which ones, if any, were human. On October 7, 1870, Allison and a group of men removed Kennedy from jail, dragged him to a nearby slaughterhouse, and lynched him.

Nearly four years later, on January 7, 1874, Allison and Chuck Colbert (or Tolbert), a ne'er-do-well and sometimes desperado and gunman who by some accounts had slain up to seven men, met at a horse race and later retired to eat at the Clifton House, a hotel and saloon alongside the Canadian River in Colfax County, near the Barlow and Sanderson

Clay Allison (El Paso Public Library)

stage route. A disagreement occurred during the meal; Colbert drew his revolver, firing as the weapon cleared the table. He missed. Clay Allison did not miss. His bullet struck Colbert over the right eye. Three days later, Charles Cooper, a friend of Colbert's, disappeared while riding toward Cimarron with Clay Allison.

The *Raton Range* (New Mexico) newspaper of July 22, 1887, gave an almost unbelievable account of how rancher Mason T. Bowman and Clay Allison drunkenly tried to prove who was the better man with a six-shooter. First, they had tried to outdraw one another, with Mace Bowman consistently proving the faster. Then they had stripped down to their underwear and danced with each other. Finally they fired a few rounds near each other's feet just to see who would flinch, or at least jump, but both showed nerve. The incident ended without a killing.

On September 20, 1875, the Rev. F. J. Tolby, a Methodist minister, was murdered while riding from Elizabethtown to Cimarron. Suspicion fell on Cruz Vega, a mail carrier, who was arrested but later released. An incensed Clay Allison and others caught Vega and threatened to hang him from a telegraph pole unless he confessed. Vega named Manuel Cardenas as the murderer, but the mob lynched him anyway, and Allison dragged his corpse through the streets.

Francisco (Pancho) Griego became incensed at Vega's murder. Griego had quite a reputation, having killed three soldiers on May 30, 1875, during a gun battle at Lambert's Saloon, in the St. James Hotel at Cimarron. On November 1, Clay Allison and Pancho Griego met at that same Cimarron hotel bar, drank together, then stepped over to a corner and talked briefly in low tones. Allison then drew his revolver and fired three shots. Suddenly the lights went out, and when someone finally reentered the room, Griego lay dead with three of Allison's bullets in him.

Allison's maniacal rages now became the terror of Cimarron. He raided a ranch to steal military mules; when nearby soldiers chased him off, he drunkenly shot himself in the foot. He later threatened to shoot not only the doctor who treated him but various employees at the courthouse as well.

Allison and friends rampaged through the *Cimarron News and Press* offices on January 19, 1876, dumping expensive printing equipment into the Cimarron River. Since one side of one page had already been printed, Allison wrote on the blank side "Clay Allison's edition" and distributed copies throughout the community. Upon sobering, he returned to the newspaper office and made restitution of $200.

Less than a month later, on February 21, 1876, New Mexico governor Samuel B. Axtell posted a $500 reward for Allison's head with regard to the disappearance of Charles Cooper. Nobody collected.

On March 25, three Negro soldiers were slain by unknown cowboys in Lambert's Saloon. Suspicion fell on Allison as one of the killers, so the sheriff and a detachment of black cavalry arrested Allison and took him to Taos for trial. An indictment as an accessory did not hold up; the territory failed to prove even Allison's presence in the saloon.

The territory then charged Allison with the murders of Chuck Colbert, Charles Cooper, and Francisco Griego. However, a grand jury again refused to indict, suggesting that the territory had made its case primarily on emotion rather than facts.

On December 21, 1876, Clay and his brother John were celebrating an early Christmas at the Olympic Dance Hall in Las Animas, Colorado. When a disturbance started, Bent County deputy sheriff and constable Charles Faber grabbed shotguns and deputized two bystanders. They entered the dance hall, where Faber wounded John Allison; Clay then shot Faber four times, killing him. The deputies fled. Sheriff John Spiers now hurried over and arrested both Allisons. A grand jury charged John with murder and Clay with manslaughter. John got off because of a lack of evidence. Clay was released when no witnesses showed up to testify.

Allison thereafter lived briefly in Dodge City and Hays City, Kansas, then moved to Hemphill County, Texas, where he became known as the Wolf of the Washita (River). Here in 1881 he married Dora McCullough. They had two children, both girls, Patsy and Clay.

Allison also owned a ranch near Pecos, Texas. On July 1, 1887, he was in the process of hauling in supplies when a sack of grain tumbled off the wagon. Attempting to recover it, Allison stumbled and fell between the wheels. The startled horses shifted forward a step or two, and a rear wheel rolled across Allison's neck; he died in less than an hour. He is buried in the Pecos Cemetery.

ALLISON, William Davis (a.k.a. Dave Allison)
(1861–1923)

Originally from Ohio, William Davis Allison, usually called Dave, was a sheriff in West Texas who joined the Texas Rangers, serving under the renowned Capt. John R. Hughes. Meanwhile, the Arizona legislature in 1903 increased the strength of the Arizona Rangers to 26 men. Allison subsequently left Texas and on April 27 pinned on his Arizona badge. Before long he became a first sergeant at a pay of $110 per month. Each man provided his own horse, saddle, and pack outfit, a Colt .45, and a .30-40 carbine.

His boss, Capt. Thomas Rynning, remarked of Dave Allison's nerve, "Cool as ice he was, and he'd left school before he learned to spell the word 'fear.' He was a grand party when it come to any kind of a scrimmage." The captain and Dave once arrested a man who had slain a schoolteacher near Galeyville,

Arizona, and was "holed" up in an old rock house. When the two Arizona Rangers crashed through the door, the suspect dived for his six-gun. The lawmen responded, wounding the man and dragging him to jail. Dave and his boss walked away unscathed.

Unfortunately, Dave Allison had a weakness for gambling, and his love for the turn of a card eventually cost him his job with the Arizona Rangers, driving him to take work as a hired gun south of the border. Since 1899, the Cananea Consolidated Copper Company had been operating in Sonora, Mexico, employing Mexican laborers working for mine owner Col. William Cornell Greene. With currents of revolution flowing beneath the surface, a movement to improve working conditions at the mine gained momentum. Sensing trouble, Greene put gunman Dave Allison on the payroll as a security measure. On June 1, 1906, the emotional lid blew off when a management employee turned a high-pressure water hose on protesting laborers. What began as a noisy demonstration exploded into a riot with several people killed. Telephone calls and telegrams flooded high levels of the U.S. and Mexican governments, and soon a hurriedly organized management rescue force arrived from north of the border. It found Allison and his cohorts desperately short of ammunition, and the 300 arriving volunteers dispersed the rioters.

On another occasion, in Culberson County, Texas, Dave Allison, now a range detective, led a posse across West Texas in pursuit of Mexican revolutionary leader Pascual Orozco. Catching up with Orozco and his four compadres, Allison and the hard-riding lawmen and ranchers struck like a thunderbolt, killing all five of the revolutionaries. Amid charges of political assassination, a grand jury indicted 11 members of the posse, including Dave Allison, for murder. In October 1915 a jury found them not guilty.

Meanwhile, Allison and fellow field inspector Horace L. Roberson had been gathering cattle-rustling evidence against Hill Loftis and Milt Good. Loftis was better known in West Texas and New Mexico as Tom Ross. He had been a rustler near the New Mexico/West Texas line, specifically around Lovington, Seminole, and Carlsbad. Good, in addition to being a suspected rustler, was a well-known rodeo performer and championship steer roper. The case came to trial on April 1, 1923, at Seminole, Texas, with trial participants jamming the hotel lobby. Allison and Roberson were seated in chairs and quietly chatting when Tom Ross and Milt Good walked in with revolvers and shotguns and killed both men.

From upstairs, Allison's wife, Martha, heard the shooting, realized immediately what it meant, raced down to the lobby, found her dead husband on the floor, removed his .25-caliber revolver, dashed to the screen door, and commenced firing at Ross and Good as they entered a getaway car. One bullet bounced off the belt buckle of Ross, and tore into his stomach. Another bullet hit Good in the arm. The two men were now hurt and bleeding; when their car ran out of gas just a few miles out of town, they surrendered. Both were sentenced to the Texas Penitentiary, but they escaped on November 29, 1925.

Milt Good was arrested in Antlers, Oklahoma, and returned to the penitentiary. After being pardoned later, he wrote a book entitled *Twelve Years in a Texas Prison*. Around 1960, while he was opening a fence gate, his car slipped out of gear, rolled forward, and crushed him to death. As for Tom Ross, he assumed the name of Charles Gannon and went to work for the Frye Cattle Company on the Blackfoot Indian Reservation near Browning, Montana. On February 2, 1929, he argued with ranch foreman Ralph Haywood, shot and killed him, proceeded to the bunkhouse, wrote a suicide note, and then shot himself in the head.

ALVORD, Albert Wright (a.k.a. Burt Alvord; Tom Wright) (1867–1909)

Burt Alvord, the son of Gold Rush parents, a lawman turned renegade outlaw, was born in Susanville, California. By 1882 he had moved to Tombstone, Arizona; in 1877 he became a deputy sheriff to John Slaughter, and for several years he was a deputy sheriff in Cochise County. In 1896, he married the 19-year-old Lola Ochoa and adopted the Catholic faith. They moved to Wilcox, Arizona, where Burt won election as a constable in July 1897. Four months later he shot and killed William King under conditions and circumstances far from clear; a coroner's jury no-billed him.

Meanwhile, two train holdups took place, one on September 9, 1899, and the other on February 15, 1900. The first was successful, the second a disaster, as express messenger Jeff Milton shotgunned one of the bandits. The other bandits were soon rounded up, and one of them was Constable Burt Alvord. He went into jail but broke out on April 7 and fled to Mexico, although he returned in September and surrendered to the Cochise sheriff. Burt subsequently pleaded guilty to attempting to rob the U.S. Mail and received two years in the Yuma Territorial Prison. Before he could be transferred, however, he broke jail on December 17, 1903. He fled across the border into Mexico but for unexplained reasons kept returning briefly to the United States. On February 20, 1904, Sheriff Albert Lewis and a posse caught up with Alvord, shot him in the leg and wrist, and locked him in the Tombstone jail. Two weeks later they transferred him to the Yuma prison. However, his prison sojourn did not last long, and he was released on October 9, 1905. Meanwhile, his wife Lola had divorced him on grounds of desertion. They had no children.

With a few federal charges still pending against him, Burt changed his name to Tom Wright and fled to Panama, where he worked on waterfront piers before drifting farther south to work on a railroad project near the Amazon River, where he contacted malaria. He was shipped to British Barbados for rest and recuperation. He died there on November 23, 1909.

ANDERSON, William C. (a.k.a. Bloody Bill Anderson) (1840?–1864)

Bloody Bill Anderson was born in Jefferson County, Missouri, fated to become one of the most bloodthirsty outlaws of the Confederacy. His story did not start so much with him as with his sister, Josephine Anderson. Union brigadier general Thomas Ewing Jr. decided that one of the best ways to root out Missouri guerrillas was to jail women who provided them with food, shelter, and comfort. So he rounded up a dozen or so female relatives and incarcerated them on the second floor of a dilapidated Kansas City building. The floor collapsed, and five women died, including Josephine (some accounts say three of these women were Anderson sisters). When brother Bloody Bill Anderson—riding with William Quantrill—heard the news, his frail hold on sanity grew even weaker.

He rode into Lawrence, Kansas, with Quantrill and participated in the notorious bloodletting of August 21, 1863. Then the psychotic Anderson followed Quantrill into Texas, where the bushwhackers—man killers who hid behind bushes and "whacked" their victims with rifle bullets—spent much of the winter quarreling among themselves. Anderson caroused in Sherman, Texas, with a saloon girl while his followers drank and argued. When Quantrill, trying to exert discipline, had one of Anderson's men shot, a rift opened that became unbridgeable. Anderson and 20 horsemen subsequently broke away from Quantrill and rode toward Bonham, Texas, with Quantrill trying to coax them back. In the end, both groups returned to Missouri by separate trails.

During the summer of 1864, near Huntsville, Missouri, Anderson's men shot and scalped two Union soldiers. A month later they killed seven soldiers, scalping four and slitting the throats of three. On September 26, Anderson and his "army" rode into Centralia, Missouri, and burned the town. Several bushwhackers poured whiskey into their boots and forced townspeople to drink it. Learning that a train was due, they piled ties on the track, stopped the train, and ordered everybody out, including 25 unarmed federal soldiers on their way home. The soldiers were ordered to strip and were shot as they stood naked on the railroad platform.

A few hours later, as word of Anderson's presence reached him, Maj. A. V. E. Johnston led his 100 Union recruits in pursuit, but the wily guerrilla sprung a trap. Most of the recruits died, including Johnston, who was shot through the head by a 17-year-old boy named Jesse James. The bodies of the recruits were mutilated.

However, on October 26, 1864, still another Union column overtook Anderson, this time near Orrick, Missouri. He and his bushwhackers charged, as usual, and they broke through the line, as usual. But this time Anderson did it the hard way—he carried two Union bullets in the back of his shaggy head. Bloody Bill was dead before he hit the ground. That same head was chopped off and placed on a spiked telegraph pole at Richmond, Missouri.

See also: JAMES BROTHERS; QUANTRILL, WILLIAM CLARKE

ANGEL, Frank Warner (1845–1906)

Frank Angel was born in Watertown, New York, and in 1868 graduated with a degree in law from the Free Academy of New York. He was admitted to the bar in 1869. From April 15 through October 5, 1878, he served as a special investigator for the Department of

Justice in the murder of Englishman John Tunstall during New Mexico's bloody Lincoln County War. During this same period he was appointed assistant district attorney for the eastern district of New York. He later became fire commissioner for Jersey City, New Jersey. Angel died in Jersey City on March 15, 1906.

See also: LINCOLN COUNTY WAR

ANGEL, Paula (a.k.a. Pablita Martin; Pablita Sandoval)

Not much is known about Pablita. She lived a few miles north of Las Vegas, New Mexico, somewhere around the Sapello River. Early in 1861 she stabbed and killed Juan Miguel Martin, her husband or perhaps boyfriend. A judge sentenced her to hang on April 26, 1861.

Paula wasn't particularly likable; the Miguel County sheriff, Antonio Herrera, by some accounts, reminded her each afternoon of the number of days remaining in her life. At the time of execution, Herrera did not even bother tying her hands, so when the wagon rolled out from under her, she reached up, grabbed the rope and simply swung back and forth. The sheriff tried to pull her hands away and even added his own weight, grabbing her around the waist and swinging along with her. By this time the crowd, developing sympathy for her, began yelling that enough was enough, that she had been hanged, and that was all the law demanded. At that moment, however, another person in the crowd reminded the audience that the death warrant called for her to be hanged by the neck until dead—and she wasn't dead. Following that assessment, the sheriff wrestled her back inside the wagon, tied her arms securely, and once more led the wagon out from under her. This time Paula went without a fuss.

ANTRIM, William Henry Harrison (1842–1922)

William Antrim was born near Anderson, Indiana, on December 1, 1842. He worked as a teamster in Philadelphia and then served with Indiana volunteers during the Civil War. Antrim filed a successful court action against the government for drafting him when it wasn't supposed to. In later life he lived in Kansas, New Mexico, and California, becoming essentially a wanderer, a man best known as the stepfather of

Billy the Kid. He died at Adelaida, California, on December 10, 1922.

See also: BILLY THE KID

APACHE Kid (1860?–?)

The Apache Kid was likely born around 1860 in a wickiup near the Gila River in Arizona. He probably belonged to the group known as White Mountain Apaches. His given name was Haskay-Bay-Nay-Ntay. Somewhere around 1875, the government rounded up his family and others and moved them to the San Carlos Reservation, in eastern Arizona. There he learned to speak fair English and essentially adopted the white man's ways, becoming a cowboy and wearing boots, spurs, and hat. No white man could pronounce his name, so everyone called him "Kid." The name became more distinctive by broadening it to "the Apache Kid." Al Sieber, chief of scouts at San Carlos, made the Kid a scout, and he served almost continuously from 1882 through 1886. In 1887, he became first sergeant of the Indian police, but he was dishonorably discharged a few months later for drinking too much at a party and then killing a man allegedly involved in some kind of a triangle with the Kid's mother.

Apache Kid (Robert G. McCubbin Collection)

7

Apache Kid (Robert G. McCubbin Collection)

The Kid and others returned to San Carlos, where Al Sieber attempted to place most of the scouts, including the Kid, under arrest. During the resultant uproar and confusion, the Kid shot Sieber in the left leg below the knee. At that instant the Apache Kid and 16 cohorts were on the run. The cavalry pursued, but after a few days the Kid sent word to Gen. Nelson Miles that he and the others would surrender if Miles would call off the troops. Miles agreed. A court-martial followed, and all the scouts were dishonorably discharged, forfeiting pay and allowances. The Kid got 10 years. Troops escorted him to Alcatraz, where after a brief period he was released and allowed to return to San Carlos.

Meanwhile, the Supreme Court, in a decision known as *The United States v. Captain Jack,* stipulated that Indians found guilty of crimes would serve their sentences in territorial prisons rather than federal ones. Arizona and the military then concocted a plan to retry these Indians and sentence them to "ter-

ritorial" prisons for crimes for which they had already served time.

The Apache Kid was retried and given seven years in the territorial jail at Yuma. However, on November 2, 1899, a coach hauling prisoners was moving uphill toward a railroad, and the sheriff ordered everyone to walk up the grade. The Indian prisoners and lawmen piled out, but the Indians then overpowered and killed the two lawmen, shot the stage driver, Eugene Middleton, and disappeared. The army tracked down a few and captured or killed them. Someone even allegedly chopped off an Indian head and displayed it on a pole at agency headquarters.

Over time, rewards for the Apache Kid alone totaled $15,000. He was accused of murders, rapes, and thefts. Travelers across the Southwest were heavily armed. Boundary employees at the U.S.-Mexico border traveled together for safety. But what happened to the Apache Kid, no one knows. He kept southwestern travelers scared and walking on their toes for years, but no one ever caught sight of him. Did he go to Mexico? Did he die in the wastelands? The fate of the Apache Kid is as mysterious and controversial today as it was a century ago.

See also: HOLMES, W. A.

ARIZONA Rangers

On March 13, 1901, the Arizona legislature, favorably impressed by the success of the Texas Rangers in curbing lawlessness, created the Arizona equivalent, the Arizona Rangers. The unit consisted of a sergeant and 12 privates, usually former cowboys, since the job required considerable time on horseback. Their commander was rancher Burton C. Mossman, who had drafted much of the enabling legislation and agreed to serve only one year. The state paid the privates $55 a month. The sergeant received $75, and Mossman $120.

In 1903, the ranger unit expanded to 26 men. The units served without uniform, although everyone had a badge. For the most part they carried .30-40 lever-action Winchester rifles, model 1895, and used single-action Colt .45 revolvers. On October 8, 1901, rustlers killed Pvt. Carlos Tafolla, the only Arizona Ranger ever slain in the line of duty. How many outlaws were killed by the Arizona Rangers is unknown.

Thomas H. Rynning took over from Mossman, after one year, but Rynning resigned in 1907, and Harry Wheeler, who had come up through the ranks, replaced him. Arizona Republicans had created the unit, and altogether 107 men served before Arizona Democrats, having achieved the necessary power and numbers, disbanded the lawmen on February 15, 1909.

See also: ALLISON, WILLIAM DAVIS; WHEELER, FRANK S.; WHEELER, HARRY

ARMSTRONG, John Barclay (1850–1913)

This renowned Texas Ranger was born in McMinnville, Tennessee, the son of a physician who moved to Missouri and Kansas, and then Texas. John became a member of the Travis Rifles during the 1870s, and on May 20, 1875, he signed on with the Special Force of Texas Rangers, led by Leander McNelly. He took part in the so-called Las Quevas War, fighting Mexican bandits along the Nueces Strip. After being promoted

John Armstrong was the famous Texas Ranger who captured noted outlaw John Wesley Hardin (Author's Collection)

to sergeant, he chased cattle thieves along the Mexican border, and in December 1875 he killed John Mayfield in Wilson County.

After McNelly stepped down, Armstrong moved up to second lieutenant under Lee Hall. In particular, he worked the Eagle Pass area, frequently crossing the Mexican border in pursuit of outlaws, and in April 1877 arresting the noted gunman/lawman/outlaw John King Fisher. Then, in Goliad, Texas, Armstrong accidentally shot himself in the groin. While recovering he tracked the noted outlaw and gunman John Wesley Hardin east from Texas to Pensacola, Florida, where on August 23, 1877, Armstrong caught Hardin on board a train, clubbed him to the floor, put him in chains, and returned him to Texas. A year later, in July 1888, Armstrong rode with the Rangers into Round Rock, Texas, where the lawmen shot and killed the outlaw Sam Bass.

Armstrong was afterward stationed in Cuero, Texas, where he retired from the Rangers, thereafter becoming a U.S. marshal. Not long afterward, he turned away from law enforcement, for nearly 20 years earlier he had married Mollie Durst. They had seven children. In 1882, he established a 50,000-acre ranch in Willacy County. John Armstrong died on May 1, 1913.

See also: BASS, SAM; HALL, JESSE LEIGH; HARDIN, JOHN WESLEY; MCNELLY, LEANDER H.; TEXAS RANGERS

ARRINGTON, George Washington (1844–1923)

This famous Texas Ranger and rancher was actually born John C. Orrick Jr. in Greensboro, Alabama. At 16 he enlisted in the Confederate army but rode with Mosby's guerrillas. When the war ended, he tried to join Maximilian in Mexico but failed. In 1867, he allegedly murdered a black businessman in Greensboro, then moved to Texas, where he became George Washington Arrington. (His mother's maiden name had been Arrington.) Following that he farmed briefly, worked in a business house, and as a cowboy trailed a herd of livestock to Brown County. There, in 1875, he joined the Frontier Battalion of the Texas Rangers, and tracked down so many fugitives that he quickly rose to sergeant and then first lieutenant.

In 1877, he became captain of Company C and within a brief period broke up a vigilante movement at Fort Griffin before moving into the Panhandle. There he established Camp Roberts and mapped much of the area, in particular the region around

Yellow House Canyon. He brought law and order to such Panhandle towns as Tascosa and Mobeetie.

In 1882, Arrington resigned from the Rangers in order to do some Panhandle ranching, in the process also becoming sheriff of Wheeler County. In November 1877, he shot and killed John Leverton, whom he had accused of cattle rustling. Leverton's wife charged Arrington with murder, but a jury called it self-defense.

Arrington resigned as sheriff in 1890, preferring thereafter to devote his time to ranching, as he now owned considerable land—although many residents suspected he had used both legal and illegal methods to acquire it. He now joined the Masons and became a Shriner, although he remained involved in law enforcement. A man named George Isaacs had slain Hemphill County sheriff Thomas McGee; after a jury convicted him, Arrington escorted the prisoner to the Texas penitentiary at Huntsville.

During his final years, "Cap" Arrington practically always carried a gun. He suffered terribly from arthritis and often visited the hot baths at Mineral Wells, Texas. During one of those trips he suffered a heart attack. He died on March 31, 1923, and was buried in the Panhandle, at Mobeetie.

See also: MCNELLY, LEANDER H.; TEXAS RANGERS

ATEN, Ira (1862–1953)

This Texas Ranger and Texas Panhandle lawman, the son of a Methodist minister, was born in Cairo, Illinois, but grew up on a farm near Round Rock, Texas. As a young man, he witnessed the demise of outlaw Sam Bass and himself became a Texas Ranger shortly thereafter, serving in Company D under Capt. Lamar P. Sieker. In 1877, Aten and famed Texas Ranger John R. Hughes trailed and killed outlaw Judd Roberts, allegedly a member of the Butch Cassidy gang, and a long way from home. Aten thereafter quickly rose to sergeant and was instrumental in putting down Fort Bend County's Jaybird-Woodpecker feud.

He married in 1892, he and his wife living at a dugout ranch in Dimmitt, Texas. In 1893, he became sheriff of Castro County, organizing 20 local cowboys into a ranch police force. He and his family moved to California around 1904, and by 1923 he had become a member of the Imperial Valley District Board. In 1945, his memoirs were published in *Frontier Times Magazine,* which touted him as "the last

of the old Texas Rangers." On August 5, 1953, he died of pneumonia. His burial took place at El Centro's Evergreen Cemetery.

See also: CASSIDY, BUTCH; HUGHES, JOHN REYNOLDS; JAYBIRD-WOODPECKER WAR; TEXAS RANGERS

ATKINS, David (1874–1945)

David Atkins, fated to be an outlaw, was born in San Anglo, Texas, on May 8, 1874, the son of a buffalo hunter and wolf trapper who died of pneumonia in 1877. The family thereafter moved often, Dave becoming a cowboy at the age of 15 and marrying in December 1894. Marriage did little to settle him down. He and Tom Ketchum, plus others, shot and killed John N. "Jap" Powers, who lived south of Knickerbocker, Texas. Atkins and Ketchum were indicted for the crime. They fled the state but returned later, and no charges were filed.

On March 20, 1897, Atkins and a friend named Sam Moore were drinking in a Knickerbocker saloon. They had no sooner left, however, than shots rang out. Both men reentered the saloon, where they started arguing over whether Moore had done the shooting outside. As the discussion heated, a local merchant named Tom Hardin entered the saloon and complained about the gunfire, claiming that bullets were apt to shatter glassware in his store. Atkins then commenced arguing with Hardin, the latter placing his hand on Atkins's shoulder in an effort to reason with him. But the effort failed. Atkins shot Hardin twice in the head; he died within minutes.

As the bartender went to find the sheriff, Atkins and Moore rode out of town. Atkins headed for Mexico, although he changed his mind and returned to Knickerbocker, hiding out in the brush, or staying at the ranch of outlaws Dave and Will Carver. By mid-December 1897, Atkins had teamed up with the Tom "Black Jack" Ketchum gang. They rode north and west, robbing the Southern Pacific Railroad at Stein's Pass near the Arizona–New Mexico border. Ed Bullion, a gang member, gave up his life there.

Not long afterward, however, a posse caught up with Ed Cullen, Leonard Alverson, and Dave, and all three went to prison in Santa Fe. But they were shortly released, only to strike the Southern Pacific at a water stop on May 14, 1898. The following July, the gang struck again, hitting a train near Midland, Texas. During the next year, seven more train robberies took place, not all of them successful. By early

1900, Dave had been caught and tossed into the Tempe, Arizona, jail, where a Texas Ranger recognized him. The ranger notified the Butte, Montana, authorities that one of their robbers was doing time in Arizona. Atkins therefore went to Montana, but he spent only a brief time in jail before he was extradited back to Texas to be tried for the death of Tom Hardin.

Surprisingly, when the trial was delayed in getting under way, the authorities placed Atkins under house arrest in Knickerbocker. That could not hold him long either; Dave left home in May 1901 and sailed to Great Britain, where he volunteered for the war against the South African Boers. So he spent 84 days at sea, to be followed by numerous battles against the Boers. The war ended in May 1902, and Atkins found himself back in Texas by that December. Two years later he sailed for British Honduras, but the only thing he got there was yellow fever.

Back in Texas by 1905, he became a cotton farmer, married, and then ran out of luck in 1911, when Texas gave him a five-year prison term for killing Tom Hardin. In 1932, he was charged with assault and wound up as a mental patient in the Wichita Falls State Hospital. He spent 32 years in the hospital, dying there at the age of 93 on June 12, 1964.

See also: KETCHUM, SAMUEL W.; KETCHUM, TOM

BACA, Abram (?–1881)

Abram Baca was born and grew up in and around Socorro, New Mexico, but little was known about him until a Christmas Eve service at the local Methodist Church in 1880, when he and his brother, Enofrio, plus a cousin, Antonio, placed muddy boots on the shawl of a young lady sitting in front of them. A commotion quickly started, and parishioners, led by A. M. Conklin, editor of the *Socorro Sun*, escorted the boys from the building. An hour or so later, however, when everyone left the church, the Bacas were waiting. They pinned Conklin to the church wall and shot him to death.

The boys scattered, but on December 29 an Anglo posse captured Antonio and placed him in the Socorro jail. Within a couple days, however, someone slipped a revolver through the jail bars to Antonio, who promptly shot and wounded jailer Jack Ketchum. The deputy drew his own weapon and killed him.

Abram and Enofrio were subsequently identified sitting on the porch of a local county judge at Ysleta, near El Paso, Texas. The rangers arrested Abram and returned him to Socorro.

Meanwhile, Enofrio fled across the Rio Grande to Zaragoza, Chihuahua, Mexico, where he was captured by Texas Ranger James Gillett, transported to Socorro, New Mexico, and lynched. Abram was tried for murder and acquitted.

See also: GILLETT, JAMES BUCHANAN

BACA, Elfego (1865–1945)

Elfego Baca was born in Socorro, New Mexico, but he spent his first 15 years in Topeka, Kansas. He spoke English with hardly an accent but occasionally had problems with his Spanish. In February 1881, he broke his father out of the Los Lunas, New Mexico, jail.

By January 1883, Baca seems to have shifted to the law enforcement side. Elfego shot at a group of cowboys who had been firing indiscriminately while riding through Escondito, New Mexico. In doing so Baca killed a cowhand named Townsend.

During October 1884, Baca became a sheriff's deputy in Socorro County and was assigned to a tiny (271 population) community called San Francisco Plaza, located on the upper San Francisco River. Tensions here had existed for some time between Anglo stock raisers (cowboys) and local Hispanic sheep raisers.

On October 28, Deputy Baca arrested Charles McCarthy, a cowboy working for the nearby Slaughter Ranch, on charges of disturbing the peace. That night 12 cowhands demanded McCarthy's release. Shooting started, and Baca killed a cowpoke named Young Parham. On the following day, 40 to 50 cowboys (Baca later claimed 80), all angry, approached the plaza and demanded that Baca surrender himself. Baca took refuge in a tiny picket cabin belonging to Geronimo Armijo. In the meantime, Justice of the Peace William Wilson, a cattleman, deputized several men as constables; cowboy William B. Hearne was one of them. Hearne approached the cabin, demanded entrance, received no response, kicked the door, and was shot in the stomach by Baca, the bullet passing through the door. Hearne died shortly afterward.

The standoff between the cowboys and Baca lasted slightly more than 24 hours. While the events were dramatic, later writers, although ably assisted by Baca's florid personal accounts, habitually stretched the intensity and the reality too far. There were no hundreds of cowboys present, there were no thousands of rounds fired, there was no cooking of meals by Baca while trapped inside. Instead, Baca surrendered to Deputy Frank Rose. Baca went briefly to jail in the Socorro County Courthouse.

In the spring of 1885, a grand jury indicted Baca for murder, but he was acquitted. A second grand jury indicted him, and again he was acquitted. He also campaigned for and was elected to the position of Socorro County clerk. Later he became a school superintendent. He served in the Republican Party and considered himself an attorney-at-law. He even opened a detective agency. Baca continued to carry a deputy sheriff's badge and sometimes took to the field. But most of all he loved to talk, and talking often became his stock in trade. Never one to be self-effacing, Baca even suggested he had the inside track on the White Sands, New Mexico, unsolved murders of Col. Albert Jennings Fountain and his eight-year-old son, Henry. But after he discussed his "information" with Pinkerton detectives assigned to the case, one of them dismissed Baca as "a frontier confidence man."

As an attorney, Baca achieved considerable renown, although he never successfully defended 19 men charged with murder, as he claimed. Still, he was good enough by March 1905 for Governor Miguel Otero to appoint him as the district attorney for Socorro and Sierra Counties. Baca became a prominent politician, sometimes supporting and sometimes denouncing the Mexican Revolution. In El Paso, Texas, on January 31, 1915, Baca shot and killed Celestino Otero, a Mexican revolutionary sitting in a car.

In 1918, Baca became sheriff of Socorro County, New Mexico, and served one controversial term. After that he became chief bouncer in the Tivoli Gambling House in Ciudad Juarez, across the Mexican border from El Paso. In 1921, President Hard-

ing's secretary of the interior, Albert B. Fall, pulled strings, and Baca became an Interior Department agent. When Fall fell into disgrace Baca tried to become a judge, failed at that, campaigned for election as New Mexico governor in 1934, and failed at that. He died in Albuquerque on August 27, 1945. He is buried there, in Sunset Memorial Park.

See also: FOUNTAIN, ALBERT JENNINGS

BACA, Saturnino (1830–1925)

Saturnino Baca never killed anybody, but his name is a thread running through New Mexico's Lincoln County War. He was born on November 29, 1830, at Cebolleta, Valencia County, New Mexico. At the time of his birth, New Mexico belonged to Old Mexico. On September 15, 1855, he married Juana Chávez. The marriage survived 50 years, and the couple had nine children. Prior to the Civil War, Baca worked as a surveyor. He joined the Union army, specifically the First New Mexico Cavalry, rose to lieutenant, and saw action at Valverde, New Mexico.

After the war he and his family resided in La Placita, near Fort Stanton, where he served in the territorial legislature and introduced the bill that created Lincoln County. La Placita thus became Lincoln. In 1875, Baca became sheriff of Lincoln County, hanging William Wilson on December 18, 1875. However, Wilson showed signs of life in his casket, so Baca's deputies dragged him out and hanged him again.

In July 1876, Baca arrested Jesús Largo for horse theft. A few days later Baca learned that nearby ranchers intended to hang Largo, so Baca and several deputies attempted to move the prisoner to the safety of nearby Fort Stanton. Along the way, the vigilantes caught up with the lawmen, forcibly removed the prisoner, and lynched him.

William Brady captured the sheriff's office during the next election, and Baca went back to farming, raising sheep, and raising children. During the Lincoln County War, Baca resided in a rental house owned by attorney Alexander McSween at a time when the McSween home was under siege and receiving rifle fire from a sheriff's posse. Baca permitted the sheriff's riflemen to take cover in the nearby torreon (stone fort) and thus shoot at his landlord. McSween ordered both Baca and the torreon occupants off his property. When the "war" ended with the death of McSween, Baca requested military protection, stating that the McSween Regulators (private individuals who banded together to counter perceived wrongs) held him responsible for the presence of troops. Baca insisted that several McSween desperados had already fired several rounds through his tent. He filed charges of attempted murder against some of his neighbors, but nothing came of it.

In 1889, he lost an arm in a shooting incident. Saturnino Baca lived to be 95, however. He died in Lincoln on March 7, 1925, at the home of his granddaughter.

See also: LINCOLN COUNTY WAR

BADLANDER

A badlander is an inhabitant of the badlands. While the name often has an evil connotation—a reference to someone bad, usually an outlaw—in reality both good guys and bad guys tended to avoid places like this.

BADLANDS

Badlands exist in various places around the West, but the largest and best-known district is the 244,000-acre Badlands National Park, east of the South Dakota Black Hills. While many people believe the name refers to a region containing desperados hiding from the law, it generally alludes to a remote region of peaks, ridges, plateaus, gullies, eroded buttes, and mesas with little water or rainfall, minimal human and animal life, and practically no vegetation. Outlaws (as well as settlers) could exist only marginally in such a terrain, because there was little to steal, no way to farm, ranch, or operate a business, and very little to sustain life. These areas are called badlands not because of their inhabitants, if any, but because day-to-day survival there is difficult.

BADMAN

Badman can be spelled as one word or two, and in its most-used, broadest sense refers to someone outside the law, an outlaw. "Badman" in the Old West, generally meant someone wild and dangerous, a person to avoid. In modern times—in reference to the Old West—we often think of a badman as a romantic figure, a good man gone wrong, usually through bad things he had to do in order to achieve a good cause. Billy the Kid, Jesse James, and Sam Bass often fall

into this category. John Wesley Hardin thought he belonged in that group too, which is why he wrote his autobiography. Movies have also helped shape public opinion, the silver screen often depicting a badman as someone forced to flee after killing an intruder bent on some evil deed. Movies in particular are responsible for changing such groups as the Wild Bunch from badmen (meaning thugs) into "romantic" badmen, meaning misunderstood good old boys. The word "badman" was seldom used during the mid- to late 1800s.

BAD Medicine

Bad medicine originally referred to an Indian concept of spirits or dreams. Bad medicine in this case would not necessarily be evil, although that was the usual implication. Bad medicine was a strong indication that it was not a good day to commence a battle, get married, or undertake anything of any complexity or challenge.

Bad medicine in the Old West usually referred to certain individuals, people one needed to avoid. A particular lawman, for instance, might be bad medicine for outlaws.

BAKER, Cullen Montgomery (1835–1869)

The well-known Texas desperado Cullen Baker was born in Weakley County, Tennessee, but by 1839 he and his family had moved to Cass County, Texas. He married Mary Petty in January 1854, but marriage did not improve the disposition of the quarrelsome, hard-drinking man. By the Civil War, when his wife died, he had already murdered two men. During that conflict he served in various cavalry units and reportedly led a band of Arkansas guerrillas. He married Martha Foster in 1862, but she died four years later. Baker turned his fury on the Union occupation of Texas, venting his wrath in particular on the Freedmen's Bureau, which sought to help blacks make the transition from slavery to independence. Baker reportedly killed numerous black men and women, as well as soldiers of the occupying U.S. Army.

On January 6, 1869, in Cass County, Thomas Orr, whom Baker had once tried to hang, allegedly killed him by lacing Baker's liquor with strychnine. Many years later, author Louis L'Amour memorialized Baker in his novel *The First Fast Draw*.

See also: LONGLEY, WILLIAM PRESTON

BAKER, Theodore (?–1887)

Theodore Baker isn't known for much. He wasn't a lawman or a desperado, and his only fame hinges on the fact that he was hanged twice for the same offense. The story opened with Frank Unruh, a Colfax County, New Mexico, farmer, who happened to meet a new friend in Springer, New Mexico, named Theodore Baker. Unruh invited Baker to stay at his house, apparently because his wife, Kate, needed someone to talk to while he (Unruh) was away on surveying business.

After awhile Unruh started becoming suspicious, although he did little except argue with the couple and then get drunk in the basement. When he came out the last time, he and Baker argued again and came to blows. The dispute ended with Unruh being shot twice. He stumbled outside; Baker followed him and shot him several more times. Baker then went into Springer, turned himself in, claimed self-defense, and was placed in jail. However, on the following night, outraged residents removed him from jail, took him to the nearest telegraph pole, and lynched him.

Someone cut Baker down too soon, and he recovered. Within a week Baker was loaded on a train and sent to the New Mexico State Penitentiary for safekeeping. During a newspaper interview, he provided this interesting statement: "The noose was thrown over my head and I was jerked off my feet. My senses left me for a moment and then I awakened to what seemed to be another world. The sensation was that everything about me had been multiplied a great many times. It seemed that my five executioners had grown in number until there were thousands. I saw what seemed to be a multitude of animals of all shapes and sizes."

During Baker's murder trial in San Miguel County, Mrs. Unruh turned state's evidence and went free. But her testimony sent Baker back to the territorial gallows, the difference being that this hanging would be legal.

During the afternoon of May 6, 1887, in a ceremony witnessed only by state officials, Baker spoke for a half-hour, then, tiring, turned to the executioner and said, "Let her go." This time, after Baker was cut down, he was promptly buried.

BALD Knobbers (1885)

Of all the vigilante groups in the Old West, the Bald Knobbers were the cruelest. They took their name from Snapp's Balds, a treeless hilltop west of Kirbyville, Missouri, where on April 6, 1885, 100 or so men gathered to discuss methods of bringing law and order to Taney County. Their chieftain, a Springfield, Missouri, saloon owner named Nathaniel N. Kinney, would organize them into the largest most heartless vigilante group in western history. Under Kinney's leadership they lashed sinners (Kinney was also a preacher), in particular those accused of arson, stealing hogs, or adultery. Kinney was strongly against adultery.

Less than two weeks after the initial organizational meeting, the Bald Knobbers lynched Frank and Tubal Taylor for wounding one of the vigilantes. Yet lashing remained the group's favorite pastime. The vigilantes also scared residents out of the county just by riding past their house at midnight and tossing a bundle of switches on the porch. The switches in themselves carried a strong message.

As killings, beatings, and terror rode the land, an anti–Bald Knobbers group arose, a group knowing it could never prevail against the vigilantes so long as Nathaniel Kinney led them. Therefore, the anti–vigilante leaders, five or six men, resolved to settle their dilemma with a game of poker—the loser would kill Kinney. Billy Miles, a young farmer, evidently had no poker skills at all. His quest would take two years. Meanwhile, the Missouri adjutant general, James Jamison, warned both groups that their organizations were illegal. As a result the Bald Knobbers passed a meaningless vote to disband, and as might be expected, did not.

But angry times were coming for the Bald Knobbers. On New Year's Day of 1888, James Berry, a merchant and mail carrier, began setting up a series of trysts with a Kansas woman. However, Mrs. Berry learned of it and retained George L. Taylor as her attorney. This infuriated James, who accused his wife and her attorney of having an affair. On February 28, 1888, Berry met Taylor on the street and threatened him with a revolver. Berry was arrested but was soon released. On April 5, the two men traded shots in the middle of a public street.

On August 18, hearings began regarding the cohabitation suit against Mrs. Berry and Taylor, and that brought out both the Bald Knobbers and the anti–Bald Knobbers, everyone carrying revolvers and rifles. For whatever reason, Kinney had inadvertently gotten himself in the middle of this quarrel; the preacher and the vigilante in him struggled for primacy. By order of the court, he took charge of the Berry store and began inventories. This brought the Bald Knobbers and anti–Bald Knobbers out into the street; Kinney bragged that the Berry possessions would soon go on sale.

On the morning of August 20, 1888, at about 10 o'clock, Billy and Jim Miles walked up the street toward the Berry store. The employees, except for Kinney, hurriedly left, and it was just as well. Both men drew weapons, and Billy Miles put a .44 slug in Kinney's forearm. Miles then shot him again, knocking the giant Kinney to the floor behind the counter. Then Miles stepped to the counter, braced himself, and shot Kinney three more times. Miles walked outside, announced that he had killed the 45-year-old Bald Knob leader in self-defense, and turned himself in to the sheriff.

Miles and Berry went on trial separately. Berry was acquitted of first degree murder but was convicted of felonious assault. He was sentenced to five years but escaped after three months and disappeared. On March 22, 1890, Billy Miles went on trial for murder and was acquitted. As for the Bald Knobbers, with their giant leader Nate Kinney dead, they disbanded.

BARNETT, J. Graham (a.k.a. Bush) (1890–1931)

This mean-spirited man was born in Files Valley, near Fort Worth, Texas, and for unknown reasons moved even farther west into West Texas to become a cowboy. In Langtry, Bush Barnett and another hand, Reid House, took to arguing while rounding up cattle. It seems that Reid had only one good eye, and Bush shot it out. Some friends then hustled Bush on board a train to Del Rio, Texas, where he surrendered. A jury in Fort Stockton set him free.

Within the year Bush shot three Mexican *vaqueros,* but nothing came of that either. By 1916 he had signed on for a brief stay with the Texas Rangers, and while on the job he killed a hack driver at Big Lake, Texas. Nobody complained, so it wasn't until December 6, 1931, that fate finally caught up with Barnett, in Rankin, Texas. Two accounts exist regarding this shootout. Some claimed that Bud Fowler, the Upton County sheriff, was trying to blackmail Barnett, while other accounts say Barnett was trying to blackmail Fowler. At any rate, both men were in town at the same time and driving Model As. At the town's one major intersection, they

happened to come eyeball to eyeball on a busy street. Bush Barnett got his six-shooter to cracking, but it was no match for Fowler's submachine gun. The feud was over.

BASS, Sam (1851–1878)

Sam Bass was born on July 21, 1851, on a farm near Mitchell, Indiana. His mother died in 1861, his father in 1864. The court appointed his uncle, David Sheeks, guardian of the seven children. In 1869, Bass left home. Before long he appeared in Denton, Texas, where he worked as a farm laborer for Sheriff Thomas J. Egan, better known as "Dad Egan." Around 1874, someone described Sam as about five feet eight inches tall, stooped in the shoulders, with a sallow complexion and dark hair. He rarely looked anyone in the eye and seldom spoke. When he did speak, it was in a sharp, nasal twang.

That same year he met Henry Underwood, five years older than Bass, a Union army veteran who had killed a man and then moved to Denton County, Texas. Meanwhile, Bass and Armstrong Egan, the sheriff's brother, plus Underwood, purchased a gray mare, historically known as the Denton Mare. But winning racehorses attract unsavory characters, as the owners found out when they brought in the 26-year-old Joel Collins, who had previous indictments for theft on his record, as well as assault with intent to kill.

The group showed up in San Antonio during 1876, likely sold the Denton Mare, and then grabbed a herd of cattle that they promptly drove north and sold in the Black Hills. But the money they earned they just as quickly gambled and drank away in Deadwood, South Dakota. So they started considering other trades, notably stage and train robbery. The gang during these forays included Sam Bass, Joel Collins, Robert McKimie (Little Reddy or Little Reddie), Bill Potts, Jim Berry, Jack Davis, and Tom Nixon. They called themselves the Collins Gang.

First they stole saddle horses. Then on March 25, 1877, they hit the Cheyenne and Black Hills stage, killing the driver, John Slaughter. The only worthwhile thing that came out of this awkward holdup was that the outlaws weeded out Little Reddy, suggesting that he leave the group and join another gang. Meanwhile, stage robbing in the area proved epidemic; various other parties started practicing the same trade. The Collins Gang switched to trains.

On September 18, 1877, they stopped the Union Pacific a few hours out of Cheyenne at a town called Big Springs. The robbers beat one person senseless and rode away with several thousand dollars, much of it in passenger "contributions." However, although the robbery had gone off perfectly, someone had recognized Joel Collins. A week later, with posses scouring the countryside, the bandits divided the loot and split. A sheriff's posse caught up with Collins and Potts near Ellis, Kansas, and killed them. The law also caught up with Berry near Mexico, Missouri, and filled one leg with buckshot. He died of gangrene.

Within a month or so of the robbery, Sam Bass was back in Denton, Texas, renewing his friendship with Francis M. "Frank" Jackson and Henry Underwood. On December 22, 1877, the three men robbed the Concho stage. Underwood was quickly captured, but that did not slow Bass and Jackson. On January 26, 1878, they hit the Weatherford and Fort Worth stage. Meanwhile, Seaborn Barnes, a slender cowboy with a prominent nose, and Tom Spotswood, a cowboy with a glass eye, joined the gang. On February 22, the robbers held up the Houston & Texas Central at Allen, Texas, netting a few thousand dollars in cash. Although it was a successful robbery, the law captured Spotswood within four days.

On March 18, the gang robbed a train at Hutchins, and on April 4, around midnight, it struck the Texas and Pacific at Eagle Ford, Texas. The holdup netted only a few hundred dollars. Bass now planned a train robbery on April 10 at Mesquite, near Dallas, so he brought in two additional associates, Albert G. Herndon and Samuel J. Pipes. Even that proved insufficient, however, as resistance was heavy. Barnes was severely wounded, and Pipes received a minor wound. Furthermore, the Texas Rangers were getting active. Before long, Elijah Mayes, Herndon, and John Skaggs were in jail. Mayes was acquitted; Herndon got life in prison.

Bass no longer had time to worry about finding additional trains to rob; the Rangers had him concentrating on his life. Posses seemed to be everywhere. At Salt Creek, near Cottondale, in Wise County, the train robbers made the mistake of roping their horses together. Arkansas Johnson died as he tried to mount. The remaining outlaws fled into nearby thickets and escaped.

Following that fight, Bass switched his strategy to banks, not realizing he had a traitor near him. While Jim Murphy toyed with joining the gang, he was sending messages to the Rangers regarding the outlaws' whereabouts. It was Murphy who suggested the Williamson County Bank in Round Rock as an easy place to rob. The desperadoes set the time for July 20 at 3:30 in the afternoon, after the day's receipts had been deposited. Shortly after noon, Sam Bass and friends casually rode into town—and the Rangers were waiting.

As Bass, Seaborn Barnes, and Jackson entered a store to purchase tobacco, Williamson County deputy sheriffs A. W. "Caige" Grimes and Maurice Moore also walked inside. Grimes stepped up behind Bass and asked if he was carrying a weapon. Sam jerked it out and started firing. Grimes was shot dead; Moore took a bullet through the lungs. The outlaws, uninjured during the fusillade except for Bass, who lost two fingers from his right hand, rushed outside.

By now the Texas Rangers were closing in, forcing Barnes, Jackson, and Bass down an alley. Ranger Dick Ware killed Seaborn Barnes, and Ranger George Harold gave Sam Bass his fatal bullet. Jackson nevertheless helped Bass mount. The two outlaws galloped out of town. The traitor, Jim Murphy, identified the dead Barnes.

Jackson and Bass rode three miles until Bass could ride no farther. Jackson went on without him and vanished. On the following day, the Rangers found a man lying under a tree who gasped as they rode up, "Don't shoot. I surrender." He admitted to being Sam Bass, and he died of his wounds on Sunday, July 21, 1878, his 27th birthday.

Sam Bass and Seaborn Barnes are buried side by side in the Round Rock Cemetery.

See also: HAROLD, GEORGE; WARE, RICHARD CLAYTON

BAYLOR, George Wythe (1832–1916)

George Wythe Baylor was born on August 2, 1832, in Indian Territory (Fort Gibson, Cherokee Nation), the eighth child of Dr. John Walker Baylor, an assistant surgeon of the Seventh U.S. Infantry. In 1836, the father left the military and moved to Natchez, Mississippi, where he died. The family then settled at Fort Gibson, where George went to school. Later he attended Baylor University before climbing on a mule in 1854 and striking out for the goldfields of California. There he killed a desperado during a gunfight near Santa Rosa. In 1856, he joined the San Francisco Vigilance Committee, but by the fall of 1859 he was living with his brother John Robert Baylor in Weatherford, Texas. The two men led a group of gunmen into Paint Creek, in Parker County, where they slew and scalped nine marauding Comanches. In the 1860 census for Parker County, Texas, George listed his occupation as "Indian killer."

On March 17, 1861, three days after the fall of Fort Sumter, George and his brother John joined the Second Texas Mounted Rifles, which marched on West Texas. The force easily entered El Paso, friendly Confederate territory, then moved north along the Rio Grande and took Mesilla, New Mexico, which was Union territory. Baylor thereafter pulled out of West Texas and joined Gen. Albert Sidney Johnston at the Battle of Shiloh in Tennessee. It ended with Baylor holding the wounded Johnston in his arms as he died. The 30-year-old Baylor, now a colonel, returned to Texas and married 21-year-old Sallie Sydnor on April 22, 1863. Baylor then waged a successful cavalry assault against Union forces during the Red River campaign, receiving praise for his gallantry during battles at Pleasant Hill and Mansfield.

Baylor now anticipated he should be promoted to brigadier general, but instead he was ordered to serve under Col. David Smith Terry. Baylor refused and took his case on April 6, 1865, to Gen. John Austin Wharton. Wharton and Baylor exchanged insults at Gen. John B. Magruder's headquarters in the Fannin Hotel at Galveston. Wharton slapped Baylor, and Baylor shot and killed the unarmed Wharton. Baylor might have been executed, but the South surrendered soon thereafter, and the affair became a civilian matter. In 1868, a jury found Baylor not guilty of murder.

For the next three years Baylor did little but twiddle his thumbs, prior to writing Texas governor Oran N. Roberts in February 1879 and requesting a Texas Ranger commission. It arrived within days, and Baylor found himself on his way to Ysleta, Texas, the seat of El Paso County. For weeks Baylor and his Rangers chased Victorio, a prominent Apache leader, back and forth through the mountain canyons of West Texas, southern New Mexico, and northern Chihuahua—there apparently being no international problems about entering Mexico as long as it was Indians that Baylor pursued. Baylor even extended an invitation to the Mexican militia to ride north across the border and "kill all the reservation Indians they could find." On January 29, 1881, Baylor

caught up with six Mescalerao Apaches who had previously overrun a stage near Ysleta, Texas, killing the driver and a passenger. Because the Indians wore blankets, the Rangers could not make distinctions between male and female. So all of the Apaches were slain, except for one woman and child.

In 1882, Baylor campaigned for sheriff of El Paso County but fell short. In early 1883, Baylor's Rangers, operating out of their territory, broke up portions of the John Kinney gang of cattle rustlers operating around Rincon, in southern New Mexico. By late 1883, Captain Baylor had the El Paso jail so full of thieves and rustlers that some had to be chained to trees in the Ranger camp at Ysleta. Meanwhile, over in the Texas communities of Toyah, Alpine, and Pecos, Ranger forces were stretched thin enforcing the law. Nevertheless, Texas now needed Baylor at central Texas, northwest of Austin, where fence cutting had become epidemic. Baylor (who had been promoted to major) soon had the situation under control and returned to El Paso County.

On April 15, 1885, the Ranger unit in El Paso disbanded, and George Baylor resigned. Turning to politics, Baylor was elected to the Texas House of Representatives from El Paso in 1886. His bill created Brewster County, eventually the largest in Texas.

Baylor's bid for reelection failed in 1888. Thereafter he held various other political posts, such as district and circuit court clerk in El Paso County. He ran for mayor of Ysleta, failed to achieve it, and then slapped the man who did. A court fined him $5.45. In 1905, he commenced writing articles for the *El Paso Daily Herald* as well as the *Galveston Daily* and the *Semi-Weekly News*. Baylor lived in Guadalajara, Mexico, for a while; following that, he moved to San Antonio, Texas, where he died on March 17, 1916. He was buried there in the Confederate cemetery.

See also: GILLETT, JAMES BUCHANAN; JONES, FRANK; KINNEY, JOHN

BEHAN, John Harris (1845–1912)

If—as is frequently believed—Wyatt Earp has been overrated as a frontier lawman, quite possibly his personal and political adversary, John Harris Behan, has been underrated and mischaracterized. Much of the primary source material soundly supports a conclusion that Behan, on balance, left a record of worthy achievements.

Born in Westport, Missouri, a jumping-off point for the Santa Fe Trail, on October 23, 1845, John Harris Behan, a man of medium height, the progeny of respected parents and grandparents, made his way across the plains. By 1863, the same year Arizona became a territory, he made it his home. John found employment in Tucson delivering freight to military installations. Around 1865 he moved north to Prescott and engaged in prospecting and real estate speculation. He also operated a sawmill. Newspapers made frequent favorable mentions (such as "nervy") of his Indian-fighting abilities. Yavapai County sheriff John P. Bourke appointed him as a deputy. He resigned later to campaign for county recorder and was elected. Behan served the community as a representative of the Arizona Territorial Legislature on two occasions. He married Victoria H. Zaff in 1869 and had a son, Albert Price Behan, on July 6, 1871. However, law enforcement was in Behan's blood, so in 1871 Johnny Behan became the Yavapai County sheriff.

In 1875, Yavapai County granted Victoria Behan a divorce on the grounds that her husband had "openly and notoriously visited houses of prostitution . . . and that he did cohabit with the inmates." A judge ordered John Behan to pay $16.66 per month in support of Albert, their son.

When John moved to Tombstone in September 1880, he engaged in the livery-stable business and then became a Pima County deputy sheriff. Following the creation of Cochise County, territorial governor John C. Fremont appointed Behan as its first sheriff.

Behan is generally remembered for his role as Wyatt Earp's foil during the tragic events leading up to, and the aftermath of, the bloody confrontation usually dubbed the "Gunfight at the OK Corral." However, Behan's actual participation is usually skewed. On the night before the OK Corral gunfight, Sheriff John Behan, Tombstone chief of police Virgil Earp, Tom McLaury, and Ike Clanton played poker all night in the Occidental Saloon. While Behan was on speaking terms with Virgil, he apparently had hostile feelings toward Wyatt; the problem likely stemmed from Josephine (Josie, Sadie) Sarah Marcus, an aspiring actress by some accounts, an attractive saloon woman by others. She and Behan had had a common-law relationship that dissolved somewhere around July 1881, when her affections switched to Wyatt Earp. Some opinions indicate that

Sheriff John Behan (Ben Traywick Collection)

Josephine left John Behan because of Behan's continuous philandering. Whatever, Wyatt welcomed her into his life, a fact that could not help but trouble future relations between the two men.

Be that as it may, on October 26, 1881, Sheriff Behan slept late and awoke to learn of impending trouble between the Earps and the cowboys. Behan shaved and found Virgil Earp on the street, where they discussed what was happening. Behan then went in search of the cowboys and found them near the corral—the fight did not take place in the OK Corral, although that was the closest identifiable landmark. He spoke briefly with them, then saw the Earps and Doc Holliday approaching and moved to them, obviously hoping to defuse the situation and prevent bloodshed. It was too late.

Behan later arrested Wyatt Earp and Doc Holliday, charging them with murder. Following that, he dropped out of most Tombstone affairs.

In October 1887, Johnny became assistant superintendent for the Arizona Territorial Prison at Yuma. Shortly thereafter he, along with others, performed heroically during a prison break in which several inmates were slain. He killed an escapee, and his quick action saved a guard's life. On April 7, 1888, Behan was elevated to prison superintendent, a post he maintained throughout considerable political turmoil until July 1890.

On June 3, 1893, Behan became an inspector of customs at El Paso, Texas. Shortly thereafter (March 12, 1894), he received a 50 percent pay increase and was promoted to Chinese exclusion agent. For the next several years Behan traveled extensively throughout the Southwest arresting illegal Chinese immigrants and performing investigative assignments relating to U.S. Customs violations.

At the outbreak of the Spanish-American War, when he was 53 years old, Behan volunteered and became the corral master at Tampa, Florida. In Cuba he was promoted to superintendent of transportation. When the conflict ended, trouble in the Far East erupted, and once again Behan (at age 55) served his country during an overseas entanglement. Some reports describe him as a "secret agent" during the Boxer Rebellion.

Back in the United States, Behan returned to El Paso and found employment as a purchasing agent for Texas Bitulithic, a firm engaged in street paving. While in El Paso (1908), Johnny Behan campaigned for sheriff but was defeated. On December 14, 1910, the acting governor of Arizona Territory commissioned Behan as a railway policeman for the Southern Pacific. In conjunction with this employment, Behan accepted responsibility for the Commissary Department during expansion operations in Mexico. Later, he supervised engineering parties repairing levee breaks on the lower Colorado River.

On June 7, 1912, he died of natural causes in a Tucson hospital and was buried in the Holy Hope Cemetery.

See also: COWBOYS; EARP, MORGAN; EARP, VIRGIL; EARP, WYATT BERRY STAPP; GUNFIGHT AT THE OK CORRAL; HARTLEE, B. F.; HOLLIDAY, JOHN HENRY

BELL, James W. (a.k.a. Jim Long) (1853–1881)

The sudden tragedy that ended James W. Bell's life has overshadowed other aspects of his biography. In 1875, Bell, who was originally from Maryland, made his way to the Lone Star State, where at the age of 22 he enlisted in Capt. Dan W. Roberts's Company D, Frontier Battalion, Texas Rangers.

Bell and two other rangers approached Captain Roberts for permission to visit Austin. Given the OK, the three rangers collected money from comrades willing to "pony up," their purpose being to purchase the relatively recent and highly prized Model 1873 Winchesters—$50 for a rifle, $40 for a carbine. The trip accomplished, J. W. Bell's marksmanship was noted when he returned from the river with "six or eight wild geese and a dozen mallard ducks." Otherwise, Bell rode on numerous scouts and led an exhilarating life.

In the spring of 1879, Bell dropped out of the Rangers and joined O. W. Williams on an overland trip to Colorado to seek his fortune from "the immense beds of carbonate ore." Both men later returned to Texas, although Bell turned around and rode on to White Oaks, New Mexico, a mining hot spot in Lincoln County. Not long afterward, Bell acquired dual law enforcement commissions as a deputy sheriff and a U.S. deputy marshal.

On November 27, 1880, Bell rode with a White Oaks posse, engaging Billy the Kid and others in a standoff at the "Whiskey Jim" Greathouse Ranch. The posse sent in a note demanding that the outlaws surrender, and the outlaws responded by inviting the posse's leader, Jim Carlyle, to step inside and discuss it. Carlyle refused until Whiskey Jim agreed to surrender himself to the posse while Carlyle went inside to negotiate with the fugitives. In this manner, negotiations for the peaceful surrender of outlaws progressed. The criminals now had Carlyle; the lawmen had Greathouse. However, becoming concerned because of passing of time and fearing something might go amiss for Carlyle, the posse threatened to shoot Whiskey Jim if Carlyle were not forthwith allowed to leave the ranch house. Reportedly, J. P. Eaker, a posse member, accidentally discharged a gun. Carlyle heard the shot and thought Greathouse had been executed; he panicked and jumped through a window. Who killed him is not clear, but bullets from the outlaw guns likely cut him down. However, there is circumstantial evidence that his nervous comrades outside might have shot him to death, mistaking him for one of the outlaws. Either way, Jim Bell lost a friend.

Ultimately, Pat Garrett's posse captured the Kid and others at Stinking Springs, New Mexico. The

Kid went to trial in Mesilla, New Mexico, and was convicted and sentenced to death for the Lincoln, New Mexico, murder of Sheriff William Brady. Deputies returned him to Lincoln County on April 21, 1881, confining him on the second floor of the courthouse, the old Murphy-Dolan general store. The guards were James Bell and Robert Olinger. Folklore records Bell as mild-mannered, polite, and friendly toward his prisoner, while big Bob was overbearing, bullying, and insensitive. The truth is likely somewhere in between; certainly there is no evidence to indicate Bell was abusive, but it is somewhat inconsistent to think he would have sympathized with someone suspected of killing his friend Jim Carlyle. At any rate, as history indelibly records, on April 28, 1881, Bell walked the manacled Kid downstairs to the outside privy, where the prisoner either acquired a six-shooter from under the toilet seat or stripped Bell's from him as they started back up the stairs. Either way, in a desperate attempt to escape the Kid shot Bell on the inside courthouse steps. Bell stumbled outside and died in the arms of the caretaker. The Kid then killed Bob Olinger, legend claiming he did it with Olinger's own shotgun. Olinger was buried at Fort Stanton, James Bell at White Oaks, New Mexico.

See also: BILLY THE KID; GARRETT, PATRICK; LINCOLN COUNTY WAR; OLINGER, ROBERT

BENDER, John (?–?)

The Bender family saga is one of the great mysteries of the West. It consisted of John Bender, his wife (unnamed), John Bender Jr. (likely a stepson), and Kate Bender. John Sr. and Mrs. Bender spoke practically no English, whereas John Jr. and Kate spoke English rather fluently but with German accents. Kate was the most fluent in English. A wanted notice in 1873 described Kate as "24 years of age, dark hair and eyes, good looking, well formed, rather bold in appearance, fluent talker." She also claimed to be a medium, able to commune with spirits and cure diseases. John, the father, was about 60 years of age, his wife around 50, and John Jr. perhaps 27. Somewhere around the year 1870, the family opened a wayside inn along the Osage Trail a few miles north of Cherryvale, Kansas.

The ramshackle wooden inn contained two rooms divided by a canvas curtain. The front room had a table for meals. A trapdoor under the table emptied into a dugout cellar. Guests sat with their backs against the curtain, their heads making perfect targets for a heavy hammer. A butcher knife to the throat or a bullet to the head in the cellar finished the job. The authorities estimated that the Benders murdered a dozen or so people, including one child. The evidence was the bodies, buried in the yard.

In May 1873, Governor Thomas A. Osborn posted rewards offering $500 each, or a total of $2,000 for the Bender family. A posse tracked them back and forth across the state and into Indian Territory (Oklahoma). Either of two things happened: (1) the Benders had reached safety in Mexico, or some other part of the United States, and were never heard from again; (2) the posse tracked down the Benders, likely in Kansas, executed them on the spot, and dumped their bodies into a common grave. *¿Quién sabe?*

BILLY the Kid (Henry McCarty, a.k.a. Henry Antrim; Kid Antrim; William Bonney) (1859?–1881)

Although Henry McCarty, alias William Bonney, alias Kid, alias Kid Antrim, alias Billy the Kid, is generally said to have been born in New York City on November 23, 1859, the alleged "facts" are at best only partly true. Although New York is the generally accepted birthplace of Billy the Kid, there is no absolute proof of his birth there. Probably the best evidence is a Secret Service statement written in early 1881 during the Kid's incarceration in Santa Fe, New Mexico. The Kid was interviewed with regard to a mail theft. The brief, scrawled, practically illegible handwritten interview made no mention of mail theft; and obviously the interrogator considered the subject as a person of no significance. He did state, however, that the Kid "talked like he came right off the streets of New York where he was born."

Prior to this, in 1880 the Kid told a Fort Sumner, New Mexico, census taker that his name was William Bonney and he had been born in Missouri. This statement may have been truthful, but it also has never been proved. If the census-recorded date of birth was correct, when he was slain in 1881 the Kid would have been 24 or 25, depending upon the month and day of birth.

In any case, the widow Catherine McCarty, with "friend" William Henry Harrison Antrim, and her

Billy the Kid (Bettmann/Corbis)

two sons, Henry and Joseph, moved to Indiana, and from Indiana moved to Wichita, Kansas, in 1871. From there the family shifted to Santa Fe, New Mexico, where Catherine and William Antrim married on March 1, 1873. The Antrims then settled in Silver City, New Mexico, where William Antrim worked as a miner. The two boys attended school, young Henry becoming known locally as Kid Antrim. Catherine died of tuberculosis on September 16, 1874, and was buried in Silver City. William Antrim thereafter became a wanderer, dying at Adelaida, California, on December 10, 1922. Joe died in Denver, Colorado, in 1930. When no one claimed the body, it went to a medical school.

Young Henry fell in with "Sombrero Jack," and together they burglarized a Chinese laundry in Silver City. Henry got caught. Sheriff Harvey Whitehill locked him in jail, but on September 25, 1875, he escaped by crawling up the chimney.

Young Antrim fled to Camp Grant, Arizona, specifically a suburb of the San Simon Valley known as Bonito (Pretty). He spent most of his time gambling. On August 17, 1877, in a cantina near Fort Grant, a local blacksmith named Frank "Windy" Cahill called the Kid a pimp, and the Kid called Cahill a sonofabitch. The two wrestled. The Kid shot him in the belly, stole a horse, and headed for New Mexico. Cahill died the next day.

Billy likely spent a short period around Mesilla, New Mexico, and may have briefly ridden south to San Elizario, Texas—a distance of about 70 miles from Mesilla—to break a friend, Melquiades Segura, out of the local jail. The Kid and Segura subsequently parted ways. The Kid moved northeast toward Lincoln and Fort Sumner, New Mexico, probably not realizing that he would soon become involved in the Lincoln County War.

The Kid hired on as a cowboy and gunman for Englishman John Tunstall, although the Kid had hardly gotten started when Tunstall was slain by gunmen working for the House of Murphy. During the subsequent Lincoln County War, the Kid participated in the capture and slaying of two accused Tunstall murderers, Frank Baker and William S. "Buck" Morton. Both men were shot and killed on or about March 9, 1878, an uncertainty still existing as to whether they were executed by their captors or slain by the Kid and a few others during a running fight.

The Kid and his friends blamed Lincoln County sheriff William Brady for the death of Tunstall. On April 1, hearing of a disturbance at the opposite end of the street, Sheriff Brady and deputies George Hindman, Billy Mathews, and George Peppin hurried to investigate. Inside an adobe corral, however, waited Billy the Kid and several gunmen, all of whom opened fire as the lawmen passed by. The wall suddenly disappeared in a cloud of blue-white smoke. Mathews and Peppin were out in front and thus escaped. Brady fell instantly dead, whereas Hindman staggered a few feet before dying. The Kid ran out either to take Brady's rifle or to slip an arrest warrant from the sheriff's pocket, but he was driven back by fire from the other deputies. Some stories also have it that the Kid was wounded on the inside of one leg, making it impossible to ride. He spent the rest of the day hiding under the floorboards of a nearby house.

Three days later, at Blazer's Mill on the Sacramento River, a gang calling themselves the Regulators, of which Billy the Kid was a member, rode in shortly before noon. They were eating when someone noticed the approach of Andrew L. "Buckshot" Roberts, one of the slayers of Tunstall. Regulator Frank Coe went out to talk him into surrendering, but shooting started. When it ended, the Regulator leader, Dick Brewer, was dead, Frank Coe had lost a finger, and Roberts was suffering a stomach wound from which he would die within hours. The Kid didn't do much more than become a scrambling witness and get nicked by a bullet.

Other than engaging in a little long-range skirmishing, the Kid remained reasonably out of sight until July 15–19, 1878, when he and the Regulators, including Alexander McSween, underwent a five-day siege at Lincoln. The Kid would later appear as a witness before a court of inquiry regarding the siege, but unfortunately the questions asked and the answers given were not particularly informative. He testified that Harvie Morris, a McSween law clerk, had exited the house in front of Billy and had been shot dead. When Billy dashed out minutes later, three soldiers had fired at him, but he had safely reached the nearby Bonito River.

For the next few months, Billy the Kid did not drop out of sight, but he did not make any headlines either. On November 13, 1878, New Mexico governor Lew Wallace issued a proclamation of amnesty to all participants in the Lincoln County War, and that amnesty included Billy the Kid.

On February 18, 1879, Huston Chapman, a one-armed attorney working primarily for Susan McSween, was murdered on the streets of Lincoln, New Mexico. Governor Wallace demanded to know who had been responsible. Billy the Kid offered to testify if Wallace could quash indictments against him. The governor and the Kid thus met in the Lincoln home of a justice of the peace, John B. "Squire" Wilson. They hammered out an agreement whereby the Kid would submit to arrest and testify before a grand jury regarding what he knew about the murder of Chapman. For all this, Billy's past New Mexico legal sins would be forgiven. However, the governor did not altogether follow through with his part of the bargain. On June 17, Billy, suspecting he had been betrayed, walked out of the jail, climbed on his horse, and put Lincoln, New Mexico, and Lew Wallace's promises behind him.

On January 10, 1880, the Kid killed ne'er-do-well Joe Grant in a Fort Sumner saloon, allegedly after examining the intoxicated man's six-shooter and setting the hammer to fall first on an empty chamber. Four days later Pat Garrett married Apolonaria Gutiérrez in Fort Sumner, and he perhaps got to know the Kid as well. On November 2, Pat Garrett became sheriff of Lincoln County, with his office and jail in the Lincoln courthouse. His first order of business was to either jail or bury Billy the Kid. The Kid then wrote Governor Wallace on December 12 and asked for amnesty. Three days later Governor Wallace offered a $500 reward for Billy the Kid.

On December 19, the Kid and several outlaw friends rode through the hard-crusted snow into Fort Sumner after dark. Pat Garrett and a posse were waiting. The lawmen killed Tom O'Folliard, thinking he was Billy the Kid. The desperadoes scattered into the hills. Four days later on December 23, Garrett and his posse trapped Billy the Kid and gang at Stinking Springs. Charlie Bowdre was slain, again

Tom O'Folliard (University of Texas at El Paso Archives)

because the posse thought he was Billy the Kid. The remaining outlaws surrendered that afternoon.

Garrett jailed the Kid at Santa Fe, but the territory transferred him to Mesilla to stand trial on May 8, 1881. The territory charged Billy with the murder of Sheriff William Brady. Throughout the entire war, Billy was the only one of those seven or eight assassins to face a jury. He was found guilty on April 13 and sentenced to be hanged in Lincoln on Friday, May 13, between the hours of 9 A.M. and 3 P.M. Billy the Kid now sent Governor Wallace three letters protesting his innocence and pleading with him to honor his earlier promise of amnesty. Wallace ignored the mail.

On April 15, the county began transferring the Kid by buckboard from Mesilla to Lincoln. Seven riders surrounded the vehicle. On April 21, the procession reached the courthouse jail. The Kid was incarcerated on the second floor, northeast corner, overlooking the Wortley Hotel across the street.

On May 27, Garrett left his deputies James Bell and Bob Olinger guarding the Kid while he rode over to the mining village of White Oaks to collect taxes. Early in the afternoon of the following day, Olinger placed his shotgun in the gun cabinet and escorted a few prisoners across the street to the Wortley for a bite to eat. He left Bell and the Kid playing cards.

A few minutes later Billy asked to visit the outside privy. Bell checked Billy's leg irons and wrist cuffs, then led him downstairs to the toilet. Coming back inside the courthouse, Billy started upstairs with Bell following. When about halfway, the Kid either snatched Bell's revolver out of its holster or had a six-shooter inside his shirt, having most likely removed the weapon from under the privy seat. The Kid turned and shot Bell once, perhaps twice. The deputy stumbled downstairs, through the door, and into the yard. He expired in the arms of caretaker Gottfried Gauss.

The Kid then hobbled over to the gun cabinet, removed Olinger's shotgun, stepped to the window overlooking the street, and waited for the other deputy. When Olinger came running up, Billy allegedly said, "Hello, Bob," then fired both barrels.

It took Billy the Kid until three o'clock to get out of town, primarily because he spent so long getting a leg iron removed from one ankle. Even so, the swinging metal caused the horse to buck him off repeatedly. The Kid finally tied the iron to his leg and rode away.

Everyone now assumed the Kid would go to Mexico or perhaps disappear somewhere in Texas.

Instead, the Kid went to Fort Sumner, perhaps out of a death wish. Garrett had once lived in Fort Sumner and knew everybody there. Pat Garrett's wife had been born and raised there. How could Billy possibly expect to hide in that community? Billy perhaps had a girlfriend there, as so many biographers believe, or he may have just wanted to be around friends.

Nevertheless, somewhere around June 11, Garrett received word that the Kid was indeed in Fort Sumner. On the afternoon of June 13, Garrett and two deputies, Thomas C. "Kip" McKinney and John William Poe, reached Fort Sumner. After scouting around until well after dark, the three men went down to the old officers' quarters to wake up and talk with Pete Maxwell, who seemed to know everything and everybody in town. Maxwell came closer than any citizen in the area to being in charge. Garrett left his two deputies outside on the porch while he went inside, sat down on the edge of the bed, slid his holster around to near the middle of his back for comfort, woke Maxwell up, and began questioning him.

As midnight approached, Billy the Kid came stepping briskly down a path, hopped up on the porch, and walked toward the deputies, reportedly to cut off a slice from a side of beef hanging nearby. The porch roof cast heavy shadows due to a full moon, but the Kid knew his way and was moving along when he stumbled across two unrecognizable Anglos a few minutes after midnight. Jerking out his gun, the Kid asked in a strained and worried voice, "Who are you?" The two men asked the same question.

Obviously hesitating to kill strangers, men he must have assumed were friends of Maxwell, the Kid turned and entered Pete Maxwell's bedroom. With his gun in his hand, and stepping to the foot of the bed, he suddenly noticed a figure sitting there. He paused, again hesitating to perhaps kill a friend of Maxwell. So the Kid cocked his weapon and hoarsely whispered, "*¿Quién es? ¿Quién es?*" (Who is it? Who is it?)

It is doubtful that he ever heard the roar of Garrett's six-shooter.

Henry McCarty, alias Henry Antrim, alias Kid Antrim, alias Kid, alias William H. Bonney, alias Billy the Kid is buried in the Fort Sumner Cemetery.

See also: ANTRIM, WILLIAM HENRY HARRISON; BELL, JAMES W.; BOWDRE, CHARLES; COGHLAN, PATRICK; EVANS, JESSE J.; GARRETT, PATRICK; LINCOLN COUNTY WAR; OLINGER, ROBERT; WHITEHILL, HARVEY HOWARD

BISBEE Massacre

Daniel Dowd, generally known as "Big Dan," had terrorized southern Arizona and was wanted for cattle theft as well as a stage holdup near Benson. But on December 8, 1883, he and four gunmen—Owen W. Sample, James "Tex" Howard, Daniel Kelly, and William Delaney—pulled their guns and entered the Goldwater/Casteñada Store in Bisbee with intentions of robbing it. The event has since been known as the Bisbee Massacre. Depending upon which accounts one reads, the robbers left with between $900 and $3,000. They also left behind four dead innocent bystanders, who had happened to be in the wrong place at the wrong time. One of them was a woman, Anna Roberts, and another was a deputy sheriff, Tom Smith. A fifth person, Albert Nolly, would die later of his wounds.

The gang itself scattered, but Bisbee deputy sheriff William A. "Billy" Daniels picked up the scent and would not give up. Posses finally quit traveling with him, but Daniels methodically kept to the scattered trails, snatching Daniel Kelly at Deming, New Mexico. A Mexican informant led him across the border to Sabinal, a tiny town north of Corralitos, Chihuahua. Daniels, disguised as an ore buyer, entered Sabinal, arrested Dowd, and soon had him jailed in Tombstone, Arizona. At Minas Prietas, Sonora, he put leg irons on William Delaney. Meanwhile, other officers arrested Red Sample and Tex Howard near Clifton, Arizona. All these prisoners went to trial in Tombstone, Arizona, were found guilty, and were sentenced to be hanged. The territory erected a five-man scaffold, an instrument of death that Dowd called "a regular choking machine." The five men were all hanged at the same time, the leader Dowd strangling before his neck broke.

BITE The Dust

To die, ordinarily to die quickly, unexpectedly, violently, and out in the open; to fall forward on one's face and die—although the term can (rarely) apply to a natural death, most people who bite the dust are victims of a gunfight or other forms of violence. Only men are said to bite the dust, the term not generally applying to women and children. Early western movies and books made this expression popular.

BLAIR, John (?–?)

As a member of the Double Dobie gang of cattle thieves, John Blair hung around Tombstone, Arizona. When he caught smallpox, however, his rustler comrades isolated him in an adobe shack remote from the outlaw hangout and paid a Mexican woman to care for him. Within a week he died. His epitaph at the Tombstone boothill reads: *Johnny Blair. Died of smallpox and a cowboy threw a rope over his feet and dragged him to his grave.*

BLAYLOCK, Celia Ann (a.k.a. Mattie) (?–?)

Mattie Blaylock was probably a Dodge City prostitute who became the common-law wife of Wyatt Earp in 1878. She moved with Earp to Tombstone, Arizona, where Wyatt cast her aside and chose another woman, Josephine Marcus.

Mattie stayed with Wyatt's parents for a while, then returned to Arizona and resumed her former trade. She died in Pinal, Arizona, on July 7, 1888, from an overdose of laudanum (opium and alcohol). She was buried in Pinal.

See also: EARP, WYATT BERRY STAPP

BOLES, Charles E. (a.k.a. Black Bart) (1828?–1917?)

Charles Boles was reportedly born in England, his family taking him to New York in 1830. Boles (often spelled Bowles) grew weary of life as a farmer, so it did not take much coaxing to involve him in the California gold rush. When that didn't work out, he wound up near Decatur, Illinois, where he married and then joined the Union army. Following his 1865 discharge, he left his family and drifted up through Montana and Idaho, then back into California.

This time he went to work with a flour-sack mask and a double-barreled shotgun, performing his first stage holdup on July 26, 1875, somewhere around Sonora, California. He pulled two more stage robberies that same year, the task apparently becoming so much fun that on August 3, 1876, he not only robbed another California stage but left the driver a piece of poetry so awful it was almost good:

I've labored long and hard for bread
For honor and for riches,

But on my corns too long you've tred
You fine haired Sons of Bitches.

Black Bart, the PO 8

With the number of his stage robberies now numbering in the twenties, Black Bart was becoming quite a familiar figure to California authorities, who considered him polite. Oddly he was a bandit who traveled primarily on foot. He carried an axe for busting open strongboxes, plus a sharp knife for slicing mail bags.

Of course, robbing stagecoaches was a risky business, and Black Bart stopped a few bullets along the way, although nothing serious. His most grievous error turned out to be dropping his own handkerchief during a stage robbery on November 3, 1883. California private detective Harry Morse traced the laundry mark through San Francisco right back to Charles E. Boles. James B. Hume, a Wells Fargo detective, assisted by Morse and city police, arrested Bart at his San Francisco home. On November 21, 1883, he entered San Quentin for a six-year term, becoming a model prisoner. The state released him in January 1888. What happened to him after that is anyone's guess.

According to Wells Fargo, Black Bart had robbed them of about $7,000. No one ever estimated how much he took from the passengers.

See also: HUME, JAMES B.

BOND, Jim (a.k.a. Jack) (1853?–1881)

Jim Bond was a Texas cowboy who signed on with the Frontier Battalion, Texas Rangers, at El Paso. However, Bond and fellow lawman Len Peterson were terminated by Capt. George W. Baylor after Baylor learned that the pair had secretly given information to a band of rustlers led by Frank Stevenson, an outlaw later sent to prison. Bond and Peterson stole a "fine pair of carriage horses" from El Paso's mayor and fled west. Bond alighted in New Mexico's San Simon Valley, where he rustled cattle. During a riotous spree at Deming, Bond rode his horse up onto a porch separating the Harvey House Restaurant from the Wells Fargo & Co. offices at the railroad depot. Frightened patrons frantically hollered for help; Deputy Dan Tucker and his shotgun responded. When confronted, Bond jerked out his six-shooter, but Tucker blasted the would-be badman out of the saddle, killing him instantly. A newspaper reporter chided Bond for his attempt to shoot it out, writing, "He failed to get there, and now he peacefully sleeps beneath the daisies."

See also: BAYLOR, GEORGE WYTHE; TUCKER, DAVID

BOOT, Joe (1871–1901)

Joe Boot has a claim to fame that nobody knows—his true name. Regardless of how his mother christened her son when he was born in Ohio, Boot goes down in the history books only as a 28-year-old stagecoach robber, and an inept one at that. When he finally made his mark, it was with a female outlaw named Pearl Hart. Pearl is how and why Joe Boot is remembered.

On July 15, 1899, Boot and Pearl robbed the Globe-Phoenix stagecoach. During their getaway, completely frazzled, the pair crawled into some brush for a quick nap. When they awoke they found themselves staring up at a dozen Winchester muzzles, with the grim eye of a posseman staring down each sight. Being captured so easily, however, was only part of Boot's embarrassment. Newspapers as well as the officers started poking fun at this desperado with a girl boss. Who could respect an outlaw like that?

Joe Boot received a sentence of 30 years in the Arizona Territorial Prison, but after two years, on February 6, 1901, he became a trustee and then escaped, presumably into Mexico. No one ever heard from him again, so maybe he wasn't so stupid after all.

See also: HART, PEARL

BOOT Hill

The name "Boot Hill" can apply to any cemetery where residents or visitors have died with their boots on. The hill usually refers to a hill of dirt covering a grave, but it can also refer to a hilltop where bodies are buried. The Boot Hill association requires, however, that death must have occurred by gunfire, hanging, or lynching. A locality can even have more than one Boot Hill.

The first and most famous western Boot Hill is in Tombstone, Arizona. Boot Hill is its actual name, although only a small percentage of its residents were gunmen. The same applies to the Boot Hill at El Paso, Texas. It is but a small chunk of Concordia Cemetery, because only a minority of residents buried there actually died with their boots on.

On any particular day in Tombstone, dozens of people can be found wandering past weatherbeaten graves scattered among the rocky mounds and sagebrush. Tombstone historian Ben Traywick expressed the scene perfectly when he wrote, "In this old cemetery ravaged by time and the elements of nature, are the last resting places of those who made Tombstone fascinating, colorful and exciting; the young and the old, the coward and the brave, the weak and the strong, the merchant and the gunfighter, the miner and the gambler, the murdered and the murderer, the prostitute and the wife, and the scripture reader and the drunkard."

See also: GUNFIGHT AT THE OK CORRAL

BORDER Draw

Sometimes known as the "cross draw," in this technique the six-shooter is holstered on the left hip with the butt forward but reached with the right hand. (For left-handed people it would be just the opposite.) Such a rig would also be particularly advantageous for gamblers (or gunmen) sitting in chairs with arms on each side. It could be useful for anyone wearing a long coat while standing, riding, or walking. As a practical matter, however, while the border or cross draw looks good in the movies, few lawmen or outlaws practiced it.

BORDER Shift

A border shift is the passing or tossing of a six-gun from one hand to the other. This looks flashy in the movies and on television, and it sounds great in pulp fiction. Reality was something else, however. Long-haired Jim Courtright was the only gunman ever acknowledged to have used the border shift. He allegedly tried it on Luke Short, who shot him dead for his trouble.

See also: COURTRIGHT, TIMOTHY ISAIAH; SHORT, LUKE

BOUNTY Hunter

This term refers to someone who hunts outlaws for the bounty, the reward on their head, the money usually being paid by federal, state, or county officials, although bankers and railroad tycoons tended to get involved also. The bounty was generally offered for capturing or killing the wanted individuals. Practically all law enforcement officers, from U.S. marshals down to constables and Texas Rangers, considered bounty hunting as part of their job, a supplement to their income. Where life had little value, death often had a price. Thus came the bounty hunter.

BOWDRE, Charles (1848–1881)

Charlie Bowdre was a pal of Billy the Kid, but he was also a man caught between desires to be a fighter and to be left alone so he could farm. He was born in Mississippi around 1848. He and Josiah "Doc" Scurlock arrived in Lincoln, New Mexico, around 1875, and purchased (on terms) a ranch on the Ruidoso River. He married Manuela Herrera, probably of Fort Sumner, San Patricio, or Lincoln, New Mexico. Calling Charlie "indecisive" would be an understatement. He evidently tried to be a peacemaker, but he was to be as awkward at that as at being an outlaw.

Sheriff Pat Garrett and his posse, after ambushing the Billy the Kid gang in Fort Sumner, New Mexico, on December 19, 1880, and killing gang member Tom O'Folliard, closed in on Bowdre and others at an isolated, one-room rock cabin, in bitter cold, at Stinking Springs. The lawmen surrounded the building at about two o'clock in the morning of December 23. The structure had no door; the outlaws were sleeping inside, and their horses were tethered outside. As the sun came up, Charlie Bowdre stepped through the doorway, a nose bag in his hand, intending to feed his horse. Garrett and the posse members immediately commenced firing, hitting Bowdre in the leg and body. Bowdre reeled toward the lawmen, his hands outstretched, saying words like "I wish, I wish . . ." Then he collapsed and died in the snow. The remaining outlaws surrendered.

Garrett sent a wagon for Bowdre's body and informed Manuela, Charlie's wife, of his death. Pat paid for a burying suit out of his own pocket. Charlie Bowdre is buried in the Fort Sumner cemetery alongside Billy the Kid and Tom O'Folliard.

See also: BILLY THE KID; GARRETT, PATRICK; LINCOLN COUNTY WAR

BOWE, Thomas (1847?–1884)

Bowe is an enigma, due to a dearth of data. Nevertheless, there is sufficient documentary evidence to reveal that Tom Bowe often reveled in unnecessary violence. A newspaper account offered a brief physical description, noting that Bowe "is about 30 years of age, five feet 5 or 6 inches in height, slim build, dark complexion with dark hair and mustache, generally goes with head and eyes cast down, and wears his hat low down on his forehead. He is Irish and talks with a slight Irish accent. Usually wears dark shirt and clothes, and goes without shirt collar."

An unsubstantiated rumor said he killed a man at Pueblo, Colorado, in 1872 and fled to Santa Fe, only to be run out of town for fractious misbehavior. Bowe next turned up in Arizona, where he was suspected of stagecoach robberies but was never arrested.

With two other ne'er-do-wells, Tom Bowe debuted in Silver City, New Mexico, during the winter of 1874. During the following spring, he entered Ward's Dance Hall and argued with Jack Clark. Tom jerked out his six-shooter and fired. Clark died on the spot. Although Tom fled to the surrounding hills, Grant County sheriff Harvey Whitehill and a squad of citizen volunteers soon had him in tow. However, all charges were dropped.

On the night of October 5, 1877, Bowe went on a gambling spree with the respected Silver City saloon operator Richard "Dick" Howlett. According to newspapers, the pair had been amicably consorting for several days, but on this particular night—during a card game that also included Grant County's first sheriffs, Richard Hudson and John Justice—Bowe's stack of chips dwindled. Unwisely, though in a jesting, friendly fashion, Howlett chided Bowe's card-playing ability, behavior that Hudson cautioned him about. With a particularly large pot on the table, which Bowe was attempting to win, Howlett called Bowe's bluff. Bowe lost. Incensed at what he perceived as ridicule and agitated at his monetary misfortune, Tom Bowe pulled his six-gun and shot Richard Howlett dead.

Bowe fled to the nearby hills, where friends "helped him to a horse, blankets, food, arms and ammunition." Reportedly he fled to Mexico, then to California, and finally to New York City. Later he "tired of life in the metropolis" and left for Montana. Seven years after the murder of Richard Howlett, Thomas Bowe was arrested and extradited from Montana to New Mexico Territory, where his murder case was ultimately dismissed.

See also: WHITEHILL, HARVEY HOWARD

BRAZELTON, William "Bill" Whitney (1851?–1878)

Bill Brazelton, originally from Missouri, by the age of 15 had reportedly killed a man. By the age of 26, this ex-circus performer had drifted throughout California and then down to Tucson, Arizona Territory, where he found employment at Robert Leatherwood's corrals. Exceedingly strong and a crack shot, Bill gained the admiration of several rough-and-tumble Tucsonites. He teamed up with a fellow employee at the corral, and the youthful pair left for work in a gristmill. But hardworking and industrious as the boys appeared to be, Brazelton had a secret occupation, that of stagecoach robber. Just over the territorial line in southwest New Mexico, this flour-sack-wearing bandit had been plying his trade. Nobody seemed to notice, or especially care, that Bill Brazelton was frequently absent from the gristmill.

Before long, however, investigative leads started pointing in the direction of Brazelton's buddy at the mill, David Nemitz. Nemitz was finally arrested, but he blamed Brazelton for the holdups and offered Pima County sheriff Charles Shibell a deal—he would help the lawmen trap Brazelton. On the night of August 19, 1878, the officers secreted themselves along the road in the surrounding brush. When Brazelton arrived to make preparations for holding up the incoming stage, the lawmen ordered him to surrender. Other stories indicate that they simply shot him. At any rate, shotgun blasts cut him to pieces, and he died on the spot. Further investigation implicated Brazelton in at least nine stagecoach robberies in Arizona and New Mexico. The coroner's jury exonerated the lawmen, and the outlaw was laid to rest on August 20, 1878. This time he did not wear his flour-sack mask.

BREAKENRIDGE, William M. (a.k.a. Uncle Billy) (1846–1931)

One of the West's most famous lawmen, Tombstone's deputy, William "Uncle Billy" Breakenridge, came out of Wisconsin, where he had been born on Christmas Day, 1846, became a deputy sheriff at Phoenix, Arizona, and then went to work as a civil engineer in the mines at Huachuca, Arizona. By January 1880 he had moved to Tombstone, Arizona, and become a deputy sheriff.

On the night of March 15, 1881, a group of highway men struck the Benson-bound stage, killing the driver, Eli Philpot, and a Montana passenger, a miner named Peter Roering. Two posses set out in pursuit, one led by two Earp brothers and another by the Cochise County sheriff, John Behan. Breakenridge rode with Behan. Neither group caught the outlaws.

On June 22, a whiskey barrel exploded in the Arcade Saloon, and half the business district of Tombstone burned. Breakenridge did as much as anybody to put out the flames and afterward became a founding member of the rescue hook-and-ladder company. By now Tombstone seemed alive with Cowboy/Earp factions, some of which Breakenridge managed to avoid while retaining his position as a deputy.

On the night of March 25, 1882, a group of Cowboys descended upon the Tombstone Mill and Mining Company to rob it, which they did, but they also killed employee Martin R. Peel. On March 28, Sheriff Behan sent Breakenridge and a posse to the Chandler Ranch in hope of bringing in Billy Grounds and Zwingle Hunt. Breakenridge reached the ranch, where his posse trapped both men inside a cabin. As the deputies shot it out with someone at the back door, Billy Grounds tried to escape through the front. He and Breakenridge commenced firing at one another; Breakenridge took a wound in the hand, but Grounds was still no match for the deputy's shotgun. Grounds died on March 30, the *Tombstone Nugget* noting that "he was an outlaw, a robber, and possibly an assassin, but that did not justify the undertaker in burying him in a perfectly nude condition, with the blood from the wounds in his head dry and clotted on his face."

Billy Breakenridge continued as a deputy, making numerous arrests, acting as census enumerator, and even unsuccessfully campaigning for Cochise County sheriff. After his defeat, his career as a deputy ended. During the late 1920s, with the assistance of author William Macleod Raine, he wrote an autobiography that appeared in 1928. It was entitled *Helldorado: Bringing the Law to the Mesquite,* an account definitely pro-Cowboy and anti-Earp. Its strength was its first-person commentary of events, points of view different from the norm; its weakness was a tendency to misstate, twist, or omit known facts. Uncle Billy Breakenridge died in Tucson at the age of 84 on January 31, 1931.

See also: BEHAN, JOHN; EARP, WYATT; GROUNDS, WILLIAM A.; HUNT, ZWINGLE

BROCIUS, William (a.k.a. Curly Bill) (1845?–?)

No one knows when or where Curly Bill Brocius (whose legitimate name may have been Graham or Bresnaham) was born or called home; some reports say Henry County, Indiana, others Missouri. It could have been in or around El Paso, Texas. On May 20, 1878, he and a man named Robert "Dutch" Martin attempted to rob an army stage carrying a Lieutenant Butler and two soldiers the 45 miles between El Paso, Texas, and Mesilla, New Mexico. In the process, the gunmen wounded the enlisted men, got no money, and were themselves pursued into Mexico, where the desperados were arrested by Mexican authorities and handed over to the Rangers. Lt. John B. Tays of the Texas Rangers described the outlaws as members of the John Kinney gang, operating north of Mesilla in the Rio Grande Valley. Tried and sentenced to five years in the Texas penitentiary for robbery and attempted murder, Brocius and his two accomplices dug under the adobe wall and escaped from the Ysleta jail on November 2, 1878. When next heard from, in the late 1880s, Brocius was in southern Arizona.

On October 28, Brocius and friends were drunkenly wandering through Tombstone and firing revolvers in the air. City marshal Fred White pursued Brocius off Allen Street to the rear of a building, where he demanded Brocius's gun. Wyatt Earp came running up, throwing his arms around Brocius from behind just as Curly Bill pulled his weapon from its holster, apparently intending to surrender it. White grabbed the gun barrel, and the weapon fired, the bullet striking the marshal in the left part of his groin. Earp clubbed Brocius to the ground and arrested him. White died a day later, but the shooting was declared accidental. Brocius went free after spending two months in jail, but within weeks he had ridden into Charleston, a Cowboy (that is, rustler) hangout. Brocius slung two belts of cartridges over his shoulder and, with a revolver in one hand and a Henry rifle in the other, shot up the town. No one openly said a word.

On May 19, 1881, Curly Bill tangled with Cowboy Jim Wallace, himself a desperado. Wallace put a bullet through the neck of Brocius. It exited through the cheek, luckily missing all the bones.

In early December, Pima county indicted William Brocius and three others on charges of stealing 19 head of cattle worth $285. On March 25, 1882, the *Tombstone Epitaph* published a highly questionable account of the Whetstone Mountains killing of Curly

Bill Brocius by Wyatt Earp. Questionable it may have been, but the fact was that no one ever saw Curly Bill again.

See also: COWBOYS; EARP, VIRGIL; EARP, WYATT; GUNFIGHT AT THE OK CORRAL; HOLLIDAY, JOHN HENRY

BROWN, Henry Newton (1857–1884)

Henry Newton Brown was born at Cold Spring Township near Rolla, Missouri, but became a buffalo hunter in Texas during the early 1870s. Around 1876, he worked for The House, the political and financial machine run by Lawrence Murphy in Lincoln, New Mexico. After that he became a cowboy for John Chisum and then joined the Regulators, frequently riding in company with Billy the Kid during the Lincoln County War. When the Kid and several others shot down Sheriff William Brady and Deputy George Hindman on April 1, 1878, questions arose as to whether it was Henry Newton Brown who had created the disturbance at the Ellis Store that lured the lawmen into walking up the street, or whether Brown, with the Kid and possibly six others, had been participants in the execution of the lawmen. Three days after the Brady killing, on April 4, Brown, the Kid, and others were involved in the Gunfight at Blazer's Mill, during which Buckshot Roberts and Dick Brewer died. Brown was also a survivor of the McSween home during the Five-Day Siege in July 1878. Shortly after that, Brown went to work as a cowboy for George Littlefield's XIT Ranch, near Tascosa, Texas.

Brown allegedly did not smoke, drink, or gamble. One person described him as around five feet six inches tall with brown hair and blond mustache. He frequently wore something akin to a business suit, with his trousers outside the boots but a kerchief tied around the neck, cowboy style. He was quiet but sometimes surly and was easily provoked.

Following his stint on George Littlefield's ranch, Brown worked as a deputy sheriff in Oldham County, Texas, as a constable in Tascosa, and in July 1882 as a city marshal in Caldwell, Kansas. He left the last position in January 1883, the grateful townspeople giving him a gold-mounted Winchester rifle.

In March Brown returned to Caldwell, resumed his duties, and killed two men, one an Indian who was ordered to leave town and didn't, the other the son of a gang leader whom lawmen had chased into Hunnewell, Kansas. On March 24, 1884, Brown married a local girl, Alice Levagood, but on April 30, 1884, he and his deputy Ben Wheeler, with two confederates named William Smith and John Wesley, robbed the bank at Medicine Lodge, Kansas. During the uproar Wheeler shot cashier George Geppert, and Brown killed the bank president, E. W. Payne. In their rush to escape, the desperadoes ignored the money but surrendered to a posse a brief distance from town. Shortly after dark, a mob stormed the jail, which was nothing more than a small house. Following a scuffle, Brown made it to an alley, where a shotgun blast nearly tore him in two. A wounded Wheeler and the other two bank robbers were dragged to a tree and lynched.

See also: BILLY THE KID; LINCOLN COUNTY WAR; WHEELER, BENJAMIN F.

BROWN, James Madison (?–1892)

Brown's place of birth and early life are obscure, although he likely was born in Alabama and grew up in Texas. He enters historical focus on February 15, 1876, after being elected sheriff of Lee County. Following a fairly quiet initial two months in office, for reasons unknown, several men ambushed him with shotguns, leaving him severely wounded but alive.

Nearly a year later, on May 4, 1877, Brown killed Hugh McKeown, the marshal of Giddings, Texas (the seat of Lee County). Brown did allow McKeown's small son to step away from his father before shooting the man at close range with a shotgun blast to the head. The newspapers muttered something about a feud between the two, although McKeown's name never surfaced in terms of the earlier Brown ambush. Anyway, a jury acquitted Brown.

Thirteen days later Brown killed attorney S. S. Brooks. Perhaps because shooting lawyers wasn't all that serious a crime in San Saba, no indictments were handed down, and Brown never faced a jury.

Brown then legally hanged longtime outlaw and gunman William Preston Longley, better known as Bill Longley. On October 11, 1878, Longley dropped through the trapdoor and from there went straight to the Giddings cemetery.

On January 10, 1880, Sam Sparks followed Longley to the cemetery, Sam being one of the shooters accused of ambushing Brown with shotguns back in 1876. Local opinion had it, however, that Brown had hired two men to kill Sparks. While the evidence seemed sufficient, a local grand jury never acted upon it.

The next shooting fray occurred on April 22, 1881, when Henry H. Wessen attempted to kill his ex-wife. Brown and a posse hurried out to Yegua Creek to seek the old man. The lawmen trapped him in a corn crib, and during a wild gunfight, they shot him to death.

In the meantime, one of Brown's daughters had eloped; Brown apparently killed William Owens, the young suitor. Following this slaying, in November 1884, Brown left office, deciding to make his living thereafter through a stable of racing horses. His animals raced in all the better-known eastern tracks, and James Brown eventually became a "turfman." Folks respectfully referred to him as "Colonel Brown."

On September 3, 1892, Brown shot it out with the Chicago police as they conducted a series of raids on Garfield Park. He killed two officers but was himself slain in the process. He was buried in Oakwood Cemetery at Fort Worth.

See also: LONGLEY, WILLIAM PRESTON

BROWN'S Park

Brown's Park—after the Hole-in-the-Wall—became the most popular rendezvous for men running from the law. It comprised a rugged, 40-mile-long, six-mile-wide area along Wyoming's Green River, overlooked by the Diamond and Cold Spring Mountains. The Wild Bunch in particular utilized Brown's Park (oftentimes called Brown's Hole). Brown's Park overlapped portions of Utah, Colorado, and Wyoming, which meant that the possibility of lawmen from all three states being in that particular area at one time was small. Tales are still told of how the Wild Bunch would throw parties, particularly around Thanksgiving, inviting the local residents over for turkey and trimmings. The outlaw Harry Tracy, following his escape from a jail in Utah, spent a brief time here in 1898.

See also: CARVER, WILLIAM RICHARD; CASSIDY, BUTCH; HOLE-IN-THE-WALL; KILPATRICK, BENJAMIN ARNOLD; LAY, WILLIAM ELLSWORTH; LOGAN, HARVEY; PARKER, ROBERT LEROY; ROBBERS ROOST; SUNDANCE KID; WILD BUNCH

BRYANT, Charles (a.k.a. Black Face Charlie) (?–1891)

"I want to get killed in one hell-firin' minute of action," Charlie Bryant once said. He would get his wish.

His odd nickname stemmed from black-powder burns seared into his face during his youth by a weapon fired perhaps accidentally, or perhaps intentionally. At any rate, he was born in Wise County, Texas, and by 1890 had become a member of the Dalton Gang. On May 9, 1891, he assisted the Dalton brothers in train robbery near Wharton, Oklahoma. Shortly afterward, the gang held up another train, at Red Rock.

Charlie became seriously ill and never arrived with the Dalton brothers in Coffeville, Kansas. The gang dropped him off at a hotel in Hennessey, Oklahoma; it wasn't long before U.S. Deputy Marshal Edward Short got the news that on outlaw happened to be holed up in the hotel. The officer walked in, arrested the suspect, placed him in handcuffs, and on August 3, 1891, locked him in the express car of a train bound for Wichita, Kansas, where the nearest federal court was located.

Bryant seemed so ill that neither Short nor the express messenger paid him much attention. When Short visited the rest room, he handed his six-shooter to the messenger, who merely stuck it in a pigeonhole. Then, as the employee busied himself sorting mail, Bryant eased over and jerked the weapon out of the mail slot, just as Short reentered the car carrying his rifle. Both men began shooting, Bryant emptying the revolver, Short working his rifle lever. Short went down with several bullets in him; he would die within minutes, but not before putting a rifle bullet through Bryant's chest. The slug broke Bryant's backbone on its way out, causing instant death. When the train stopped at Waukomis, Oklahoma, both bodies were laid out on the station platform.

See also: DALTON BROTHERS

BUFFALOED

The term refers to being struck across the head with a revolver barrel. Lawmen were essentially the practitioners of this technique. If done solidly, it had the practical effect of instantly taking the fight out of an opponent. Of course, lawmen risked the possibility of the weapon accidentally discharging and wounding or killing their opponent, or even an innocent bystander. Furthermore, lawmen often ruined their own weapon in the process, an act that could have serious personal consequences, especially if the intended victim emerged unhurt or his friends decided to intervene.

BULL, John Edwin (1836–1929)

John Bull, a gunman and a gambler, was also an Englishman, although when and why he arrived in the United States is uncertain. He wandered from the Great Lakes to Seattle, but his trail wasn't first identified and studied until 1862, during the Salmon River gold rush in California. He was a rather short man with a dark, full beard, and dark eyes. In August 1862 he and a man named Fox rode into Gold Creek, Montana, posing as lawmen in quest of three horse thieves. They captured one, C. W. Spillman, without resistance, but William B. Arnett and B. F. Jermagin seemed split as to whether to run or fight; Jermagin stuck up his hands, while Arnett reached for a weapon. Bull killed him with a shotgun. Oddly, Arnett was lowered into his grave still clutching monte cards in his left hand and a six-shooter in the other. Of the two prisoners, Jermagin convinced a miner's court that he was a good, honest fellow at heart, and so he was released. Spillman did not seem repentant, so the miners lynched and buried him alongside Arnett. The name Gold Creek thereafter became Hangtown.

Four years later, in 1866, Bull put in an appearance at Virginia City, Nevada, not as a lawman but as a gambler. There he met another English gambler named, Langford Peel, who had served in the U.S. Army and then entered the gambling profession. Unlike Bull, Peel was tall and slender, with blue eyes and blond beard. He had also killed a man, faro dealer Oliver Rucker, in 1858 at Salt Lake City. The two antagonists had shot each other down with revolvers, then continued firing until their weapons clicked empty. Once both had fallen to the saloon floor, Peel squirmed and crawled over to his still gasping opponent and buried a Bowie knife in his chest. Rucker died.

Peel went to Virginia City, Nevada, reportedly killing at least six people there and in different localities around the state. In 1867, he and John Bull teamed up as gambling partners. The two men for a lot of reasons did not like one another, but they gambled their way through Virginia City to Salt Lake City, and on to Helena, Montana. There in the Greer Brothers' Exchange Saloon on the night of July 22, 1867, the jealousy between the two started smoldering and then flaming. Remarks were exchanged, the men took to slapping one another. Bull finally yelled that he was unarmed but that he would get armed and return in a few minutes. With that he left the table.

Bull ran to his room, wrote letters to family and friends, scratched out a makeshift will, then went back downstairs, only to learn that Peel had gone down the street with his girlfriend, Belle Neil, to Chase's Gambling Hall. As the two lovers stood together, Bull walked up, shot Peel three times, then stood over the fallen man's body and shot him again, in the head. The murder trial ended in a hung jury, and Bull never faced the judge again. Bull now rode the Union Pacific Railroad from one town to the next, gambling and then moving on. At Promontory Point, Utah, Bull married. His wife bore three of his children; what happened to them is anybody's guess, since Bull was soon back on the road again, spending considerable time in Omaha with gamblers and confidence men.

In 1872, Englishman Tom Allen and German-born Ben Hogan fought in Omaha for the so-called heavyweight championship of the world. Bull backed Hogan, but during the third round, Hogan, who was taking a pummeling, sank to the floor holding his groin and claiming foul. Bull leaped into the ring screaming victory for his man, but only the hand of Allen was raised. Fights started outside the ring, and a man was killed.

By 1879, Bull had reached Denver, where he was repeatedly arrested for gambling and running confidence games. His life continued in that fashion until reaching Spokane, where in 1898 he and Frisky Barnett left the People's Theater in good humor. Yet within a block Barnett had jabbed the lighted end of his cigar into Bull's eye, and both men pulled pistols. When the smoke cleared, a female bystander lay seriously wounded, Barnett had lost a finger, and Bull lay sprawled on the sidewalk with four bullets in him. Barnett paid a fine of $10, the woman finally recovered, and Bull's bullet-mangled left arm was amputated at the shoulder. He recovered.

In 1921, a doctor at Excelsior Springs, Missouri, removed the last of Barnett's bullets from alongside Bull's windpipe. Eight years later, at Vancouver, British Columbia, on September 9, 1929, John Bull died at the age of 93.

BURDETT, Robert Lee (1882–1915)

Born in Travis County, Texas, after an undocumented stint as a city police officer somewhere, Burdett joined Company C of the Texas Rangers. He spent most of his time working around Fabens, 30 miles downstream along the Rio Grande from El Paso.

During the evening of June 8, 1915, after returning to South El Paso, he and his partner encountered a group of Mexican *braceros* (laborers) who had taunted them earlier in the day. The *braceros* now disappeared into an El Paso alley, only to be followed by the rangers, who decided to search them for weapons. At this point the shooting started, and the 32-year-old Robert Lee Burdett stopped a bullet with his chest. His body was shipped home to Austin.

See also: TEXAS RANGERS

BURNS, Edward (a.k.a. Bymes; Big Ed) (1855?–1930?)

"Big Ed" Burns was an enigmatic frontier personality. On his life there is a paucity of substantiated material, but he has nevertheless his meager place in history as a disreputable conman, desperado, gambler, and all around ne'er-do-well. He is thought to have been born in the Midwest. Later, however, "Big Ed" Burns would find a home near any town along the railroad tracks, as long as there were "tenderfeet" and natural-born suckers in the vicinity waiting to be taken.

His nickname was no misnomer. "Big Ed" stood over six feet tall and weighed over 200 pounds. With his fierce reputation for violence and mayhem and his short fuse, it was surprising that he did not thrash the local Deming, New Mexico, newspaper editor who publicly characterized him as a "notorious top and bottom fiend."

Burns had earned this reputation by using loaded dice to dupe players into betting against the possibility that the tops and bottoms of three rolled dice would total 21. Naturally, real sports were keenly aware that the tops and bottoms would add up to 21 every time—with honest dice. But chumps needed cheatin', or so thought "Big Ed."

Although always at odds with the law and frequently antagonistic toward people of his own ilk (he had difficulties with the Earps and J. J. "Off Wheeler" Harlan), Big Ed by most accounts survived

to old age, dying of natural causes in California during the Prohibition era.

BURNS, James D. (1860–1882)

On August 23, 1882, 22-year-old part-time Grant County, New Mexico, deputy sheriff James Burns arrived in Silver City from Paschal, a copper mining camp in the Burro Mountains. Normally the transplanted Texan (some accounts say he had been a deputy sheriff in Brown County) was well behaved, and he was considered an efficient officer. However, on this occasion James Burns arrived in Silver City in a drunken condition, at a time when the town's peace-keeping duties had temporarily been assigned to Deputy Sheriff Mahony, who was acting in the absence of Marshal G. W. Moore. At Sam Eckstein's Saloon, Burns either intentionally flourished or inadvertently exposed his six-shooter. Whether Mahony made the observation himself or responded to a citizen's complaint is undetermined, but in either event, he approached Burns, advising him to divest himself of the revolver. Burns declined, protesting that since he also was a deputy, he could tote a six-shooter. Mahony left the barroom, presumably to either get help or check on Burns's official status.

Mahony never returned, and Burns indulged in a spree that lasted all night and into the next day. On the following night, August 24, in the Centennial Saloon, Burns fired a shot that attracted the attention of Marshal Moore, who by now had returned to the city. Moore investigated and found a drunken Burns in the taproom gambling with Frank Thurmond (Lottie Deno's husband). Moore ordered the young man to accompany him outside. Burns refused, so Moore recruited Deputy William (Billy) McClellan and reentered the saloon through a side door. When Burns noticed the officers approaching, he jerked out his pistol. Standing nearby, however, was "Dangerous Dan" Tucker, also a Grant County deputy sheriff. All three lawmen now pointed weapons at their uproariously drunk brother of the badge, and had it not been for the intervention of John Gilmo, himself an ex-lawman (and future convict), shooting might have started. As it was, Gilmo talked Burns out of his weapon, and the explosive situation eased.

John Gilmo inexplicably later returned the six-shooter to Burns, and the inebriated deputy again commenced making threats against anyone attempting to arrest him. An exasperated Marshal Moore and Deputy McClellan quickly obtained a warrant for Burns and located their suspect inside the Centennial. This time they found Burns arguing with lawman Dan Tucker. At the words "We've got papers for you," Burns turned and commenced firing. Tucker, Moore, and McClellan fired simultaneously, but not wildly. Burns died on the spot.

As it turned out, the late Jim Burns did have friends, and they pooled their monetary resources for a prosecution fund. Eventually all three lawmen were arrested. Tucker was released on a $2,000 bond, and charges against him were dismissed. Moore and McClellan eventually went to trial and were acquitted.

See also: TUCKER, DAVID

BURNS, Tom (1854–1901)

Tom Burns, of English-Irish parents, was born in Boston, Massachusetts, but does not enter the historical record until March 9, 1881, at Visalia, California, when, during a saloon brawl, he tried to kill a man but merely shot the sombrero off his head. Burns was arrested for assault, and a judge subsequently sentenced him to two years in San Quentin. The state released him in January 1883. By 1886, Burns was in Arizona, and by 1893 in San Francisco, California, working for the Morris Detective Agency. Meanwhile, desperadoes Chris Evans and John Sontag had executed a series of train robberies in California's San Joaquin Valley. Lawmen had been slain. Rewards were being offered. Naturally, the Morris Detective Agency expressed an interest, and it sent operative Samuel Black to investigate. In May 1893, detective Tom Burns joined him. However, during a shootout on May 23, Black was severely wounded and retired from the chase. The outlaws escaped.

Wells Fargo detective John Thacker now became involved. He, U.S. Marshal George Gard, several Fresno County deputies, and Tom Burns moved into the San Joaquin Valley and on June 11 fought an all-night gun battle with Chris Evans and John Sontag. Come morning, the posse found a badly wounded John Sontag, helpless and immobilized, in a pile of manure and straw. A seriously wounded Evans stopped at a house a few canyons away and pleaded for help. The parties within reported him to the sheriff's office. Sontag died, and Evans was convicted of murder and sentenced to Folsom Prison for life. Although who killed whom became confusing in

terms of the bad guys, Tom Burns accepted the newspaper credit.

Burns filed for a share of the reward, afterward quarreling about it on the rear platform of a train with another operative, George Witty. Burns shot Witty in the hand, whereupon the two wrestled and fell off the train, the impact knocking both unconscious. Burns recovered first and thought he had killed Witty, but both men survived. Each put the incident behind them, although as time passed Burns acquired a reputation as a bully. A Pinal County, Arizona, housewife charged him with rape in August 1899.

Later, as an Arizona cowboy, Burns argued with a young ranch hand named Wallace. The youth shot Tom Burns off his horse, killing him instantly. The *San Francisco Chronicle* of June 20, 1901, described Burns as "Arizona's most Famous Gunfighter," but it noted that everyone was so happy to see Burns dead that the mourners "danced on his coffin."

BUSCADERO

A term originally applied to lawmen, it stems from the Spanish *buscador*, or *busca*, meaning to search, seek out, hunt, or pursue. Lawmen in particular often adopted this moniker, but American usage also applied it to fugitives hiding out in brush country.

Early American movies also invented the buscadero six-gun rig. The basic elements were a Mexican holster threaded through a slot in a wide cartridge belt. These looked flashy on such movie actors as Tom Mix, Buck Jones, William S. Hart, and Ken Maynard, although Bronco Billy Anderson became the first star to wear one, strapping it on during a 1903 western called *The Great Train Robbery*. Of all these individuals, Tom Mix should have known better, but he too was caught up in what he thought the public wanted. What the Hollywood studios primarily wanted was eye-catching flamboyance passing for reality. No genuine gunman, outlaw, or lawman ever wore anything remotely resembling the latter-day buscadero rig.

Hollywood also put together the tie-down rig, a picket string tying the holster tip to the wearer's leg. Original Western holsters never had holes in the tip. Guns riding low on the hip or leg, especially if tied down, made it difficult and uncomfortable for a wearer to mount and dismount a horse. Riders carried the gun belt high on the waist or wrapped it around the pommel; after dismounting, if anticipating trouble, they would loosen the belt to drop the holster down, not necessarily to accommodate a fast draw but for more comfortable, confident, and easy drawing and firing. An old-time gunman would have been less interested in a fast draw than in a secure and steady one. Incidentally, these rigs were not made for fist-fighting scenes. Guns fall out; holsters and belts get twisted and uncomfortable. To avoid this, movie actors usually had their gun rigs sewn to their clothes so that everything would stay in place during the brawling scenes. Revolvers would be fastened inside the holsters to keep them from falling out.

BUSHWHACKED

The term refers to ambushing someone from cover, specifically from behind trees, rocks, bushes, or brush. The assault is unexpected and usually at a distance, delivered with a rifle or shotgun. Guerrillas and marauders during the Civil War were particularly adept at bushwhacking, although manhunters like Tom Horn practiced it as a necessary part of their trade. It was simpler to kill a wanted man or an enemy than to risk being killed yourself in trying to capture him.

See also: HORN, TOM

CALAMITY Jane
See CANNARY, MARTHA JANE

CANNARY, Martha Jane (a.k.a. Calamity Jane)
(1844?–1903)

Martha Jane Cannary (the last name is sometimes spelled with one "n") is better known in history as "Calamity Jane." During her early teens, the family moved from Missouri to Wisconsin, where her father, Robert Cannary, became such a heavy drinker that after the Civil War she left home, supporting herself primarily as a prostitute. She later claimed to have been a stage driver, scout, and guide, but evidence—except for her word—is nonexistent. By 1876, probably in Wyoming, she acquired the name Calamity Jane, although why she got it historians haven't proved. Nevertheless, the two words "Calamity Jane"—and her alleged relationship with Western gunfighter Wild Bill Hickok—combined to make her a world-famous figure for over a century after her death.

What we know about her isn't much. There are no known photos of her in early life, and those that survive from later times reveal a woman in her forties or fifties, husky, muscular, short-haired, gruff, a mannish-appearing woman who cursed like a mule-skinner and had more miles on her than the San Francisco stage. There are no smiles in any of these photos; the truth is that she probably had very little to smile about. She was frequently jailed, had no par-ticular skills, and was such a poor gambler that she usually supported herself by prostitution. That she drank in excess and could spit tobacco juice farther than most men seems to be a given. Yet above all, she was a survivor—rugged, adventurous, independent, flamboyant, and strong minded.

She claimed to have ridden with Gen. George Crook's column into Montana, evidently posing as a man—but again evidence for this, other than her word, is lacking. In 1885 she supposedly married Clinton Burke, an El Paso, Texas, cab driver, although no records exist. They allegedly had a daughter, whom she reportedly turned over to St. Mary's Convent in Sturgis, South Dakota. (Other stories mention two children.) Otherwise, any of her marriages would have been the common-law variety.

Although Jane traveled occasionally with Buffalo Bill's Wild West show, history associates her primarily with Wild Bill Hickok, perhaps because Hickok often appeared as effeminate as Jane was mannish. Whether Jane and Wild Bild even met is debatable. All we know for certain is that she expressly wished to be buried beside him and came close to getting her wish. But that too is a puzzle. At one time their tombstones were pictured as side by side, but they now lie head to toe, Calamity Jane in the upper grave. Regardless, the facts are that she was, is, and remains one of the most recognizable females in western/frontier folklore.

See also: HICKOK, JAMES BUTLER

CANNON, A. B. (a.k.a. Add) (1865?–?)

Choosing a life of crime at a reasonably early age, A. B. "Add" Cannon, originally from Buffalo Gap, Texas, accompanied by a 19-year-old accomplice, Joe Brown, hijacked and shot a drummer (salesman) traveling between Abilene and Anson, Texas, on October 25, 1885. Apparently pleased with their new career as desperadoes, the pair waylaid and robbed a stagecoach on the following night as it traveled between Abilene and San Angelo. Now bent on a life of crime but imbued with a degree of calculating caution, the pair rode 200 miles south, to Kendall County, where on December 2, they held up a stagecoach.

The robberies aroused George Scarborough, the Jones County sheriff, as well as the Mitchell County sheriff and future U.S. Marshal Richard C. "Dick" Ware. They pursued the outlaws, capturing Cannon and Brown near Sweetwater, Nolan County, Texas. Charged with robbing the U.S. Mail, the robbers went to trial at San Antonio before a U.S. District Court.

The proceedings commenced on May 25, 1886, but the jury deadlocked. The two men made bail and were about to be released when Scarborough placed them under arrest for the Jones County robbery. On July 23 he incarcerated them in the Jones County jail at Anson.

Slightly over a month later, on the night of August 31, 1886, "Add" Cannon surprised the temporary jail guard William C. Glazner and beat him severely with a lead pipe wrapped in a towel. With his man down and unconscious, Cannon grabbed Glazner's revolver and fled the jail clad only in his underwear. Although Scarborough organized a posse early the next morning, the diligent search proved futile. Five days after the violent escape, Glanzer died of skull fractures.

A. B. "Add" Cannon was never apprehended.

See also: SCARBOROUGH, GEORGE ADOLPHUS

CANTLEY, Charles (1858–1895)

Charles L. Cantley first saw the light of day at Palestine, Anderson County, Texas, on May 5, 1858. Reportedly serving a stint with the Texas Rangers, Cantley, at the age of 25, moved to Silver City, New Mexico.

Grant County sheriff James Woods retained the youthful Texan as a deputy sheriff and jail guard, but on the morning of March 10, 1884, Cantley and another deputy, Steve Wilson, were overpowered by train robbers "Kit" Joy, Frank Taggart, Mitch Lee, George Washington Cleveland, convicted murderer Carlos Chávez, and suspected horse thief Charles Spencer. The desperadoes locked Cantley and Wilson in a cell and escaped, shooting their way out of town, although a posse captured them within hours. When Cantley caught up with the posse, he found Taggart and Lee on the verge of being lynched. Cantley grabbed a rifle and screamed that he would not permit a lynching so long as he was armed. So the posse disarmed him. Taggart and Lee were quickly suspended by the neck until dead.

Cantley continued as a deputy under Sheriff Woods's administration and later under his successor, Andrew B. Laird. Following elections of May 1890, Charles Cantley was elected marshal of Silver City, a position he retained for five successive terms.

Cantley did an admirable job of maintaining order and carrying out his duties, but he developed an addiction to liquor. In time he became aggressive and arbitrary. The more he drank, the more he enforced the law *his* way. On October 10, 1895, policeman Cantley approached attorney James S. Fielder in the White House Saloon. Cantley, obviously befuddled by drink, berated Fielder and challenged him to go for his gun, drawing his own revolver and firing two shots. Both missed. Fielder now commenced shooting, knocking Cantley to the ground with the first bullet. A second bullet finished him off. A coroner's jury ruled the killing justifiable, and so the city fathers began accepting applications for a new town marshal.

CANTON, Frank (a.k.a. Joe Horner) (1849–1927)

Frank Canton was born Joe Horner in Richmond, Virginia, but sometime in midlife he changed his name to Frank Canton; he has been known as Canton ever since. After the Civil War he moved to Texas, drove cattle to Nebraska, and some time around 1880 he served a couple of terms as sheriff of Johnson County, Wyoming. Along the way he became a detective for the Wyoming Stock Growers Association. In this field he played a preeminent role in the Johnson County War; he was later accused of the murder of John Tisdale, a rancher said to be a rustler.

From Wyoming Canton moved back to Oklahoma, where he served as a deputy sheriff and U.S.

deputy marshal. On one occasion he arrested a Lon McCool and during a struggle shot McCool in the face. McCool lived. During 1897, Canton showed up as a U.S. marshal in Alaska but reportedly went snowblind a year later. In 1907, when the territory of Oklahoma became a state, he became adjutant general of the national guard.

See also: JOHNSON COUNTY WAR

CAP-AND-BALL Gun

This single-shot revolver was loaded with loose powder and a ball; the weapon was fired by a percussion cap placed on the nipple of the chamber. The process could be slow and tedious, so each shot had to count. Nevertheless—movies, magazine illustrations, and expectations to the contrary—the cap-and-ball continued in the West for years after the Civil War, because metal cartridges were expensive. Later, as metal cartridges became less expensive and more easily available, most cowboys, lawmen, and outlaws made the transition.

CARNES, Herff A. (1879–1932)

Herff Carnes was born at Fairview, Wilson County, Texas, on May 23, 1879. During his youth Carnes must have heard exciting tales of lawmen versus outlaws, for on February 13, 1903, Herff enlisted in Capt. John R. Hughes's Company D, Texas Rangers, at El Paso, Texas.

One particular incident in 1906 caught Captain Hughes's attention. Violence associated with labor disputes had always been a concern of state law enforcement agencies, and the oilfields at Humble, Texas, were fertile ground. Rangers Herff Carnes, J. C. White, and Milam Wright were detailed to the scene to prevent loss of life as well as to prevent rioting and the destruction of property. In enforcing the law, those three men went up against 300 strikers and the strikers backed down.

After an eight-year stint with the Texas Rangers, during which he earned a distinguished law enforcement reputation, Herff Carnes joined the U.S. Mounted Customs Service and quickly became immersed in an extremely dangerous encounter and a very public controversy. Pascual Orozco, a general in the Mexican revolutionary forces, was arrested by U.S. Justice Department federal agents on June 27, 1915 at Newman, New Mexico, 20 miles northeast

of El Paso, Texas. Agents had earlier raided a warehouse and recovered 14 machine guns, 500 rifles, and 100,000 rounds of ammunition. Orozco was charged with Neutrality Act violations and posted a $7,500 bond. Three days later, the agents made another raid and recovered 346 rifles and 46,000 rounds of ammunition. The border area surged with rumor, innuendo, and conspiratorial gossip; the international line became a powder keg. Orozco jumped bail and with four friends fled east into the rugged and barely populated stretches of unfenced ranch country of West Texas.

After they butchered a calf belonging to rancher Dick Love, the bandits' trail was picked up by pursuing possemen, one of whom was Herff Carnes. On August 30, 1915, the posse caught up with Orozco at his camp near High Lonesome Mountain, nine miles from the Mexican border. The battle—or as some later claimed, the ambush—was over in a few minutes. Orozco and his four partners were dead. The 11-man posse was indicted for murder, but a Culberson County jury found the defendants not guilty.

At twilight on December 1, 1932, attempting to arrest suspected liquor smugglers crossing the Rio Grande downstream from Ysleta, Texas, U.S. Mounted Customs Inspector Herff A. Carnes was gunned down in an ambush. On December 3, at an El Paso hospital, the seasoned 53-year-old lawman died of his wounds.

See also: ALLISON, WILLIAM DAVIS; HUGHES, JOHN REYNOLDS

CARSON, Joe (1837–1880)

Originally from Knoxville, Tennessee, Joe Carson had ambled his way through northern Texas and reportedly hunted for gold in Colorado's Rocky Mountains before finally settling at East Las Vegas, New Mexico Territory, in 1879. There, due to the exceptionally corrupt city and county administration, he teamed up with the disreputable Hyman G. Neill, better known as "Hoodoo Brown," a leader of the legendary Dodge City Gang. Neill appointed Joe Carson as city marshal and Dave Mather, better known as "Mysterious Dave," as his chief deputy.

On January 22, 1880, Joe Carson and a part-time police buddy, Jack Lyons (later shot and killed at Rincon, New Mexico), attempted to quiet four cowboys. Thomas Jefferson House (also known as

Tom Henry), a 22-year-old Texan, seemed to be the leader of the heavily armed men. They may have been in the general area planning a raid on unattended livestock, as some residents suspected, but that night Tom and his pals, John Dorsey, Anthony Lowe, and "Big" Bill Randall, seemed to be relishing the saloons.

All four entered Close and Patterson's Saloon but failed to check their six-shooters. When 43-year-old Joe Carson stepped inside and attempted to disarm the party, the shooting started, most of it into the body of Carson. As he fell, Carson returned the fire. By some accounts, as many as 40 rounds altogether were expended.

Carson died with nine bullets in his body. "Big" Bill Randall was killed. Anthony Lowe had been shot through the middle and was unable for the moment either to run or die. Tom House and John Dorsey were both wounded but managed to flee.

A posse later surrounded the two wounded desperadoes at a farm house near Mora, New Mexico, and accepted their surrender. Returned to the vicinity of Las Vegas, and in the company of the wounded Anthony Lowe, who was removed from his jail cell, all three were led to the infamous "hanging windmill." As ropes were being placed around their necks, Joe Carson's widow—with a rifle in her hands—opened fire on the trio. Not to be outdone by a member of the fairer sex, the mob also opened fire. Joe Carson's killers died in the fusillade.

See also: MATHER, DAVID

CARVER, William Richard (a.k.a. News Carver; George W. Franks) (1868–1901)

Will carver was born in Wilson County, Texas, and as a young man worked as a cowboy on the Sixes Ranch in Sutton County, working with Sam and Tom Ketchum, and with Ben and George Kilpatrick. He grew up to become a gun-carrying member of the "old" as well as the "new" Black Jack Ketchum gang, a difference being that the difficult Tom Ketchum (Old Black Jack) tended to alienate his followers, whereas his brother Sam Ketchum (New Black Jack) had more personality. Both the old and the new Black Jack Ketchum gangs operated in Texas and New Mexico; the Wild Bunch in Montana and Wyoming provided a conduit whereby disgruntled members could shift back and forth between the two groups. Butch Cassidy, for instance, rode briefly with the Ketchum group as he waited for things to cool off up north.

Will Carver, as his friends called him, married Viana Byler, the 17-year-old daughter of Jake, in early 1892, but within months she died during pregnancy. It wasn't long before he took up with Laura Bullion, who was related in some way to his former wife's family. As for Sam Ketchum, he and Will Carver once operated a gambling house in San Angelo, Texas. During this period, Carver killed a man named Oliver C. Thornton.

During July 1899, the Black Jack gang held up a train near Folsom in New Mexico's northeast corner. The outlaws escaped with considerable money, eventually killing two lawmen who had pursued them into Turkey Creek Canyon, near Cimarron. Will Carver left the area, settling in with Butch Cassidy and the Wild Bunch in time to rob the First National Bank at Winnemucca, Nevada, on September 19, 1900. From there, Carver—taking Laura Bullion with him—went to Fort Worth with the Wild Bunch. There, on November 21, he posed with Butch Cassidy, the Sundance Kid, and two others for a famous photo displayed prominently in the photographer's outdoor window. Carver is standing on the left, in the derby hat. He was the first person in that photo to be recognized. Around this time, on December 1, 1900, Carver married Callie May Hunt, also known as Lillie Davis, who worked in a San Antonio brothel as one of Fannie Porter's girls. As for Laura, she took Lillie's place in the brothel.

The gang split up shortly afterward, Cassidy and Sundance going to South America and Carver rejoining the Black Jack Ketchum gang in the Southwest. Although never indicted, Will Carver is believed by some authorities to have been one of the slayers in 1896 of U.S. Deputy Marshal George Scarborough, killed at Triangle Springs in Triangle Canyon (later called Outlaw Canyon), approximately 20 miles southwest of San Simon, Arizona.

Will Carver drifted back to Texas, where he and George Kilpatrick (probably a brother to Ben Kilpatrick, the Tall Texan) entered Sonora, Texas, and while casing a bank, sought grain for their horses. Word reached Sheriff Elijah S. "Lige" Bryant on April 2, 1901, that these might be the men responsible for Thornton's slaying. The sheriff and four deputies stepped into the grain store, called on the two desperadoes to surrender, and the shooting started. One bullet hit Carver in his gun hand, and after that the killing was easy. Both men were shot to pieces, although Kilpatrick, with 14 wounds, survived and was released. Their horses were sold to pay for Carver's funeral; he was buried in the local Sonora cemetery.

See also: CASSIDY, BUTCH; KETCHUM, SAMUEL W.; KETCHUM, TOM; LAY, WILLIAM ELLSWORTH; SCARBOROUGH, GEORGE ADOLPHUS; SUNDANCE KID; TURKEY CREEK CANYON, BATTLE OF; WILD BUNCH

CASH, Edward (1873–1894)

Ed Cash wasn't your typical gunfighter, and in fact he probably wasn't a gunfighter at all. But his neighbors in this southeastern part of Coryell County, Texas, considered him difficult, mean at times, a person who took your cattle secretly, one at a time, and then dared you to do something about it. But even timid people who look the other way when someone walks off with their cows will sooner or later take a stand.

When Ed's neighbors decided they had enough, they picked an interesting night to take action. Cash's wife was giving birth, and on hand was a doctor, plus a couple of local women, all of whom must have looked aghast on April 9, 1894, when seven masked men came knocking on the door. They subdued Cash, led him outside to a large oak tree, put a noose around his neck, threw the rope over a stout limb, and pulled him up. When satisfied that he was dead, each man put a bullet in him, and then they went home. The crime was never solved, but the livestock thefts stopped, and perhaps that was sufficient.

CASSIDY, Butch (a.k.a. Parker, Robert Leroy) (1866–1937)

Robert Leroy Parker was born in Beaver, Utah, on April 13, 1866, the oldest of 13 children in a Mormon family. In 1878, the group moved to Circleville, Utah, and ranched. Young Parker came into contact with a cowboy named Mike Cassidy. Just where Cassidy came from and what happened to him isn't known, but he obviously threw a wide loop, especially around the necks of cattle that did not belong to him. Parker admired Cassidy enough to adopt his name, and since Parker often worked as a butcher, the name Butch also came naturally. Butch Cassidy thus became a household name somewhere around 1890, a name destined to echo down the smoky corridors of the Wild West.

Cassidy raced horses, and then graduated to working in the mines around Telluride, Colorado, and then to developing an inner circle of outlaw comrades known today as the Wild Bunch. Matt Warner and Tom McCarty had been Cassidy's primary stalwarts, but as they dropped by the wayside, others took their place—such as Henry "Bub" Meeks; Harry Longabaugh (the Sundance Kid); Harvey Logan, often known as Kid Curry, the most dangerous manslayer in the group; William Ellsworth Lay, the amicable one of the bunch, known as Elza, probably because of that middle name; and George Sutherland Curry, usually called Flat Nose Curry, because of a flat portion (due to lack of cartilage) of his broken nose.

On June 22, 1889, Cassidy and a couple associates struck the Telluride bank and fled to Brown's Park, then over to Robbers Roost, and from there to the Hole-in-the-Wall. One crime followed another, of course, and in due time he was caught. On July 15, 1894, Butch Cassidy entered the Wyoming State Penitentiary at Laramie. He did not leave until January 19, 1896. On August 13, he and several confederates walked into the Montpelier, Idaho, bank, put on their masks, and robbed it. Afterward, they hardly stopped running until they reached Brown's Park, from there they went on to the Roost. It was somewhere around this time that the Wild Bunch came into existence, the name probably stemming from the gang's wild antics when it rode into various towns for fun and relaxation. On June 24, 1897, the gang robbed the bank in Belle Fourche, South Dakota.

Following that escapade, Cassidy traveled, especially in New Mexico, in his spare time hitting banks as well as trains. At Tipton, Wyoming, his gang stopped the Union Pacific out of Omaha, and then on September 19 it robbed the First National Bank at Winnemucca, Nevada. By now the Pinkertons were after them, so the fall of 1900 seemed like a good time to pack up and go to Fort Worth, Texas, for relaxation. Here (or in San Antonio) Harry Longabaugh met Etta Place, a lady of many loves and occupations; "Etta Place" may or may not have been her real name. Also in Fort Worth, five of the outlaws, buying the best in spiffy suits and derby hats, posed for photographs in the studio of John Swartz. Evidently, John liked the photo too, since he posted it in a window for advertising purposes. Fred Dodge, a passing Pinkerton detective, recognized one of the "gentlemen." The police now had a picture of everybody who was anybody in the Wild Bunch: Harry Longabaugh, Will Carver, Ben Kilpatrick, Harvey Logan, and Butch Cassidy. Butch, Sundance, and Etta—apparently unaware they had been identified—extended their vacation to New York City, made plans for sailing to South America, and then headed west for one last robbery—a big one. They hit the *Coast Flyer* of the Great Northern Railroad near Wagner, Montana, on July 3, 1901. Some reports say the gang took $40,000 when it left. By the end of the year Butch Cassidy, Harry Longabaugh, and Etta Place were either in Argentina, living in the Cholila Valley, or soon would be. Harvey Logan appears to have joined them later. Meanwhile, during the next couple of years, a series of Argentine banks went down.

By late 1907, Harry and Butch had reached San Vicente, Bolivia, where, after a few mining robberies, their luck ran out. In November 1907, sometime between the 5th and the 8th, they shot it out with a Bolivian army patrol. Some accounts suggest that when down to their last two bullets, Cassidy shot Sundance in the head and then took his own life. Their bodies were dumped into unidentified graves. Other accounts suggest that Cassidy lived and returned to the United States.

See also: BROWN'S PARK; CARVER, WILLIAM RICHARD; CURRY, GEORGE SUTHERLAND; HOLE-IN-THE-WALL; KILPATRICK, BENJAMIN ARNOLD; LAY, WILLIAM ELLSWORTH; LOGAN, HARVEY; ROBBERS ROOST; SUNDANCE KID

CATTLE Rustling

The Old West has numerous staples: gunfighters, cattle towns, High Noons, outlaw gangs, Indians, gamblers, shady ladies, heroic sheriffs and city marshals, ranchers, cowboys, cattlemen, and cattle rustlers. Cattle rustling commenced primarily after the Civil War, and it substantially ended with the advent of barbed wire and the railroads. Texas was the hardest hit with regard to widespread cattle theft, if for no other reason than the fact that its vast expanse of grasslands offered almost unlimited opportunities. Furthermore, the Mexican border from Arizona across New Mexico and Texas to the Gulf of Mexico provided quick exits for cattle from one nation to another.

Most cattle thieves were out-of-work cowboys who took advantage of the winter months, when few line riders could be found. Branded cattle were generally disposed of quickly, usually to slaughterhouses that were not picky about ownership. Livestock theft peaked during the late 1870s and 1880, after which it was reduced by the advent of fencing, plus the employment of range detectives and brand inspectors by cattle associations and corporate ranchers. The Texas Rangers also added strong law enforcement resources to the suppression of cattle theft.

See also: CATTLE TOWN

CATTLE Town (a.k.a. cow town)

Western cattle towns are an intricate part of the lawman/outlaw/gunfighter story. All cattle towns, for the purposes of this encyclopedia, arose in the western United States. They were generally small, usually sat astride major cattle trails twisting north out of Texas, and they practically always had rail connections to eastern slaughterhouses.

Some of the better-known cow towns were Abilene, Dodge City, Ellsworth, Newton, Wichita, Kansas City, and Caldwell, these communities being fed by such Texas trails as the Goodnight-Loving, Chisholm, and Western. Trail drives usually lasted between two and three months, periods plagued by frequent bad weather, equally bad food, and unending monotony. The towns catered to the Texas cowboy, particularly in the late spring and summer, but had few facilities other than saloons, gambling houses, and brothels. The community administration was generally primitive; the towns wavered somewhere between resenting, even detesting the wild and frequently unrestrained cowboy, yet at the same time they were dependent upon him for a living. The cowboys, usually unmarried youths between 15 and 30 years of age, often hit the towns like thunderbolts. The cow-town boom times lasted from roughly 1867 to the early 1880s.

Because of large amounts of cash floating around, the presence of professional gamblers, and wild cowboys, many games and no few arguments were frequently resolved by way of the six-shooter. The towns therefore hired fast and deadly guns to keep the peace, and out of this arose the romanticized legend of the fast-drawing marshal, plus High Noons practically without end.

CHADBORN, Daniel Joseph (a.k.a. Buck)
(1879–1966)

Although born in central Texas, Daniel J. "Buck" Chadborn made his historical mark in the Trans-

Pecos region, as well as in southern New Mexico, along the international border. Chadborn was one of the many overlooked transitional frontier personalities who lived through thrilling adventures during both the 19th and 20th centuries. As a youth, necessity forced him to travel by horseback; in later years, he traded leather reins for a steering wheel, chasing smugglers with an automobile.

Chadborn had married Nita Johnson, the daughter of Annie Frazer Johnson, who had in a second marriage tied the knot with the notorious southwestern gunman Barney Riggs. However, the Annie–Barney Riggs union ended in a bitter divorce, amidst accusations of physical violence. By marriage, Chadborn had been thrust into this uncomfortable situation. A court even named Chadborn as the trustee for Annie, designating that he would receive periodic cash payments from Barney Riggs on Annie's behalf. However, the court order created so much animosity between Buck and Barney that Chadborn finally went to the judge and declared, "I want out, and you get somebody else."

On April 7, 1902, Chadborn and Riggs met on a Fort Stockton, Texas, street, Chadborn seated in a buggy, Riggs standing on the sidewalk. During an exchange of heated words, Riggs gestured wildly in the face of the much younger and less worldly Chadborn. Exactly what the movement intended remains a mystery, but suddenly Riggs reached toward his back pocket. Chadborn interpreted the move as a reach for a six-shooter. Buck jerked his revolver from the buggy seat and shot the unarmed Barney Riggs in the chest. Barney staggered back, collapsed, and died. Buck was indicted by a grand jury for second-degree murder. A change of venue subsequently shifted the trial to Alpine, Texas, where on October 14, 1903, a jury returned a verdict of "not guilty" following 15 minutes of deliberations.

After the shooting of Riggs, Buck operated a livery stable in El Paso, but by February 1909 he was in Columbus, New Mexico, in the cattle business and also working as a deputy sheriff. On March 9, 1916, Pancho Villa made his famous predawn raid. During the ensuing battle and subsequent chase after the fleeing Villistas, Buck with other civilian residents engaged in "mop-up" operations, killing Mexican stragglers and taking prisoners. Buck's scorecard in this man-killing escapade is impossible to tally, although one of his cohorts reportedly killed 12 of Villa's raiders. A few months later, in his role as a deputy sheriff, Buck participated in the legal hanging at Deming, New Mexico, of six Mexican prisoners convicted of taking part in Villa's cross-border incursion.

During 1921, Buck entered the U.S. Customs Service as a mounted patrol inspector, an assignment involving both equine and horseless-carriage operations. On the border, especially throughout the Prohibition era, Buck participated in numerous arrests, seizures, and an occasional car chase and shootout.

On his 62nd birthday Buck Chadborn retired from law enforcement. At Deming, New Mexico, on March 30, 1966, the 86-year-old ex-border lawman passed over to the other side.

See also: RIGGS, BARNEY

CHADWELL, William (a.k.a. William Stiles) (1857–1876)

This desperado, born in Missouri, rode with the James gang and participated in the Otterville, Missouri, train robbery of July 7, 1876. Chadwell then reportedly talked Jesse James into the Northfield, Minnesota, robbery of the First National Bank on September 7, 1876. It turned into a fiasco; the James boys barely escaped, and most of their associates were killed or captured.

Chadwell was one of the dead, his body being taken by Henry M. Wheeler, a young medical student who had fired the shot. When Wheeler later commenced his medical practice, Chadwell's skeleton went on display. It may or may not have been good for business, but it certainly became quite a conversation piece.

See also: JAMES BROTHERS

CHAPMAN, Huston Ingraham (1847–1879)

Huston Chapman was an attorney, not a gunman or outlaw, but guns and outlaws played a significant and terminal part in his life. He was born on April 28, 1847, in Burlington, Iowa, and a week later his family left for the Oregon Territory. As he grew older, he moved south to the California goldfields, then returned to become a founder of Portland, Oregon, as well as an Oregon legislator. He would become a U.S. attorney for Wisconsin and a prosecuting attorney for Michigan.

On May 19, 1860, he accidentally shot himself with a shotgun, losing his left arm. The injury spurred him to numerous achievements, his mushrooming law practice being the major result. By 1878, he had begun practice in Las Vegas, New Mexico; Mrs. Susan McSween became one of his clients. Her husband, Alexander McSween, also an attorney, had been slain during the Lincoln County War, and Mrs. McSween sought retribution.

Chapman told New Mexico governor Lew Wallace that he intended to file criminal proceedings against Col. Nathan Dudley, commander at Fort Stockton, for arson and murder. Other people would also be charged. On February 18, a year to the day after Englishman John Tunstall had been slain, his death setting off the Lincoln County War, Huston Chapman was in Lincoln on Susan McSween's legal behalf. Due to the effect of the cold weather on his severe neuralgia, he had bound his face with bandages. On the Lincoln streets that evening, however, as he sought a poultice to ease the pain, he encountered gunmen who days before had been enemies of each other but now seemed to be friends. They were James Dolan, Henry McCarty (Billy the Kid), Billy Mathews, Jesse Evans, William Campbell, and several others. All were drinking, carousing, looking for trouble, and Chapman was it. Dolan and Campbell pulled six-shooters, blocked Chapman's path, taunted him, and then shot him to death. They stood so close that their gunpowder set his clothes afire. His death was hardly investigated. No serious arrests were made, and no one ever went to trial.

See also: BILLY THE KID; EVANS, JESSE J.; LINCOLN COUNTY WAR

CHÁVEZ y Chávez, José (1851?–1923?)

José Chávez y Chávez was probably born in Ceboleta, New Mexico, and spent much of his life as a day laborer and desperado. San Patricio, New Mexico, residents elected him constable in 1874 and followed that by making him a justice of the peace. He became a sheriff's deputy in Las Vegas, New Mexico. Although he rode as one of the Lincoln County War "Regulators," Chávez does not come into historical focus until fleeing the burning McSween house in Lincoln, New Mexico, on July 19, 1878. While he certainly was an active participant in the Lincoln County War—he claimed to have fired one of the bullets into Sheriff Brady—very little is known regarding his activities.

A decade later he became a member of the little-known *La Sociedad de Bandidos* (Society of Bandits) and *Las Gorras Blancas* (White Caps), led by Jesús Silva—cruel and little-known organizations devoted as much to killing as to anything else. On October 22, 1892, the group lynched Patricio Maes at the behest of Silva, and in February 1893, it killed Silva's brother-in-law, Gabriel Sandoval, because Gabriel had asked too many questions about Maes. The (perhaps) insane Silva then murdered his own wife, because she also asked too many questions about her brother. He ordered Chávez and others to dig her grave. However, his gang, suspecting Silva might kill them next, shot Silva and buried him with his wife in the same hole. The authorities eventually got wise, of course, and arrested the gang, capturing Chávez at Socorro, New Mexico, on May 26, 1894. Following his second trial, a jury sentenced Chávez to hang on October 29, 1897. His attorney arranged a stay of execution, and on November 20, Governor Miguel Otero commuted the sentence to life in prison. Sometime afterward, a riot occurred in the Santa Fe territorial prison, and since Chávez assisted the guards, Governor George Curry pardoned him on January 11, 1909.

Chávez returned to Las Vegas, where he afterward bragged about killing Col. Albert Jennings Fountain and his young son Henry. A problem with the confession, however, was that the murders had occurred in 1896, while Chávez was in jail.

Various accounts say Chávez died at Milargo, New Mexico, on July 17, 1923.

See BILLY THE KID; FOUNTAIN, ALBERT JENNINGS; LINCOLN COUNTY WAR

CHENOWTH, Howard (a.k.a. Carl Martin) (1881–1947)

At just 23 years of age, Howard Chenowth, the son of a prominent Arizona family, made his memorable mark during a drunken rampage at Silver City, New Mexico. Otherwise—aside from these horrific killings—he led a long and peaceful life.

After spending two years in college, Howard Chenowth skipped all further education and did what some youngsters do best—he became a cowboy, working for the Diamond-A Cattle Company in southwestern New Mexico.

On the night of August 27, 1904, Chenowth, his boss Pat Nunn, and several Diamond-A cowhands were winding up festivities in the Silver City gin mills. At about two o'clock in the morning, Nunn yelled that it was time to ride back to camp. Chenowth's cowboy buddy, Mart Kennedy, started arguing. What started out as a heated verbal exchange between Nunn and Kennedy ended up as a fight. Deputy Sheriff Elmore Murray rushed into the fracas, intent on separating everybody. That brought Chenowth into the fray. He grabbed Nunn's six-shooter and began to shoot at its owner. Three times Chenowth fired at Nunn. One bullet missed, one shattered Nunn's watch, and the last carved a nasty but not fatal furrow across Nunn's forehead. Nunn, blood streaming down his face, retired from the brawl.

As the commotion continued, Perfecto Rodríguez, a former Grant County lawman, rushed to aid deputy Murray, but Chenowth, drunkenly cocking and snapping the hammer, happened to snap it with Rodríquez in front of the end of the barrel. The former lawman dropped to the floor, shot through the heart, stone dead. Meanwhile, Murray persisted in doing his job, struggling with Chenowth, who by now had been joined by Kennedy. City Marshal W. H. Kilburn jumped into the melee but fell almost instantly with a mortal wound; the drunken Chenowth had snapped off another round. At this point, everyone fled.

Kennedy was soon arrested. Chenowth was caught hiding behind shipping crates. He refused to surrender and in the resultant skirmish was wounded by a charge of birdshot fired by Deputy Sheriff John Collier. Chenowth went to the hospital and then to jail, by now charged with the double murder of Kilburn and Rodríguez. Howard Chenowth was convicted and sentenced to 50 years in the penitentiary, but remained in jail at Silver City only until Christmas Day 1905. Then, with unknown assistance, Chenowth was liberated at gunpoint and disappeared.

Years later the story broke that Chenowth had been "rescued" by his uncles, that he had spent time hiding in Alabama, then worked for the famous King Ranch holdings in Brazil, where he became known as Carl Martin. He also married and fathered seven children. With the death of his wife in 1927, Chenowth returned to New Mexico, where after considerable effort he received a governor's pardon. Thereafter he worked for area ranches in New Mexico and Arizona until he passed away at Tucson in

1947 at age 65. Except for that one voyage on a whiskey river many years ago, Chenowth's life had been honorable and productive.

CHEROKEE Strip

By the time of the Civil War, most of what is now the state of Oklahoma was devoted to different Indian tribes. A strip of land 25 miles wide and roughly 200 miles long, having Kansas as its northern border, extended west in a straight line across northern Oklahoma from Missouri. The property's official name became the Cherokee Outlet. Directly across the line in Kansas, an equally long line—but this one only two and a half miles wide—bordered the northern portion of the Cherokee Outlet. Thus this narrow piece of Kansas land became known as the Cherokee Strip, effective as of a treaty of July 19, 1866.

The strip, with high grass and few settlers, became a major holding ground for Texas cattle, which paused here to be fattened up before being driven into one of several nearby cattle towns. Over time, various cattlemen started claiming and fencing in portions of the strip. This led to legal conflicts, first with the Cherokees, and then with the Boomers—white people, generally farmers, who were short on funds and sought to settle on what they regarded as free land. The area, with so little government, attracted numerous renegades, some of them part Indian. By 1886, Boomers and others commenced setting vast regions of the prairie afire. The Cherokee Strip thus became lawless, dangerous area. Although the army repeatedly forced Texans, Boomers, and others out of the territory and tore down many of the fences, the momentum finally proved unstoppable. With Indians threatening to go on the warpath, the government gave up. Fences gradually started coming down, while others started going up, as the Cherokee Strip reluctantly gave way to legitimized settlement.

CHRISTIAN, William T. (a.k.a. Black Jack Christian) (1871–1897)

The desperado Black Jack Christian did not enter the historical record until April 27, 1895, when he and others killed deputy sheriff Will Turner near Burnett, Oklahoma. During Christian's escape from jail at Oklahoma City, two other men died during the shooting, and others were to fall during the breakout across Oklahoma, New Mexico, and into Arizona, where Christian formed a new gang. The desperadoes held up stores and post offices, graduating to stagecoaches and trains, killing people along the way before briefly disappearing into Sonora and Chihuahua, Mexico. On April 28, 1897, after Christian ventured out into Arizona again, someone, perhaps Tom Horn, shot him dead.

See also: HORN, TOM; MUSGRAVE, GEORGE

CHRISTIANSEN, Willard Erastus (a.k.a. Mormon Kid; Matt Warner) (1864–1937)

This Mormon desperado was born at Ephraim, Utah, around 1864 and at an early age learned to herd cattle and break horses. He fought a boy named Andrew Hendrickson when he was 13; he hit Hendrickson with a rock and thought he had killed him. It was time to leave, so he headed for Brown's Hole in Colorado, Wyoming, and Utah, where he joined Elza Lay and Tom McCarty, taking the name of Matt Warner. He also met Leroy Parker, better known as Butch Cassidy, and from this time on he was a Wild Bunch desperado.

Warner and Tom McCarty (who had married Matt's sister) likely held up the First National Bank of Denver on March 30, 1889. Warner, Cassidy, and McCarty hit the Telluride Bank on June 24. The outlaws then circled Jackson Hole and spent the winter at Star Valley, where the 25-year-old Matt married before robbing a bank at Roselyn, Washington.

In 1896, one E. B. Coleman, who claimed to have struck it rich in the Black Hills, hired Warner and one William Wall to protect him, claiming that three men—David Milton and Dick and Isaac Staunton—were harassing and threatening to kill him for his money. On May 7, 1896, Warner and Wall fired into a tent containing the three suspects, killing Milton and Dick Staunton. Warner and Wall then spent considerable time trying to convince the prosecuting attorney that it was self-defense, but they still spent three years in the Utah Penitentiary for manslaughter.

Upon being freed, Warner settled in Price, Utah. His first wife had died; Warner was accused of having abused her. He remarried, was elected justice of the peace, and might have settled down completely except that he read the book *Outlaw Trail: The Story of Butch Cassidy and the Wild Bunch,* by Charles Kelly. Kelly repeated the story of the wife

abuse, which so infuriated and depressed Warner that he reportedly drank heavily. He died in 1937.

See also: BROWN'S PARK; CASSIDY, BUTCH; WILD BUNCH

CHISHOLM Trail

The Chisholm Trail was the most-used Texas cattle pathway, long celebrated in song and story. Like most trails, it had feeder branches to small settlements. The Chisholm essentially wound from San Antonio, Texas, through Fort Worth and north across Oklahoma to Kansas, specifically to Caldwell, Wichita, Newton, and Ellsworth. A herd might range in size from several hundred head of cattle to several thousand. The Chisholm opened around 1866 and closed in 1884.

CLAIBORNE, William Floyd (a.k.a. Billy the Kid Claiborne) (1860–1882)

Most reports indicate that William "Billy" Claiborne at some point in his youth stepped from the quagmire and swamps of one of the southeastern states and fine-tuned his cowboys skills in the employ of cattleman John Slaughter. Stories existed that he killed two men in Texas, but in any event he moved with John Slaughter to the territory of Arizona in 1879.

Shortly afterward he left the cowboy life behind and reportedly worked as a teamster, a miner, and even as a waiter in a Galeyville saloon. In 1881, in the tumultuous community of Charleston, he shot down a James Hicks (Hickey) at the Queen Saloon. The authorities jailed him, but "cowboy" friends bailed him out. He was ultimately acquitted of the Charleston killing.

By most accounts he was a good friend of the Clantons, as well as of John Ringo and the McLaury brothers. Although he did not get involved in the Gunfight at the OK Corral, he did testify during Justice of the Peace Spicer's preliminary hearing.

During the following year on November 14, 1882, in Tombstone's Oriental Saloon, he quarreled bitterly with Buckskin Frank Leslie, one of the thoroughly dangerous characters of Tombstone, Arizona. Apparently Claiborne was unarmed at the time, so he left the premises to get his rifle, mentioning to anyone who listened that he intended to kill Buckskin Frank.

The two men met within the hour, and Billy the Kid Claiborne fired. He missed. Leslie did not miss.

George Parsons, who kept a journal of these Tombstone years, noted that Buckskin Frank's cigarette did not even go out during the encounter.

See also: GUNFIGHT AT THE OK CORRAL; LESLIE, NASHVILLE FRANK; TOMBSTONE, ARIZONA

CLANTON, Newman Haynes (a.k.a. Old Man Clanton) (1816–1881)

Newman Clanton was born near Nashville in Davidson County, Tennessee. Following the War of 1812 the family moved to Missouri, where Newman acquired a farm and on January 5, 1840, married the 16-year-old Mariah Kelso. Three children were born:

Newman H. ("Old Man") Clanton (Robert G. McCubbin Collection)

John Wesley, 1841; Phineas (Phin) Fay, 1845; and Joseph Isaac (Ike), 1847.

Although Newman joined the gold rush to California, he found no wealth and stayed just long enough to see his farm being sold for debt on his return. Clanton then took the family to Illinois, where Mary Elsie was born in 1852. The next stop was a farm and ranch near Dallas, Texas, where two more children were born, Esther Ann (1854) and Alonzo (1859). In 1861, the family moved to Hamilton County, Texas, where William Harrison (Billy) Clanton was born. Both Newman and his son John Wesley Clanton, joined the Confederate army and had undistinguished, if checkered, careers. Newman was described as six feet one inch with blue eyes, fair complexion, and light hair. He deserted and reenlisted so many times that it appears he was joining just for the bonus money.

In 1865, the Clantons showed up in Fort Bowie, Arizona, but within a year left for California. Mariah died along the way. By 1873 the Clantons had returned to Arizona, settling in the Gila Valley; then they shifted to grazing land on the San Pedro River, not far from Charleston and Tombstone. Before long the McLaury brothers, Robert and Thomas, moved nearby. By now Newman had become "Old Man Clanton," and so far as is known, no one ever referred to him as anything else. By now a "Rustlers Trail" (actually a system of routes) extended up from Mexico through the San Pedro, Sulphur Springs, and Animas Valleys, across ranches, through mountain passes, and into towns and railroad stops.

The trails also produced other advantages as well. On August 1, 1881, Old Man Clanton, Ike and Billy Clanton, John Ringo, and a half dozen others ambushed a group of Mexican smugglers guarding a mule train of Mexican coins passing through Skeleton Canyon, about one mile south of the international border. The canyon walls ran red, and the killers divided the money.

Old Man Clanton in the meantime purchased stolen Mexican livestock—at a cut rate, of course, since it had cost the raiders nothing—and planned to sell them in Tombstone. However, Old Man Clanton and his riders (none of the Clanton children were along) were ambushed on the trail on August 13, 1881. The dead Mexican vaqueros were now avenged. By some accounts the ambush had been set up by the Earp brothers and Doc Holliday. The killings help explain the subsequent enmity between the Clantons and the Earps, an enmity that became a factor in the forthcoming Gunfight at the OK Corral.

Be that as it may, the family initially buried Old Man Clanton on a knoll inside the Gray Ranch in the Animas Valley. In early 1882, Ike and Phin Clanton reburied their father in the Boot Hill Cemetery at Tombstone.

See also: BOOT HILL; BROCIUS, WILLIAM; COWBOYS; EARP, WYATT BERRY STAPP; GUNFIGHT AT THE OK CORRAL; HOLLIDAY, JOHN HENRY; RINGO, JOHN PETERS

CLEVELAND, George Washington (1860?–1884)

On November 24, 1883, George Washington Cleveland, a black cowboy, along with accomplices A. Mitchell "Mitch" Lee, Frank Taggart, and Christopher "Kit" Joy, robbed a Southern Pacific train near Gage Station, 15 miles west of Deming, New Mexico. They escaped with approximately $800 in cash plus assorted contributions from frightened passengers. In the process they killed Theopolis C. Webster, the train's engineer. A footsore brakeman finally stumbled into Gage Station and reported the holdup. That brought Grant County deputy sheriff Dan Tucker and a posse hastily to the scene, but as the newspapers later noted, "the desperadoes had too far a start and were too well mounted."

Wells Fargo and the Southern Pacific Railroad offered rewards of $2,200 per head for the capture of the outlaws, a sum bringing former Grant County sheriff Harvey Whitehill out of near retirement. Whitehill stumbled across a discarded edition of an out-of-territory newspaper, ultimately tracing the newspaper back to a legitimate subscriber, an area storekeeper who had wrapped foodstuff in the paper for a local black cowboy named George Washington Cleveland. The identification of Cleveland as a suspect also focused attention on his three known associates.

Whitehill tracked Cleveland to a restaurant in Socorro, New Mexico, where the suspect worked, and where Whitehill arrested him. Acting as if astonished Cleveland demanded to know why he was being jailed; Whitehill bellowed, "For killing that train engineer. I already have your partners and they talked." It was a bluff! A confused and bewildered Cleveland blurted out, "It wasn't me that killed him, it was Mitch Lee." Under the impression that his criminal cohorts were in custody, Cleveland made a full confession during his trip to Silver City, furnish-

ing lawmen with the possible whereabouts of the remaining outlaws.

Frank Taggart was arrested near St. Johns, Arizona Territory, and Mitch Lee and Kit Joy were snared in a line cabin near Horse Springs, New Mexico. All four of the desperadoes went to the Grant County Jail pending trial, three of them very angry that their companion had confessed.

On March 10, 1884, the four train robbers, accompanied by a convicted murderer and a suspected horse thief, overpowered their guards, seized an armload of weapons, and escaped. A jail witness noted that Mitch Lee swore "they would do away with the negro Cleveland before they were many miles from town."

Pursuit started quickly. A short distance out on the Fort Bayard road, a posse overtook the outlaws, who immediately hid in the desert brush beside the road. As the posse scrambled to higher ground, they fired a withering fusillade into everything that moved, killing Cleveland and wounding Mitch Lee. However, Taggart and Spencer, out of ammunition, surrendered. Only Kit Joy escaped, in the process ambushing and killing posse member and Singer sewing-machine salesman Joseph N. Lafferr. During the fruitless search for Joy, the body of Chávez (the murderer) was found.

On their way back to Silver City, the posse decided to dispense with additional legal proceedings. It lynched Mitch Lee and Frank Taggart. Spencer was returned to jail. Kit Joy was eventually captured and imprisoned.

See also: JOY, CHRISTOPHER; LEE, A. MITCHELL

COE, Philip Houston (1839–1871)

Phil Coe, born in Gonzales County, Texas, is best known for two things: he was one of the best known gamblers in the West, and he was the last person known to have been slain by Wild Bill Hickok.

On March 24, 1862, Private Coe enlisted in Company D, Wood's Regiment, Texas Cavalry. On September 21, he became a first lieutenant. A month later he was demoted to private and was listed as absent without leave. He reenlisted in December with another unit, where, after spending a month in the Houston hospital with gonorrhea, he became a lieutenant again.

Somewhere while in the army Coe met the (later) well-known gunfighter Ben Thompson. There is some evidence, but mostly conjecture, that Coe and

Thompson briefly signed on with the Emperor Maximilian in Mexico.

After the war, Coe opened a gambling hall in Austin, probably in partnership with Ben Thompson. He moved around the area, getting to know gunfighter John Wesley Hardin during a trip to Brenham, in Washington County, Texas. Hardin liked to gamble almost as much as Coe, and it was Coe who gave Hardin the nickname of "Young Seven Up," the phrase stemming from a popular card game of the time. In his autobiography, Hardin described Coe as "notorious" but failed to explain further.

By spring 1871, Coe and Thompson were in Abilene, Kansas, where they opened the Bull's Head, a saloon and gambling hall. It was a profitable enterprise, since Texas cowboys and trail herds were already arriving at the railhead. However, Thompson may not have spent much time in Abilene that summer, due to injuries reportedly suffered in a buggy accident.

Be that as it may, undisclosed hard feelings arose between Coe and Abilene city marshal Wild Bill Hickok. On Thursday evening, October 5, Coe and 20 or 30 friends had been wandering the evening streets, sometimes dragging friends into saloons and forcing them to buy drinks for the crowd. At other times, they walked into the bars and tossed those not offering to buy drinks over the counter.

Sometime during that evening, probably not long after dark, Coe shot at a dog. Hickok came on the run, a confrontation arose . . . and a gunfight started. When the smoke cleared, Mike Williams, a special deputy hired by the Novelty Theater, lay dead, shot by Hickok by mistake. The marshal had a bullet hole in his coat where a bullet passed through. Another bullet had passed between his legs. As for Phil Coe, he lay moaning, a bullet in his stomach; he would die in agony three days later. The remains were shipped to Brenham, where he today lies in the Prairie Lea Cemetery.

See also: ABILENE, KANSAS; HARDIN, JOHN WESLEY; HICKOK, JAMES BUTLER; THOMPSON BEN

COGHLAN, Patrick (1822–1911)

Pat Coghlan, an Irish immigrant who reached American shores in 1845, enlisted in the U.S. Army and was discharged in 1852 at San Antonio, Texas. For a while he tried his hand at farming and trading cattle in the Texas counties of Mason and Menard. By 1873, he had migrated to New Mexico Territory, settling at Tularosa, where he began acquiring land at Three Rivers, 20 miles north of Tularosa, on the western slope of the Sierra Blanca Mountains. By whatever questionable means, Coghlan always had plenty of cash. He built a substantial adobe house with walls three feet thick and obsessively persisted in efforts to acquire land and cattle, eventually carving out an empire, over which he ruled with an iron fist and seemingly—at least for a while—with legal impunity. While it lasted, Coghlan was indeed "king of the Tularosa," a name bestowed upon him by local and regional newspapers.

With headquarters at both Tularosa and Three Rivers, and property that included a store, saloon, and wagon yard, town lots and ranches, and herds of cattle, Coghlan concentrated on living the good life. He smoked fine cigars, drank aged whiskey, raced purebred horses, and took occasional trips to California and Ireland.

Coghlan in fact dealt primarily in stolen cattle, the well-known gunman and cattle rustler Billy the Kid supplying much of his beef. Coghlan owned his own slaughterhouse and had lucrative contracts to supply beef to the military unit at nearby Fort Stanton. However, Coghlan had his detractors, one of them livestock detective Charles Siringo, who submitted sufficient evidence (hides of freshly butchered cattle with Texas brands) to cause John William Poe, sheriff and U.S. deputy marshal, to arrest him. Due to legal shenanigans and prosecutorial timidity during the 1882 spring court session at Mesilla, New Mexico, Coghlan was offered a plea bargain, a one-count guilty plea in exchange for a fine of $150. He accepted the deal. Noted southwestern attorney Albert J. Fountain, representing the cattlemen's interests, filed a $10,000 civil suit against Coghlan after the plea was entered.

During extended legal machinations, on April 17, 1882, George Nesmith (a prosecution witness against Coghlan), his wife, and his little girl were brutally murdered near White Sands. Maximo Apodaca and Rupert Lara were tried for the killings. Lara was hanged. Maximo Apodaca confessed and received a life sentence (he committed suicide in prison). The prosecutors tried to implicate Coghlan in the slayings, but the effort failed for lack of evidence.

Coghlan's legal problems continued to cause such financial woes that gradually he ceased to be "king of the Tularosa." In poor health and with a personal estate by then figured at $4,300, Coghlan died in El Paso, Texas, on January 22, 1911. El Paso newspapers made no mention of his past exploits and relationships, instead referring only to his extraordinary strength, describing him as one of the strongest men in the region. He is buried in El Paso's Concordia Cemetery.

See also: BILLY THE KID; FOUNTAIN, ALBERT JENNINGS; GARRETT, PATRICK FLOYD JARVIS; LINCOLN COUNTY WAR; POE, JOHN WILLIAM

COLT Revolver

In February 1836, Samuel Colt patented a repeating, hand-held firearm based on a revolving cylinder. It became the No. 5 Belt Revolver and was sold to the Texas Rangers. During the Mexican War, Samuel Walker, a Texas Ranger, helped Colt design what became the Colt-Walker Revolver, better known as the Walker Colt. In 1851, Colt introduced the .36 caliber Navy Revolver. Colt's Single-Action Army Revolver, popularly known as the "Peacemaker," remains the icon of the American Wild West.

See also: WALKER COLT

COMANCHEROS

Comancheros were Spanish-Mexicans permitted in Comanche camps for purposes of trade. Of course, often they lived there and raised children. Anglo-Americans generally thought of Comancheros as half-breeds and renegades. A Comanchero, however, did not have to have Comanche blood, although through intermarriage many of them did. As a general rule, the Comanchero made his living by ransoming Mexican or American captives and by trading firearms to the Indians. In short, the Comancheros became middlemen between the Spanish and the Indians, trading hides from one party for guns from another and brokering plunder and captives, regardless of who the buyers or sellers were.

Over time, the Comancheros often became valuable to Americans, as in the case of Rachael Plummer, taken captive by Comanches and brutalized for years. She was returned to her family only when New Mexico Americans learned of her fate and commissioned a group of Comancheros to ransom her.

Comancheros remained active even beyond the Civil War, in particular trading rifles from New Mexico and Arizona ranchers for livestock driven in from Texas by raiding Comanche warriors. These actions brought about such bitterness toward Comanches, however, that ultimately the Texans destroyed the Comanches as a people. Only the middlemen, the Comancheros, survived. Over time they integrated in mainstream society, perhaps becoming Main Street businessmen.

CONSTABLE

The position and power of constables in the law enforcement chain varied from state to state, but as a general rule constables served elective or appointive four-year terms. Justices of the peace often appointed their own constables or served in the position themselves. The constable's duties generally included serving processes, attending court sessions, and otherwise performing the usual, established duties of precinct peace officers. Constables often served concurrent as well as overlapping terms as town marshals, police chiefs, or deputy sheriffs. In their own jurisdictions they served as the precinct counterpart of the county sheriff. They also earned fees for serving writs; summoning juries, witnesses, or grand juries; for attendance in court; for travel; and even for hanging sentenced prisoners. Most constables in the Old West carried firearms and frequently used them. Constables also could be powerful allies, one example occurring during the Lincoln County War. While the House of Murphy enjoyed the support of sheriffs in Lincoln County, New Mexico, the opposing faction, nominally led by attorney Alexander McSween, had the support of a justice of the peace, John Wilson. Wilson appointed deputy constables so as to give legitimacy to the McSween cause.

See also: LINCOLN COUNTY WAR

CONTENTION City

This site lies 12 miles northwest of Tombstone, Arizona, on the San Pedro River. It is a former tiny mining community with the requisite saloons and brothels. Its claim to fame arrived with the nighttime Tombstone stage on March 15, 1881. The stage carried eight passengers and $26,000 in gold, but three masked men stopped it. During the resultant shootout, one passenger and a shotgun guard were slain. The outlaws were driven off, one of them wounded.

The crime was never solved, although Kate Elder, former bedmate of John "Doc" Holliday, later signed an affidavit swearing that Doc had participated in the robbery. Nothing came of it.

See also: HOLLIDAY, JOHN HENRY; TOMBSTONE, ARIZONA

COOK, Thalis Tucker (1858–1918)

Born in Uvalde County, Texas, Thalis Tucker Cook enlisted in Company F, Frontier Battalion, Texas Rangers on June 4, 1874, under the command of renowned Capt. Neal Coldwell. At the time he signed on, Cook was 16 years old, the youngest lawman ever to serve in the unit. In contrast to the rough lifestyle of many frontier lawmen, Thalis Cook throughout his career remained a serious Bible student and led a fervently religious life. He no doubt even prayed for his wayward cousin in New Mexico Territory, one of Billy the Kid's buddies, Tom O'Folliard, later slain by a posse headed by Lincoln County sheriff Patrick Floyd Garrett.

An epileptic, Thalis Cook trained his horse to stand completely still during his seizures and resultant losses of consciousness. Once an attack passed, it was back to normal for man and beast. In fact, the disability affected Cook hardly at all. Throughout West Texas he was a crack shot with both rifle and six-shooter, and a demonlike fighting man when he had to be.

After two separate enlistments with the ranger service, Cook signed on as a deputy sheriff in Presidio County, the Big Bend country of Texas. His best remembered gunfight occurred on January 31, 1891, while he was working in conjunction with Texas Ranger Jim Putman in the Glass Mountains north of Marathon, Texas. The lawmen had been seeking Fine Gilliland, wanted for the murder of H. H. Poe. As these things sometimes happened, the two lawmen literally collided with Gilliland. As the desperado watched them approach, he eased a cocked six-shooter into his hand, the weapon obscured under a coat draped across the front of his saddle. Upon recognizing Cook and Putman as peace officers, Gilliland fired, the bullet smashing Cook's knee. Another shot downed Cook's horse. Nevertheless, the officers killed Gilliland during that exchange of gunfire.

Cook's leg mended stiff and straight, making it difficult thereafter for him to mount and ride. In exasperation Cook asked a doctor to rebreak the leg and reset it slightly bent, to allow him to sit properly in the saddle once again.

On September 27, 1896, while tracking outlaws through the Glass Mountains and farther west into the Davis Mountains, Cook, along with ranger captain John R. Hughes and a small group of other rangers, shot it out with cattle rustlers. Two of the rustlers were slain. One escaped. The lawmen recovered the pilfered livestock.

Thalis Cook in his twilight years moved to eastern Texas, where he died near Marshall on July 21, 1918.

See also: GARRETT, PATRICK FLOYD JARVIS; HUGHES, JOHN REYNOLDS

COOK, William Tuttle (a.k.a. John Williams; John Mayfield) (1873–?)

Bill Cook lived an interesting if dangerous life. His mother died early, and Bill grew up in the Cherokee Nation (Oklahoma), where he had been born, near Fort Gibson. He worked initially as a federal and military scout, but he got into trouble in 1893, when federal judge Isaac Parker gave him a month in jail for selling liquor to the Indians.

Within a year Cook had organized an outlaw gang calculated to terrorize Oklahoma. The outlaws

William (Bill) Cook (Robert G. McCubbin Collection)

slashed back and forth across the territory, robbing trains, banks, and businesses, as well as travelers. Tenacious federal marshals and local lawmen gradually decimated the desperadoes, killing many of them and capturing the rest, including Crawford Goldsby, better known as Cherokee Bill.

Oddly, Cook himself wasn't known positively to have killed anyone, so when Borden County, Texas, sheriff Thomas D. Love and Chaves County, New Mexico, sheriff C. C. Perry overtook Cook near Fort Sumner, New Mexico, on January 11, 1895, he surrendered without a fight. A month and one day later, on February 12, Judge Isaac Parker found Cook guilty of bank robbery. He handed Cook a 45-year sentence, to be served in Albany, New York. Cook died in prison.

See also: GOLDSBY, CRAWFORD; PARKER, JUDGE ISAAC.

COOMER, Daniel (a.k.a. Dan) (1846–1890)

Dan Coomer falls into that genre of frontier personalities not actually classified as lawmen but who could always be relied upon to jump into a fray on the "right" side. Cattle rustlers, thieves, and jail escapees all too late learned that it didn't pay to mess with Dan or his livestock.

Born in Washington County, Tennessee, Dan moved with his family to Van Buren, Arkansas, where at the outbreak of the Civil War he volunteered for the Confederate army but was rejected due to his age. However, he worked as a teamster hauling military supplies for troops until the close of the conflict. After that, in the spring of 1867, he and his brother, Jesse, took up cattle ranching on the Mimbres River in southwestern New Mexico.

By 1872, Dan Coomer had moved closer to Silver City, by now ranching in the Santa Rita Mountains. A local newspaper editor wrote:

This was at that interesting time in the history of Grant county when thieves had things pretty much their own way. Mr. Coomer's strong ideas of right and wrong caused him to make a relentless war on that class of people. Single-handed and alone he followed the thieves for days and nights without stopping. He always recovered his stock and in several instances started the thieves on the road to a better life.

During September 1879, rustlers departed with 65 head of Coomer's cattle. Coomer contacted Grant County sheriff Harvey Whitehill, who for unknown reasons declined to offer assistance. Coomer and a fellow rancher therefore pursued the thieves, picking up the trail near Silver City. Coomer followed it through the Burro Mountains, down the Gila River, across the Carlisle Mountains, down the Gila once again, and on to Pueblo Viejo. The trail extended all the way to Fort Grant, Arizona Territory, and then doubled back into the Burro Mountains, where after a grueling 24 days Coomer finally caught up with the beleaguered thieves.

There are two versions of what happened next. One account says the rustlers were slain while resisting a citizen's arrest; the other says they were shot down while trying to escape. Either way, two outlaws were dead. Back at Silver City, Coomer looked up Deputy Sheriff Dan Tucker and inquired if there had been any warrants issued for his arrest involving the dead outlaws. There hadn't been, nor would there be.

During the following year of 1880, rustlers made off with 20 head of Coomer's livestock and sold them to a civilian butcher at Fort Cummings. At first the butcher remained tightlipped as to the source of the beef. His hesitation ended, however, when Coomer shoved an "eared-back" Winchester in his face. He quickly named men called Bud Rice and Johnson. When the thieves learned Coomer was hunting them, they sent him a spate of death threats. Nevertheless, at Fort Bayard, Dan Coomer and Bud Rice came face to face. Rice died with a bullet in his head and two in the torso. Johnson disappeared.

On March 10, 1884, a wild jailbreak occurred at Silver City, New Mexico. Kit Joy, Mitch Lee, Frank Taggart, and George Washington Cleveland, all imprisoned for a murderous train robbery near Gage Station, plus convicted killer Carlos Chávez and suspected horse thief Charles Spencer, seized weapons, overpowered their guards, stole horses, and fled. A citizen, J. C. Jackson, jumped on his horse and followed the escaping prisoners, being careful to stay out of rifle range. Two or three miles out of town Jackson was joined by three posse members, one of them Dan Coomer. While Jackson and the others deployed in a flanking movement, Coomer charged the fugitives. Spotting Coomer alone and unaided, the outlaws did an about-face and began firing. They all missed. Dan Coomer coolly dismounted with his rifle, took aim, and killed Chávez's horse. The outlaws again turned and ran, Chávez now riding double.

In a brief time the posse overtook the outlaws. Coomer wounded Mitch Lee. Cleveland was killed, while Taggart and Spencer were captured. Chávez was found dead in the underbrush. Only Kit Joy escaped, killing posse member Joseph N. Lafferr, a sewing-machine salesman and respected Silver City resident. The wounded Mitch Lee and Frank Taggart surrendered and were lynched. A local newspaper editor remarked: "Taggart died hard of strangulation—a throat disease that is becoming extremely common among their ilk in this section." Spencer was returned to jail. Days later, Joy was shot and captured. He went to the penitentiary after a trial at Hillsboro.

For his outstanding performance and extraordinary courage, Coomer received a $500 reward. Yet before he could spend it, Dan Coomer led an assortment of ranchers after a quartet of Mexican outlaws who were butchering the wrong beeves. He arrested José López, Alaris Frescas, Danacio Gonzáles, and Julio Castillo. The prisoners were hustled before a local justice of the peace, who set their bonds at $2,000 each. How they managed to escape cow-country justice (lynching) is indeed a mystery.

Coomer later established a successful sawmill and lumber business in Grant County, but on a trip back to Arkansas in May 1890, he passed away of natural causes. Among other things, his obituary stated, "Daniel Coomer did much towards putting down the lawless element of the country, and in a short time his name became a terror to thieves. His and his neighbor's property was let alone."

See also: JOY, CHRISTOPHER; TAGGART, FRANK; TUCKER, DAVID; WHITEHILL, HARVEY HOWARD

COUGHLIN, Patrick (?–1896)

Patrick Coughlin appears in the record as a young man perhaps in his twenties or thirties in 1895, when he and an equally obscure friend, Frederick George, stole two horses in Summit County, Utah, and rode them to Salt Lake City, where they teamed up with an equally obscure youth named A. D. Bruce. Bruce, however, changed his mind about the relationship, returned to Salt Lake City, and reported the two men, plus their horse-thieving and house-breaking activities, to the authorities.

On July 26, a posse caught up with the thieves along the Webber River in Summit County. The factions traded rifle fire, injuring no one. Four days later a gunfight between another posse and the youngsters

occurred at the Palmer Ranch, near Evanston, Wyoming. This time two lawmen died—Constable Thomas Stagg and N. E. Dawes, an ex–Evanston city marshal. One of the great territorial manhunts now commenced. In early August, word arrived that the outlaws were hiding in South Willow Canyon, which was in Utah but near Grantsville, Wyoming. A posse immediately converged, fired into some brush when they saw it moving, and flushed out Patrick Coughlin. He was ordered to yell for his companion. Within a brief time, Frederick George surrendered.

On August 13, the two prisoners, charged with the murder of Stagg and Dawes, appeared in an Ogden, Utah, court. On October 30, a jury found Coughlin guilty of murder in the first degree, sentenced him to death, and set the date of execution as December 15, 1896. Another jury found Dawes guilty and gave him life imprisonment. He was paroled on December 20, 1909.

Coughlin had a choice regarding his method of execution: hanging or firing squad. Coughlin said, "I'll take lead." However, he did (unconvincingly) appeal his conviction through the courts. To avoid crowds, on December 15 Coughlin was slipped by wagon to a remote outdoor location in Rich County. There the prisoner, dressed in dark clothes, was seated, hooded and bound, in an ordinary straight chair fastened securely to the snow-covered ground. At least 200 onlookers watched. In a few minutes, a tent flap opened perhaps 50 yards in front of the condemned. Five riflemen cocked their weapons. One of them had a blank. At the count of three, they all fired into a piece of white paper pinned over Coughlin's heart. The execution went off without a hitch.

COURTRIGHT, Timothy Isaiah (a.k.a. Longhaired Jim Courtright) (1848–1887)

Jim Courtright was born in Iowa, scouted for the Union army, then moved to Texas and became the Fort Worth city marshal in 1876. Hints of corruption seemed to follow him around, however, so he drifted west to New Mexico, where some stories claim he killed two men, then fled to South America for two years. Upon returning during the mid-1880s, he again showed up in Fort Worth, this time opening the Commercial Detective Agency, and began a career of shaking down business establishments. On February 8, 1887, he clashed with Luke Short, the gambler owner of the White Elephant. The two men shot it out; Short, who should have died, got lucky and put two bullets in Courtright. A rather sleazy David had slain Goliath.

See also: SHORT, LUKE

COWBOYS

"Cowboy" is a generic term generally taken to mean a western American male who spends considerable time in the saddle and works with livestock. A cattleman can also be a cowboy, but "cattleman" generally connotes extensive ranch and livestock ownership.

However, the term "Cowboys" (frequently spelled with a capital C, although often with a lowercased "c" or hyphenated, "cow-boys") in southern Arizona during the 1870s and 1880s meant "rustlers." John Ringo epitomized the Cowboy, as did Curly Bill Brocius, Ike Clanton, and the McLaury brothers. Of course, they were cowboys too in the accepted sense of the word; "Cowboys" were considered riders who made their living by stealing cattle. Over time many of these Cowboys had drifted in from Texas, New Mexico, and Colorado, and they each had long histories of participation in feuds and range wars. They were as good with the gun as they were with the rope, and they liked southern Arizona primarily because of the nearby refuge of the Mexican border.

In modern times, the cowboy image has been blurred in with the gunfighter images, but in most parts of the American West, the two were not the same. Lawmen came far closer to fulfilling the term "gunfighter" than did cowboys. Most American cowboys carried weapons to shoot snakes or to shoot "Old Paint" should the horse fall on the rider and the rider not be able to get up. The image of the ordinary Western cowboy as a fast and accurate gunfighter has practically no validity.

See also: BROCIUS, WILLIAM; EARP, WYATT BERRY STAPP; GUNFIGHT AT THE OK CORRAL; RINGO, JOHN PETERS

COX, William Webb (a.k.a. W. W. Cox)
(1854–1923)
William Cox's father, James W. "Captain Jim" Cox, a recognized leader of the Sutton faction in Texas's Sutton-Taylor troubles, succumbed to 19 buckshot and a slashed throat, all of it inflicted by members of the Taylor faction.

On September 19, 1876, the Sutton followers killed Dr. Philip Brassell and his son, James W. Bras-

sell, at their home in Shiloh Mills, DeWitt County. A 23-year-old William Webb Cox, along with other partisans, was arrested for the murder and then released on bond. Murder indictments were returned in December, and papers were placed in the hands of Texas Ranger Lee Hall. He and a posse surrounded the Cox home just as a wedding commenced— Melissa Cox, W. W.'s sister, was getting married. Hall demanded the immediate surrender of those seven defendants formally charged with homicide. A discussion took place, and everyone agreed that insistence would cast a pall over the festivities. So the wedding ceremony continued, the Texas Rangers maintained vigilance, and the next morning the wanted men surrendered. Taken before a judge, expecting to post a nominal bond, the defendants were stunned by being remanded to jail pending trial. Ultimately, after convictions, appeals, new trials, and administrative errors, William Webb Cox, was allowed to post bail. Cox fled to the Big Bend of Texas.

Oliver Milton Lee, Cox's brother-in-law, urged Bill to relocate to New Mexico Territory. Stepping across the line and out of Texas jurisdiction seemed like good advice to Bill Cox. Although characterized as an "expert cusser," a tobacco-chewing connoisseur, and a man with a fiery temper, Cox, at least in New Mexico, seemed a changed man, developing an enviable reputation for public service and sound business investments. The Texas criminal charges, worrisome but not now aggressively pursued, were ultimately dismissed.

In 1893, Cox purchased the Shedd Ranch (later called the San Augustin Ranch) at San Augustin Springs on the east side of the Organ Mountains, one of the largest ranches in that part of New Mexico. (The Union's Fort Fillmore had surrendered at this site to Confederate forces in July 1861.) With the communities of Mesilla and Las Cruces just over the Organ Mountains to the west, and Oliver Lee's huge Circle Cross Ranch across the Tularosa Basin to the east, William Webb Cox became a political and economic powerhouse in the region, developing relationships with a number of the Southwest's famous, and infamous, characters.

One of the former was Col. Albert Jennings Fountain, whose strange disappearance in February 1896, along with his eight-year-old son Henry, is still hotly argued today. Rumors cast suspicions on Oliver Lee and, by implication, on his brother-in-law, W. W. Cox.

The tall Patrick Floyd Garrett was another of these infamous characters, a former Lincoln County, New Mexico, sheriff and the well-known slayer of "Billy the Kid." Garrett became a rancher, a neighbor of Cox, and as sheriff of Dona Ana County once helped kill a wanted outlaw in Cox's house. But Pat hadn't drawn a financially solvent breath in years. W. W. Cox held the mortgage on the ex-lawmen's real estate. When Garrett was murdered in 1908 on the western slope of the Organs by Cox's employee Wayne Brazel, inevitable rumors of conspiracy and intrigue arose and persisted. Some tales even had Cox himself rising up out of the sand hills and murdering Garrett.

Cox served two terms as Dona Ana County treasurer and collector (1911–13), and after failed ventures at wildcat oil drilling in the Jornada del Muerto and the Tularosa Basin, he divided much of his time between his Elk and Masonic Lodge associations. In particular, Bill Cox concentrated his activities on his renowned ranch holdings. The Cox Ranch house still stands and can be easily seen from the nearby White Sands Missile Range headquarters complex. On December 23, 1923, William Webb Cox died a natural death. He is buried not far from Pat Garrett in the Masonic Cemetery at Las Cruces, New Mexico.

See also: LEE, OLIVER MILTON; GARRETT, PATRICK FLOYD JARVIS; SUTTON-TAYLOR FEUD

CRABTREE, William (a.k.a. Bill) (1853–1878)

Bill Crabtree, like so many youths of the frontier West, simply got in over his head. The McLennan County (Waco), Texas, cowboy wanted to be a desperado. Reports indicate he was tried and acquitted for one murder and arrested by noted Texas Ranger Jim Gillett for unlawfully carrying a six-shooter. Ranger lieutenant N. O. Reynolds arrested him for suspected crimes in Navarro County (Corsicana). Sheriff Groesbeck arrested him for stealing a horse. Furthermore, when he married a Dixon girl in 1878, Bill Crabtree forevermore aligned himself with the Horrell faction of the bloody Horrell-Higgins feud.

On May 28, 1878, Bill Crabtree, in the company of John Dixon, John Holt, and Tom Bowen, set off to execute a high-dollar robbery plan in Bosque County (Meridian), Texas. The masterminds, Mart and Tom Horrell, established an alibi elsewhere.

Meanwhile, at his place on Hog Creek in the southern portion of the county, James Theodore "Dorrie" Vaughn, who sometimes acted as a local banker, had no idea that trouble was riding his way. At half-past eight o'clock in the evening, Dorrie opened his store to accommodate four rough-looking travelers. For this courtesy he was mercilessly gunned down by Tom Bowen, who operated under the theory that "dead men tell no tales." Exchanging a few shots with neighbors, all the outlaws got away, even though about a mile from the store Bill Crabtree's horse collapsed, the result of a bullet wound.

The posse cut off one foot of the dead horse, shopped it around to area blacksmiths, and discovered the horseshoe nailed to the hoof could be positively identified as one put on Crabtree's mount. Bill Crabtree was arrested and turned over to Bosque County sheriff Jack J. Cureton, a former Texas Ranger and well-known Indian fighter. Crabtree talked. As a result, Mart and Tom Horrell were arrested as accessories in Dorrie Vaughn's death and were later jailed at Meridian. Wanted fugitives, the other participants splashed across the Rio Grande and forever faded away.

On November 28, 1878, Bill Crabtree testified against the Horrells. That night, as he walked alongside the Bosque River (by some accounts he was leaving town), Crabtree was nearly cut in half by shotgun blasts from the underbrush. No official investigation was deemed necessary. On November 30, in a new suit of clothes, the wannabe badman was laid to rest. Vigilante justice later dealt the Horrells—Mart and Tom were gunned down while still behind bars.

See also: GILLETT, JAMES BUCHANAN; HORRELL BROTHERS; HORRELL-HIGGINS FEUD

CROCKETT, David (1853–1876)

Davy Crockett, named after his grandfather—the famous frontiersman—was born in Tennessee but spent much of his youth in central Texas, where his father operated a toll bridge across the Brazos River. As a young man in the company of Peter Burleson, Davy moved to the vicinity of Cimarron, New Mexico, where he engaged in small-scale ranching before selling out to devote his attention to more pleasurable pursuits. Crockett maintained a reasonably good relationship with Cimarron townsmen, but his sidekick and former business associate, a quarrelsome Gus Heffron, did not.

Local folklore placed Davy Crockett in the company of Clay Allison, a member of the party that lynched Elizabethtown serial killer Charles Kennedy and then decapitated the scoundrel. They placed his head on a corral fence post as a warning to others contemplating such behavior. Whether the aforementioned actually took place remains debatable, but beyond dispute is the fact that all three—Davy Crockett, Robert Clay Allison, and the murderous Charles Kennedy—were cut from rough cloth.

On March 24, 1876, at Cimarron's St. James Hotel, Crockett in a drunken rage shot and killed three black soldiers and wounded another, all of them on leave from Fort Union. Crockett fled the scene and hid near a local ranch until arrangements were made for a favorable hearing before a sympathetic justice of the peace. Ultimately, Crockett's crime was excused because he was inebriated during its commission. He was admonished with a small fine for unlawfully carrying firearms.

Later, and usually in the company of Heffron, Davy Crockett terrorized Cimarron's peaceful population with sporadic gunshots, rambunctious behavior, and brazen threats. He cowed the local sheriff, Isaiah Rinehart, on one occasion ordering himself a new suit of clothes and sending the bill to the lawman. Another account claimed Crockett once stuck his six-shooter in the sheriff's face and forced him to guzzle drinks until he was stupefied. A humiliated Rinehart finally sought assistance from area rancher Joseph Holbrook as well as the Cimarron postmaster, John McCullough. On September 30, 1876, the sheriff and his two deputies armed themselves with shotguns and challenged Crockett and Heffron, who, just finishing up a spree, were mounted and leaving town. Deputy Holbrook called on them to halt; mockingly and mistakenly, Crockett challenged Holbrook to shoot. Holbrook did! So did the sheriff and McCullough. Crockett's frightened horse broke into a gallop that didn't end short of the Cimarron River. When the lawmen approached, they found Davy Crockett slumped dead in the saddle. As for Heffron, the lawmen arrested him, but he later broke jail and disappeared into the vastness of Colorado's snow-capped Rockies. The sheriff and his two "deputies" were acquitted of causing Crockett's death.

See also: ALLISON, ROBERT A.

CRUGER, William R. (a.k.a. Bill) (1840–1882)

In 1874, Bill Cruger migrated to the "Clear Fork Country," in what would later be organized as

Shackelford County, Texas. It was the site of Fort Griffin and a nearby ramshackle civilian community officially named Albany but better known as "The Flat." Albany became the Shackelford county seat, Cruger naming it in honor of his birthplace in Georgia.

Serving as a deputy under Sheriff John Larn, Cruger was involved in a horrific shootout at the Bee Hive Saloon. On January 17, 1877, gunmen Billy Bland and Charlie Reed drunkenly galloped into The Flat amid yells and popping six-shooters. Pulling back hard on their reins, the pair made a sliding stop in front of the saloon, jumped down, and vanished inside. Although the saloon was a roisterous dive at best, patrons in the Bee Hive were rightfully alarmed when Bland and Reed began shooting out the lamps. Taking note of the disturbance, Deputy Sheriff Bill Cruger, accompanied by the county attorney and two Shackelford County officials, entered the bar. Cruger hollered "hands up!" Bland whirled and fired at the deputy. Cruger fired back, joined by his cohort, William (Robert?) Jefferies. Bland's buddy Reed chimed in with his six-gun. Unfortunately, the quarters were close, and the barroom full. Bystanders Dan Barron, who had just been married, and a Lieutenant Myres, recently discharged from the army at Fort Griffin, attempted to retreat from the blistering melee—but not quickly enough. Barron caught a bullet in the forehead. Myres suffered a mortal wound in the back. Cruger was slightly wounded, and Jefferies received a wound through a lung, but survived. What of the instigator, Billy Bland? One of Cruger's bullets knocked him to the floor, where he painfully lingered, begging for someone to put him out of his misery. They didn't, so he died on his own within minutes. Charlie Reed disappeared during the excitement and wisely quit the area.

John Larn, Cruger's boss, resigned, and Cruger was appointed sheriff on March 20, 1877. Later, previous criminal misdoings by Larn came to light, and he was assassinated by vigilantes while a prisoner in the county jail. Cruger's involvement in the mob justice remains speculative. His name appeared on the vigilante list.

Although later elected to the position of Shackelford County sheriff, Cruger resigned on July 20, 1880, and with his wife and son moved to Princeton, Tennessee. There, while serving as city marshal, on May 29, 1882, just one day before his 42nd birthday, Bill Cruger was fatally gunned down while attempting to overpower a drunken prisoner who had secreted a revolver.

See also: FORT GRIFFIN, TEXAS, VIGILANTES; LARN, JOHN; SELMAN, JOHN HENRY

CURLY Wolf

A dangerous individual known to have a short temper and a quick fuse. While the term sometimes applied to lawmen, it primarily applied to outlaws and gunmen known to be constantly on the prowl, seeking trouble.

CURRIE, James (?–?)

This obscure Irish-born desperado, whose real last name might have been Curry, had found work in Marshall, Texas, as a detective for the Texas & Pacific Railroad. At about midnight on March 19, 1879, Currie, full of liquor, wandered into Marshall's White House lunchroom, where he encountered three New York show personalities—Miss Nellie Cummins, Benjamin C. Porter, and Maurice Barrymore, having an evening meal prior to catching the train to Hot Springs (later Truth or Consequences), New Mexico, for a performance. Back in New York, Barrymore and a Frederick Warde had formed a road company called the Warde-Barrymore Combination; Cummins, Barrymore, and Porter were taking a play called *Diplomacy on Tour* across the West. They had just finished a performance in Marshall.

During this meal, James Currie strolled through the room, pausing by the Barrymore table to make an insulting reference to the sexuality of Miss Cummins. Porter took offense and asked Currie to leave, which he did, going to a nearby table. Later, upon finishing his own meal, he passed by again, making more crude remarks regarding Miss Cummins. This prompted Barrymore, who had been a well-known middleweight boxer in England, to jump up and start removing his coat.

Currie glanced at him, drew two pistols, fired one and missed, then fired the other, and shot Barrymore in the left shoulder. The actor ran out of the room, through the kitchen, and into the backyard.

Porter now leaped to his feet, only to be shot in the stomach. Clutching his stomach, he staggered out the front door and collapsed on the sidewalk, where he died less than an hour later. Shortly after that, Sheriff Arch Adams arrested Currie and without inci-

dent locked him in jail. As for Porter, his body was shipped back to New York.

Barrymore, with a bullet lodged near his spine, was placed in the Marshall, Texas, Pacific Hotel, where Miss Cummins nursed him until Mrs. Barrymore arrived. Oddly, one of Barrymore's frequent visitors turned out to be Currie's brother, Andrew, the mayor of Shreveport, Louisiana. He offered to help Barrymore in any way possible, while insisting that his brother deserved to be freed.

The case went to trial in June 1879. Currie swore that he, Barrymore, and Porter had been gambling with others that afternoon, and the three men had won $30. The three then went to dinner where an argument started, and he shot Barrymore in self-defense. However, since none of Currie's "witnesses" showed up at the trial, the case was continued until November 26, by which time both Barrymore and Miss Cummins were on the stage back east. Subsequently, no trial occurred until June 10, 1880. This time Currie took the stand and claimed temporary insanity, swearing he had been drinking heavily on the evening of the shooting and that his delirium tremens had unbalanced him. The jury thus brought in a verdict of not guilty by reason of temporary insanity.

Currie thereafter wandered over to Lincoln County, New Mexico, where during a spree in White Oaks he stabbed and killed his roommate. A New Mexico jury gave him six years, although the governor soon pardoned him. After that, he dropped from sight.

As for Barrymore, by 1889 he had grown more unbalanced. As time passed, his erratic, irrational actions finally cost him his acting career. The state eventually committed him to the Amityville Sanitarium on Long Island, New York, where he died on March 25, 1905.

CURRY, George Sutherland (a.k.a. Flat Nose Curry) (1864?–1900)

George Curry (frequently spelled "Currie") was born on Prince Edward Island, Canada, but when he was a boy his family moved to Chadron, Nebraska. Some authorities believe he was an uncle to the Logan boys—Harvey, John, and Lonie. They rustled cattle together, but a kick in the face by a horse earned George the moniker of "Flat Nose Curry." The kick may also have contributed to his slight stoop when he walked.

On April 13, 1897, he and the Logan brothers allegedly killed Deputy Sheriff William Deane of Johnson County, Wyoming. Somewhere around this time they joined the Wild Bunch, participating in train and bank robberies. In 1899, he was caught changing the wrong brand and was shot to death by Sheriff Jesse M. "Jack" Tyler of Moab, Utah. Before dumping him into a grave at Thompson, Utah, however, souvenir hunters reportedly peeled away portions of his skin. His father later disinterred the body and moved it to Chadron, Utah, for burial.

Sheriff Tyler and Deputy Sheriff Sam Jenkins were both slain by Harvey Logan on May 27, 1900, reportedly in retaliation for the killing of Curry.

See also: CASSIDY, BUTCH; LOGAN, HARVEY

CYPRIAN

This is a word almost never used by ordinary people in the Old West. An exception was newspaper men, and they loved the expression. It meant prostitute.

See also: SOILED DOVES

DAKE, Crawley P. (1827–1890)

Crawley P. Dake was born at Kentfield, Ontario, Canada, but while still a youngster, he relocated to New York, along with his parents. By the time he was 28, he had moved to Michigan, where he tried his hand as a retail merchant. At the outbreak of the Civil War, Dake raised a company of volunteers and received a commission in the Fifth Michigan Cavalry. Major Dake fought at Gettysburg and in other stirring engagements until he was wounded and forced to retire in August 1864.

Dake returned to Michigan and accepted an appointment as chief deputy marshal of Detroit. He was also appointed as Michigan's collector of internal revenue. Up until now, Dake had been known more for his administrative roles than as an enforcer, but that was about to change, because on June 12, 1878, President Rutherford B. Hayes appointed Dake as the U.S. marshal for the Arizona Territory.

From the very beginning, two problems plagued Dake. First he complained, and with justification, that he was not provided sufficient funds for an efficient federal operation. In fact, for 1879 the U.S. Congress failed to appropriate any money at all for federal law enforcement. Secondly, sometimes the public questioned his selection of deputies—namely, Joseph W. Evans, because of his perceived involvement in the death of Jack Swilling; and later the brothers Virgil and Wyatt Earp, for their question-

able activities at Cochise County's booming mining town of Tombstone.

General lawlessness plagued Arizona during its formative years, highlighted by a spate of stagecoach robberies. Bureaucratic red tape further hampered Dake's efforts to field posses. Supervisors in Washington viewed each robbery as a separate exception to the rule of law and insisted that funds for pursuing lawbreakers be requested and approved after each offense. Furthermore, the Department of Justice typically became weary of hearing bad news, and bad news included Dake's continuing complaint, "If I am to protect the people, I must have the funds to do it." Even the murder of deputies J. H. Adams and Cornelius Findlay (Finely) by a band of desperadoes south of Tucson failed to persuade certain political leaders in the nation's capital that law enforcement problems on the southwestern frontier were a festering sore in need of lancing.

Adding to Dake's enforcement headaches was Arizona's proximity to the border with Mexico. Admittedly, Anglos were crossing the border and rustling Mexican livestock, but from Dake's perspective problems of greater weight were illegal incursions onto American soil by Mexican bandits. In truth, fugitives from each country simply stepped across the line to avoid capture by their respective governments.

Nevertheless, in spite of inherent political, geographical, and cultural adversities, Crawley Dake during his first term fielded seven posses, five of which captured or killed at least one outlaw. Dake, fully recognizing the importance of effective communications for law enforcement made extensive use of the telegraph. He also fostered a positive working relationship with Wells Fargo and Company. Somewhat unfairly, however, Dake's legitimate successes were often overshadowed by the chaotic unraveling of events at Tombstone. The friction between rival political, economic, and cultural factions in the mining camp, plus the eye-popping street fight of October 26, 1881, and its bloody aftermath, in effect were death knells for Dake's tenure as U.S. marshal.

Despite 20th-century glamorization, Dake's appointment of Virgil and Wyatt Earp as U.S. deputy marshals, even though their service lasted only two months, did not meet with universal public approval. Complicating the already abrasive state of affairs was Dake's failure to maintain a tight rein on these part-time, highly partisan deputies, a situation noted by many in the community of Tombstone, especially the Democrats. Furthermore, Dake's continual remonstrations regarding finances exacerbated an already severe public loss of confidence stemming from his lack of efficient record keeping, his pressuring of private companies for investigative funds, and his alleged mingling of government monies with his personal finances. An official Washington investigation ultimately resulted in the charge that Dake had "feloniously converted" over $50,000 of official funds to his own personal use. It led to his forced resignation and the filing of charges. In 1886, the controversy ended with a negotiated settlement.

After Washington replaced him with Zan L. Tidball, Crawley P. Dake resided in Prescott, Arizona Territory, where he developed mining and business interests. On April, 9, 1890, he died at Prescott from natural causes. Certainly from a purely objective point of view, his law enforcement activities could be characterized, at least in part, as innovative and progressive during a time when investigative support was not forthcoming from headquarters at Washington.

See also: EARP, VIRGIL; EARP, WYATT BERRY STAPP; EVANS, JESSE J.; GUNFIGHT AT THE OK CORRAL

DALTON Brothers: Bob, Emmett, Frank, Grattan, Mason

Of the 15 Dalton children, two died in infancy. Three were girls. Four sons went bad. Their father, Lewis

Dalton, had been a fifer during the Mexican War but otherwise spent his life operating saloons and betting on slow horses. The mother, Adeline, a tiny woman distantly related to the Youngers, held the family together, although she and her husband got along like Sitting Bull and George Armstrong Custer. When the boys grew older, the four black sheep followed their father throughout the racing circuit, particularly in California.

Although Grattan (Grat), born in 1861, was the oldest of those who went wild, Bob (born 1869) seemed the smartest. Mason, better known as Bill (born 1863), seemed the most devious, as well as the most articulate and in odd ways the most ambitious. Emmett (born 1871) was the youngest and most impressionable. He tagged along with the others because he looked up to them.

Bill, properly Mason Frakes Dalton, would spend a majority of his life in California. During the mid-1880s he worked as a ranch foreman in Merced County, California, married the boss's daughter, had his own spread, and entered politics. He supported the local Democratic Party and worked as a party officer.

As for Frank (born around 1865), he caught the attention of Isaac Parker, a Fort Smith, Arkansas, "hanging judge" who commissioned Frank a U.S. deputy marshal. Deputies in those days picked up two dollars for every prisoner delivered and six cents a mile for travel expenses. The work was so dangerous that almost one-third of Parker's men—65 out of 225—died in the line of duty. Frank died during a shootout in 1887 while chasing whiskey smugglers; he killed three bootleggers. Frank thus became the first Dalton to die with his boots on. Bob Dalton, meanwhile, had become police chief of the Osage Nation, but he and Grat did little more than rustle cattle and shake down bootleggers and other nefarious characters. By 1890, when it seemed like they might become residents of their own jail, they resigned their positions and went to visit their brother Bill. Safe at Bill's ranch, their big question seemed to be: How can we make a good living without working for it?

Train robbery, if the Wild Bunch successes were any indication, seemed an easy way to put bread on the table. Thus in mid-February 1891, Bob, Grat, and Emmett struck the Southern Pacific near Alila, California. They killed a fireman but were driven off without getting any money. Bill Dalton may or may

Bob Dalton and his sweetheart in 1889 (Author's Collection)

not have been along on this attempted heist, although he was arrested along with Grat Dalton and charged with the robbery. Grat was convicted and sentenced to 20 years in San Quentin, but in September he broke jail and took refuge in Indian Territory (Oklahoma), where Bob and Emmett were hiding.

The Dalton gang now recruited mean and ambitious help: George "Bitter Creek" Newcomb, "Black Face" Charlie Bryant, Dick Broadwell, Charley Pierce, Bill Doolin, and Bill McEhanie. In early 1891, they hit the Texas Express near Wharton, Oklahoma. With no resistance offered, the outlaws rode away with $14,000. Black Face Charlie celebrated too much, however, and was captured. He escaped but died in August of that same year when he and a U.S. marshal shot each other to death.

Meanwhile, Bob Dalton's girlfriend, Eugenia Moore, made inquiries regarding the safety of property she planned to ship by rail. She therefore had a pretty good concept regarding railroad security, and she passed the information along to Bob. On September 15, 1891, the Dalton gang successfully struck a train near Lellietta, Oklahoma. On July 1, 1892, the gang stopped a train in the Cherokee Strip, and again without resistance cleaned out the cash. On September 15, at Adair, Oklahoma, the Daltons not only raided the depot and the cash box but backed a wagon up to the express car of the Missouri-Kansas

& Texas train just as it pulled in. They quickly convinced the guard to open up, but when the doors swung open, the Daltons encountered Indian police and railroad detectives, who opened fire. The outlaws escaped without a scratch, leaving behind one official dead and three wounded.

Bob Dalton decided that it was time to switch tactics. With lawmen concentrating on protecting trains, Bob considered it a perfect chance to rob a bank. In fact, why not rob two at the same time? While much has been made of the fact that robbing two banks at once would be an accomplishment even Jesse James could not pull off, whether the Daltons had that thought in mind is questionable. Bob probably saw the two banks solely as targets of opportunity, a chance to make a huge, final cash withdrawal—and then retire.

So the Daltons turned their horses toward Coffeyville, Kansas, where Bob had once lived. He knew about the Condon and First National Banks, so Bob, Grat, and Emmett, Bill Powers, Bill Doolin, and Dick Broadwell rode north and east. On the day they approached the community, Bill Doolin's horse came up lame, so he turned toward the last ranch seen in order to make a swap. At 9:30 A.M., still minus Doolin but undaunted and convinced of their infallibility, the outlaws fastened on false beards, rode down Maple Street, and secured their mounts in an alley between Walnut and Maple. Bob and Emmett then entered the First National, while Powers, Broadwell, and Grat strolled into the Condon.

Surprisingly, the two men had better luck than the three, although all five ultimately had no luck at all. While Bob covered the bank employees and customers, Emmett stuffed money in a grain sack, by some accounts over $21,000. Across the street, Grat was having trouble. A clerk claimed the cash was inside a safe with a time lock and that it would not open for another three minutes. Grat agreed to wait.

Meanwhile, the outlaws had been recognized, and the street was filling up with citizens loading rifles. Bob Dalton, who saw the congestion, and of course noticed bullets flying through the windows, yelled, "Out the back door!" The two brothers headed that way, Emmett carrying the money. Bob, with a rifle, shot down Lucius Baldwin, a bank clerk who had armed himself.

From both banks the outlaws now poured into the street, guns blazing, heading for the horses in the alley. Bob killed three men along the way, although some of those deaths could have been attributed to the firepower of the other outlaws, or even the excited townspeople.

The desperadoes reached their horses, but that was all they reached. Riflemen were approaching from both ends of the alley. Bill Powers was shot out of the saddle, stone dead when he hit the ground. Dick Broadwell vaulted into the saddle and galloped through the crowd to the end of the alley, but he was dead before he got another 50 feet. The town barber, Carey Seaman, fired a shotgun blast into Bob Dalton from less than five feet. City Marshal Charles Connelly and Grat Dalton began closing and firing at one another. Both men went down; Grat did not get up. Emmett, repeatedly wounded, managed to climb on his horse, reportedly pausing to help his brother Bob. At that instant, another shotgun blast blew him out of the saddle. Emmett

would be the only survivor, if one doesn't count Bill Doolin, who, reportedly, heard the gunfire while approaching Coffeyville, turned his horse, and disappeared in the direction of Oklahoma. The Dalton gang had ceased to exist.

The dead gang members were duly propped up, photographed, and buried. As for Bill Dalton, he moved to Oklahoma, teamed up with Bill Doolin, and killed Marshal Lafe Shadley during a shootout at Ingalls, Oklahoma. In late the May 1894, the Dalton/Doolin makeshift gang robbed a bank in Longview, Texas. A posse killed Bill Doolin on June 8.

That left Emmett Dalton as the only survivor. He was tried for murder and received a life sentence. In 1907, the governor pardoned him for good behavior. He married his childhood sweetheart and lived as a model citizen until his natural death in 1937.

See also: BRYANT, CHARLES; DOOLIN, WILLIAM M.

Emmett Dalton was the only survivor of the Coffeyville Bank robbery. (Author's Collection)

DALY, John (?–1864)

John Daly, by most accounts, was born in New York and wound up in California by way of Canada. In late 1862, at somewhere around 25 years of age, with a string of dead men reportedly in his past, John Daly rode into Aurora, Nevada. The Pond Mining Company at Last Chance Hill hired him to protect its interests. Daly therefore brought together a group of thugs going by the names of John McDowell—alias Three Fingered Jack—Italian Jim, William Buckley, and Jim Sears. In the fall of 1863, John Daly also became a deputy city marshal. At this point one murder followed another. Honest merchants were shaken down by dishonest lawmen.

Meanwhile, William Johnson, who owned a way station on the West Walker River, had asked one of his employees to recover a stolen horse, and the employee had killed the thief. It took Daly time to get his revenge, but on February 1, 1864, Daly and associates clubbed Johnson to the earth with revolvers, shot him in the head, and cut his throat.

Such a senseless murder enraged the town. Aurora formed a Citizens Protective Order, essentially a vigilante committee. Italian Jim confessed and was given immunity. John Daly, Three Fingered Jack, James Masterson, and William Buckley were arrested and jailed. But the vigilantes broke them out and led them to a scaffold. Daly took a swig of whiskey. At 1:30, they were all jerked into eternity.

DEADFALL

As used by cowboys and some city folks, a deadfall was a gambling or drinking establishment of low repute. Patrons never had a chance of winning, or even of leaving sober.

DEADWOOD, South Dakota

Deadwood, South Dakota, might not be remembered at all had not Wild Bill Hickok been slain there in the No. 10 Saloon on August 2, 1876. His name and fate alone have brought thousands of visitors to this community. Buried first in the Ingleside Cemetery, he was later transferred to the Mount Moriah Cemetery. Calamity Jane lies near him, and her grave also has been a tourist draw.

Prostitution dens and gambling halls (often called the Badlands) once lined the streets of this Black Hills community, which otherwise made its living from the rich and plentiful ore that lay underground nearby. Also, some of the Wild Bunch broke jail here on October 31, 1897. At present the town is attractive, pleasant to stroll through, and modern yet old.

See also: CALAMITY JANE; HICKOK, JAMES BUTLER; WILD BUNCH

DEMING, New Mexico, Hangings (1916)

On the night of March 9, 1916, the Mexican insurrectionist leader Pancho Villa raided the sleeping village of Columbus, New Mexico. Ten American civilians were slain, as well as eight soldiers. Other Americans killed at least 100 of Villa's partisans and captured seven, all of them wounded. They were all indicted for the murder of Charles D. Miller, James Dean, J. L. Moore, and Cpl. Paul Simon.

The indicted were: Juan Sánchez, age 16; José Rodríquez, 20; Taurino García, 21; Francisco Alvarez (age unknown); José Rangel, 23; Eusebio Renetería, 24; and Juan Castillo, 26. All were single, although one (Castillo) was a widower. All were Catholics from southern Mexico, and none could read or write.

Since the attack had been against not a military post but a peaceful New Mexico community, jurisdiction in this murder trial went to the state of New Mexico. The trial began promptly on April 19, 1916, nearly six weeks after the Columbus attack. Burl R. Wood acted as defense attorney, but his defense was neither spirited nor articulate. A doctor testified that

while he was treating their wounds the raiders had admitted to being in Columbus, although none had realized that Columbus was part of the United States. Nevertheless, the territory did not have to prove that any of these men had killed anyone. All it had to prove was that these individuals were in Columbus during the commission of a felony, which made irrelevant the excuse that most of the accused claimed to merely be holding and watching horses.

José Rodríguez testified that the Villistas had forcibly inducted him into the rebel army. Renetería stated that he had been pressed into the federal Mexican army for five years. After discharge, Yaqui Indians had taken him prisoner for 14 months. Following that he had found employment unloading ore from boxcars, but after Villa raided the ore station, Renetería found himself suddenly in his army.

Rangel testified from a cot and said that while working as a vaquero on a Chihuahua ranch, he had been purchasing supplies in Chihuahua City. Villa's men had snatched him off the street and inducted him into their forces.

Castillo claimed that he had been a private soldier with the federal army and had been locked in a house for eight days before agreeing to join Villa.

García insisted he had been on his way home to Oaxaca when Villa partisans surrounded and beat him with a spade until he agreed to enlist.

At the trial, both sides rested early on the morning of April 21, 1916. At 11:30 the jury rendered its verdict: all were found guilty of murder in the first degree. The judge sentenced each one to be hanged by the neck until dead, their execution to take place between the hours of 6 A.M. and 6 P.M. on Friday, May 19, 1916. While their appeals were being heard, the prisoners were transported to the Santa Fe Penitentiary, where the governor delayed their execution until June 9, 1916. On that date, Francisco Alvarez and Juan Sánchez were taken to Deming and hanged. The others received a 21-day reprieve. It had been three months and 21 days since the Columbus raid.

On June 30, Governor William C. McDonald commuted the sentence of José Rodríguez to life imprisonment. Rodríguez was released from the penitentiary in February 1921. The remaining four—Renetería, García, Castillo, and Rangel—were brought to Deming, New Mexico, and hanged side by side on June 30. They went calmly to their deaths and today lie in remote, unmarked graves in the Deming Cemetery.

DENO, Charlotte (a.k.a. Lottie) (1844?–1934)

Lottie Deno, one of the West's great lady gamblers, was well known and highly respected, one reason being that she was also mysterious. By some accounts, she was born Carlotta J. Tompkins in Warsaw, Kentucky, on April 21, 1844. Her parents called her Charlotte, but everyone else called her Lottie. The financial shock of the Civil War ruined her parents. She was rumored to have married Johnny Golden, reportedly a jockey who turned to gambling—and so did she. In Texas he reportedly killed a man during a card dispute, then fled the state. The buxom redhead was thereafter on her own. Gambling was about all she knew. She lived for a while in San Antonio, where she adopted the moniker "Lottie Deno," the name being, according to historian Robert DeArment, a twist on a crude English/Spanish phrase, "Lotta Dinero," meaning lots of money. She worked in such high-class gambling houses as Jack Harris's Vaudeville Saloon, the Comanche Club, and the Jockey Club. In 1876, this tastefully dressed lady, now in her early thirties, stepped off the stagecoach at Fort Griffin, Texas, and became a gambler in the Bee Hive Saloon.

She stayed nearly two years; then suddenly she was gone, marrying Frank Thurman, a gambler and owner of the University Club in San Antonio. At that time, she dropped the name Lottie Deno and became Charlotte Thurman. The two of them worked in the Gem Saloon at Silver City, New Mexico, spending a couple of years there until moving on to the mining town of Kingston, New Mexico, where Charlotte reportedly won $9,000 in one evening.

These two gamblers, however, knew when to quit. She and her husband moved to Deming, New Mexico, where they spent the remainder of their lives. Frank died in 1908 and Charlotte in February 1934.

See also: HOLLIDAY, JOHN HENRY; THURMOND, FRANK

DERRINGER

Henry Derringer Jr. developed this pocket pistol in 1825. The barrel length ranged from a half-inch to four inches, and the guns were usually sold in matched pairs of .33 to .50 caliber. Primarily because of its size, which made it easy to conceal, the Derringer became a favorite of ladies of the evening, as well as of gamblers and holdup artists.

DESPERADO

Desperadoes were desperate, dangerous outlaws of the early American West. They were usually mounted. Examples were the Dalton brothers and the James boys. Singular desperadoes would have included such figures as John Wesley Hardin, Billy the Kid, and Butch Cassidy. The desperado era had basically run its course by the late 1880s.

DIE With Their Boots On

To die with one's boots on is to die bravely in battle. It is a way of saying that someone fought all the way to the end, accepting death on the field of combat rather than dying in bed with a cover over his or her head. Those who die with their boots on never surrender, preferring not to die as a victim. People who die with their boots on have reached the point where all they have left to give is their life, so they give it too.

See also: BOOT HILL

DIME Novels

Dime novels—cheap 10-cent sensationalist books printed by the thousands for a mass audience—go all the way back to the 1860s. Through a series of adventure formulas, these paperbacks brought a fascinating string of characters to life; in fact, they created figures that real-life individuals seemed to fit. Calamity Jane and Deadwood Dick got their start as dime-novel figures. The public in particular thrived on melodramatic western stories with heroines of purity and heroes of virtue and bravery. Thanks to dime novels, such individuals as Buffalo Bill and Wild Bill Hickok catapulted from little-known people into world-famous ones. Unfortunately, neither truth nor realism ever became an essential component of dime novels.

DIXON, Simpson (a.k.a. Simp Dixson) (?–1870)

Simp Dixon, who may or may not have been related to John Wesley Hardin through Hardin's mother's side of the family, was likely born in northeast Texas, never served in the Civil War, and was probably only about 18 or 19 years old when he died. Hardin referred to Dixon as a member of the Ku Klux Klan and called him "a man who had sworn to kill [the occupying] Yankee soldiers for as long as he lived."

Hardin mentioned that he and Simp had once been engaged in a thicket shootout with Yankee soldiers that left two dead.

In February 1870, however, life ran out for Simp Dixon. He died during a Limestone County shootout with Union soldiers led by Sergeant Dash. The soldiers buried him in the Fort Parker Memorial Cemetery near Mexia, placing him oblique to the other graves because he was "crossways with the world." John Wesley Hardin described Simp as "one of the most dangerous men in Texas."

See also: LEE-PEACOCK FEUD; HARDIN, JOHN WESLEY

DODGE City, Kansas

Dodge City, Kansas, began as a cow town, perhaps the most famous cow town of them all. Taking its name from the nearby Fort Dodge, the community began as a buffalo-hide collecting and shipping point. By 1873, as the Atchison, Topeka, & Santa Fe Railroad entered the neighborhood, and as Texas cattle followed the western extension of the Chisholm Trail, the time seemed ripe for the creation of a high-flying community serving a variety of needs.

Texas cattle arriving in Dodge City led to the establishment of restaurants, saloons, barber shops, and grocery stores. The Dodge House became one of the West's better-known hotels, and Front Street the wildest and most active part of town. When the crime rate started to soar, the city taxed its saloons, brothels, and gambling casinos to pay for law enforcement.

Although the town's gunfighting reputation was blown somewhat out of proportion (the wildest years occurred between 1876 and 1885, but only about 15 killings took place), several lawmen made reputations for themselves. These included the Masterson brothers (James, Ed, and Bat) plus Wyatt Earp. Doc Holliday never shot anyone in Dodge, but he did spend some time in and around the Long Branch Saloon. So did "Mysterious Dave" Mather, who was more lethal. Still, although shootings did occur, none fit the movie-classic mode of *High Noon.*

It took the Texas fever to kill Dodge City as a cow town. In 1884, the governor quarantined the state, and the cattle drives abruptly halted.

See also: EARP, WYATT; HOLLIDAY, JOHN HENRY; MASTERSON, EDWARD JOHN; MASTERSON, JAMES; MASTERSON, WILLIAM BARCLAY; MATHER, DAVID; SHORT, LUKE

DODGE City Gang

As Dodge City, Kansas, cleaned out some of its better-known unsavory individuals, many of them, along with reckless individuals—gamblers, gunmen, and fugitives from cow camps and railroad yards—fled to East Las Vegas, New Mexico. The shallow Gallinas River, easily crossed by anyone over two feet tall, separated East Las Vegas from West Las Vegas. So the two towns formed one tiny community; still, each lived in its own different, unique world.

By mid-1879, East Las Vegas, a railroad town, had essentially arrived. The unincorporated town had saloons, brothels, a few restaurants, and no few wild and woolly residents. The Earp brothers and Doc Holliday joined in the festivities. Holliday opened the last dental office of his career but soon closed it and substituted a saloon and gambling hall.

But the man who controlled the unincorporated town of East Las Vegas turned out to be Hyman G. Neill, a confidence man most folks knew as "Hoodoo Brown." He became the acting coroner and justice of the peace, and he considered himself not only the mayor but the town council. His police force consisted of former Dodge City, Kansas, gunfighters and confidence men, Brown paying them by shaking down local merchants. Thus the Dodge City Gang, as most residents and visitors referred to it, actually controlled East Las Vegas during its formative period. Brown retained a right-hand man called John "Dutchy" Schunderberger. With his almost unpronounceable name, Dutchy had to be good with his fists and his guns, and he was.

Still, the Dodge City Gang and its iron-fisted rule over East Las Vegas had started to fade by early 1880. The Earps and Holliday drifted off to more lucrative pastures in Arizona. Hoodoo Brown's town marshal, Joe Carson, was slain in a gunfight, and the job passed to "Mysterious Dave" Mather, who shot some of the wrong people before he again got mysterious and vanished. Among his other talents, Hoodoo Brown went on to become an administrator for the estate of the recently murdered Michael Kelliher, killed by J. J. Webb, one of Brown's violent policemen. Webb and Brown, of course, both skipped town, Webb charged with murder, and Hoodoo with larceny (since Brown had taken all of Kelliher's money, estimated to be at least $2,000).

Webb escaped from prison on December 3, 1881, and is thought to have died of smallpox in Arkansas during 1882. As for Hoodoo Brown, there are stories of his being in El Paso, Texas, as well as in Deming, New Mexico, but neither he nor the remnants of the Dodge City Gang ever again controlled anything. How and where Hoodoo Brown died is anyone's guess.

See also: EARP, WYATT; HOLLIDAY, JOHN HENRY; MATHER, DAVID; SHORT, LUKE.

DODGE City War

During the early and mid-1870s, a group of merchants, gamblers, and saloonkeepers created, or became known as, the Dodge City Gang, led by Mayor James H. Kelley, better known as "Dog" Kelley. The Masterson brothers—Ed, Jim, and Bat—handled law enforcement. They also operated various saloons. Wyatt Earp arrived primarily to gamble but also served as a policeman and city marshal. An 1878 law against gambling and prostitution did not arouse much opposition, especially since sin paid salaries for law enforcement personnel. However, an open city did extract its penalties. While trying to disarm a drunken cowboy in 1878, City Marshal Ed Masterson had been slain.

In 1879, an antigang movement called the Reformers arose. It defeated Bat Masterson as the Ford County sheriff, and he left town. By 1881, Mayor Kelley and his council had been thrown out by the voters, and the new mayor, Alonzo B. Webster, who also had fingers in saloons and brothels, posted a warning to the gang:

To all whom it may concern: All thieves, thugs, confidence men, and persons without visible means of support, will take notice that the ordinance enacted for their special benefit will be rigorously enforced on and after tomorrow.

Although the council dismissed Masterson as city marshal, someone wrote Ben's brother, Bat Masterson, and asked him to come to Dodge and help. Bat arrived in mid-April 1881, and immediately got into a shooting spree with saloon gunmen A. J. Peacock and Al Updegraff, the participants firing rounds at

Dodge City Peace Commission. (Standing in rear) W. H. Harris, Luke Short, Bat Masterson; (sitting) Charles E. Bassett, Wyatt Earp, M. F. McLane, and Neil Brown (Kansas State Historical Society)

each other in the business district, although only Updegraff was wounded. Bat was arrested and paid an eight-dollar fine, plus court costs.

To further complicate the situation, the fashionably dressed gambler Luke Short arrived in town within the year (1882), and by February 1883 he had purchased a half-interest in the Long Branch Saloon. He and the Mastersons were long-time friends, and with the Mastersons' support, Short's partner, William H. Harris, campaigned for mayor against reform candidate Lawrence E. Deger. Deger won.

When Luke Short complained, he and five gamblers were arrested too, marched to the railroad depot, and given a choice of taking the train east or west. Short went east, complaining every step of the way that conditions in Dodge were out of control. Newspapers across the nation picked up on the excitement, and stories started appearing that referred to the disturbance as the Dodge City War.

Talk arose of troops being raised, but that came to nothing. Fortunately for Short, he had friends, and it wasn't long before six of them, including Wyatt Earp, along with Short, began strutting through the city streets. Accommodations were reached. No one shot anyone, of course, and there was more laughter than intimidation around the public square and on Front Street. In 1890, once things quieted down, the seven, who remained friends, including Short, had their photo taken. The picture, with tongue in cheek, has historically been dubbed "The Dodge City Peace Commission." Meanwhile, Dodge City continued with Mayor Deger's somewhat modified reform movement.

See also: EARP, WYATT; MASTERSON, WILLIAM BARCLAY; SHORT, LUKE.

DOOLIN, William (a.k.a. Bill) (1858–1896)

Bill Doolin was born and raised in Arkansas. He worked mostly as a cowboy but joined the Dalton Gang around 1891. It robbed three trains in Indian Territory (Oklahoma), one at Lelietta, one at Red Rock on June 1, 1892, and the third at Adair on July 13. Afterward, the gang headed for Coffeyville, Kansas, its intentions being to rob two banks at once, but Doolin's horse reportedly came up lame, and he dropped out. Had Doolin remained with the Daltons, Coffeyville would probably be the end of his story.

Instead he married and then reorganized the gang with himself as leader, including in it such individuals as Dynamite Dick Clifton, George "Bitter Creek" Newcomb, Charley Pierce, George "Red Buck" Weightman, Little Dick West, and several others. By mid-1893, they were robbing trains and stagecoaches. The lawmen on their trail would not be denied. On the afternoon of September 1, 1893, the outlaws slipped into Ingalls, Oklahoma, and had to shoot their way out.

Three famous lawmen—Chris Madsen, Heck Thomas, and Bill Tilghman—continued the pursuit, over time whittling down the Doolin gang members. At Eureka Springs, Bill Tilghman captured Doolin at a bathhouse and dragged him to Gutherie, Oklahoma, where the whole town turned out to cheer as Doolin was led down the street. Nevertheless, within a short time he led a jail break and again disappeared.

The lawmen now adopted another tactic, that of watching the home of Doolin's father-in-law near Lawton, Oklahoma, where the outlaw's wife and child lived. Thus on the night of August 25, 1896, as Doolin walked toward the house leading his horse, Heck Thomas called on him to surrender, then killed him with a shotgun.

See also: DALTON BROTHERS; MADSEN, CHRISTIAN; THOMAS, HENRY ANDREW; WEST, RICHARD

DUANE, Charles P. (a.k.a. Dutch Charley) (1829–1886)

Dutch Charley Duane was born in Tipperary, Ireland. The family moved to Albany, New York, around 1837, and within another five years Charles had become a wagonmaker as well as a local athlete, excelling in prizefighting. A German competitor gave him the name of "Dutch Charley," and it followed him all the way west, where he arrived in San Francisco during the height of the Gold Rush in January 1850. Throughout the next few years, Duane became quite the man's man around town engaging in boxing matches, but also being repeatedly hauled into court for brawling. He frequently knocked an opponent unconscious before the man even realized that the fight had started. On February 17, 1851, he not only attended a masked ball but beat one man senseless and then shot him in the back. Dutch Charley escaped prison only because the victim recovered.

On July 27, the courts gave Duane a year in jail for injury to another person, but because of political connections the governor secretly pardoned him. He was again arrested for brawling on April 5, 1852. The court fined him $50. On June 6, 1853, perhaps for the first time, he found serious work, becoming assistant chief of the San Francisco fire department. Three years later, however, the vigilance committee reorganized. It hanged four thugs and ordered Dutch Charley (who had not reformed) out of town. Duane hustled east to Washington, D.C., where he unknowingly drank liquor containing wood alcohol. It nearly killed him, weakening his legs in particular. So when he returned to San Francisco in 1860, though he still started brawls, now there was a difference—he usually lost.

During that same year, William Ross took possession of a piece of San Francisco land that Dutch Charley claimed. The two men argued about it, and Dutch Charley shot Ross in the back. On October 22, 1866, Duane went on trial for murder. The jury found him not guilty.

Dutch Charley Duane never changed much even after that. His end came in May 1886, when he fell out of a buggy. He died of his injuries.

DUBLIN, Richard (a.k.a. Dick Dublin) (?–1878)

Richard Dublin was born, and grew up with his brothers Dell and Role, on a small farm along the South Llano in Kimble County, Texas. All the youngsters became outlaws. Dick, the oldest, was described as "a large man, stout and of dark complexion, who looked more like the bully of a prize ring than the cowman he was." Although the motive remains murky, Dick and a partner in crime, Ace Lankford, killed two men at a country store in Coryell County. Combined county and state rewards totaling $700 went out. Dick Dublin, boasting he would never surrender, fled to the mesquite and chaparral thickets, becoming a desperate and much-wanted fugitive.

Adding to the mix, Dell Dublin killed Jim Williams and also took to the brush, later locating and joining up with brother Dick. After an intensive search by Texas Rangers, Dell was arrested at Luke Stone's ranch and was immediately transported to the Llano County jail for safekeeping. But for whatever reason, the authorities released him in 1877.

On more than one occasion, Dick was almost captured by Texas Rangers but managed to escape after blistering exchanges of gunfire, causing the irate ranger lieutenant N. O. Reynolds to chastise his subordinates, snapping that his black cook could have done a better job in dealing with Dick Dublin, and that the outlaw had become a "regular Jonah" to the ranger company.

At last, on the morning of January 18, 1878, taken completely off guard and fleeing on foot, Dick Dublin was fatally gunned down at the Mack Potter ranch by the second shot from Ranger James Gillett's lever-action rifle. Since the reward was for arrest and conviction, not dead or alive, the money was never paid. Reportedly Dell and Role Dublin made serious, but in the end empty, threats against the Texas Rangers for killing their brother.

Meanwhile, a series of stagecoach holdups had occurred near Peg-Leg station, a stop on the San Saba River in particularly rough and isolated country midway between Fort McKavett and Fort Mason. Texas Rangers had been assigned to ride shotgun on stagecoaches, but the tactic had been abandoned in order to handle other demanding law enforcement missions. Finally, a break came when Bill Allison, Jimmy Dublin's son-in-law, "snitched" to Texas Rangers Dick Ware and Jim Gillett. Warrants were issued for Dell and Role Dublin, Mack Potter, and Rube Boyce. In the end, all were rounded up, both Dublin boys being shot in the process. The bandits received 15 years in the penitentiary. The Peg-Leg robberies ceased.

See also: GILLETT, JAMES BUCHANAN

DUEL

In the eastern and southern United States, a duel involved two men standing back to back, pistols in hand, stepping off 10 paces, turning, and firing at each other. In the western United States, a gun duel took place without the formalities. There were no High Noons, in the strict sense of the metaphor. A duel referred to two or more men firing at each other, frequently from opposite sides of a street, with various calibers and types of weapons, and often from behind cover. Sometimes several parties were injured or slain, including innocent bystanders.

DUFFIELD, Milton B. (1810–1874)

Born in Wheeling, West Virginia, Milton Duffield drifted at an early age over to Ohio, where he worked as a merchant. There he married, fathering four children, all of whom he abandoned. He ended up at Tuolumne County in California (1852), where he sought his fortune in real estate and gold-mining claims. In these gold camps, Duffield won many a drink with his steady hand and sure six-shooter aim.

As time passed, the foul looking, hard-drinking Duffield became an utterly audacious frontier personality, a person many were offended by and most were afraid of. Adding to his intemperate behavior were well-grounded suspicions about questionable business dealings.

Absolutely fearless with regard to his own personal safety, deliberate and cool in any desperate encounter, it wasn't long before the hulking (six foot three inches, 220 pounds) Duffield found his trouble. In 1854, Duffield was attacked by James G. Lyons, Tim Hazelton, and a man known as Scott. The trio commenced firing at Duffield as he walked down a public street. Seemingly possessed with raw nerve, Duffield jerked one of his own revolvers and shot down Lyons. Hazelton and Scott fled.

At the outbreak of the Civil War, Duffield returned east and may have made an exploratory trip to Nicaragua for the U.S. government. Later, after the Arizona Territory had been carved from New Mexico, Milton B. Duffield, on March 6, 1863, at 53 years of age, became the territory's first U.S. marshal.

When Duffield arrived in Tucson, the town was just starting to live up to its stereotypical image as a wild and woolly frontier community. There was an overabundance of loose livestock, loose women, loose tops on whiskey barrels, and loose interpretations of how the law should be enforced. Yet Milton Duffield, silk hat atop his balding head, an arsenal concealed in his clothes, felt at home amid the boisterous *bailes* and the dirt-floored saloons. "He drew weapons from the arm-holes of his waistcoat, from his boot-legs, from his hip-pockets, and from the back of his neck . . . On a war-footing, nothing less than a couple of Gatling guns would have served to round out the armament." Those who witnessed Duffield's personal artillery inventory chose to remain silent about the marshal's "eccentricities."

During one well-publicized dispute with a former Confederate officer, a Lieutenant Colonel Kennedy, Duffield knocked the man to the ground and kicked him in the head. When the befuddled antagonist regained his feet and fled, the marshal pulled out a derringer and shot him in the buttocks, a painful but nonfatal wound. On another occasion, "Waco Bill," a teamster and a Texan full of rot-gut whiskey, declared he wanted his own personal piece of the new lawman in town. He was obliged. Waco Bill had hardly reached for his six-shooter when Duffield's bullet struck him in the groin.

Duffield's extreme hatred for ex-Confederates and their sympathizers fed his unrelenting attacks on southerners. This made it difficult for territorial officials to heal old wounds. The marshal made a lot of people happy when, enormously dissatisfied with delays in financial compensation, he tendered his resignation on November 25, 1865, to become effective on April 1 of the following year. No one tried to change his mind.

Seeking other work, and weary of wrangling about past expense accounts, Duffield secured an appointment as special postal agent for Arizona, New Mexico, and Colorado. The officials replaced him in March 1870 due in large part to his "high-handed conduct."

In a dispute with newspaper editor Pierson Dooner, who was holding a pistol in each hand, both aimed at Duffield's chest, the ex-marshal stared him down. Nothing happened. On another occasion Duffield challenged Tucson mayor Fred Maish to a duel. The district attorney (McCaffry) approached him from behind, placed a small pistol against his back, and pulled the trigger. The gun misfired. Duffield had to be the luckiest man in the West.

In June 1870, two Mexican men entered his residence while he slept and tried to kill him with a hatchet and a knife. A blow to the shoulder awakened him, and Duffield dispersed his attackers, later commenting, "I sprang up in my bed and fought them, and in grasping a large knife my right thumb was cut off. That prevented me from cocking my pistol although I finally got one shot. They retreated, but not till they had made some 31 wounds on my person."

Duffield continued to be the focal point for numerous brawls, his life coming to an abrupt end on June 5, 1874. During a dispute with Joseph T. Holmes over a piece of real estate, Holmes with a double-barreled shotgun stood firm as Duffield advanced toward him. Duffield should have heeded repeated warnings to back off. He didn't, and he died.

DUNLAP, John (a.k.a. Three Fingered Jack) (?–1900)

"Three Fingered" Jack Dunlap is something of a Western enigma. Of the fact that indeed he was at one time a real, live bad guy, there is no historical question or doubt. Presumably he was handed his nickname because of a missing digit. Specific details regarding his origin and antecedents are sparse, and while he lived, Jack wasn't worth much. Dead, though, he occasionally made it into the history books.

Three Fingered Jack Dunlap allegedly was a product of the Colorado Penitentiary for some unknown criminal mischief, and whether he just wanted a change to a warmer Arizona or was running from Rocky Mountain policing authorities will possibly remain a not very significant mystery.

A couple of Three Fingered Jack's misadventures, however, are not clouded in ambiguity, one being his August 6, 1896, abortive robbery of the International Bank of Nogales in Arizona Territory. By most accounts Three Fingered Jack was the gang's leader, but plans went awry when Fred Herrera, a sharp-witted bank cashier, grabbed his six-shooter and started firing, although all he killed were a couple of horses in the street.

Later, after tedious and time-consuming posse work on the part of Cochise County sheriff C. S. Fly and Pima County sheriff Bob Leatherwood, the outlaws and lawmen closed for a skirmish. The outlaws killed a U.S. mounted customs inspector named Frank Robson and then fled.

Three Fingered Jack now dropped out of sight until 1900, when the Alvord/Stiles gang recruited him for a southeastern Arizona train robbery scheduled for February 15. As expected, the train chugged across the international line from Sonora, Mexico, and steamed into Fairbank, Arizona Territory, with a Wells Fargo & Co. guard Jeff Milton on board. Waiting were Three Fingered Jack Dunlap, former West Texas cowboy Bob Brown, "Bravo Juan" Yoas, and the Owens brothers, George and Lewis. They hit the train hard, severely wounding Jeff Milton in the arm. Thinking Milton out of tactical commission the desperadoes advanced on the express car, but Milton steadied his double-barrel shotgun with his good arm and banged away. Three Fingered Jack took most of the charge and collapsed, while some of the remaining pellets punctured Bravo Juan in the back, causing painful though not life-threatening wounds. Jack's condition was much worse. Helping Jack into the saddle, the five fled into a dark desert night. Three Fingered Jack was ultimately abandoned by his partners. When a posse finally stumbled onto Jack Dunlap, they uncorked a bottle of liquor for him. He drank, he talked, and he died. His pals were soon captured and sent to the Yuma Territorial Prison in chains.

See also: ALVORD, ALBERT; MILTON, JEFFERSON DAVIS; YUMA TERRITORIAL PRISON

EARP, Morgan (1851–1882)

Morgan Earp was born in Pella, Iowa, but was in Wichita, Kansas, by the mid-1870s. By July 1880, he and his common-law wife Louisa (known as Lou) met Wyatt Earp in Tombstone, where Morgan and others joined a group of soldiers trailing mule thieves. Morgan later became a shotgun guard for Wells Fargo. During his off hours in mid-August 1880, he captured George Perrine, the accused murderer of Mike Killeen. Shortly afterward, Virgil Earp became Tombstone's chief of police as well as a U.S. deputy marshal.

Along with Doc Holliday, Morgan acted as one of Virgil's special deputies during the OK Corral gunfight. Morgan likely shot Billy Clanton in the chest and was himself seriously wounded, shot horizontally through both shoulders.

On March 18, 1882, someone assassinated Morgan. He had been playing pool at Campbell & Hatch's on Allen Street. A glass door opened into the alley, and parties unknown fired through the glass. Dr. George Goodfellow later noted that "the bullet entered the body just to the right of the spinal column in the region of the left kidney emerging on the right side of the body in the region of the gall bladder. It passed through the left kidney, the liver and injured the spinal column." The bullet finally lodged in the thigh of onlooker George A. Berry.

Bystanders carried Morgan 10 feet to the doorway of the card room, where Doctors Matthews, Millar,

and Goodfellow did what they could, knowing it wouldn't be enough. Morgan's last words were, "This is the last game of pool I'll ever play." His body went to Colton, California, for burial. The slayers were never positively identified but were believed to be Pete Spence, Frank Stillwell, Frederick Bode (alias John Doe Freeze or Freis), and two Indians, one called Charlie.

See also: EARP, VIRGIL; EARP, WYATT BERRY STAPP; GUNFIGHT AT THE OK CORRAL; HOLLIDAY, JOHN HENRY

EARP, Virgil (1843–1905)

Virgil Earp was born in Hartford, Kentucky, although the family moved to Illinois and then to Iowa. To say Virgil's love life was somewhat convoluted is something of an understatement. His first marriage was to a girl named Ellen Ryadam, but her parents had the marriage annulled. He then enlisted in the Union army, served without injury for three years, and was discharged in June 1865. In the meantime, however, his first wife had decided he was dead and moved to Oregon, where she gave birth to a daughter and then remarried. Virgil never knew he had a daughter until she was grown. Anyway, Virgil married Rozilla Draggoo in Lamar, Missouri, in 1870, but she disappeared when Virgil left Lamar for Council Bluffs, Iowa, where he reportedly drove a stage. In Council Bluffs, he met Alvira

(Allie) Sullivan. There is no evidence that they ever married, although she lived with him for 32 years.

From Council Bluffs, Iowa, Virgil and Allie showed up in Dodge City, Kansas, where by some accounts he became a member of the police force. Following that, he lived in Prescott, Arizona, and became a deputy sheriff. Crawley Dake, the U.S. marshal for Arizona, appointed Virgil as a deputy marshal. Virgil Earp then migrated to Tombstone.

After Curly Bill Brocius shot Tombstone's first city marshal, Fred White, the city council appointed Virgil as the temporary marshal. However, in a special election a man named Ben Sippy won the position. Undeterred, Virgil hung on to his deputy U.S. marshal position until June 1881, when Ben Sippy left town, throwing the city marshal position back to Virgil. Earp now wore two hats, city marshal and U.S. deputy marshal, and he took his positions seriously, making arrests and generally cracking down on lawbreakers. He even arrested Kate Elder, Doc Holliday's mistress, charging her with being drunk and disorderly. After the town burned on June 22, 1881, Virgil became a leading spokesman for getting a professional fire department. Meanwhile, relations between the Earps and the Clantons (cowboys/rustlers) deteriorated.

On October 26, Virgil Earp walked up behind Ike Clanton on Fourth Street and pistol-whipped Ike, knocking him against the wall. Virgil confiscated Ike's weapons, then arrested him for carrying firearms in town. A judge fined and released Ike Clanton, and Ike, Billy Clanton, and Tom and Frank McLaury walked from Allen Street through the OK Corral to the vacant lot alongside Fly's Photography Studio, a stone's throw from the OK Corral. As they stood there cursing the Earps and Doc Holliday and discussing what to do, Marshal Virgil Earp, his brothers, and Doc Holliday approached the lot. The most famous gun battle in Western history was only seconds away.

When the gunsmoke cleared less than two minutes later, the two McLaury brothers were dead, Billy Clanton was just minutes from death, Morgan Earp had been seriously wounded, and Virgil had a bullet hole in the right calf of his leg.

However, for Virgil the famous gunfight was only a prelude. That wound stung, but it was nothing compared to five shotgun blasts at near midnight as he left the Oriental Saloon on December 28, 1881.

One round badly shattered his left arm. Friends raced for the doctor, while others carried Virgil to his room at the Cosmopolitan Hotel. He would never again fully use that arm. Although suspects were all over the place and arrests were made, witnesses swore that the accused had been in Charleston at the time of Virgil's shooting. All suspects were acquitted.

Virgil remained a U.S. deputy marshal until April 1882, and although he never completely recovered from his wounds, he became the first town marshal of Colton, California, and later an Esmeralda County, Nevada, deputy sheriff. He died of pneumonia at Goldfield, Nevada, on October 19, 1905.

See also: BROCIUS, WILLIAM; CLANTON, NEWMAN HAYNES; DAKE, CRAWLEY; EARP, MORGAN; GUNFIGHT AT THE OK CORRAL; HOLLIDAY, JOHN HENRY

EARP, Wyatt Berry Stapp (1848–1929)

Wyatt Earp is best known for the Gunfight at the OK Corral in Tombstone, Arizona, but he lived a long and colorful life that began at Monmouth, Illinois, where he was born on March 19, 1848. His father, a Mexican War veteran, moved the family to the Dutch community of Pella, Iowa, around 1850. In 1864 the family headed for California, but in 1869 it turned around and moved to Lamar, Missouri, where Wyatt became a constable. He also married Urilla Sutherland on January 24, 1870. Urilla died of unknown causes within the year. By now, the lean, tall Wyatt was in bond trouble, and he left Missouri in March 1871; within a month, the authorities in Indian Territory (Oklahoma) had arrested him and others for horse theft. All charges were dropped, with the exception of those against Wyatt. He posted bail and then forfeited it when he disappeared.

For a couple of years Wyatt Earp reportedly hunted buffalo before becoming a policeman in April 1875 on the Wichita, Kansas, force. He served without distinction, and in fact raised eyebrows because of his money-collection practices and alleged takes. Within a year Wyatt moved to Dodge City, where on June 5, 1878, Mayor James H. Kealy appointed Earp as an assistant city marshal. Wyatt put in his time credibly but without any particular prominence. He also took up with Celia Ann "Mattie" Blaylock, who became his common-law wife. A month later, on July 27, Earp and officer James Masterson shot at several cowboys in the act of disturbing the peace while leaving for camp. The fusillade hit a cowboy named George Hoy in the arm, and he tumbled off his horse, dying a month later. Either of the two officers may have fired that shot. At any rate, Wyatt resigned his seasonal job in September 1879 and drifted to Las Vegas, New Mexico, with his brothers Virgil, Morgan, and James. By December they were all in Tombstone, Arizona.

The three brothers filed mining claims and purchased lots in town. In July 1880 Wyatt became a deputy sheriff, a lawman dealing faro in his spare time. Virgil became a U.S. deputy marshal in 1879. Morgan rode shotgun for Wells Fargo.

On October 27, 1880, Deputy Wyatt Earp happened to be in Billy Owen's Saloon when he heard several shots fired a block up the street. Earp and his brother Morgan reached the scene only to find City Marshal Fred White ordering Curley Bill Brocius to surrender his revolver. Brocius pulled the six-shooter from its holster just as Earp threw his arms around him. At the same time, White snatched the pistol from Brocius's hand. The gun fired, the bullet striking White in the groin. He would die of peritonitis.

Wyatt Earp (Creative Publishing Co.)

In the meantime, Officer Earp clubbed Brocius over the head with his revolver and hustled him to jail. A judge freed Brocius.

Wyatt resigned his office on November 9, 1880, just as Sheriff Charles Shibell won his third term. Shibell appointed John Behan to Wyatt's old position, and Behan soon afterward became sheriff, due to the creation of Cochise County and the naming of Tombstone as the county seat. By some accounts, Behan had promised Wyatt the position of chief deputy, but that didn't happen, one reason perhaps being that Behan had previously taken up with "actress" Josephine Sarah Marcus, better known as Sadie or Josie. It did not take long for Earp to move in, although that created a problem with Mattie, Earp's common-law wife. Nevertheless, Mattie was out, and Sadie was in. Of course, Earp also failed to get the job as Behan's deputy.

On March 15, 1881, unknown parties stopped the Wells Fargo stage 10 miles west of Tombstone and, during a botched robbery attempt, killed the driver and a passenger. Sheriff Behan and the Earp brothers rounded up only one suspect, and he escaped. Since then, suspicion has focused on John Henry "Doc" Holliday as one of the bandits. In June Virgil Earp became Tombstone's chief of police, usually referred to as city marshal.

Six months later, on September 8, the Bisbee stage was held up by several masked men. City Marshal Virgil Earp and Deputies Wyatt and Morgan Earp arrested cowboys Pete Spence and Frank Stilwell. These arrests set the stage for what would later become known as the Gunfight at the OK Corral. Following the arrests, Morgan and Virgil Earp walked up behind Ike Clanton on Allen Street, and Virgil whacked Ike across the head with a six-shooter. After charging Ike with illegally carrying a gun, they marched him to a court. Wyatt Earp entered the room and began taunting Clanton. Ike did not take the bait but paid a $25 fine.

Wyatt then encountered Tom McLaury on the street. Earp asked if he were armed; upon learning that he wasn't, Earp slapped him, bounced a pistol off his head, and left him bleeding in the dirt. Within minutes, Ike and Billy Clanton, plus Tom and Frank McLaury, had gathered in a vacant lot on Fremont Street a few doors distant from the OK Corral. Billy Clanton and Frank McLaury had apparently made up their minds to go back to the ranch. Their saddled horses stood beside them.

But it was now too late to leave, since Wyatt, Morgan, and Vigil Earp, plus Doc Holliday, were bearing down on them. They were all armed, Doc Holliday out of the ordinary way, in that he toted a double-barreled shotgun under his long coat. One of his party, probably Wyatt, screamed, "You sons of bitches, you have been looking for a fight!" Virgil followed by yelling for the cowboys to throw up their hands. The shooting started.

Wyatt likely shot Frank McLaury in the stomach. Holliday killed Tom McLaury with a shotgun blast. Billy Clanton stumbled to the ground fatally wounded, and Ike Clanton, not having a weapon, dashed over to Wyatt, screamed something to the effect that he wanted no part of this, and fled unmolested.

In seconds the gunfight was history. Frank McLaury was dead; Billy Clanton and Tom McLaury were dying. Morgan Earp had been wounded in the back; Virgil had a hole in his lower right leg; and Doc Holliday had a smarting hip where a bullet had grazed it. The lawmen would recover.

A coroner's inquest essentially did not pass judgment, although warrants were issued for the three Earps plus Doc Holliday, all of whom were bonded out. However, Wyatt and Holliday's bonds were revoked, and they remained jailed.

During the hearing, on November 16, 1881, Wyatt read several pages of a long, often rambling statement going back over every conversation and threat made toward him during the last few months. He then presented the court with a good-character testimonial signed by 49 Dodge City civic leaders. He followed that with a shorter endorsement signed by seven Wichita, Kansas, politicians. Wyatt then sat down, not having been cross-examined.

Judge Wells Spicer rendered his verdict—longer than Wyatt Earp's statement—in which he also seemingly went over every bit of evidence and found Earp and Holliday not guilty of murder. He ordered their release.

Public opinion both supported and condemned the gunfight victors, but some citizens were more than vocal. On December 28, 1881, shortly before midnight, as Virgil Earp walked toward the Golden Eagle Brewery in the Cosmopolitan Hotel, a shotgun blast shattered his left arm.

On the following day Wyatt Earp wired U.S. Marshal Crawley Dake and asked to be appointed deputy marshal. The request was immediately granted.

Nearly three weeks later, on January 17, Doc Holliday and John Ringo confronted each other in the middle of a crowded street. Tombstone's acting police chief, James Flynn, along with Wyatt Earp, broke up the confrontation.

Deputy Marshal Wyatt Earp on January 23 pulled together a posse that included his brother Morgan, his reliable sidekick Doc Holliday, and five other men. Their intent was to apprehend "diverse persons," meaning primarily the Clantons and John Ringo, desperadoes they hoped to find in nearby Charleston. However, after disrupting lives and making threats, the posse returned to Tombstone near the end of the month with no arrests and no battles to show for their efforts. On February 1, 1882, Virgil and Wyatt resigned as U.S. deputy marshals, but the resignations were not accepted. They were instead arrested and taken to nearby Contention, Arizona, for possible trial regarding the slaying of Billy Clanton. However, the judge found no valid reason for retrying the incident.

The Earps' troubles were far from over. On March 18, 1882, in Campbell and Hatch's Billiard Parlor in Tombstone, as Wyatt Earp sat in a chair, his brother Morgan Earp prepared to sink a ball in the outside pocket. At that instant, two assassins fired through the window. One bullet had Wyatt Earp's name on it, but it thundered into the wall over his head. The other bullet passed through the body of Morgan Earp. He lived perhaps an hour. A jury believed the assassins to be Frank Stilwell, Pete Spence, and Frederick Bode.

On March 20, Morgan's body was loaded onboard a California-bound train. The wounded and weak Virgil accompanied it, as did a heavily armed Wyatt and his brother Warren Earp, Doc Holliday, Sherman McMasters, and Jack Johnson, better known as "Turkey Creek." When the train arrived in Tucson later that day, the Earp party encountered Frank Stilwell, whom they followed alongside the train and shot to death. Florentino Cruz became number two on the list; the Earp party trailed him into the Dragoon Mountains and shot him too. In the meantime, the authorities in Tombstone arrested and jailed Pete Spence and Frederick Bode for investigation into Morgan Earp's murder. Charges were later dropped for lack of evidence.

Five days later the *Tombstone Epitaph* printed a sensational story that Curley Bill Brocius had been slain by Wyatt Earp in the Whetstone Mountains. All that is known for certain is that at this time Curley Bill dropped from sight. Opinion is hotly divided as to whether he was actually slain or chose to disappear. Wyatt claimed to have killed Brocius, but Wyatt told different stories at different times.

Earp left Arizona in April 1882 for Gunnison, Colorado, returning to Dodge City, Kansas, in 1883. The next year found him in Shoshone County, Idaho, where he did some legitimate mining as well as some illegitimate claim jumping.

Earp continued his wanderings, finding himself in San Francisco, California, on December 2, 1896. There he would become known as the referee who "threw" a crucial heavyweight fight. Heavyweight champion contenders Tom Sharkey and Bob Fitzsimmons met that day in the Mechanics Pavilion. Fitzsimmons, better known as "Ruddy Bob," was an Englishman, a former blacksmith, and now a professional boxer. Sharkey was an Irishman, a former seaman, and like Fitzsimmons had fought several notable opponents. The two men would battle for the privilege of meeting the heavyweight champion of the world. The winner would also receive a certified check for $10,000, the money to be handed over by the referee at the close of the fight.

When the contestants could not agree on a referee, promoter Andrew "Long Green" Lawrence suggested his bodyguard, Wyatt Earp. Although a controversial figure in his own right, Earp obtained the job even though the police chief, noticing a bulge in Earp's coat, stepped into the ring and demanded Earp's six-shooter. Wyatt handed it over, and everybody settled back in their seats.

For seven rounds both men fought hard, each going once to the canvas. Both seemed to be tiring. In the eighth round, Fitzsimmons landed a left to the body and a right to the chin, and Sharkey went down, rolling over and holding his groin. Earp at that instant declared Sharkey the winner on a foul. He handed him the check and left the ring. A riot started.

The Athletic Club stopped payment on the check. Two doctors examined Sharkey for evidence of a groin injury. Each disagreed with the other's diagnosis. Two other physicians examined Sharkey and agreed that he had been injured but not sufficiently to halt the fight.

In the meantime, Earp made no effort to recover his gun, although four officers arrested him for carry-ing a concealed weapon. He posted a $50 bond. Sharkey kept the $10,000 purse.

So, was the fight fixed? Was Sharkey struck below the belt? Did Wyatt Earp actually see the foul, or was he somehow involved in a kickback scheme? The answers are not in, and never will be. Only the questions linger.

Wyatt Earp continued his wanderings, establishing a Dexter Saloon partnership at Nome, Alaska, in late 1899. He also managed to get arrested for interfering with an officer and so left Alaska in 1901. He and Josephine lived mostly in Los Angeles, he at times being arrested for various confidence schemes.

Wyatt Earp died in Los Angeles on January 13, 1929, and was cremated. When Josephine died in 1944, her ashes joined Earp's in the Marcus plot inside the "Hills of Eternity," the Jewish section of the Colma, California, Cemetery.

See also: BLAYLOCK, CELIA ANN; DODGE CITY WAR; EARP, MORGAN; EARP, VIRGIL; GUNFIGHT AT THE OK CORRAL; HOLLIDAY, JOHN HENRY

EAST, James Henry (a.k.a. Jim East) (1853–1930)

James Henry East dreamed of being a cowboy, and his dream came true. Although born at Kaskaskia, Illinois (Missouri by some reports), by the time he was 15 years old East had reached the Lone Star State. After the Civil War he rode for the well-known Tom Ranch in South Texas, as well as for the King Ranch's founders, King and Kennedy. East made several cattle drives to Kansas and at least one to Nebraska. Reportedly, on occasion he raided for horses in Old Mexico, which was not an uncommon practice for youthful and exuberant cowboys.

Along the line he found the Texas Panhandle area appealing, signing on with the LX outfit in 1880. At this point, his career careened in a new direction. Ranch manager W. C. "Outlaw Bill" Moore, himself a questionable character, ordered Charlie Siringo (later to become a famous cowboy detective) to gather a posse of fighting cowboys and run Billy the Kid and his gang to the ground. This posse was to recover cattle that the outlaws had "liberated" from the LX herds as well as from other area ranches. Twenty-seven-year-old Jim East was one of those riders. On November 16, 1880, a posse consisting of East, Lee Hall, Lon Chambers, Cal Polk,

Frank Clifford, and Siringo began their manhunt. Along the way they were reinforced by additional manpower, including Frank Stewart, Bob Roberson, Tom Emory, Bob Williams, and Louis "The Animal" Bozeman (Bousman).

In New Mexico Territory, the posse encountered Lincoln County sheriff Pat Garrett and one of his deputies, Barney Mason. Garrett was seeking assistance in his quest of capturing or killing Billy the Kid. Jumping at the chance, Jim East, Lee Hall, and Lon Chambers from the LX outfit volunteered, joined by Tom Emory, Bob Williams, and "The Animal," Bousman. On the night of December 19, 1880, at Fort Sumner, Garrett deployed the men and waited. At about eight o'clock the outlaws rode in single file into town and into the possemen's bullets. Riding in the lead were Tom O'Folliard and Tom Pickett, followed by Dave Rudabaugh, Billy Wilson, Charlie Bowdre, and Billy the Kid. For a few seconds the exchange of gunfire was blistering, and to this day it is debatable as to whose bullet inflicted what damage. In the end, only Tom O'Folliard, with a bullet in his chest, slumped from his horse. With an about-face the other outlaws fled. O'Folliard was laid out on East's blankets. Jim brought the wounded desperado a drink of water, and then O'Folliard "lay back, shuddered and was dead."

On December 22, the posse surrounded a rock house at Stinking Springs. At daylight, Bowdre stepped from the house, was mistaken for the Kid, and was gunned down. Jim East and Tom Emory then slipped to the rear of the fortification and fired a few shots into the house to convince the outlaws inside that chipping through the rock wall was not a viable option. With no hope of escape, the outlaws surrendered. If the reports are indeed true, East and Lee Hall, at gunpoint, prevented Barney Mason from executing Billy the Kid, an act very much appreciated by the young hoodlum, who gave Jim East his Winchester for the favor. East had his comeuppance at Fort Sumner, however. With the prisoners in tow, and Charlie Bowdre's body bouncing in a wagon, a grieving as well as furious Mrs. Manuela Bowdre struck East over the head with a branding iron, fortunately inflicting no damage except for painful knots.

On the return trip to Texas, Jim East decided that police work was more to his liking than being a cowboy, and during the elections of 1882, with considerable ranch-hand support, he won an election as the second sheriff of Oldham County. As sheriff, East suffered the usual trials and tribulations of frontier law enforcement: Ed Norwood, charged with murder, escaped from jail. After suffering through a bitterly cold surveillance, East courageously arrested an exceedingly desperate Bill Gatlin. East aroused the cattlemen's ire, however, when he collected the "drift tax" (a fee paid for the collection of stray cattle). He sorted out the gory details of March 21, 1886, when colliding cowboy factions clashed in old Tascosa and four were killed. Later, in 1889 he killed a local gambler named Tom Clark during a fierce gun battle in a saloon.

After stepping down as sheriff, East operated a detective agency in Amarillo, and then, in 1903, at the age of 50, he moved to Douglas, Arizona Territory, and accepted the position of town marshal. Later he served as municipal judge. On June 30, 1930, the old cowboy closed his eyes and dreamed of days gone by as he peacefully rode the last trail to the other side.

See also: BILLY THE KID; GARRETT, PATRICK FLOYD JARVIS; HALL, JESSE LEE; SIRINGO, CHARLES ANGELO

ELLSWORTH, Kansas

Ellsworth, one of the Kansas cow towns, displayed little of its wild nature until the Kansas Pacific Railroad arrived. That, of course, encouraged Texas cowboys, weary from long months on the trail, but they had no sooner hit town than they collided with the three-man Ellsworth police force. In 1873, a fiery cowboy named Billy Thompson killed Sheriff Chauncey Whitney with a shotgun. The police then killed a cowboy named Cad Pierce. The Texans had now killed two of the three policemen. Where it all might have ended is impossible to say, except that the rails kept moving west, and so did the cattle. Ellsworth, thus, became little more than a blip on the Wild West scene. By 1874 its day had essentially passed.

See also: THOMPSON, WILLIAM J.

EL PASO Salt War

For many years of its early life, El Paso, Texas, in the far western corner of the state, slept peacefully. It was awakened by rumbles caused by salt beds 90 miles east of town. Salt, of course, had a multitude of uses, especially in the silver mines in Mexico. For centuries the salt trails had curled north out of Mexico, and southwestern residents had made a fair living by supplying the product. El Pasoan Albert J. Fountain and others organized a "Salt Ring" in 1868, laid claim to the salt beds, and commenced charging a fee. Fountain then went off to Austin as a state senator; learning that some of those people whom he was charging money actually voted, Fountain thus organized the "Anti–Salt Ring." This led to problems with his former associates, and on December 7, 1870, a shootout occurred in downtown El Paso. Two men died, and

Fountain subsequently moved 40 miles north to Mesilla, New Mexico. His death, on February 2, 1896, still remains the Southwest's greatest murder mystery. His body was never recovered.

By 1876, Missouri attorney Charles Howard had arrived in El Paso, and it wasn't long before he filed on those same salt lakes in the name of his father-in-law. This brought him into conflict with Louis Cardis, a supporter of the salt gatherers, plus Father Antonio Borrajo, the San Elizario village priest. San Elizario was a Rio Grande community about 30 miles downstream from El Paso. Most of the salt gatherers lived there.

Digging salt during the El Paso Salt War. These salt flats are approximately 90 miles east of El Paso, Texas (University of Texas at Austin Archives)

On October 10, 1877, Howard caught Cardis inside an El Paso store and killed him with a shotgun. On the following day, the details of the murder reached San Elizario and sent the entire valley into an uproar. The state dispatched Texas Ranger major John B. Jones to investigate, and within a week Jones had set about organizing Company C of the Texas Rangers. He put El Pasoan John B. Tays in charge. While Tays no doubt was a good man, he had no competence in terms of leadership. As for the rangers, many were toughs recruited from Silver City, New Mexico. According to historian C. L. Sonnichsen, "Not a one of them could have been a ranger under normal circumstances."

Meanwhile, soldiers, most of them from Fort Stanton, began marching on the El Paso Valley. They would not reach San Elizario in time. Howard, acting to protect his salt interests, entered San Elizario with a ranger escort on December 12. His timing could not have been worse.

San Elizario storekeeper Charles Ellis, under suspicion of being an Anglo, was dragged around the plaza and knifed to death. Howard and the rangers timidly watched the affair from their quarters a short distance away and did nothing. At midmorning the next day, Sergeant C. E. Mortimer, patrolling outside, was shot and killed by a sniper. Still the rangers did nothing. Thus the siege continued for several more days, each morning the line of encroaching riflemen drawing closer to the ranger quarters.

The rangers surrendered to the mob, the only time in history that such a thing occurred. The lawmen were disarmed and shoved into a building. As for Howard, he was removed to an open field to face a ragged firing squad. He himself gave the command to fire. After the lead knocked him down, the mob rushed in with machetes and finished the job.

Civilians John Atkinson and John McBride were led out next, and they too fell wounded before the volleys. The mob likewise hacked them to death. All the bodies were tossed in a well. The rangers were then released to find their way home as best they could.

Within days, troops reached San Elizario. Additional ranger recruits had arrived from Silver City. The lower El Paso Valley now became a madhouse, as lawless Texas and New Mexico thugs committed rape and murder with maddening frequency. Most residents, as well as the San Elizario murderers, fled across the Rio Grande into Mexico.

On January 22, 1878, a four-man board conducted a congressional investigation of the recent Salt War. A subsequent grand jury indicted six men, and the governor of Texas offered rewards. But all had found refuge south across the Rio Grande.

See also: EL PASO, TEXAS; FOUNTAIN, ALBERT JENNINGS; JONES, JOHN B.

EL PASO, Texas

El Paso, in far West Texas, dates back to 1598 but did not become a community until 1849, and it did not become El Paso until 1859. The Civil War led to turmoil and shooting, but the El Paso Salt War of 1877 proved the initial bloodletting of significance. It started with a couple of killings downtown and then expanded when a group of Silver City, New Mexico, thugs were recruited by the Texas Rangers to restore order in the lower El Paso Valley.

With the arrival of the railroads in 1881, gunmen, desperadoes, outlaws, and lawmen saw El Paso and the nearby Mexican border as their last refuge. El Paso thus became the man-killing capital of the American West, an era that lasted from roughly 1881 to roughly 1896. Some of the figures were John Wesley Hardin, John Selman, George Scarborough, Jeff Milton, Dallas Stoudenmire, Mysterious Dave Mather, Jim Miller, Wyatt Earp, Pat Garrett, James Gillett, John R. Baylor, and Mannen Clements.

Within 10 years of its desperado period, El Paso entered its Mexican revolutionary era. El Paso's sister city, Ciudad Juarez, Chihuahua, changed hands six times during the revolution, making it perhaps the most fought-over city in North America. Mexican revolutionaries and American soldiers of fortune thus became familiar sights on El Paso streets: Pancho Villa, Francisco Madero, Pascual Orozco, Victoriano Huerta, Giuseppe Garibaldi, Red López. Thousands of Mexican refugees took refuge in El Paso, and many of their descendants still live there.

Because of the Mexican Revolution, El Paso's Fort Bliss, originally an infantry post, expanded to the largest cavalry post in the United States. In World War I it became the largest artillery post in the United States, and later the largest air defense center in the world. Today El Paso, along with its Mexican neighbor Ciudad Juarez, are the two largest cities on the Mexican border. The border ruffians are gone, although smuggling, drugs, and illegal immigration currently provide federal, state, and local authorities with plenty of work.

The El Paso, Texas, police force in 1895 (Author's Collection)

EMORY, Thomas (a.k.a. Poker Tom) (?–1902?)

Tom Emory was involved in two of the most notable happenings in the Old West—the capture of Billy the Kid and the 1866 shootout at Tascosa, Texas. During the late 1870s, a short, sandy-haired man rode into George Littlefield's XIT Ranch near Tascosa, in the Texas Panhandle. He said his name was Tom Emory, and he needed a job. He found it as a working cowboy.

In December of 1880, Lincoln County, New Mexico, sheriff Pat Garrett pulled together a posse composed of Jim East, Lee Hall, Cal Polk, Bob Williams, Lon Chambers, Barney Mason, Louis Bousman, and Tom Emory. Garrett sought Billy the Kid, but at Fort

Sumner all he got was Tom O'Folliard. On December 23, Garrett's posse trapped the Kid and others at Stinking Springs. Desperado Charles Bowdre died. The Kid and others surrendered and were taken to Santa Fe by way of Las Vegas.

A few months later, in February 1881, Tom Emory and detective Charles Siringo rode into Fort Stanton, New Mexico, looking for signs of rustled cattle held by suspected thieves. That proved inconclusive, so Emory returned to the ranch after an absence of seven months. Shortly after that, Littlefield sold out, and Emory left the ranch to become a professional gambler in Tascosa. There he and a handful of others became involved on March 20, 1866, in what became known as "the big shootout." Three men died, and Emory was one of those charged with murder. Their first trial ended in a hung jury, the second in an acquittal.

Tom Emory subsequently followed his vocation as a gambler in Las Vegas, New Mexico, and then in Roswell. When his health started failing during the mid-1890s, he moved to El Paso, Texas, where on his sickbed he talked with Pat Garrett, the tall slayer of Billy the Kid and now the collector of customs in El Paso. Tom asked Garrett to send for Tom's brother, hoping that maybe the brother would take him back home to die. Garrett did as requested, and Emory returned home, where he shortly passed away. He had played out his last hand.

See also: BILLY THE KID; GARRETT, PATRICK FLOYD JARVIS; LINCOLN COUNTY WAR; HALL, JESSE LEIGH; TASCOSA SHOOTOUT

EVANS, Jesse J. (1853?–?)

Jesse Evans is one of the many enigmas relating to the Wild West. He claimed to have been born in Missouri in 1853. One who knew him, Frank Coe, believed he was half Cherokee. Otherwise, Jesse Evans was blessed, or cursed, with a common name. A belief even exists that Jesse Evans was a graduate of the College of Washington and Lee in Virginia.

Evans arrived in New Mexico around 1872 and worked as a cowboy for John Chisum. By 1875 he was a suspect in the Shedd Ranch murders of the Mes brothers in the Organ Mountains of southern New Mexico. On New Year's Eve, 1875, he and three other gunmen brawled with Fort Selden troopers at a dance. The soldiers won, but Evans and his friends returned around midnight and commenced shooting through the windows. A soldier and a civilian were killed; another civilian and three soldiers were wounded.

Two weeks later, on January 19, Quirino Fletcher bragged that he and two friends had killed and robbed two Texans in Mexico. Later that night, a person assumed to be Evans put six bullets in Fletcher. In the meantime Billy the Kid fled Arizona, where he had killed Frank Cahill; while on his way to Lincoln, New Mexico, he paused for a few months in the Mesilla Valley, where he took up the practice of horse thievery. Both Billy and Jesse Evans may also have become involved in the subsequent El Paso Salt War, but at any rate the Kid went on to Lincoln and became a regular, while Jesse put in off-and-on appearances during the Lincoln County War. Jesse, for instance, signed up as a Lincoln County deputy and was one of the posse members who put bullets in Englishman John Tunstall. A grand jury indicted Evans for murder, he being first on the list. At the trial, Jesse testified that he had not even been in the vicinity of the Tunstall shooting—and went free.

Shortly afterward, in mid-March, Jesse and Tom Hill tried ransacking the nearby sheep camp of a German herdsman, whom they shot and assumed they had killed. The herdsman made it to his rifle, however, and killed Hill. Then he shattered Jesse's right arm. Evans took refuge in the Shedd Ranch and from there was taken under arrest to Fort Stanton. He was released soon afterward.

On February 18, 1879, Evans and friends met with Billy the Kid in Lincoln. The Lincoln County War was over by this time, its major participants either dead or scattered. The Kid sent Jesse Evans a note at Fort Stanton suggesting a talk. The two men, plus friends, met that evening in Lincoln and essentially agreed that from that moment on neither side would threaten or harm the other. Then, to celebrate the pact and to prove they were great friends, they went on a drunken spree, bumping into Huston Chapman, an attorney representing Susan McSween. By some accounts, Jesse Evans shot him, by others it was Billy the Kid. In this instance, not only did the bullet kill Chapman, but the powder set his clothes afire.

On March 5, Jesse Evans was arrested, charged with Chapman's murder, and jailed at Fort Stanton. Within days he escaped. He now fled to Fort Davis,

Texas, robbed a store, and on July 3, 1880, engaged in a gunfight during which he killed a civilian and a Texas Ranger, George Bingham. The rangers captured Evans and tried him for murder. He entered the Huntsville, Texas, penitentiary on December 1, 1880. Then in May, while on a work detail, he escaped and vanished. All efforts to trace him from that moment on have come to naught.

See also: BILLY THE KID; CHAPMAN, HUSTON INGRAHAM; EL PASO SALT WAR; LINCOLN COUNTY WAR

FAN A Gun

This happens only with a revolver: the shooter pulls the trigger all the way back and holds it there, while with the other hand he fans the hammer. The practice permits rapid but very inaccurate fire, except at point-blank range. The tactic is popular in Western fiction and movies, but as a practical matter no known outlaw or lawman was stupid enough to try it.

FARO (a.k.a. Bucking the Tiger)

Faro was hands down the most popular gambling game in the Wild West, although gamblers rarely play it now. The game had its origins with King Louis XIV and entered the United States through New Orleans around 1840. It peaked in popularity during the 1880s.

The game required three distinct pieces of equipment, beginning with a green cloth having an entire suit of spades painted on, all arranged in a shape similar to a horseshoe. A dealer's box, which never left the dealer's hand, was only slightly larger than the deck of cards inside. Finally, the dealer had a device called the "case keeper" that kept track of the cards when dealt from the box. The object of the game was to bet on the rank of the cards as they were dealt from the box, so odds and evens usually spelled the difference between winning and losing.

Faro was an easy game to learn, and players came up with all kinds of occult systems, none of which

helped but continuously sparked interest and gave hope. So why did the game die out? That was due primarily to the development of the "crooked box," permitting the dealer to slip two cards out at a time instead of one. Furthermore, Wyatt Earp is said to have taken the crooked box even a step farther, placing tiny pin holes in the center of each card, one that could be felt by the finger but was tiny enough not to be seen by the eye. When playing odds and evens, the dealer knew which was coming up next. Nevertheless, the game of Faro added picturesque phrases to the language, many of which are still used today—"bucking the tiger," "you picked a sleeper," "a square deal," and "keeping tab."

See also: EARP, WYATT BERRY STAPP

FAST Draw

The fast draw is equated in the popular mind with the High Noon walkdown, made famous by movie star Gary Cooper. Two men stand roughly 50 yards apart, facing each other in the street, hands poised over six-guns holstered to the hips. Then at a certain signal, such as the ringing of the village clock, they draw their weapons and fire. The faster draw wins.

Although Old West gunmen such as Wild Bill Hickok, Billy the Kid, John Wesley Hardin, and a few others are generally thought of as "fast guns," speed actually had little or nothing to do with their success or number of killings. Guns were awkward and sometimes undependable. Holsters were fine for saddle work, but in town most men carried their weapons in coat or trouser pockets, and sometimes inside their shirt. Most communities had laws, and most saloons had rules, against the open carrying of weapons, although many men kept pocket weapons conveniently out of sight. To draw quickly meant the possibility of a gun's hanging up in the clothes. The fast draw therefore was a myth. Who lived following a shootout usually depended upon who was the luckier. Some men just seemed to have more luck than others.

FEDERAL Marshals and Deputy Marshals

New territories in the American West invariably called for federal courts and for U.S. marshals and deputy marshals. They were the only lawmen. Initially, they handled every variety of crime, from shoplifting to train robbery, from rape and embezzlement to assault and murder. As areas became settled, however, with counties organized and civilian government taking over, U.S. marshals and deputy marshals became primarily officials of the federal courts.

Public opinion to the contrary, the position of U.S. marshal in the opening of the West was practically always a political appointment, a reward that did not always have anything to do with law enforcement experience or ability. The post frequently became a political payoff to washed-up politicians, lawyers, or brothers-in-law, and the incumbent changed only through death or when political parties or personalities shifted in Washington. The toughest thing most marshals did was defend their congressional requests for more money, and explain away inquiries and accusations of fraud and embezzlement. In short, professional lawmen were almost never chosen for the position of U.S. marshal.

U.S. deputy marshals, however, were appointed by federal marshals, and these officials usually handled the law enforcement caseload. These individuals were paid on a mileage and fee basis, and likely as not had steady jobs as deputy sheriffs, sheriffs, city marshals, or deputy marshals. These city and county lawmen considered the U.S. deputy marshal position and pay as supplemental income. Sometimes these deputy marshals held dual commissions for months or several times a year. While the public tends to think of them as enforcing federal laws, for the most part they eased the transition from territory to state,

located witnesses, served subpoenas, sold condemned property, took the federal census, moved prisoners back and forth, and kept order during federal trials.

In places such as Indian Territory (Oklahoma), U.S. deputy marshals provided practically the only law enforcement. Bass Reeves, a black man, did an exceptionally fine job. Some better known (occasional) U.S. deputy marshals were Wild Bill Hickok, Pat Garrett, and the Earp brothers.

See also: EARP, MORGAN; EARP, VIRGIL; EARP, WYATT BERRY STAPP; GARRETT, PATRICK FLOYD JARVIS; HICKOK, JAMES BUTLER; REEVES, BASS

FEELY, J. H. (1868–1912)

J. H. Feely, a father of six children, and the first sheriff of Culberson County, Texas, in the far western reaches of the state, miscalculated on just how hot the partisan political cauldron could boil during a crisp February afternoon at the county seat of Van Horn.

J. Y. Canon, the Culberson County judge, had a long-standing political dispute with O. J. Hammit. One afternoon the hard feelings boiled over. The judge ducked behind a telegraph pole near the Texas and Pacific depot and commenced firing his Winchester at Hammit, who was himself armed with a double-barreled scatter-gun. Bullets were zinging, and buckshot was belching, all with little effect until Sheriff Feely, a dedicated lawman, intervened in an attempt to restore sanity to the town. However, the sheriff stepped between the two men, and Judge Canon's rifle put a bullet through his heart. At about the same time, Hammit staggered and fell, a bullet in his right testicle and groin. Judge Canon, wounded in the hand from one of those shotgun pellets, dropped the Winchester.

Famed cowboy preacher L. R. Millican eulogized at Feely's memorial service. In the meantime, Hammit and Judge Canon posted $5,000 bail bonds, while Culberson County citizens pondered the wisdom of seeking elected office.

FERGUSON, Lark *See* SPENCE, PETE

FENCE-CUTTING War

In 1883, fence cutting became epidemic in Texas, as some cattlemen preferred to graze on open range, while others purchased or otherwise acquired land and wanted to fence it in with barbed wire. In general, the fences encircled regions containing grass and water, which meant that neighbors who might have used that grass and water for decades were denied access. So when fences went up, a man's neighbors tended to cut those fences—and the war was on. By the end of 1883, damages were estimated at $20 million. At least three people had been slain, and the Texas Rangers were called out to restore order in some counties. In 1884, the Texas legislature made fence cutting a felony, and its punishment between one and five years in prison.

See also: BAYLOR, GEORGE WYTHE; TEXAS RANGERS

FEUDS

These can best be classified as wars between families, although sometimes just between individuals. They happened in all parts of the American West, though Texas seemed to have more than its share. Examples were the Sutton-Taylor feud, the Pleasant Valley War, and the Earp-Clanton feud.

FIMBRES, Manuela (1868–?)

Manuela Fimbres was the only female to serve time in the Arizona Territorial Prison as the result of a murder conviction, and while incarcerated she gave birth to a bouncing baby boy.

Juan Enríquez and Manuela were escorted under the strap-iron sally-port gate and delivered to prison officials on March 30, 1889. The pair had been convicted of the cold-blooded murder of Ah Foy, a.k.a. "Sullivan of Tucson," a wealthy Chinese businessman. Enríquez was sentenced to 30 years. Manuela received 15. At the time she entered prison, Manuela had a secret—she was pregnant. The prison superintendent, John Behan, gave her the run of the prison, but when the pregnancy could be hidden no longer, Republicans gleefully pointed partisan fingers at Democratic prison administrators, implying that they, or perhaps one of the prisoners, had fathered the child. Obviously that had not happened, as a normal boy was born to Manuela on October 26, only six or seven months after she entered prison.

Despite a plea to the governor from the Catholic Church, Manuela at first failed to obtain an early release. But on September 24, 1891, when the prison was under Republican control, Governor Murphy granted her and her son a pardon. His stipulations were that she "immediately go beyond the boundary lines of this Territory [Arizona], and that she remain forever outside its limits, otherwise this grant of freedom and pardon shall be void."

A kindly prison executive's wife gave Manuela and the boy a week's provisions. They disappeared without a trace, but no one ever completely quashed the rumor that she was pregnant again when she walked out of the prison gate to freedom.

See also: BEHAN, JOHN

FISHER, John King (a.k.a. King Fisher)
(1854–1884)

John King Fisher was a frontier dandy, but not a superficial one. With black hair, strong teeth, and mustache, he stood about five foot ten or eleven and weighed about 185. One of his friends described him like this:

Fisher was the most perfect specimen of frontier dandy and desperado that I ever met. He was tall, beautifully proportioned, and exceedingly handsome. He wore the finest clothing procurable, the picturesque, border, dime novel kind. His broad-brimmed white Mexican sombrero was profusely ornamented with gold and silver lace. His fine buckskin Mexican short jacket was heavily embroidered with gold. His shirt was of the finest and thinnest linen and open at the throat, with a silk handerchief knotted loosely around the wide collar. A brilliant crimson sash wound around his waist, and his legs were hidden by a wonderful pair of chaparejos—or chaps as cowboys called them—leather breeches to protect the legs while riding through the brush.

He was born in Fannin County, later Collin County, Texas, but when he was 16 the family moved to Goliad. There the authorities arrested him for theft. He got two years, but the governor shortened it to four months. He drifted over to the Nueces Strip, then to Pendencia, Texas, where he reportedly vanquished the local rustlers, settled on his own land, hired desperate men as cowhands, rustled cattle to stock the ranch, and posted a sign along one route, saying, "This is King Fisher's Road. Take the other one."

Although Fisher reportedly killed seven men, his most famous shootout occurred with Fisher's own *vaqueros* at the Pendencia Ranch. Some accounts say the men were stealing from him, others that the *vaqueros* wanted better pay. Whatever, King cracked one man across the head with a branding iron, killing him, then shot and killed three more before they could jump off a fence.

Over time, Fisher was indicted for various murders and had classic confrontations with Texas Ranger chieftains Leander McNelly and Capt. Lee Hall. For a while the rangers confined Fisher inside the Bat Cave Jail in San Antonio. Lee Hall alone processed over 20 indictments against Fisher, but he gave up when six juries in a row failed to convict. By then Fisher had become his own worst enemy, shooting himself in the leg by accident in 1879.

King became a deputy sheriff of Uvalde County, then in 1884 decided to campaign for the office. By now he was practically legitimate; he was in Austin seeking information on the unlawful act of fence cutting. There he bumped into an old friend, Ben Thompson, who had just arrived from San Antonio after killing Jack Harris, proprietor of the Vaudeville Variety Theater. After drinking too much, and for whatever reason, the two men returned to San Antonio and walked into the Vaudeville Variety Theater, where Ben picked up where he had left off, threatening now to shoot some of the staff. Fisher backed away, saying something about avoiding trouble, but it was too late. Thompson was shot nine times; Fisher took 13 bullets in the head and body. He died immediately—simply because he was there.

See also: THOMPSON, BEN

FORD, Robert and Charles (1861–1892); (1857–1884)

Bob Ford owes his small niche in history to the poem and the song about "the dirty little coward who shot Mr. Howard, and laid Jesse James in his grave." It isn't certain where Ford was born or grew up, although some accounts credit Ray County, Missouri. Like so many frontier figures, he led a nondescript life, a difference being that he became famous by way of a singular, notorious act of murder—the slaying of outlaw Jesse James.

By 1879, Bob Ford and his brother Charles had become new recruits to the James gang, learning the outlaw trade through the experience of train and bank robberies. By some accounts, Bob usually held the horses. On September 7, 1881, the James gang halted the St. Louis Express near Blue Cut, Missouri. When the cache turned out to be less than expected, the outlaws pistol-whipped the express car messenger, then handed the conductor two silver dollars and rode off.

Back home in Kansas City, Jesse moved from Ninth Street to Troost Avenue. By the end of the year he was living near the outskirts of St. Joseph, Missouri, where he adopted the alias of Tom Howard. His wife, Zee (who went by the alias "Josie"), apparently hoped he would settle down and give more "traditional" guidance to the two children, Jesse Edward and Mary.

Jesse's remaining associates were for the most part recent converts, people like the brothers Charlie and Bob Ford, gunmen lacking a sense of solidarity, people for whom the word loyalty had no strong meaning. True, Dick Liddil had been around for a while, and he seemed reliable. Then, in January 1882, Dick Liddil and Wood Hite—cousins of Jesse's—decided to hide out temporarily at the home of Bob Ford's widowed sister, Martha Bolton. While the three men—Bob Ford, Hite, and Liddil—sat at her table, however, Hite

Robert Ford, who shot Jesse James in 1882 (Author's Collection)

and Liddil started arguing, then drew their weapons and commenced shooting. Neither man seemed to be getting high marks for accuracy; as gunsmoke filled the room, Liddil received only a slight wound and Hite a bullet in the right arm. Ford, who was uninvolved, apparently liked Liddil more—perhaps because Liddil had been romancing Martha—so he calmly drew his revolver and fired one round, the bullet striking Hite in the head and killing him instantly. Ford then loaded the body on a mule and buried it in the woods a mile or so from the house.

Rather than face Jesse after killing his cousin, Liddil decided it was safer to give himself up to the law. On January 24, 1882, he surrendered to Sheriff James Timberlake of Clay County, Missouri. At roughly the same time, Bob Ford—apparently with the blessings of his brother Charlie—contacted Henry Craig, the Kansas City police commissioner. On February 22, Craig arranged a meeting between Ford and Governor Thomas H. Crittenden in Kansas City. The governor promised Bob and Charlie Ford a dead-or-live reward of $10,000 for Jesse James. In the meantime, Jesse, Zee, and Charlie Ford had been evaluating a large farm at Franklin, Nebraska, where Jesse contemplated settling down. Bob joined the group on their return home.

The Ford brothers and Jesse James finished their breakfast in Jesse's house at St. Joseph, Missouri, on April 3, 1882. The three men then strolled into the living room, where Jesse reportedly removed his gunbelt, placed a chair under a picture with the caption "God Bless Our Home," and stepped up on the chair in order to straighten the picture and dust it. His head then hit the wall as Bob Ford fired a .45-caliber Smith & Wesson.

On April 17, 1882, a grand jury indicted the Ford brothers for murder, Bob in the first degree and Charlie with aiding and abetting. They pled guilty and were sentenced to be hanged, the sentence being set aside that same afternoon when Governor Crittenden provided the promised amnesty. Whether they received all, part, or none of the $10,000 reward is unclear.

A distraught Charles Ford, tormented by conscience, committed suicide by gunfire near his home in Richmond, Missouri, on May 6, 1884. As for Bob Ford, he married Nellie Waterson, a chorus girl, and spent considerable time on tour. During the first half of his stopovers, he told the audience how and why he killed Jesse James. During the second half of the presentation, the audience usually booed him off the stage. Bob also traveled with P. T. Barnum for awhile and apparently accumulated sufficient funds to open a saloon in Las Vegas, New Mexico. It flopped. He then moved to Creede, Colorado, where he opened a tent saloon but drank too much of his own product. On June 8, 1892, he accused Edward Capeheart O'Kelley of stealing his diamond ring. O'Kelley raged that he did not; to punctuate his point and accentuate his integrity he walked into Bob Ford's saloon with a shotgun and killed him.

See also: JAMES BROTHERS

FORT Griffin, Texas, Vigilantes

Texas had several vigilante movements, most in cattle country as warnings to stock thieves. For instance, in 1887, three horse thieves were hanged from a tree limb in Grayson County. A note pinned to one body read, "Cattle Thieves Doom."

However, the West Texas civilian community of Fort Griffin, known as "the Flats," probably held the state record in terms of lynchings. A reporter for the *Dallas Herald* in April 1876 described one lynching as "So far, so good," and noted that this positive action of the vigilantes "has the well wishes of every lover of tranquility."

Another column that same month, with a dateline of Fort Griffin, noted that horse thief number five had been lynched, with an afterthought, "Shall horse thieves rule the country?"

The Fort Griffin vigilantes, however, put themselves out of business when John M. Larn was elected sheriff of Shackelford County that same month. Larn was popular, an excellent sheriff, but a man who couldn't stay away from cattle belonging to other people. The vigilantes forced his resignation and tried to warn him. He ignored those efforts and was soon locked in the county seat jail at Albany, Texas, where on the night of June 27, 1877, the vigilantes, who allegedly included some of Larn's in-law relatives, walked into the cells after midnight and shot him to death. Cattle rustling at this point slacked off in Shackelford County, and there is no further record of vigilante action.

See also: CRUGER, WILLIAM R.; LARN, JOHN

FORT Sumner, New Mexico

Fort Sumner is best known as the burial place of Billy the Kid, but the California Column (troops from

California who rode east to New Mexico to fight in the Civil War) established it in 1862 as a post for the Union at Bosque Redondo, on the east bank of New Mexico's Pecos River. Kit Carson later brought in 7,000 Navajos as well as hundreds of Apaches. Except for the cemetery, the post was abandoned in 1868 and then purchased by Lucien Maxwell, by then the second-largest individual landowner in the United States. His son, Pete Maxwell, lived in the community of Fort Sumner, and it was at Pete's house that Sheriff Pat Garrett killed Billy the Kid at practically the stroke of midnight on July 14, 1881.

Fort Sumner today is a tiny community living primarily off the tourist trade. The pleasant-looking cemetery holds the remains of numerous historic figures, although the graves of Billy the Kid, plus his two partners, Tom O'Folliard and Charles Bowdre, lie side by side and are the most visited. The stone says "PALS."

See also: BILLY THE KID; BOWDRE, CHARLES; GARRETT, PATRICK FLOYD JARVIS, LINCOLN COUNTY WAR

FOUNTAIN, Albert Jennings (1838–1896)

Some authorities cite Canada as the birthplace of Albert J. Fountain, but more solid evidence suggests Staten Island in New York on October 23, 1838. During his early years he traveled in Canton and Calcutta, and as a reporter for the *Sacramento Union* he visited Nicaragua to write a story on the Walker filibustering expedition. He gained admittance to the bar in San Francisco, and during the Civil War he joined the First California Volunteer Infantry. He rode east to New Mexico with Carleton's California Column, and along the way fought a two-day battle at Apache Pass with Cochise and his Chiricahua Apaches. As part of the Union army, he helped occupy El Paso, then decided to remain. Perhaps in El Paso, Texas, but probably in Mesilla, New Mexico, he fell in love with 14-year-old Mariana Pérez and married her on October 27, 1862. They would have 12 children.

In El Paso, Texas, Fountain worked as a lawyer, but he was also a spellbinding speaker, an organizer of amateur theatricals, a resourceful coordinator. He was a brave, fascinating individual, a radical Republican who was also at times a tiresome windbag. In El Paso, Fountain became a district surveyor and a collector of internal revenue. He was elected to the Texas state senate from El Paso, became Speaker of the House, and organizer and head of the El Paso

Albert Jennings Fountain (Robert G. McCubbin Collection)

Salt Ring, a group of men laying claim to the salt flats 90 miles east of El Paso. By 1869, however, he had become an organizer of the Anti–Salt Ring, and this caused trouble with his former El Paso cohorts.

On December 7, 1870, Fountain wandered into El Paso's Ben Dowell Saloon and encountered one of his former "salt" friends, Benjamin F. Williams. Williams opened fire with a derringer, hitting Fountain twice, while Fountain rained blows on him with his walking stick.

Williams, his weapon empty, dashed next door to get his shotgun. Fountain walked two blocks to get his rifle, on the way pausing to tell Judge Gaylord Judd Clarke what had happened. Clarke enlisted state policeman Albert French to assist in an arrest, but as they reached the saloon, Williams killed Clarke with the shotgun. From down the street, Fountain fired a rifle round into Williams, and

French finished the job with a couple of revolver shots to the head.

Fountain now underwent a storm of charges, ranging from fraudulent election practices to theft in office. Although acquitted, he stepped aside from Texas politics and moved with his family to Mesilla, New Mexico. There he became editor and publisher of the *Mesilla Valley Independent,* as well as district attorney for the Third Judicial District. He also became a powerful voice against rustlers, making accusations in particular against Dog Canyon rancher Oliver Lee, who lived near Alamogordo, New Mexico.

In late March 1896, Fountain and his eight-year-old son Henry traveled by buggy from Mesilla to Lincoln, New Mexico, where Fountain obtained several cattle-rustling indictments against Oliver Lee, plus cowboys Jim Gilliland and William McNew. However, during their return home on April 1, 1896, Albert J. Fountain and Henry disappeared from the face of the earth, somewhere between Tularosa and Mesilla, New Mexico, most likely within a couple miles of today's White Sands Missile Range headquarters complex. Their bodies have never been found, and the question of who killed them still remains New Mexico's greatest murder mystery.

See also: EL PASO SALT WAR; GARRETT, PATRICK FLOYD JARVIS; LEE, OLIVER MILTON

FOWLER, Joel A. (1849–1884)

Leaving a respected family in Indiana, Joel Fowler in his mid-twenties relocated to Fort Worth, Texas, where he lived with his uncle. There Fowler met a charming young Texas belle. They married, but if rumors are true, the bride proved unfaithful. Joel Fowler shot and killed her paramour.

Fowler vanished for parts unknown, eventually alighting in Las Vegas, New Mexico Territory, in 1879. Opening a saloon and dance hall, Joel married one of his employees. Later the pair moved to Santa Fe, where on February 27, 1880, Joel loaded up on bad whiskey. He treed practically the entire town with a shotgun until being overpowered and transported to jail. After being released, he moved to White Oaks, a mining camp in Lincoln County, where on May 31, 1880, he encountered two miners, Virgil Cullom and Joe Askew, both of whom were drunkenly shooting up the town. A group of timid citizens who thought they ought to do something fired an ineffective volley at the two men. Joe was

wounded, but a besotted Cullom foolishly attempted to save his pal. At that moment, Fowler fatally shot Cullom.

While Fowler occasionally partook of drunken sprees, he had his sober moments. By 1881, Fowler had entered the ranching business in Socorro County and had become financially secure. But he hated theft. On one occasion, accompanied by a ranch employee, Fowler trailed three suspected rustlers. Catching up with the trio, Joel Fowler's shotgun killed "Whiskey Jim" Greathouse and a man named Forrest Neal. His partner shot and killed the third suspect, Jim Finley. Fowler later swore out warrants for C. F. Blackington, the deceased men's boss. Blackington counter-sued, although the matter was amicably settled over drinks at a nearby saloon. Fowler was cleared during an inquest regarding the suspected rustlers' demise.

During an 1883 incident, Fowler allegedly killed "a gambler and bad man" commonly known as "Butcher Knife Bill" (William Childes) from Fort Griffin, Texas. During the melee, another desperado, "Pony" Neal, the brother of Forrest Neal, killed earlier by Fowler, hid out in a house and refused to surrender. In disgust, Fowler set the house on fire, asserting later that Pony had committed suicide.

Fowler sold his ranch soon afterward and promptly whooped it up in Socorro, New Mexico, discharging his six-shooter and making some townspeople dance. Others he ordered to stand on their head. In the middle of all this, Fowler stabbed James E. Cale, a drummer (salesman) by some accounts, and an Engle, New Mexico, saloon owner by others.

Arrested and jailed, Fowler waged an expensive legal defense but was nevertheless convicted of first-degree murder and sentenced to death. Meanwhile, stories about Fowler's past crimes spread around the community, arousing local vigilantes who feared either an escape attempt or a rescue by cowboys from Texas hired by Fowler's uncle. So the townspeople took the law into their own hands. They lynched Joel Fowler on January 22, 1884.

FRAZIER, Sam (1853–1878)

Little is known regarding the origin or early life of Sam Frazier, other than that he was from North Carolina. He drifted to the Lone Star State, and at the age of 24 enlisted in Company C, Frontier Battalion,

Texas Rangers, at San Elizario, El Paso County, Texas, on November 21, 1877. There, along the Mexican border, it did not take him long to become a tough hombre and a remorseless enemy. He and several of his counterparts were often described as "hard-faced and battle scarred."

During outrages committed by both factions in what has generally became known as the "El Paso Salt War," Frazier was suspected of participating in the murder of two men named Durand and Iragoen. Later reports mention that Frazier acknowledged killing the two men for their money.

During another incident, Frazier claimed he was shot while rifling a San Elizario house. He removed what appeared to be a spent pistol ball from his boot. Incensed Rangers shot and killed the suspect, in the process severely wounding his wife.

Throughout the riotous melee, Sam Frazier's violent behavior earned him the scorn of a Hispanic population on both sides of the Rio Grande. The bitter and sometimes violent Catholic priest Father Borrajo allegedly placed a reward of $1,000 for the heads of Frazier and another ranger. If so, there were no takers.

During the racial strife, Frazier's commander, J. C. Ford, passed over Frazier for promotion to first sergeant of the company. Simple jealousy now festered in Frazier's breast, as he became more and more insubordinately belligerent. He threatened Ford's life. When Ford, following orders, advised Frazier that he would have to leave his six-shooter in camp before venturing into town, Frazier declared that Company C was "not big enough to hold both of us." The Texas Rangers predicted trouble.

On January 31, 1878, as Frazier returned to camp and dismounted, Ford called out his name. When Frazier turned around, Ford fired one barrel of his shotgun. The buckshot knocked Frazier to the ground in a sitting position. The second blast missed Frazier completely. Frazier screamed at Ford to quit shooting, but Ford approached the wounded Frazier and emptied the contents of a six-shooter into his head.

A coroner's inquest cleared Ford of wrongdoing, indicating his actions were justified due to Frazier's earlier threats and dangerous disposition. Later, a respected historian remarked that other homicides might have taken place in El Paso County had not these rangers been mustered out of service.

See also: EL PASO SALT WAR

FREDERICKS, William (1872–1895)

William Fredericks was born in Germany and still had his heavy German accent when he showed up in California. In May 1890, masked and carrying a shotgun, he stopped a Mariposa County stage, found the strongbox empty, and got only a few pennies from the driver and one female passenger. Within a week he was caught and given four years in Folsom Prison. For a bandit, this was not an auspicious beginning.

Three years later, practically to the day, the prison released him for good behavior, but Fredericks had learned little. He arranged for friends still in prison to get guns so that they might escape, but all were killed during the attempt.

Fredericks then fled to Nevada, riding as a train hobo. However, he shot a crew member trying to evict him, and on June 30, 1893, killed Nevada sheriff William H. Pascoe, who sought him for questioning. Although a statewide manhunt commenced, no success came until March, when Fredericks appeared back in California at the San Francisco Savings Union, handing a note to a teller demanding money or the building would be blown up. That confrontation ended with Fredericks killing the teller, then fleeing down the street, where he tried to hide by crawling under an empty house. Officers flushed him out. In April 1898, he went on trial for murder, was found guilty, and was sentenced to be hanged.

On the day of his execution he borrowed some paper, wrote an account of his crimes, and tried to sell them for $100. After lowering the price to $20 and still getting no takers, he tore up the confession. On July 26, 1895, he went quietly to his death.

FREE, Mickey (1847?–1915)

This celebrated scout was born in Santa Cruz, Sonora, Mexico, his last name being Martínez. After his father died, his mother moved to the Sonoita Valley of Arizona, where she remarried. On January 27, 1861, wandering Apaches stole the boy and raised him as a Western White Mountain Apache. Sometime during his youth, he was blinded in his left eye, the disfigurement giving him a lifelong vicious appearance. He married four times, fathered four children and was never known to have killed anyone, although many stories have circulated otherwise.

The name "Mickey Free" was the name he gave when he joined the Apache Scouts on December 2,

1862. He became a first sergeant, rode repeatedly with the noted scout Al Sieber, and was considered a fine interpreter and spy (scout). He rode with Gen. George Crook during the Sierra Madre expedition of 1883. In 1885, he accompanied Chatto and other Apaches to Washington, D.C. He reportedly died in the summer of 1915.

FUSSELMAN, Charles (1866–1890)

Although born on July 11, 1866, at Greenbush, Wisconsin, Charles Fusselman moved with his family to Nueces County, Texas when he was four years old. In May 1888, he enlisted as a private in Company D of the Texas Rangers. In June 1889, Fusselman—now a corporal—traveled by train to the isolated whistle stop of Maxon Spring (near Marathon), Texas, where he and wanted outlaw Donanciano Beslinga blazed away at each other without effect during a violent thunderstorm. The two met again at sunrise, and this time the ranger fired eight rounds into Beslinga, who did not survive. A year later the state promoted Fusselman to sergeant and transferred him to Presidio, Jeff Davis, and Brewster Counties. He frequently made courtroom appearances in and around El Paso, Texas.

On April 17, 1890, as Fusselman lounged in the El Paso sheriff's office talking with Deputy Frank Simmons and police officer George Herold, rancher John Barnes dashed in and breathlessly reported a theft of cattle at Mundy Springs in the Franklin Mountains, eight miles north of El Paso.

Fusselman, Herold, and Barnes rode in pursuit and entered an east-side canyon, where they easily captured Ysidoro Pasos, a rustler rear guard. A half-hour later the lawmen unexpectedly blundered into the outlaw camp, where, during a brief gun battle, the rustler leader, Geronimo Parra, shot Fusselman twice in the head with a rifle, killing him instantly. The rustlers escaped. The lawmen retreated back to town and later returned with a large posse. They recovered Fusselman's body. A funeral home packed Fusselman in ice and shipped him to Lagarto, Texas, for burial. Today this tragic canyon, the largest in the Franklin Mountains, is called Fusselman Canyon.

See also: HUGHES, JOHN R.

GAINESVILLE Hangings

An example of fear, ignorance, war, racism, lack of communications, and man's inhumanity to man occurred at Gainesville in Cooke County, Texas, during mid-October 1866. What became the "Great Gainesville Hangings" had their initial roots in North-South bitterness before and after the Civil War.

Gainesville, about 60 miles north of Fort Worth and Dallas, and 10 miles south of the Red River, had begun as a small community eventually reached by the Butterfield Overland Stage Company. The small community of Gainesville turned into a continental crossroads. Here in northern Texas, Union sentiment ran high, since only about 10 percent of the population owned slaves. Furthermore, Cooke and most of its neighboring counties voted against seccession, arousing the fears of farmers and cattlemen who did own slaves. Making matters worse, Kansas abolitionists (known as Jayhawkers) had been active in this part of Texas. While they found much of the population desiring only to be left alone, these Jayhawkers aroused considerable sentiment for turning north Texas into a free state.

The Confederacy Conscription Act (generally called the Conscript Law) of April 1862 was unevenly enforced in north Texas. By some accounts, the draft leaned toward inducting Union Sympathizers into the Confederate army. Therefore, many of these individuals formed what became locally known as the Union League, or the Clan. Rumors circulated that the league planned to assault regional arsenals. Texas reacted by dispatching state troops on the morning of October 1, 1862. The 11th Texas Cavalry arrested an alleged 150 white Unionists—none of them slave owners—in and around Gainesville, holding them at Gainesville and charging them with insurrection and treason.

The military turned the prisoners over to civil authorities and returned to their encampment. At this point the community seemed to go berserk. Thomas Barrett, a local preacher who wrote memoirs of the event, recalled that "there were crowds . . . in every direction, armed and pressing forward [toward] prisoners under guard. The deepest and most intense excitement . . . prevailed. Reason had left its throne. The mind of almost every man seemed to be unhinged, and wild excitement reigned supreme. When I arrived on the [town] square, there were perhaps three or four hundred armed men . . . in sight." Although trials had not yet started, Barrett mentioned that "a [hanging] tree [in the public square] had already been selected," a "historic elm with long and bending limbs."

The jailed prisoners next went before a citizens court of 12 jurors, seven of them slave owners. In this court, the jurors needed not a unanimous vote but only a majority vote of seven. Therefore, by majority vote several of the suspected Unionists were released, but the jury still convicted seven leaders of the accused, most of whom confessed, after a fashion, allegedly admitting plans for an attack on the town in coordination with Kansas Jayhawkers. They spoke of secret handgrips, various oaths and degrees of membership, special words with double meanings, and distinctive motions made with the hands or eyes or feet, one of them a particular way of tugging on the ear. They allegedly confessed that men, women, and children would be slain during a forthcoming uprising.

The seven—one at a time, after being found guilty—were turned over to the outside mob and taken to a huge elm tree in the Gainesville public square and hanged. Not satisfied, however, the mob within hours sent word that 14 more men had to be hanged, or else everyone in the building would be killed, including the jury. Therefore, the intimidated jury called for a list of names, chose 14, then handed the list to the jury foreman, saying, "Maybe this will satisfy them [the outside mob]." The 14 men were then locked in a separate room and told they would be hanged during the following day, Sunday.

During the next morning the condemned were loaded into a wagon and hauled down California Street to the Public Square, where at the direction and insistence of the mob the military carried out the executions, hanging each man from a branch of the elm. However, even the larger limbs would not support several bodies at once, so the hangings took all day, darkness finally approaching as the last man died. Barrett noted in his memoirs that the mob did not permit wives and children to observe the executions, but he also wrote that "the sun set that night on fourteen widowed families."

A killing lust satisfied, at least temporarily, the remaining 60 to 80 prisoners, now considered innocent, would be released, likely within the week. But other tragedies intervened. Within days, unknown but suspected Union assailants ambushed and killed Confederate colonel William C. Young, the officer charged with originally rounding up the insurrectionists. They also killed a local resident named James Dickson. None of the slayers were identified or ever apprehended, but an enraged community still had the remaining prisoners as targets for its rage. These men were now hustled from jail back to the courtroom and retried on the original charges. Two-thirds (about 50 or 60) were released, but 19 were convicted and promptly taken by heavily guarded cart to the same public square and hanged from the same elm on the following Sunday. Altogether, 40 men had

now died in the Gainesville Square at the end of a rope.

The Texas government paid expenses for the military's part in rounding up the accused and in general applauded what came to be known as the "Great Gainesville Hangings." Many state newspapers provided supportive editorials. However, after the Civil War ended, a few of the jurors were tried by a Union government for murder. All but one were acquitted.

GARLICK, William Henry (1868–1913)

In the annals of Western history, the name William Henry Garlick is seldom mentioned, but a careful investigation reveals that this steady and fearless lawman was a highly regarded and respected El Paso County deputy sheriff during trying times at the westernmost tip of far West Texas. Aside from serving a satchel full of routine arrest warrants, scuffling with drunks, calming family disputes, and serving subpoenas, William Henry Garlick had the Mexican Revolution to worry about.

During the heady days of the topsy-turvy revolution, *Federales,* revolutionaries, and mercenaries were creating mischief and murder along the turbulent border. Sometimes their motives were pure, and at other times their intentions were personal and larcenous. Area lawmen maintained a constant guard, sometimes jumping back and forth across the international line.

On numerous occasions, famed Texas Ranger captain John Hughes, the "Border Boss," detailed Sgt. C. R. Moore and Pvt. Charles Webster to parallel the movements of revolutionists operating from across the Rio Grande and prevent any unwarranted and unwelcome intrusion onto Texas soil. Knowing they indeed had their hands full with this dicey assignment, the pair of rangers sought the help of a salty border veteran, 45-year-old W. H. Garlick.

The trio of lawmen shadowed the movements of Pascual Orozco's army. The Mexicans no doubt looked to the American side of the Rio Grande and postulated that the three lawmen posed little threat, yet, for whatever reason, the insurgents moved on, wary of testing them. Later, however, other rebels decided to splash across the line for piracy and pillage. Three made a bold attempt to ford the river but were turned back by an officer's admonition. With reinforcements, the rebels wheeled about and charged back across the river toward the lawmen and just as suddenly opened fire. Undaunted, Moore, Webster, and Garlick returned the shots. Three bandoleer-wearing bandits tumbled from flat-horned Mexican saddles. With news of the incident in hand, the Texas governor instructed Captain Hughes, "You give an account of the experience of Sergeant Moore and Private Webster and Deputy Sheriff Garlick in their brush with the rebels. I think the time has come when the State should not hesitate to deal with these marauding bands of rebels in a way which they will understand."

After the shootout, Deputy Garlick was clearly tagged a ranger cohort and supporter, although nothing happened until the middle of June (1913), when he and Texas Ranger Scott Russell arrested Sabino Guadarrama, Will Hill, and L. Dominguez for stealing cattle. The defendants made bond and threatened revenge.

Then on June 23, Garlick and Russell entered the Guadarrama family business, the "del Barrio Libre" grocery and butcher shop, a suspected site for selling meat from stolen, butchered beeves. Garlick and Russell were not overly concerned, as both "were considered excellent pistol shots and were quick on the draw," at least so reported the *El Paso Morning Times*. However, for the moment both dropped their guard, and suddenly each was struck from behind by a heavy meat cleaver (an ax by other reports) in the hands of Mariana Guadarrama, Sabino's mother. And, at almost the exact instant that the two officers fell to the floor bleeding copiously from massive head wounds, Juan Guadarrama, another of Mariana's sons, riddled the face-down lawmen with lead, firing nine shots. However, in a wickedly sour twist of fate, during the chaotic fracas somehow Juan shot his own mother, the ax-wielding Mariana, in the stomach. She died on the floor, inches from Garlick and Russell.

Scott Russell's remains were shipped to his birthplace, Stephenville, Erath County, Texas. Garlick was survived by a pregnant wife and four children, and he was later interred at Valentine, Jeff Davis County, Texas. Juan Guadarrama went to the penitentiary.

See also: HUGHES, JOHN REYNOLDS; TEXAS RANGERS

GARRETT, Patrick Floyd Jarvis (a.k.a Pat Garrett) (1850–1908)

Pat Garrett is best remembered as the slayer of Henry McCarty, a.k.a. William H. Bonney, a.k.a. Billy the Kid. Garrett came into the world as one of eight children at Chambers County, Alabama, on June 5, 1850, the son of John and Elizabeth Garrett, farmers. Three years later the family moved to Claiborne Parish, Louisiana, where Pat grew up. Due to a family dispute, Garrett left home in 1869 and became a buffalo hunter on the Texas plains. In November 1876, Garrett shot and killed buffalo hunter Joe Briscoe during a campfire altercation. At Fort Griffin, Texas, a grand jury declined to prosecute.

On February 1, 1877, a Comanche band struck the buffalo hunters' camp near present-day Lubbock, Texas, inflicting damages. Shortly afterward, Garrett left the buffalo range, rode into Fort Sumner, New Mexico, briefly entered the hog business, and married Apolinaria Gutiérrez. They would have eight children.

Pat Garrett and his wife, Apolinaria, in a photo likely taken on their wedding day (Author's Collection)

New Mexico's Lincoln County War commenced in 1877–78. In November 1880, Pat Garrett became the Lincoln County sheriff. On December 19, 1880, at Fort Sumner, New Mexico, Pat Garrett and his posse killed Tom O'Folliard, a friend and outlaw associate of Billy the Kid. Early the next morning, December 20, Garrett trapped Billy the Kid and gang remnants in a rock house at Stinking Springs, several miles from Fort Sumner. During a shootout the posse killed gang member Charlie Bowdre. Several hours later the Kid and the others surrendered and were transported by buckboard and train to the territorial prison in Santa Fe. From there the Kid was moved to Mesilla, New Mexico, tried for murder, found guilty, and was sentenced to be hanged at Pat Garrett's jail in Lincoln, New Mexico. But that never happened, because while Garrett was collecting taxes at White Oaks, New Mexico, the Kid killed two guards and escaped. Then, shortly before or right after midnight on July 14, 1881, Sheriff Pat Garrett fired two revolver shots in Pete Maxwell's bedroom at Fort Sumner, New Mexico. One bullet struck the wall; the other buried itself in the heart of Billy the Kid. It took Garrett another six months to collect the $500 reward.

A biography then appeared with the mind-numbing title of *The Authentic Life of Billy the Kid, the Noted Desperado of the Southwest, Whose Deeds of Daring Have Made His Name a Terror in New Mexico, Arizona and Northern Mexico.* Pat Garrett's name went on the cover as author, but Garrett's journalist friend Ash Upson claimed that he (Upson) wrote every word of it.

Garrett could not get reelected sheriff, although he continued dabbling in territorial politics. In 1884, with rampant cattle rustling occurring in the Texas panhandle, the LS Ranch retained Pat Garrett to organize a force of Texas Rangers and suppress the outbreaks. By 1885 much of the rustling had ceased, so Garrett disbanded the lawmen. Thereafter, he worked briefly for the Cree Ranch in New Mexico, but within a year, due to drought and a pullback of foreign investment, Garrett was again out of work.

Garrett moved his family to Roswell, New Mexico, where in cooperation with various financiers, he engaged in irrigation schemes along the Pecos River. By 1893, however, due to a financial depression, Garrett was forced out. Bitter, he left New Mexico, moving to Uvalde, Texas, where he gambled and raced horses with John Nance Garner, who would be

vice president of the United States during the first two FDR administrations.

Meanwhile, back in New Mexico, Col. Albert Jennings Fountain, a prominent Mesilla resident, and his young son Henry had been traveling by buggy across the desolate 70-mile stretch between Alamogordo and Mesilla, New Mexico. Somewhere near White Sands, they disappeared. The territory feared murder, and once again New Mexico needed Pat Garrett. He returned to become sheriff of Dona Ana County in early 1896. In doing so, he switched from the Democratic to the Republican Party.

During the course of the Fountain murder investigation, Garrett zeroed in on three suspects: Oliver Lee, Bill McNew, and James Gilliland, ranchers and cowboys living in the Tularosa Basin of southern New Mexico. Before dawn on July 12, 1898, Garrett and several deputies rode to Wildy Well, a ranching line-camp near present-day Oro Grande, New Mexico. The posse dismounted a quarter-mile distant from the shacks, approached, and broke into the bedroom of a rancher and his wife. The suspects were not there. During the search that followed, Tularosa, New Mexico, school teacher and deputy Kent Kearney placed a ladder against the roof of a shack. The outlaws shot him off it when he climbed up to look around. He died shortly afterward. The gunmen on the roof, in control of the high ground, forced the sheriff and his deputies to surrender and relinquish their weapons before leaving.

A sheriff had now been humiliated, three outlaws were loose and running, and the whole Southwest was in an uproar. However, two of the Fountain murder suspects, rancher Oliver Lee and cowboy Jim Gilliland, subsequently surrendered and were taken to Hillsboro, New Mexico. During an 1899 trial that made newspapers all over the country, Lee and Gilliland were acquitted.

A discouraged Garrett now dropped the Fountain investigation but learned that Norman Newman, an Oklahoma fugitive with a price on his head, was working at the San Augustine Ranch owned by W. W. Cox in the foothills of the Organ Mountains in Dona Ana County, New Mexico. Garrett and deputy José Espalin rode out to make the arrest and found Newman inside the Cox house. The wanted man put up a struggle, and the family dog, which had been sleeping on the porch, jumped through the open window. The arrest then turned into a wild melee of yells, screams, barks, growls, profanity, and the clatter of bodies crashing into walls and furniture. It ended with Espalin shooting the wanted man dead.

Meanwhile, President Theodore Roosevelt, who had always had an affinity for rugged men of the West, in December 1901 appointed Pat Garrett as collector of customs at El Paso, Texas. For a variety of reasons the collectorship did not become a happy experience. The always cantankerous, sarcastic Garrett antagonized practically everyone who dealt with him. He engaged in a fist fight on an El Paso street corner with a discharged employee, Charles Gaither. A disturbed President Roosevelt subsequently ordered Garrett to meet and confer with him during a 1905 Rough Rider convention in San Antonio. Garrett agreed and took with him his best friend, Tom Powers, owner of the Coney Island Saloon in El Paso.

Garrett introduced Powers as a West Texas cattleman. Pictures were taken and released to the press. Upon learning that he had been deceived, Roosevelt did not dismiss Garrett but simply refused to appoint him to another two-year term. So in December 1905, out of work and down on his luck, Garrett moved his family back to New Mexico, settling on a ranch on what is now the White Sands Missile Range.

He subsequently cosigned a banknote for his property with two other men, and they defaulted. The county threatened to repossess his land and cattle. In desperation Garrett mortgaged his property to Las Cruces businessman Martin Lohman, but Pat then could not make the payments. W. W. Cox picked up the note, but Garrett couldn't and didn't pay Cox either. To make matters worse, one of Garrett's sons, Poe Garrett, back in 1905, had leased the Bear Canyon portion of the Garrett ranch to local cowboy Wayne Brazel, who placed goats on it.

In 1908, Garrett tried to sell the ranch, but his only offer came from Jim Miller, better known as "Killin' Jim Miller," or sometimes "Deacon Jim Miller." Miller needed a remote area to graze Mexican cattle prior to shipping them to market, so he made a conditional offer for the ranch, stipulating that the goats must go. (Miller likely also wanted the land to hide Chinese illegally smuggled into the country from Mexico.)

Garrett promised to meet and negotiate with Jim Miller in Las Cruces, New Mexico. Garrett and Carl Adamson, a brother-in-law of Miller's, left the Garrett ranch on February 29, 1908, and headed by buckboard for Las Cruces. On the way they over-

took Wayne Brazel on horseback. About halfway to town, Pat Garrett stopped the buckboard to urinate. While standing there in the desert sand, someone shot him in the back of the head. Wayne Brazel confessed to the shooting but claimed self-defense. A jury acquitted him. Pat Garrett's death still remains a point of controversy. He is buried in the Masonic Cemetery at Las Cruces, New Mexico.

See also: BILLY THE KID; BOWDRE, CHARLES; COX, WILLIAM WEBB; FOUNTAIN, ALBERT JENNINGS; MILLER, JAMES; LINCOLN COUNTY WAR

GILLETT, James Buchanan (1856–1937)

James B. Gillett was born on November 4, 1856, a fourth child of James S. Gillett (an adjutant general under Texas governor Sam Houston) and the former Bettie Harper. By 1870, he had never been more than 12 miles from Austin, Texas. By the early 1870s, he had become a West Texas cowboy in the vicinity of Lampasas, Texas. He saw his first man killed in 1873, when two cowboys, Jack Perkins and Levi Dunbar, began arguing—and Perkins shot Dunbar to death.

On June 1, 1875, in Menard County, Texas, James B. Gillett enlisted in Company D of the Texas Rangers, his salary being $40 a month. He also received a .50-caliber Sharps carbine and a .45-caliber Colt revolver, the cost to be deducted from his first month's pay. In August of that same year he had his first Indian fight. By 1877, the Indian wars were mostly over, so the rangers began concentrating primarily on Texas feuds, such as Horrell-Higgins. These were also years in which filibusters (private armies) used the Texas border with Mexico as a supply, recruitment, and jumping-off point for invading northern Mexico. The rangers had the task of locating and breaking up these expeditions when possible.

In September 1877, James B. Gillett helped escort a heavily shackled and handcuffed John Wesley Hardin out of the Austin jail and over to Comanche, Texas, where Hardin was tried for the murder of Brown County deputy sheriff Charles Webb. As Gillett described the experience, "The boy who had sold fish and game on the streets of Austin was now guarding the most desperate criminal in Texas."

Following this the rangers went after Dick Dublin, who lived and operated along the South Llano River and had a $700 reward on his head. In January

1877, as Gillett and a squad of rangers closed in on his ranch, Dublin made a run for it, bent over and skimming along the ground. Gillett fired a Winchester rifle, the bullet striking Dublin in the hip, slicing through his body and exiting at the collar bone. Although he was dead practically upon striking the ground, another ranger rode up and put two additional bullets in the body. As for the reward, no one collected. The conditions had been specific: it would be paid for Dublin's arrest and incarceration, not his death.

By September 1879, Gillett had arrived in Ysleta, Texas, with Lt. John R. Baylor, and although they had missed the recent El Paso Salt War, the last Indian fights in Texas were still in their future. The rangers repeatedly tangled with Victorio's Apaches, driving them back into Chihuahua, Mexico, where Mexican forces killed Victorio and most of his people.

In the meantime, a Christmas Eve 1881 murder occurred in Socorro, New Mexico, when the two Baca brothers killed A. M. Conklin, editor of the *Socorro Sun News*. The men fled to Ysleta, Texas, where one was captured and returned. The other, Enofrio Baca, had found employment in Zaragoza, Mexico, across the Rio Grande from Ysleta. With a reward of $500 on Baca's head, Gillett and another ranger crossed the river and found their prey working in a store. A female patron fainted when they stuck a revolver in Baca's ear and marched him to a horse. They raced two miles to the international border with a Mexican posse in pursuit. Gillett then hustled the man to Socorro, turned him over to the vigilantes, collected his reward, and saw Baca dangling from a rope as his train left the Socorro station, heading south.

The kidnapping, however, created an international uproar. Mexico brought pressure on the United States, which brought pressure on Texas, which brought pressure on Capt. John R. Hughes, Gillett's commanding officer. Gillett therefore left the rangers, moved to El Paso, and married the attractive 16-year-old Helen Baylor, daughter of Capt. John R. Baylor. Gillett became an assistant city marshal under Dallas Stoudenmire. When Stoudenmire was shot to death on September 18, 1882, Gillett became "the" marshal. Six months later in March 1883, Marshal Gillett accused El Paso mayor pro tempore Paul Keating of being too intoxicated to perform his duties. Keating responded by accusing Gillett of not properly accounting for fines and fees. Gillett coun-

tered by bouncing a six-shooter off Keating's head—and the city council dismissed the marshal.

By now, Gillett's personal troubles were mounting. He and Helen, in spite of two children—one of whom became Harper Lee, a noted Mexican bullfighter—did not have a happy marriage. She charged him with adultery and sued him for divorce. He left El Paso for the Big Bend in April 1885. There he remarried, entered the ranching business around Marfa, Texas, and founded the world famous Cowboy Camp Meetings. He died on June 11, 1937, in Temple, Texas, and is buried in Marfa.

See also: HARDIN, JOHN WESLEY; JONES, FRANK; STOUDENMIRE, DALLAS

GILMO, John W. (a.k.a. Gilmore) (1850–1895)

The name John W. Gilmo attracts little historical attention, although for a time throughout New Mexico and Arizona he was known as one of those blue-eyed men who are simply devoid of fear. Seldom did anyone question his courage, although on occasion his judgment served him none too well. Some say he hailed from Maryland, but he didn't come to the law's attention until Grant County sheriff Harvey Whitehill gave the 29-year-old Gilmo a deputy's commission on February 28, 1880.

On May 13, 1880, Gilmo was appointed the Silver City town marshal, a position he held until resigning on December 10. He also turned over his Grant County deputy's badge. Then for reasons not altogether understood, he was rehired as a deputy on February 7, 1881. In July, he was again removed from office, this time replaced by A. G. Ledbetter.

The removal stemmed from Gilmo's shooting and killing of Walter M. Harvey, a cook at the Southern Hotel. The details are sketchy, but for whatever reason, Harvey failed to lay down a kitchen knife quick enough to suit the marshal. Gilmo shot him in the head, left breast, and side. All of this lead seemed a little extreme to many residents, who believed Gilmo had fired too soon, that the shooting was unjustified. With public pressure building for prosecution, Gilmo stole some Silver City money and vanished. On July, 19, 1881, Judge Warren Bristol issued an arrest warrant, and Sheriff Whitehill ordered deputy J. W. Fleming to find Gilmo. Fleming pursued Gilmo past Duck Creek to the west, and on to Clifton, Arizona Territory, before he gave up and returned to Silver City. Three weeks later, on August 6, 1881, however,

Gilmo returned to Silver City on his own, surrendered to authorities, and was released on a $5,000 bond. Although indicted on a charge of murder, Gilmo was freed.

By the end of the next month, however, Gilmo had returned to the public spotlight. At Silver City's Centennial Saloon, an uproariously drunk James Burns, himself a deputy sheriff, created a disturbance. Gilmo subsequently talked Burns out of his six-shooter, which was a wise move, although later during an unwise lapse of good judgment he gave it back. On the night of July 25, 1882, Burns picked up where he had left off, and in an argumentative mood he gambled with the poisonously dangerous Frank Thurmond. The two argued, and when Deputy Sheriffs Dan Tucker and Billy McClellan and Town Marshal G. W. Moore approached, Burns drew his revolver and was shot and killed. The shooting was indeed sensational—three officers killing another officer. At the preliminary hearing, John W. Gilmo testified that Burns's gun hand had been near his waist. Eventually, charges against Tucker were dismissed, and Moore and McClellan were found not guilty by a court in Mesilla.

Meanwhile, south of Silver City, near Gage, on November 24, 1883, a Southern Pacific train was robbed and the engineer slain. The suspects were Frank Taggart, George Washington Cleveland, Mitch Lee, and Christopher "Kit" Joy. An intense manhunt started.

With hopes of monetary rewards, John Gilmo accompanied ex-sheriff Harvey Whitehill to the vicinity of St. Johns, Apache County, Arizona, a former home of suspect Frank Taggart. Regrettably, Taggart had just departed for Socorro, New Mexico. Taking a Mexican guide with him, Gilmo set off in pursuit, overhauling Taggart and returning him to Silver City. Near Horse Springs, the other suspects, Mitch Lee and Kit Joy, were also captured. Whitehill arrested Cleveland at Socorro. With several bounty hunters involved in the four arrests, questions now arose as to how the $8,000 was to be divided. Len Harris, the well-known Southern Pacific Railroad detective, credited Gilmo with Taggart's arrest, a fact that Whitehill did not dispute. Gilmo subsequently got two-thirds of Taggart's reward money, $2,666.66.

In partnership with George Chapman, Gilmo entered the saloon business in Clifton, Arizona, but by November 1882 the brief undertaking had failed.

Gilmo returned to Grant County, New Mexico, settling in at the Burro Mountain copper camp of Paschal, a bustling community with a 50-ton smelter, stores, saloons, and nearly 1,000 residents. Gilmo was soon doing assessment work on mining claims.

Never far removed from trouble, however, in a row with a drunken companion, Gilmo was wounded, although not seriously, when a gun fired prematurely. After his recovery Gilmo briefly served as town marshal for Kingston, a mining camp on the eastern slope of the Black Range Mountains. Meanwhile, Gilmo was promised a reward if he arrested Charley Small, suspected of an Arizona train robbery. In September 1887, Gilmo encountered Small at the Deming, New Mexico, depot, but Small pulled his six-shooter. Only the prompt arrival of Deputy Dan Tucker stopped a shooting. Wisely, Small submitted to Tucker, and while the deputy was sorting out the mess, Gilmo skipped out for Mexico, a few miles south. Dan Tucker determined that there was no evidence against Small, turned him loose, and swore out a warrant for Gilmo's arrest. Nothing came of it.

By 1892, Gilmo was in Graham County, Arizona Territory, most probably in Clifton, where he was convicted of assault with a deadly weapon. On April 25, 1892, John W. Gilmo (under the name Gilmore) entered the territorial prison at Yuma to begin a four-year sentence. Three years later, on February 2, 1895, Gilmo received a pardon from Governor Hughes. Where he went from there remains a mystery.

See also: TUCKER, DAVID; WHITEHILL, HARVEY HOWARD

GLEASON, Harvey (a.k.a. Teton Jackson)
(1855–1927)

Teton Jackson was believed born in Rhode Island. He had a tussle with the law in Joplin, Missouri, and later claimed to have scouted for Gen. George Crook during the Sioux campaign of 1876. He may or may not have been born a Mormon, but if not, he converted to one. Frank Canton, a Wyoming sheriff who later put irons on Jackson, noted, "I have never seen a man of his description before or since. He was about 45, over six feet in height, weighed 190, stubby beard, rawboned, coarse features, flaming red hair, red face, and eyes as black as a snake." Canton said he stole government mules, killed several soldiers plus some U.S. deputy marshals, and was a member of the Mormon "Destroying Angels." Biographer Robert DeArment wrote that Jackson "escaped capture for years by using his Mormon religion to gain the help and protection of Mormon families in the region."

Teton Jackson took this nickname from the Wyoming mountains where he lived and circulated. The "Jackson" came from the Jackson Hole country, especially what is now the National Elk Refuge, an area he seldom strayed from. Otherwise, killing people wasn't so much a priority as it was a necessity: Teton Jackson was a horse thief. He never robbed trains, stages, or banks. He and a dozen or so followers just liked good horseflesh, the kind one didn't have to pay for. The stolen animals were usually sold or traded in Wyoming or South Dakota, and stories during the height of his career had them numbering in the hundreds. The trade flourished for roughly eight years. Lawmen could never find the thieves during the summer, and in the winter a heavy snow closed all the passes into and out of the Tetons.

In February 1884, Jackson and a confederate went to Eagle Rock, Idaho, and reported that in defense of their lives they had killed a man named Robert Cooper at Badger Creek. Sheriff Ed Winn rode out to take a look, found a body frozen stiff, and since he had no way to transport it, he simply chopped off the head and brought it in as evidence. Jackson was indicted and tried for murder but was acquitted.

Within months, livestock associations all over Idaho and Wyoming were posting rewards for the capture and conviction of horse thieves, one Idaho notice offering $800. By October of that same year, Sheriff Canton had tracked down Jackson and had him in handcuffs and on his way to the Buffalo, Wyoming, jail. On November 5, 1885, the Idaho authorities sentenced him to 14 years in prison at the Boise Federal Penitentiary. Meanwhile, various posses had gradually reduced the gang's numbers and effectiveness through death and capture.

On August 17, 1886, Teton Jackson escaped from the Boise prison, returned to his old haunts and trade, and managed for two years to avoid the authorities. However, in April 1888, he was recaptured near Billings, Montana, and returned to prison at Boise, where he spent four more years, being pardoned on April 6, 1892.

By now, times had changed. The outlaw chieftain had outlived most of his friends, as well as his enemies. He married a Shoshone woman, lived in Fremont County, Wyoming, and found occasional work as a guide. He died in 1927 at the county home in Lander, Wyoming.

See also: CANTON, FRANK

GOLDEN, Johnny (1846?–1877?)

By most accounts, Johnny Golden was originally from Illinois (or Boston, or Georgia) but later drifted to Kentucky, where he became a jockey for a well-known racehorse owner. Aside from his role in the sport of kings, Johnny's employer (if the rumors are true) was also the father of a daughter he christened Carlotta (Charlotte) J. Thompkins. Westerners would come to know her as Lottie Deno, the most prominent female gambler in the Southwest.

Reportedly, Golden and Charlotte Thompkins tied the matrimonial knot, although the assertion has not been substantiated by official documentation. Nor do all historians believe it. But one thing is sure—the pair tried their luck at one of the roughest towns in Texas: Fort Griffin. A nearby civilian settlement was The Flat, and the couple arrived either at separate times, or as complete strangers. At least one writer, concentrating on the feminine side of the relationship, declares that Golden, by the time he reached Fort Griffin, was a wanted criminal, and indeed a list of 1870s Texas fugitives does mention a John Golden as being indicted for assault to kill and for theft at Travis County (Austin) in February 1876. Another author simply reports, Golden "knifed a man to death and skipped out, leaving his wife penniless." But in the end, all accounts concur: Johnny Golden, by now a professional gambler, ended up in the "Clear Fork Country," specifically at The Flat. Johnny Golden's arrival at Fort Griffin's Bee Hive Saloon was wanted not by Lottie Deno or by any of her current or potential suitors.

So it wasn't long before Constable William C. "Bill" Gilson and Deputy Sheriff Jim Draper arrested Johnny Golden as a fugitive from justice. Rather than throw him in the local jail, the pair set off with their prisoner into the darkness, later saying they were delivering Golden to the nearby military installation's guardhouse. At any rate, Johnny Golden never arrived. The powder burns on his body more or less told the story, and although murder was never proved at the inquest, Lottie skipped off to New Mexico Territory.

See also: DENO, CHARLOTTE

GOLDSBY, Crawford (a.k.a. Cherokee Bill) (1876–1896)

Goldsby had a touch of every color in him: white, black, and Hispanic, which meant that he belonged nowhere. Born at Fort Concho, Texas, he grew up quick, mean, and tall, once killing his brother-in-law after being told to feed the hogs. He then wandered off to Oklahoma, where in 1894 at Fort Gibson he shot and wounded Jake Lewis, a black man, following a dispute over a woman.

The law now took up the pursuit, and Goldsby, on the run, fell in with William and James Cook, leaders of a wild Oklahoma band of desperadoes. It would be William Cook who anointed young Goldsby with the moniker Cherokee Bill. It would also be these two men who led Goldsby into his next killing, as law officers in pursuit of the three lost a man to Cherokee Bill's deadly aim. The killing again sent Bill into hiding, the young gunman taking refuge in the home of his sister, Maud Brown. But that did not work either, because Cherokee Bill shot and killed her husband, reportedly when he (the husband) took a whip to her.

Back with the Cook brothers, young Goldsby and others in mid-1894 rode into Nowata, Oklahoma, stopped at the railroad station, killed the station agent, waited for the next train, and when it chugged in hammered on the express door until the express agent opened it. The agent took a bullet in the head, the brakeman took one in the leg, and Cherokee Bill left.

A short time later, Cherokee Bill, with Cook and other friends, attempted to rob a general store in Lenapah, Oklahoma. Bill killed an innocent bystander, then fled to the home of a Cherokee girl who, unknown to him, also happened to be the cousin of lawman Isaac Rogers. The lawman overpowered Goldsby, disarmed him, loaded him in a buggy, and hauled him to Fort Smith, Arkansas, where, on February 26, 1895, Judge Isaac Parker tried him for the murder of the innocent bystander in Lenapah. Parker sentenced him to die on June 25, 1895. Goldsby's attorney, however, won repeated delays.

In the meantime, a jail trustee smuggled in a gun to Goldsby, and on July 26, Bill ordered a guard to open his door. Instead, the officer reached for his own weapon, and Cherokee Bill killed him. That slaying sent Goldsby back before Judge Parker, who again sentenced him to death, this time on December 2, 1895. Appeals delayed this trip to the hangman also,

and the date was rescheduled for March 17, 1896. A subsequent appeal to the president went nowhere.

On St. Patrick's Day, March 17, Cherokee Bill sang ditties and whistled as he walked up the stairs, reportedly saying, as the knot was being adjusted around his neck, "This is about as good a day to die as any." He is buried at Fort Gibson, Oklahoma.

See also: COOK, WILLIAM TUTTLE; PARKER, JUDGE ISAAC

GOOD, Milton Paul (a.k.a. E. Kyle) (1889–1960)

Milton Paul Good was a fine steer roper, but a dismal thief. He was also a murderer. Born near Tularosa in what was then Lincoln County, New Mexico Territory, on March 17, 1889, he moved with his family back to Texas from whence they had earlier come. Milt's father, Isham J. Good, was once described by a Texas Ranger as a "notorious cow thief," while his uncle, John Good, had a somewhat deserved man-killing reputation. A cousin, Walter Good, ultimately would be gunned down in a New Mexico dispute involving the always interesting and sometimes controversial cowman Oliver Lee. So, as a bad hombre, Milt Good could be proud of his lineage.

Milt Good worked as a cowboy on various West Texas ranches and over time, by whatever means, established himself a small rancher, but a rancher in serious financial difficulty due to drought. Turning to rodeo, Milt Good in 1920 captured the title of "world champion steer roper" during a contest held at Shreveport, Louisiana.

Returning to West Texas with a pocketful of prize money, Milt started trading in cattle, only a few of which he had legitimate title to. The other livestock belonged to his neighbors.

On one occasion, Texas and Southwestern Cattle Raisers Association inspectors W. D. Allison and H. L. Roberson caught him with 516 head of stolen livestock. They filed criminal charges.

Common sense now gave way to panic, and operating with one of the West's truly callused cow-country characters, Hillary U. Loftis, Good murdered the inspectors on Easter Sunday, April 1, 1923, at Seminole, Texas. The two dead men had planned on meeting with a grand jury the following day. After shotguns and .45 automatics were emptied into the bodies of the cattle inspectors, the killers fled, although they later surrendered. Following a scandalous and sensational public trial, the defendants were locked away in the state prison at Huntsville, Texas.

Two years later the prisoners, along with others, overran a guard and escaped. As fugitives, Good and Loftis went on a minor crime spree in the Northwest before splitting up in Oklahoma. Good subsequently was captured and was returned to the Texas prison. Once again he sought illegal liberation, this time through a tunnel. The authorities caught on to that one too.

Finally the governor pardoned him, and that was both good and bad news. He was at last out of prison, but on July 3, 1960, near Cotulla, Texas he was caught and crushed between the bumper of his vehicle and a pasture gate. The death was ruled an accident.

See also: LEE, OLIVER MILTON

GORDON, Jack (a.k.a. Peter Worthington)
(1822–1864)

Peter Worthington was born and raised in Virginia or Maryland. At the age of 17 he headed for the Rocky Mountains after killing a man. During the Mexican War he served with Col. Alexander Doniphan, killed a man in Ciudad Juarez, across the Rio Grande from El Paso, and then joined an Apache tribe, killing and raiding his own people and taking an Apache wife. Soon afterward, he abandoned her and fled west to California, where he served with state rangers in pursuit of Joaquin Murrieta.

For the next few years he was suspected of ambushing isolated California travelers, killing them, and taking their goods and money. By 1864 he had teamed up with Confederate guerrillas, then he briefly mined and later butchered hogs near Tailholt, California. But he never stayed anywhere long, on one occasion returning to El Paso, Texas, where he killed a man on El Paso Street in front of Mayor Ben Dowell's saloon. Following that he returned to California, raised hogs on the side, clashed with a grizzly bear, and almost lost his life before teaming up once again with a band of highway robbers. In December 1864, he and Samuel Groupie, another hog raiser, shot it out at Tailholt, California. Gordon died of his wounds.

GRAND Lake Shootout

The Fourth of July celebration in 1883 at Grand Lake, Colorado, turned out to be dramatic beyond expectations. The buildup had started three years earlier, in 1880, when Grand County voters moved the county seat from Hot Sulphur Springs to the community of Grand Lake. But Hot Sulphur Springs screamed foul, recounted the votes, and claimed vindication. The Colorado Supreme Court thought long and hard, and decided in May 1882 that Grand Lake was actually the county seat after all.

County judge John Gillis Mills, from Vermont, a self-proclaimed mining attorney who had allegedly killed two people earlier in Mississippi, had supported the Grand Lake move. He denounced the other commissioners for fraud, insisting they had stolen and revised relevant county records, particularly the vote count. During a following election, however, Edward P. Webber, a Chicago lawyer, campaigned for commissioner, won, and replaced Mills as the commission leader, although Mills remained on the board. Mills and Weber now began a personal vendetta against each other. Weber had the most commission support, so before long the other commissioners started meeting without the knowledge of Mills. However, Mills had strong backing in Undersheriff William Redman, who when peeved refused to allow the commissioners access to the courthouse.

Everything came to a head on July 4, 1883, when county commissioners E. P. Webber and Barney Day, plus commissioner and county clerk T. J. Dean, were walking toward town. They were ambushed by between three and five gunmen. Webber died instantly. Commissioner Dean took a bullet in the hip and the brain. Commissioner Day was also shot dead, but he fired one round before he died. His bullet killed John Gillis Mills. So four officials were now dying and dead in almost as many seconds.

Sheriff Royer began an immediate investigation but hit a stone wall everywhere he turned. Undersheriff Redman appeared to drop out of sight. Royer struggled for cooperation and assistance from the governor, and perhaps with good reason got little. Then on July 17, Royer committed suicide, a bullet to his head, leaving a note saying he had "killed Barney Day, my best friend—and I have decided to make short work of the whole mess."

In August, the tragedy reached closure when travelers found the body of Undersheriff William Redman near the Colorado-Utah border. His six-shooter, with one bullet missing, lay alongside.

The story, or perhaps the best estimate of what happened back on July 4, goes something like this. A group of men including lawmen Royer and Redman, Commissioner John Mills, and others met and concocted a plan to "scare" the other commissioners into resigning from office. It didn't work, and the scare got out of hand, perhaps when the approached commissioners became frightened and started shooting.

As for the county seat, following an election in 1888, Hot Sulphur Springs took back the title from Grand Lake. The seat has remained Hot Sulphur Springs ever since.

GRAVES, William (a.k.a. Whiskey Bill) (?–1864)

Not much is known about Graves except that he rode with Henry Plummer's band of Montana cutthroats. Plummer's escapades, of course, led to the rise of a Montana vigilante movement, which began thinning out the desperadoes. Graves therefore is best remembered for his manner of death. The vigilantes tied a rope to a tree limb, knotted the noose around his neck, then set him astraddle a horse behind a vigilante member. At a given signal, the vigilante shouted "So long, Bill," and galloped under the limb.

See also: PLUMMER, WILLIAM HENRY

GREATHOUSE, James (a.k.a. Whiskey Jim Greathouse) (?–1881)

Just how much liquor "Whiskey Jim" Greathouse could drink is undetermined, but that he would sell firewater to Indians, trade in stolen livestock, and associate with reprobates and rascals is beyond historical question. The origin of his backtrail is murky. Some speculate he was from Texas, specifically San Saba County; others theorize he may have come from Arkansas, because he was occasionally referred to as "Arkansas Jack." Of course it is not impossible that both guesses are correct. But by 1874, by whatever route, "Whiskey Jim" was in the vicinity of Fort Griffin, Texas, "already well known—but not favorably known—as a notorious whiskey peddler to the Indians." Prodded to move on by threats from Gen. Ranald S. MacKenzie, Greathouse inched a little farther west.

On the Staked Plains, Greathouse hunted buffalo and participated in the infamous buffalo-hunter skirmish with Comanches during February 1877 at Yellow House Canyon. Later during July he may have been part of a group campaigning with Capt.

Nicholas Nolan, an adventure that almost ended in disaster from thirst and starvation.

Two years later (1879), "Whiskey Jim" Greathouse had established a rather large ranch in Lincoln County, New Mexico Territory, reasonably near the mining boom town of White Oaks. There he and a partner operated a store and stopover for travelers between Las Vegas and White Oaks, and it was there also that he gave a "wink and nod" to outlaws who not too secretly dealt in cattle with questionable titles. It was at this ranch of dubious reputation that during November 1880 possemen surrounded the Greathouse main building and held Greathouse as a semihostage until negotiations broke down, resulting in the death of Jim Carlyle. Greathouse's buildings were burned in retaliation.

Afterward, "Whiskey Jim" traveled as far north and west as Socorro, New Mexico. With friends Jim Finley and Jim Kay, Greathouse rustled cattle from Socorro County rancher and a genuine hard case, Joel Fowler, in December 1881. On the trail, Fowler and his foreman, Jim Ike, came upon the trio of thieves who had already sold the steers at Georgetown and were on their return trip. Feigning to be running from the law, Fowler put the outlaws at ease, then blasted "Whiskey Jim" with a charge of buckshot before turning the other barrel on Finley. He too died. Jim Ike, in the ensuing seconds, killed Jim Kay. "Whiskey Jim" Greathouse, without doubt, in death left behind an indisputable Western legacy. Too bad it was not a reputable one.

See also: BELL, JAMES W.; FOWLER, JOEL A.; LINCOLN COUNTY WAR

GRIMES, Albert Calvin (1855–1908)

Al Grimes is usually overlooked, possibly because his older brother, a former Texas Ranger, Ahijah W. "High" Grimes, has received numerous historical mentions for his role as the Williamson County deputy sheriff who was gunned down by the Sam Bass gang during the furious shootout at Round Rock, Texas.

The law enforcement career of Albert Grimes began at Coleman, Texas, where he enlisted as a private in Company C, Frontier Battalion, of the Texas Rangers on September 1, 1877. In the Texas Panhandle, Grimes made a name for himself tracking fugitives throughout the area, as well as in the isolated reaches of eastern New Mexico. His faithful dedication to service resulted in promotion to lieutenant; Grimes's courage was never questioned. On March 26, 1884, he shot and killed a bank robber at Wichita Falls, Texas. Later, in southern Texas, he fought desperadoes and cattle rustlers, again achieving a degree of law enforcement fame. On January 17, 1887, near Cotulla, he and fellow Texas Ranger Walter Durbin, while on a stakeout, shot and killed a man wanted for the murder of Sheriff McKinney in La Salle County.

Grimes saw service as a mounted patrol inspector along the Rio Grande. Still later, with a well-earned no-nonsense reputation, he efficiently guarded Bexar County prisoners at San Antonio. He died in San Antonio of natural causes.

See also: BASS, SAM

GROUNDS, William A. (a.k.a. Billy the Kid Grounds; Arthur Boucher) (1862–1882)

Born in central Texas and more than likely involved in a blood-letting altercation with Sam Good, young Grounds fled to southwestern New Mexico Territory, frequently drifting into and then out of the rough-and-tumble mining camp of Shakespeare, a favorite hangout for a whole cast of nefarious characters who would earn or steal their individualized places in the history books.

At Shakespeare, "Billy the Kid" Grounds associated with such notables as "Curly Bill" Brocius, Joe Hill (Olney), John Peters Ringo, Sandy King, Johnny Barnes, William Rogers "Russian Bill" Tettenborn, Frank and Tom McLaury, "Slim Jim" Crane, the Clantons, Charles "Pony Deal" Ray, Billy Leonard, and Jimmy Hughes, but most notably with Zwingle (Zwing) Richard Hunt, from the Lone Star state.

In letters to his mother back in Dripping Springs, Texas, Grounds boasted of involvement in a "shooting scrape" and of buying a horse from the notorious (at least locally) Johnny Ringo. He left out any references or assertions regarding his participation in rustling livestock, robbing Mexican smugglers, or the time he and his cohorts stripped a Mexican church of its valuables.

Rambunctious raids and indiscreet shenanigans aside, it took a more murderous crime to write Grounds's name onto the Who's Who of western badmen and into the tally book of Boot Hill burials. On March 25, 1882, civil engineer M. R. Peel was killed while sitting in his office at the Tombstone Mill and Mining Company near Charleston, Arizona. The crime was thought to have been a bungled robbery rather than an assassination. Investigators were stymied, but suspicion soon fell on Zwing Hunt and his sidekick "Billy the Kid" Grounds.

When information was received in Tombstone that Grounds and Hunt were at John Chandler's ranch a few miles out of town, deputy sheriff E. A. Harley handed Deputy Billy Breakenridge the task of making arrests and enforcing livestock-rustling warrants. The deputy rounded up jailer Hugh Allen and a posse that included John Gillespie.

On the morning of March 29, 1882, the lawmen secreted themselves around the ranch house and hollered for the inhabitants to surrender. Several innocents emerged from the house, and then the shooting started. During the gun battle, Grounds was mortally wounded by a blast (he died the next day) from Breakenridge's shotgun, and Hunt was severely wounded. Gillespie was killed, and posse members Hugh Allen and Jack Young were wounded. Later, Zwing Hunt, with the help of his brother, fled the Tombstone hospital in which he was being confined.

See also: BREAKENRIDGE, WILLIAM M.; HUNT, ZWINGLE RICHARD

GUNFIGHT at Ingalls, Oklahoma

Ingalls, Oklahoma, a tiny community east of Stillwater, wasn't much of a town, and it doesn't occupy much space on today's maps either, but on September 1, 1893, the greatest outlaw/lawman gun battle in Western history took place inside it.

One might have assumed that the day of the Wild West was about over. The Daltons had recently gone down; the James gang was no longer in business; Wild Bill Hickok was dead; Billy the Kid was dead; and John Wesley Hardin was in prison. Yet tough remnants survived, among them William "Bill" Doolin, George "Bitter Creek" Newcomb, and Charley Pierce, who were still loose and running—and rapidly finding most communities closed to them. These former cowboys, now whiskey-smuggling, night-riding graduates of terror, killing, and robbery, had become Oklahombres, along the way shedding old comrades through death or prison but picking up new, little-known converts such as Jack Blake, better known as "Tulsa Jack," George Weightman, Dan "Dynamite Dick" Clifton, and William Marion Dalton, a Dalton brother.

The opposition consisted of men who wore badges, stalwart lawmen like U.S. Marshal Evett Nix. Nix wanted to obliterate or jail this "last of the outlaws," and for the task he had assembled seasoned lawmen: Chris Madsen, Heck Thomas, Bill Tilghman, Lafe Shadley, Jim Masterson, Dick Speed, H. A. "Hi" Thompson, John Hixon, and Tom Hueston.

Why the outlaws chose Ingalls, Oklahoma, for a rendezvous will likely never be known for certain, except that it was remote and rugged, an obscure land-rush community. So after dark on August 31, two wagons, looking like ordinary "Sooner" wagons—a single driver in front, lawmen (altogether 13) in the interior—rolled into town, one from Stillwater, Texas, and the other from Guthrie, Oklahoma. The plan was to reach town before midnight and to hang around and collar the outlaws after they had gone to bed. It wasn't much of a plan, but it was all they had. No contingency plans existed, perhaps because the town was so new, the population so rowdy and unsettled. So when the Guthrie wagon did not arrive until well after midnight, the arrest plans were put off until the following morning, September 1. The lawmen even sent for 11 additional associates but didn't wait for them to arrive.

With practically no information about the location of anybody, the lawmen waited until midmorning, then slowly drove their wagons from two different directions into town, not knowing where to go, who exactly was there, or even what most of the outlaws looked like. At about 9 A.M., one of the lawmen, Dick Speed, asked a 14-year-old boy who it was that was coming toward them on horseback. The boy stopped, turned and pointed, saying, "Why, that's Bitter Creek."

The outlaw saw and heard it all. Bitter Creek jerked out his rifle, and the battle commenced. Speed fired, his bullet hitting Newcomb's rifle and sending splinters into the outlaw's hands, arms, and body. Newcomb turned and lurched for cover, while his associates in Ransom's Saloon commenced firing, pinning down the lawmen. Meanwhile, at the OK Hotel, Arkansas Tom looked out the window, saw what was happening, and from the window put a bullet in Speed, who went down wallowing in blood.

The lawmen now tried circling the saloon, ordering those inside to surrender. The firing just got heavier. As it was, the lawmen—though they shot the saloon into splinters—could not see the south side of the saloon and so never saw the desperadoes fleeing to the stable. There, Doolin and Dynamite Dick

managed to saddle their horses and escape, while lawman Tom Hueston went down with several bullets in his body.

The outlaws scampered out of town; only the wounded remained. Arkansas Tom, who from his hotel room had provided such remarkable cover for his outlaw friends, was soon forced to surrender and was taken into custody.

With that, the battle ended. It had lasted an hour or so, and the dirt streets had blood all over them. Speed was dead. Shadley and Hueston were seriously wounded; both died within 24 hours.

As for the outlaws, the captured Arkansas Tom received 50 years in prison. He was released after several years but then robbed a bank, dying in 1924, when lawmen shot him to death. They did the same for Tulsa Jack Blake. Charley Pierce and Bitter Creek Newcomb were killed by friends named Dunn who wanted the reward money. Dynamite Dick Clifton lived until 1897, when a party of U.S. deputy marshals shot him to death. On September 25, 1895, the marshals surprised Dalton, who leaped through a back window and tried to run. He got only a few steps. As for Bill Doolin, Heck Thomas and a posse caught up with him in Oklahoma, where Thomas riddled him with 20 buckshot pellets fired from an eight-gauge shotgun. He was buried in a Stillwater, Oklahoma, cemetery, a buggy axle for a monument.

The era of wild, hard-riding outlaws and lawmen had ended. As for Ingalls, it could not outlive its reputation. The only two churches couldn't stop quarreling until somebody dynamited one of them. Then the Atchison, Topeka & Santa Fe chose a different route for its track, so the end of a town came that few would dispute was already dead anyway.

See also: DALTON BROTHERS; DOOLIN, WILLIAM M.; MADSEN, CHRISTIAN; NEWCOMB, GEORGE; THOMAS, HENRY ANDREW; TILGHMAN, WILLIAM MATTHEW JR.

GUNFIGHT at Newton, Kansas

The western gun battle that killed the most men took place in Newton, Kansas. In July 1871, the railroads reached Newton, a cow town of perhaps 15,000 residents, the most wicked community in Kansas. Arthur Dulaney (or Donovan), known in Kansas as Mike McCluskie, a former section boss for the railroad, became the night policeman. On August 11, 1871, an important city bond election took place, and the village hired Texas gunman William Bailey

(Baylor) to oversee it, the difficulty being that Bailey was too soused to oversee anything. So McCluskie was brought in to oversee the overseer and wound up cussing him out. Later that evening, in the Red Front Saloon, Bailey picked a fistfight with McCluskie. The brawl terminated in the street, with McCluskie shooting and killing Bailey.

McCluskie thereafter left town for a few days, then returned, hoping things had blown over. He headed initially for Perry Tuttle's Dance Hall, where he proceeded to drink and gamble. It didn't take long for a group of Texas cowhands, led by Hugh Anderson, who had come up from Salado, Texas, on a cattle drive, to seek an opportunity to avenge Bailey's death. At some time after midnight on August 20, Anderson found McCluskie in the dance hall. After a brief argument punctuated by profanity, Anderson shot McCluskie in the neck. At this minute the gunfire became general, seeming to erupt from everywhere. When McCluskie's six-shooter misfired, Anderson and perhaps others shot him a few more times. A couple of railroad men, perhaps friends of McCluskie's, also went down. A young, scrawny, teenage tubercular named James Riley saw his friend McCluskie sprawled on the floor, so Riley locked the saloon door, pulled his own revolver, and commenced shooting. He hit Anderson once in each leg, then killed two cowboys and wounded two others.

McCluskie died the next morning. Hugh Anderson survived, thanks to good medical attention. Altogether, five were dead, and three were wounded. The wildest shootout in western history had ended. Perry Tuttle spent hours mopping up the blood. The story itself did not end, however, for another two years, in June 1873, at Medicine Lodge, Kansas. It seems that McCluskie had a brother named Arthur who tracked Hugh Anderson across the West and eventually to Medicine Lodge. He sent out a challenge, and the two men met on a grassy lot at 20 paces. The two shot each other practically to smithereens, then fell to the ground with guns empty, unable to rise. While the whole mesmerized town watched, they painfully crawled toward one another and finished the fight by killing each other with knives.

As for Jim Riley, he simply disappeared.

GUNFIGHT at the OK Corral

In this, the most famous gunfight in western history, it is well to point out that it was not a shootout between good guys and bad guys. Although one side wore badges, it was also not a battle between the law and the lawless. It was a battle of personal animosities between two groups; hate was the common denominator. The participants on one side were Virgil Earp, chief of the Tombstone police, and deputies Wyatt Earp, Morgan Earp, and Doc Holliday. The other group consisted of two sets of brothers, all Cowboys—Ike and Billy Clanton, and Frank and Tom McLaury.

The events started when Ike Clanton and Tom McLaury left the range and reached Tombstone on October 25. While Ike (who would claim to have been unarmed) was eating lunch in the Occidental Saloon, Doc Holliday entered the room, cursed him, and dared him to go for his gun. Ike declined and left the building. Later on, Ike along with Virgil Earp, Tom McLaury, and others gambled the night away. Ike was up early enough to commence his morning by making threats against his enemies.

At about noon, Morgan and Virgil Earp walked up behind Ike Clanton on the street, pistol-whipped him against the wall, then hustled him off to a justice of the peace who fined him $25 for carrying a weapon.

At about 1:30, Tom McLaury checked his gun, then started up the street with both hands in his pockets, only to bump into Wyatt Earp. Wyatt slapped him, struck him across the head several times with a revolver, then continued on his way. In the meantime, Frank McLaury and Billy Clanton reached town, heard what happened, and apparently not being armed, purchased revolvers. It was now midafternoon, and the Clantons and McLaurys met in a vacant lot on the south side of Fremont Street, a few steps from, but not in, the OK Corral.

The two groups—Earps and Holliday, and the Clantons and McLaurys—now cursed each other from their respective locations, a major difference being that the Earps and Holliday were moving toward the Clantons and McLaurys. The Earps and Holliday wanted a showdown; the Clantons and McLaurys probably just wanted to leave. To ease the latter possibility along, Sheriff Johnny Behan searched and conferred with the Cowboys, stating later that he found only Billy Clanton and Frank McLaury armed.

Behan, seeing the Earps approaching, hurried over to say that he had disarmed the Cowboys and they were departing. Wyatt Earp brushed him aside.

As the two sides came together, the words flew, and suddenly the guns started to pop. Frank McLaury went down with a bullet in his stomach. Billy Clanton took a bullet in the chest. Everybody seemed to be firing at once. Only Ike Clanton fled, rushing up to Wyatt Earp and screaming he wasn't armed before disappearing into the nearby Fly's Photography Studio. Under any other circumstances, Tom McLaury might have looked hilarious as he scrambled around trying to get his rifle out of the saddle boot, his frightened horse bucking in terror. Doc Holliday emptied a shotgun into him.

The shootout lasted perhaps 30 seconds. It ended with 19-year-old Billy Clanton down, still trying to shoot, gasping out his last breaths, only seconds away from death, and by some accounts begging unseen individuals for more ammunition. Thirty-three-year-old Frank McLaury was dead, and his 28-year-old brother Tom was only seconds away from death. Only Ike Clanton had escaped.

As for the Earp side, Doc Holliday had a minor hip wound. Morgan had a serious but not fatal hole through both shoulders. Virgil took a wound in the calf of his right leg. Wyatt emerged unscathed. Most of the wounds had come from Billy Clanton.

The funerals took place at Boot Hill on October 27. The bodies were laid side by side, the headboard inscription reading, "Murdered on the Streets of Tombstone." Two days later, Mayor John Clum and his city council suspended Virgil Earp as chief of police. Ike Clanton filed murder complaints, and Sheriff Behan arrested Wyatt Earp and Doc Holliday and kept them behind bars for a month. The other Earps were not arrested, since they were confined to bed with wounds.

On November 30, 1881, Judge Wells Spicer stated, among other things, "I am of the opinion that the defendant Virgil Earp, as chief of police, by subsequently calling upon Wyatt Earp and J. H. Holliday to assist him in arresting and disarming the Clantons and McLaurys, committed an injudicious and censurable act; and although in this he acted incautiously and without proper circumspection, yet when we consider the condition of affairs incident to a frontier country; the lawlessness and disregard for human life; the existence of a law-defying element in our midst; the fear and feeling of insecurity that has existed; the supposed prevalence of bad, desperate and reckless men who have been a terror to the country, and kept away capital and enterprise, and con-sidering the many threats that have been made against the Earps, I can attach no criminality to this unwise act. Considering all the testimony together, I am of the opinion that the weight of evidence sustains and corroborates the testimony of Wyatt and Virgil Earp, and that their demand for a surrender was met by William Clanton and Frank McLaury drawing their pistols. Upon this hypothesis my duty is clear." He then read further, but at length Judge Spicer found Earp and Holliday not guilty of attempted murder and ordered them released.

Who was to blame for this gunfight? Probably everyone involved was. Who emerged as the good guys? When the smoke cleared, the Earps and Doc Holiday were practically the only ones standing, so they all provided supportive points of view. Only Ike Clanton and John Behan had something to say for their side, but by then almost no one was listening. The Gunfight at the OK Corral now belonged to the historians and the mythmakers.

See also: BOOT HILL; EARP, MORGAN; EARP, VIRGIL; EARP, WYATT BERRY STAPP; HOLLIDAY, JOHN HENRY

GUNFIGHT at Poplar Grove, Washington

This shootout took place at Kennewick, Washington, on October 31, 1906, between several rows of poplar trees at the south end of the Northern Pacific Bridge. It was Halloween night.

The story begins a night earlier with the burglary of two Kennewick stores, one handling general merchandise and the other hardware. The report reached Kennewick's marshal, Mike Glover, who telegraphed Sheriff Alex G. McNeal, who arrived by train at 10 A.M. At this time Glover, McNeal, Deputy Sheriff Joe Holzhey, and an unarmed townsman named H. E. Roseman decided to check out Poplar Grove first, it being the local hobo jungle.

As the lawmen approached the campfire, some words were shouted, and then shooting commenced. Roseman scampered away as Holzhey dropped at the first shot. Glover also fell, and McNeal, although wounded, answered the fusillade until his gun clicked empty, at which time he eased back toward the railroad tracks. Roseman meanwhile had located Sheriff McNeal and steered him back toward Kennewick, where a posse quickly formed and galloped toward the grove. It found Glover dead and Holzhey severely wounded. He would die the next day.

The posse also located the body of outlaw Jacob Lake, but the second gunman had vanished. By dark of the following day, a Walla Walla prison guard and a pack of bloodhounds arrived, and now a posse of 200 men took up the search and chase. It became an epic, tragic affair. A 24-year-old posse member named Forrest Perry became the first to intercept the outlaws. Perry shouted, "Throw up your hands." The other posse members, coming along behind, heard him shout, did not recognize his voice, and fired into the brush. Perry died three hours later, and the last outlaw, Kid Barker, surrendered shortly after that, denying he had shot anyone. He went to jail but escaped shortly afterward. Barker was never recaptured.

GUNFIGHTER

In the broadest sense, a gunfighter was anyone highly skilled with weapons who fought with guns, specifically the Colt revolver. The term is most frequently applied to western American lawmen like Wild Bill Hickok and Wyatt Earp, although it can also be applied to outlaws, such as Billy the Kid and John Wesley Hardin. The gunfighter era began essentially with the discovery of gold in California, and the era had pretty well run its course by 1900. However, dime novels and western movies have lumped almost every western lawman/outlaw figure into the heroic/gunfighter category. The terms themselves, along with a similar word, *shootist*, seem to have been rarely used in the American West.

See also: GUNMAN

GUNMAN

A gunman is someone who packed a gun and did not hesitate to use it. Although the term applied primarily to outlaws, it could also include lawmen. Unlike *gunfighter*, the word *gunman* carried no heroic or esoteric overtones.

See also: GUNFIGHTER

GUNSLINGER

A gunslinger was a Hollywood showoff, since neither the term nor the person existed in the Wild West. This film gunslinger implied a desperado or lawman swinging his six-shooter out of its holster and firing it, still moving, with deadly accuracy. It never happened, and the term and the Hollywood act demonstrated little more than how silly people can be in depicting history.

See also: GUNMAN

HALL, Jesse Leigh (a.k.a. Lee Hall) (1849–1911)

This Texas Ranger and military man started life in Lexington, North Carolina. Around 1869 he changed his middle name to Lee and signed on as a school teacher in Texas. Perhaps the job was too dull, because he quickly switched occupations, making one suspect that he had friends somewhere in high places. He just as quickly became a sergeant at arms in the Texas senate, as well as a deputy sheriff at Denison.

He yearned for action, however, so he signed on as a second lieutenant in Leander McNelly's Special Force of Texas Rangers. After flushing out the Nueces Strip, he and his men transferred to Goliad, where he arrived too late to prevent a bank robbery, but not too late to drive the robbers into Mexico and then disperse a group of vigilantes. In the meantime, McNelly had stepped aside due to poor health, so Hall assumed command, one of his first tasks being to bring the Sutton-Taylor feud at least under temporary control. His report "The agony is over," wasn't quite correct, but he had the situation at least easing and moving toward peace. Then in January 1877, Texas moved Hall's forces to Victoria, reorganized the unit, and promoted Hall to first lieutenant.

Hall subsequently scattered his men along the Nueces Strip to reduce lawlessness. Along about this time in 1880 he married Bessie Weidman, who intensely disliked the rangers and the part he played in them. When in March 1881 the Special Force merged with the Frontier Battalion, the new designation being Company F, Hall knew it was time to leave. Looking back, in terms of his marriage, one could argue that he was a fair success, raising five daughters. Certainly, in terms of law enforcement he had been one of the best. But in terms of cattle and business he was a dismal failure. He managed the Dull Ranch, and whether he gave it that name or someone else did is anyone's guess. But he did resolve some illegal fence-cutting activities. The government appointed him as an Anadarko Indian agent and then indicted him for embezzlement. The case was thrown out of court.

During the Spanish-American War, Hall raised two companies of volunteers. After the war, Hall reenlisted as a first lieutenant, supervising and leading the Macabebe Scouts in the Philippines. Following his discharge in October 1900 he seemed at loose ends, unable to refind his way. He turned to the bottle and died on March 17, 1911. He is buried in the National Cemetery at San Antonio.

See also: MCNELLY, LEANDER H.; SUTTON-TAYLOR FEUD; TEXAS RANGERS

HANGING Windmill

Back in 1876, the good citizens of Las Vegas, New Mexico, erected a wooden windmill in the plaza. It consisted of two parts. Four stout posts roughly 20 feet high supported a large platform, itself perhaps

20 feet by 20 feet square. A tapering superstructure rose another 20 feet above that, and a wooden ladder connected the entire piece to the windmill near the top, the axis of the windmill being about 40 feet off the ground. Otherwise the plaza remained barren, but the windmill at least provided a conversation point as well as something for young boys to play on.

The windmill wasn't meant to be anything other than a curiosity, a talking piece for residents enjoying the park. Three years passed, and the windmill still served its purpose, dozens of children hundreds of times having crawled all over it. Meanwhile, on June 4, 1879, Manuel Barela had taken too much of the available saloon sauce and proceeded to make a nuisance of himself. He mentioned to someone standing at the bar that he could shoot the third button off the shirt of a man standing near the door. To prove it, Barela pulled a gun, aimed, and fired, the bullet striking Jesús Morales in the face but not seriously wounding him. At this time, the situation went totally out of control; a friend of Morales's, Benigno Romero, angrily denounced Barela for the unprovoked attack. Barela then shot Romero twice, killing him.

Barela went to jail, and at midnight a few dozen other men joined him, although not just to cheer him up, or keep him company. They shoved the guards aside, removed Barela, and on second thought also removed another prisoner, Giovanni Dugi, an Italian also awaiting trial on a murder charge. Both men were dragged to the windmill in the center of the town plaza, Barela being hanged first and Dugi second. The *Las Vegas Gazette* noted, "In half a minute after the hangings were accomplished, the plaza was clear of people and the town was as quiet as a graveyard." No one ever went to trial for the two lynchings.

As for the windmill, it came down on February 9, 1880, the *Las Vegas Optic* saying that its dark influence and bad memories were too much for the children, many of whom had tried to hang their dogs from the windmill.

See also: DODGE CITY GANG

HANKINS, John Henry (a.k.a. James Jenkins; James W. Smith; Six-Shooter Smith) (1856?–1882)

Like so many of the less-well-known men of the gunfighting era, John Henry Hankins, alias James W. "Six-Shooter" Smith, is somewhat of a puzzle.

Most reports simply indicate that he was probably a Texas or a Missouri product and that he had formerly lived in Kansas. Rumors gave him credit for being at least a hanger-on or maybe a full-fledged member of the disreputable "Dodge City Gang," then primarily operating out of the wicked railroad town of East Las Vegas, New Mexico. Whatever, Hankins was adept at con games, at robbing hoboes, gambling, and whoring. Hankins specialized in popping off bullets at unsuspecting neophytes, just to see how close he could come without actually hitting them.

By 1881, "Six-Shooter" had moved near to Deming, New Mexico, where he set up his own modest saloon at the Rio Mimbres water tower stop. Accompanied by some nefarious individuals, Smith declared himself the law. A Deming newspaper referred to him as "the big dog with the brass collar." All of this neither amused nor frightened Grant County sheriff Harvey Whitehill, who rode down to the water tower with his truly dangerous deputy, Dan Tucker. That quieted down the atmosphere at Deming, and "Six-Shooter" Smith meandered off to Benson, Arizona, and then to Colorado, where he was arrested and convicted at Durango on October 12, 1881, for carrying a concealed weapon.

Not long after that, Smith walked away from a work detail and returned to Texas, where he adopted the nickname "California Jim" and found employment in a Laredo restaurant. When Smith and his boss argued about how much to charge a customer, the Laredo city marshal attempted to quell the disturbance. "Six-Shooter" Smith shot him dead. Smith then fled to San Antonio, where he robbed a nearby station master at Cactus, Texas. That led to a shootout with lawmen Charley Smith and Wesley DeSpain when they tried to arrest him near Cibolo, Texas. Smith shot and disabled DeSpain but was mortally wounded by Charley Smith. On June 23, 1882, the "bloody, naked body" of John Hankins, alias "Six-Shooter" Smith, "was placed in a rough pine box, and lowered into a shallow grave in the brush."

See also: DODGE CITY GANG; TUCKER, DAVID; WHITEHILL, HARVEY HOWARD

HARDCASE

This refers to a tough individual, someone who ordinarily cannot be broken, an outlaw who will not confess or implicate his associates.

HARDIN, John Wesley (1853–1895)

This greatest of all Texas gunmen entered the world on May 26, 1853, by the Red River at Bonham, Texas, the second of 10 children of James and Elizabeth Hardin. His devout Protestant parents (the father was a Methodist preacher, a circuit rider) named him for John Wesley, the founder of Methodism. Young Hardin grew up wild and restless, stabbing Charles Sloter, a schoolmate (who survived), when the two were 10 years old. In November 1868, Hardin and a cousin entered a wrestling match with a black freedman named Major (Madge) Holshousen. It ended in a brawl. On the following day, Hardin stalked Madge and shot him dead during a trailside confrontation.

John Wesley Hardin now became a fugitive from the Texas Reconstruction government, which charged him with murder. In December of that same year, in Trinity County at Hickory Creek Crossing, Hardin killed three Union soldiers, two with a shotgun and one with a revolver. Nearby farmers buried their bodies in the creek bed.

From that time on, Hardin killed people as a regular thing. He shot and killed Jack Helm, sheriff of DeWitt County and a former state police captain. Hardin shot Benjamin Bradley during a quarrel over a card game. This slaying earned Hardin a place in the 1878 *List of Texas Fugitives from Justice*, often known as *The Ranger's Bible*. On January 20, 1870, he killed a jealous boyfriend (or husband) who had interrupted Hardin during a sexual tryst. According to Hardin, that was number eight. By this time, Phil Coe, a Texas gambler, had given Hardin the moniker of "Young Seven Up," the Seven Up referring to a card game popular among gamblers.

Between shootings, Hardin frequently taught school and even Sunday school. Nevertheless, killing people remained his primary talent. On January 22, 1871, Hardin killed lawman Jim Smalley, near Waco, Texas, and escaped from two other officers. Less than two weeks later, he killed three additional Texas lawmen in their sleep, officers he identified only as Smith, Jones, and Davis. Smith and Jones died in front of a shotgun. Davis went down under a six-shooter.

Hardin now decided to leave Texas for a while, so he hired on as a cowhand during an Abilene, Kansas, trail drive. Along the way Hardin killed two Indians (he said they were stealing cattle) and five Mexican *vaqueros*, the latter during a wild, dramatic shootout

John Wesley Hardin (Robert G. McCubbin Collection)

on the banks of the Little Arkansas River. These later deaths forever gave John Wesley Hardin the sobriquet of "Little Arkansas." Many writers since have incorrectly assumed the "Little" referred to Hardin's height; the stocky Hardin stood about five foot 10, average or slightly above for the time.

In Abilene, Hardin became a two-gun man, wearing his weapons openly in spite of City Marshal William "Wild Bill" Hickok's admonition against it. Yet, the two became friends, often drinking, gambling, and chasing girls together. Hardin killed two Abilene rowdies in separate incidents, and Hickok hardly flinched. Then came two of the most controversial occurrences ever to dog Hardin's backtrail.

Hardin had been in Abilene several weeks, constantly wearing his guns in spite of a city ordinance to the contrary. One afternoon Marshal Hickok decided that enough was enough. He ordered Hardin to hand over his weapons. Hardin stuck them out, butts forward, then spun them around in his hands and covered Hickok, forcing the marshal to back down. The question therefore becomes, did the incident really happen? The only evidence is Hardin's own controversial narrative. Passionate, knowledgeable advocates can easily be found who support the incident as either fact or fiction.

The second alleged event involves "shooting a man for snoring." Hardin, his cousin Gip Clements, and Texas cattleman Charles Cougar had been out on the town, drinking heavily. They returned late at night to their side-by-side, second-story hotel rooms. Hardin and Gip shared one room; Cougar had the one alongside. Hardin's memoirs do not mention the friend. He notes that late in the night, a sneak thief eased into his darkened room and picked up Hardin's trousers. The thief had barely reached the door when Hardin shot him dead.

However, Abilene newspapers never mentioned an intruder. They stated that it was Cougar, Hardin's friend in the next room, who was shot, and that he was shot while sitting in his own bed reading a newspaper. Shortly afterward, a story started circulating that Hardin had killed a man for snoring. The evidence thus points to the possibility that Hardin may have yelled for his neighbor friend to "roll over." After that happened a couple or three times, Cougar may have sat up in bed to read a newspaper and stay awake. He fell asleep again, started snoring, and an exasperated Hardin fired a shot through the wall to "really" wake him up. Hardin "probably" never meant to kill Charles Cougar, but he did—and at that point Hardin hastily departed for Texas.

Back in eastern Texas, Hardin married Jane Bowen on February 29, 1872. Although Wesley Hardin spent more time sleeping on the ground than in Jane's bed, the marriage produced two daughters and one son. Meanwhile, John became deeply involved in the Sutton-Taylor feud, and the killings started to mount. The deaths culminated in the May 25, 1874, slaying of Brown County deputy Charles Webb on the streets of Comanche, Texas. Hardin had now likely notched his 32nd victim.

A few days later, vigilantes hanged John Wesley Hardin's attorney brother, Joe, plus two other relatives. Over in DeWitt County on June 21, a midnight mob lynched additional Hardin relatives and supporters. On January 20, 1875, the Texas legislature placed a $4,000 reward on the head of John Wesley Hardin, making him the most wanted outlaw ever in the state of Texas. For that kind of money the Texas Rangers would follow Hardin across the ice cap, and

Hardin knew it. He, his wife, and children fled east (with a few killings along the way) to Florida, where the rangers took him prisoner onboard a train at Pensacola on August 23, 1877. Hardin was returned to Texas, tried for murder in the second degree of lawman Charles Webb, and sentenced to 25 years in the state penitentiary at Huntsville.

Hardin attempted to escape several times and was brutally beaten. He then started cooperating, becoming head of the debating team and the Sunday school class. He studied law. Hardin's wife, Jane, died of undisclosed causes on November 6, 1892, at the age of 35. A year and three months later, on February 17, 1894, John Wesley Hardin walked out of prison after 15 years and eight months behind bars. He went to Gonzales County to practice law and see his children, but the relationship seemed strained. He then moved to the Texas Hill country, where the 41-year-old Hardin married 15-year-old Callie Lewis on January 9, 1895. The marriage lasted less than a week, and by some accounts only an hour. Hardin returned her to her parents. There was no divorce, no annulment.

John Wesley Hardin moved on to El Paso to practice law, his only client being New Mexico cattle rustler Martin Mrose. Martin sought refuge in Ciudad Juarez, Mexico, across the Rio Grande from El Paso, and sent his wife, Beulah, into El Paso to get him an attorney. She got John Wesley Hardin, but within a week the attorney/female relationship had blossomed all too well, and she wasn't returning to her husband. When the husband began threatening his attorney, Hardin encouraged several El Paso lawmen—former chief of police and now U.S. Deputy Marshal Jeff Milton, U.S. Deputy Marshal George Scarborough, Texas Ranger Frank McMahan, and (perhaps) El Paso constable John Selman—to lure Mrose across the Rio Grande and shoot him to death.

At Hardin's dictation, Beulah commenced an autobiography entitled *The Life of John Wesley Hardin as Written by Himself*. However, their own lives quickly deteriorated into drunken brawls, threats, and arrests.

On August 19, 1895, John Wesley Hardin, and Constable John Selman argued on a San Antonio street. Later that night at about 11 o'clock, Hardin walked into the Acme Saloon in San Antonio, bellied up to the bar, picked up the dice for a game of Ship, Captain, and Crew, rolled them down the bar, turned to a grocer beside him, and softly said, "Brown, you have four sixes to beat." At that instant Selman stepped through the door and shot Hardin four times, the first bullet taking effect in the back of the head.

So far as is known, Hardin had never killed anyone after he left prison. As for the total string of dead men haunting his backtrail, the figures range somewhere between 20 and 50.

John Wesley Hardin is buried in El Paso's Concordia Cemetery. Beulah paid the entire funeral cost, $77.50. The grave has a Texas state historical marker, and is one of the most visited tourist attractions in the El Paso area. As for Beulah, she moved to California, dying in Sacramento a few years later of acute alcoholism.

See also: HICKOK, JAMES BUTLER; MILTON, JEFFERSON D.; MROSE, HELEN; MROSE, MARTIN; SELMAN, JOHN HENRY; SUTTON-TAYLOR FEUD

HAROLD, George (1840–1917)

If George Harold attended school, either he didn't pay attention to his lessons or the educational experience was short-lived. He was illiterate in the ways of readin' and writin', but make no mistake, the fluently bilingual George Harold was not an ignorant man—especially when the subject matter was outlaws and thieves. Born south of Richmond, Virginia, George had somehow made it to Texas in time for the opening salvo of the Civil War. He signed up with the Second Texas Field Artillery Battery and saw active service.

After the conflict, Harold signed on as chief of police at Laredo, but in October 1877 he made a career move and enlisted in the Texas Rangers. On July 19, 1878, Harold found himself posted on surveillance at Round Rock, Texas, sitting on a bale of hay in Highsmith's livery stable, awaiting the arrival of outlaw Sam Bass and his gang of robbers. Harold wasn't to be disappointed. Three of the outlaws ambled into town, and were approached by officers. Then the fireworks started. Harold took up a position between the members of the gang, who were all still afoot, and their horses. When Bass attempted to mount his horse, Harold shot him in the side, the bullet punching through a kidney and then exiting close to Sam's belly button. Bass and Frank Jackson managed to get out of town, but the outlaw leader couldn't make it far. He was later captured and

returned to Round Rock, where he died. Jackson escaped.

A coroner's jury ruled that George Harold had killed Sam Bass and that fellow Texas Ranger Dick Ware was responsible for the death of Seaborn Barnes, another outlaw.

Just before the new year dawned in 1880, George Harold was mustered out of the Texas Rangers. Reportedly, he pulled some gendarme duty in Old Mexico, but by 1883 he was in El Paso, where six years later he signed on with the city police force. On April 17, 1890, an area rancher, John Barnes, dashed into town and alerted officers that Mexican thieves were running off a herd of his livestock. The sheriff was unavailable, so Texas Ranger Charles Fusselman, aided by policemen George Harold and Barnes, galloped north. Eight miles away, in the Franklin Mountains, the trio of lawmen picked up the rustler's trail and captured Ysidoro Pasos, the rustler's rear guard. Shortly thereafter the trail took a tragic turn. Riding ahead of the other lawmen, the 24-year-old Ranger Fusselman unexpectedly stumbled upon the rustlers. A furious gun battle erupted; Fusselman was shot in the head and was killed instantly. Harold fired back, at the same time attempting to grab Fusselman, who he thought might still be alive. The opposing thieves, however, continued shooting, forcing Harold and Barnes to race back to El Paso for reinforcements. The bandits escaped. Years later, Geronimo Parra was hanged in El Paso for his role in Fusselman's death.

Harold continued with the El Paso Police Department, retiring in 1916. He maintained his residence at El Paso until his death from natural causes a year later, on December 11, 1917. George Harold was remembered as a genuine "terror to thieves" and a "first class fighting man." He is buried in El Paso's Evergreen Cemetery on Alameda Street.

See also: BASS, SAM; EL PASO, TEXAS; FUSSELMAN, CHARLES; WARE, RICHARD CLAYTON

HARRIS, Jack (?–1875)

Jack Harris was reportedly born in Massachusetts, spent some time at sea, and then lived in Marysville, California. By 1860, he had reached Nevada and was married in Carson City. He also became a saloon operator. In late 1865, the Nevada authorities arrested Harris and several companions for the August 28, 1865, holdup of the Pioneer stage between Placerville, California, and Silver City, Nevada. Harris was acquitted and then moved briefly to Washington, D.C., where evidence suggests that he worked as a city policeman. Nevertheless, he was back in Virginia City, Nevada, by October 31, 1866, that being the date he stopped a stage, robbed the passengers, and took the strongbox. On June 10, 1868, he and another man carrying double-barreled shotguns robbed the Overland stage. Much of the holdup money he spent on opening and operating saloons, and sometimes opening mines, but neither was as successful or as lucrative as robbing stages.

He proved it in May 1871 at Pioche, Nevada. Two mining companies drilling in the same mountain opened tunnels and each claimed ownership of whatever ore they found. When one tunnel intersected another, barricades went up as well as tensions. On one occasion the two companies, with Harris egging them on, waged a 24-hour gun battle inside the shaft. Since both sides used black powder, the smoke drifted everywhere. The fight ended with four dead and a half-dozen wounded, Jack Harris being neither one nor the other.

Over time, most of the Jack Harris stage-robbing associates were shot dead, in various gunfights. Jack Harris, often referred to as the Comstock Bandit, died in bed at Pioche, Nevada, of apparent natural causes in May 1875.

HART, Edward (a.k.a. Little Hart) (?–1878)

Edward "Little" Hart likely migrated with the Horrells to New Mexico from Lampasas, Texas, for he was certainly there by December 1, 1873, when a race war broke out at Lincoln County. He also may or may not have been with the Horrell partisans on the night of December 20, when those riders fired six-shooters into a wedding party at Lincoln, killing four Hispanics and wounding three others.

Near the end of January the following year, during Horrell's retreat from New Mexico Territory, several of their cohorts, Hart included, tormented the area residents. Little Hart, Bill Applegate, Zack Crompton, and an accomplice identified only as Still were driving stolen horses and mules when they paused at Picacho, New Mexico. At this point, Hart, learning that local rancher Joe Haskins had a Mexican wife, casually remarked, "Well, we'll just go over there and kill the fellow." As Haskins

opened his door to greet the strangers, Hart shot him down.

New Mexico ranchers, in a state of fury about the murders and thefts, organized a posse led by Aaron and Frank Wilburn. They took their revenge at Hueco Tanks, just across the Texas line, 40 miles northeast of El Paso, Texas. On February 20, finding the outlaws still in their bedrolls, the volunteer vigilantes showed no mercy. Zack Crompton and Still were shot dead in their blankets. Applegate and Edward "Little" Hart escaped.

Edward Hart was indicted for the murder of Joe Haskins but was never apprehended. Instead, after a four-year stopover in Texas, Little Hart returned to New Mexico, aligning himself with the Murphy/Dolan faction in the Lincoln County War, specifically fighting as a member of "Peppin's posse" during the Five Day Battle at the McSween home. Afterward, Hart teamed up with such notables as the ever-dangerous John Selman, his brother Tom "Tom Cat" Selman, Bob Speakes, Reese Gobles, Jake Owens, Marion Turner, and "Rustling Bob" Irwin. However, he had ambitions for leadership, so while awaiting supper late one afternoon, "Uncle" John Selman's thumb cautiously cocked a Colt hammer. He pulled the trigger, and the bullet crashed up through the flimsy boards, tearing off the top of Edward "Little" Hart's head.

See also: HORRELL BROTHERS; LINCOLN COUNTY WAR; SELMAN, JOHN HENRY

HART, Pearl (1874?–1955)

Pearl Hart (not likely her real name) was born in Ontario, Canada, but her name did not become a part of American history and folklore until 1899, when she and Joe Boot robbed the Globe stage at Cane Spring, Arizona. She wasn't much more than a five-foot-three-inch wisp of a woman, who admitted (without details) to having been married and having two children. She had dark hair, grey eyes, weighed maybe 100 pounds, and possessed a certain grace and elegance. A little makeup would have done wonders, of course, as would have letting her hair grow longer and wearing dresses instead of men's clothing. But she was a working girl, and working girls looked like men—especially when robbing stage coaches. Of course, she robbed stages for various reasons: putting food on the table and, especially, feeding her seemingly insatiable appetite for morphine and cigarettes.

On July 15, 1899, driver Henry Bacon stopped the Globe-Phoenix stage for a short rest and found himself covered by two bandits, Pearl Hart and Joe Boot, who robbed not only him but the passengers also. The bandits then headed for Benson to catch a train, but being tired from all that exertion they stopped to rest in a thicket, went to sleep, and were captured by a posse. Joe went to Florence for incarceration, while Pearl went to the Pima County jail in Tucson, which had facilities for women.

Ed Hogan, serving time for drunk and disorderly conduct, happened to be in an opposite cell, and he and Pearl managed to communicate. During the night of October 12, 1899, someone forgot to lock a door leading to the outside. Hogan escaped. Once free, however, he broke back in again, knocked a hole in the wall and took Pearl (who had not yet even gone to trial) with him. She and Logan got as far as Deming, New Mexico, where U.S. deputy marshal George Scarborough arrested both and returned them to the Arizona jail.

Although Pearl had admitted in writing the details of the stage holdup, a Florence jury found her innocent. A furious court ordered her retried for taking the driver's revolver, and for this she got five years in the territorial prison. As for Joe Boot, he received 30 years, Pearl Hart writing, "Why the fellow hadn't an ounce of sand. While I was going through the passengers, his hands were shaking like leaves. Why if I hadn't more nerve than that, I'd jump off the earth." A newspaper account wasn't any kinder to Joe: "Boot is a weak, morphine depraved specimen of male mortality, without spirit and lacking intelligence and activity. It is plain that the woman was the leader of this partnership."

On December 2, 1902, she left prison, thanks in large part to intervention by the Arizona governor. The *Arizona Sentinel* said she walked out in good health, free from the opium habit. She briefly toured the theater circuit and wrote some remarkably good poetry; by 1903 she was running a cigar and tobacco stand in Kansas. She died on December 30, 1955, at 84 years of age.

See also: BOOT, JOE; SCARBOROUGH, GEORGE EDGAR, JR.

Pearl Hart in her stagecoach-robbing days (University of Oklahoma Archives)

HARTLEE, B. F. (a.k.a. Frank Hartlee)
(1830?–1901)

Frank Hartlee is not well known outside the circle of western aficionados interested in gunfighting men of the Southwest, but Hartlee's reputation for raw courage and decisiveness were unquestioned by anyone—lawman or bad guy, Republican or Democrat.

By one contemporary newspaper account, Frank "was one of the most noted characters on the Pacific Coast" and "a man of extraordinary coolness and wonderful nerve which he always maintained under the most exciting and trying circumstances." While early accounts confirm that Frank spent several years as a Los Angeles resident and participated in several desperado-chasing posses, Hartlee is best remembered for the law enforcement role he played in territorial Arizona.

During this period, correctional officers and policemen were considered by the public as one and the same. Frank Hartlee went to work as a guard at the Arizona Territorial Prison at Yuma. Numerous were his exploits, but one instance overshadowed all others.

On the morning of October 27, 1887, eight convicts attempted to escape. Taking prison superintendent Thomas Gates hostage, the desperate men charged into the administrative offices in an effort to acquire arms. Realizing that a major security breach was at hand, John H. Behan, the assistant superintendent, rushed to the strap-iron front gate, locked it, grabbed a rifle, and dashed to the aid of a guard who was being assaulted by one of the inmates. He recaptured the perpetrator.

From his water-tank guard station, Frank Hartlee successfully sorted out guilty parties from innocent bystanders and, with remarkable marksmanship using a short-barreled carbine, killed three attempted escapees. Prison secretary Richard Rule shot another prisoner. Meanwhile Superintendent Gates, struggling for control of the institution, was stabbed in the neck, only to be saved by prisoner Barney Riggs, who snatched a six-shooter off the floor and killed the convict. (Riggs later obtained a Christmas Day pardon for his heroic act.) When the shooting ended moments later, four convicts lay sprawled on the ground. Another would die in the prison hospital. Thomas Gates resigned as superintendent for health reasons. The territory then appointed John H. Behan as prison superintendent. It promoted Frank Hartlee to assistant superintendent.

Still, the prison went through endless rounds of political turmoil. John Behan resigned, and Frank Hartlee was demoted, these events not being fair but anticipated, since prison positions were usually awarded along political party lines. After a 13-year career with the prison, on December 3, 1898, Frank Hartlee tendered his resignation.

Hartlee planned to retire in Puerto Rico but settled for Nogales, Arizona. When past his 70th birthday, Frank was serving as a local constable when he died of a heart attack on November 3, 1901. Throughout the Southwest he was remembered as a "square-shooter" in his personal dealing and an absolutely "dead-shot" with a short-barreled carbine.

See also: BEHAN, JOHN HARRIS; RIGGS, BARNEY

HAYS, John Coffee (a.k.a. Coffee Jack Hays)
(1817–1883)

One of the great Texas Rangers of his time, a soldier, surveyor, and politician, John Coffee Hays was born at Little Cedar Lick in Wilson County, Tennessee. He

John Coffee Hays, Texas Ranger (Library of Congress)

became a Mississippi surveyor but joined the Texas battle for independence, fighting with Thomas Rusk and helping bury the victims of the Golliad massacre. Following that he joined the Texas Rangers, serving under Erastus "Deaf" Smith. He quickly rose to the rank of sergeant, then captain and major. Hays became one of the first ranger commanders to adopt the Colt revolver as an effective Indian-fighting weapon; after the Texas war for independence, the big enemy proved to be Comanches. Decisive battles at Plumb Creek, Painted Rock, and Bandera Pass enhanced his reputation. He helped stop the Mexican invasion of 1842. Otherwise, he recruited and trained men in Indian fighting and frontier warfare. Captains who served under him were Big Foot Wallace, Ben and Henry McCulloch, and Samuel Walker.

Hays later led his rangers (called the First Regiment, Texas Mounted Rifles) into the Mexican War, fighting alongside the U.S. Army as it marched through Mexico. The Hays units were particularly effective in repulsing Mexican guerrillas near Veracruz.

Following the war, Hays dropped out of the rangers, tried to open a trade route between San Antonio and El Paso, and then went west, where in 1850 he founded Oakland, California, and became sheriff of San Francisco County. He died in 1883 and is buried in California.

See also: TEXAS RANGERS

HEATH, John A. (1854?–1884)

Little is known regarding the origins or early upbringing of John A. Heath, but somewhere along the line, John "bowed his neck" and ignored the good advice of his parents—who, in the absence of information to the contrary, we will credit as being reasonably honest and righteous people. By whatever route in the early 1880s, Heath reached the banks of the Trinity River at Dallas, where as a youth he was arrested for burglary on one occasion and cattle rustling on another. He also underwent police scrutiny because in partnership with a locally notorious mulatto prostitute, Georgia Morgan, Heath operated a bordello and later a downtown saloon. For reasons subject only to speculation, Heath then headed farther west and by 1883 had established a dance hall in Bisbee (other accounts say Clifton), Arizona.

On December 8, 1883, five heavily armed desperadoes—Dan "Big Dan" Dowd, Owen W. "Red" Sample, James "Tex" Howard, William Delaney, and Daniel York "Yorkie" Kelly—robbed the Goldwater and Casteñada Store, which controlled the payroll for the Copper Queen Mine. However, once inside, the bandits discovered with befuddlement that the payroll funds were yet to arrive and that the safe contained only $600. Of course, they took it—as well as a pocket watch from one of the employees.

Out in the street, the outlaws shot down five more or less innocent bystanders, including an expectant mother, Annie Roberts. The gunmen escaped.

A well-armed and thoroughly infuriated posse took the field. Some of the manhunters were Cochise County sheriff Jerome Ward, ex-sheriff Johnny Behan, deputies "Billy" Daniels, and Sy (Ci) Bryant. The town newcomer, John A. Heath, participated. After a while though, it seemed to certain posse members that Heath might be trying to misdirect them, and those suspicions were confirmed. The

store's owner stated that five men had recently been in the area dividing up cash and then leaving in different directions. Curiously, according to the lawmen's intelligence information, and according to the rancher, the murderous thugs had earlier been observed conversing with John Heath.

Heath, protesting his innocence, was placed under arrest. In the meantime Grant County, New Mexico, Deputy Sheriff Dan Tucker arrested York Kelly at Deming and held him for Arizona lawmen. "Red" Sample and "Tex" Howard were arrested near Clifton, Arizona Territory, still in possession of the stolen and easily identifiable pocket watch, although the timepiece had actually been given to a girlfriend. Deputy Daniels finally tracked down "Big Dan" Dowd in Old Mexico, and Mexican authorities sweetened the pot by throwing in William Delaney, whom they had recently captured. The suspects were now locked in the Cochise County jail.

All five of the subordinate bandits were tried, convicted, and sentenced to be hanged. Heath, identified as the ringleader, argued for a separate trial but was convicted of murder in the second degree. A jury sentenced him to life in the territorial prison at Yuma, although he served only one day.

Local citizens considered the punishment too puny, so they forcibly removed Heath, shirtless and shoeless, from jail and lynched him from a Tombstone, Arizona, telegraph pole. His last words were, "Don't mutilate my body or shoot me full of holes."

Dr. George Goodfellow drafted the coroner's jury report: "We the jury, find that John Heath came to his death from emphysema of the lungs, a disease very common at high altitudes. In this case the disease was superinduced by strangulation, self-inflicted or otherwise."

On March 28, 1884, the remaining five defendants were adorned with black hoods at Tombstone and given their "final launch into eternity." They, along with Heath, lie in the Tombstone Boot Hill.

See also: BEHAN, JOHN HARRIS; TUCKER, DAVID

HELL'S Half-acre

This was a generic name for red-light districts all over the American West from Civil War times until the early 1900s. None was more famous, however, than the one in Fort Worth, Texas, even though its residents and clients often reduced the name to "the Acre." Social and business activities included prostitution, gambling, horse racing, cock fighting, brawling, and gunfights. The area sprawled across four of the city's north-south thoroughfares, occupying roughly four acres, although the boundaries were never formalized. While war was often declared on the Acre by reform-minded editors and mayors, much of the ire was aimed at dance halls and brothels where men and women congregated, rather than at saloons, which were basically an enclave of males. The Acre also proved a home to such gunmen as Luke Short, Long-Haired Timothy Courtright, and the Wild Bunch. By 1919 the Acre had largely become history, a victim of military off-limit restrictions and religious, political, and newspaper attacks.

See also: CASSIDY, BUTCH; SHORT, LUKE; WILD BUNCH

HENDERSON, William (a.k.a. Bill Henderson)
(?–1876)

Bill Henderson had an easily identifiable identity: he was a charter member in, some say leader of, as roguish a band of "cut-throats, robbers and cattle rustlers" as ever operated out of the Wichita Mountains near Fort Sill, Indian Territory (Oklahoma). The outlaws survived as long as they did by constantly changing legal jurisdictions, mostly by jumping back and forth across the Red River, to avoid apprehension.

With tiresome regularity they plied their trade southward to the vicinity of Fort Griffin, Texas, where citizens weary of continually replacing stolen livestock finally had their fill of inactive court processes and lame excuses. The Tin Hat Brigade, the Fort Griffin vigilantes, captured three of Henderson's men: Charles McBride, Jim Townsend, and a man known only as Brownlee. The vigilantes left all three dangling from the same tree limb.

Meanwhile, Bill Henderson murdered a rancher in nearby Jones County, Texas, then drove his horses toward Kansas. However, a telegraphed message reached Dodge City before the outlaws and their 26 stolen horses did. Bill Henderson and Hank Floyd were arrested by Kansas authorities practically as soon as they showed their dust-covered faces. Under guard, they were shipped to the Shackleford County jail at Albany and locked away on June 1, 1876. During the next night, June 2, 70 men disarmed the jail guards and escorted Bill Henderson and Floyd to a tree overlooking Hubbard

Creek, perhaps a quarter-mile from the courthouse. A newspaper editor noted that "if hanging didn't put the 'kibosh' on the criminal class, maybe cremation would."

See also: LARN, JOHN

HICKOK, James Butler (a.k.a. Wild Bill Hickok)
(1837–1876)

The child who would become Wild Bill Hickok, perhaps the West's best known pistoleer, was born on May 27, 1837, at Homer (later Troy Grove), Illinois, the fifth of seven children by William Alonzo Hickok and Polly Butler. James grew to be slightly over six feet tall, with long auburn hair, broad shoulders, blue-gray eyes, lean hips, a flat stomach, and a straw-colored mustache. By some accounts he also had a high-pitched voice, although if so, no one ever laughed. His primary biographer, Joseph Rosa, noted that his great passion was gambling, particularly poker. That, plus his fondness of liquor and his overabundance of human frailties, brought him both good and bad times. They also brought him death. But before he fell, his two ivory-handled Colt 1851 Navy revolvers made him famous.

James Hickok headed west in 1856 and soon became known along the Missouri/Kansas border, little realizing that practically within the decade, in January 1867, *New Monthly Magazine* would feature his exploits, factual and otherwise. In the meantime, he worked as a wagon master and quartermaster. The Union army retained him as a contract scout. He briefly served during the Civil War as a government detective on the provost marshal's staff at Springfield, Missouri, his assignment being to "hunt up personal property." By the time the war ended, Wild Bill was a recognizable name in the states of Missouri, Arkansas, and Kansas. Hickok also briefly became a U.S. deputy marshal. He saw service with the Seventh Cavalry for four months in 1867.

While an accurate tally of men dead at Hickok's hands throughout his career is impossible to establish, rounding the figure off at between five and 10 would place any curious individual in the ballpark. The fight that firmly established Hickok's reputation became known as the Rock Creek, or McCanles, Massacre. The site was a Nebraska Territory Pony Express relay station operated by Russell, Majors, and Waddell. Hickok's station duties consisted primarily of stock tending. When the firm went bankrupt, the property owner, David C. McCanles, ordered everyone to vacate. No one left, so McCanles, his son William Monroe McCanles, and two employees, James Good and James Gordon, rode over on July 12, 1861, to expel them. What happened next is confused, and the facts in the years since have become tenuous at best. A shotgun blast—probably fired by Hickok from inside the house—killed David McCanles. When someone else clubbed Good over the head with a hoe, he died. Gordon ran into the brush, where a shotgun killed him. Only McCanles's son escaped. A trial took place in Nebraska Territory, and the house defendants, including Hickok, were released because of insufficient evidence. As for who shot whom, no one is certain—but Hickok got most of the credit.

Hickok kept wandering, and on July 21, 1865, in Springfield, Missouri, he and David Tutt argued. The 26-year-old Tutt, like Hickok, had been a scout (but a Confederate one) and had a string of violence haunting his own backtrail. The two men argued over a gambling debt. Hickok paid $40 and promised to ante up the additional $35 in a brief time. Tutt said Hickok owed him not $35 but $40. As an added insult, he picked up Hickok's watch as security. Tutt promised to wear the watch in the public square the following day.

Both men put in an appearance on Friday, 6 P.M. July 21. When somewhere between 50 and 100 yards apart, they pulled their guns and fired. Tutt missed. Hickok did not. He then turned on his heel and challenged any of Tutt's friends to take up the quarrel. None of them did. Hickok went to trial on August 5 and 6 and was acquitted.

A few years later, Hickok became marshal of Hays City, Kansas. On August 22, 1869, not long after he entered office, Hickok shot John Mulrey during an argument of which Mulrey was the instigator. He died a few hours later.

On September 27, 1869, Samuel O. Strawhun—the name has been spelled various ways— practically destroyed a beer hall. Hickok walked in and shot him dead.

Hickok lost a Hays City reelection bid on November 2, 1869, and appears to have worked as a U.S. deputy marshal for a while. He returned to Hays City just in time on July 17 to become involved in a gunfight with two Seventh Cavalry troopers, John Kile and Jeremiah Lonergan; the

James Butler ("Wild Bill") Hickok (Robert G. McCubbin Collection)

shootout took place inside the Paddy Welche Saloon. Hickok probably entered first. As he stood leaning against the bar, Lonergan grabbed him from behind and wrestled him to the floor while Kile ran up alongside, pulled a .44 Remington, stuck it in Hickok's ear, and jerked the trigger. The weapon misfired. Meanwhile, Hickok had managed to draw one of his own weapons. He jammed it against Lonergan's knee and blew it away. Lonergan naturally let go, at which time Hickok rolled over and shot Kile twice, once in the body and once in the arm. Hickok, apparently figuring the whole roomful of people was trying to kill him, jumped through a window and dashed to his hotel room. There he grabbed additional weapons and hid out in the local Boot Hill for the rest of the night, that particular

116

hideout being the last place troopers would expect to find him. Meanwhile, Kile died.

Hickok subsequently disappeared from Hays City, only to reappear in Abilene, where the city council in April 1871 appointed him town marshal. In the process the council created a tinderbox. Texas trail herds would be arriving soon, and most cowboys were southerners, whereas Hickok was a northerner, a Yankee. Since neither faction showed much tolerance or respect for the other, trouble would be the only outcome.

At about 9 P.M. on October 5, a group of Texas cowboys led by gambler Phil Coe stumbled down the street, occasionally ordering drinks from saloon patrons, throwing over the bar bystanders who did not offer to pay. Coe even fired at a stray dog, which brought Hickok on the run. A street-corner confrontation occurred in front of the Alamo Saloon; it ended with both Hickok and Coe blazing away at each other from a distance of eight to 12 feet. Coe fired four rounds. Hickok banged away with both six-shooters, each man creating clouds of gunsmoke; Coe missed completely, but Hickok scored twice. He shot Coe in the stomach, a wound from which Coe died three days later. Hickok also accidentally shot his own deputy, Mike Williams, who came running up at the wrong time. Coe and Williams would be Hickok's last killings. His best-known biographer, Joseph Rosa, believes Hickok killed eight men altogether, at the maximum.

Within a few weeks Hickok also confronted Texas gunman John Wesley Hardin. The marshal had made it illegal for anyone in Abilene to wear guns; when Hardin kept his strapped on, Hickok supposedly ordered Hardin to take them off and hand them over. Hardin's story was that he performed the Road Agent Spin on the marshal and forced him to back down.

Did such an event actually happen? Probably. At any rate, when Hardin shot a man a few weeks later, he did not wait around for Hickok to come knocking on his door. Hardin "borrowed" the first fast horse going south to Texas.

As for the marshal, when the cattle-shipping season ended, the Abilene city council dismissed him. Hickok had by this time acquired a dime-novel reputation. *Harper's Magazine,* among others, made him a violent, straight-shooting, romantic hero. Bill reinforced the image by performing in Buffalo Bill's Wild West Show from 1872 to 1874. Hickok became one of the "Scouts of the Prairie."

But Hickok had sobriety problems, especially when acting. Furthermore, he seemed temperamentally unsuited to show business. He left the Buffalo Bill Show in March 1874 and spent the next two years in and around Cheyenne, Wyoming. There he acquired what appeared to have been trachoma, an eye disease.

In Cheyenne, on March 5, 1876, he married Agnes Lake Thatcher, the widow of a circus owner. They honeymooned in Cincinnati, Ohio. Hickok left almost immediately afterward for the Black Hills in South Dakota, where gold had reportedly been discovered.

Here he likely met Martha Jane Cannary, better known as "Calamity Jane," a mannish-appearing, nearly middle-aged prostitute. Bill may have indulged himself briefly, but there is little evidence of any serious association.

Anyway, on August 2, 1876, as he sat playing poker in Deadwood's Nuttall and Mann's No. 10 Saloon, Jack McCall walked up behind and shot the gunfighter in the back of the head. Hickok died instantly. The bullet went through Wild Bill's skull and embedded itself in the wrist of a fellow poker player.

The reasons for the slaying are speculative. Furthermore, there were no aces and eights clutched in Hickok's fingers, the so-called Dead Man's Hand. In fact, no one recorded his cards. McCall was tried for murder and hanged. Wild Bill was buried in Deadwood, where he remains the town's top tourist attraction, almost as well known in death as in life. Calamity Jane lies in the next tier, directly above Hickok.

See also: BUFFALO BILL; CALAMITY JANE; COE, PHILIP HOUSTON; HARDIN, JOHN WESLEY

HIGGINS, John Calhoun Pinckney (a.k.a. Pink Higgins) (1848–1914)

Pink Higgins was born in Georgia but in 1857 moved to Lampasas County, Texas. He fought Indians, joined the Ku Klux Klan, and in 1874 killed two Horrell Ranch cowboys, Ike Lantier, and Zeke Terrell. In January 1877, Higgins killed Merritt Horrell during a saloon fight in Lampasas. In March of that same year, a group of men, including Higgins, ambushed but failed to kill Sam and Mart Horrell. During a subsequent June 14, at Lampasas, the Horrell and Higgins clan shot at each other for several hours, killing only a Higgins brother-in-law, Frank Mitchell.

One month later the Higgins bunch invaded the Horrell Ranch, but ran out of ammunition within two days. Still, it took the Texas Rangers to push them out. The rangers also forced both sides to sign a peace treaty.

Higgins now briefly took his anger to the Mexican border town of Ciudad Acuna. There he shot and killed a man who had not fulfilled a horse deal. Higgins swam north across the Rio Grande and escaped.

Higgins apparently loved his feuds, but feuds eventually did him in. In Kent County, Texas, on October 4, 1903, he and Texan William Standifer, each on horseback, shot it out with rifles. Standifer shot the Higgins horse; Higgins shot Standifer through the heart.

In 1914 Pink Higgins died of heart failure.

See also: HORRELL BROTHERS; STANDIFER, BILL

HIGH Noon

High Noon is arguably the most famous western movie of all time. Gary Cooper portrayed a lone man standing up to evil at high noon while others in his town cower in the shadows. Producer-director Stanley Kramer released this western. The message movie portrayed an American West not of reality but of imagination. No real-life American West lawman or outlaw ever faced this kind of storybook situation. It's a real history versus Hollywood scenario, in which Hollywood wins out.

HODGES, Thomas J. (a.k.a. Tom Bell) (1830?–1856)

Desperado Tom Hodges was known practically all his life as Tom Bell. Born in Tennessee, he served as a medical assistant during the Mexican War and afterward headed for California, where he became a mule thief. That got him five years in 1851, the initial part of his sentence likely being served on board a rickety anchored ship, used as a jail, in San Francisco Harbor. Anyway, he and others broke out in 1855. Bell formed a gang that for a brief period amounted to perhaps 30 individuals. Its members shot and killed without mercy, robbing stagecoaches, mines, and miners. They even stationed a thug in the Mountaineer Hotel at Auburn to notify the outlaws of guests with bulging pockets.

The end came when lawmen caught Charlie Hamilton, a black associate of Bell's. Charlie talked, and on October 3, 1856, a posse shot up Bell's gang. Bell and some of the others escaped, but gang member Juan Fernandez led the lawmen to a San Joaquin River ranch and hideaway where Bell had established his headquarters. So this man who might have become a respected doctor was instead captured, led to a tree, given an opportunity to write two letters, and hanged.

HOLE-IN-THE-WALL

The Wild Bunch outlaws had their favorite hideouts, one of the best known being the Hole-in-the-Wall, in Johnson County, Wyoming, near what is now Kaycee. Actually, it never was a hole in the canyon wall as has been touted but rather a notch, a path taken by an ancient river that had left behind red granite cliffs. From the top of that notch a person could see for miles, making it easy to spot approaching posses, friends, or enemies. Herds of cattle could be driven in or out through that notch. Butch Cassidy, a founding member of the Wild Bunch, believed a dozen men could hold off an army from that vantage point—which of course was not quite correct but makes a point.

Not many people lived in that remote area, and they were never of the inquisitive type. Today, the region is still out of the way, remote, a park for visitors, campers, and those who want to experience a long-ago atmosphere of the Old and Wild West.

See also: CASSIDY, BUTCH; SUNDANCE KID; WILD BUNCH

HOLLIDAY, John Henry (a.k.a. Doc Holliday) (1851–1887)

John Henry Holliday (named for both his uncle and his father), but forever known as Doc Holliday, was born on August 14, 1851, in Griffin, Georgia, of well-to-do parents; his father, Henry, was a druggist. Dr. John Holliday, Henry's brother, made the delivery. He also performed cleft-palate surgery on the youngster. Nevertheless, the boy spent much of his youth in intensive speech therapy. In 1864, when John Henry Holliday reached 12, the family moved to Lowndes County, Georgia, settling near Bermiss. Sometime during this period young John Henry decided to become a dentist, and although his and

John Henry ("Doc") Holliday (Robert G. McCubbin Collection)

a few rounds at each other. Holliday was charged with assault with intent to murder, but a jury found him not guilty.

For a while he lived in Denison, Texas, but showed up in Fort Griffin, Texas, in 1875; there he was charged with gambling and drinking. By summer he had reached Denver, where he used the alias of "Tom Mackey" and dealt faro at the Theatre Comique. Doc was now becoming a drifter as well as a gambler. On February 5, 1876, he arrived in Cheyenne, Wyoming, and from there moseyed over to Deadwood, South Dakota. But Deadwood could not hold him either, and he now began a gambling odyssey that carried him back and forth and up and down in the West and Southwest, pausing briefly at a dozen or so towns before reaching Breckenridge, Texas, in summer 1877. There, on July 4, he caned Henry Kahn, a local gambler, and Kahn put a little round hole in Doc Holliday. It took Doc time to heal, but before long he reappeared in Fort Griffin, Texas. Here he met Kate Elder, better known historically as "Big Nose Kate." She was well traveled, educated, and 26 years old. She also worked in a brothel, but she gave that up to follow Doc Holliday as his common-law wife.

Doc and Kate moved to Dodge City, where Doc hung out his shingle as a dentist but spent much of his time gambling. The two moved to Las Vegas, New Mexico where he found Wyatt Earp and his brothers, whom he had first met somewhere along the route, probably in Dodge City or Abilene, Kansas. Wyatt mentioned new gold strikes in Arizona. So in 1879, the Hollidays and the Earps arrived in Prescott. Here, although Doc cemented his relationship with the Earps, he and Kate found that they had about all they could stand of each other. Still, they reached Tombstone together in September 1880. There Doc continued to be in and out of trouble—gambling, liquor, and pistol work being at the root of it.

On March 15, 1881, eight road agents attempted to rob the Wells Fargo Tombstone-to-Benson stage, killing the driver and a passenger. Rumors immediately surfaced regarding Doc's involvement, and the fallout between him and Kate made the robbery and murder accusations more serious. On July 5, 1881, Kate testified before Judge Wells Spicer that Doc Holliday had in fact participated in the stage holdup and murders. Holliday was arrested, but the charges were dropped when the district attorney asked that the case be dismissed. Kate left town.

his family's feelings ran high against the North, everyone agreed that the best training could be had at the Pennsylvania College of Dental Surgery in Philadelphia. In 1870, young John paid the $105 fee and enrolled. He graduated on March 1, 1872, with a degree of Doctor of Dental Surgery. He opened his practice in Atlanta.

Somewhere along the way, perhaps since early childhood, he developed a nagging cough diagnosed as pulmonary tuberculosis. The only cure—move west to a drier climate. In September 1873 he took a train to Dallas, Texas, and opened his new office at 56 Elm Street. Before long, remote from his family, he became aware of the many Dallas saloons and of gambling. Doc Holliday began spending more time with dice and cards than with teeth. By May 12, 1874, when the city charged him with gambling, he knew dentistry was a lost cause; he would never go back. In January 1875, Doc Holliday and saloon keeper Charles Austin broke the monotony by firing

Holliday continued as before, drinking, gambling, and occasionally fighting. He participated with the Earps at the so-called Gunfight at the OK Corral on October 26, 1881. Doc carried a nickel-plated revolver in his pocket and a double-barreled shotgun concealed under his long coat. When the shooting started, either Wyatt or Doc put a revolver bullet into the belly of Frank McLaury. Doc then emptied his shotgun into Tom McLaury, who was desperately trying to get his rifle out of a saddle scabbard. In the meantime, someone's bullet bounced off Doc's hip. In the uproar that followed the killings and the funeral, Wyatt Earp and John Henry Holliday went to jail for roughly 30 days before being released.

On January 17, 1882, Holliday and John Ringo met in the middle of Allen Street and cursed one another. Ringo had his hand on his hip; Holliday had his in his breast pocket. Lawmen broke it up. Furthermore, following the wounding of Virgil Earp and the slaying of Morgan Earp, Holliday rode with the Earps during their various vendettas. He allegedly participated in the slaying of Frank Stillwell.

In 1882, Holliday arrived in Denver, Colorado, where he was arrested. He was soon released, and moved to Leadville, Colorado, where his tuberculosis caught up with him. This time the only medicine was whiskey, and it prodded him into shooting Billy Allen, a murder being prevented only when bystanders wrestled him to the floor. In 1887, at Glenwood Springs, Colorado, Doc was too sick to support himself either by gambling or dentistry.

During the morning of November 8, 1887, John Henry "Doc" Holliday died at the Hotel Glenwood in Glenwood Springs, Colorado. His last words were, reportedly, "This is funny." He lies in an unmarked grave in Glenwood's Linwood Cemetery. Kate was by his side when he passed on.

See also: DENO, CHARLOTTE; EARP, VIRGIL; EARP, WYATT BERRY STAPP; GUNFIGHT AT THE OK CORRAL; HORONY, MARY KATHERINE; RINGO, JOHN PETERS

John Henry ("Doc") Holliday (Ben Traywick Collection)

HOLMES, W. A. (a.k.a. Hunkydory) (1833?–1889)

Originally from Texas, Holmes was drawn to the Southwest in search of gold. He made it to Arizona Territory, where sometime around 1863 he earned a living as a "hawker" of church-owned tracts of land. He found the work dissatisfying, however, and returned to prospecting around Safford.

He reportedly struck it rich with a very successful silver mine, the Daisy Dean, in the vicinity of Globe, but he was forced to expend his newfound wealth on a legal defense. It seems that a fellow prospector, Banjeck Marco, if Holmes's account is accurate, tried to jump his claim. Heated words escalated to the point where Holmes killed the alleged claim jumper. The trial cost him his fortune, but the jury freed him.

Thereafter he remained in the vicinity, a well-liked figure locally known as a staunch Democrat. He was also something of an entertainer, as well as a reasonably skilled poet. One of his poems was entitled "Hunkydory"—thus the nickname.

In the meantime, an ex-scout commonly known as the Apache Kid and several cohorts were convicted of shooting and wounding Al Seiber, the Army's renowned chief of scouts. The responsibility of getting the prisoners to Yuma Prison fell upon the shoulders of Apache County sheriff Glenn Reynolds.

Reynolds deputized Holmes for the journey, and on November 1, 1889, the two men loaded the prisoners into a private stagecoach hired for the trip to Casa Grande. From there the group would proceed by train. The sheriff armed the stage driver, Eugene Middleton, with a revolver. Reynolds carried a double-barreled shotgun as well as a six-shooter, and Holmes had a lever-action Winchester and a six-shooter.

The first night passed without incident. On November 2, however, the trip turned tragic. At the steep Kelvin Grade, the prisoners were herded out of the coach in order for the team to be able to make the pull. The Apache Kid, whom the lawmen considered extremely dangerous, was ordered to stay in the coach, along with another Apache, Hoscal-te.

The coach started the tortuous climb, the remaining six prisoners walking behind. Having concocted a plan, the prisoners gradually positioned themselves, and then at a designated signal overpowered Reynolds and Holmes. Sheriff Reynolds was shot to death. "Hunkydory" Holmes either had a fatal heart attack (he was in his fifties) or was killed by gunfire, all depending on which version is believed. During the melee, stage driver Middleton was wounded in the mouth and neck, but he survived. The prisoners fled into the Arizona landscape to make their own histories. Holmes, a bachelor, was buried at Globe in an unmarked grave.

See also: APACHE KID

HORN, Tom (a.k.a. James Hicks) (1860–1903)

Tom Horn was born in Scotland County, Missouri, the fourth in a family of four boys and four girls. In 1874 he left home, primarily to escape his father's beatings, and within a couple of months was working for the Santa Fe Railroad in Kansas City. A few months later he was in Santa Fe driving stages to Prescott, Arizona, for the Overland Mail. He became fluent in Spanish, a skill that led the Fifth Cavalry to retain him. Tom worked frequently with Al Sieber, chief of scouts, Sieber teaching him the mule-packing trade. Horn and numerous others often rode with Gen. George Crook tracking and pursuing Apaches back and forth across the deserts, the mountains, and the border between the United States and Mexico. Horn would write extensively about himself, giving himself most of the credit for capturing Geronimo; in fact, he was little more than a witness.

After the Indian wars ended, and the army no longer needed scouts and packers, Horn became an occasional lawman as well as a rodeo rider. Although particularly apt at steer-roping, that skill did little more than put coffee on the table, so he reverted to his old trade of man hunting. The Pinkerton Detective Agency, out of Denver, hired him to help prevent stock theft, and the Swan Land and Cattle Company of Wyoming retained him in 1894 to be a stock detective, a phrase that was in this case a euphemism for hired assassin. He allegedly killed two Laramie ranchers for $600 each. Business was so good that Horn made a pretty fair living. Working primarily out of Wyoming, he shot and killed Bob and Bill Christian, then put his career on hold while he signed on as a mule packer with the U.S. Army during the Spanish-American War. He left the army in 1900, changed his name briefly to James Hicks, then killed stock rustlers Isom Dart and Madison Rash, thieves operating out of Brown's Hole in Colorado. At about the same time, he quarreled with a Wyoming hard case named Neut Kelley and received a severe knife wound in the stomach.

Horn recovered, but not as the same person. On July 19, 1901, he ambushed and shot 13-year-old William Nickell as Willie opened a corral gate at his father's ranch near Iron Mountain, Wyoming. Horn had meant to kill the father but from a distance mistook one for the other. Almost two weeks later on August 4, Horn shot the father, Kels Nickell, but only wounded him.

These Nickell shootings had now attracted the attention of U.S. Deputy Marshal Joe LeFors. In January 1902, LeFors took Horn on a saloon crawl through Cheyenne, Wyoming. It ended with both men bragging about their accomplishments. Horn in particular wound up allegedly talking about the Nickell shootings. He was immediately arrested.

In October 1902, at Cheyenne, Wyoming, Tom Horn went on trial for murder, although he denied it. The jury turned a disbelieving ear and sentenced him to hang on January 9, 1903. The date was later moved to November 20, 1903. After a failed escape attempt, Horn met the hangman right after breakfast. An hour or so later he dropped four feet to his doom. He is buried in Columbia Cemetery at Boulder, Colorado.

See also: BROWN'S PARK; PINKERTON NATIONAL DETECTIVE AGENCY

HORNER, Joe (a.k.a. Frank M. Canton) (?–1927)

Frank Canton, actually born Joe Horner, could have come from either Indiana or Virginia, as he seems to have claimed both at one time or the other. At any rate, the family moved to Missouri and from there to Denton, Texas. He seems to have served briefly as a Texas Ranger as well as a cowboy, and worked as a guard during the Texas trial of Big Tree and Satanta for their parts in the 1871 Warren Wagon Train Massacre. Around Jacksboro, Texas, he became a cattleman as well as a rustler. In 1874, he killed his first man during a saloon shootout in Fort Richardson, Texas.

Three men on January 6, 1876, robbed the Comanche, Texas, bank. Although Horner denied involvement, a March 1877 jury gave him 10 years. Horner promptly broke out of jail and robbed a stagecoach. This earned him another 10 years at Huntsville. However, on August 4, he escaped again, this time heading for Wyoming, where Joe Horner the man killer became Frank Canton the man hunter.

By 1882, Canton had become sheriff of Johnson County. He also married Annie Wilkerson. He brought in the murderer Teton Jackson, although Canton's involvement in the capture seems to have been controversial. He was reelected sheriff in 1884, attended the Democratic National Convention in Chicago, was defeated in 1886, and subsequently became a U.S. deputy marshal, on November 3. Throughout his life Canton remained a supporter of big cattlemen and a strong enemy of small ranchers (read "rustlers"). The responsibility for several killings was laid at the Canton doorstep.

In March 1892, various cattlemen began meeting in Cheyenne, planning an invasion of Johnson County. Twenty-four professional gunmen were hired and brought in from Texas. A couple of dozen Wyoming cattlemen, including Canton, joined the force; in fact, Frank Canton seems to have been the expedition leader. Whoever was in charge, the expedition foundered. The force wasted too much time killing alleged rustler Nate Champion, and then bumbled and stumbled until the invasion ran out of steam. The invaders themselves wound up incarcerated at Fort D. A. Russell. At the trial in Cheyenne, Canton accidentally dropped his revolver and shot himself in the foot, which seems to sum up a sorry episode.

Canton later applied for a position as U.S. marshal in Alaska, and when that failed, he turned south, trying to get a pardon for the man he had once been, a fugitive known as Joe Horner. Governor James Hogg granted a full pardon. Canton then moved to Oklahoma, became a deputy sheriff as well as a U.S. deputy marshal, and was involved in the killings of Lon McCool and Bill Dunn. Shortly after that, Canton resigned as deputy marshal because of expense voucher irregularities. Canton then moved to Alaska, becoming a deputy marshal, but once more financial irregularities caught up with him.

Time was also catching up with him. He encountered Will Foster, a former enemy, on the Buffalo, Wyoming, streets. Foster clubbed Canton to the ground. Canton's life throughout the next few years seems something of a mystery, although in 1907 he became adjutant general of Oklahoma. In 1911, he called out guardsmen to prohibit illegal prizefighting, and in 1914 he stopped a rodeo that had violated Oklahoma's blue laws.

Frank Canton retired in 1917 and died in Edmond, Oklahoma, on September 27, 1927.

See also: JOHNSON COUNTY WAR

HORONY, Mary Katherine (a.k.a. Big Nose Kate) (1850–1940)

Big Nose Kate, best known as the consort of Doc Holliday, was born in Pest, Hungary, in 1850. Family traditions say her father emigrated to Mexico, but she moved north and took the name of Kate Fisher. Certain evidence places her in St. Louis where she may have been widowed. She reportedly spoke several languages and acted aristocratically as if to the manor born. How she got the name "Big Nose Kate" is a mystery, as her photos do not reveal a nose out of the ordinary in size.

In Fort Griffin, she teamed up with the homicidal and tubercular Doc Holliday and accompanied him to Tombstone, Arizona, where they evidently had a serious falling out. On March 15, 1881, three men attempted to hold up the Wells Fargo stage, killing the driver and a passenger. The holdup men escaped, but Big Nose Kate broke the story with a statement to the *Daily Nugget* that Doc had been the slayer of Bud Philpot, the driver. This of course led to speculation—or confirmation—that she acquired the nickname Big Nose not because of a large nose but because, as some people may have seen it, of sticking her big nose where it did not belong.

Sheriff Behan arrested Holliday and placed him in jail. Meanwhile, the Earps argued that Kate had been under the influence of the sheriff and that she had been intoxicated when she made her statement. On July 9, Virgil Earp arrested Kate, charging her with being drunk and disorderly. She paid a $12.50 fine and fled to Globe, Arizona. However, she obviously returned a short time later, because on October 26, 1881, from the window of Fly's Photography Studio, she witnessed the most famous shootout in western history, the Gunfight at the OK Corral.

When Holliday left Tombstone for the sanitarium in Glenwood Springs, Colorado, Kate visited him; she was there when he died. In March 1890, she married a prospector, George M. Cummings. They lived for a while in Bisbee, Arizona, where Kate operated a bakery. George worked in the mines and beat his wife on occasion. Fortunately, he died, and in 1899 she became a housekeeper for John J. Howard, a well-to-do eccentric, who treated her well. She stuck with him, living in obscurity, until he passed away.

Big Nose Kate Horony died at the Arizona Pioneers Home on November 2, 1940. She is buried in the Prescott Cemetery.

See also: BEHAN, JOHN; EARP, VIRGIL; GUNFIGHT AT THE OK CORRAL; HOLLIDAY, JOHN HENRY

HORRELL Brothers: William C. (1839–?); John W. (1841–1868); Samuel L. (1843–1936); James Martin (1846–1878); Thomas L. (1850–1878); Benjamin F. (1851–1873); Merritt (1854–1877)

The Samuel and Elizabeth Horrell family had eight children, all born in Alabama. By 1867, the family had moved to Lampasas, Texas. In 1868, they drove a trail herd of 1,000 cattle west, selling the animals at Las Cruces, New Mexico. Some of the family now went to work. John Horrell was killed by Early Hubbard following a wage dispute. In January 1869, the father, Samuel Horrell, was slain by Apaches at San Agustin Pass in the nearby Organ Mountains. Later that year, the family moved back to Lampasas, where every one of the boys—except Merritt—married. Only Tom failed to have children.

Four years later on March 14, 1873, Capt. Tom Williams of the Texas State Police and several other officers rode into Lampasas, where they clashed with Merritt Horrell and other clan members. Captain Williams and four officers died in a saloon shootout.

James Martin Horrell, better known as Mart, was badly wounded but was jailed, as were three desperado companions. In September, the Horrells broke their brother and friends out of the Georgetown jail. The Horrells now rounded up cattle and headed for Ruidoso, New Mexico, where the so-called Horrell War broke out.

In Ruidoso Country, the troubles were racial as well as concerned with water rights. On December 1, 1873, Ben Horrell and friends shot up Lincoln, New Mexico, and killed the town constable, Juan Martín. The constable's friends retaliated, killing David Warner, a Horrell friend. They then pursued Ben Horrell and Jacob C. Gylam down to the river, where they shot Gylam 13 times and Ben Horrell nine. Neither survived.

On September 5, Sheriff Alexander H. Mills took a posse of 40 men down to Eagle Creek and demanded that the Horrells surrender. They did not; after each side had fired a few harmless volleys, the posse returned to Lincoln.

Events became bloodier on December 20, when the Horrells and friends rode into Lincoln around midnight. When they rode out, they left behind four dead Hispanic males and two wounded women.

On January 7, 1874, the governor offered a $100 reward for each of the three Horrells. A posse subsequently shot up the Horrell ranch and drove off livestock. On January 25, the posse returned and burned the house. On January 30, the Horrells and other Texans split into two groups and began reprisals. One group killed five Hispanic wagoneers doing nothing more than hauling corn. The other group stole livestock. Then they all went back to Texas, where they were tried for the murder of Thomas Williams and were acquitted. Otherwise, things stayed relatively quiet until 1877.

In January of that year, a nearby rancher, John Calhoun Pinckney Higgins, better known as "Pink Higgins," accused the brothers of stealing his stock. On January 22, he killed Merritt Horrell in the Gem Saloon in Lampasas. On March 26, the Higgins party ambushed Tom and Mart near Battle Creek, east of Lampasas. Both men were hit, Tom seriously. Mart single-handedly dispersed the attackers.

On June 7, both factions happened to be in Lampasas at the same time, and the street fighting began. Frank Mitchell, a cousin of Pink Higgins's wife, was slain. Jim Buck Miller, a newcomer to the Horrell gang, was shot dead. Meanwhile, a citizens' committee convinced both sides to withdraw, and shortly afterward the Texas Rangers swept in and temporarily stood between the combatants. Maj. John B. Jones talked both sides into signing documents saying the feud was a "bygone thing."

The Horrells had one final fling in western history. Mart and Tom Horrell were jailed in Meridian, Texas, charged with the murder of storekeeper J. T. Vaughn. On December 15, 1878, while they were behind bars awaiting trial, a mob forced its way inside and shot the prisoners to death.

Sam Horrell, the last surviving brother, the one who never seemed to bother anybody, moved his family to Oregon in 1882 and died peacefully in California on August 8, 1936. He is buried in Eureka, California.

See also: HORRELL-HIGGINS FEUD

HORRELL-HIGGINS Feud

Six Texas-born Horrell brothers—Benjamin, John, Mart, Merritt, Sam, and Tom—walked away intact from the Civil War, only to become New Mexico and Texas feudists. Tom died early, slain in Las Cruces, New Mexico, but his brothers teamed up with Texas rancher John Calhoun Pinckney ("Pink") Higgins near Lampasas, Texas. In 1872, that friendship terminated during an 1872 joint cattle drive when Pink Higgins and Tom Horrell argued, Higgins accusing the Horrells of stealing his cattle.

A year later at Lampasas, Texas, state police captain Tom Williams and seven officers tried to arrest Bill Bowen, a Horrell brother-in-law in Jerry Scott's Saloon. Of course, the Horrell brothers joined in; when the fight ended, Mart Horrell lay badly wounded and four state policemen, including Williams, lay dead. Upon recovering, Mart went to the Georgetown jail, where his brothers broke him out. The family then rounded up a herd of cattle and headed for Lincoln County, New Mexico, where they settled until the so-called Horrell War, a "war" the Horrells likely instigated. At least 17 men died, one of them being Ben Horrell. While he lay dead, someone chopped off a finger to get his gold ring. Nearly three weeks later, on December 20, the Horrell boys retaliated by shooting their way into a Lincoln wedding, wounding two guests and killing four. They then returned to Lampasas but were shown to the state line by an angry army of Hispanics.

In February 1874, the state of Texas tried the Horrells for the murder of Capt. Thomas Williams but acquitted them. The Horrells now renewed their antagonisms with Pink Higgins, who on January 22, 1877, shot and killed Merritt Horrell in the Gem Saloon at Lampasas.

Meanwhile, on March 26, the Higgins gang ambushed Tom and Mart Horrell. Although wounded, both men escaped, Mart providing enough firepower to drive off his enemies.

Two months later, on June 7, both factions collided in a Lampasas street shootout that lasted three hours. The Horrells wounded Bill Wren, a friend of Higgins, and killed a Higgins brother-in-law, Frank Mitchell. However, the Horrells lost Jim Buck Miller, a hired gun. A furious Higgins retaliated on July 25. He and 14 cowboys shot up the Horrell ranch for two days until the Higgins faction ran short of ammunition and retreated.

Maj. John B. Jones and the Texas Rangers now stepped in, convincing both sides (they actually got the Horrells out of bed) to negotiate and sign a peace treaty. That ended this particular feud, although as an aside, in 1878 Tom and Mart Horrell were arrested for allegedly robbing and murdering a Bosque County merchant. A vigilante mob shot them to death in their jail cell as they awaited trial. This left Sam as the only Horrell left.

Sam moved to Oregon in 1882 but died in California in 1936. As for Pink Higgins, he went to work for the Spur Ranch in Texas as a range detective. He died of a heart attack in 1913.

See also: HORRELL BROTHERS

HORSE Theft

Horses have added romance, color, drama, and speed to the history of the American West. In short, the West as we know it could not have existed without the horse.

A horse was indispensable, but since not everybody had a horse or could afford to purchase one, horse theft became a major activity. Indians, especially Comanche, were renowned for their horse-thieving abilities. During the Spanish period, Santa Fe became a major market for the trading, buying, selling, and stealing of horses. Mountain men like Peg-Leg Smith and Dutch Henry Born became notorious for the vast numbers they drove off and sold. If they could not grab them before the brands went on, they would steal them from one army post and sell them to another.

The Wild Bunch always found themselves in need of horses; fortunately, they had a ready-made pen behind the Hole-in-the-Wall. Harry Longabaugh served seven months in jail at Sundance, Wyoming, for horse theft. He lost the horses, of course, but he picked up a nickname that would serve him well for generations to come—the Sundance Kid.

Billy the Kid, when not shooting or running from lawmen, made a lifestyle out of stealing and selling horseflesh. Furthermore, the Rio Grande area north of El Paso, Texas, became a haven for horse thieves. As for the horse-theft penalty, depending on where you were, it could range from being lynched, or shot on the spot, to up to 10 years in prison.

HUGHES, John Reynolds (a.k.a. Border Boss) (1855–1947)

This well-known Texas Ranger was born near Cambridge, Illinois, on February 11. His family moved around the state before settling in Mound City, Kansas, where John worked on a ranch, and then moved to Oklahoma, where for several years he lived in the Indian Nations among the Comanche, the Choctaw, and especially the Osage. He knew Quanah Parker. He went to work for Art Rivers, an Indian trader who provoked a fight with the Choctaw. Hughes was struck on the right arm, an injury that never properly healed. The arm remained so weak that Hughes learned to draw and shoot a revolver with his left hand.

With his brothers, Will and Henry, John Hughes established the Long Hollow Ranch—their brand being the Running H—in Travis County, Texas, 33 miles northeast of Austin. There they ranched peacefully until May 4, 1886 when rustlers took 16 head of livestock, plus a stallion named Moscow. John tracked the horses to near Silver City, New Mexico, where, after enlisting Sheriff Frank Swafford and a deputy, they killed four of the rustlers during a gunfight. Upon returning to Texas, however, Ranger sergeant Ira Aten warned Hughes of a threat upon his life from a man named Roberts. Within a few days Roberts and Hughes shot it out, and Roberts went to the graveyard. Following that, the 32-year-old Hughes signed on as a Texas Ranger, and was assigned as a private to Company D near Uvalde.

Hughes and several other rangers went under cover during the fence-cutting wars. Hughes was assigned to Navarro and McLennan Counties, arriving on May 14, 1888. Nevertheless, it became a frustrating assignment, and Hughes asked to be reassigned: "It will be no use for me to work after them any more as they are the best organized band that I ever worked after. They keep spies out all the time. The big pasture men [big ranchers] live in town, and the people in the county are almost all in sympathy with the wire cutters."

The rangers promoted Hughes to corporal and reassigned him to Presidio County, Texas, specifically to the silver-mining community of Shafter, where he broke up a silver-smuggling group and was promoted to sergeant, replacing Sgt. Bass Outlaw, who had been dismissed for heavy drinking. Shortly afterward, the rangers transferred Hughes to Marfa, but events were already cooking near El Paso. Events there would involve Hughes. Texas Ranger sergeant Charles Fusselman had been slain in the El Paso Franklin Mountains by Geronimo Parra on April 17,

John R. Hughes, Texas Ranger (Robert G. McCubbin Collection)

1890. Hughes left Marfa on temporary duty to investigate the killing but lost the trail in New Mexico, where he had no jurisdiction. Hughes then returned to Marfa, only to learn that Texas Ranger captain Frank Jones, headquartered at Ysleta, near El Paso, had been slain while in pursuit of the Bosque Gang along the Rio Grande downstream from El Paso. Jones had lost his life during a shootout at Tres Jacales, a controversial island in the Rio Grande claimed by both the United States and Mexico. Hughes was then reassigned to El Paso as Jones's replacement, although Sergeant Outlaw argued for that position also. It went to Hughes on July 4, 1893. Hughes then took command of the Ysleta camp, only to learn that Fusselman's slayer, Geronimo Parra, was in the New Mexico Territorial Penitentiary. Hughes failed to get Parra extradited.

Pat Garrett, the Dona Ana County, New Mexico, sheriff, rode into the ranger camp one day. Garrett was trying to solve the disappearance and likely murder of New Mexico's Col. Albert Jennings Fountain. Garrett sought a fugitive named Pat Agnew, loose somewhere in Texas—so the tall sheriff and Hughes struck a deal. Hughes would find and turn Pat Agnew over to Garrett if Garrett would use his influence to extradite Parra from the New Mexico prison. It worked, and Hughes helped (legally) hang Parra in the El Paso County jail.

Hughes continued to serve admirably, retiring after 23 years in June 1915. His ranger service was the longest in history, and he retired only because incoming Texas Governor James Ferguson announced a plan to sell ranger commissions.

Hughes never married. Always a frugal man, he bought river bottom land near Ysleta, Texas, the price of which soared after the creation of New Mexico's Elephant Butte Dam. Hughes then sold the land at a huge profit and used the funds to create the Citizens Industrial Bank in Austin. This man, who had been dubbed the "Border Boss," now led many Sun Bowl parades in El Paso, as well as the Texas Centennial Parade in Dallas in 1936. In 1928 he purchased a Model T Ford, driving it until he reached the age of 92. On June 3, 1947, he entered his garage at the home of his niece in Austin and committed suicide by shooting himself in the head. He is buried in the state cemetery in Austin.

See also: FENCE-CUTTING WAR; FUSSELMAN, CHARLES; GARRETT, PATRICK FLOYD JARVIS; JONES, FRANK; OUTLAW, BASS; TEXAS RANGERS

HUGHES Brothers, Ben and James

The Hughes brothers were born in Missouri but came early to Texas and lived near Strawn, in Palo Pinto County. To earn a living, they robbed trains with an associate named Sam Baker, a.k.a. Harvey Carter. On December 1, 1886, the gang robbed the Fort Worth & Denver train in Clay County, Texas. On January 29, 1887, they robbed the Texas & Pacific at Gorman, Texas, as it paused to take on fuel. On June 3, along with Baker, they robbed the Fort Worth & Denver at Ben Brook, Texas.

On August 14, authorities picked up the brothers, jailed them in Dallas, and tried them in Graham, Texas, in November. A jury found both boys guilty and sentenced each to 99 years at hard labor. However, a new trial set them free, a local newspaper reporting that "a speech made by James Hughes made a profound impression on the court." Shortly afterward, the Hughes boys joined their father, James Hughes, in Indian Territory (Oklahoma) but continued their nefarious careers while posses, including U.S. marshals and Texas Rangers, repeatedly tracked them back and forth. In a shootout near Checotah, Oklahoma, James Nakedhead, an Indian, a deputy with the Cherokee Indian Police and a guard at the Muskogee jail, took a Hughes bullet in the head and died on the spot.

No disposition of the resulting trial has been located, but the accused were apparently acquitted of train robbery. It remained for Judge Isaac Parker, the famous "hanging judge" at Fort Smith, Arkansas, to try both men for the murder of Nakedhead. That proved a fiasco too; once more the Hughes luck held. Since the posse lacked train-robbery warrants during their assault upon the Hughes home and had not announced its presence and purpose prior to the shooting, the accused went free. They returned to their Oklahoma ranch, which subsequently became a rendezvous for additional thieves and murderers.

In 1903, Ben and Jim Hughes were again arrested, this time for participating in the lynching of Louis Houston, the brother of Ben's ex-wife. Both were acquitted. Finally, Ben was charged with grand larceny, and in 1911 he was sentenced to four years in the Oklahoma State Penitentiary. He served five months. In 1923, his brother Jim was sentenced to four years for transporting a stolen vehicle across state lines. He served 37 months.

Uncle Ben Hughes died in 1945 at the age of 84. Jim Hughes died of natural causes in 1949 at the age of ninety.

See also: PARKER, JUDGE ISAAC

HUME, James B. (a.k.a. James Hughes)
(1827–1904)

Although born in New York, James B. Hume spent his youth in Indiana but as a young man migrated to California in 1850. As a speculating miner Jim was not overly successful, at least not enough to achieve financial independence and personal satisfaction. Therefore, Hume energetically turned to law enforcement, and there he stayed for the remainder of his life.

At Placerville, El Dorado County, California, on March 4, 1860, Hume was appointed deputy tax collector. Two years later he was appointed city marshal, and on April 21, 1863 Hume was elected marshal by a substantial margin. Then, longing for more meaningful police work than collecting fees, catching dogs, and arresting drunken miners, on March 4, 1864, Hume went to work as a deputy for Sheriff William H. Rogers.

Deputy Hume quickly began making a name for himself. He engaged in a shootout with jail escapees during May 1864, wounding Ike McCollum. During the following month he solved a Nachman Store robbery case. Come July of that same year, Deputy Hume chased stagecoach robbers who had murdered a lawman; the outlaws had given him the slip until Tom Bell Poole, a wounded outlaw who had been left behind, decided to talk. With his information in hand Hume arrested a whole cadre of accomplices, the newspapers nothing that they all claimed to be Confederate "freedom fighters."

In another case, Hume shot it out with rustlers, wounding one and capturing another. Because of his distinguished service to the county he was generally well liked, but not enough to become sheriff. He came in third in a three-way race. Undaunted by his political defeat, Hume went back to work, joining other officers courageously engaging outlaws Hugh DeTell and Walter Sinclair, and a man named Faust. During the gunfire exchange Hume was wounded. Faust died of bullet wounds, but Sinclair and DeTell were captured. A short time later, in November 1867, Hume arrested four suspects and solved the murder of Joseph F. Roland, a miner of French extraction.

With numerous, well-publicized cases to his credit, in the November elections of 1868 Hume was elected sheriff of El Dorado County, but he served only one term. Because of his fame as an investigator, Hume was hired in March 1872 to head the Wells Fargo & Co.'s new detective bureau, but he almost immediately requested, and received, a one-year leave of absence to serve a hitch as deputy warden for the Nevada State Penitentiary. Mired in political upheaval, plagued by terrible morale, staffed by ineffective guards, and populated wholly by unmanageable prisoners, the Nevada prison indeed needed work. Whether Hume's objectives as prison administrator were actually met is historical guesswork, but after a new warden had been appointed, Hume returned to his Wells Fargo assignment.

From the outset, his investigative expertise was in overworked demand for capturing notorious outlaws. Just as importantly, at least from the company's perspective, Hume's attention also focused on dishonest employees embezzling corporate funds. Hume successfully apprehended Richard Perkins, a.k.a. Dick Fellows, a.k.a. Richard Kirtland. He tracked down the Marysville-Downieville stage robbers, Ephraim White and George Rugg. He accurately deduced that Bob and Bill Hamilton had assisted "Big Jack" Davis in attempting to rob a stagecoach at Willow Station, 40 miles south of Eureka, Nevada—a robbery abruptly aborted when a shotgun blast killed Davis. Finally, he was triumphant in the battle of wits with the legendary stagecoach robber and highwayman Charles E. Boles, more widely known as Black Bart.

But for whatever reason, Hume was frequently characterized as a blundering victim of stagecoach robbers rather than their nemesis. On January 7, 1882, Hume was a passenger aboard the "Sandy Bob" stage when masked highwayman stopped it halfway between Tombstone and Contention in Arizona Territory. Nine male travelers, including Hume, were highjacked at the point of a shotgun. He lost two fine revolvers and $70 in cash.

The aging manhunter and detective accepted assignments as far east as Cleveland, but age gradually took its toll, although he continued working for Wells Fargo almost to the end. He died at 77 at his California home on May 18, 1904.

See also: BOLES, CHARLES E.

HUNT, Zwingle Richard (a.k.a Zwing Hunt)
(1858–1882?)

Zwing Hunt is believed to have been born in central Texas and later to have drifted to eastern New Mexico and western Arizona. He became a frequent presence around the Shakespeare mining community, as well as a close associate of well-known borderland rogues. He allegedly participated in numerous cattle-stealing schemes and raids across the international border. Hunt was considered an excellent shot and utterly fearless. A newspaper writer once remarked, "Zwing would do to go tiger hunting with."

In 1882, a Cochise County, Arizona, cattle-theft warrant started circulating for Zwing Hunt. On March 29, 1882, murder joined the theft charge, and Hunt subsequently became involved in a furious gunbattle in which his partner, "Billy the Kid" Grounds, and a lawman were killed. Two posse members were wounded.

Hunt, shot through the chest, was hospitalized at Tombstone. Acquiescing to the desires of a renowned physician, Dr. George Goodfellow, who thought the wounded Hunt was too seriously injured to be removed to the county jail, the authorities permitted the prisoner to remain at the medical institution pending partial recovery.

During the night of April 27, 1882, however, the prisoner's brother, Hugh, arrived from Texas and loaded Zwing into a waiting buggy. The pair simply drove out of Tombstone town. A posse later returned empty-handed. Then the rumors started.

Hugh reported that he and his brother had been attacked by Apache and that Zwing had been killed. Supposedly the scout Jim Cook had found Zwing's remains and buried the body beneath a juniper.

Reportedly a military command exhumed the body, made an examination and declared it was indeed the escaped prisoner. The soldiers reburied the body and departed what was then known as Russell's Canyon but is now known as Hunt's Canyon. (The story is unsupported by official documents, but the site is identified by an official historical marker). Other tales have Zwing managing to make it back to Texas, where he suffered forevermore from his wounds. All in all, it is now safe to say that Zwingle Richard Hunt is dead.

IVERS, Alice (a.k.a. Poker Alice) (1851–1930)

Alice Ivers was born in Sudbury, England, on February 17, 1851. Her family immigrated to America during her teens, and the petite blonde married Frank Duffield, a mining engineer who took her to the western slopes of the Rockies. There she watched her husband gamble, although she frequently participated. When he died in a mining accident, gambling was about all she knew. In fact, she became so proficient that she acquired the nickname of "Poker Alice." She gambled in Leadville, Alamosa, Georgetown, and at any other spot in the road wide enough to hold a gambling table. In Silver City, New Mexico, she broke the bank. She lived for a while in New York City, until her money ran out.

She gambled in Indian Territory (Oklahoma), at Clifton, Arizona, at Crede, Colorado, and wherever else she happened to land. As Bob DeArment, one of her biographers, says, "She took her booze straight, smoked cigars, packed a .38 on a .45 frame, and could cuss like a mule skinner." At Deadwood, South Dakota, she met and married W. G. Tubbs, and they settled down, almost. Tubbs caught pneumonia and died. Alice drove his frozen body to Sturgis, South Dakota, the nearest town, and pawned her ring to pay for the funeral. She then hired on at the nearest gambling hall and won sufficient money to redeem the ring.

Later she married George Huckert, who had previously been a hired hand working around her house.

"Poker Alice" Ivers (Robert G. McCubbin Collection)

As she said later, it was cheaper to marry him than to pay him. He died within a few years.

Alice, in her seventies, with a cigar clenched tightly between her gums, operated a roadhouse between Sturgis and Fort Meade, South Dakota. Most of her patrons were soldiers. One afternoon she fired a gun through a closed door in order to quiet down a ruckus and killed a drunken soldier. A jury acquitted her, but the authorities closed down the roadhouse.

She died on February 27, 1930. The Catholic Cemetery at Sturgis, South Dakota, accepted her body.

IVES, George (1836–1863)

George Ives seems to have been born at Ives Grove in Racine County, Wisconsin, but turned to California mining by 1850. Before long he took to gambling and drinking. Then he moved to Washington State, where he herded government mules before becoming an intense gambler, a rowdy, and a rustler. By 1862 he had drifted over to Montana, where he functioned as a lead thug in the Henry Plummer gang, operating around Bannack and Virginia City. During the following year, however, he and others held up a stage and within another month or two murdered Nicholas Tbalt, a young German. The vigilantes now took action, capturing Ives and taking him to Nevada City, Montana, where he was tried by an impromptu jury of 24 men and promptly hanged.

See also: PLUMMER, WILLIAM HENRY.

JAILS and Prisons

To be jailed in the American West up until well after the Civil War often meant being tied or chained to a tree. At best, jails were little more than crude wooden buildings, which explains why so many prisoners could break free. It also explains why various townspeople often took the law into their own hands, either lynching lawbreakers before authorities could incarcerate them or simply approaching the jail, usually after dark, and removing the prisoners for execution. Most lawmen perhaps did not approve of mob action, but few lawmen put up more than a perfunctory resistance to it.

A sheriff's office was often built over a deep pit, perhaps an old cistern, locally known as "the hole." Deputies working the night shift often sat (or slept) in a chair over the hole, which meant that a prisoner could not escape without rousing the lawman.

Jails ordinarily lacked full-time security. They were usually heated (if at all) by wood or coal, and the fires were rarely stoked after dark. There was no running water, no toilet facilities, no recreation room, no cooling, no heating. Coal-oil lamps in a wooden facility were too risky, so inmates sat in the dark. Meals were skimpy and medical attention practically zero. Prisoners who were lucky had a jail mate to talk to; if they were unlucky they had too many jail mates to talk to, and so inmates had to take turns sleeping on the floor. The stench was awful. Very few jails had facilities for women.

"Rehabilitation" was unheard of. People were in jail, or prison, not to be reformed but to be punished. Such concepts as "prisoner coddling" were almost a century distant.

In 1868, the federal government built the Canon City, Colorado, territorial penitentiary. Twenty years later, it built another one at Rawlins, Wyoming. What made these detention buildings so different from others was that they had separate, individual cells, not particularly large but modern and humane according to standards of the time. For the first time, a prisoner had at least a touch of privacy, at least until the government started incarcerating two to three prisoners to a cell.

JAMES Brothers: Frank (1843–1915) and Jesse (1847–1882)

American history has few parallels to Frank and Jesse James. They were train, stage, and bank robbers; terrorists, guerrillas, and night riders; and national heroes. Both were born in Clay County, Missouri, Frank on January 10, 1843, and Jesse on September 7, 1847. Their Baptist preacher father died in California, where he had gone to mine gold; the mother married twice again, the last time to a gentle physician, Dr. Reuben Samuel. The clan supported the Confederacy, kept slaves, and believed it was their right. During the Civil War, both boys fought under guerrilla leaders William Clarke

131

Jesse James (Robert G. McCubbin Collection)

Quantrill and William "Bloody Bill" Anderson. The two James brothers shot their way through some of the bloodiest, most brutal, and fiercest guerrilla conflicts along the Missouri/Kansas border. In fact, they owed their later acclaim and success as colorful outlaws to this guerrilla training—the tactics of surprise, take no prisoners, swoop and shoot, get in and get out, and careful planning combined with the element of terror and surprise.

When the Civil War ended, Jesse tried to surrender on April 15, 1865, but took a bullet through the lungs as he rode into Lexington, Missouri, under a white flag. After recovering, he and the James and the Younger brothers had the option of going back to farming or continuing as they had during the last few years. They agreed to take up bank and train robbing. Oddly, although Jesse was the baby of the bunch, he was also the unquestioned leader. On February 13, 1866, the James boys and the Youngers robbed the Clay County Savings and Loan in Liberty,

Missouri. The only casualty was a 19-year-old boy who happened to run across the street at the wrong time. Otherwise, the bleak countryside swallowed up the outlaws. On October 30, they robbed a bank in Lexington, Missouri. Other banks also went down. In the confusion, no one could say whether the Youngers and James boys had been involved.

By now the Pinkerton National Detective Agency had been called in, and from this moment on, for a lot of reasons, bank robbery suddenly became a more dangerous occupation. Still, on December 7, 1869, Jesse, Frank, and Cole Younger hit the Daviess County Savings Bank in Gallatin, Missouri. Shooting started, people died, Jesse's horse threw him in the middle of the street, and Frank went back to get him. Everyone made it safely out of town. A bank robbery in Columbia, Kentucky, followed. Then as the countryside began concentrating on protecting banks, the gang changed its style by throwing in an occasional train robbery.

The Pinkertons retaliated. In 1875, two men thought to be Pinkerton agents fire-bombed the James homestead, mutilating the arm of Zeralda James (now Zeralda Samuel) and killing Archie Samuel, the nine-year-old half brother of Jesse and Frank. Meanwhile, both Frank and Jesse had married in 1874; both now had families. When not out killing and robbing, the two were attentive fathers and husbands. Jesse even wrote frequent letters to the newspapers denying he had robbed such and such a bank or train.

The gang now headed to Northfield, Minnesota, where on September 7, 1876, they robbed the First National Bank, wounded the teller, and killed the cashier and a bystander. The gunfire alerted the community, however, and the gang had to shoot its way out of town. In the process, outlaws Clell Miller and William Stiles were killed, and Bob and Cole Younger were wounded, Bob the more seriously. The outlaws fled, only to be pursued by a relentless posse in what became one of the West's most intense manhunts. Since the Youngers could not keep up, the James boys struck out on their own. Within days, the pursuing posse killed Charlie Pitts and captured Jim, Bob, and Cole Younger.

All three Youngers went to the Minnesota State Prison at Stillwell. Bob died there of tuberculosis in 1889. Cole and Jim were released in 1901. Jim committed suicide. Cole sold insurance, ran a Wild West show with Frank James, and lectured against evil.

Whether Jesse and Frank ever robbed another bank or train isn't certain. Jesse changed his name to Thomas Howard, and with his family he probably lived in Tennessee or Kentucky. By 1881, he had moved to St. Joseph, Missouri, still dreaming of the old days and occasionally accepting new gang members, such as Robert Ford. On April 3, 1882, as he stood on a chair to straighten a picture on the wall, Ford shot him in the back of the head—for the reward money and the publicity. Six months later Frank surrendered to the governor of Missouri; over time, he was acquitted of all his crimes.

The body of Jesse James was removed to town, identified, photographed, and viewed by hundreds. It was then transported to the James/Samuel farm, where his stepfather and mother, Zeralda, buried it in the yard. The tombstone inscription read:

Jesse James in death (Author's Collection)

"Devoted Husband and Father, Jesse Woodson James. September 5, 1847, murdered April 3, 1882 by a traitor and coward whose name is not worthy to appear here."

After Jesse's mother and stepfather passed away, the outlaw's son, Jesse Edward James, disinterred his father's body and reburied it alongside Zee in the Mt. Olive Cemetery in Kearney, Missouri. In 1995, his remains were exhumed by a George Washington University forensic team, given DNA testing, and positively identified as Jesse James. On October 28, he was reinterred.

As for Frank James, he lived another 30 years, doing all kinds of odd jobs, including running a James-Younger Wild West Show in partnership with Cole Younger. Frank's wife cremated his body when he died in 1915 and kept the ashes in a bank vault until she died in 1944. Their ashes are now mixed together and buried as one in a Kansas City cemetery.

See also: ANDERSON, WILLIAM C.; FORD, ROBERT AND CHARLES; QUANTRILL, WILLIAM CLARKE; WELLS, SAMUEL; YOUNGER BROTHERS

JAYBIRD-WOODPECKER War

This war of 1888–89 involved a feud between political/racial factions in Fort Bend County, Texas. Perhaps 40 white residents (the Woodpeckers) had gained control of the county during the Reconstruction era. One of the odd aspects of the feud was that they claimed to be Democrats but campaigned as Republicans. The Woodpecker political strength

Joseph Heywood was killed by Jesse James in a Northfield, Minnesota, bank holdup (Author's Collection)

therefore stemmed from the support of a large black population that voted Republican, because black people perceived the Republicans as the ones who had set them free.

On August 2, 1888, someone shot and killed J. M. Shamblin, leader of the Jaybirds who opposed the Woodpeckers and represented the majority of whites in the county. Henry Frost, another Jaybird was wounded a month later. The Jaybirds then held a mass meeting and warned selected black people to vacate the county. Most accepted that advice.

As Texas Rangers took up quarters in Richmond, county elections took place, and the county turned out its largest vote in history. Yet because of the black turnout the Woodpeckers won again; all sides started arming themselves. On June 21, 1889, the Woodpecker tax assessor, Kyle Terry, shot and killed L. E. Gibson. Gibson's brother, Volney, killed Terry a week later.

All this was too much for everyone involved, and so the Battle of Richmond began, on August 16, 1889. Most of the fighting took place around the National Hotel and the courthouse. For nearly a half-hour the firing continued, the Woodpeckers finally holing up in the courthouse. Jaybirds now controlled the city. The casualties are unknown but were reported as "heavy."

On the following day, August 17, Governor Lawrence Ross dispatched the Houston and Brenham Light Guards to restore order. He himself arrived and negotiated a political change. As a result, all the Woodpecker country officials either resigned or were forced from office, and the Jaybirds took political control for the first time in 20 years.

On October 3 and again on October 22, 1899, the Jaybirds met and drafted a constitution giving county control to white people, the "real" Democrats. That political situation continued for decades. But at least the shooting stopped.

See also: TEXAS RANGERS

JAYHAWKERS

The name "Jayhawker" once denoted terror, and this terror had its birth in Kansas during the Civil War. It commenced with men named James Montgomery and Charles R. "Doc" Jennison, Montgomery being the cruel idealist and Jennison the implementing

hammer. Jennison organized raiders he called "Jayhawkers," and Montgomery used them to raid Missouri slave owners. From the outset of the Civil War, this group teamed up with James Henry Lane, who called himself "the Great Jayhawker." Thus the Independent Mounted Jayhawkers, as they termed themselves, murdered and burned their way through Kansas and Missouri, their reasons lost in the looting and killing.

Another group of Jayhawkers, this one referring to itself as the "Red Legs," slashed its way along the Missouri border. Like the others, these raiders took advantage of Civil War chaos; military units, both Confederate and Federal, were distant, fighting a traditional war. As a result, Missouri thugs retaliated when William Clarke Quantrill organized what he called "the bushwhackers," raiders who cast fire and lead upon the Kansas Jayhawkers, making no distinction between legitimate targets and families. The Youngers and the James brothers both got their start here.

The Jayhawkers and Bushwhackers went out of business with the demise of the Civil War and the return of stable, effective government.

See also: JAMES BROTHERS; LANE, JAMES HENRY; QUANTRILL, WILLIAM CLARKE

JOHNSON, Edwin W. (1853–1931)

Johnson was born in Clark County, Arkansas, became a deputy sheriff at Arkadelphia, Arkansas, and by 1880 had moved to Clay County, Texas, where as a lawman he tried to suppress fence cutting. By 1889, he had became a U.S. Deputy Marshal working in Texas and Oklahoma, losing his right arm due to a Wichita Falls, Texas, gunfight with a Bob James. Undeterred, Johnson learned to shoot with his left hand. In mid-1888, he helped arrest Charles, George, Llwellyn, and Alf Marlow. It took but a brief time for the Marlow brothers to escape from the Graham, Texas, jail but they were recaptured during a gunbattle that cost the life of one officer. At this time, January 19, 1889, the lawmen started herding the Marlows on a 60-mile trip to Weatherford, Texas, believing it to be a more secure jail. However, a gang of desperadoes, perhaps trying to lynch the Marlows, perhaps trying to free them, waylaid the caravan. Five men died, a chief deputy, two of the attacking bunch, and two of the Marlows, Llwellyn and Alf.

During the resultant uproar, Johnson, who had his good left hand mangled by gunfire during the shootout, was charged with being one of the outlaws. He was finally exonerated, and in 1916 moved to Los Angeles, California, where he became a deputy sheriff. Fourteen years later he died in Los Angeles.

JOHNSON, John (a.k.a. Turkey Creek Johnson) (1872–?)

Johnson was one of those obscure outlaws who popped up out of nowhere, achieved a measure of notoriety, and then faded into the background, never again to be positively identified. There is some suspicion that while acting as a city marshal in Newton, Nebraska, he killed Mike Fitzgerald. With perhaps a couple more dead men on his backtrail, he showed up next in Tombstone, Arizona, where he became one of the Wyatt Earp stalwarts. There seems little doubt that he helped Earp kill Frank Stillwell in the railroad yards at Tucson on March 20, 1882, and Florentino Cruz 48 hours later. What happened to him then? Who knows?

See also: EARP, WYATT BERRY STAPP

JOHNSON County War

In 1892, Johnson County, Wyoming, became the last of the great cattle conflicts. The problem stemmed from numerous small ranchers in that area appearing to help themselves to the nearby "big" ranchers' cattle. Large cattlemen, especially those along the Powder River in Wyoming, had grown fat, rich, and comfortable after years of ranching, now profits were down and cattle were disappearing, especially in Johnson County, where many small ranchers lived. Ordinarily, these big cattlemen might have felt themselves relatively powerless, but since big ranchers controlled the Wyoming government, they decided to act. The result became the Johnson County War.

The cattlemen hired gunmen from Texas, and on April 5, 1892, a special train left Cheyenne for Casper. On board was Frank Canton, a detective for the Wyoming Stock Growers Association, retained to provide muscle to remove the small cattlemen. With him were 23 gunmen, 22 of them from Texas, five additional stock detectives, two newspaper reporters, and 19 cattlemen. Canton no doubt carried a death list of rustler names, and the governor had already been advised to ignore any calls for assistance from Buffalo, the seat of Johnson County. In fact, Canton ordered the telephone wires cut.

At Kaycee, Wyoming, the invaders disembarked and trapped accused rustlers Nate Champion and Nick Ray inside their shack. The Texans shot Ray when he ran and killed Champion after setting his house afire and flushing him out. Meanwhile, word of the fighting reached Buffalo, so Sheriff Red Angus rounded up 200 Buffalo residents, met the invaders along the line of march, and forced them to seek shelter in a TA Ranch barn, 10 miles short of Buffalo.

There, the Canton raiders called frantically for assistance, and the cavalry from Fort McKinney responded. Canton and the others were taken as prisoners to Cheyenne, where the case was dismissed several months later because Buffalo County could not raise sufficient funds to continue with the prosecution.

Since then, numerous books, fiction and nonfiction, plus a couple of movies—*Heaven's Gate* and *Shane*—have been loosely based on the Johnson County War. It is a war still argued around prairie campfires as well as in the halls of academia.

See also: CANTON, FRANK

JONES, Frank (1856–1893)

One of the great Texas Rangers, Frank Jones was born in Austin, Texas, and joined the rangers in September 1875, serving in various locations until 1882, when he joined Company D, at that time serving in southern and southwestern Texas. He became a ranger captain in May 1886. Jones married in 1885; his wife died in 1889. In 1892, he married Helen Baylor Gillett, daughter of Texas Ranger captain George W. Baylor, as well as the ex-wife of former ranger and later El Paso city marshal, James Gillett.

In 1893, Jones and five other rangers pursued Mexican bandits and rustlers into the Rio Grande thickets, an area frequently known as "the island" or "Pirate Island," a strip of isolated land in contention between the United States and Mexico. As they approached a brush village known as Tres Jacales (three shacks), a gunfight erupted on June 30. It ended with Jones's death. His body was not returned to El Paso for several days. He was buried with

Texas Ranger Captain Frank Jones died in a Bosque gun battle in 1893 near San Elizario and Ysleta, Texas (Author's Collection)

Masonic honors on the George Baylor property at Ysleta, Texas.

See also: BAYLOR, GEORGE WYTHE; GILLETT, JAMES BUCHANAN

JONES, John B. (1834–1881)

John Jones, the man most responsible for the creation of the Texas Rangers—in fact, a man deserving of the title "Mr. Texas Ranger"—moved from South Carolina, where he had been born, to Texas when he was four years old, his family settling in Travis County. After attending college in South Carolina, he enlisted for the Civil War in the Eighth Texas Cavalry, then became a captain in the 15th Texas Infantry. By war's end he had become a major.

When the Texas legislature in 1874 authorized the Frontier Battalion, with its five companies of Texas Rangers, Governor Richard Coke needed a man to lead the organization who could stop the Indian raids as well as the increasing outlawry. During his first six months on the job, Jones led his rangers in 14 Indian engagements. During the second six

months, the battles were down to four. His largest battle occurred on July 12, 1874, when Jones led approximately 40 rangers into battle against 125 Apache, Kiowa, and Comanche.

During 1877, Jones found himself in El Paso, Texas, trying to quell the El Paso Salt War. He failed in that respect but served on an international commission to mediate the difficulties.

Jones brought about a truce in the Horrell-Higgins feud. His men destroyed the Sam Bass Gang at Round Rock, Texas. One year later, in 1879, Jones became adjutant general of Texas in addition to remaining commander of the Frontier Battalion. He died in Austin on July 19, 1881, and is buried in Oakwood Cemetery.

See also: BASS, SAM; EL PASO SALT WAR; HORRELL-HIGGINS FEUD; TEXAS RANGERS

JOY, Christopher (a.k.a. Kit) (1861–1884?)

A Texas cowboy, well known around Silver City, New Mexico, and a former employee of ex-Grant County

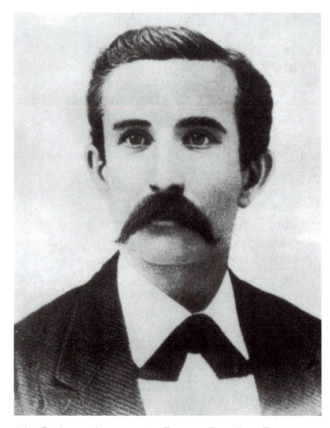

John B. Jones, Commander, Frontier Battalion, Texas Rangers (Library, University of Texas at Austin)

sheriff Harvey Howard Whitehill, Kit Joy (along with Frank Taggart, Mitch Lee, and George Washington Cleveland, a black cowboy) robbed a Southern Pacific train near Gage Station, west of Deming. During the robbery, one of them killed the train engineer. After an intensive search and competent investigation, Joy was identified as one of the outlaws, and he was subsequently arrested with Lee near Horse Springs, New Mexico Territory. The authorities locked him up at Silver City. On March 10, 1884, Joy and others, including his train-robbing companions, overpowered the guards, stole firearms from the sheriff's office, and fled. However, a posse caught up with the outlaws outside of town, and during an ensuing gun battle all were captured or killed except Joy. He managed to escape in the heavy underbrush, in the process fatally ambushing posseman Joseph N. Lafferr, a Silver City resident. As for the other outlaws, Cleveland was shot, some say by Joy, for "snitching." Lee and Taggart were caught and lynched.

Joy hid out along the Gila River until posse member "Rackety" Smith's buffalo gun shattered his leg below the knee. Doctors amputated it at Silver City.

On a change of venue, a jury at Sierra County, Hillsboro, New Mexico, found Joy guilty of second-degree murder, the prosecuting attorney acknowledging that it could not be proved that Joy himself had killed the engineer, nor could any premeditation to commit homicide be proved. Although sentenced to life, Joy eventually walked free from prison, and dropped out of sight somewhere around Bisbee, Arizona.

See also: CLEVELAND, GEORGE WASHINGTON; LEE, A. MITCHELL; TAGGART, FRANK

KELLY, Ed (?–1904)

Ed Kelly was likely born in Harrisonville, Missouri, and he married a relative of the Younger brothers. Although considered a tough, even desperate character, he is historically remembered today only as the slayer of Bob Ford, who, of course, is known only as the slayer of Jesse James. Bob Ford and Ed Kelly evidently roomed together briefly in a Pueblo, Colorado, hotel (men usually bunked together in order to save money), and during the night Ford's diamond ring disappeared. Ford loudly and repeatedly accused Kelly of stealing.

An angry Kelly stormed into Ford's tent saloon in Creede, Colorado, and killed Ford with a shotgun on June 8, 1892. Kelly received a life sentence but was released. On January 13, 1904, he became involved in a street fight with an Oklahoma City policeman, and the policeman shot him to death.

See also: FORD, ROBERT AND CHARLES; JAMES BROTHERS

KEMP, David Leon (1863–1935)

David Kemp was born on March 1, 1863, in Coleman County, Texas, but went with his parents to Hamilton County shortly after the Civil War. When he turned 17, he defended a friend during an altercation and by some accounts wound up killing a man. Although sentenced to 25 years, he obtained an early release when he helped prevent a prison break.

Kemp moved to Eddy County, New Mexico, where he was elected sheriff in 1890 and served until 1894. Later he had disputes with a brand inspector, Les Dow, who became sheriff in 1896. On February 16, 1897, the two men fought a duel, Dow's gun hanging up in his holster and Kemp's working perfectly. He shot Dow in the mouth, and Dow died the next day. An 1898 jury found him not guilty of murder. David L. Kemp remarried (twice more), served on the school board, and moved his Kemp & Lyell's Silver King Saloon in Phenix, New Mexico, to Eddy and renamed it The Central. But hard times were coming. His son, Leon, was shot to death by a mail carrier while Leon stood on his own front porch. Kemp spent much of his later life as a recluse, dying of a heart attack on January 4, 1935. He is buried in the Heart Cemetery at Booker, New Mexico.

KENEDY, James W. (?–?)

Kenedy, son of a respected Texas patriot, Mifflin Kenedy, drove cattle to Ellsworth, Kansas, where on July 27, 1872, during a gambling argument, he shot the Texas cattleman Print Olive. Olive's trail boss, Nigger Jim Kelly, then shot Kenedy. Nevertheless, Kenedy was soon up and about, at least in shape to make an attempt on the life of Dodge City mayor James H. (Dog) Kelley. The shooting likely had something to do with Kelley's relationship with actress and saloon and dance hall queen Dora Hand, whom Kenedy allegedly shot and killed on the following day. Pursuers then chased Kenedy through a snowstorm, killed his horse, and wounded him in the shoulder before returning him to Dodge City. However, Kenedy was acquitted after a "private" trial. He afterward returned to Texas. What happened to him after that is anybody's guess.

See also: OLIVE, ISOM PRENTICE

KETCHUM, Samuel W. (a.k.a. Black Jack) (1854–1899)

Sam Ketchum was born on Richland Creek in San Saba County, Texas. He and his younger brother Tom both had the nickname of "Black Jack," although why is obscure. Sam worked as a cowboy before turning hardcore outlaw by the mid-1890s. He and Tom gathered a gang, including now and then members of the Wild Bunch, an outfit that on occasion killed but became primarily known for stage and train robberies, mostly committed in Arizona, New Mexico, and Texas.

On July 11, 1899, the Ketchum outlaws held up a train at virtually the same site, near Folsom, New Mexico, where Sam had robbed one in 1897. This time, however, a posse chased the fugitives into Turkey Creek Canyon, in Colfax County, where a brisk fight occurred. The desperadoes killed Sheriff Edward J. Farr and wounded five of the eight posse members, one of whom, Henry Love, died. For their part, the posse wounded Sam Ketchum and William Ellsworth Lay (Elza Lay). The two forces now went their separate ways, each to attend to its wounded and dead. Sam Ketchum made it to a ranch in Ute Park, where gangrene set in. A farmer and his wife amputated the arm. New Mexico lawmen picked Ketchum up shortly afterward. He died not of his wounds but of amputation shock on July 24, 1899, in the Santa Fe prison.

See also: KETCHUM, TOM; LAY, WILLIAM ELLSWORTH; TURKEY CREEK CANYON, BATTLE OF

KETCHUM, Tom (a.k.a. Black Jack) (1863?–1901)

The outlaw Tom Ketchum was born on Richland Creek in San Saba County, Texas, as the youngest of three boys. During his early years he seems to have wandered West Texas and New Mexico, usually working as a cowboy but early on realizing that cowboy wages would have to be supplemented. He was

tall and muscular, with dark hair, a handlebar mustache, and piercing dark eyes. In late 1895, he and some friends shot and killed John N. "Jap" Powers, a Knickerbocker, Texas, rancher. Mrs. Powers assisted. She went to jail. Ketchum fled to New Mexico.

There is uncertainty regarding the name "Black Jack," as it seems to have been applied to his brother Sam as well. There was also a Black Jack Will Christian, a bandit operating along the New Mexico/Arizona border. The moniker "Black Jack" seemed to apply to all three, but after Christian was slain in Graham County, Arizona, it was easier for lawmen to sort out the other two.

To make matters worse, various members of the Black Jack gang and the Wild Bunch in the Wyoming, Colorado, and Montana area had a habit of frequently moving back and forth, of interacting, of being in one area of the country for a while and then appearing somewhere else. However, Wild Bunch members like Will Carver and Elza Lay seemed to prefer Sam Ketchum's leadership to that of the more awkward and less thorough Tom.

Although the gang robbed stagecoaches, even Tom realized that trains carried more money, so the focus shifted to the rail transportation category. On May 4, 1896, the Black Jack Tom Ketchum gang held up a train in Terrell County, Texas. A few months later they hit the *Texas Flyer* and took the strong box but had to lay a slaughtered beef across it when they applied dynamite, the weight of the beef holding everything together. However, much of the money was blasted to smithereens, along with the beef.

In December 1896, Tom assaulted the Southern Pacific as it crossed Stein's Pass, near the New Mexico/Arizona border. However, Wells Fargo agents were waiting, and they killed Ed Cullen, one of the bandits. A couple of years later, Sam Ketchum died of gangrene after being wounded during a train robbery.

At Cape Verde, Arizona, on July 2, 1899, Tom Ketchum made his worst mistake. He killed two miners during an Arizona saloon fight, the murders making him eligible for the death penalty. Shortly thereafter, on August 16, 1899, his string of robberies ended when Ketchum single-handedly held up the Colorado & Southern train near Folsom, Arizona. He shot a mail clerk through the jaw after calling on him to open the baggage car doors. At that moment, Frank Harrington, the conductor, armed

Hanging of Tom Ketchum, 1901 (Author's Collection)

with a shotgun, approached Ketchum, and they exchanged rounds. Both men wounded the other, but Ketchum took a load of buckshot in his right arm. He reeled off into the darkness, to be found the next morning lying propped against a tree, flagging down a train, once a symbol of ill-gotten gains but now a vehicle of mercy.

Doctors amputated his arm, and in September 1901, the territory tried him for train robbery, found him guilty, and sentenced him to hang. Tom heartily denied the charges and appealed the conviction to the U.S. Supreme Court, which upheld the verdict. In the Clayton, New Mexico, jail he gave numerous interviews, saying he "expected to go straight to hell after his death." Otherwise, his life's philosophy could be summed up in a brief paragraph he wrote on April 26, 1901, the hanging date: "My advice to the boys of the country is not to steal either horses or sheep, but to either rob a train or a bank when you have got to be an outlaw, and every man who comes in your way, kill him; spare him no mercy, for he will show you none. This is the way I feel, and I think I feel right about it."

During his time in prison, Black Jack Ketchum had gained weight, but the rope was not adjusted proportionally to account for it. As a result the drop decapitated him. He was the only man ever hanged in the United States for train robbery.

See also: KETCHUM, SAMUEL W.

KIDDER, Jeff P. (1875–1908)

Jeff Kidder never wanted to be anything other than a lawman, so this South Dakota–born cowboy in 1903 joined the Arizona Rangers, taking with him an unfortunate tendency of pistol-whipping men he didn't like or intended to arrest. These actions cost him $50 for one such offense in Bisbee, Arizona.

Kidder rose rapidly to sergeant and traveled with Capt. Thomas H. Rynning on a futile search for three Americans in Mexico. Upon returning, Kidder killed Tom Woods during a Douglas gun battle, the reason not being entirely clear. Then on April 4, 1908, Kidder crossed into Naco, Sonora, Mexico; 300 yards south of the international border he shot it out with Mexican police. He killed one officer and wounded two others but was himself seriously wounded while trying to recross the border. Mexican police threw him in jail, where he died of his wounds.

See also: RYNNING, THOMAS H.

KILBURN, William Harvey (1864–1904)

W. H. Kilburn was from Livingston County, Missouri, but at 18 he headed west for Leadville, Colorado. Shortly thereafter he traveled to the booming silver camp of Lake Valley, New Mexico Territory, where he worked at odd jobs until he amassed an amount sufficient to engage in the cattle business. Moving over to Grant County, Kilburn staked out a ranch and systematically increased his herd. Later he founded successful mercantile enterprises in Hanover and Silver City.

During 1888, W. H. Kilburn signed on with the Grant County sheriff's office, in the process serving as the Silver City town marshal for various terms: 1889–91, 1895–99, and 1903–04. Kilburn was fearless, although he exercised good judgment, usually.

An exception occurred on the night of August 27, 1904, when, in his capacity as town marshal, Kilburn assisted Deputy Sheriff Elmore Murray during a desperate struggle with Howard Chenowth, a local cowboy who had just shot his foreman, Pat Nunn. Before the bloody melee ended, Kilburn lay in the street mortally wounded. Deputy Perfecto Rodríguez was killed outright.

Suffering a neck wound that severed the sixth cervical vertebrae, W. H. Kilburn died on September 4, 1904, succumbing to the irreversible injury done to his 40-year-old frame. Local newspapers described Kilburn as a prime example of the "Western Man" and then shrugged off the shooting incident with the headline "A Cowboy Runs Amuck."

See also: CHENOWTH, HOWARD

KILPATRICK, Benjamin Arnold (a.k.a. the Tall Texan) (1874–1912)

Ben Kilpatrick was born in Coleman County, Texas, and grew up as a six-foot two-inch cowboy who joined the Black Jack Ketchum gang as well as the Wild Bunch. Whether he ever killed anyone is questionable, although he never hesitated to draw and fire. He participated in the Wild Bunch double robbery of the Union Pacific, the first in 1898 and the second in September 1900. Following that, he assisted with a bank heist at Winnemuca on September 19, at the conclusion of which the gang decided to take some time off and visit Fort Worth. Kilpatrick participated and became part of the celebrated photograph of November 21, 1900, featuring himself, Will Carver, Butch Cassidy, the Sundance Kid, and Harvey Logan.

During this same period Will Carver married Laura Bullion, an attractive Fort Worth prostitute. When Carver died later during a shootout, Laura transferred her affections to the Tall Texan and became his common-law wife. In the meantime, the Wild Bunch struck again on July 3, 1901, robbing the Great Northern train at Wagner, Montana. With the countryside by now swarming with posses, Cassidy and Sundance fled to New York and from there to South America.

As for the Tall Texan and Laura, they visited St. Louis, where detectives arrested them on November 5, 1901. On December 12, a judge sentenced Kilpatrick to 15 years in the Atlanta penitentiary. Laura got five years in a women's prison in Tennessee and was released on September 19, 1905. She waited in Birmingham, Alabama, for Ben to be released. Although scheduled to be released on June 11, 1911 the authorities instead transferred Ben to Paint Rock, Texas, and tried him for an earlier murder; the case was eventually dismissed.

Upon getting out of prison, the Tall Texan briefly waited for his cell mate, H. "Ole" Beck, to be released also. Then on the night of March 12, 1912, both men climbed aboard the *Sunset Flyer,* traveling between Dryden and Sanderson, Texas. When the train stopped for water, they entered the express car with the intention of robbing it, but long years in prison had sapped Kilpatrick's timing and judgment. The guard, David A. Trousdale, let them in, then picked up a heavy mallet used for crushing ice. He struck Kilpatrick on the head, and the Tall Texan died on the spot. Trousdale then grabbed Kilpatrick's rifle and shot Beck dead. At Dryden, Texas, the two bodies were tossed out onto the baggage platform,

then were propped up erect with the help of bystanders and photographed. They were buried together in a common grave at the Cedar Grove Cemetery.

As for Laura, she moved to Memphis, Tennessee, lived under the alias of Mrs. Fredia Lincoln, and died on December 2, 1961.

See also: CARVER, WILLIAM RICHARD; CASSIDY, BUTCH; KETCHUM, SAMUEL W.; KETCHUM, TOM; SUNDANCE KID; WILD BUNCH

KIMBELL, Russell G. (a.k.a. Rush) (1855–1954)

Rush G. Kimbell was born at Memphis, Tennessee, and relocated to the Lone Star State in 1870, winding up in Limestone County. Eight years later, Kimbell signed on with the Texas Rangers, not because he was seeking a "higher calling" but to satisfy the desires of the girl he wanted to marry. She had demanded that Kimbell pull a stint with the Texas Rangers before she would accept his proposal. So in exchange for wedded bliss, Rush became a lawman.

Enlisting at Austin, Kimbell initially accepted guard duty in the capital city but was soon transferred west, where he engaged in the pursuit of, and occasional skirmishes with, Indian raiders and outlaws.

Kimbell rose rapidly to sergeant. During one raid he led fellow rangers in a demanding chase after horse thieves Jim and John Potter, a father-and-son team who had taken livestock from the vicinity of the abandoned Fort Terrett, 30 miles east of Sonora. Following special instructions from Capt. Dan Roberts, Kimbell vowed to maintain his pursuit as long as the outlaws "stayed on top of the ground." Kimbell and his six-man squad followed a hunch and picked up the suspect's trail near Fort Lancaster. However, at Horsehead Crossing on the Pecos River, Kimbell reluctantly ordered five rangers with run-down horses to return to the ranger station.

With ranger assistant Bill Dunham, Kimbell continued the chase, swapping run-down horses at the Hash Knife ranch, where cowboy Billy Smith joined the two-man posse. After an exhausting night's ride, it dawned on Kimbell that he had probably gotten ahead of the brigands in the dark. So he backtracked. Shortly afterward, Jim and John Potter were observed riding toward the lawmen. Kimbell deployed his two men, advising the civilian cowboy to "just play where he saw he was needed the most." After coming within

Ben Kilpatrick, "The Tall Texan" (Robert G. McCubbin Collection)

shouting distance, Kimbell flashed his badge. Everyone pulled rifles, and the battle opened. Each side lost a horse in the blistering exchange of gunfire. When the smoke cleared, Jim Potter lay on the ground with a serious leg wound, his son beside him with a bullet through the chest. The lawmen survived unscathed. Kimbell left the prisoners under guard and rode toward Fort Stockton, 130 miles away. Arrangements were quickly made via telegraph communications, and a wagon was dispatched to retrieve the wounded rustlers. The effort was too late, however, at least for Jim Potter, who died waiting for help. John Potter was eventually turned over to local authorities in Kimble County, but he died of mob justice before he could stand trial. Sergeant Kimbell and his compadre had chalked up 1,118 tortuous miles during the pursuit.

Kimbell subsequently resigned from the Texas Rangers, and true to her word, his sweetheart accepted his marriage proposal. They tied the knot in October 1881. Kimbell eventually settled in Oklahoma, where he became a respected retail merchant. On January 18, 1954, Rush Kimbell, nearly 100 years old, died of natural causes. The ride for the bride—well, the results of that became an enduring success!

KING, Sandy (a.k.a. Red Curly; Sandy Ferguson) (1859–1881)

By some accounts Sandy King was born at Allegheny City, Pennsylvania. However, when the 22-year-old was booked into the Grant County, New Mexico, jail (1881) he told the registrar of prisoners that he was from Kansas. One writer claims that Sandy King may have been the Luther King who walked out of the Cochise County jail as a prisoner being detained for the murder of stagecoach driver Eli "Bud" Philpot, during a robbery of March 15, 1881.

He was sometimes described as a "hard, dangerous man of courage and a record" as well as a "pure-quill badman." These characterizations fitted the bill, since Sandy King spent his life as a desperado of note, having served time at Silver City for "wanton homicide." Regardless of exact details, Sandy King was in fact a hanger-on, a minor outlaw who staked out an unofficial claim at the legendary mining camp of Shakespeare, New Mexico Territory. Without repeating a roll call of reprobates and misfits stumbling up and down Avon Street, suffice it to say that Sandy King was one.

Although there is scant evidence, it is generally assumed that King was a friend of another Shakespearean, William Rogers "Russian Bill" Tettenborn, a gentlemen of noble birth who had gone bad. Whether or not they were actual pals, they were to share one experience—their last.

In what was to be a one-man act at a two-man show, Sandy King got drunk, ordered a new scarlet neckerchief, and instead of paying for the scarf with U.S. currency, shot the shopkeeper's finger off and fled. The authorities arrested him, but since the town had no jail, he was placed in a room under guard. At about the same time, "Russian Bill" stole a horse and headed east. At Deming, Deputy Sheriff Dan Tucker took him into custody. Tettenborn was returned to Shakespeare and tossed into the same cell with Sandy King. Tucker returned to Deming.

What then happened is best explained by a quick review of the *El Paso Lone Star*:

Two "rustlers," "Russian Bill" and "Sandy King" from the southern part of Grant county, were arrested last week by Deputy Sheriff Tucker and lodged in jail at Shakespeare last Monday. They were taken from jail that night by citizens who overpowered the guards, and hanged. "Russian Bill" has often declared that no man living could arrest him, but when he found Tucker was on his track he gave himself up without resistance. Their fate has no doubt engendered the enmity of the element to which they belonged against Shakespeare and the people there will organize a safety committee as a means of protection. The two men hanged were noted horse and cattle thieves.

There the little story should end. In the absence of handy trees in the desert area, the two owl-hoots were hanged from a ceiling beam in the dining room of the Grant Hotel, where they dangled all night. The next day, a passenger fresh off the stagecoach asked what had happened, and the stationmaster simply pointed and remarked, "One was hung for stealing a horse, the other one for being a damned nuisance." Whether the little anecdote is historically factual, Sandy King was dead.

See also: TUCKER, DAVID

KINNEY, John (1847?–1919)

John Kinney probably was born in Massachusetts, most likely in 1847 or '48. At Chicago, on April 13, 1867, he enlisted in the Third U.S. Cavalry and listed his occupation as laborer. The records described him as five feet five inches tall, with hazel eyes, brown hair, and ruddy complexion. He spent time around Fort Selden, near Mesilla, New Mexico, participated in several Apache Indian expeditions, and was discharged at Fort McPherson, Nebraska, in 1873. Within a brief time he reappeared in southern New Mexico, clashing on January 1, 1876, at a dance with a number of soldiers. The soldiers won and returned to the bar, only to be shot to pieces by a group of cowboys, of which John Kinney was one. Two soldiers died, and three others were seriously wounded.

Kinney thereafter became a cattleman with other people's cattle, his rustling empire extending along the Rio Grande Valley north through Mesilla and centering around Rincon. Newspapers described him as "King of the Rustlers," a title he aptly deserved. He and gunman Jesse Evans made life difficult for honest ranchers, since the outlaws, also referred to as "the Boys" by the press, operated almost without interference in that isolated portion of the valley. Kinney established a butcher shop in Mesilla and operated it until a Dona Ana County grand jury indicted him on several counts of "larceny with meat cattle." In November 1877, the grand jury indicted him again, this time for the murder of Sheriff Ysabel Barela.

By now the El Paso Salt War had broken out. John Kinney led a band of New Mexico roughnecks—which probably included Billy the Kid—to San Elizario, Texas, where they terrorized more than they helped. Kinney reportedly killed four Mexicans. Even the Texas Rangers, themselves a rather rowdy group, did not speak in flattering terms of the New Mexico contingent.

Following the Salt War, John Kinney opened the Exchange Saloon in El Paso, the press describing it as "a hangout for the most parasitical." Kinney was indicted for a killing; charges were dropped, and Kinney and his Mesilla Valley warriors rode north and became involved in New Mexico's Lincoln County War. He and his boys helped torch the Alexander McSween home, causing Mrs. McSween to accuse him of arson and murder.

After the "war," Kinney returned to the Mesilla Valley and went on trial for the murder of Sheriff Barela. A jury found him not guilty. During the following year, when Billy the Kid was tried in Mesilla after a change of venue for the murder of the Lincoln

John Kinney (Robert G. McCubbin Collection)

County sheriff William Brady, John Kinney became part of the guard escorting the Kid to Lincoln for a hanging that never took place.

Kinney returned to Rincon, reactivated "the Boys," and continued selling beef to outlying slaughter houses. Pretty soon there wasn't a steer to be found anywhere around Mesilla; residents protested, and the governor sent Col. Albert Jennings Fountain to investigate and halt the thefts. With the pressure on, Kinney tried slipping into Mexico via the rail junction at Lordsburg. However, New Mexico authorities caught him on March 5, 1883, and escorted him in irons to Las Cruces for trial. A jury took eight minutes to find John Kinney guilty. It assessed a $500 fine and five years in prison.

In 1886, Kinney appealed for a new trial and was released from prison. Charges were dropped before the case even returned to court. Kinney subsequently moved to Prescott, Arizona, where he died of Bright's disease on August 25, 1919. His newspaper obituary described him as "one of the most daring and courageous . . . of men who were sacrificing and unflinching to preserve law and order."

See also: BILLY THE KID; EL PASO SALT WAR; EVANS, JESSE J.; FOUNTAIN, ALBERT JENNINGS; LINCOLN COUNTY WAR

KIRCHNER, Carl (1867–1911)

This Texas Ranger started life in Bee County, Texas, and became a first sergeant in July 1895. He worked primarily from far West Texas to the Big Bend area, killed several men, and was with Capt. Frank Jones when Jones gave up his life during a gun battle with Mexican desperadoes at Pirate Island, near El Paso, Texas, on June 30, 1893.

Kirchner retired shortly afterward and opened the Silver King Saloon in El Paso, after marrying a lady from San Antonio. In 1911, he crossed the Rio Grande into Ciudad Juarez, Chihuahua, Mexico, to view the stacks of dead left by the First Battle of Juarez during the Mexican Revolution. He caught typhus from them and died at his El Paso home on January 28. He is buried in El Paso's Concordia Cemetery.

See also: JONES, FRANK

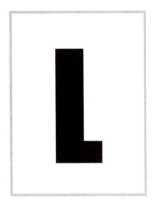

LANE, James Henry (1814–1866)

James Lane, a six-foot, lean, and cadaverous politician, was born in Lawrenceburg, Indiana, lived there half his life, developed fiery oratorical abilities, became lieutenant governor of the state, practiced law, served in the U.S. House of Representatives as well as the Lawrenceburg City Council, and became a colonel during the Mexican War. He moved to Kansas in 1855. He also joined and led the Free State Party, sometimes known as Lane's Brigade. There he became the "Grim Chieftain." Here also he met Charles R. "Doc" Jennison, whose antislavery pillagers became better known as "Jayhawkers." Jennison and his marauders joined Lane's Brigade, pillaging Fort Scott, Kansas, in a sweep that took them all the way to Osceola, Missouri. By now the maniacal Lane had taken to calling himself "the great Jayhawker." He advocated an expedition through Oklahoma and into Texas, the stated purpose being to free slaves wherever found.

Kansas became a state in 1861. Lane became a colonel, a U.S. senator, and a brigadier general, all the while recruiting men for his "Independent Mounted Kansas Jayhawkers," a guerrilla collection of brutes more interested in blood than freedom. Their activities brought them into conflict with the Missouri Bushwhackers, an odious opposition force supporting the Confederate cause. The Bushwhackers and the Jayhawkers, practically all of them murderers, arsonists, and looters, brought multiple miseries to Kansas.

As the Civil War closed down, with Unionists placing the various states under Reconstruction government, the crazed Senator Lane correctly perceived himself as declining in leadership and influence. During a black depression, he shot himself in the mouth and died 10 days later.

See also: ANDERSON, WILLIAM C.; QUANTRILL, WILLIAM CLARKE

LARN, John (1849–1878)

John Larn was reportedly born in Mobile, Alabama, but drifted out to Colorado in his early teens and killed a rancher over the ownership of a horse. In the summer of 1871, when he was 22 years old, he became a trail foreman for Bill Hays, a well-known stockman around Fort Griffin, Texas. During that same year he and 11 cowboys drove a herd of 1,700 cattle north along the Goodnight-Loving Trail to Colorado markets.

Henry Griswold Comstock, a Wisconsin native, wrote an account of the Larn and Hays trek many years later, describing it as a drive that bypassed the inspection stations and was punctuated by frequent murders. According to Comstock, Larn killed two Mexican drovers who were simply passing through and tossed their bodies into the Pecos River to "feed the catfish." Near Fort Concho, Texas, he had a confrontation with "buffalo" (black) soldiers seeking a better count of his cattle. The soldiers finally backed down. Larn later killed a Mexican sheepherder for no other reason than that he was there.

In Colorado, Hays had trouble selling the stock and couldn't leave, so he sent Larn back to Texas to protect his cattle interests. When Hays returned to Texas, however, he noticed that Larn owned practically as many cattle as he did, so Hays and his brother John took most of them and left. When he was 40 miles from Fort Griffin, Texas, however, Larn caught up with him. During a wild battle, both Hays boys were killed. Four cowboys surrendered; within days they were slain "while trying to escape."

Back home near Camp Cooper, Texas, John Larn married Mary Matthews, the daughter of a prominent Shackelford County cattleman. They settled on land soon known as the Camp Cooper Ranch.

Shackelford County in those days had its Old Law Mob, better known as the OLM, a group of vigilantes who evolved into the Tin Hat Brigade. Larn was a member, and so was John Selman, a would-be gunman and cattleman who had recently moved into the area with his wife and children. On February 15, 1876, Larn became sheriff of Shackelford County, and William Cruger and John Selman were his two deputies. On April 2, 1876, Larn and deputies (vigilantes) caught up with the Bill Henderson gang of rustlers. Those who were not shot were lynched. One of those lynched had a sign pinned on his shirt: "He said his name was McBride, but he was a liar as well as a thief." On June 2, the Tin Hat Brigade took two men out of Larn's jail and lynched them too. On December 28, 1876, the *Austin Statesman* noted, "No wonder the highwaymen are seeking security east of the Colorado. Eleven men were hanged ten days ago at Fort Griffin, and four more are enroute to that merciful village."

On the evening of January 17, 1877, two of Larn's friends and associates, Billy Bland and Charlie Reed, thoroughly intoxicated, came riding into Griffin, swearing, yelling, and firing six-shooters. Dismounting, they stomped inside the Bee Hive Saloon, where they continued their rampage. The evening ended with Bland dead, Reed leaving the country, and several more or less innocent bystanders wounded and dead. First Deputy William R. Cruger had done much of the shooting but Larn blamed Cruger for Bland's death.

Larn resigned as sheriff on March 17, 1877, and Cruger took his place. On April 28, Larn and John Selman were appointed deputy inspectors of hides and animals for Shackelford County. It was a license to steal, a permit to shake down ranchers and brokers. However, a rift grew between Larn and Selman on one side, and the other ranchers and businessmen on the other. Larn and Selman withdrew in anger from the Tin Hat Brigade. Even Larn's father-in-law, the well-known and highly respected rancher Joseph Beck Matthews turned against his son-in-law.

Selman had sense enough to pack up his family and leave the county. Larn knew he had troubles, but hoped he could overcome them through relationships and ties. He couldn't. On the night of June 22, 1878, a group of Tin Hat members gathered while Sheriff Cruger and deputies took Larn into custody and transported him to the Albany jail, where chains and shackles were fastened to his legs. Late that night, he was awakened by masked men—some say nine, some say more. At least one was a brother-in-law. Because they knew him, they decided not to lynch him. Instead, nine rifles cracked in the night air. Larn's wife Mary took the body home and buried it in the backyard of the Camp Cooper ranch house, where a tombstone marks the grave today.

See also: CRUGER, WILLIAM R.; SELMAN, JOHN HENRY

LAUSTENNEAU, W. H. (a.k.a. Three Fingered Jack) (1869–1906)

W. H. Laustenneau was a firebrand. The Austrian's hand had been damaged in an industrial accident or a bare-knuckles barroom brawl of undetermined origin, but because of the deformity, Mexicans called him *Mocho* (crippled hand). Americans dubbed him "Three Fingered Jack." Otherwise, some folks called him a desperado, while others simply used the term "agitator." But wherever he went, Three Fingered Jack Laustenneau either stirred up trouble or inspired others to do so.

He debuted at the Morenci copper mines in southeastern Arizona Territory, at the behest of an anarchistic extremist group based in Chicago. With Progressive movement gaining strength throughout the United States, the Arizona legislature in 1903 passed an eight-hour workday limitation for underground miners "except in cases of emergency where life or property were in eminent [*sic*] danger." The resultant consequence of shorter workweeks naturally led to a decrease in wages, facts agitating to the miners and labor union activists. Labor demanded more money. Management resisted. All the while, Three Fingered Jack fueled the fires of discontent.

On June 1, 1903, roughly 3,000 miners walked off their jobs as Three Fingered Jack extolled the virtues of union membership. He advocated the destruction of mine and railroad property, as well as the pillaging of company-owned stores. Threats like this brought the Arizona Rangers as well as the Arizona National Guard to the scene. The federal government dispatched troops from Forts Grant and Huachuca. A military contingent of soldiers arrived from Texas.

Arizona Rangers Johnny Foster and Bud Bassett swiftly arrested Three Fingered Jack Laustenneau, while a horrific thunderstorm helped cool the other boiling tempers. In the end, that thunderstorm probably saved lives, even though up to 20 local residents drowned in the torrential downpour. Three Fingered Jack continued to organize convicts, activities earning him two years in the Yuma Penitentiary. There he incited work stoppages and threatened to clog prison administration with frivolous lawsuits. Those threats earned him solitary confinement. As he sweated and stewed for nearly three months in the dungeon, Laustenneau plotted. Finally, he was returned to the prison mainstream, but he was not a broken man.

On April 28, 1904, accompanied by 14 other prisoners, Three Fingered Jack led an assault on the lockup's armory, in the process taking Superintendent Frank S. Griffith and his assistant hostage. Alert guards, however, fired into the rioting prisoners. They wounded three. The others, including Jack, surrendered.

For his leadership and participation in the attempted outbreak, Three Fingered Jack received an additional 10 years. However, two years later, on August 20, 1906, Laustenneau died in the prison hospital. The jail physician said he died of "apoplexy caused by inner rage at his personal confinement."

See also: ARIZONA RANGERS

LAW And Order

As a general rule, a sheriff was the chief law enforcement officer of every county in every state. He generally had as many deputies as county finances would allow. As for the communities, they generally had a chief of police or city marshal, who also had as many assistant marshals or policemen as finances would

allow. A city marshal or sheriff's duties in the old days often involved shooting stray dogs, keeping order in the saloons, showing up at legal hangings, rounding up jurors, and occasionally clearing stray cattle off the streets. A lawman may or may not have had a badge, and except in the larger cities he seldom wore anything that could be identified as a uniform. Residents generally recognized their officers by sight, and those who did not usually got acquainted in a hurry.

Every hamlet and large city also had its justices of the peace, these officers having a smattering of legal experience. While they could make arrests, as a general rule they handled the paperwork after arrests were made.

A few states, such as Texas, had rangers, a system that worked quite well; the Texas Rangers still exist. Other states, such as New Mexico and Arizona, tried similar ranger law enforcement systems but discarded them after a brief period.

United States marshals, and deputy marshals dealt with crimes that were federal in nature; these lawmen were especially active in the territory of Arizona and in the Oklahoma Territory. Once a territory became a state, the marshal's power diminished somewhat; he now had jurisdiction only for federal offenses, such as selling liquor to the Indians and mail robbery.

Execution in the American Wild West practically always meant hanging, firing squads coming in a very distant second. Trials tended to be quick, appeals even quicker. The period between verdict and execution could range from several weeks or months down to hours or even minutes. Jail and prison conditions ranged from dismal to brutal. There was no such thing as rehabilitation, except as a well-meaning but obscure concept.

See also: ARIZONA RANGERS; FEDERAL MARSHALS AND DEPUTY MARSHALS; JAILS AND PRISONS; SHERIFFS; TEXAS RANGERS

LAY, William Ellsworth (a.k.a. Elza Lay; William McGinnis) (1868–1934)

Elza Lay—the "Elza" no doubt coming from his middle name—was born in Mount Pleasant, Ohio, on November 25, 1868. Soon after his birth, his farming family began moving west until it reached Colorado. By that time Elza was old enough to strike out on his own. He drifted into Vernal, Utah, probably met Butch Cassidy, and opened a gambling hall, where he allegedly passed counterfeit money. The government closed that down, so in 1896 he wandered over to Brown's Park, where he and Butch Cassidy reportedly peddled counterfeit currency smuggled in from Canada.

By some accounts Elza Lay, and not Butch Cassidy, masterminded the initial string of Wild Bunch train and bank robberies. On August 13, 1896, the Butch Cassidy gang, still in the process of formation, rode into Montpelier, Idaho, and robbed the bank. On April 21, 1897, the gang robbed the Pleasant Valley Coal Company. Elza now drifted south, hooked up with the Black Jack Ketchum outlaws, and in July 1899 helped rob a train at Folsom, New Mexico. By most accounts, the outlaws rode away with $70,000, but also with a posse in pursuit. During a wild shootout in Turkey Creek Canyon, two lawmen died, and the outlaws Sam Ketchum and Elza Lay were badly wounded. Sam was captured but died later of his wounds.

In August of that same year, Sheriff Cicero Stewart captured Lay in Eddy County, New Mexico. A jury convicted him of the murder of Huerfano County, Colorado, sheriff Edward J. Farr, killed during the gun battle in Turkey Creek Canyon. A jury gave him life in prison, but in 1906 the governor pardoned him in return for helping quell a prison riot. He married, raised two daughters, worked as a gambler in Mexico, became head watermaster for the Imperial Valley Irrigation System, and spent a period on Skid Row in Los Angeles. He died at Los Angeles on November 10, 1934, and is buried in Forest Lawn Cemetery.

See also: BROWN'S PARK; CARVER, WILLIAM RICHARD; CASSIDY, BUTCH; CURRY, GEORGE SUTHERLAND; KETCHUM, SAMUEL W.; KILPATRICK, BENJAMIN ARNOLD; LOGAN, HARVEY; SUNDANCE KID; TURKEY CREEK CANYON, BATTLE OF WILD BUNCH

LAZURE, Charley (a.k.a. Charley Hadley, T. H. Thorne; Long Necked Charley; Rattlesnake Dick) (1859–1887)

Little is known about the origins of Charley Lazure, and even less about his exit from the panoramic western stage. Maybe that's the way history intended it to be, since he was an outlaw and evidently not a successful one. From the best information at hand, it appears that "Long Necked Charley," among other aliases, was born in Cincinnati, Ohio. At the age of 16, the tall and skinny lad drifted to southwestern

New Mexico Territory, via short sojourns in Colorado and Santa Fe, during 1882. Somewhere along the line, he either shot himself in the thigh or someone did it for him. The details are a mystery.

Reportedly, he worked in the mines at Eureka in southern Grant County, but he later chose the life of a rustler, becoming a working member of what was often referred to as the Old San Simon Gang. If in fact he was the guilty party who stole a horse and a mule from a Mr. Dobbins, he gave the pursuing posse the slip somewhere in the Sulphur Springs Valley of Arizona.

On August 15, 1883, at Tombstone, his luck ran out. Officers accompanied the manacled prisoner during the train trip back to New Mexico, where at Separ, the no-nonsense Deputy Dan Tucker took custody of "Long Necked Charley." At the next day's hearing, the complainant failed to show, so Lazure was released, to the displeasure of townsmen grown tired of rustlers and thieves.

At Silver City, in 1885, he and a man named Cunningham involved themselves in a gun duel. The authorities again arrested Long Necked Charley, but he was released on a bond posted by the ex-sheriff of Grant County, Harvey Howard Whitehill.

Charley showed up next 11 miles west of Silver City at the bubbling mining camp of Fleming, a rough town doing its best to keep Chinese and Mexicans from working there. Here Charley stole two horses from Thomas Kendall, one of Fleming's founding fathers. The young outlaw then rode to Socorro, New Mexico, where he was arrested at D. Z. Moor's livery stable by Sheriff Charles T. Russell. It was a case beyond reasonable doubt, since Charley still had the two stolen steeds. Delivered back to the county seat at Silver City for trial, he was found guilty and sentenced on August 2, 1885, to two years in the territorial penitentiary at Santa Fe.

Two years later, Long Necked Charley Lazure, granted a governor's pardon on May 4, 1887, heard the prison door close behind him. Thereafter he either kept a low profile and dropped from sight or changed his name again.

See also: WHITEHILL, HARVEY HOWARD

LEE, A. Mitchell (a.k.a. Mitch) (1863–1884)

This Texas cowboy entered history for the first and only time when he drifted into western New Mexico and recruited associates named Christopher "Kit" Joy, Frank Taggart, a black cowhand, and George Washington Cleveland. They robbed the Southern Pacific train near Gage Station on November 24, 1883. In the process, they murdered the train engineer. Lee was soon arrested, but on March 10, 1884, he and his friends broke out of the Silver City jail, only to be recaptured swiftly. Surrounded by irate posse members, with a rope around his neck, and urged to get right with Jesus, an exasperated Lee finally blurted out "Well, by God! I did kill that train engineer." At that moment the wagon rolled out from under him, and Lee swung out into eternity.

See also: CLEVELAND, GEORGE WASHINGTON; JOY, CHRISTOPHER; TAGGART, FRANK

LEE, Beauregard (1868–1900)

Born in August 1868 in Virginia to James and Susan Lee, Beauregard moved with his family to Raton, New Mexico, where he grew into a tall, dashing, and very enterprising detective working for the Atchison, Topeka & Sante Fe Railroad. By March 1895, he already had quite a reputation for careful police work and fearlessness when he decided to try his hand at tracking the New Mexico desperado Martin Mrose and his wife, Beulah. Although every competent lawman in Arizona, New Mexico, and Texas was looking for the pair, Beauregard Lee was smart enough to stake out the hotels in Ciudad Juarez, Mexico, across the Rio Grande from El Paso, Texas. He soon spotted an attractive woman, with a four-year-old daughter, who fit the description. Keeping the woman under surveillance, he learned she had purchased a train ticket deeper into Mexico. Lee enlisted the help of Mexican policeman Francisco Haro, and on April 6, 1895, the two boarded a train and followed the woman. In Chihuahua City a large man resembling her husband approached and embraced her, and Lee rushed up and placed him under arrest. It was one of the most sensational arrests of the day.

The authorities released Beulah Mrose, and she moved to El Paso, Texas, to live with her attorney, John Wesley Hardin. Martin Mrose went to jail in Juarez but was later freed. He was shot to death on June 29, 1895, by officers after he crossed the Mexican railroad bridge into El Paso.

Beauregard Lee made several trips to El Paso after that, appearances no doubt having a lot to do with the reward money. In 1897, he married in Raton, New Mexico. He and his wife separated after a couple of years, and she took their young son to Chicago.

According to family tradition, Lee was slain by outlaws sometime in 1900.

See also: HARDIN, JOHN WESLEY; MILTON, JEFFERSON; MROSE, HELEN; MROSE, MARTIN; SELMAN, JOHN HENRY

LEE, Oliver Milton (1865–1941)

New Mexico rancher and accused murderer Oliver Lee started life at Buffalo Gap, near Abilene, Texas, and in 1884 moved to New Mexico, settling on a ranch near Dog Canyon on the west side of the Sacramento Mountains, only a short distance from Alamogordo, New Mexico. A series of feuds soon developed, and Lee came under suspicion regarding

Oliver M. Lee (Author's Collection)

150

the deaths of several ranchers, even though his Dog Canyon Ranch and Circle Cross brand quickly became dominant in the region. On February 12, 1893, Lee and nearby rancher William McNew killed cowboys Matt Cofelt and Charles Rhodius near El Paso, claiming both had been rustlers.

Three years later, in February 1896, near Chalk Hill, on today's White Sands Missile Range in New Mexico, Col. Albert J. Fountain and his eight-year-old-son, Henry, turned up missing. Oliver Lee, William McNew, and Jim Gilliland became the immediate suspects, the reasoning being that Fountain had recently obtained cattle-rustling indictments against Lee.

Pat Garrett, the Dona Ana County, New Mexico, sheriff, now took to the field in search of these men but was himself captured, and a deputy was slain, when both tried to slip up on the outlaws at Wildy Well on the Lee Ranch.

Lee and New Mexico state senator A. B. Fall now arranged for the creation of Otero County in southern New Mexico, where the wanted men could surrender to Sheriff George Curry. Nevertheless, Garrett still took Lee and Gilliland to trial in Hillsboro, New Mexico, for the Fountain murders. Both were acquitted. On February 29, 1908, when Garrett was mysteriously slain while traveling in a buckboard not many miles from the Lee Ranch, Oliver Lee's name surfaced as a murder suspect. However, no indictments ever came down.

Lee later became a New Mexico state senator, well known around the state and in the Southwest. He had nine children and died in Alamogordo.

See also: FOUNTAIN, ALBERT JENNINGS; GARRETT, PATRICK FLOYD JARVIS

LEE-PEACOCK Feud

The renowned historian C. L. Sonnichsen, in his Texas feuds book *I'll Die Before I'll Run,* discussed the "Lee-Peacock feud," but the struggle itself was much broader than that—in fact, so broad that the Lees and Peacocks almost get lost in it. In a sense it began with John Hugh "Irish Jack" Dixon, who moved from Indiana to Illinois to Missouri, and in 1858 migrated into Pilot Grove in Grayson County, Texas, where he farmed. Grayson, Fannin, Hunt, and Collin Counties intersected at Four Corners, near that site; there thickets lured renegades, desperadoes, Union sympathizers, and Confederate deserters. During Reconstruction, Jack entered the freight-hauling business with his sons Billy, Simpson (Simp), Bob, and Charles, plus Dick Johnson, a half-brother.

Bob Lee, one of John Dixon's cousins, a handsome, tall, and muscular man, had fought in the Confederate army under the brilliant cavalry commander Gen. Nathan Forrest. Back in Texas, Lee clashed verbally as well as physically with Lewis Peacock, a former Missouri wagon maker who lived near Pilot Grove. Peacock also organized the Union League; one of the men he recruited was Henry Boren, a Unionist but also a cousin of Bob Lee.

As the feud heated up, on June 6, 1868, Bob Lee wrote a letter to the *Texas News* accusing the Union men led by Lewis Peacock of dragging him out of his sickbed and leading him into the thickets near Pilot Knob, where they took his mule, saddle, bridle, and a $20 gold piece. He had then agreed to leave the country forever after signing a note to them for $2,000 in gold. The note was written by mixing water with gunpowder for ink and using a toothpick for a pen. Lewis Peacock had then shot Bob Lee in the face, left him for dead, and shortly afterward murdered a doctor who treated him.

Reprisals came quickly. Peacock was wounded, and two supporters, Dow Nance and John Baldoc, slain. The U.S. Army then became involved, with Gen. J. J. Reynolds posting rewards for Bob Lee, dead or alive. A year later, in June 1869, as Bob Lee left his ranch house, cousin Henry Boren shot him dead on the porch. Henry then rode home to a dance already in progress in his house.

A day later, Bill Boren, a cousin of Henry's who had served with Bob Lee in the Confederate cavalry, rode up to Henry Boren's home, called Henry out, and shot him dead on the porch. He later explained it with a letter written to Henry's brother:

I know that you are aware that my feelings were against the Union, and Henry was with us at the first . . . I felt no anxiousness when Henry joined the Unionist cause as we had never seen eye to eye on matters anyway, and I though that this was just another dispute, but this friendliness with the Peacock faction against Cousin Bob Lee was a thorn in all our sides. Still I felt no anxiousness. Then Henry stained the proud Texas name of Boren with the blood of cousin Bob Lee.

Bill Boren also mentioned costs paid by other families. "Haven't we all lost a brother in this cause?" he asked. "I know you will recall that my brother Isham died at the hands of the same Unionists and war mongers that Henry saw fit to join up with."

Meanwhile, the Dixons fared just as harshly as the Borens. They too had supported the Bob Lee faction. Peacock partisans and U.S. soldiers surprised 16-year-old Billy and Charlie while the Dixons were hauling cotton to Jefferson, Texas. They captured both brothers at Hog-Eye, lashed them to a wagon wheel, and whipped them. Billy died, and his slayers looted his body, taking even his spurs.

The Peacock faction next ambushed Jack Dixon and his sons, Bob and Charlie, plus Dick Johnson, while the Dixons were cutting timber at Black Jack Grove. Bob and Charles died. Jack and Dick, wounded, crawled into the brush and escaped. After the assassins had left, Dick loaded the two dead family members into an ox cart and took them home for burial.

A few years later Johnson had his revenge. On June 28, 1871, a Galveston newspaper called *Flake's Bulletin* wrote *finis* to the Lee-Peacock feud, writing that "we are credibly informed that the famous Lewis Peacock, formerly commander-in-chief of the Peacock Party, was shot to atoms this morning in his yard. May God grant this sinful world, peace."

See also: DIXSON, SIMPSON; HARDIN, JOHN WESLEY

LEES, Isaiah Wrigles (1830–1902)

This famous San Francisco detective was born in England but migrated to New Jersey, where he became a mechanical engineer. By 1849 he had arrived in California in the Gold Rush. There he worked as a miner before a chance encounter with a San Francisco policeman led him to solve a murder that resulted in San Francisco's first legal hanging, that of José Rodríquez in December 1852. A year later Lees joined the police department and rose quickly to captain as well as detective. He started a rogues' gallery, taking daguerreotypes of arrested criminals. He studied cause and effect, clipping crime stories out of newspapers and magazines, taking care to record names, ages, descriptions, and modus operandi. He poured over criminal materials and corresponded with detectives around the world.

His crime library numbered over a thousand volumes. These and scrapbooks altogether consumed a large room, where one could always find him actively at work. It all paid off as he cracked one celebrated case after another, even traveling to other countries in response to requests for his expertise. In many instances he made his own arrests, being shot, clubbed, kicked, punched, and stabbed on several occasions. When he retired as chief of the San Francisco Police in 1900, he was a legendary figure, one of the world's best known detectives. William Pinkerton called him "the greatest criminal catcher the West ever knew." He died on December 21, 1902, and is buried in San Francisco's Laurel Hill Cemetery.

LeFORS, Joe (1865–1940)

This lawman, one of six children, originally came out of Lamar County, Texas, but grew up in Indian Territory (Oklahoma). LeFors made several cattle drives to Kansas, hauled mail, fought Indians, and worked as a trader. By the mid-1880s he was driving cattle into Dodge City, running wild horses, and hiring out to the Wyoming Land and Cattle Company. He learned to speak Sioux and to talk in sign language. As a livestock inspector, however, he went after the cattle rustlers. In particular, he led cattleman invasions into the Hole-in-the-Wall country, sometimes being driven out himself and sometimes recovering batches of livestock and shooting a few rustlers. At one time he had 17 men locked in the Newcastle, Wyoming, jail.

Due to his successes, he became a U.S. deputy marshal with headquarters in Cheyenne, Wyoming, and began concentrating on train robbers. Meanwhile, the famous scout and manhunter Tom Horn had come under suspicion for the slaying for hire of 15-year-old Willie Nickel. Horn mistakenly had killed the son instead of the father. Horn and LeFors sat in a room drinking and talking, discussing aspects of their careers; but unknown to Horn, LeFors had stationed a court reporter and a U.S. deputy marshal in an adjoining room. They took notes regarding the conversation, and although Horn denied he ever confessed to killing Willie, he went to the hangman's rope.

In 1908, Joe LeFors went to work for the Wool Growers Association and did his best to bring peace between sheep men and cattlemen. After that he lived briefly in Argentina before returning to California.

He then moved back to Buffalo, Wyoming, where he died on October 1, 1940.

See also: HOLE-IN-THE-WALL; HORN, TOM

LeROY, Kitty (1849–1870)

This actress, or "jig dancer," as some called her, had moved from Dallas to Deadwood, South Dakota, during the 1870s. There she allegedly married 27 men while still finding time to dance in all the community's major gambling houses and theaters. She then married faro dealer Sam Curley, who apparently knew little or nothing about her background. Sam killed her when he found out; he later shot himself.

LESLIE, Nashville Franklin (a.k.a. Buckskin Frank Leslie) (1842–1920?)

By some accounts the gunman Buckskin Frank Leslie was born in Galveston, Texas, although he once claimed that his father's name was Kennedy and his mother's name Leslie. He was an army scout during the 1870s, serving in the Dakotas, Oklahoma, and Texas. By 1878 he had hit San Francisco, where he attended bar and opened his own saloon before drifting to Tombstone, Arizona, arriving with Tom Horn around September 1880. Here he filed on several mining claims and worked as a bartender in the Oriental Saloon, reportedly the finest saloon between St. Louis and San Francisco. In his off hours, for sport, Leslie supposedly shot flies off the ceilings of less prominent Allen Street saloons. Leslie also had a bent for painted women, and in Tombstone he became involved with Mrs. Mike Killeen. When the husband objected, Frank and a friend, George Perrine, on June 22, 1880, put several bullets in him. The husband died a few days later. A couple of weeks after that, the widow married Buckskin Frank.

On March 15, 1881, someone held up the Bisbee stage, killing the driver and a passenger. Buckskin Frank led the posse, but for all his tracking skills, the posse just went in circles. Leslie later reportedly told Wyatt Earp that Sheriff John Behan had paid him to lead the posse astray. Leslie remained friends with Earp, but he was never a close associate. As for the feud between the Earps and the Clantons, Leslie did his best to avoid involvement.

Two years later in July, Leslie reportedly killed the famed gunman John Ringo. However, that slaying remains as mysterious now as it was then, and few historians believe Leslie pulled the trigger. Leslie had always been noted for embroidering on the truth.

On November 14, 1882, he killed the red-headed, hot-tempered William Claiborne, often known as Billy the Kid Claiborne. The Kid had challenged Leslie outside Tombstone's Oriental Saloon. The two met in the middle of the street in something akin to a classic "high noon" walkdown. Claiborne fired first, but Leslie fired straight.

Leslie lost his job at the Oriental and turned to ranching in the Swisshelm Mountains, 20 miles south of Tombstone. Growing bored with that, he scouted for the army during the Indian wars. In 1886, he worked briefly as a mounted customs inspector before returning to ranching. His wife, the former May Killeen, divorced him for adultery in September 1887. (She returned to Tombstone, married a freight hauler, moved with him to the West Coast, and died in Banning, California, on March 27, 1947.)

Leslie now spent much of his time in the Tombstone Birdcage Theater, where he met a bosomy, hard-drinking singer named Mollie Bradshaw. She already had a boyfriend, but when the fellow turned up dead in an alley, she and Buckskin retired to his ranch. However, when Leslie rode home on the evening of July 10, 1889, he found Mollie and a hired man called "Six Shooter Jim" wrapped up in each others arms on the front porch. Leslie shot Mollie first and Jim second. Jim survived to testify, and on January 9, 1890, Leslie was sentenced to life in the Yuma Territorial Prison. In prison he worked as a druggist and practiced good behavior. Governor Franklin gave him a full pardon on November 17, 1896. Two weeks later, on December 1, the 55-year-old Leslie married the 39-year-old, divorced Belle Stowell, who had corresponded with him.

At this point, Buckskin Frank Leslie seems to have dropped from sight. Stories are that he became a drifter, living and drinking and fighting in San Francisco, trying his luck in the Alaska gold rush, and mopping saloons in California. Rumors exist, but there is no evidence that he committed suicide around 1922. In any case, no one ever recalled seeing him again.

See also: EARP, WYATT BERRY STAPP; HORN, TOM; RINGO, JOHN PETERS; YUMA TERRITORIAL PRISON

LEVY, James H. (1842–1882)

Back at the turn of the 20th century, when journalists and moviemakers first captured America's attention with thrilling exploits of western heroes and badmen, they passed over James H. "Jim" Levy. They shouldn't have.

Levy, a Jew, was born in Ireland but emigrated to the United States. Before long he reached eastern Nevada, stopping at Pioche, a rough and tumultuous mining camp. By 1871, Jim was considered a gambling man with a bad attitude. In front of Freudenthal's General Store, during an argument over $5,000, Levy shot Mike Casey, then violently battered him with a six-shooter into permanent unconsciousness. In retaliation, Dave Neagle, an up-and-coming gunfighter, commenced shooting at Levy, one bullet puncturing both of Levy's cheeks and shattering his jaw. From that point forward Jim Levy's poisonous disposition matched his evil-appearing exterior. In 1873, Jim Levy was arrested for killing Thomas Ryan, although he got cleared of the charges due either to a lack of evidence or because no one was foolish enough to testify against him.

Levy now left for Virginia City; in 1876 he moved to Deadwood, in the Black Hills country of Dakota Territory. During March of 1877, Jim made appearances at Cheyenne, on one occasion getting into a row at the Shingle & Locke Saloon with fellow gambler Charlie Harrison. Although accounts vary, it appears that Harrison didn't like Irishmen, or Jews, and he unwisely boasted of that to Levy's face. The two quarreled. Harrison left, only to return and find Levy leaning against a post in front of French's Saloon at the corner of Eddy and 16th Streets. Harrison quickly pulled his revolver and emptied it. Unflinching and unscathed, Jim Levy dropped Harrison with one shot, then casually walked over to the prostrate and helpless cardsharp and shot him again. Levy stuck his six-shooter in his waistband, strolled around the corner, and ordered oysters for supper. There he was arrested; he was later released.

By 1882, the thoroughly dangerous Jim Levy moved to Tombstone and then to Tucson, where he and faro dealer John Murphy quarreled in the Fashion Saloon. Intermediaries broke it up but not before both parties agreed to fight a duel south of the border, in Old Mexico, at dawn. However, that night, accompanied by Bill Moyer and Dave Gibson, Murphy noticed Levy standing in front of the Palace Hotel. He immediately opened fire. Levy ducked the wrong way, running into, rather than away from, the fusillade. He died as a result of the miscalculation.

LEYBA, Marino (1859–1887)

This horse thief and mankiller was born in New Mexico and was said to have been an associate at times of Billy the Kid. During 1880, he killed, or at least helped kill, Charles Porter in Bernalillo County, New Mexico, and on December 10, 1880, he attempted to kill Lincoln County sheriff Pat Garrett who, in turn shot, wounded, and arrested Leyba in Puerta del Luna. Leyba got seven years for trying to kill Garrett and one month for trying to steal livestock, but he was pardoned on July 21, 1886. A year later, on March 29, he and others killed three ranchers in San Miguel County. Leyba was himself slain shortly afterward near Golden, New Mexico, by Deputy Sheriffs Joaquin Montoya and Carlos Jacomo.

See also: GARRETT, PATRICK FLOYD JARVIS

LINCOLN County War

The Lincoln County War is easy to understand and yet very complicated. It was primarily a mercantile war, but it was also a range war. In 1866, two army officers, Lawrence G. Murphy and Emil Fritz, stationed at Fort Stanton, New Mexico, took their discharges and set up a mercantile business (known as "the House") in Lincoln, New Mexico. They were supported by the Santa Fe Ring, which—politically and to a large extent economically—controlled the entire territory. Thomas B. Catron, a U.S. attorney and Ring organizer, had his political imprint all over New Mexico. The House became something of a Ring subsidiary.

Within a brief time, Lincoln attorney Alexander McSween and wealthy Englishman John Tunstall arose in opposition to the House. Tunstall opened a store and his own bank in Lincoln. To complicate matters further, cattleman John Chisum established a ranch near the village of Fort Sumner, New Mexico, and essentially aligned himself with the McSween/Tunstall faction. Both the House and Tunstall/McSween envisioned profits in dealing with the post of Fort Stanton and the adjacent Mescalero Apache Indian reservation.

When Emil Fritz died in Germany, a young, feisty Irishman named James J. Dolan took his place in

John Tunstall (University of Texas at El Paso Archives)

the firm. Until now, relations between the Lincoln parties had been fairly amiable, so much so that Dolan and Murphy retained McSween to collect the $10,000 Fritz life insurance money. McSween did so and settled up with everybody, except for $2,000 he held back in case other claimants also filed for the money.

The House demanded the $2,000, and as charges and countercharges swept across the community, as court suits piled one on top of another, both sides began hiring guns. The House controlled Sheriff William Brady, who dispatched deputies to the Tunstall Ranch to "recover" horses. Along the way the group collided with another from the ranch. Tunstall's cowboys, Billy the Kid and others, outnumbered, knew enough to flee. Tunstall did not. He foolishly rode up to the "posse" and was shot dead.

Tunstall's body reached Lincoln on the following day, and Justice of the Peace John B. Wilson issued murder warrants for posse members: Jesse Evans, James J. Dolan, Frank Baker, George Hindman,

William Morton, Thomas Hill, and others. The town constable, Atanacio Martínez, and deputies Fred Waite and Billy the Kid, attempted to serve those warrants but were rebuffed by Sheriff William Brady. Instead, the sheriff threw Martínez and his deputies briefly into the pit jail.

A few days later, Wilson deputized Dick Brewer as a special constable. His deputies were Henry Brown, Sam Smith, Jim French, John Middleton, Fred Waite, Doc Scurlock, Charlie Bowdre, and Billy the Kid. They called themselves "the Regulators." The Lincoln County War, although no one ever referred to it as that at the time, had begun. The Regulators almost immediately caught two Tunstall slayers, William Morton and Frank Baker. They shot the accused to death on March 9 under circumstances still obscure.

On April 1, 1878, Sheriff William Brady, with deputies George Hindman alongside and Jack Long, George Peppin, and Billy Mathews bringing up the rear, began walking along Lincoln's main street toward a reported disturbance at the opposite end. Off to the side, behind adobe walls, an assortment of gunmen—including Jim French, Fred Waite, Henry Brown, John Middleton, and Billy the Kid—rose up and commenced firing. They killed Brady and Hindman and wounded Mathews. The gunmen escaped.

Three days later, on April 4, the Regulators, with Dick Brewer as leader, showed up at Blazer's Mill in the Sacramento Mountains. While eating, they noticed Andrew Roberts (historically known as Buckshot Roberts) approaching. A confrontation started. Charlie Bowdre shot Roberts in the stomach, and Roberts commenced firing also. A bullet slightly wounded the Kid, and still another ricocheted off the cartridge belt of Charlie Bowdre and tore a finger off George Coe.

With the regulators scattering, Roberts stumbled inside the building, pulled a mattress to the doorway, and sprawled across it. Dick Brewer sought a clear line of fire from across the canyon, but as he was preparing to fire, Roberts killed him with a long shot to the forehead. The demoralized Regulators now rode away. Roberts died the next day. He and Brewer were buried side by side on a nearby hill.

During mid-April, the Lincoln County commissioners nominated John Copeland for sheriff, and 10-man grand jury handed down roughly 200 indictments. Frank McNab became captain of the Regulators. However, on April 29, a group of Seven Rivers men ambushed and killed McNab. Doc Scurlock now assumed command of the Regulators. Then on May 28, Governor Samuel B. Axtell removed the pro-McSween John Copeland from the office of sheriff and installed George Peppin, a pro-House man.

Peppin and his posse chased the Regulators through the mountains and finally drove them into Lincoln on July 15, 1878. McSween and several fighters occupied the 12-room McSween home, while the others took refuge in the nearby Tunstall, Ellis, and Montano stores. Since nobody surrendered, Sheriff Peppin and roughly 40 deputies put the McSween group under siege. He requested and received military assistance from Fort Stanton. Thirty-five soldiers (a company of infantry and one of cavalry), a Gatling gun and a 12-pound mountain howitzer took up positions in the street. The military thus patrolled back and forth, making it difficult for McSween supporters to shoot over their heads, but easy for the deputies to fire into the buildings.

The final day of battle, July 19, found the Regulators' numbers reduced, as McSween's forces had quietly deserted the other buildings and vanished. McSween now had perhaps 10 or 15 people left, each in his own house. Three were women, who were permitted to leave.

Sometime during that morning, a fire started in the kitchen. All day long the flames ate their way through the wood, forcing the men from one room to another. Shortly after dark, generally one at a time, the defenders dashed through the smoke and flames toward the safety of the Bonito River. Most of them, including Billy the Kid, made it.

From the house, Alexander McSween called out that he wished to surrender. Bob Beckwith, a respected member of the community, offered to accept. But as they came together, gunfire echoed from everywhere. McSween and Beckwith died on the spot. McSween was buried near where his house had once stood; the exact grave site has never been determined.

The Lincoln County War thus ended with dramatic suddenness. Within a brief time, buffalo hunter Pat Garrett would be elected sheriff of Lincoln County. His number-one job would be to hunt down Billy the Kid.

See also: BILLY THE KID; BOWDRE, CHARLES; EVANS, JESSE J.; GARRETT, PATRICK FLOYD JARVIS

LOFTIS, Hillary U. (a.k.a. Hill Loftis; Tom Ross; Charles Gannon) (1871–1929)

At an early age, this future outlaw left his birthplace in northeastern Mississippi and went to Texas, working on the famed Dan Waggoner ranch in the Red River country, north of Vernon, in Wilbarger County. For whatever reason, Loftis joined several Dalton/Doolin Gang veterans, like George "Red Buck" Weightman, ex-Panhandle lawman and proven mankiller Joe Beckham, and a pitiless cowboy named Elmer "Kid" Lewis. On December 24, 1895, the quartet robbed the Waggoner company store, beat the clerk severely, and then proceeded to a nearby store and post office for more pillage.

Afterward, the outlaws, seeking shelter, holed up in a line-rider's dugout but were eventually surrounded by a posse led by a Texas Ranger sergeant. In an ensuing shootout and siege, Joe Beckham was killed, but the posse, because of extraordinarily cold weather, forfeited the battlefield. "Red Buck," Lewis, and Hillary Loftis escaped under cover of darkness. The following comments regarding Loftis went into *The Ranger's Bible*, a list of desperately wanted Texas fugitives:

Wanted for highway robbery, Hill Loftis. Age about 32, height 5 feet 9 inches, weight 160 pounds. Has a very peculiarly shaped head, being very long behind with a high forehead. Occupation, cowboy. Probably in New Mexico. Indicted in 1896. Reward by sheriff of Wilbarger County.

Hillary Loftis assumed a new name, Tom Ross, and then rode hard for parts unknown to the locals. After spending time in Canada, he returned to the Texas/New Mexico border and immersed himself in the cow business, working as a foreman during area roundups, even establishing a ranch of his own that straddled the state line. Learning of his whereabouts and his new identity, Sheriff Charles Tom and Capt. John H. Rogers of the Texas Rangers went to arrest the fugitive. Captain Rogers reports what happened next:

In June 1904, while scouting in the plains country near the line of New Mexico, I made an unsuccessful attempt to arrest Hill Loftis, alias Tom Ross; he ran out of shooting distance from me, thereby avoiding arrest. Later in the day he waylaid me, shooting my horse in the jaw, getting the drop on me with a big Winchester, while I had only a pistol. I was completely in his power; and it looked as if he would kill me in spite of all I could do or say. This party is an old time robber of a hard gang.

Meanwhile, two Texas and Southwestern Cattle Raisers Association inspectors, Horace Roberson and Dave Allison, filed indictments against Loftis in eastern New Mexico and were in the process of preparing a cattle-thieving case against "Ross" on the Texas side of the line. Gathering up one of his partners in crime, Milt Good, plus shotguns, rifles, and revolvers, "Ross" proceeded to Seminole, Texas, where on the night of April 1, 1923, he murdered Roberson and Allison. Later, after a lengthy trial in Lubbock, Texas, he was sent to the Texas penitentiary.

Two years later in the company of Milt Good, and others, Loftis/Ross escaped and fled to the Northwest. After several trips back to the Southwest, he and Good parted company, and Loftis/Ross, this time under the name of Charles Gannon, became a Canadian cowboy. There, according to newspaper reports, he killed a Chinese cook and fled back into the United States, where he took a job on the Frye Cattle Company's Blackfoot Reservation operation near Browning, Montana. Loftis, a.k.a. Ross, a.k.a. Gannon, got into a dispute with ranch foreman Ralph Haywood and settled the dispute by shooting him dead. Knowing he would have to answer to new murder charges, and knowing full well he was still a much-wanted fugitive from the Lone Star State, Hillary U. Loftis entered the bunkhouse and committed suicide.

See also: ALLISON, WILLIAM DAVIS; GOOD, MILTON PAUL

LOGAN, Harvey (a.k.a. Kid Curry) (1865–1904)

Of all the Wild Bunch figures, one of the least known but most dangerous was Harvey Logan, often known as Kid Curry, a part–Cherokee Indian born in Kentucky. He was primarily raised by an aunt in Missouri, drifted to Wyoming, became involved in the Johnson County War, and joined the so-called Red Sash Gang. He appeared next in Landusky, Montana, driving a herd of stolen cattle. There he quarreled with Pike Landusky, the town's founder, humiliated him inside a saloon, knocked him down, and while he was trying to get up, shot him to death.

A year later, in January 1896, Harvey and his two brothers, John and Lonie, assaulted the Jim Winters ranch house, but Winters was waiting and killed Johnny Logan with rifle fire. Harvey was the one who fled this time, moving over to the Hole-in-the-Wall country, where he and his brother Lonie teamed up with Butch Cassidy's Wild Bunch. Logan actually became the wildest of them all, in particular becoming a cohort of George "Flatnose" Curry—which was probably where the Logan alias "Kid Curry" came from. On September 24, 1897, Curry had his horse shot out from under him, was captured, and was jailed in Deadwood, South Dakota.

On September 31, he broke jail and disappeared, participating next in a Wilcox, Wyoming, train robbery on June 2, 1899. Three days later, Sheriff Joe Hazen of Converse County and a posse surprised the outlaws while they were eating. Logan put a bullet in the sheriff's stomach. Hazen died a few hours later. Meanwhile, the fugitives escaped by swimming the rain-swollen Powder River. Logan probably also took part in the July 11 train robbery near Folsom, New Mexico. On April 5, 1900, lawmen George Scarborough and Walter Birchfield trapped Logan in Triangle Canyon south of San Simon, Arizona, but Kid Curry shot Scarborough through the leg. That ended the battle. Scarborough died a few days later. On May 27, 1900, Logan killed Sheriff Jesse M. Tyler and Deputy Sam Jenkins of Moab, Utah, in retaliation for Tyler's killing of George Curry.

Near Thompson, Utah, a posse seeking Logan split into two groups. On May 26, one of them encountered Logan but did not immediately recognize him. Meanwhile, Logan shot two deputies in the back, killing both as they ran toward their horses. Kid Curry then headed toward Paint Rock, Texas, where he killed a local citizen following an argument, and then raced north to Montana, where on July 26, 1901, he killed Jim Winters, who had five years earlier slain his brother, Johnny. Figuring now that he had no place to hide west of the Mississippi, Logan meandered into Knoxville, Tennessee, where within an hour he had shot it out with several saloon customers. He himself took a wound in the shoulder, and a posse caught him 10 miles from town. On June 27, 1903, Harvey Logan broke out of the Knoxville jail.

A year later, on June 7, 1904, near Parachute, Colorado, he held up a small train but got only a few bills for his trouble. On the following day, June 8, a posse caught up with him, shot him in the shoulder, and closed in to find Harvey Logan dead with a bullet in his head. Whether a posse bullet had killed him or he committed suicide is an open question.

See also: CARVER, WILLIAM; CASSIDY, BUTCH; CURRY, GEORGE RICHARD; DEADWOOD, SOUTH DAKOTA; HOLE-IN-THE-WALL; KILPATRICK, BENJAMIN ARNOLD; LAY, WILLIAM ELLSWORTH; LOGAN, LONIE; SUNDANCE KID; WILD BUNCH

LOGAN, Lonie (1871–1900)

Lonie Logan and his brothers came from a star-crossed family. Their aunt reared them in Dodson, Missouri. As the Logan boys grew older, they sought less than honest employment. The brothers Lonie and Johnny followed their brother Harvey to Wyoming, where they hired out their guns to Nate Champion's Red Sash Gang in Johnson County during the war there. After Nate Champion was slain, the brothers turned to rustling cattle, acts that upset local authorities, to say nothing of the ranchers. This brought the Pinkertons into the area, so Lonie moved to Harlem, Montana, and purchased a saloon. When the law closed in, he sold out and fled back to Dodson, Missouri, where he took refuge in his aunt's home.

On February 28, 1900, with several inches of snow on the ground, a posse surrounded the house. Logan dashed out the back door, taking cover behind a mound of snow. He and the deputies then briefly exchanged shots before he jumped up and charged the lawmen. Lonie Logan died in a hail of gunfire.

See also: LOGAN, HARVEY

LONGABAUGH, Harry (a.k.a. Sundance Kid; Harry Place) (1867–?)

Harry Longabaugh was born in Pennsylvania; the exact month and day are not known. By 1884, the family had moved to Cortez, Colorado, where Harry worked as a horse wrangler. He then drifted to the Black Hills, passing through Sundance, Wyoming. He used the aliases Kid Chicago and Harry Alonzo. The authorities arrested the youth in Miles City, Montana, during 1887, jailing him in Sundance for

18 months and charging him with several counts of grand larceny. On February 4, 1889, Governor Thomas Moonlight granted him a full pardon. Longabaugh rode away from Sundance as the Sundance Kid.

Within a month the Kid had somehow aligned himself with Butch Cassidy, Matt Warner, and Tom McCarty, a group calling themselves the Wild Bunch. On June 24, 1889, they struck the San Miguel Valley Bank in Telluride, Colorado, and got away with roughly $20,000. By now the Pinkertons had a description of Sundance—slim, six feet tall, a man who walked with downcast eyes, combed his hair in a Pompadour style, was bowlegged, and walked with feet wide apart. He carried his arms straight at his side, fingers closed, thumbs sticking straight out.

Sundance made his next appearance on November 29, 1892, at Malta, Montana, where he and two confederates robbed the Great Northern Railroad. A couple of days later, all three were rounded up by lawmen. Two went to prison, but Sundance escaped. Meanwhile, over in Belle Fourche, South Dakota, Flatnose George Curry, Tom O'Day, Walt Punteney, and Harvey and Lonie Logan hit the local bank on June 28, 1897. Following a helter-skelter, inept robbery that netted only $97, the outlaws fled, except for O'Day, who had come into town to scout out the bank but had gotten drunk and wasn't even present at the holdup. O'Day took cover in a nearby outhouse and was captured. Harvey Logan and Punteney galloped for the Colorado/Wyoming border, teamed up again with the Sundance Kid, and from there all four drifted to Lavina, Montana, where they were captured, returned to South Dakota, and locked in the Deadwood jail. On October 31, 1897, all four prisoners (including O'Day) broke out of the Deadwood jail, although only Sundance (posing in jail as Frank Jones) and Lonie Logan actually made a getaway. The other two were recaptured within hours. Oddly, O'Day was tried for the robbery and acquitted. The state released Punteney.

A year later, on July 14, 1898, Sundance, Kid Curry, and Flatnose George Curry held up the Southern Pacific coming into Humbolt, Nevada. They blew apart the express car door and escaped with $450 in cash, plus jewelry. On April 3, 1899, the same men and others of the Wild Bunch walked into the Club Saloon in Elko, Nevada, and robbed it of between $1,000 and $3,000. Then a Wilcox, Wyoming, Union Pacific holdup netted between $30,000 and $60,000 on June 2, 1899. Although large posses, including such stalwarts as cowboy detective Charles Siringo, tracked them for days, little came of it except tired men and horses. The gang escaped, only to appear at Tipton, Missouri, where on August 29, 1900, they robbed the Union Pacific, this time blowing the roof, sides, and end out of the express car as well as wrecking the car behind it. Three weeks later, on September 19, the gang hit the National Bank at Winnemucca, Nevada, and escaped with $32,000. This time, after days of hard riding, the gang split up.

Sundance went to California, Logan and Carter to Texas, and Butch Cassidy possibly to Wyoming. Once they felt free, they gathered at Fort Worth, Texas, where on November 21, 1900 Harvey Logan, Butch Cassidy, the Sundance Kid, Ben Kilpatrick, and Will Carver posed for a photograph in John Swartz's studio at 705 Main Street. Since they had been earning money and not spending much during the last few months, they had bought nice clothes. The photographer, very proud of his ability, placed a copy on display in his front window. Within a week Pinkerton detective Fred Dodge recognized Will Carver. Soon the Pinkertons knew the name of every individual in that photo.

In the meantime, Butch Cassidy, Harvey Logan, and Ben Kilpatrick moved back to their old haunts, robbing the Great Northern Train near Wagner, Montana. On April 2, 1901, Will Carver died by a sheriff's bullet in Sonora, Texas. As for Sundance, he met a mysterious young lady known as Etta Place, who had a variety of names. She stood about five foot five, had dark hair, and was perhaps 24 years old. Her occupation was unknown, although almost certainly she was a San Antonio prostitute. When and how Sundance met her isn't known. By some accounts they married. They also toured the eastern United States, visiting his Pennsylvania family and seeing all the sights, including Niagara Falls. Then, on February 20, 1901, they took ship for Buenos Aires, Argentina, where they rendezvoused with Butch Cassidy and Harvey Logan (Kid Curry). All at least initially resided in Bolivia.

After a few years, however, either the money ran out or the men grew restless, or both. They seem to have resorted to additional robberies and to have been shot to death on November 8, 1908, at San Vicente, Bolivia. Some reports indicate that Etta Place later made it back to the States, and disappeared.

See also: BROWN'S PARK; CARVER, WILLIAM RICHARD; CASSIDY, BUTCH; HOLE-IN-THE-WALL; KILPATRICK, BENJAMIN ARNOLD; LOGAN, HARVEY; LOGAN, LONIE; ROBBERS ROOST; SIRINGO, CHARLES ANGELO; WILD BUNCH

LONGLEY, William Preston (1851–1878)

Bill Longley, born in Austin County, Texas, grew into one of the state's most feared gunmen, a man describing the first steps of his own career as "disobedience, next whiskey drinking, next carrying pistols, next gambling and then murder." Like many Texans of his time, Longley began his killing profession by shooting black men, the first ones in December 1868. By 1870, the state had a standing offer for Bill Longley's head.

The young outlaw now moved east and teamed up with Cullen Baker, leader of an eastern Texas/Louisiana gang that prowled the piney woods in search of victims as well as money. It committed theft, rape, and murder, in numbers impossible to establish. They shot the women just as easily as they shot the men.

In order to escape encroaching posses, Longley joined a cattle drive heading for Kansas, racking up bodies along the way. During the early 1870s, he wandered as far north as Wyoming and as far east as Missouri and Arkansas. On June 22, 1870, he even joined the army; military accounts described him as nearly six feet tall, spare of frame, with black hair and whiskers, slightly stooped in shoulders, a man "easily recognized by his penetrating eyes." Longley had enlisted for five years but deserted within two weeks. He was caught, served some time pounding big rocks into little ones, then was returned to duty—only to desert again, this time for good on June 8, 1872. He made it back to Texas, allegedly committing rape and shooting Indians, black men, and fellow gamblers along the way.

Up until now, most of the people allegedly slain by Longley had been little missed, but then he killed George Thomas, probably in Lee County, Texas. He next shot it out with Lou Shroyer in mid-January 1876 and killed him. Much of eastern Texas now had rewards out for Bill Longley, some as high as $250. On June 6, 1877, in De Soto County, Louisiana, as Longley, one of the most dangerous gunmen in Texas was hoeing, unarmed, in the middle of a cotton field, three lawmen took him into custody. The lawmen loaded Longley into a wagon and hustled him across the state line into Henderson, Texas. From there he went to Giddings and was locked in the Lee County jail.

While in jail Longley wrote his memoirs for the *Giddings Tribune*, claiming to have killed 32 men. (He later dropped the figure to eight, saying some of the people he shot did not die.) He was found guilty, sentenced to be hanged, and baptized in the Catholic faith. He filed a string of appeals. On October 11, 1878 the day of his hanging, he sang "Amazing Grace" in his cell, prayed, and told stories. As for the hanging, it turned into a strangulation because his feet hit the ground. Bill Longley is buried in Giddings, Texas.

LOVE, Harry (1810–1868)

Harry Love was born in Vermont but ran away to sea before returning and enlisting in Zachary Taylor's army during the Mexican War. Following the war he spent time in Texas, then followed the Gold Rush to California, where he mined around Mariposa. When several bandits robbed and killed Allen Ruddle, Love raised a posse for what turned into a futile pursuit. He captured only one gang member, killing him when he tried to escape.

The California legislature now prevailed upon Love to lead a posse of California Rangers in pursuit of Joaquin Murrieta, a noted Mexican bandit upon whom the state had placed a reward of $1,000. Actually, there were five bandit gangs, each one of them headed by a man whose first name was Joaquin. Undeterred by the ambiguities, Love led a ranger posse forth, and on July 25, 1853, fought a battle with a Mexican force, killing four gang members and capturing two. Two of the dead allegedly were Joaquin Murrieta and his most trusted associate, Three Fingered Jack García. Both were beheaded for evidence. The reward was duly paid.

Within a year Love married one Mary Bennett, who owned a sawmill near Santa Cruz. The marriage

tended to be rocky. A flood washed away the mill, and the house burned. Love ran unsuccessfully for justice of the peace in 1867. He began to drink heavily, as Mrs. Love took up with Chris Eiverson, a handyman hired by Mrs. Bennett. On June 19, 1868, as Eiverson and Mary returned from a buggy trip to town, Love met them at the gate with a revolver and a shotgun. The men commenced shooting at one another, the fight spilling over into the house and ending when Love took a severe pistol wound in the right arm. A doctor arrived and decided to amputate the arm, but overdosed his patient with chloroform. Love died. He is buried in the Santa Clara Mission Cemetery.

See also: MURRIETA, JOAQUIN

LOWE, Joe (a.k.a. Rowdy Joe) (?–1899)

Joe Lowe, better known as Rowdy Joe Lowe, was a beefy individual with receding hairline, mustache, and goatee. He came out of Florida, but was in Missouri when the Civil War started. For a while he served in the Second Missouri Light Artillery, and after the war acted briefly as a civilian scout. Following that he opened a series of gambling and dance halls in Kansas, where he acquired the moniker "Rowdy Joe." Lowe and gambler Jim Bush were once arrested in Ellsworth, Kansas, for drugging and robbing a man, and in 1874–75 they were repeatedly indicted for gambling. Rowdy Joe reportedly married seven women, the first appropriately known as Rowdy Kate. When Joe shot and killed E. T. Beard (better known as Red Beard), his chief gambling hall competitor in Wichita, Kansas, he and Rowdy Kate fled to Luling, Texas. Over the next few years, Joe opened various gambling enterprises across the state. In 1899, a former police officer shot him to death in a Denver saloon.

LYNCHING

A hanging in the Old West usually referred to a legal execution by rope, whereas a lynching involved illegal mob action. Lynching parties favored tree limbs, although rafters, railroad bridges, windmills, saddle horns, wagon tongues, windows, and large rocks or cliffs were also utilized. Lynchings generally stemmed from a community breakdown in law and order, but

Lynch mob hanging in Ada, Oklahoma. On the left is Killin' Jim Miller, then men named Joe Allen, B. B. Burwell, and Jesse West. Note the onlookers in the back, especially the children. (University of Texas at El Paso Archives)

they were not as common as media hype would lead readers to suspect. Prosecutions against participants were extremely rare, however.

LYNN, Wiley (1900?–1932)

Lynn was probably born in Oklahoma, where he lived most of his life and worked primarily as a Prohibition agent. He is best known for the November 1, 1924, killing of one of the three Oklahoma Guardsmen—Bill Tilghman, who was trying to arrest Lynn. The slaver went free on a plea of self-defense.

Lynn then quit his job and moved to Madill, Oklahoma, where he drank heavily and accosted Crockett Long and others on the Madill police force. During a shootout, Long and a bystander died, another bystander was seriously wounded, and Wiley Lynn could not survive his wounds. He is buried in Madill.

See also: TILGHMAN, WILLIAM MATTHEW, JR.

McCALL, John (a.k.a. Jack; Buffalo Curly; Bill Sutherland) (1852–1877)

John McCall is remembered for one incident—he killed Wild Bill Hickok. He was born near Jeffersontown, Kentucky, but rambled about the West for years, reportedly working as a buffalo hunter as well as for a stage company. He arrived in Deadwood, South Dakota, probably by mid-1876. There he found employment at odd jobs.

On August 2, 1876, as Hickok played poker in the No. 10 Saloon, the medium sized, cross-eyed McCall stepped up behind him and fired one shot. Hickok died instantly.

A miner's jury found him not guilty, but since Deadwood was not a legally constituted community, the trial was declared illegal and moved to Yankton, South Dakota. On November 9, 1876, McCall tried to break jail, failed, and went once more to trial on December 4. A jury on January 3, 1877, sentenced McCall to hang, and the sentence was carried out on March 1.

See also: HICKOK, JAMES BUTLER

McCARTY, John Thomas (1850?–?)

John Thomas McCarty was born in Union County, Iowa, the son of a physician who after the Civil War moved first to Montana and then to Utah. There young Tom met and married Christina Christiansen, although he rarely showed up except to impregnate her. Otherwise, he spent his time stealing livestock. She died following the birth of their third child. Tom hardly noticed, and in 1877 he spent a short stretch in the Nevada State Prison for robbing a ticket agent of the Central Pacific Railroad. Following this, he teamed up with his wife's brother, Willard Erastus Christiansen, later to become better known as Wild Bunch member Matt Warner. Matt had been riding with Butch Cassidy, and through his association with Tom McCarty, the three men had made contact with one another. In 1889, the gang successfully struck the Telluride, Colorado, bank, and the Wild Bunch was in business. For a few months the gang hid out in Robbers Roost and Brown's Park, and then Warner and McCarty branched out on their own, hitting several banks, becoming so successful that the outlaws (19 of them) posed for a group photograph in Rawlins, Wyoming Territory.

Within a brief time they were joined by Tom's brothers and nephew: George (who was caught early and served some jail time), Bill McCarty, and his son, Fred. However, more disaster followed, for in 1893 when they hit the Delta Bank in Colorado, the local residents killed Bill and Fred McCarty.

As for Tom, he allegedly fled into Utah and disappeared, although the *Denver Times* of March 12, 1899, noted that $5,000 had been set aside for the capture or destruction of Tom McCarty's Blue Mountain Gang, reputed to number at least 200.

During this time, however, Tom McCarty vanished, and all efforts to trace him have come to naught.

See also: BROWN'S PARK; CASSIDY, BUTCH; CHRISTIANSEN, WILLARD ERASTUS; LAY, WILLIAM ELLSWORTH; ROBBERS ROOST; SUNDANCE KID; WILD BUNCH

McCULLY, Thomas (a.k.a. James Henry; Jackson) (1833?–1865)

During the 1850s, Tom McCully reached California from Virginia, where he is thought to have been born, he and his brother Ed settling in Tuolumne County. Instead of becoming miners, however, the brothers concentrated on petty theft and brawling. During one saloon fight near Shaw's Flat, they injured a man named Fair. The case went to court, where a man named Bonds testified for Fair. (Bonds subsequently died of a knife wound administered by Edward and Tom McCully.) At their trial, Tom was sentenced to nine years at San Quentin, while Ed was lynched, with a couple of others, on December 11, 1857.

By 1863, Tom was back in circulation, teaming up with groups who specialized in robbing mining camps populated mostly by Chinese. After being chased off by vigilantes, however, the thugs split up. McCully, who repeatedly changed his name back and forth, reportedly killed an isolated sheepherder and a stage attendant, plus others, in an orgy of murder. The California governor in late 1864 offered a $1,000 reward for Tom McCully, describing him as riding a "large, flea-bitten grey horse," (stolen, of course) and wearing "an old black coat with many holes in it." McCully may have been murderous, but he was not a prosperous murderer.

McCully could not run forever though, and in mid-September 1865 a posse of soldiers and civilians tracked him down and shot him to death. His body briefly went on display in San Bernardino and presumably was later buried somewhere in the vicinity.

McDANIELS, James (1852–1881?)

On one certificate of record, Jim McDaniels asserted that he was a farmer. Certainly the auburn-haired lad from Tennessee was not lying; he did in fact farm out his gun, farmed out other peoples' livestock, and farmed out his own brand of frontier justice. It is doubtful that Jim McDaniels ever raised a tomato or planted a row of corn.

The biographical details of the McDaniel's early life are sketchy, but Jim landed one of his first jobs at John Chisum's Home Creek Ranch in Texas. By 1872, he was riding the range in New Mexico for the "Cattle King of the Pecos." Here he earned his spurs, and tarnished them.

McDaniels allegedly quieted a cattle camp commotion by simply shooting a black cowboy between the eyes. While working for Chisum, McDaniels both stole and recovered horses from the Mescalero Apache Reservation. McDaniels took custody of the notorious Mes brothers, who were later executed near Shedd's Ranch, on the east side of the Organ Mountains. Somewhere along the line, however, McDaniels and Chisum had a falling out, by most accounts over wages, and McDaniels ambled west toward the Rio Grande.

On New Year's Eve in 1875, at Las Cruces, New Mexico, a bunch of Eighth Cavalry soldiers thumped the heads of a small group of cowboys. After midnight, the vanquished returned to the scene of the dance. Poking their six-shooters through the windows, McDaniels, John Kinney, Jesse Evans, and Charles "Pony Deal" Ray opened fire. Five men inside hit the floor, three with serious wounds and two killed outright. Local authorities looked the other way.

During mid-1877, at the McDaniels mining camp of Jicarilla, Ben Reinhardt and the combatants cut each other to pieces with knives, although somehow both survived. McDaniels later in the year showed up in El Paso as a mercenary in what has been commonly referred to as the "El Paso Salt War." There he allegedly committed murder, rape, robbery, and general mayhem. In February of the following year (1878), Jim McDaniels wounded a man named H. Martin in the neck during a shooting incident at Mesilla, New Mexico.

In July of that same year (1878), McDaniels accompanied John Kinney to Lincoln, New Mexico, and was present during the infamous "Five Day War," in which Alexander McSween and others were killed. Federal investigator Frank Warner described McDaniels as a "desperado."

McDaniels was arrested on several occasions but died from unknown causes. One report says he died on March 2, 1881, while another indicates he returned to Texas and was killed by lawmen in Bexar County during an 1885 shootout. No doubt at some point he was declared dead, but while he lived, Jim

McDaniels was a formidable adversary and a dangerously violent frontier personality.

See also: EVANS, JESSE J.; KINNEY, JOHN; LINCOLN COUNTY WAR; RAY, CHARLES T.

McMASTER(S), Sherman W. (1853?–?)

This lawman/outlaw started life in Galena, Illinois, the son of a businessman. He left home, apparently wandering for a while, perhaps visiting New Mexico, and by 1878 winding up in West Texas as a member of John Kinney's Silver City (New Mexico) Rangers. After that he switched to the James Tays Detachment of Company C, the Texas Ranger battalion stationed at Ysleta, Texas, the seat of El Paso County. McMaster had dark hair, eyes, and complexion, and stood about five feet seven inches. Practically all descriptions referred to him as short, very short. McMaster spent much of his Texas time chasing cattle rustlers and Indians, serving honorably and well, and was discharged at Ysleta on April 12, 1879.

Shortly after, McMaster became one of the slipperiest individuals in western history, over time becoming a Wells Fargo undercover agent, an informant, a criminal, and a lawman, but always a hired gun. After leaving Texas he teamed up with another discharged ranger named Pony Diehl. By July 30, 1880, both men had been mentioned in connection with the theft of army horses in Arizona, and by January 1881 they were being referred to as members of a Wyatt Earp posse that prevented a lynch mob from hanging "Johnny Behind the Deuce." McMaster went from there to assist with a Globe, Arizona, stage robbery on February 25, 1881, an action that later made him the subject of various Tombstone manhunts; every law officer available, including Virgil Earp and John Behan, claimed to be looking for him. As it turned out, the stage robbery charges were dropped, and from this time on McMaster gave his undying allegiance to the Earps. He would become one of their bodyguards; the Earps in turn persuaded the government to make McMaster a U.S. deputy marshal.

Back in Tombstone on March 18, 1882, McMaster and Morgan Earp walked into the Hatch Saloon, and Earp, at least, engaged in a game of billiards. From somewhere two gunshots rang out, and Morgan Earp collapsed. McMaster dropped immediately to the floor but saw nothing to shoot at.

On March 20, the Earps, Doc Holliday, Sherman McMaster, and the body of Morgan left for California. During a stopover at Tucson, the party caught sight of Frank Stillwell moving among the train cars and shot him to death. Upon returning to Tombstone, however, the Earps organized a posse consisting of at least seven men, including McMaster, and on March 22 they caught up with Florentino Cruz, whom they promptly executed. Two days later, that same posse killed Curly Bill Brocius, although during the shootout McMaster avoided death only by a hair's breadth when a bullet passed unimpeded through his clothing. Another cut the straps off his field glasses.

What happened to McMaster after this isn't known. Some stories say he was killed in the Philippines during the Spanish-American War. Other people claim he died in Colorado some time around 1892.

See also: BEHAN, JOHN HARRIS; EARP, WYATT BERRY STAPP; EARP, MORGAN; EARP, VIRGIL; EL PASO SALT WAR; KINNEY, JOHN

McMURTRY, William (1802–1892)

William McMurtry started life in Kentucky and became a doctor. The lure of gold proved strong, however, so in 1849 he took his wife and five children to Oroville, California. They opened a restaurant and hotel, but William and his brother, James, in partnership with Richard Kimball, had even greater dreams. They staked a gold claim called the Larimer.

A man named Alexander Griffin opened a nearby claim, and in 1858 the two parties started arguing over who owned what. Gunfire commenced, and James McMurtry and Richard Kimball went down.

Dr. William McMurtry, not a man of violence, proved it when he jerked a revolver out of his belt and it tangled up in his suspenders. Still, he was resourceful, and once he freed the weapon, the good doctor proved to be dangerous. His first two shots killed men called Carney and Holland. Then three more men went down almost as quickly. Another gunman, known only as Coyote Jack, died later. McMurtry, a country doctor, had now fired six times and killed or seriously wounded six opponents.

He then bent down to retrieve his fallen brother's revolver, and at this point the opposition, or what was left of it, departed. When the newspapers got the story about what became known as "the Osborne Hill gunfight," they published accounts that conflicted in every way except one—the good doctor never missed.

William McMurtry lived a quiet, uneventful life thereafter, practicing medicine almost until he died at 91 on March 6, 1892, in Oakland, California.

McNELLY, Leander H. (1844–1877)

This relentless, fighting Texas Ranger was born in Virginia but got to Texas as soon as he could and joined the Confederate army. He fought in the New Mexico campaign as well as the Battle of Galveston before fighting his way across southern Louisiana, in the process being seriously wounded, although he later captured several Union soldiers at Brashear City, Louisiana.

After the war, he return to farming in Texas, married, and became one of the four captains in the Texas State Police until it was disbanded in 1873. In July 1874, he became captain of the Seventh Company of the Texas Rangers, being assigned to duty in DeWitt County to suppress the Sutton-Taylor feud. Governor Richard Coke described the process as "making friends." As for McNelly, he reported that "a perfect reign of terror existed as armed bands of men made predatory excursions through the country, overawing the law-abiding citizens." At the end of four months, McNelly was assigned to other troubles. He said the Sutton-Taylor feud would restart once he was gone. Of course, it did.

In early 1875, McNelly raised a 40-man company to patrol the Nueces Strip between the Rio Grande and the Nueces Rivers. This time it wasn't necessary to make friends, so for two years (1875–76) along that remote area McNelly shot the bad guys and stacked their bodies in the town plazas. He made several illegal crossings south into Mexico, shot up various outlaw ranches, and wasn't gentle in coaxing information from captured Mexican *vaqueros*. On one occasion the U.S. Army had to cover McNelly's retreat back into Texas. The Texas governor finally relieved him in 1876 with Jesse Lee Hall. McNelly subsequently retired to a farm in Burton, Texas, and died of tuberculosis on September 4, 1877.

See also: HALL, JESSE LEIGH; SUTTON-TAYLOR FEUD; TEXAS RANGERS

MADSEN, Christian (a.k.a. Chris Madsen) (1841–1947)

This soldier of fortune and Denmark-born lawman served in the Danish army at 14 and with the French Foreign Legion in 1870 during the Franco-Prussian War. He reached the United States in 1876 and joined the cavalry before becoming a U.S. deputy marshal in Oklahoma during 1891. He, Bill Tilghman, and Heck Thomas became the legendary "Three Guardsmen," pursuing outlaw gangs and doing everything from battling whiskey smugglers to extraditing fugitives. Madsen in particular became well known for his pursuit of the Dalton brothers and his breakup of the Doolin gang in Oklahoma. He joined Teddy Roosevelt's Rough Riders in 1898, and in 1910 he received a temporary court appointment as a U.S. marshal. He died quietly at Guthrie, Oklahoma, in 1947.

See also: DOOLIN, WILLIAM M.; THOMAS, HENRY ANDREW; TILGHMAN, WILLIAM MATTHEW, JR.

MALEDON, George (1834–1911)

This hangman was born in Detroit, served in the Union army, then moved to Fort Smith, Arkansas, where he became a U.S. deputy marshal assigned in 1875 as "the" executioner for the "hanging judge," Isaac C. Parker. Although he did not execute all 79 of those sentenced to die by Judge Parker, he handled most of them.

His executions invariably went off without a hitch. The sad-faced Maledon oiled and tenderly prepared his ropes; he sent all condemned men to their graves in new suits and clean coffins. To Maledon, there was nothing personal in his executions. On one occasion, six men at once did what the newspapers called "the dance of death." Following that, the government ordered executions closed to casual visitors. It then became Maledon's additional job to arrange a barricade around the execution platform and to issue official passes.

When his executioner days ended, Maledon briefly went on the road, displaying ropes and telling dry stories. However, the audience just wasn't there. George Maledon died on May 6, 1911.

See also: PARKER, JUDGE ISAAC

MARTIN, Charles (?–?)

Little is known about Charlie Martin, although he was likely born in Missouri. All that's recorded is that he arrived in Cheyenne, Wyoming, in mid-1867. He and a man named Andy Harris subsequently opened a dance hall, but the two partners had a falling out, and Martin killed Harris. A jury acquitted Martin, but the finding outraged the local vigilantes. They hanged him.

MARTIN, William A. (a.k.a. Hurricane Bill) (?–1881)

Hurricane Bill was a character, and like most characters he acted and cherished the part. The army accused him of stealing horses; he had allegedly shot a policeman, somewhere; and had spent considerable time in the Black Hills, as well as in Dodge City. The Texas Rangers had arrested him once, charged him with an attempt to kill, then couldn't prove it and turned him loose. Everybody seemed to know Hurricane Bill, and most people seemed to like him. He spent a lot of time around Fort Griffin, Texas, even marrying an interesting prostitute known as Hurricane Minnie.

Notwithstanding a reputation like this, the little community of Otero hired him as a deputy sheriff. It had no jail, so Bill tied everyone he arrested to a telegraph pole. After three months, the community dismissed him for "incompetency and drunkenness." Then, sometime around mid-1881, Hurricane Bill vanished.

MASON County War (Hoodoo War)

No other state had cattle feuds quite like Texas. Mason County in particular seemed to be settled primarily by Germans, Americans, livestock, and an insidious group of cattle rustlers. To keep order, Governor Richard Coke was asked to dispatch troops.

In early 1875, Sheriff John Clark incarcerated nine alleged rustlers, of whom four promptly escaped. This was too much for local stock grazers, so on February 18, 1875, 40 very angry men removed the remaining prisoners from jail and led them to a site near Hick Springs, where all kinds of confusion took place. The Texas Rangers managed to intervene, but two men were still lynched. Another had been lynched but was still alive. A fourth had escaped, and the fifth had been shot and would soon die.

Three months later, on May 13, Mason County deputy sheriff John Worley rode to Castell, Texas, to take custody of an alleged cattle thief, Tim Williamson. While returning to Mason, however, they were stopped by 12 men with blackened faces, who killed Williamson. The Mason County War was now under way.

Scott Cooley, a former ranger turned rancher and a friend of Williamson's, now rounded up a group of colleagues, one of them named John Ringgold, a man who would be in and out of Texas jails during the following few years. After learning the names of the Williamson assassins, Cooley and his band began methodically exterminating them, initially killing John Worley, who was not only shot but scalped. A week or so later they killed John Cheney, who was preparing breakfast when death overtook him.

Governor Coke now called out the Texas Rangers to restore order, sending Maj. John B. Jones, with portions of Company A and Company D. The rangers rode into Cold Springs, Texas, where they encountered Sheriff Clark and perhaps 20 riders, who explained they had organized because Scott Cooley and his cohorts planned to "burn out the Dutch," meaning the Germans. So the days passed with numerous killings. Some men disappeared, some were wounded, and some obviously left the area.

In the meantime, Major Jones discharged several of his rangers after learning they sympathized with the Cooley faction. Several arrests took place; the cases were usually dismissed, or the subjects were found not guilty. So as the war wound down, the county had over a dozen unsolved murders on its hands, for which no one was ever convicted, although several men went on trial for various crimes in different counties. Cooley himself took refuge in Blanco County, where he reportedly died of brain fever. John Ringgold fled Texas for Arizona, winning fame as John Ringo. As for a gun/rope-weary Mason County, it seemed to have forsaken killing by late 1876, although in January 1877 someone burned the courthouse, destroying the records.

See also: JONES, JOHN B.; RINGO, JOHN PETERS

MASTERSON, Edward John (1852–1879)

Ed Masterson was the first of seven children born to Thomas Masterson and Mary McGurk in Quebec, Canada. The family began moving in 1861 and by 1871 had reached Wichita, Kansas, where it farmed on 80 acres while Ed, Bat, and James became buffalo hunters. By 1873, Ed had arrived in Dodge City, working as a grading contractor as well as a hide man, trading in buffalo skins. In April 1877, Mayor Jim Kelley appointed Larry Deger as city marshal of Dodge City. Ed Masterson became Deger's assistant in May. On July 12, Deger arrested a friend and supporter of Kelley's and ignored the mayor's demand that the man be released. Kelley ordered Ed Masterson to arrest Deger, but the marshal pulled a gun. Masterson talked him down and placed him under arrest. He also arrested Mayor Kelley. A court later dropped charges against both Kelley and Deger.

On the day before Bat Masterson became sheriff of Ford County, a resident named Bob Shaw accused a local citizen named Texas Dick of stealing $40. Ed Masterson arrived at the Lone Star Saloon and asked for Shaw's gun; Shaw refused to give it up. As a result, Masterson cracked Shaw across the head with a revolver, but Shaw hardly blinked. Instead he shot and grazed the marshal's chest. In falling, the marshal fired and wounded Shaw in the left leg and arm. During the melee, Texas Dick took a bullet in the groin, there being some uncertainty about who had fired it, Masterson or Shaw. A month later, the city council removed Deger as marshal and replaced him with Ed Masterson.

Late in the evening of April 9, 1879, Marshal Ed Masterson entered Dodge City's Lady Gay Saloon and noticed several cowhands whooping it up at the bar. One of them, Jack Wagner, had a holstered gun, and Ed walked over to advise him that wearing weapons was illegal, that the six-shooter would have to be checked. Wagner offered no resistance, so Masterson handed the gun to Alf Walker, the trail boss.

Masterson walked outside. A few minutes later the cowboys followed, the marshal noticing immediately that Wagner had his six-shooter back. The marshal stepped in close to take it away, and a scuffle started; Wagner drew the weapon, stuck it against Masterson's side, and pulled the trigger. Not only did the round go all the way through Masterson's body, but the flame set the marshal's clothing afire. Trail boss Walker now pulled his own weapon and aimed it at the marshal, but Masterson fired three times, one shot striking Walker in the chest. The cattleman staggered through the saloon and out the back door.

The marshal now turned from the smoke and fury, stumbled across the plaza and into Hoover's Saloon, where he collapsed, dying in less than an hour. Wagner died during the following day. Walker finally recovered.

Marshal Ed Masterson was initially buried in the Fort Dodge cemetery. The body was moved a year later to the Prairie Grove Cemetery, and later still to the Maple Grove Cemetery. The exact burial plot cannot now be determined.

See also: MASTERSON, JAMES; MASTERSON, WILLIAM BARCLAY

MASTERSON, James (1855–1895)

James Masterson was born in Henryville, Iberville County, Quebec, Canada, on September 16, 1855, the third of the seven Masterson children. In 1861, the Masterson family arrived in New York; they then drifted to Illinois and perhaps to Missouri. In 1871, the Mastersons ended up near Wichita, Kansas. Later that year or shortly afterward, Jim joined his brothers Bat and Ed Masterson on the buffalo range.

Jim hunted buffalo until 1878, and a year later opened a Dodge City saloon. Shortly afterward, his brother, Dodge City marshal Ed Masterson, was slain in a gunfight.

On June 1, 1878, Jim became an assistant marshal. On November 4, 1879, he became the city marshal. During this period, someone sent his brother Bat a telegram: "Come at once. Updegraff and Peacock are going to kill Jim." Bat did come, but no attempted killings occurred. By 1882, he lost an election; Jim was without a job.

He drifted over to Trinidad, Colorado, and became an assistant city marshal, losing the position when his brother Bat became city marshal. By late 1884, he had moved south to Raton, New Mexico, where he became undersheriff. A month later, Masterson became a captain in the New Mexico Territorial Militia, a quasi-military group whose purposes were to keep the peace in Colfax County. A Texas gunman named Dick Rogers and a band of men invaded a saloon one evening on January 30, 1885. They backed Masterson against the wall and made him dance while they peppered the floor around his feet with gunshots.

Jim apparently swallowed hard and then jumped into another silly—and dangerous—confrontation, the war between the Kansas communities of Ingalls and Cimarron over which would be the Gray County seat. Only six miles separated the two towns. On January 12, 1889, a half-dozen gunmen, including Jim Masterson, Ben Daniels, Neal Brown, and Bill Tilghman, slipped into town. Masterson and three others went to the second floor, grabbed boxes of records, and were hauling them out to a wagon when several Cimarron residents started shooting. The people in the wagon, although shot up, escaped. The four men inside the building commenced firing. During a six-hour siege, they wounded four Cimarron residents and killed J. W. English. Then they surrendered under a white flag and were permitted to leave town. Masterson was acquitted in the English slaying.

Jim Masterson immediately left the state, soon afterward participating in the Oklahoma land rush before becoming deputy sheriff of Logan County (Guthrie, Oklahoma). In May 1890, as the Oklahoma Territory was being carved out of Indian Territory, Jim Masterson became a U.S. deputy marshal. In the meantime, Bill Doolin and his gang had robbed a train and holed up in Ingalls, Indian Territory, 30 miles north of Guthrie. A federal posse with Masterson second in command converged on the community during September 1, 1893, arriving in covered wagons so as to obscure the fact that they were lawmen.

However, outlaw Bitter Creek Newcomb happened to be on the street when he heard someone speak his name. He immediately started firing. Lawmen Dick Speed, Tom Hueston, and Lafe Shadley died. Bill Doolin, Bill Dalton, and several other gang members escaped.

Only Arkansas Tom was now left behind, but he threw up his hands when Jim Masterson produced two sticks of dynamite and threatened to blow up the building sheltering him. He was the only outlaw captured.

On March 31, 1895, James Masterson died of consumption. He was 39 years old. There is no evidence that he ever killed anybody.

See also: DALTON BROTHERS; DOOLIN, WILLIAM M.; MASTERSON, WILLIAM BARCLAY; TILGHMAN, WILLIAM MATHEW, JR.

MASTERSON, William Barclay (a.k.a. Bat)
(1853–1921)

Bat Masterson started life on November 26, 1853, at County Rouville, Quebec, Canada, but the family moved to Sedgwick County, Kansas, in June 1871. Bat and his brother, Ed, hired on as buffalo skinners for an outfit operating near the Salt Fork of the Arkansas River. Here Bat met many men who would influence him throughout his life. In the meantime, the Masterson brothers rode into Adobe Walls, Texas, just in time to repulse an assault by Comanche chief Quanah Parker. Masterson thereafter became a civilian scout for Gen. Nelson Miles. By October 1874, he decided he had had enough.

Masterson drifted over to Sweetwater, near Dodge City, where he ran awry of Cpl. Melvin King of the

William B. ("Bat") Masterson (Robert G. McCubbin Collection)

Fourth Cavalry, stationed at nearby Fort Elliott. King had been born Anthony Cook in Quebec, Canada, in 1845. Because of rowdy behavior (drunkenness and fighting), he had left the U.S. Army and reenlisted on several occasions until being dishonorably discharged in 1869. He had reenlisted a couple months later as Melvin King and had risen to corporal. On the night of January 24, 1876, he, Bat Masterson, and a soiled dove named Molly Brennan came together in confrontation.

Apparently, Corporal King resented the intrusion of Masterson regarding the affections of Molly. She and Bat caroused in several saloons during the evening. Sometime around midnight, the two wandered into Charlie Norton's place and closed the doors. King glanced through the window, witnessed what was going on, and began hammering on the front door. Bat opened it, and King came charging in. Corporal King fired two shots, one hitting Molly, who apparently—and probably unintentionally—had gotten between the two men. The other bullet hit Masterson. Masterson fired one shot at King.

King died, and Molly died, and Masterson seemed about to die but did not. There is some argument as to whether the incident even happened, but regardless, King, if indeed Bat shot him, would be Masterson's only shooting victim.

Bat Masterson moved to Dodge City in 1876. There he opened a saloon, became a deputy city marshal, a year later a deputy sheriff, and then the full-fledged sheriff of Ford County. Some authorities believe this is where the moniker "Bat" came from. He usually carried a cane, perhaps because of the King shooting; he frequently mentioned that the cane was useful for "batting" rowdies over the head.

In April 1878, his brother Ed—the town marshal—died in a Dodge City gunfight, but Bat continued as a busy and efficient law enforcement officer. A year later Bat Masterson became a U.S. deputy marshal, which primarily meant making additional money by serving papers, rounding up jurors, and arresting fugitives with prices on their head.

The Atchison, Topeka & Santa Fe Railroad retained him to haul a party of gunmen to enforce the company's right of way through Raton Pass, on the border of Colorado and New Mexico. However, the opposing railroad bought him off. Perhaps because he had ignored and abandoned his job as sheriff while assisting the railroads, Bat was defeated at the polls in the next election.

The following years found Bat Masterson making his living primarily by gambling and promoting horse races and prize fights. Wandering to Kansas City, drifting over to Ogallala, and involving himself in the essentially nonviolent Dodge City War, he finally made his way to Tombstone, Arizona, and from there up to Denver.

On November 21, 1891, he married song-and-dance performer Emma Walters in Denver. There is some indication, but no proof, of earlier marriages, one perhaps even to Emma. Nevertheless, Bat's real interests remained in sports, especially boxing promotion. The usual sports speculation and controversies surrounded him wherever he went. Somewhere around 1907 he moved to New York City, where he became a sports reporter for the *Morning Telegraph*. He died at his desk on Tuesday, October 25, 1921, and is buried in New York's Woodlawn Cemetery.

See also: EARP, WYATT BERRY STAPP; MASTERSON, JAMES

MATHER, David (a.k.a. Mysterious Dave) (1845–?)

Mysterious Dave Mather was born in Connecticut; by some accounts he was a lineal descendant of clergyman Cotton Mather. By 1873 he had migrated to Dodge City, Kansas, where he gambled and hunted buffalo. For reasons unknown, someone knifed him in the ribs, but he survived to become a part-time peace officer in Dodge before moving on to places like Mobeetie, Texas. Mather later showed up in Las Vegas, New Mexico, where in 1880 he became a deputy marshal. Here, he and city marshal Joe Carson took on the Henry gang. Carson died in the shootout, but Mather killed one man and wounded two. Two others escaped but were captured in Mora, New Mexico, and returned to Las Vegas. They were jailed along with their partner, the wounded James West, but not for long. Mather led an assault upon the jail, and all three men were dragged out and lynched.

Mather left Las Vegas shortly afterward. He drifted from town to town, likely serving a brief time as an El Paso deputy marshal before moving on to Dodge City, where he and another assistant marshal, Tom Nixon, quarreled over the affections of Mrs. Nixon. One afternoon Mather walked up behind Nixon and shot him six times in the back. A jury apparently felt Nixon had gotten what he deserved, for it acquitted Mather.

Lone Pine, Nebraska, in 1887 proved to be Mather's last known stopping place. Whatever happened to him after that is speculation. Folks didn't call him Mysterious Dave for nothing.

MATHEWS, Jacob Basil (a.k.a. Billy) (1847–1904)

During the Civil War, J. B. Mathews served in the Fifth Tennessee Cavalry Regiment, enlisting on October 19, 1863. After the war, Mathews briefly returned home to Cannon County and then headed west to the mining camps at Russell Gulch, Colorado, and a few months later to Elizabethtown, New Mexico.

Mathews, growing tired of searching for gold, decided to raise cattle and moved to eastern Lincoln County. By the fall of 1873, he had acquired a small farm. Still later he moved west to the Rio Penasco and started a ranching operation.

In April 1877, "Billy" Mathews bought a silent share in the firm of J. J. Dolan & Company, in the village of Lincoln. Mathews also became the company clerk. Connected with the Dolan faction during New Mexico's Lincoln County War, Mathews found

Jacob B. (Billy) Mathews (Robert G. McCubbin Collection)

himself, probably willingly, embroiled in a conflict with John Tunstall and Alexander McSween. Acting as a deputy sheriff, Matthews was responsible for the posse (to use the word loosely) that murdered Englishman John Tunstall, although Matthews was not at the crime scene. He was later indicted as an accessory to murder for the killing, but he took advantage of the territorial governor's amnesty.

On April Fool's Day of 1878, it was no joke when members of the opposition forces, including Billy the Kid, hid behind an adobe corral wall and waited until Sheriff William Brady and deputies ambled into their rifle sights. The ambush killed Brady and George Hindman. The remaining pedestrians—Matthews, George Peppin, and John Long—scattered. Matthews took refuge in a private dwelling, and when "Billy the Kid" dashed out toward the sheriff's body, supposedly to recover a rifle, Matthews levered one round in the chamber of his .44-40 Winchester, took aim, and slipped a bullet through the outlaw's thigh, a serious but not fatal wound.

Matthews participated during the subsequent "Five-Day Battle" in Lincoln (July 15–19, 1878) and later in Mesilla testified against the "Kid" regarding

the murder of Sheriff Brady. He was also a member of the armed guard that escorted the defendant to Lincoln from the trial site in Mesilla, New Mexico.

After the Lincoln County War, Billy Matthews continued in the cattle business while seeking elective office. He became postmaster at Roswell on May 19, 1898, a position he held until his death from natural causes on June 3, 1904.

See also: BILLY THE KID; LINCOLN COUNTY WAR; GARRETT, PATRICK FLOYD JARVIS

MAVERICK

In the word's purest sense, a maverick is a wild, unbranded calf belonging to no one. However, the word goes back to a Texas lawyer named Samuel A. Maverick. One story has it that back in 1845, in accepting payment for a debt, Maverick took possession on Matagorda Island of a herd of Longhorn cattle. Not knowing what to do with them, he simply left them to multiply. Of course, all unbranded calves belonged to Maverick. Even after arriving on the mainland, these unbranded calves remained Maverick's. Cowboys referred to the unbranded calfs as "Maverick's." On the other hand, men who stole or branded these calves differently became "maverickers." Thus the name "maverick" passed into the language.

With regard to people, the name "maverick" took on a deeper meaning. A maverick had no allegiance. He was different, often temperamental, capable of extremes, frequently a loner, a man not to be trifled with. A maverick person tends to be wild, unsettled, and irresponsible, often an outlaw not bound by the rules and mores of society.

MEADE, William Kidder (1851–1918)

A Virginian by birth, William Kidder Meade became an Arizonan and a Democrat. Aside from that, the energetic, opinionated, and ambitious Meade arrived in Arizona during the early 1870s as a mining speculator. He then served two terms in the 10th and 11th Territorial Legislatures. During 1884, he traveled to Chicago as a delegate to the National Democratic Convention. After the election of Grover Cleveland, Meade campaigned for an appointment as governor of Arizona Territory, an unsuccessful effort, although as a reward for his hard work and party loyalty he was appointed as a U.S. marshal for Arizona Territory on July 8, 1885.

On February 22, 1888, someone robbed a Southern Pacific passenger train near Steins Pass, just across the line in New Mexico Territory. The prime suspects, already headaches for Arizona lawmen, were Larry Sheehan, Tom Johnson, Dick Hart, and Jack Blount. Exactly whose technical jurisdiction these thieves had violated made no difference to Marshal Meade. Accompanied by deputies and lawmen Will Smith, W. G. Whorf, the Pima County undersheriff Charles Shibell, and Sheriff M. F. Shaw, as well as several Papago Indian trackers, Meade set off in pursuit.

Shaw and Whorf dropped out of the chase after a couple of days. The remaining cadre of lawmen pressed on across the international border and deep into Mexico. At Janos, in the state of Chihuahua, 65 miles south of the border Marshal Meade contacted a Mexican official, a Lieutenant Martínez, in charge of the customshouse. To Meade's dismay, he and his party were arrested. So after a meandering pursuit of 400 miles the lawmen themselves were now the prisoners, whereas the train robbers, just two hours ahead, kept riding south. Back in the United States,

verbal barbs flew back and forth, some people defending Meade's actions, others condemning his incursion onto foreign soil. After protests, diplomatic parlays, and possibly even a bribe, William Kidder Meade and his posse were released after a 14-day ordeal, minus their arms and horses. Adding to Meade's embarrassment, a Southern Pacific Railroad detective named Bob Paul, a former sheriff of Pima County, obtained Mexican permission to continue the chase. At a farmhouse near Cusihuirachic, Paul engaged the outlaws in a peppery gunbattle and killed three of the highwaymen.

Not long afterward, on May 11, 1889, a band of American outlaws ambushed U.S. Army paymaster Joseph Wham in Graham County, wounding several soldiers. The thieves escaped with $29,000. Meade directed the investigation. Based on informant information, a number of arrests took place. Several of those jailed were Mormons, and in a climate where the Edmunds Act (outlawing polygamy) was enforced, a perception of persecution permeated the air. However, the jurors refused to convict anyone for simply "robbing the Government and shooting a few black soldiers."

Under political pressure, much of it from the Mormon community, Meade stepped down from the U.S. marshal's position on March 4, 1890, and became superintendent of the Yuma Territorial Prison on April 24, 1893. Scarcely a month later, however, the 17th Territorial Legislature failed to confirm his appointment. Later in the year, Grover Cleveland reappointed Meade to the position of U.S. marshal for Arizona Territory. During this second posting. Meade arrested individuals earlier involved with the aforementioned Wham payroll heist. Several of those men received prison sentences.

On June 15, 1897, Meade reluctantly tendered his resignation. He then traveled to Alaska and briefly dabbled in mining interests, then returned to Arizona, where he was a caustic voice in Democratic politics. He died at Tombstone on March 14, 1918.

See also: FEDERAL MARSHALS AND DEPUTY MARSHALS

MEAGHER, Michael (1843–1881)

This lawman was born in Ireland but became city marshal of Wichita, Kansas, on April 13, 1871. His brother John, also from Ireland, acted as an assistant, and between the two of them they bounced

U.S. Marshall William K. Meade (Arizona Historical Society)

back and forth, one then the other becoming marshal or assistant marshal. However, during his last term as city marshal in Wichita, Kansas, he shot and killed Sylvester Powell, allegedly in self-defense.

Meagher then moved to Caldwell, campaigned for mayor, and won the election of April 1880. However, a month later, on June 19, he shot and killed George Flatt. This time the district attorney charged Meagher with complicity in the slaying. A jury freed him. He did not seek reelection; instead, he went to Caldwell, Kansas, and was immediately named city marshal. There he and a man named George Speers were slain by five cowboys, most of whom were never tried, or were tried and acquitted. The stories seemed to revolve around a conspiracy that was never proved.

MEEKS, Henry (a.k.a. Bub Meeks) (1869?–1903?)

Bub Meeks, as most folks called this Mormon desperado, was born in Utah near Walesburg. He cared little for ranch life, and as a young man he drifted over to the Lost Cabin area of Wyoming, where he became acquainted with Butch Cassidy. He apparently signed on with the Wild Bunch, with whom he started his training by guarding horses at Montpelier, Idaho, while Cassidy and Elza Lay robbed the bank and customers. All three escaped with a reported $16,500.

The three outlaws then struck the Castle Gate coal mine on April 21, 1897; this time Meeks cut the telegraph wires as well as held a relay of horses several miles distant from the heist. Cassidy and Lay acquired an estimated $8,000 before barreling away alongside a railroad track. Pursued at first by a locomotive, the two outlaws finally veered from the tracks and met Meeks. All three escaped.

The three men now split up, Cassidy and Lay riding south and Meeks heading to Wyoming, where he was arrested for robbing a train. The authorities extradited him to Bear Lake County in Idaho, where on September 4, 1897, a jury sentenced him to 35 years in the Idaho State Penitentiary. Prison records described him as five foot eleven inches, with a dark complexion, black hair and mustache, 170 pounds, and green eyes. Four years later the Board of Pardons commuted the sentence to 12 years, but on December 24, 1901, he broke out, only to be recaptured the next day. The authorities attached another 12 years to the sentence.

On February 2, 1903, he broke loose again, running through the gate. He might have made it had not Deputy Warden R. H. Fulton noticed the attempted break and shot him in the left leg. Doctors had to amputate, and not long after that Meeks attempted suicide by leaping from a 35-foot wall. When that failed, he tried to stab himself with a pair of shears. That wasn't successful either. On April 22, 1903, the authorities transferred him to State Hospital South, the insane asylum at Blackfoot, Idaho. On August 9, 1903, he broke out, and from there the trail vanished. It is generally believed that Bub Meeks went back to Wyoming.

See also: CASSIDY, BUTCH; LAY, WILLIAM ELLSWORTH; WILD BUNCH

MILLER, Clell (1849–1876)

The desperado Clell Miller started life in Kentucky but moved to Missouri and fought alongside Bloody Bill Anderson as a guerrilla during the Civil War. Union forces wounded and captured him near Albany, Missouri, and he spent the remaining war years in captivity. In 1871, he rode with the James gang at Corydon, Iowa, when it struck the bank. There he was caught and tried. Acquitted, he rejoined the gang and was slain during a subsequent James gang job at a bank in Northfield, Minnesota. The University of Michigan medical school claimed the body and returned it for burial in Missouri.

See also: ANDERSON, WILLIAM C.; JAMES BROTHERS; YOUNGER BROTHERS

MILLER, James (a.k.a. Killin' Jim; Deacon Jim) (1861–1909)

Jim Miller was born in Van Buren, Arkansas, and lived to raise the art of bushwhacking and ambush practically to a science. His tools were a shotgun and occasionally a rifle. By some accounts, he killed between 20 and 50 men, although such figures defy documentation. Jim Miller was literally a shotgun for hire, his first two victims being his grandparents. He went to live with his sister and her husband, Jim Coop, but Coop proved to be troublesome. So Miller killed him too.

Miller became a town marshal in Pecos, Texas, as well as a deputy sheriff, a likable figure who never smoked, drank, or swore. He spoke softly and politely to women, loved old hymns, and could always be counted on to be in church, ever active in

James Brown Miller, better known as "Killin' Jim Miller"
(Bill James Collection)

the Amen Corner. Otherwise, he had just one noticeable idiosyncrasy: he wore a heavy black frock coat. Folks did not pay much attention to it in winter, but some did consider it strange in July.

Miller had his ups and downs with Sheriff Bud Frazer, one reason being that Frazer—who had gone to El Paso, Texas, on business—learned in his absence that Miller had more or less turned the town over to thugs. Frazer therefore brought the noted Texas Ranger John R. Hughes back to Pecos with him. Within hours Miller was in jail, charged with attempted murder. A jury set him free.

On April 12, 1894, Frazer walked up behind Miller and fired his revolver. The bullet bounded off Miller's black coat, courtesy of an iron plate sewn there. The sheriff fired again and disabled Miller's right arm. Miller also began shooting but only wounded a bystander. Frazer fired again, hitting Miller in the groin, and that ended the fight. Miller recovered.

Frazer lost his reelection bid and left town for Eddy (Carlsbad), New Mexico, only to return a few months later and encounter Miller on the street. Both men drew weapons, and Frazer shot Miller in the arm and leg—then rushed in to kill him with a bullet to the heart. However, Miller now had an iron plate sewn in the coat front, and the bullet bounced.

Miller swore out a charge of attempted murder against Frazer. The case, tried in El Paso, ended in a hung jury. On September 13, 1896, the feud reached its conclusion at a gambling table in Toyah, Texas. Miller laid a shotgun across the top of the saloon door and with one blast killed Frazer, who was dealing. A jury forgave him. However, a Joe Earp testified against Miller; three weeks after the trial, someone killed Earp with a shotgun.

In Ward County, Texas, during the summer of 1902, Miller claimed to have caught three men rustling cattle. He killed two; the other one escaped. In 1904, he killed Lubbock attorney James Jarrott, a successful lawyer fighting for nesters (farmers who raised fences unpopular with cattlemen) against big ranchers. The big ranchers paid Miller to kill him. Later that year at Fort Worth, Texas, Miller fulfilled a contract on Frank Fore, killing him in the restroom of a local hotel. On August 1, 1906, Miller murdered U.S. deputy marshal Ben Collins near Emet, Oklahoma. The Pruitt family paid for that one, although the authorities caught and indicted Miller.

Out in Las Cruces, New Mexico, on February 29, 1908, someone shot the famed New Mexico sheriff Pat Garrett. A popular myth had it that Killin' Jim Miller was the actual slayer; however, local cowboy Wayne Brazel confessed, went to trial, and was acquitted.

Of course, Miller's luck finally ran out. On February 26, 1909, three of rancher Gus Bobbitt's neighbors paid Jim Miller to kill him. Miller complied, killing Bobbitt with a double-barreled shotgun near Ada, Oklahoma. However, someone talked. Miller hid out in Fort Worth, but authorities caught him and sent him back to Ada for trial. On the night of April 19, 1909, a mob broke Miller and the three accomplices out of jail and lynched all four in a nearby barn.

See also: GARRETT, PATRICK FLOYD JARVIS; HUGHES, JOHN REYNOLDS

MILTON, Jefferson Davis (1861–1947)

Milton is remembered primarily as a lawman. Born the son of a Florida governor, he reached Texas around 1877 and joined the rangers in 1880. After three years, he followed a law enforcement carrer in New Mexico, becoming a range detective as well as a cowboy and a deputy sheriff before signing on with U.S. Customs. He left around 1890 to become a Pullman conductor before being appointed chief of police on August 10, 1894, at El Paso, Texas.

In mid-March 1895, John Wesley Hardin arrived in El Paso and within a week had taken up with Beulah Mrose. That upset her husband, Martin, living in Ciudad Juarez as a New Mexico fugitive charged with cattle rustling. Martin demanded that Beulah return his money, and Hardin arranged a rendezvous between the two in El Paso. He even lined up U.S. Deputy Marshal George Scarborough to guide Martin across an old railroad trestle and into town. However, Hardin also arranged for Constable John Selman, Texas Ranger Frank McMahan, and Chief of Police Jeff Milton to meet Martin on the U.S. side of the Rio Grande. Milton carried a shotgun, and the three lawmen executed Mrose as soon as he stepped onto Texas soil. Their pay was the New Mexico reward money, rumored to be $350.

Milton now drifted back to Arizona where he again became a U.S. deputy marshal as well as a Wells Fargo agent assigned to the Southern Pacific Railroad. In 1900, a botched holdup caused Jeff Milton some serious wounds. Nevertheless, he retired as a U.S. immigration agent in 1932. He died in Tucson.

See also: HARDIN, JOHN WESLEY; MROSE, HELEN; MROSE, MARTIN

William (Bill) Miner (Robert G. McCubbin Collection)

MINER, William (1846–1913)

Bill Miner was born in Ingham County, Michigan, and reached California as soon as he could, about 1860. He joined the Second California Cavalry in May 1864 but deserted two months later. In 1866, authorities convicted him of horse theft. He spent the next four years at San Quentin, being released on July 12, 1870. Six months later, in 1871, Miner and two friends held up a stagecoach and took the Wells Fargo box. Miner and one of his partners, "Alkali Jim" Harrington, were captured and tried in Calaveras County. Each received 10 years. However, because they had been forced to wear leg irons in court, the case was appealed and a new trial ordered. This time each man received a 13-year sentence, which should have told Miner something about complaining too much. In 1879, Miner and a fellow convict named Gibson brutally beat another convict. Both were flogged.

Miner took his release papers in 1880 and headed for Colorado, where he and Arthur Pond, and later Pond's brother, held up several stages. A posse captured all three, but Miner managed to slip away. A furious posse lynched the Pond brothers.

In March 1881, Miner and Stanton Jones robbed the Del Norte stage. Sheriff William Bronough of Saguache County caught them, but Miner broke loose, grabbed a gun, and wounded both the sheriff and his deputy. Then Miner headed for California, where a Wells Fargo detective captured him. A jury dispatched him back to San Quentin in 1881 for another 25 years.

In 1892 Miner tried another jail break, a futile attempt that earned him a mouth and neck full of buckshot. Still, the state released him in June 1901.

After some brief, stagnant attempts at honest work, he and three others held up a train near Portland. One of his companions died in the shootout, but Miner escaped to British Columbia, where in 1904 he and others successfully robbed a couple of trains of an undetermined amount of money. A week later the Northwest Mounted Police captured him. A jury sentenced him to life imprisonment. But jails were made for breaking out of, sometimes, and on August 7, 1907, he and others slipped over the wall. The others were recaptured. Miner just kept running and didn't stop until reaching Pennsylvania, where he lived as George Anderson. He showed up next in Georgia, where on February 18, 1911, he and Charles Hunter held up a Southern Express train. He hadn't gotten 20 miles when the law caught up with him again. A Georgia jury gave him 20 years in the state prison at Milledgeville. This time, in spite of several escape attempts, he broke out only through death on September 2, 1913. No relative or friend claimed the body, so it lies today in the Milledgeville City Cemetery.

MITCHELL, William (a.k.a. Baldy Russell; John Davis) (1850–1928)

The remarks of Bill Mitchell's biographer tell the story: "He could not read books, but he could read sign. . . . He would not run from anybody and refused to let anyone 'run over' him . . . ready for fight or a frolic." On the western frontier there may have been scores of "Bill Mitchells," but none produced a better story than Bill Mitchell from Hood County, Texas. The Mitchell story is one of a feud and its resultant killings. After that, the feud evolves into a 47-year odyssey of "life on the dodge."

In a struggle over land, pride, and probably factors yet to be understood, the Mitchell clan went to war with the Truitts. The two factions couldn't agree about anything important or even trivial. They agreed only that they despised each other.

After a bitter court conflict described as "vexatious litigation," on March 28, 1874, the case became deadly serious. In a sense it started outside of Granbury, Hood County, Texas, when James, Sam, and 17-year-old Isaac Truitt galloped past the Mitchell party hurling jeers and insults. The irked Mitchells grabbed their horses and caught up with the Truitts at Contrary Creek, where the family had

stopped for water. At this point the yelling and cursing turned into gunfire that left Sam and "Little Ike" Truitt dead. Brother James had a gaping hole in his shoulder.

From this moment on, Bill Mitchell and his friend Mit Graves were fugitives. Other Mitchells were arrested, although they probably never fired a shot. Nevertheless, the authorities locked them in "close confinement and well guarded."

A judge sentenced Nelson "Cooney" Mitchell, the family patriarch, to be hanged. The judgment was affirmed, his appeal denied. Bill Mitchell chose not to come in and take the blame for what he himself had done. On October 7, 1875, Nelson's youngest son, who no doubt was attempting to come to his father's aid, was slain by jail guards after dark as he prowled around jailhouse walls, armed with a double-barreled scattergun and a brace of Colt revolvers. Two days later, the state executed the 79-year-old prisoner.

Bill Mitchell remained a fugitive in the wild brush country north of Del Rio, existing on what the land could provide, trading animal pelts, and collecting county bounties for the skins of wolves and cougars so he could purchase provisions. During the early 1880s, Bill Mitchell moved over to New Mexico Territory, hanging out at Seven Rivers in the Pecos Valley. There on April 28, 1884, he married a divorcee, Mary Jane Beckett Holliday.

By 1888, Mitchell, now using an alias of John Davis, managed to elude capture. Soon it was time for another name change—Henry "Baldy" Russell was born. He moved farther west, this time to Magdalena, New Mexico, a wild and woolly, wide-open, and wide-awake frontier town described as "behind the beyond." Later he sought and obtained employment in the mines near Silver City, but there were just too many people there for "Baldy." He headed in 1892 for the Jornada del Muerto (Journey of Death), an exceedingly hostile and desolate patch of real estate, eventually settling on the Jornada at the northern edge of the Tularosa Basin, but still in New Mexico.

Completely cut off from the rest of the world, Mitchell would make but two or three trips to town every year for supplies, while his wife and two daughters, Maude and Belle, remained behind to do chores and tend livestock. At home, "Baldy" Russell always carried a six-shooter. Mary Jane stood guard on the roof with a rifle cradled in the crook of her arm and scanned the horizon through binoculars. A fugitive's life was hard on all.

But trouble, when it came, was not necessarily going to be easy to see. On March 23, 1907, H. M. Denny, sheriff of Otero County, New Mexico Territory, was notified of the fugitive in his bailiwick. Accompanied by one of his deputies, Ben Wooten, he set out to arrest "Baldy" Russell. Assuming an undercover role, the pair of lawmen lured Russell away from his residence on the pretext of examining mining property. Within a brief time, Baldy was in irons and on his way back to Texas.

As the next three years dragged by, Mitchell spent time in jail, at trial, out on bond, back in jail, out again, and back in New Mexico, first at one place and then the other. On March 25, 1912, Bill Mitchell entered the Texas prison at Huntsville, sentenced to life imprisonment 38 years after the murders. But Mitchell possessed the instincts of a wily coyote. He escaped on July 14, 1914, and once again assumed the role of John Davis. For the next 14 years, the accomplished fugitive carefully guarded the secrets of his past as old age began to hobble his movement. In April 1928, Bill Mitchell, with a failing heart, surrendered at a hospital in Douglas, Arizona—and there he died.

MORCO, John (a.k.a. Happy Jack) (?–1873)
John Morco was a cross between a good guy and a bad guy. He allegedly killed four men in California when they tried to prevent him from beating his wife. He next showed up as a policeman in Ellsworth, Kansas, where in the Joe Brennan Saloon he was involved in the Billy/Ben Thompson confrontation that led to the death of Sheriff Chauncey Whitney.

Morco thereafter left town after allegedly stealing a pair of six-shooters. He returned to Ellsworth in 1873. There he and policeman Charles Brown argued; Brown shot him twice, killing him.

See also: THOMPSON, BEN; THOMPSON, WILLIAM J.

MORENO, María (1880–1899)
The story of Arizona Territorial Prison inmate 1224 does not revolve around the exploits of a six-shooter-packing dynamo. Near her Yuma picket-house, at 10 o'clock on the morning of July 2, 1896, María Moreno, armed with a double-barreled shotgun, killed her 15-year-old brother, Alberto, blowing off one side of his face. Alberto had been critical regarding her unbecoming behavior at an area dance. The 16-year-old María, not wishing to listen, shot him dead.

María was held without bond, though her crime was reduced to manslaughter. A jury sentenced her to prison for one year and one month, the youngest female prisoner ever sent to the Yuma Territorial Prison. She served her sentence and was released.

A year later, on July 25, 1899, María Moreno died. "María was demented and was not responsible for her acts," reported the *Arizona Sentinel*, citing facts apparently already widely known. Life could prove tough for teenagers, especially poor ones!

MORTON, William Scott (1856–1878)
This Lincoln County War gunman was born near Richmond, Virginia, and somehow wound up in Lincoln County, New Mexico, where he went to work for the House of Murphy. In March 1877, he became foreman of the Murphy-Dolan cow camp on the Pecos River; stories still exist that he killed at least two men there. As a member of Sheriff William Brady's posse, on February 18, 1878, Morton helped ignite the Lincoln County War by being one of the group that killed Englishman John Tunstall. Less than a month later, Morton and another slayer, Frank Baker, were captured by the Regulators, among them Billy the Kid. Morton subsequently wrote a letter to a friend in Richmond, Virginia, saying that he expected to be killed. And he was killed, probably by execution.

See also: BILLY THE KID; LINCOLN COUNTY WAR

MOSSMAN, Burton (1867–1956)
This lawman came out of Minnesota, where he had been born, to survey the Sacramento Mountains in southern New Mexico, as well as to become a cowboy. During the next few years he moseyed over to Colorado and Kansas before becoming in 1897 manager of the Hash Knife outfit near Holbrook, Arizona. In 1901, he became the first captain of the Arizona Rangers, one of his earliest and greatest cases being his pursuit into Sonora, Mexico, and the capture of the murderer Augustino Chacón, who by his own admission had killed 52 men. Chacón was hanged at Solomonville, Arizona, on November 21,

1902. Mossman later entered the cattle business around Roswell, New Mexico, where he died. He is buried there.

See also: ARIZONA RANGERS

MROSE, Helen Beulah (1872–1904)

She was born Helen Williams on November 1, 1872 at Berry Creek, Williamson County, Texas. In 1884, the family moved to northern Mason County, Texas, where she met Steve Jennings. They married on March 21, 1889, and in spite of a rocky marriage had three children, only one of whom—a daughter—survived. The daughter, who in photos resembles a boy, has been referred to as "Albert.") In October 1884, Helen and her daughter moved to Eddy County, New Mexico, to be closer to kin. She had never been divorced from her first husband, but she took the name of Helen Beulah and married Martin Mrose, a local cowboy. Martin unfortunately had several local complaints pending against him, including one for cattle rustling. After being arrested—but jailed only briefly—in Midland, Texas, he fled to Mexico. In Chihuahua, both he and Beulah were arrested by a Santa Fe Railroad detective named Beauregard Lee, who arranged to incarcerate Martin briefly in Ciudad Juarez. However, Martin bribed his way out and filed for Mexican citizenship. Mrose now needed an attorney, so Helen took Martin's cash and crossed the river into El Paso, where she retained the services of lawyer and former Texas gunfighter John Wesley Hardin. Within a week, however, Hardin had both her and much of her money, and she was not returning to her husband. From across the Rio Grande, an enraged Martin Mrose demanded his funds. Hardin pretended to arrange a clandestine meeting between the husband and wife on the El Paso side of the river. Hardin convinced U.S. Deputy Marshal George Scarborough to lure and guide Mrose across the Rio Grande. Once Mrose was on the Texas side, George Scarborough, Texas Ranger Frank McMahan, former El Paso police chief Jeff Milton, and possibly El Paso constable John Selman shot him to death.

Beulah lent John Wesley Hardin roughly $1,000 to purchase a half-interest in El Paso's Wigwam Saloon, and Hardin retained her as his secretary to write his memoirs. Still their lives and times together were not happy. He once ordered her to write a letter saying she was committing suicide, while she once kept him at bay in their apartment by threatening to kill him with his own six-shooter. She even filed a $100 peace bond against Hardin on August 7, 1895. Nevertheless they had a need for one another and perhaps even shared some affection. She left him once and took a train to Arizona. At Deming, New Mexico, through some premonition, no doubt a sense of doom, she wired him, "I fear you are in trouble and I'm coming back." She did return, but their life was not any better, and she left again.

A few days later, on August 19, 1895, Constable John Selman killed John Wesley Hardin in the El Paso Acme Saloon. Beulah returned and paid the funeral costs of $77.50. She also laid claim to the Hardin estate, insisting that she had a right to it, primarily because of unpaid secretarial services regarding his autobiography.

In the end, she was outlawyered, got nothing, and left again. In February 1896, she and her daughter moved to the San Francisco/Oakland area, where between May and July she relinquished her daughter to a Catholic orphanage and likely never saw her again. In California, Helen probably worked at prostitution and as a drink hustler, being reduced to little more than a panhandler when she collapsed in an alley and then died in a Sacramento hospital on September 11, 1904. Helen Beulah Mrose is buried in Sacramento, California, probably in the East Lawn Cemetery.

See also: HARDIN, JOHN WESLEY; MILTON, JEFFERSON DAVIS; MROSE, MARTIN; SELMAN, JOHN HENRY

MROSE, Martin (1856–1895)

Martin Mrose (the last name is spelled in various ways) was born in 1856 at the struggling Wendish colony of Serbin, Texas. By 1879 he had become a horse wrangler, working for rancher Mahlon McCowan in Atascosa County. Later, the well-known New Mexico figure Charles B. Eddy retained him as an employee for the Eddy-Bissell Cattle Company, with ranches in New Mexico and Colorado. Martin eventually became Eddy's trail boss and chief wrangler, although in the financial panic of 1893, Martin was released. He bought a small ranch of his own five miles east of Eddy, homesteaded on another tract, and stocked each with cattle, some of it rustled. He married in November 1894 Helen Jennings, a young lady who subsequently became Helen Beulah

Mrose. Meanwhile, although he was never specifically charged with selling pilfered livestock, a grand jury indicted him for receiving $24 in stolen property. The young couple sold out and moved to Midland, Texas, where Mrose learned that rewards on his head were now circulating across southern New Mexico. Helen fled to Ciudad Juarez, Mexico, across the Rio Grande from El Paso, and Martin quickly followed. The Mexican police arrested him on a train in Chihuahua, but he fought extradition back to the United States.

In the meantime, Beulah crossed into El Paso and sought the legal services of attorney and former gunslinger John Wesley Hardin. Beulah and Hardin subsequently began an affectionate relationship, and she decided not to return to her husband. When Martin asked her for his money, Hardin dispatched a U.S. deputy marshal, George Scarborough, to entice Martin to the north end of the Mexican Central Railroad Bridge on the pretense of meeting Beulah. There the two men were met on June 29, 1895, by former El Paso chief of police and now U.S. deputy marshals Jeff Milton and George Scarborough, Texas Ranger Frank McMahan, and (quite possibly) El Paso constable John Selman. These four lawmen (including Scarborough) shot Martin full of revolver rounds and shotgun pellets. He was buried the next day in El Paso's Concordia Cemetery, three graves north of where John Wesley Hardin would soon lie.

See also: HARDIN, JOHN WESLEY; MILTON, JEFFERSON DAVIS; MROSE, HELEN BEULAH; SCARBOROUGH, GEORGE ADOLPHUS; SELMAN, JOHN HENRY

MURRIETA, Joaquin (1832–1853)

Joaquin Murrieta, one of the legendary California bandits, likely was born and raised in Sonora, Mexico. He is believed to have married a Rosa Feliz in Sonora and to have taken her with him—along with several brothers and sisters—when he moved to California during the Gold Rush. By 1850, his claim had been jumped, Rosa raped, a brother lynched, and Joaquin whipped. Joaquin killed several of his enemies, and from that time on he made his living by running stock into Mexico and by robbing miners, travelers, and occasionally ranchers. In April 1882, he and his gang murdered a merchant named Allen Ruddle and escaped with $500. The gang moved toward Los Angeles, then twisted north toward San Andreas and into Mariposa County, stealing horses and occasionally robbing and killing ranchers. But Murrieta was starting to pay a price. Several gang members had been killed, and a few had been captured and lynched.

A startled California legislature met and formed a law enforcement group called the California Rangers. Harry Love became its leader, and tracking down Murrieta became one of Love's priorities. He surprised the outlaws in camp, but they escaped, Murrieta subsequently blundering into an ambush by Indians, who captured, robbed, and then released the gang members.

On July 12, 1853, Love reached San Juan Bautista and spent the next two weeks combing the area, asking questions, and making occasional arrests. Then he and his men unexpectedly encountered Murrieta and his *vaqueros* on July 24. A fight immediately started. The rangers killed four men and captured two. Joaquin Murrieta was believed to be one of the dead. Another was Three Fingered Jack, Murrieta's second in command.

Both heads were cut off and placed in jars, as was the hand of Three Fingered Jack. For years the head of Murrieta was exhibited in a San Francisco museum; it was lost or destroyed during the 1906 California earthquake.

So, did the rangers really have the head of Murrieta? Probably they did, although positive proof certainly did not, and does not, exist. The issue remains controversial, although Capt. Harry Love collected the $1,000 reward.

See also: LOVE, HARRY

MUSE, Herbert E. (a.k.a. H. E.) (1850–1935)

Certainly his is not a well-known name in the annals of western frontier marshals and sheriffs, but possibly it should be, for H. E. Muse was a veteran peace officer, and in southwestern New Mexico he was a terror to bad men. Born in Cambridge, Maryland, on June 9, 1850, Muse migrated to Texas. After acquiring cowboy skills, he wandered westward to Grant County, New Mexico, where for a while he tended cattle. It was there, though, that H. E. Muse tossed away the lariat and branding iron, accepting employment as deputy under Sheriff Harvey Howard Whitehill.

Stationed at Paschal, a copper-mining community in the Burro Mountains 12 miles south of Silver City, Muse graciously offered his house overnight to a family passing through—Judge H. C. McComas, his wife, and their six-year-old son, Charles. The McComas family declined, opting to make a few more miles before stopping. Muse was stunned when he saw them next. On March 29, 1883 in the wee morning hours, Muse at the head of a squad of 15 resolute citizens rushed to investigate reports that the McComas group had been massacred on the road to Lordsburg. At dawn, Muse who was ranging ahead of the platoon, discovered the naked and brutalized body of Mrs. McComas, slain by Apaches. Respectfully, he removed his coat and covered her before others reached the scene. Shortly thereafter the remains of Judge McComas were discovered. Little Charley McComas was a prisoner.

Two years later, in 1885, Muse became town marshal for Silver City. Over time, he arrested the notorious "Salome." He faced down Dave Cooney, who was pointing a six-shooter at him at the time; tracked down a band of burglars; and arrested a "dead hard game" Chinaman appropriately named Ah Bang. In 1886, the U.S. government appointed him as a U.S. deputy marshal.

During the course of his law enforcement career throughout Grant County, in such communities as Tyrone, Santa Rita, Paschal, Pinos Altos, and Silver City, Muse "won a widespread reputation. Few had the temerity or reckless judgment to question his authority. Those who did, without exception, regretted it and some who elected to fight it out with Muse paid with their lives, as he was a dead shot and devoid of fear." So said the local newspaper reporter.

At the time of his death on October 14, 1935, at age 85, Muse was the court crier for the Grant County District Court.

MUSGRAVE, George (a.k.a. Jesse Williams; Jeff Davis; Jesse Miller) (1874–1947)

This outlaw, born in Texas, associated himself early with the Black Jack Christian and the High Fives outlaw bands. On October 19, 1896, he killed George Parker during a Diamond-A roundup along the Rio Feliz, near Roswell, New Mexico. After Black Jack Christian died, Musgrave was arrested at Fronteras, Mexico; he was not released until December 1897. At that point he dropped out of sight, not reappearing until being arrested on the North Platte in Nebraska during late 1909. He went to trial for the earlier killing of Parker but was acquitted.

NAVY Colt 1851

This weapon is called the "Navy Colt" because of an engraved scene on the cylinder depicting a naval encounter. One loaded this percussion revolver from the front of the cylinder and aligned its chamber with the barrel by cocking the hammer. When loaded with 25 grains of black powder and a round lead ball, the 1851 Navy Colt had the punch of a modern .38 Special.

NEAGLE, Dave (?–1925)

This lawman didn't reach the historical spotlight until he showed up in Tombstone, Arizona, as one of Sheriff John Behan's deputies during 1881. When town marshal Virgil Earp was wounded in 1881, Neagle replaced him as the chief of police. However, Neagle lost the next election. He allegedly killed a Mexican desperado in Tombstone before leaving for Montana, where he became a U.S. deputy marshal. With a judge under his protective custody in Lathrop, California, Neagle shot and killed another judge whom the lawman perceived as threatening his prisoner. Neagle died in Oakland, California.

See also: LEVY, JAMES H.

NECKTIE Party

A necktie party was a lynching, usually by vigilantes. Necktie parties generally occurred on the spot and without much deliberation.

See also: VIGILANCE COMMITTEES

NEVILL, Charles L. (1855–1906)

This Texas Ranger was born in Carthage, Alabama, but arrived in Texas at least by 1874, when he joined the Frontier Battalion of the Texas Rangers. He fought Indians and was present at Round Rock when the mortally wounded Sam Bass surrendered to him. Three years later, in 1881, Nevill rode with Capt. George Baylor when some of Victorio's Apache braves made their last stand in the Diablo Mountains. Not long afterward, Nevill, plus a surveyor and several other hearty souls, became the first ever to travel by boat down Santa Elena Canyon, in the Big Bend.

Nevill became sheriff of Presidio County, Texas, in 1882, and for a while put together a ranching partnership with former ranger James Gillett. After that he moved to San Antonio, where he died.

See also: BASS, SAM; BAYLOR, GEORGE WYTHE; GILLETT, JAMES BUCHANAN; TEXAS RANGERS

NEWCOMB, George (a.k.a. Bitter Creek; Slaughter's Kid) (1867–1895)

This desperado left home in Kansas while still a young boy and wound up as a cowboy on the Slaughter Ranch in Texas. Here he became Slaughter's Kid. From Texas he moved into the Cherokee

Strip in Oklahoma, where as a cowboy he grew to love the lyrics, "I"m a Wild Wolf from Bitter Creek, and it's my night to howl." He sang it so often that the cowboys started referring to him as Bitter Creek.

Before much time had passed, Bitter Creek Newcomb joined first the Dalton Gang, and then the Doolin Gang. In July 1892, he and the Daltons rode into Adair, Oklahoma, robbed the train depot, and then tried to hold up the train. A year later the Doolin Gang rode into Ingalls, Oklahoma, and was shot to pieces by lawmen. Bitter Creek and Bill Doolin barely escaped.

A $5,000 reward now went on Bitter Creek's head. Outlaw Charley Pierce made the mistake of tagging along when Newcomb decided to hide out near Ingalls, at the Dunn Brothers Ranch. On May 1, 1895, the Dunn brothers ambushed the outlaws for the reward money as they left their barn.

See also: CANTON, FRANK; DALTON BROTHERS; DOOLIN, WILLIAM M.

NEWMAN, Norman (a.k.a. Henry Reed) (?–1899)

This outlaw may or may not have been born in Oklahoma, but he killed a man in Greer County in Oklahoma, in November 1898. With the assistance of a neighboring farmer, Perry Cox, he broke jail. Newman fled to the San Augustine Ranch in Dona Ana County, New Mexico; the property was owned by William W. Cox, probably a brother or relative of Perry Cox. At this time Newman changed his name to Billy Reed, but that did not help any, because Pat Garrett, sheriff of Dona Ana County, tracked Newman to the Cox Ranch. During the resultant shootout on October 7, 1899, Garrett's deputy, José Espalin killed Newman.

See also: COX, WILLIAM WEBB; GARRETT, PATRICK FLOYD JARVIS

NEW Mexico Mounted Police

When Texas and Arizona organized ranger forces, dozens of outlaws from both places headed for New Mexico. There it was illegal to carry openly a six-shooter in a public place. Saloons were ordered closed on Sundays, and gambling was illegal—although these statutes were considered jokes, and

Norman Newman (University of Texas at El Paso Archives)

fines were minimal. However, to meet its territory-wide law enforcement responsibilities, New Mexico on February 15, 1905 organized what it called the New Mexico Mounted Police. This single company comprised 11 men, each enlisting for two years: eight privates, a sergeant, a lieutenant, and a captain. The privates drew $40 a month, and out of that they had to furnish their own weapons (usually a Winchester rifle and a Colt .45); the territory provided the ammunition. Each man had to supply his own mount, plus a packhorse, and pay for their care and feeding. Their uniforms resembled Rough Rider clothing; the captain wore a different-style hat. Each officer had a silver shield, although that later switched to a star and various other designs. The captain earned $200 a month, the lieutenant $100, and the sergeant $60.

John F. Fullerton, a Socorro County cattleman, took charge as captain, his lieutenant being Cipriano Baca, a U.S. deputy marshal as well as a former Luna County sheriff. The officers and one private set up their headquarters in Socorro. The remaining rangers scattered everywhere, enforcing the law across 122,000 square miles of territory. Although the unit never had any official name except the New Mexico Mounted Police, in popular parlance the group usually went by the tag of Fullerton's Rangers.

Officer Jessie Lefettie Avant (usually called Fate Avant) became the first officer to kill a man, doing so on August 24, 1905, when he shot a burglar named Bob Rusher at a Capitan store. Rusher had made a bad decision to shoot it out rather than hold up his hands and surrender. Otherwise, during this first year or so of operation, the Mounted Police killed just the one man, capturing 72.

A new governor, in a political move, replaced Fullerton with Fred Fornoff in 1906. Fornoff moved the Mounted Police headquarters to the Santa Fe capital building, where it remained for 14 years. Fornoff's boys seemed especially effective at rounding up outlaws, preventing holdups, and sometimes arresting fraudulent public officials. On one occasion during a dangerous confrontation, mounted policemen John Beal and Bob Putman cowed a mob of gamblers and others in a saloon near Mogollon.

In 1909, the territorial legislature reduced the Mounted Police to four rangers and two officers. However, these officers were augmented by a "Special" Mounted Police; none of its members were salaried. All of these individuals became state policemen a year later, however, when President William Taft granted statehood to New Mexico on January 6, 1912. A year after that, in the spring of 1913, the state police arrested several state senators and charged them with taking bribes. The state senate then refused to pass appropriations to support the state police, and on December 1, 1913, the

New Mexico state police department went out of business.

Governor William McDonald opened his contingency funds during 1914–17 to retain one state police officer for New Mexico—Fred Lambert. This officer worked the entire state. During World War I the New Mexico State War Council reactivated the force, authorizing 16 men. By 1919, there were five sergeants and 16 police patrolling the state. Later that year, all of them invaded Gallup, where they restored order during a coal mine strike. Then on February 15, 1921, the Mounted Police again bowed to the whims of politics and was abolished until the spring of 1933, when the state authorized what it called the New Mexico Motor Patrol. That also was discontinued two years later, on February 25, 1935, when New Mexico created its present state police force.

NIX, Evett Dumas (1861–1946)

This Oklahoma lawman was born in Kentucky. He moved to Guthrie, Oklahoma, where in early 1893 he became a U.S. marshal. His field deputies were a Who's Who of early law enforcement: Heck Thomas, Frank Canton, Chris Madsen, Frank Lake, John Hixon, Ed Kelly, and Jim Masterson. Although he himself never made arrests, "he directed the work . . . and his organization captured or killed more criminals and collected more rewards than did that of any other pioneer officer."

After his law enforcement career ended, Nix moved to Missouri and spent the remainder of his life in investment speculation. He died at St. Louis.

See also: CANTON, FRANK; FEDERAL MARSHALS AND DEPUTY MARSHALS; MADSEN, CHRISTIAN; MASTERSON, JAMES; THOMAS, HENRY ANDREW

NORTHFIELD Raid

People who tend dairy cows are not ordinarily considered fighters. They are inclined to be thrifty, sometimes salting money away in mattresses but generally trusting banks to do the right thing. Thus it seemed to the James-Younger gang in 1876 that the bank at Northfield, Minnesota, in the heart of dairy country, might be isolated in a sense from the rest of the state. The vault should be fat from savings, guarded by people who consumed a lot of cheese and rode fat horses, people more apt to panic than fight.

Thus the eight-man James-Younger gang rode north. The group consisted of Clell Miller, Jesse and Frank James, Jim, Cole, and Bob Younger, and a couple of others known as Charlie Pitts and Bill Styles. The plan had been to hit the bank in Mankato, Minnesota, but the outlaws noticed too many people standing in the street out front, so the gang shrugged and pushed on another 40 miles to Northfield. The decision was no doubt a good one, all things (except the end result) considered, but by far the best decision would have been to turn around and go home. The record doesn't indicate that anyone thought of that.

At Northfield, Jesse, Bob Younger, and Pitts went inside, while the others waited in the street to lay down covering fire when the three came running out. But things inside immediately went wrong. The cashier refused to open the vault, so the outlaws cut his throat and shot him. A teller was wounded when he fled for the door. Outside, a Swedish boy of 17 did not understand an order to turn around and go the other way. He was shot and killed.

Bill Styles went down, never to rise. Clell Miller, shot in the face as he tried to mount, turned his horse to leave, and at that moment a medical student shot him in the chest. He fell off his horse, dead. The Youngers and the James boys fled; Charlie Pitts—whose real name was Samuel Wells—fled with them. When the Younger brothers and the James boys decided to split up, Pitts stayed with the Youngers, dying when the posse caught up with them. The Youngers went to prison. One of the possemen cut off an ear of Pitts, and the body went to a medical school. The James brothers escaped.

See also: JAMES BROTHERS; WELLS, SAMUEL; YOUNGER BROTHERS

NYE, John A. (1832–1906)

John Nye went by many titles, farmer and merchant being perhaps the ones he preferred. But he is best known as a vigilante leader. He was born in New York but moved to Colorado and Montana at an early age. There he became one of five men to organize the state's vigilante movement. Over time they

executed many of the Plummer gang and brought a measure of peace and security to the mining camps. He joined the Black Hills gold rush in 1876 and lived all over that part of the world. He died in Deadwood, South Dakota.

See also: PLUMMER, WILLIAM HENRY

NOTCH-CUTTERS

The Notch-Cutters took their name from an East Texas forested area known as the Yegua Knobs, near McDade, Texas. This group robbed, rustled, and murdered from the early 1860s to the early 1880s. In Texas, at least, the Notch-Cutters had been the first draft dodgers of the Civil War, supporting the Union almost every step of the way, and taking advantage of eastern Texas's shortage of manpower. Three county lines intersected the thick woods of Yegua Knob, thus making it difficult for law enforcement to be effective. The Notch-Cutters took their name not only from the forested thickets but from the fact that every time they murdered someone, they carved notches in the wooden grips of their revolvers.

A group of vigilantes was formed under George Milton and Tom Bishop to oppose the Notch-Cutters, and one hanging tended to lead to another. On May 4, 1874, the Notch-Cutters hung a black man from a tree limb, then shot his body full of holes. In January 1875, the vigilantes strung up two Notch-Cutters.

Both sides tended to rustle cattle, and the nearby Olive brothers Jay and Print, in particular objected to this practice. On March 22, 1876, these ranchers discovered two beeves lying butchered on the prairie, and later that evening caught two Notch-Cutters returning to pick them up. Gunmen working for the Olives shot them, then wrapped their bodies in cowhides and left them lying on the prairie as a warning to others. In retaliation, after dark on August 1, 1876, nearly two dozen Notch-Cutters attacked the Olive Ranch, killing Jay Olive, wounding Print, and burning the house.

On June 22, 1877, at two o'clock in the morning, masked vigilantes caught four Notch-Cutters at a dance. The vigilantes rode away, leaving all four hanging from a tree limb. Things quieted down now for a while, but in 1883 the killings began again. The

Notch-Cutters killed Lee County deputy sheriff Isaac Heffington on December 1.

Then on Christmas Eve of 1883, the vigilantes took three Notch-Cutters into custody, tied their arms, helped them mount their horses, then swung them from a tree limb. On Christmas Day the blood literally flowed in McDade; gunfights roared all over town. The end result was a half-dozen or so wounded and trials that went nowhere. But this final spasm of violence had resolved something. The terror and the bloodshed had to end. On December 27, 34 vigilantes met in McDade. They agreed upon a list of all known Notch-Cutters. Each one received a visit and a message—stop the terror or die at the end of a rope. The Notch-Cutter group never held another meeting, and no additional lynchings occurred. The terror ended.

See also: OLIVE, ISOM PRENTICE

O'DAY, Tom (1862?–1930)

There were newspeople who referred to O'Day as a "Montgomery Ward bandit," and as gunmen go, he did seem awkward and fumbling. By most accounts he came out of Pennsylvania and reached Wyoming in 1893. First he tried to become a participant in the Johnson County War but arrived too late. Following that he joined the Wild Bunch and assisted with the Belle Fourche, South Dakota, robbery in 1897. At least, he tried to assist—the most common story has it that he drank too much while waiting inside a saloon and that upon hearing gunshots ran out in the street to get his horse, let the reins slip through his fingers and, instead of participating in a robbery, chased his horse in the opposite direction.

After finally arresting him, the citizens locked him in the very vault he had sought to rob. There he stayed until October 15, when he and other gang members were indicted on charges of attempted robbery. O'Day was acquitted.

But still O'Day could not stay away from horses, particularly animals belonging to someone else, so in February 1904 he was finally brought to trial in Casper, Wyoming. The first two juries failed to agree, but the third one found him guilty of stealing 135 horses. He spent four years and six months in the state penal system. Thereafter, he moved to South Dakota, reportedly married an Indian woman, and died in 1930 when a team of horses ran away with a wagon he was driving and wrecked it.

See also: WILD BUNCH

ODEN, Alonzo Van (a.k.a. Lon Oden) (1863–1910)

Originally from near Dogtown (Tilden) in McMullen County, Texas, Alonzo "Lon" Oden became a third-generation lawman when he enlisted in the Texas Rangers on March 1, 1894. Oden was one of the few early Texas Rangers to keep a diary. His Swedish grandmother had instilled in the youngster an appreciation for the written word, a rare trait for one raised in the inhospitable and bandit-infested south Texas brush country. Because of the poetic entries in his diary, Oden is often referred to as "the Rhymin' Ranger."

At Shafter, in the Texas Big Bend area, Oden and the renowned Ranger captain John Hughes, along with Ernest "Diamond Dick" St. Leon, halted silver thefts from the Fronteriza Mining Company. During an undercover investigation, St. Leon determined the plans and probable route of the thieves. The officers waited for hours in surveillance, before the outlaws arrived with their pack animals. A shootout commenced. Three desperadoes died. The rangers had no casualties.

Oden now spent considerable time in El Paso, where for seemingly inexplicable reasons he became favorably acquainted with Utah Street's notorious madam Mathilde Weiler, better known as Tillie Howard. Also during this time period, Oden formed a friendship with Baz "Bass" Outlaw, a free-spirited, hard-drinking, hell-raising Texas Ranger who would later be slain by Constable John Selman in Tillie's backyard.

Later (1893), in the Big Bend area, Rangers Hughes and Oden engaged in a furious gun battle (Oden's horse was shot out from under him) in which the brigand Florencio Carrasco was slain.

Oden tendered his resignation as a Texas Ranger on May 18, 1894. He finished his days operating the Chispa Ranch at Marfa, Texas, where he died of natural causes on August 11, 1910.

See also: HUGHES, JOHN REYNOLDS; OUTLAW, BASS; SELMAN, JOHN HENRY

OLINGER, Robert (1841?–1881)

Bob Olinger was said to have been born in Ohio, although the family soon afterward moved to Indian Territory (Oklahoma). Around 1876, he joined his brother, John Wallace Olinger, at Seven Rivers, New Mexico. Bob, often called "Pecos Bob," was a large man who wore his hair long. He stood about six feet tall and weighed 240 pounds. His favorite weapon was a shotgun. He is said to have killed several men, although the only positively known victim was Frank Hill, in March 1880. The details are sketchy.

When Billy the Kid's murder trial ended at Mesilla, New Mexico, on April 9, 1881, Pecos Bob was one of the guards who escorted the Kid on his way by buckboard to the Lincoln jail. Numerous stories have Olinger patting his shotgun and taunting the Kid, daring him to make a break. In Lincoln, the Kid was incarcerated on the second floor of the courthouse. Olinger and James Bell were the guards.

On the 28th, when Sheriff Pat Garrett left to collect taxes in White Oaks, Bob Olinger placed his shotgun in the gun rack and told Bell he was taking a few prisoners across the street to the Wortley Hotel for a bite to eat. Within minutes, the Kid asked Bell to escort him to the outdoor privy. Coming back inside the jail and starting up the stairs, the Kid either yanked Bell's gun out of its holster, or he had a six-shooter that someone had secreted under the toilet seat. At any rate, the Kid killed Bell, who stumbled down the stairs and out into the courthouse yard, where he died.

Robert Olinger, Lincoln County, New Mexico, deputy slain by Billy the Kid (University of Arizona)

The Kid then hobbled to the gun rack, removed Olinger's shotgun, hobbled over to the upstairs window overlooking the Wortley, and waited for Olinger. Across the street, Olinger heard the shots and yelled, "Bell just killed the Kid!" Then Olinger hit the door running, not pausing until directly (by many accounts) beneath that upstairs jail window. The Kid glanced down both barrels, said "Hello Bob," and pulled two triggers. Olinger died instantly.

Billy the Kid did not realize it, but he had only two more months to live himself. As for Bob Olinger, he was buried at Fort Stanton.

See also: BILLY THE KID; GARRETT, PATRICK FLOYD JARVIS; LINCOLN COUNTY WAR

OLIVE, Isom Prentice (a.k.a Print) (1840–1886)

Print Olive was born on February 7, 1840, in Mississippi, but in 1843 his parents, James and Julia Olive, moved to Texas. Around the age of 14, he participated in Longhorn cattle roundups near Brushy and Yegua Creeks in Williamson County. The meat wasn't worth much, but the hide and tallow had value.

When Texas seceded, Print joined the Second Texas Infantry Regiment and saw action at Shiloh and Farmington. The Federals captured him at Vicksburg, then paroled him. Print finished out the war guarding docks at Galveston.

Upon returning home, Olive married Lousia Reno on February 4, 1866. They would have four sons and a daughter. Otherwise, he and his brother Thomas Jefferson (Jay), Ira, and Bob began longhorn cattle drives from Williamson County to the railheads at Kansas and Nebraska. The ranch became wealthy, but it also acquired the reputation as a "gun outfit," meaning that it did not take rustling lightly. Print shot Rod Murray for rustling livestock, then nursed the man back to health and hired him for the Print Olive brand.

Sometime during 1870, Print tangled with Dave Fream during a horseback duel. Fream died on the spot, although Olive suffered heavy damage too.

During 1871, he took a trail herd to Abilene, Kansas, returning with enough money to make his ranch one of the wealthier outfits. In mid-1872, during a card-game argument at Ellsworth, Kansas, Print was seriously wounded by James Kenedy, who shot Print in the hand, the groin, and the thigh. Print might have died had it not been for his loyal bodyguard, Nigger Jim Kelly, who shot Kenedy in the leg and thus ended the fight.

In mid-1875, Print and Jay Olive ambushed and wounded W. H. McDonald, an alleged rustler. Both men went on trial for assault. Print was discharged. Jay paid a $1 fine.

In March 1876, from a tree near their ranch, the Olives hanged two cattle thieves known only as Waddell and Lane. Not long afterward, Print and his brothers caught two rustlers in the act of butchering livestock; they wrapped the thieves—James H. Crow and Turk Turner—inside the green beeve skins. It became known as "the death of the skins," since the sun gradually shrank the skins tightly around their victims, causing a slow, suffocating death. A county court acquitted the Olives of murder despite evidence of a dried skin prominently displaying the Olive brand.

During that same year at the "Olive Pens," 20 miles east of Taylor, Texas, Print and Jay tangled with rustlers in early August. Both men were wounded. Jay died on August 20. In September Print killed a man named Banks who was allegedly responsible for Jay's death. No indictments came down.

Perhaps in retaliation, other outfits struck the Olive Ranch environs. Bob Olive shot and killed alleged rustler Lawson Kelley, as well as an unknown black boy, who, according to rumor, planned to assassinate Olive. Bob later killed a local rancher named Cal Nutt in an Austin saloon. At this point in 1877, the Olives decided to move their operations, first to Colorado and then to Custer County, Nebraska. Even there, however, trouble as well as their violent reputations followed them. Bob became a deputy sheriff in 1877 and was slain by local rustlers Ami Ketchum and Luther Mitchell.

The Olives and some of their neighbors now formed the Custer County Livestock Association in

Print Olive (Author's Collection)

187

1878. Print became its first president. When a jury found Ketchum and Mitchell innocent, a lynch mob shot them to death and set the bodies afire. Other (probably more reliable accounts) say the Olives hanged them from a limb near Devil's Gap and then set their bodies afire as they dangled. From here on, Print Olive had the moniker of "Man Burner." A Hastings, Nebraska, court found him guilty of second-degree murder and sentenced him to life in prison. The case reopened a year later, and Print walked free when witnesses failed to appear.

By now the beef market had come on hard times. Print lost essentially everything and moved his family in 1881 to Dodge City, Kansas. There he invested in real estate at Trail City, Colorado, establishing a wagon yard, stable, and saloon. On August 18, 1886, he walked into the Haynes Saloon, where he and his former trail boss, Joe Sparrow, argued over a trivial sum of money. Sparrow shot him in the head. Print Olive is buried in the Maple Grove Cemetery in Dodge City, Kansas.

O'NEILL, William Owen (a.k.a. Buckey)
(1860–1898)

Buckey O'Neill did it all. He was a soldier, newspaper reporter and editor for the *Phoenix Herald*, politician, sheriff, gambler, Rough Rider, attorney, and a Populist Party candidate. He became sheriff of Yavapai County, Arizona, in 1888, hardly finding his office before he conducted a 600-mile search for four bandits who had robbed a railroad safe at Diablo Canyon. He captured the outlaws in southern Utah and returned them to the Yuma Territorial Prison. Shortly afterward, he became mayor of Prescott and adjutant-general of Arizona Territory in 1897.

O'Neill subsequently organized and became captain of the first U.S. volunteer cavalry regiment from Arizona to serve in Cuba, shortly afterward taking part in the action of June 24, 1898, at Las Guasimas. On July 1, at Kettle Hill, he died from a sniper's bullet in the head. Buckey O'Neill is buried at Arlington National Cemetery.

O'TOOL, Oscar (a.k.a. Barney; Charles Williams)
(1852–1880)

Not to be confused with another Charles Williams who frequented Shakespeare, New Mexico Territory, and who was also charged with murder, "Barney"

O'Tool, originally from Wheeling, West Virginia, was a 28-year-old who murdered a man at Georgetown in Grant County, New Mexico. Williams was sentenced to hang. A local newspaper editorial said it well:

Too many murderers have already gone unpunished in Grant County. This community cannot longer afford to allow groundless feeling of pity or a culpable indifference to stand in the way of justice. We owe it to ourselves to see that the sentence of the law is executed to the letter . . . Justice should always be tempered with mercy, but mercy like charity, begins at home. We must protect ourselves.

Complicating this picture was the fact that another prisoner, a black man named Louis Gaines, who had killed a soldier from Fort Bayard, was scheduled to hang alongside O'Tool. Many in the area, still harboring sympathy for the Confederacy's lost cause, declared that come hell or high water a white man should not be hanged alongside a black man. Rumors circulated that O'Tool would be liberated from the jail. The air was "thick with animosity."

Determined not to be intimidated, Grant County sheriff Harvey Whitehill deputized a crew of 60 well-armed citizens. Along with his chief deputy, Dan Tucker, he marched the two prisoners to the scaffold before a crowd numbering over 400. One person said later, "It looked like war for sure, even some of the women had guns."

On August 20, 1880, standing on the scaffold, O'Tool (at the time still known as Williams) insisted that his true identity would forever remain secret. Then he and Gaines, the latter having had publicly proclaimed his "entire life to have been very evil," were swung into eternity. O'Tool and Gaines dangled side by side, the crowd dispersing quietly.

See also: TUCKER, DAVID

OUTLAW, Bass (?–1894)

Bass Outlaw, an interesting name for a lawman, perhaps spelled his first name "Bazz." Bass, who was born in Georgia, left that state, where he had allegedly killed a man, and in 1885 enlisted in Company E of the Texas Rangers. From there he transferred to Company D in 1887, moved up to sergeant, and then was forced to resign by Capt. Frank Jones for being drunk on duty at Alpine, Texas. However, like most lawmen, Outlaw also carried a U.S. deputy marshal's commission, and this frequently brought him in and out of El Paso, Texas. But even so, he could not control his drinking. On April 4, 1894, he put in another El Paso appearance, still intoxicated, and this time growling threats against U.S. Marshal Dick Ware, who Bass believed had paid someone else to serve papers when the job and the commissions should have gone to him. As it turned out, Outlaw bumped into El Paso constable John Selman, and the two men discussed Outlaw's bad luck on the way down Utah Street, specifically to Madam Tillie Howard's Parlor House. There Selman seated himself on a couch while Bass visited the toilet, where in rearranging his trouser buttons he either dropped his six-shooter or accidentally fired it. The noise sent Tillie rushing into the backyard blowing her whistle, a signal that she needed police assistance.

Bass drunkenly stumbled outside and was wrestling with Tillie for the whistle when Texas Ranger Joe Coolly, in town to testify in a criminal case and now just down the street talking with a printer, came running up the block, vaulted over the fence, and separated the two combatants. By now, Constable John Selman had reached the back porch, where he watched the events.

Ranger Coolly separated the madam and Outlaw, then yelled, "Bass, why do you do things like this?" Outlaw screamed, "Do you want some too?" With that he shot the ranger in the head and then, when Coolly fell to the ground, shot him in the back.

Selman now jumped off the porch, pulling his revolver and screaming at Outlaw, who turned in that direction. Both men fired at the same time. Selman's bullet struck Outlaw directly above the heart as Outlaw's bullet zipped past Selman's head. The gunsmoke blinded Selman, who now began wandering around screaming, "I can't see! I can't see!"

Outlaw stumbled backward to the fence, braced himself, and fired another round that severed an artery in Selman's leg. Selman now stumbled from the brothel and sought a doctor.

In the meantime, Outlaw tumbled over the fence and lay thrashing around on Overland Street, where two passing Texas Rangers, recognizing him but not knowing what had happened, carried him inside the Boss Saloon and laid him on the bar. A doctor was summoned but said there was nothing he could do, so Outlaw was transferred to a backroom prostitute's bed, where he survived for four hours, screaming over and over, "Where are my friends? Where are my friends?"

One of his best friends, Lon Oden, the poet ranger, wrote upon Outlaw's funeral: "Bass Outlaw is dead. Maybe all of us knew something like this would come to Bass—Bass who was so kind; who could laugh louder, ride longer, and cuss harder than the rest of us; who could be more sympathetic, more tender, more patient, than all of us when necessary. Bass had one weakness that—at last—proved stronger than all his virtues. Bass couldn't leave liquor alone, and when Bass was drunk, Bass was a maniac."

John Selman survived, although he forever after walked with a cane and had trouble seeing, particularly at night. Selman was tried for murder and acquitted. Bass Outlaw was buried in El Paso's Evergreen Cemetery.

See also: JONES, FRANK; SELMAN, JOHN HENRY

OWENS, Commodore Perry (1852–1919)

This lawman got his name as a result of being born on the 40th anniversary of Commodore Matthew C.

Commodore Perry Owens (Robert G. McCubbin Collection)

Perry's victory on Lake Erie during the War of 1812. Although born in Tennessee, he lived as a child in Indiana. By the 1870s he had reached Texas, and then Apache County, Arizona. The citizens of Apache County didn't know what to make of this man, who wore his blond hair long, sported a huge, fancy sombrero, and carried a long-barreled Colt .45 surrounded with double belts of ammunition. The railroads hired him to discourage bandits, and in his spare time he chased Indians, on one occasion killing two of them.

Owens achieved his greatest fame as a result of the Pleasant Valley War, when he walked into the Bucket of Blood Saloon in Holbrook, Arizona. When he left a few minutes later, three men lay dead on the floor, and another was seriously wounded. The Bucket of Blood had lived up to its name.

The fame of Commodore Perry peaked as a result of this battle. Folks came to fear him, and most of those who did not fear him disliked him. Although he went on to become sheriff of Navajo County in 1895, that was substantially the end of the line. He quit his job shortly afterward, and spent the remainder of his life operating a saloon and reportedly drinking too much. He died in 1919.

See also: PLEASANT VALLEY WAR

PACKER, Alferd (a.k.a. John Schwartz)
(1847–1907)

Packer is best known as a cannibal. Born in Allegheny County, Pennsylvania, Packer served briefly in the Union army and later became a shoemaker. He learned the prospecting trade early and gained considerable experience as a guide. During the fall of 1873, which became one of the coldest winters on record, he took 21 prospecting beginners for a trek into the San Juan Mountains near present-day Montrose, Colorado. Fortunately, a group of friendly Indians saved them. Several returned to civilization, but Packer and five others pushed on through bitter, frigid weather and were lucky enough one night to find a deserted cabin. That night they all huddled together, went to sleep in sheer exhaustion, and while they slept, Packer shot them. His initial motive was perhaps robbery, and he did take what little money they possessed. He also realized, however, that he needed food and that even with money he could die of starvation before reaching civilization.

Therefore, using his hunting knife, he sliced flesh from the breast and ribs of his former companions. He pushed the flesh into his packs and for two weeks, surviving on the meat of former comrades, he worked his way toward the Los Pinos (Indian) Agency, arriving in February 1874. Here the military and civilians took in the frozen, half-starved Packer, briefly accepting his story that the others in his party had wandered off and frozen to death.

However, as Packer started recovering, he began drinking too much and spending the money of his former comrades. This led to questions about where he had obtained that kind of cash. On April 4, 1874, several strips of human flesh turned up as the nearby snow melted. This led to Packer's arrest, and a long involved tale of how the men took to fighting, how Packer had been the only survivor, and how he had sliced away the human flesh to stay alive. Packer swore that he and a man named Bell had survived, and when Bell attacked him, he had slain Bell in self-defense.

The army now ordered Packer to return to the cabin with lawmen, who would examine the scene. There it quickly became apparent that Packer was a mass murderer, but by the time the search party returned to the agency, Packer had disappeared. In fact, he vanished for over nine years until being arrested near Fort Fetterman, Wyoming, where Packer had changed his name to John Schwartz. He went on trial in Lake City, Colorado, on April 13, 1883, a jury finding him guilty of murder and sentencing him to death. After Packer sat in the Gunnison City jail for three years, the supreme court reversed the decision.

In 1889, Packer won a new trial, the charges now reduced to manslaughter. Again he was found guilty, this time being sentenced to 40 years. He entered the Canon City prison, but he behaved himself, and through efforts of two *Denver Post* publishers who wanted to exhibit him in a circus, he was released in 1901. (The publishers by this time had both been shot and wounded by an attorney named William W. [Plug Hat] Anderson, who was tried for assault three times and finally acquitted.) After that Packer worked as a cowboy, dying in a bunkhouse on April 24, 1907. As a humorous adjunct to the earlier trial, Judge Melville Gerry is reputed to have said, upon passing his death sentence, that "There was seven Democrats in Hinsdale County, and you et five of them, God Damn ye."

PACKING Iron

This means carrying weapons, concealed or otherwise. It refers specifically to six-shooters, rifles, or shotguns. Any outlaw or lawman would be considered as packing iron, even though the weapons might not be readily visible. The phrase also carries a more ominous connotation, that one is not only carrying weapons but is prepared (and perhaps eager) to use them.

PARKER, Fleming (1866–1898)

Fleming, born in California, was an ambitious man who turned to crime and spent five years in San Quentin for burglary. After being released, he headed for Arizona, where in February 1897 he and a friend robbed the Atlantic & Pacific Railroad at Peach Springs. The friend was slain, and the law jailed Parker in Prescott. During a May 9 jailbreak, Parker escaped, but not before he and others had slain the assistant county attorney. The Tuba City, Arizona, authorities arrested him, and on June 4, 1898, he became the last man hanged on the courthouse plaza at Prescott, Arizona.

PARKER, Judge Isaac (a.k.a. Hanging Judge) (1838–1896)

Hanging Judge Parker is undoubtedly the most famous judge in western American history. Born in Maryland, he moved to Ohio, received his bar appointment in 1859, and then settled at St. Joseph, Missouri, where in 1864 he became state's attorney for the 12th Judicial Circuit. In 1870, a Republican, he was elected to Congress, where he convinced President Ulysses Grant to appoint him to the judgeship at Fort Smith, Arkansas. Parker arrived on May 2,

1875, at 36, becoming the youngest judge on a federal bench. He would be there 21 years. His sector included the Indian Territory (Oklahoma) and the Western District of Arkansas, areas overrun by renegades and desperadoes. Two hundred U.S. deputy marshals patrolled this vast region, and over time 65 of them were murdered.

Parker tried 18 people for murder during his first two months on the bench. Fifteen were found guilty, and six were sentenced to death. Although never a great judicial intellect—many of his decisions were overturned on appeal—during Judge Parker's 21 years, he presided over 13,000 criminal cases and sentenced 160 of those found guilty to be hanged, the largest number ever given the death penalty by any judge in U.S. history. Seventy-nine were actually executed on the Fort Smith gallows. The president commuted 46. Two others died in jail, two were pardoned, and two were slain while attempting to escape.

Judge Isaac Parker died on November 17, 1896, shortly after Congress removed the Indian Territory from his jurisdiction. He is buried in the National Cemetery at Fort Smith, Arkansas.

PARKER, Robert Leroy

See BUTCH CASSIDY

PARRA, Geronimo (?–1900)

After rustler Geronimo Parra killed Texas Ranger Charles Fusselman in the Franklin Mountains near El Paso, Texas, in 1890, he fled to New Mexico, where authorities sentenced him to the Santa Fe Territorial Penitentiary for unrelated crimes. In the meantime, Dona Ana County, New Mexico, sheriff Pat Garrett sought Texas fugitive Pat Agnew for questioning in the murder of New Mexico's Col. Albert Jennings Fountain. The rangers agreed to find Agnew if Garrett would use his influence to get Geronimo Parra released from the Santa Fe prison and turned over to Texas authorities. The capture and swap duly took place.

Parra went on trial in El Paso for Ranger Fusselman's murder and was sentenced to be hanged in the El Paso County jail on January 6, 1900. Another convicted El Paso murderer, Antonio Flores, was ordered hanged at the same time.

The men passed their time in adjoining cells on the second floor of the courthouse. The trapdoor yawned just a few steps away. On the day of execution, in a crowded jail corridor, the cell doors were opened, and to everyone's astonishment both men charged out with homemade knives, inflicting minor injuries on several officials. The brawl ended with officers throwing Parra back into his cell and dragging Flores to the trapdoor, pulled a hood down over his head, adjusted the rope, and dropped him into the room below. As the authorities hustled Parra to the trapdoor, however, jailers below were unable to loosen the rope from the neck of Flores. Finally, they hauled Flores up, stretched him out at the feet of Parra, loosened the rope, removed it, soaped it, then slipped it around the neck of Parra and dropped him too. These were the last legal executions in El Paso County.

See also: FOUNTAIN, ALBERT JENNINGS; FUSSEL-MAN, CHARLES; GARRETT, PATRICK FLOYD JARVIS; TEXAS RANGERS

PARROTT, George (a.k.a. Big Nose George) (?–1880)

This desperado once claimed he entered the world on April 13, 1843, in Dayton, Ohio, but few took him seriously. All that's really known is that he had a reputation as a murderer and horse thief when he rode through Montana and moved into Wyoming's Powder River area in the late 1870s. He and his gang planned to rob a train, but Carbon County deputy sheriffs Robert Widdowfield and Henry Vincent were tailing them. The outlaws ambushed the lawmen near Elk Mountain, shooting Widdowfield in the back of the head and Vincent in the legs and chest. Both died, but by year's end most of the gang except for Big Nose Parrott had been captured and prosecuted.

Carbon County sheriff James Rankin subsequently took Parrott into custody, but had not even jailed his prisoner before the vigilantes threw a rope around the outlaw's neck. The sheriff intervened, and Parrott made it to trial, where a judge sentenced him to be hanged in April. Parrott quickly broke out and tried to flee, not getting far before the sheriff had him in custody again. Big Nose had no sooner been tossed back in jail, however, than the vigilantes wrestled him out and slipped a noose around his neck. They were in the process of yanking him high from the arm of a telegraph pole when the rope broke. Parrott fell and hit the ground, with most of the rope, dangling loosely over the cross-bar, trailing from around his neck. He again jumped up, turned,

and darted up a ladder leaning against the pole; the vigilantes let him climb. Grabbing the other end of the dangling rope, they pulled on it, jerked him off the ladder, and watched him swing from the crossbar. After a while he was lowered, but when a local doctor refused to pronounce him dead, the vigilantes pulled him high again. This time he pleased everyone by having died.

Someone made a plaster mask of the dead man's face, while some others cut skin from his chest and fashioned a pair of shoes from it. The brain bowl of his skull became a flower and pin pot as well as a door stop for a local doctor's office. The remainder of the body disappeared, not turning up again until September 1895, when workmen digging a foundation for a store in Rawlins, Wyoming, came across the remains sealed inside a buried whiskey barrel.

PEACEMAKER, Colt .45

The name "Peacemaker" had a lot to do with the popularity of this weapon. Peacemaker in itself said it all. This single-action army six-shot revolver became the first cartridge handgun ever made. It originated in 1871, and the army picked it up in 1873. But in 1874, civilians started clamoring for it. It used 40 grains of black power behind a 235-grain lead bullet. Civilians, however, insisted on a shorter, 4.75-inch barrel, and so the manufacturer cut almost three inches off the military model. Due to the popularity of the 1873 Winchester, most westerners wanted the same ammunition to fit both rifle and six-shooter. So the Peacemaker was retooled to a .44-40, meaning .44 caliber and 40 grains of powder.

The Peacemaker balanced well in the hand, cost only a few dollars, and could absorb incredible abuse while continuing to be dependable. It remains a popular modern weapon primarily because of movies and books, and because the "Peacemaker" still has a certain "American" ring to it.

PERRY, Samuel R. (1844–1901)

Frank Warner Angel, sent by Washington, arrived in New Mexico Territory to facilitate an investigation into the Lincoln County troubles. During this process, he interviewed Samuel R. Perry, a special investigator who noted in his papers that he considered Perry reliable but of no standing. Most newspaper editors were less charitable.

Sam Perry, a Mississippi boy, was born on the last day of July 1844. By the time he was grown, Sam sported a handlebar (killer) mustache and had an unexplained bullet wound in his hip that somewhat retarded him when walking. By whatever route, Sam then made it to New Mexico Territory in time for the chaos and confusion better known as the Lincoln County War.

Sam Perry allied himself with the Murphy-Dolan faction and rode with several posses. One posse on February 18, 1878, caught up with the young Englishman John Tunstall and murdered him. By most accounts, Perry, who was bringing up the rear, was not present when the homicide took place. He told the investigator that after "laying out" Tunstall's body he had heard pistol shots and was advised that some of the crowd "had been shooting at a mark on a tree." The shooter may have been Tom Hill (Chelson), William "Buck" Morton, or Jesse Evans. (It was later claimed that Tunstall had resisted the serving of legal papers and had fired his revolver at posse members, and that therefore he had been killed in self-defense. Perry had placed Tunstall's pistol next to the body.)

Later, during the "the Five-Day War," in which Alexander McSween was killed, Sam Perry occupied the rock tower built by early Lincolnites as a defense against Apache attack. Perry huddled there with such notables as J. B. "Billy" Mathews and the notorious and thoroughly dangerous Jimmy McDaniels. The resultant siege, strategies, fires, shootouts, allegations, and counterallegations have by this date been recorded in numerous volumes, so no attempt will be made to document them here.

Following the Lincoln County War, Perry could not stay out of trouble. He went to trial twice on rustling charges and horse theft but refuted the charges and was found not guilty.

On July 16, 1879, near Hillsboro, New Mexico, on the west side of the Rio Grande, just below the Black Mountains, Samuel Perry shot and killed a cowboy named Frank Wheeler. The generally accepted account is that Wheeler slipped some of Perry's cattle off to a sale barn and afterward refused to relinquish the proceeds to an infuriated boss. One newspaper editor said, "Now if Perry would die of remorse the honest people of this county would sleep more soundly."

Instead, Perry moved east across the Tularosa Basin, settling in the Sacramento Mountains. In his fifties, he married Eolin Bates, a sister-in-law of J. B. Mathews. But the marriage ended when Eolin's mother-in-law arrived from Mississippi and moved in with the newlyweds. On November 7, 1901, Samuel R. Perry, was found dead near Sixteen Springs, just east of present-day Cloudcroft. He had either jumped or fallen off a wagon and landed on his head. Sam Perry thus died from a cracked skull, not remorse.

See also: ANGEL, FRANK WARNER; BILLY THE KID; EVANS, JESSE J.; LINCOLN COUNTY WAR

PHENIX, New Mexico

Phenix was like a lot of once-promising western towns. It began as a speculative venture by Eddy County, New Mexico, surveyor A. B. Nymyer in November 1892. It was a reaction to the Pecos Valley Town Company's rigid enforcement of deed restrictions in the county seat of Eddy preventing the sale of alcohol within the city limits. The little town of Phenix—also called "Jagtown: Oasis of the West," or "Hagerman City,"—was located a mile south of Eddy, on the same side of the Pecos River. Its first saloon was H. A. Bennett's "The Legal Tender," but within two years the little town had developed into a Las Vegas of the Old West. Its largest saloon was Ed Lyell's Silver King, but there were at least a dozen others, including the Adobe, the Ranch, and Two Brothers. These saloons attracted brothels and cribs of the worst sort. Shootings and robberies were so common that Sheriff Dave Kemp assigned the town a permanent deputy, Lon Bass. But even so, violence continued. The saloon district burned in 1893 when a barrel of whiskey exploded, but in just a few months the town rebuilt itself, bigger and brassier than ever. Nevertheless, hard times—a financial panic, a great flood—struck Eddy County in 1893. Ed Lyell divided his business interests with his silent partner, Sheriff Dave Kemp, and relocated Phenix to the mining camp of Globe, Arizona. In 1895 and 1896, restrictions on alcohol eased in Eddy, and a few establishments relocated there. By 1900, most of the businesses—and even the buildings—in Phenix had shifted to Eddy, which is today's Carlsbad, New Mexico. The last brothel closed in 1910, as Phenix faded into the desert. Today almost nothing remains of the once-bustling community.

See also: KEMP, DAVID LEON

PICKETT, Thomas (1856–1935)

Tom Pickett was born to a religious family in Wise Country, Texas, the third of 10 children, on May 22, 1856. His father, George, owned a large ranch and became a Texas legislator as well as a justice of the peace. Tom spent a year (1876–77) in Company B of the Texas Rangers, although during this period he was charged with, but never prosecuted for three counts of cattle theft. By the fall of 1879, he had become a policeman in Las Vegas but lost his nerve on January 20, 1880, following a gunfight that did not involve Pickett but did involve Police Chief Joe Carson. Desperadoes killed the chief, and Pickett took to bed upon learning of Carson's death. Three weeks later he arose and returned to duty. The following May he resigned to become assistant city marshal at White Oaks, New Mexico. In this instance, he lasted but a month, stepping aside after an unknown party fired a shot that grazed his cheek.

Oddly, for a man who took to bed at practically the mention of blood, Tom Pickett now teamed up with Billy the Kid, apparently having met the Kid at Las Vegas or White Oaks, New Mexico. Pickett subsequently was with the Kid when Sheriff Pat Garrett surprised the gang at Fort Sumner, New Mexico, during Christmas week of 1880. Pickett escaped along with the others, only to be captured in company with the Kid shortly afterward at Stinking Springs. Garrett then herded his prisoners to Las Vegas, where the sheriff inexplicably turned Pickett loose—perhaps because of law enforcement ties they had once shared. Eight months later, in August 1880, a Las Vegas grand jury indicted Pickett for cattle theft.

Pickett left town, only to resurface with three additional desperadoes at Seven Rivers, New Mexico, in January 1884. They rode out of town a day or so later, leaving five Hispanic resident males dead in the snow.

Come October 1890, a census taker found Pickett living alone in a cabin at Graham, Arizona, where the local Democratic Party had nominated him as a delegate. Tom Pickett thereafter kept a low profile until 1902, when he ran afoul of a former Texas Ranger at Douglas, Arizona. Capt. Thomas Rynning ordered him out of town and gave him 15 minutes. Pickett heeded the warning and thereafter wandered in and out of the Southwest, staying out of serious trouble, spending years arguing for a military pension as well as medical treatment (and failing at

both). He died on May 14, 1953, at Pine Top, Arizona, and was buried in the Desert View Cemetery at Winslow, Arizona.

See also: BILLY THE KID; GARRETT PATRICK FLOYD JARVIS; RYNNING, THOMAS

PINKERTON National Detective Agency

The Pinkerton National Detective Agency is probably the world's most famous private investigative institution, and it owes its name and its success to its originator, Allan Pinkerton. He was born in Glasgow, Scotland, and began his career as a security guard for President Abraham Lincoln. He also organized the federal secret service, and became its first chief. In 1860 he opened his own business, calling it the Pinkerton National Detective Agency. Its motto: "The Eye That Never Sleeps."

After the Civil War, he furnished employees, known as Pinkerton Men, to private companies, especially firms having labor troubles. Labor unions rightfully considered them strikebreakers, and the Pinkerton name is still detested in the organized labor movement.

Pinkerton is best known for his operations against western outlaws. Although his firm was initially retained by the railroads to control workers, the Pinkertons owe much of their substantial fame to their relentless pursuit of train robbers. During this period, national police agencies such as the modern Federal Bureau of Investigation did not exist, so the Pinkertons established offices in several states and territories. They also added a roaming force of detectives who paid scant attention to state or county lines.

Mention a group of Wild West outlaws—such as the James brothers, the Daltons, the Sam Bass Gang, Butch Cassidy's Wild Bunch, or Colonel Fountain's New Mexico disappearance, plus a dozen or so other figures and events—and the Pinkerton name is bound to surface. One operative, Tom Horn, worked all sides: as a Pinkerton man, a bounty hunter, and as a loner later legally hanged for killing the wrong person. Pinkerton also possessed the world's finest and most extensive rogues' gallery, as well as the world's best, and most resilient, group of operatives. He retained a female detective, Kate Warne, at a time when women did not do such work.

One of Pinkerton's better-known western detectives was Charles Siringo, who later wrote a book entitled *The Cowboy Detective*, detailing his Pinkerton experiences. The Pinkertons suppressed it. Even Dashiell Hammett, who wrote best-selling yarns featuring dashing detectives, worked briefly as a Pinkerton operative.

Nevertheless, the Pinkerton expertise often fell short of exactitude. Training at best tended to be informal, and its investigative techniques could be sloppy and brutal. For instance, in 1875, the Pinkertons assaulted a Missouri cabin allegedly hiding Jesse James. Without being certain, the detectives tossed a fire bomb through the window. The device exploded, mutilating the arm of Jesse's mother and killing Archie Samuel, a half-brother to Jesse. As for Jesse James himself, he wasn't there, and the resultant bad publicity further stigmatized the Pinkertons. It also provided Jesse James with considerable sympathy among the American public.

Three years later, in 1888, the Pinkertons brought in strikebreakers for the Burlington Railroad. When the fighting ended, three guards and 10 strikers sprawled dead. Allan Pinkerton himself had died in 1884, after writing several autobiographical books: *Criminal Reminiscences and Detective Sketches; The Spy of the Rebellion;* and *Thirty Years a Detective.*

Today, the Pinkerton agency remains one of the world's best. It concentrates primarily on property protection.

See also: BASS, SAM; DALTON BROTHERS; CASSIDY, BUTCH; FOUNTAIN, ALBERT JENNINGS; JAMES BROTHERS; HORN, TOM; SIRINGO, CHARLES ANGELO; WILD BUNCH

PLAINS Rifle

During the 1830s and '40s the most popular and most effective weapon was the Plains rifle, if for no other reason than there wasn't anything else to compare it to. The Plains rifle (oftentimes called the Hawken) was generic. Kit Carson used this weapon, as did Auguste Park Vasquez and David Meriwether. A good mountain man never left home without one.

The plains or Hawken rifle was simply an erudite name for a muzzleloader. It weighed 12 to 14 pounds, took black powder, had a flintlock powder charge or percussion cap, needed a ramrod, and could leave you in real trouble if you needed to get a second shot off in a hurry. Generally speaking these weapons were difficult to shoot—or reload—from a horse. The good news was that they were fairly accurate at long range, capable of bringing down a buffalo, a man, or a squirrel.

PLEASANT Valley War

A 50-mile, oval-shaped valley in central Arizona, north of Globe, goes by the name of Pleasant Valley. The Tewksbury brothers—Edwin, John, and James—of mixed Indian and perhaps Negro heritage, stumbled onto it during the late 1870s and began raising purebred horses. In 1882, Ed Tewksbury met the brothers Tom and John Graham in Globe and suggested that they consider Pleasant Valley as a desirable site to raise cattle. The Grahams did so well in the valley that they brought in their brother Billy. They also hired Jim Tewksbury as a cowboy. In 1883, however, Jim noted that the Grahams had a habit of acquiring other people's livestock. He mentioned it to his own family, and the father insisted that Jim quit the brand and find honest work.

The Tewksburys did not see eye to eye with the Grahams on such matters as cattle theft. Neighboring ranchers began choosing sides. John Gilliland, a Texas-born Stinson Ranch foreman, and his nephew, rode over to the Tewksburys', where an argument started. Gilliland drew and fired, missing. Ed Tewksbury snatched a rifle and wounded both Gilliland and his nephew.

The Grahams filed charges of attempted murder against the Tewksburys in early 1884. In bitter weather the dispute went to trial in Globe, where a judge dismissed the charges, ruling that the Tewksburys had responded in self-defense. The youngest brother, Frank Tewksbury, who had ridden through bitter weather to observe the trial died shortly afterward of pneumonia. The Tewksburys blamed the Grahams for Frank's death—and the feud was on.

In the meantime, Texan Mark Blevins, who had a long-time association with the Aztec Land and Cattle Company, also known as the Hash Knife outfit, brought his family to the valley and settled alongside the Grahams. Blevins had a son, Andy, who had changed his last name to Cooper because he was selling whiskey to Oklahoma Indians and stealing cattle in Texas. Cooper's friends began stealing cattle and horses, and the Pleasant Valley situation deteriorated.

Into this caldron stepped the Daggs brothers of Flagstaff, who sought better winter grazing for their sheep. Since they were friends of the Tewksburys, they moved into the valley. The Tewksburys, already taking snide remarks because of their racial heritage, now had to contend with being supporters of sheepherders. Before long, someone ambushed a herd of sheep, killed the Basque herdsman, cut off his head, and drove the sheep over a cliff. Shortly after that, Mark Blevins, in search of horses, vanished from the earth.

On August 9, 1887, Hamilton Blevins and four Hash Knife cowboys approached a cabin belonging to the Middleton Ranch and, not realizing that Jim and Ed Tewksbury were inside, shouted for something to eat. A gunfight started. Blevins died on the spot. His four cowboy friends fled, three of them wounded, one seriously.

A week later, 18-year-old Billy Graham was riding home from Phoenix when he encountered the Basque sheepherder's brother. Billy made it home with a bullet in him and died the next day.

On September 2, a large contingent of Grahams, plus friends, occupied the high ground overlooking the Tewksbury ranch house and ambushed John Tewksbury and William Jacobs, killing both men. Inside the cabin, Ed and Jim Tewksbury, their father, and another man held off the attackers. The Tewksburys watched in helpless horror as hogs started eating bodies in the yard. The attackers later withdrew, and burials took place.

Two days later, Andy (Blevins) Cooper celebrated at the Bucket of Blood Saloon in Holbrook, Arizona. While in his cups and before leaving for his mother's home, he boasted of the killings. Those boasts quickly grabbed the attention of Commodore Perry Owens—who ordinarily dressed like a refugee from a Wild West show but nevertheless was sheriff of Apache County and just happened to be in Holbrook. A family gathering was taking place in the Blevins house; Owens walked inside and said he had a warrant for Cooper, who resisted, and Owens shot him dead. Other family members now entered the battle, one of the bloodiest gunfights in western history. When it ended, Owens still stood, but three men were dead. Another would recover sufficiently to spend five years in the Arizona prison at Yuma.

Two weeks later the Grahams made another Tewksbury raid, killing a Tewksbury friend and seriously wounding a young cowboy. The territorial governor now ordered Yavapai County sheriff William Molvenon to end the feud. On September 21, Molvenon and a 25-man posse rode to the Graham Ranch and in a gunfight killed John Graham and Charles Blevins. Tom Graham wasn't to be found. Molvenon now warned the others that once he had Tom Graham in custody he would come for the Tewksburys. That was sufficient. The two Tewksburys quickly surrendered and were released on bond. Tom Graham later surrendered. All of them went on trial, but when no witnesses appeared, charges were dropped.

One more episode remained. On August 2, 1892, Ed Tewksbury and a man named John Rhodes, shot Tom Graham off the back of a wagon. Both men went on trial for murder. Rhodes had a good alibi and went free. Ed Tewksbury also had a good alibi but no one believed it, and he went to prison. After languishing there for two years, he won a new trial—and a hung jury. The state dropped its charges, and he went free after two and one-half years in prison.

Ed Tewksbury became the last living feudist of the Pleasant Valley War. He died in bed on April 4, 1904. Zane Grey would later write a romanticized novel based on the struggle, entitled *To the Last Man*.

See also: OWENS, COMMODORE PERRY; ROBERTS, JAMES FRANKLIN

PLUMMER, William Henry (1832–1864)

Henry Plummer worked all sides of the law, and he did it as skillfully and as brutally as any outlaw/lawman who ever lived. He was born in Maine but by 1852 had arrived in Nevada City, California, where four years later he became the city marshal. In 1857, he campaigned for the state legislature but was defeated, primarily because of alleged criminal activities.

He then killed John Vedder after the two men quarreled over the affections of Vedder's wife. That earned Plummer 10 years at San Quentin, although he obtained an early release through a pardon. After killing a man in Nevada City, Plummer fled to Montana, where he became sheriff of Bannack in 1863. One of his first tasks was to build a gallows, but while doing so he organized a group of cutthroats; estimates of their numbers range from a couple of dozen to 100. They called themselves the Innocents, and their occupations were murder and robbery. Plummer himself rode with them so frequently that he was recognized during several of the holdups.

Since the miners received no help from the law, they organized vigilance committees, which lynched George Ives, one of Plumber's key operatives. They strung him up from a ridgepole supporting an adobe wall. They also hanged George Brown and Erastus Yeager. Yeager confessed before he died, implicating Plummer.

Between December 1863 and late February 1864, the vigilantes lynched 22 men, including Plummer and two associates, on the town gallows. It was a fitting end for a Dr. Jekyll and a Mr. Hyde.

See also: VIGILANCE COMMITTEES

POE, John William (1850–1923)

This buffalo hunter turned lawman, turned businessman, was born on a farm in Mason County, Kentucky. At the age of 10 he left home, worked on farms and railroads, and around 1872 settled near Fort Griffin, Texas, where he sold wolf pelts and by his own estimate killed 20,000 buffalo. In 1878, he became the Fort Griffin city marshal, and in 1879, a deputy sheriff in Wheeler County. He also held down a U.S. deputy marshal commission. He became a detective for the Canadian River Cattle Association in 1881 and accompanied Sheriff Pat Garrett to Fort Sumner, New Mexico, where on the night of July 14, 1881, Billy the Kid walked right by John Poe, neither man recognizing the other. Minutes later, Sheriff Pat Garrett shot the Kid dead.

Poe later secured indictments against Pat Coughlin, a Tularosa, New Mexico, cattle thief. Coughlin had allegedly hired assassins to murder people who might testify against him during his upcoming cattle-theft trial in Mesilla, New Mexico.

In 1882, John Poe became the next sheriff of Lincoln County, married Sophie Alberding, and in 1884 moved to a ranch near Fort Stanton. He then resigned as sheriff and moved to Roswell, New Mexico. He became a member of the Roswell Masonic Lodge and founded two banks in the city. He served on the Board of Regents of the New Military Institute and as president of the New Mexico State Tax Commission. He died in Roswell on July 22, 1923, and was buried in the South Park Cemetery. In 1936, his widow wrote and published his biography, entitled *Buckboard Days*.

See also: BILLY THE KID; COUGHLIN, PATRICK; GARRETT, PATRICK FLOYD JARVIS; LINCOLN COUNTY WAR

John Poe and his wife, Sophie (Library, University of New Mexico)

POINTER, John (?–1884)

John Pointer, born in Eureka, Arkansas, was one of those youngsters who remain perpetually in trouble. As a youth, he reportedly stabbed a neighbor friend and set another companion on fire. The behavior pattern never varied, but he finally went too far late Christmas Day, 1891, somewhere in the Choctaw Nation in Oklahoma. Pointer had been traveling with two companions, but their journey forever ended that same evening. Pointer took their horses, money, and wagon and left the two bodies in the creek. The authorities arrested him shortly afterward when he attempted to sell the gear.

Pointer went before federal judge Isaac Parker and accepted his death sentence with a chuckle, even offering, and being allowed, to name his own hour of execution. However, at 3:30 P.M. on September 24, 1894, Pointer has a change of heart. He requested and received a quarter-hour delay the better to steel his nerves for the brief trip into eternity. That was granted, but it helped little. A subsequent request for additional time was turned down.

See also: PARKER, JUDGE ISAAC

PRATT, John (?–?)

This U.S. marshal came out of Massachusetts, where he was born, becoming a Republican and a Unionist who knew how to manipulate the federal system to his benefit. To this end he curried favors from the Santa Fe Ring, which was controlled primarily by political operatives Thomas Catron and Stephen B. Elkins. Thus in March 1866, Pratt became the U.S. marshal in New Mexico, even prosecuting for embezzlement the man he replaced, Abraham Cutler. (Cutler was acquitted).

Pratt and his U.S. deputy marshals, most of them New Mexico sheriffs, in September 1868 arrested 150 alleged violators of the New Mexico peonage laws, people who allegedly kept workers in what amounted to slavery. While these cases meandered through the courts, Pratt attempted to resolve New Mexico's Colfax County War, in particular the slaying of Parson F. J. Tolby, a preacher who had threatened to expose dishonest dealings between the Maxwell Land Grant Company and a bank owned by Stephen B. Elkins. Elkins, of course, was a political powerhouse, a man whom Pratt was much more interested in placating than investigating. All of this, of course, brought conflict-of-interest charges raining down on the head of Pratt, but he survived, as did everyone else.

For service in failing to rock numerous political boats, President Ulysses Grant in May 1876 named Pratt secretary of the Territory of New Mexico.

See also: ALLISON, ROBERT A.

PRICE, Anthony (a.k.a. One Arm Price) (?–1883)

Although little is known of the origin or ending of Anthony "One Arm Price," he is vividly remembered for his ingenious defense at his murder trial. It seems that Price and Mike McCrea had engaged in a wild spree at Warder's Cafe on a hot July 1881 afternoon in Deming, New Mexico. Price had jerked a borrowed six-shooter and pointed it at McCrea. Through bloodshot eyes McCrea looked down the muzzle and foolishly slurred, "Does she pop?" It popped! Price was charged with murder.

On a change of venue, Price was taken to Mesilla, New Mexico, for trial. Grant County sheriff Harvey Whitehill and Deputy Dan Tucker handcuffed the sheriff's young son Wayne to Price's good arm for the night as an effective alarm and an efficient anchor. The two lawmen got a good night's rest, as they planned.

The well-known political powerhouse Albert J. Fountain defended Price, insisting that the revolver had been borrowed and that it furthermore had been altered to fire by merely slipping the hammer, a factor not realized by Price. Furthermore, Fountain argued, Price had been drinking whiskey in anticipation of a trip to the dentist, and the dentist had also given Price a dose of morphine. Price therefore had suffered "chemical induced amnesia" concerning the entire episode; if he had indeed shot his friend, "it was in a playful mood." Fountain's arguments were so persuasive that the jury spent but 15 minutes finding Price guilty of murder only in the fifth degree. The jurors assessed a punishment of a small fine and a few days in jail.

Not long afterward, a newspaper reported, "Andy Price—a man twice tried for murder in this county—is constable at Eureka. He is a very good officer and the rustlers give that section of the county the go-bye."

QUANTRILL, William Clarke (a.k.a. Charlie Hart) (1837–1865)

In terms of outlaw and military guerrilla tactics, William Clark Quantrill practically wrote the book. He was born in Canal Dover, Ohio, on July 31, 1837. In 1857 having briefly farmed in Kansas, he wandered west for a couple of years, prospecting and gambling along the way. Sometimes he went by the alias of "Charlie Hart." He even taught school until the advent of the Civil War. Quantrill then hung around Lawrence, Kansas, by various accounts committing a few murders and stealing a few horses. He spent a brief time in the Confederate army, then seems to have deserted—or perhaps been discharged. He began at once to recruit men in opposition to the Jayhawkers; he called his men "Quantrill's Raiders," ruffians who looted and murdered, often in support of slavery but mostly in support of anarchy.

Throughout the Civil War, Quantrill's raiders burned towns and ranches as well as Union strongholds along the Missouri-Kansas border. With him rode such soon-to-be-well-known outlaws as Frank and Jesse James, William C. "Bloody Bill" Anderson, and Cole Younger. On August 21, 1863, he led 200 men into Lawrence, killing 180 Kansas men and boys (women were spared). Quantrill lost one man during the four-hour murder and burning spree, which in addition to the deaths caused over $1 million in damages. A year later, Quantrill dressed his men in new Union uniforms, walked them into the Federal camp at Baxter Springs, Kansas, and slaughtered 101 soldiers.

Quantrill's raids made him as feared and as despised in the South as the North. His guerrillas rode into Sherman, Texas, killing Confederates as well as Unionists, an act that on March 31, 1864, got him arrested by Gen. Henry McCulloch. Quantrill broke out of confinement; his command had split into small, disintegrating groups, but Quantrill led the remnants into Kentucky. On May 10, 1865, Quantrill, down to 11 men, was at the James Wakefield farm, near Bloomfield. During a pouring rain, Federal cavalry swept in and caught Quantrill napping in a hayloft. Quantrill never quite got seated on his horse before a bullet shattered his backbone. The troops moved him to a military hospital in Louisville, where he died on June 6, 1865.

Quantrill was buried in the Catholic Cemetery at Louisville. In 1887, his mother, Caroline Clarke Quantrill, ordered his bones dug up and sold. William Clarke Quantrill was obviously his mother's son.

See also: ANDERSON, WILLIAM C.; JAMES BROTHERS; JAYHAWKERS; LANE, JAMES HENRY; YOUNGER BROTHERS

QUEEN, Samuel Dawson (a.k.a. Kep) (1860–1888)

Samuel "Kep" Queen was born in March 1860 on his family's horse farm at Queen Hill, in Williamson

County, Texas. His first cousin, John Tolliver Barber, was born around 1860, probably in Pettytown, Caldwell County, Texas. Kep, of Indian heritage, had black hair and eyes. At a youthful age the two boys joined the Brackett Cornett/William Whitley gang of bank and train robbers. Its two best known robberies were a holdup of the Missouri Pacific at McNeil, Texas, in February 1887, and a train robbery at Flatonia that occurred shortly afterward. Cornett soon left the gang and was slain on February 12, 1888 in South Texas.

John Barber and Bill Whitney ambushed Deputy Sheriff Bill Stanley near Florence, Texas, on August 6, 1887. The gang then fled to Indian Territory (Oklahoma), where they hid briefly before teaming up with Kep Queen to rob the bank at Cisco, Texas, on February 15, 1888. That brought the Texas Rangers as well as a sheriff's posse in pursuit, so the two robbers parted company. A posse shot Whitney to death near Floresville, Texas, on September 25, 1888. Barber and Queen returned to Indian Territory, where the authorities killed Queen at Claremore, Oklahoma, on November 16, 1888. Another Oklahoma posse killed John Barber in December 1889.

See also: QUEEN, VICTOR

QUEEN, Victor (a.k.a. Vic) (1870–1904)

Vic Queen, a brother to Samuel Dawson Queen, was born on his family's horse farm at Queen Hill, Williamson County, Texas about 1870. In 1890, the family moved to Eddy County, New Mexico. Queen, a medium-sized, lean man with a fondness for blustery speech, had a square head, dark hair, and mustache. In 1894, the authorities accused Vic of rustling cattle and defacing brands. He fled to Mexico, where the authorities arrested him on March 26, 1895; they jailed him in Ciudad Juarez, Chihuahua. Here he renewed his friendship with Martin Mrose who also had outstanding New Mexico cattle-theft warrants.

Mrose bailed both himself and Queen out of jail, and they applied for Mexican citizenship. On June 29, 1895, Mrose crossed the Rio Grande for a promised El Paso, Texas, rendezvous with his wife, Helen Beulah Mrose, then living with El Paso attorney John Wesley Hardin. Law officers shot Mrose to death the moment he stepped onto U.S. soil.

Queen now accused Hardin and others of outright murder but could do nothing about it. Instead he returned to Carlsbad, New Mexico, and surrendered, being released in April when no indictments came down. On December 13, 1904, parties unknown shot and killed Vic Queen in Central, New Mexico, a tiny community near Silver City. Vic is buried in the Silver City cemetery just a few yards from Catherine Antrim, the mother of Billy the Kid.

See also: HARDIN, JOHN WESLEY; MILTON, JEFFERSON DAVIS; MROSE, MARTIN; QUEEN, SAMUEL DAWSON

QUICK-DRAW Artist

The term refers to someone very adept at getting his six-shooter out of its holster in a hurry, prepared to fire. Cowboys did not ordinarily possess this attribute, although professional gunmen and lawmen often did. Three fast-draw examples usually cited are Wild Bill Hickok, John Wesley Hardin, and Billy the Kid, but they also had their bad moments. A problem with the fast draw was that it tended to be more flashy than effective in terms of hitting a mark.

QUICK on the Trigger

In a literal sense, this meant anyone who could draw or quickly fire his revolver. But in a general sense—as it was most often used—the term referred to anyone with a violent temper, a person who was argumentative, an individual constantly on the prod, quick to take offense, and always ready to fight.

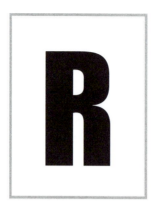

RANGER'S Bible, the (a.k.a. *List of Fugitives from Justice*; the Book; the Black Book)

This refers to the rare 1878 *List of Fugitives from Justice* in Texas. The names numbered in the hundreds. The original book was a small, black, leather-bound volume issued to Texas Rangers in 1878. As various outlaws were captured or killed, their names were crossed out, while others were continuously written in. How many copies were originally published in 1878 is not known, but new additions came out in 1882, 1889, 1891 (an addendum), 1896, and 1900.

Who wrote or compiled the original publication or any of its revisions is also not known.

The outlaws were listed randomly by county along with physical descriptions, ages, and crimes committed, the last ranging from murder and attempted murder to theft of livestock, infanticide, adultery, gambling, assault, rape, swindling, incest, and so forth. Many descriptions were specific, such as "glib with his tongue," "fleshy," "likes draw poker," and "white, very talkative and well educated."

Over time these fugitive books disappeared, with the exception of one owned by Sgt. James B. Gillett. Sergeant Gillett carried an 1878 edition in his saddlebag, making notes, scratching out names, and adding new ones. His copy was fortunately preserved. Entitled *Fugitives from Justice,* it was republished in 1997 by the State House Press in Austin, Texas.

See also: GILLETT, JAMES BUCHANAN; TEXAS RANGERS

RAY, Charles T. (a.k.a. Pony Deal; Pony Diehl) (1849–1887?)

This desperado was far better known throughout Arizona Territory as "Pony Deal" or "Pony Diehl" than he ever was by his real name. He was born at Rock Island, Illinois. He does not come into historical focus, however, until around January 1876, when he surfaced in Las Cruces, New Mexico, as a member of the John Kinney gang. Ray was one of a group that murdered two Eighth Cavalry soldiers and wounded several others by firing through windows during a dance.

Ray fled to Tombstone, Arizona, and was on the scene when Curly Bill Brocius accidently killed Marshal Fred White. Ray in particular hung around with Sherman McMasters, and he was suspected of robbing stages, some in cahoots with McMasters. Nevertheless, Pony Diehl proved to be a shadowy figure, allegedly breaking jails both in Texas and Arizona. He was one of numerous folks who never believed John Ringo committed suicide. Ray suspected John O'Rourke of the shooting, and he killed O'Rourke in retaliation.

Pony Diehl thereafter drifted around, spent time in El Paso, rustled cattle again for John Kinney, and was sentenced to five years in the territorial prison at Santa Fe. He escaped on February 20, 1885, but had only four days of freedom before being recaptured. The authorities released him on March 14, 1887; all efforts to trace his life after that have come to naught.

See also: BROCIUS, WILLIAM; KINNEY, JOHN; MCMASTERS, SHERMAN W.; RINGO, JOHN PETERS

RAY, Ned (?–1894)

As a desperado, Ned Ray remained mostly in the shadows, joining the Henry Plummer gang in Montana but (either intentionally or unintentionally) keeping a low profile. He once claimed to have escaped from San Quentin Prison, taking delight in showing friends a knot on his foot where he had been wounded. Ray is best remembered as one of two men captured with Plummer, all three being hanged by vigilantes from a single scaffold on January 10, 1894. Before he took the drop, Ray managed to free one hand and insert it between his neck and the rope—so he strangled instead of dying instantly of a broken neck.

See also: PLUMMER, WILLIAM HENRY

RAYNER, Hamilton (a.k.a. Ham Raynor) (?–1932)

Hamilton Rayner, a lawman, had been born in Texas, probably El Paso, his father being Judge Kenneth Rayner, solicitor of the U.S. Treasury in Washington, D.C. His older brother, William, was a deputy U.S. revenue collector working out of Dallas.

Rayner likely had never heard of Hunnewell, Kansas, until the spring of 1883. By then the recently created town was overflowing with Texas cowboys and ranchers. The long trail drives had ended for the year, the livestock had been sold, and there was nothing left to do but hoop, holler, and gamble until returning to Texas. Since the town needed a marshal, it picked Joe Forsythe of Dallas, and Forsythe reached out to El Paso, Texas, for his chief deputy, Hamilton Rayner. Thus during the forthcoming Hunnewell showdown, it would be Texan lawmen trying to control Texas cowboys. This brought Forsythe into conflict with the Hunnewell town fathers, who were encouraging the Texans to spend their money on sin, and then risking Forsythe's being shot when the Texans became too rowdy. As a result, in December 1883, Forsythe resigned in disgust as city marshal and returned to Dallas. Hamilton Rayner took his place as city marshal.

Rayner then telegraphed El Paso and talked former Texas Ranger Ed Scotten into becoming his assistant. Along about this same time, Raynor also fell in love with a raven-haired saloon girl. The memoirs of one local resident described her as "a peach," but "not the kind [of peach] to lead cowboys to a prayer meeting."

By August the rowdiness had steadily gotten worse. With the atmosphere sticky, the cowboys had less and less to do, and more and more time in which to do it. They took solace in gambling, drinking, and arguing, and twice Rayner had called for assistance from Sheriff Frank Henderson, at nearby Wellington. Twice the sheriff had caught a train and arrived in town with a posse. But by then things had gotten quiet.

On August 9, everything came to a head. The Halsell brothers, who owned nearby ranches, were entertaining themselves at Pat Hanly's saloon. One of the girls there just happened to be the already mentioned love of Rayner's life, and it wasn't long before Marshal Rayner and Deputy Scotten strolled into the room. They complained of noise.

The dispute carried over into a side alley, where Rayner and Scotten squared off against Oscar Halsell and Clem Barefoot, the latter two cattlemen being good friends. A short burst of profanity was followed by shooting.

Barefoot shot Rayner in a leg below the knee and subsequently grazed him with several other rounds. One of Rayner's bullets struck Barefoot in the side. As for Halsell, he shot Ed Scotten in the neck, blowing out his spine.

Halsell and Barefoot fled on foot, stopping a cowboy down by the river and taking his horse at gunpoint. After reaching Barefoot's camp, they saddled two horses and parted ways. The 27-year-old cowboy Clem Barefoot made it to camp and died there of his wounds. Halsell disappeared completely.

As for Ed Scotten, for a while it seemed that he would live, but he lasted only long enough for his mother to reach him from El Paso. She took him back to El Paso and buried him in Concordia Cemetery on September 5, 1884.

Hamilton Rayner survived and moved to New Orleans, where he became cashier for the North Central and South American Exposition of 1885. In 1902, he came to El Paso as a special railroad officer. Harry Halsell stayed on the run for two years. He finally turned himself in, was tried for murder, and was acquitted.

See also: RAYNER, WILLIAM R.

RAYNER, William R. (a.k.a. Bill Raynor) (?–1885)

Bill Rayner, a deputy U.S. revenue collector, not only dressed well but loved to gamble, specifically in El Paso's Gem Saloon. Rayner had already killed at least one man, John C. Morris, a gambler, on December 20, 1881, in Fort Worth, Texas. Now, on April 14, 1885, he and Charles "Buck" Linn, a jail guard and former Texas Ranger, started drinking early and didn't shut it down until about 11 P.M., when they wandered into El Paso's Gem Theater and Saloon, where Rayner began verbally abusing Cowboy Bob Rennick—whose nickname of "Cowboy" stemmed from a huge white hat he habitually wore. Rennick wasn't armed at the time, so he gritted his teeth and made no response. After insulting Rennick, Rayner wandered on his way, apparently assuming Rennick would shrug it off. He didn't. Rennick borrowed a six-shooter from faro dealer Robert Cahill, but he had no sooner stuck it in his pocket than Rayner learned of the transaction and started back up the street. Rennick shot Rayner in the stomach and

William Rayner (Author's Collection)

shoulder in a saloon. Several friends, including Linn, quickly gathered Rayner up off the floor and carried him to a streetcar and then to his room, where two doctors worked over him for several days. Meanwhile, Bob Rennick fled south down El Paso Street and took refuge in Ciudad Juarez, Chihuahua, Mexico, across the Rio Grande.

Other friends steered a badly shaken Buck Linn outside the boarding house where Rayner lay slowly dying. They tried to reason with him, but the distraught Linn walked back to the Gem, firing a few rounds in the air, and then stepped inside the saloon. Since Rennick had fled, Linn shot a couple more rounds into the ceiling, then called on Bob Cahill to fight because, Cahill had caused Rayner's near death by lending a weapon to Rennick. The two men screamed back and forth at each other, then the shooting started once again. Within seconds Linn was sprawled on the floor about where Rayner had fallen. According to Dr. A. L. Justice, the same physician who had attended Rayner, Linn died almost instantly sometime between midnight and one. Cahill now quickly joined Rennick in Mexico, although both returned to El Paso within a few days. Cahill was charged with murder but was released under a $10 bond. As for Rayner, he stayed remarkably alert and did not die until June 7. Both burials took place in El Paso's Concordia Cemetery.

As an aside, the famous lawman Wyatt Earp had been in town between trains, and he witnessed both gunfights. His written, sworn testimony was undoubtedly one reason why Cahill never went to trial.

See also: EARP, WYATT BERRY STAPP; RAYNER, HAMILTON.

REEVES, Bass (1840–1910)

The early years of Bass Reeves are obscure. He was a black man who appears to have grown up in Indian Territory (Oklahoma), since he fluently spoke the languages of the Five Civilized Tribes. There is talk that he may have also been a slave of Col. George Reeves, which would explain the name. At any rate, he reportedly was 22 in 1863, when Lincoln signed the Emancipation Proclamation, so he must have been around 34 in May 1875, when federal judge Isaac Parker appointed him as a U.S. deputy marshal, the first black man so honored. In those days, farmer Reeves could neither read nor write, but he was articulate, intelligent, and had the tracking instincts of a tiger.

A deputy marshal earned his living in fees and awards, getting a specified amount of money per mile traveled and arrest made. This arrangement gave incentive to Reeves; the 1880 census of Van Buren, Arkansas, listed him as having a wife and eight children. So it was fortunate that Uncle Sam paid its fees for outlaws whether alive or dead. In 1883, the government gave Bass a warrant for rancher Jim Webb, who had killed a preacher. Reeves quickly caught up with Webb, but during the shootout he killed Frank Smith, one of Webb's rustling friends. Webb surrendered, bailed himself out of jail, and then fled, only to be tracked down by Reeves and shot and killed during a running gun battle on June 15, 1884.

A few months later Reeves was meandering down the so-called Seminole Whiskey Trail when he encountered three suspects, all named Brunter. Bass shot and killed two and captured the other. During the next two years, Bass arrested nearly 100 murderers, arsonists, and whiskey peddlers. A Fort Smith, Arkansas, newspaper printed the following on October 30, 1885:

> U.S. Marshal Bass Reeves came in on Monday evening last with 17 prisoners, among whom were Hens Posey and One Deldrick, charged with murder. The others are John Robinson, assault with intent to kill; Robert Johnson, Wiley Kelly, Colbert Lasley and old man Cintop, larceny. The balance are all whiskey cases.

However, on January 19, 1886, the government arrested Reeves for the slaying of his own cook. The trial began on October 12, 1887. Three days later a jury found him not guilty.

Nearly two years later, in 1889, Reeves killed an outlaw leader named Tom Story, who had a long history of rustling, ending at the Delaware Crossing of the Red River. Ten years after that, a federal court transferred Bass to Muskogee, where he concentrated on black and Indian outlaws. On November 28, 1901, the *Chickasaw Enterprise* quoted Reeves as having been a U.S. deputy marshal for 27 years and noted that he had arrested over 3,000 men and women, one of those his own son, jailed for murdering his wife. In May 1902 alone, he brought in 24 prisoners, charging them with instigating a race war.

In November 1902, the month Oklahoma became a state, Bass Reeves retired from the federal marshals' service. With too much time on his hands, however, at the age of 67 he joined the Muskogee police force, retiring for good in 1909. He died on January 12, 1910, and is buried in the Old Union Agency Cemetery in Muskogee. Hundreds attended the funeral service.

See also: PARKER, JUDGE ISAAC

REGULATOR-MODERATOR War

This feud started in the pine country of far East Texas, just north of the Mexican border. It essentially lasted from 1839 to 1844. Charles Jackson, a former Mississippi riverboat captain and Louisiana fugitive, and Charles Moorman organized the Shelby County Regulators; Edward Merchant, John Bradly, and Deputy Sheriff James Cravens put together the Moderators. Land swindles proved the root of the troubles, with the Regulators trying to regulate transactions and the Moderators trying to moderate the Regulators.

Jackson originally organized the Regulators to prevent cattle theft. In 1840, Jackson shot a man named Joseph Goodbread at Shelbyville. When Jackson went to trial on July 12, 1841, the Regulators not only intimidated the court but burned a few houses in Shelbyville to demonstrate their power. Not long afterward Jackson and an innocent Dutchman named Lauer were assassinated, and Moorman replaced Jackson. The assassins were captured near Crockett, Texas, and following an October 1841 trial in Shelbyville, all were hanged, with the exception of one man.

Private quarrels now erupted. A man named Stanfield accused an ex-Regulator named Hall of hog theft and shot him dead. County judges now began taking sides, becoming Regulators or Moderators, and of course freeing anyone who appeared before them who happened to be of their political persuasion. It became so confusing and so bloody that during the summer of 1844, the Moderators met at Bells Springs, Texas, and renamed themselves "the Reformers," although the term never stuck. Then they announced an intention to occupy Shelbyville.

As for the Regulators they dreamed equally big, plotting to sign up everyone in Texas, and perhaps occupy the whole state. But after all that blustering, on July 24, 1844, both sides signed a truce. It lasted only sufficiently long for the ink to dry.

Murder once more followed murder. Near Shelbyville, on August 2, about 225 Moderators attacked 62 Regulators during what the Regulators called the Church Hill Battle and the Moderators called Helen's

Defeat, this latter title being a reference to Helen Daggett Moorman, who rode to spy on the enemy camp. When the smoke cleared, however, very few casualties lay on the ground. The battle proved nothing and decided nothing.

On August 15, 1844, Texas president Sam Houston ordered Travis C. Brooks and Alexander Horton to take Texas militia east and establish peace. They arrested 10 leaders from each side, put them together, and forced them to draft an agreement disbanding both groups and agreeing to peace. Except for an occasional killing here and there, the Regulator-Moderator War was over.

REYNOLDS, Glenn (1853–1889)

Born on an East Texas cotton farm, Glenn Reynolds in 1859 moved to West Texas, near the present town of Albany. Raised in the heart of Comanche country, Reynolds developed his survival skills while engaging in skirmishes with raiding Indians when he was 12 years old. But he also received an education of a more formal nature while temporarily staying with relatives at Pueblo, Colorado, and still later at St. Louis. While at the latter, he attended Jones Commercial College.

After mining in Colorado, Reynolds returned to Texas and engaged in the sheep and cattle business on a rather large scale. Additionally, he served as sheriff of Throckmorton County for a year. At least one author asserts he was probably involved as a vigilante in the killing of ex-sheriff John Larn, who had turned outlaw and was gunned down in the Albany jail on the night of June 24, 1878.

In 1885, after more or less disastrous results in the sheep business, Glenn Reynolds moved his wife, Gussie, and their five children to the Pleasant Valley area of Arizona Territory, on rangeland lying at the edge of the Tonto Basin. By 1887, the surrounding mountain valleys were echoing with the sounds of gunfire as the feud known as the Pleasant Valley War swirled about the transplanted Texan. Reynolds's involvement in the fracas remains subject to debate, although one account does have Glenn blasting participant Al Rose with a load of buckshot.

On another occasion, Glenn's infant son became violently ill, and Glenn sent one of his cowboys on a night ride to Globe. Unfortunately, someone ambushed the cowboy, thus terminating the mission. The baby, George, died. Utterly disgusted with the violent foolishness, Reynolds moved to town and campaigned for Gila County sheriff. Because he was generally well liked and considered by many to be the best shot in the Arizona Territory, he defeated the incumbent, B. F. Pascoe.

Sheriff Reynolds assisted Chief Deputy Jerry Ryan in arresting the infamous "Apache Kid" and incarcerating him at Globe. After the Kid's conviction, Reynolds hired William "Hunkydory" Holmes to guard a group of convicted prisoners (the Apache Kid included) during their journey from Globe to the Territorial Prison at Yuma. Glenn Reynolds, armed with a double-barreled shotgun and a .45 Colt six-shooter, and "Hunkydory," with a revolver and Winchester, loaded the prisoners on to a stagecoach driven by Eugene Middleton.

During the trip, on November 2, 1889, having unloaded the prisoners so that the team could pull the steep Kelvin Grade, the lawmen were overpowered and their weapons removed. The prisoners escaped after slaying both Reynolds and "Hunkydory" Holmes.

See also: APACHE KID; HOLMES, W. A.; LARN, JOHN; PLEASANT VALLEY WAR

RIGGS, Barney (?–1892)

Very little is known regarding the early days of Barney Riggs except that he worked as a cowboy in Arizona, and killed his employer during an argument over a young lady who apparently had been sharing her affections with both men. That shooting earned Riggs a life sentence in the Yuma Territorial Prison, although he was let out for doing practically the same thing that got him incarcerated. The story is that seven Mexican prisoners attempted to escape in October 1887, most of them being shot and killed by guards. One prisoner, however, stuck a knife against prison superintendent Thomas Gates and, using Gates as a shield, attempted to gain his freedom. Riggs, looking on, suddenly snatched a revolver off the floor and shot the convict twice, freeing Gates. That act of heroism earned Riggs a governor's pardon on Christmas Day, the only stipulation being that Riggs absent himself from Arizona and never return. As a result, Riggs went to Pecos, Texas, where he married the sister of Sheriff Bud Frazer. Frazer had been feuding with local gunman Jim Miller, and Riggs supported his brother-in-law, Frazer.

The word soon came down that John Denson and Bill Earhart, gunslinging associates of Miller, were in town to kill Riggs. The confrontation took place in R. S. Johnson's saloon. As the two gunmen stepped through the door, Earhart fired and missed. Riggs fired, and Earhart died on the spot. Denson then decided to run, and Riggs killed him from the doorway as the man reached the street.

In the meantime, Barney Riggs's marriage ended in a bitter divorce, the court naming Daniel Chadborn, a step-grandson, as the trustee for Annie Riggs. Chadborn and Barney subsequently met on a Fort Stockton, Texas, street on April 7, 1892, Chadborn in a buggy, Riggs standing on the sidewalk. Riggs made wild threats and also the mistake of reaching into his hip pocket. Chadborn interpreted reaching for a handkerchief to be the same as reaching for a gun, and he shot Riggs dead. Chadborn was acquitted.

See also: CHADBORN, DANIEL JOSEPH; MILLER, JAMES

RILEY, James M. (a.k.a. Doc Middleton)
(1851–1913)
Riley was born in Bastrop, Texas, but went to prison early for horse theft. He escaped a few months later, fled to Nebraska, and assumed the name of Doc Middleton. He made his living thereafter primarily by horse theft, and he wasn't particular about where the animals came from—Indians, the government, or ranchers. By 1879, he was back in prison. Later he was released and performed on an irregular basis in Buffalo Bill's Wild West Show.

RINGO, John Peters (a.k.a. John Ringgold)
(1850–1882)
John Ringo was born on March 3, 1850, at Green Fork, Indiana, and some confusion exists as to whether the family name was Ringgold. Some people always called him that. In 1856, the family moved to Missouri, then headed for California in 1864, a hope being that the sunny climate would ease the suffering of John's tubercular father. The father accidentally or intentionally killed himself with a rifle during the trip, but the family continued on to San Jose, where they lived with Coleman Younger, whose wife Augusta was the sister of John's mother, Mary.

For reasons unknown, John Ringo left California in 1869 and moved to Texas, where a judge in Burnet fined him $75 for firing a revolver across the town square on Christmas Day, 1874. Ringo subsequently became involved in the Mason County War, in which murder and cattle theft played important roles. As lynchings and gunfire led from one killing to another, former Texas Ranger Scott Cooley recruited a group of gunmen, one of them John Ringo. The Cooley faction killed perhaps a dozen people. Ringo and gunman Bill Williams killed Bill Cheney, allegedly for the murder of Mose Beard; they rode up to his home, accepted his invitation to eat, and while he was washing his face shot him to death.

Texas authorities arrested Cooley and Ringo in Burnet, and Ringo spent the next several years being transferred from one Texas jail after another until his release in 1879, when his case was dismissed. During this incarceration, gunfighter John Wesley Hardin and John Ringo became acquainted, Hardin taking an active interest in Ringo to the point of—years later—writing friends and inquiring about rumors of Ringo's death.

Ringo drifted to Arizona, where he wounded Louis Hancock at Safford on December 14, 1879. For the next year he continued to make a nuisance of himself, even returning to Austin, Texas, in May 1881. There, City Marshal Ben Thompson arrested and jailed him briefly on minor charges.

Back in Arizona, Ringo quarreled and drank, although he avoided charges of cattle rustling. He also avoided what has since become known as the Gunfight at the OK Corral on October 26, 1881, although he probably missed it only due to a serious lack of Cowboy communications, plus the fact that the gunfight was not a previously scheduled event.

On November 26, 1881, Ringo and a friend, Dave Estes, held up a saloon poker game at Galeyville, Arizona, and took $500, as well as a horse. Ringo was arrested shortly afterward, but after three successive trips before a trial judge, no witnesses showing up to testify, all charges were dropped in May 1882.

On January 17, 1882, John Ringo and Doc Holliday confronted each other on Tombstone's Allen Street, both men making references to each other's mother while keeping one hand on their gun. Wyatt Earp stood nearby poised to intervene, but Acting Police Chief James Flynn broke it up, arresting both Holliday and Ringo. A judge fined the two antagonists $30 each for carrying weapons.

On July 14, 1882, teamster John Yoast found the body of John Ringo sprawled under an oak tree in Morse's Canyon in Arizona's Chiricahua Mountains.

A revolver clutched in his hand had fired one round. A bullet on the right side of his head had gone in between the eye and the ear and exited through the top of his skull.

Ringo had been acquainted with the country and was within 200 feet of water. A road passed within 40 feet, and a house stood less than a mile distant. His rifle leaned against the tree. Oddly, he wore an upside-down cartridge belt and had removed his shoes and wrapped his feet in an undershirt. The body was buried within a few yards of where it was found. The official verdict was suicide.

See also: EARP, WYATT BERRY STAPP; GUNFIGHT AT THE OK CORRAL; HARDIN, JOHN WESLEY; HOLLIDAY, JOHN HENRY; MASON COUNTY WAR

ROAD Agent Spin (a.k.a. Border Roll)

When an outlaw surrendered, the lawman's task was to take him into custody, but this could be risky if the desperado was still armed. His weapons had to be removed, and this entailed a degree of peril. If a lawman stepped too close, he ran the risk of having his own weapons knocked aside. If a lawman ordered a desperado to drop his weapon, both lawman and outlaw ran the risk of it accidentally firing once it struck the floor or ground. To step up behind an individual to disarm him also had disadvantages, since a lawman had to holster his own guns in order to remove another man's from his holster.

A common method of disarmament was to ask for six shooters to be handed over, butts forward. However, the "road agent spin" could then occur—in which an outlaw removed his guns from his hips, extended them butts forward in surrender, then slipped his index finger inside the trigger guard, spun the weapon or weapons around in his hand, and either fired or covered the lawman.

When these things are enacted in western movies, they tend to be cute or clever. Outside of the movies, however, gunman John Wesley Hardin is the only individual recorded as being proficient at the road agent spin. According to Hardin's autobiography, he performed the stunt on Wild Bill Hickok in Abilene, Kansas, during the summer of 1871. He did not kill Hickok; he just wanted to impress him.

On October 6, 1871, John Wesley Hardin encountered Texas state policeman Green Paramore who, holding his gun on Hardin, growled, "Give me your pistols." Hardin pulled both, offered them butts forward, then spun one around and shot Paramore dead. As Hardin wrote later, "One of the pistols turned a somersault in my hand and went off."

See also: HARDIN, JOHN WESLEY; HICKOK, JAMES BUTLER

ROBBERS Roost

Robbers Roost was perhaps the third major Wild Bunch hideout, and its being only the third spoke of its ruggedness and remoteness. It lay in the thinly populated area of southeastern Utah, halfway between Moab and Hanksville. The Colorado, the Green, and the Dirty Devil Rivers formed rough boundaries. The twisting canyons were intimidating to anyone but outlaws running from the rope. The Sundance Kid once reportedly wintered at the Roost with Etta Place. Tales still revolve around hidden, buried, still-undiscovered outlaw loot.

See also: BROWN'S PARK; CASSIDY, BUTCH; HOLE-IN-THE-WALL; SUNDANCE KID; WILD BUNCH

ROBERTS, James Franklin (a.k.a. Jim) (1858–1934)

Macon County, Missouri, was the birthplace of James Franklin "Jim" Roberts, but while he was still a teenager the family moved to Tonto Creek, under the Mogollon Rim in Arizona Territory, more often described as Pleasant Valley. During the Pleasant Valley War of the late 1880s, Jim Roberts established his gunman reputation.

Originally, Roberts was content to breed horses near his isolated cabin, and indeed he was raising blue-ribbon-quality livestock, a fact noted by rustlers. After the loss of some prized steeds and the incineration of his home, Jim Roberts sided with the Tewksburys in their violent struggle with the Grahams.

It can be reasonably established that Roberts took an active part in gun battles resulting in the deaths of adversaries Mark Blevins, John Paine, and Harry Middleton and the serious wounding of Joseph Underwood. As many as 22 members of the Graham faction succumbed to partisan retribution. Just how much of the work was done by Roberts has to be regarded as suppositional at best, largely because he chose to remain closed-mouthed. All accounts, however, agree that his contemporaries believed him a poisonously dangerous adversary.

After an 1888 dismissal of a murder case against him, Roberts migrated to the gold camp of Congress, 19 miles north of Wickenburg, and from there sauntered over to Jerome, a copper-mining camp. There the Yavapai County sheriff "Buckey" O'Neill gave Roberts a deputy's commission on December 18, 1889, a position he held under subsequent administrations. He later became a Jerome constable as well as town marshal.

At Jerome, Roberts capped off two more criminal careers. For instance, Dud Crocker, after being pistol-whipped by Deputy Sheriff Joe Hawkins, found himself handcuffed to a wagon wheel for the night. While Roberts patrolled the streets, Sid Chew liberated Crocker from custody with a crowbar. Arming themselves with two stolen six-shooters, the outlaws killed lawman Hawkins and escaped on stolen horses.

Roberts calmly saddled his favorite mule and the next day located the fugitives camped in a draw. With well-placed rifle shots, Roberts killed both and returned to Jerome with the outlaw bodies strapped to the horses they had stolen.

Roberts drifted south for a few years, finding time to pull a stint as a deputy sheriff in Cochise County in 1904. After that, acting under the authority of a deputy sheriff's commission, in 1927 Roberts became a special officer with the United Verde Copper Company at Clarksdale, Arizona.

On the morning of June 21, 1928, after returning from the post office, the 70-year-old Roberts noticed a robbery in progress at the local bank. After scooping up $40,000 in cash, and restraining terrified employees, desperadoes William Forrester and Earl Nelson left the bank on the run, jumping into a waiting automobile. At that point Roberts and another local citizen engaged the outlaws in an exchange of gunfire. As the auto raced past, Roberts fatally shot the driver (Forrester) in the head, causing the vehicle to careen out of control and crash into a utility pole. Nelson was captured.

On January 8, 1934, six years later, James Franklin Roberts, still actively on the job, died of natural causes and was buried in the Clarksdale Cemetery.

See also: PLEASANT VALLEY WAR

RUDABAUGH, David (1854?–1886)

Dave Rudabaugh is said to have been born in Fulton County, Illinois. The family later moved to Ohio. David's father died during the Civil War. In 1870, the mother later moved the family to Eureka, Kansas.

David supposedly went to Dodge City as a young man, and on January 27, 1878, was involved with an unsuccessful train robbery in Kansas. Bat Masterson and a posse captured him shortly afterward. Rudabaugh turned state's evidence, or as the *Kinsley Graphic* expressed it, "Rudabaugh was promised immunity if he would 'squeal,' therefore he squole." His associates received five years in Leavenworth. Dave went free.

In 1879, Rudabaugh and another scoundrel named John Joshua Webb became policemen in Las Vegas, Nevada, but were arrested for stage robbery. Nothing came of the charges. However, on March 10, 1880, Webb killed a cattleman in a Las Vegas saloon. Webb was sentenced to be hanged. Rudabaugh tried to break him out of jail but succeeded only in killing the jailer. Webb later broke free of his own accord, killing three jailers in the process. As for Rudabaugh, he now teamed up with Billy the Kid and was allegedly one of the gunmen responsible for the death of James Carlyle at the Greathouse Ranch in Lincoln County, New Mexico, on November 27, 1880. Sheriff Pat Garrett later tracked the gang to Fort Sumner, killing Tom O'Folliard on December 19, 1880, and Charlie Bowdre at Stinking Springs on December 25. During that latter day, Garrett also accepted the surrender of the Kid as well as those of Rudabaugh and Billie Wilson.

Garrett incarcerated the prisoners in Santa Fe, where Rudabaugh on December 28 pleaded guilty to robbing the U.S. mail. He received life imprisonment, although that was put on hold until his murder trial had been completed. On May 7, 1881, he was escorted to Las Vegas for trial, and on December 3 he escaped by tunneling out of jail.

Rudabaugh now dropped from sight, allegedly going to Mexico, where on February 18, 1886, he allegedly killed two men and wounded another during a cantina fight in Parral. An angry mob killed him, cut off his head, and paraded it around the plaza on a pole. The mob then left his head for the birds.

See also: BILLY THE KID; BOWDRE, CHARLES; GARRETT, PATRICK FLOYD JARVIS; GREATHOUSE, JAMES; WEBB, JOHN JOSHUA

RUNNING Iron

This was a short, straight iron, usually with a crook on one end, carried by cattle thieves. They used it to cross out or change brand markings on cattle or to create fictitious brands where none had existed.

RYNNING, Thomas H. (1866–1941)

This lawman earned most of his fame with the Arizona Rangers. Born in Christiana, Norway, he came to the United States when he was two. In 1885, he joined the U.S. cavalry, fought in numerous Indian engagements, and was with Gen. Leonard Wood at the surrender of the Apache leader Geronimo. Rynning later pursued Sitting Bull into British Columbia. He left the army in 1891, having notched 17 Indian battles. Following that, he could not resist joining the Rough Riders and participating in the charge up Kettle Hill in Cuba.

In 1902, Tom Rynning seemed a natural to succeed Burt Mossman as captain of the Arizona Rangers. Rynning's first concern was bringing order to such mining towns as Morenci, Globe, Bisbee, and Douglas, where racial tensions in the mines ran especially high. The Clifton strikes in particular seemed severe, yet Rynning brought the rioting there under control.

Throughout his brief career as a leader of the Arizona Rangers, he feuded with county sheriffs and their deputies, considering them gun-toting, flashy individuals for the most part incapable of honest work. He believed sheriffs and their deputies were upset because rangers, with the power to arrest anywhere, deprived county officers of fees and mileage.

However, Rynning's major problem stemmed from the Cananea Copper Mines, 30 miles south of the Arizona border in Mexico. Strikers demanded $5 an hour, Mexican money. Col. William C. Greene, the mining manager, had wired the U.S. government as well as officials in Arizona, insisting that troops be sent to protect American workers and families. From the south, Mexican Rurales rushed toward the scene. From the north, the Arizona government sponsored a special train carrying Captain Rynning, 24 armed Arizona Rangers, and a large number of armed civilians. At the border the train

Captain Thomas Rynning, ex-captain of the Arizona Rangers, 1903 (Arizona Historical Society Library)

bluffed its way past Rurale Col. Emilio Kosterlitzky, steamed into Cananea, took command of a strategic hill, and later moved out with American civilians, transporting them north toward and across the international border.

Rynning's reward for all this was a promotion to superintendent of the Yuma Territorial Prison where by all accounts he served honestly, honorably, and well. Thomas Rynning died in 1941.

See also: ARIZONA RANGERS; WHEELER, HARRY; YUMA TERRITORIAL PRISON

SALOONS

A saloon was an entertainment establishment, a drinking, gambling, and social enterprise whose heyday lasted only 60 or 70 years. Yet it played an indispensable role in the history of the American West. The first saloons were eastern and southern colonial inns and taverns that moved west and changed with the times. They were places of comfort, of small talk, where cowboys could gripe about bosses and trail drives, soldiers could curse their sergeants, and business and professional men could find solace in the problems and failures of other establishments. In a sense saloons were the last refuge of the male, although hurdy-gurdy girls and dance-hall queens frequently enriched the smoke-drenched, fly-swarming atmosphere.

Saloons served beer and whiskey ranging from the best ale to the worst rotgut. Some saloons were clean and neat, ornate and opulent, lively and well lit, with big mirrors marching around the interior. Others were dark and dank, with dirt floors, smoky lanterns, log or mud walls, and clients and staff who had not bathed in years.

Most saloons made their money off gambling and drinks. A few also rented upstairs rooms either for sleeping or casual sex.

Because saloons stayed open late and encouraged both drinking and gambling, violence, particularly as the night wore on, tended to result. Although most saloons had rules against the carrying of weapons, many men packed firearms in their hip or front pockets, holsters being too obvious. Since patrons tended to be young men away from home, many of them soldiers or cowboys, drink and losing money often led to violent arguments that sometimes ended in the street, or on the saloon floor. Practically every person mentioned in this encyclopedia at one time or another frequented saloons and occasionally either engaged in brawls or shootouts or observed them. Not many visitors ever left a saloon where a brawl was pending, all of which proves only that there wasn't much to do in a cow town except eat, sleep, and drink. You took your excitement where you found it, and saloons were the best game in town.

SANDERS, Wilbur Fiske (1834–1905)

This attorney turned vigilante was born in New York, studied law, fought in the Civil War, and moved to Montana, where he practiced law in 1863. With rampant lawlessness all around, he first prosecuted murderers, but when the cases got to be too many for the justice system to function well, he switched to working with the vigilantes. Lynch ropes were much more effective than courtroom arguments.

He later became a U.S. senator, eventually dying in Helena, Montana.

Saloon gambling (Arizona Historical Society)

SAN FRANCISCO Vigilantes

Although self-styled vigilantes existed practically all over the American West, nowhere do they seem to have been better organized or to have had a clearer sense of purpose than in San Francisco.

The California Gold Rush started in 1849, and it drew to the West Coast the best and the worst that America had to offer. By 1851, San Francisco in particular had undergone a surge of lawlessness and a series of fires. A Committee of Vigilance, with 700 members, swiftly formed, its target being the common criminal. Historian John Boessenecker claims it hanged four criminals in 1851 and chased others out of town. But that was just the beginning.

By 1855, the crises shifted to governmental corruption, an issue creating so much outrage that 8,000 men reorganized as vigilantes, specifically 50 companies or units. They frequently wore militia uni-forms and carried rifles. They had access to cannons and were headquartered in a two-story building called Fort Gunnybags, a massive structure surrounded by sandbags.

These vigilantes were largely the elite of the city, business and professional people with political power, leaders who gave their victims trials with lawyers and prosecutors. The hangings—and the vigilantes hanged only four in 1856—drew large and appreciative crowds. (Two were hanged from second-story windows of the "fort.") Most criminals, however, either went on a blacklist with instructions to leave town or were outright forced on board a ship and deported to whatever port of call happened to be next.

When the vigilantes finally cleaned up their city, they disbanded.

See also: DUANE, CHARLES P.; VIGILANCE COMMITTEES

SCABBARD

A scabbard can be a sheath or container for a knife or a holster for a six-shooter. These early scabbards, or holsters, came complete with a flap. It kept the gun inside and kept the dust and rain out. By the early 1870s, the flap had disappeared, but the holster wasn't cut away for a faster draw until shortly afterward. The double-action six-shooters in particular needed cutaways. By the 1880s and '90s, holsters started being designed to fit particular guns, and if there was such a thing as the classic quick draw, it was the holster as much as the weapon that made it possible.

The term *scabbard* is also frequently associated with rifles, especially when carried on horseback. The scabbard is designed not only to keep out the dust and rain but to make the weapon readily available when needed.

SCARBOROUGH, George Adolphus (1859–1900)

This well-known frontier peace officer was born in Natchitoches Parish, Louisiana, moved to Texas in 1874, and worked as a cowboy in McCulloch County. He married Mary McMahan, and they had seven children. George Scarborough Jr. became a noted lawman in his own right. In November 1884, the voters elected the elder Scarborough sheriff of Jones County, reelecting him in 1886. On October 15, 1887, in controversial circumstances, he killed an outlaw named A. J. Williams in Haskell; he was tried for murder and acquitted. Nevertheless, he lost his

San Francisco as it looked during the time of the vigilante movement (Institute of Texian Cultures, San Antonio)

213

1888 reelection bid. He found employment as a stock detective before being appointed as a U.S. deputy marshal in 1893.

Two years later, Martin Mrose, an accused southern New Mexico cattle rustler, fled to the Mexican border town of Ciudad Juarez, Chihuahua, and sent his wife Helen Beulah to retain attorney John Wesley Hardin across the Rio Grande in El Paso. Hardin subsequently retained George Scarborough to lure Mrose across the river on an old railroad bridge on the night of June 29, 1895. Once on the El Paso side, Scarborough, plus former El Paso police chief Jeff Milton, Texas Ranger Frank McMahan, and (probably) El Paso constable John Selman, shot Mrose to death. Scarborough and the others were tried for murder, and Scarborough was acquitted. Late at night on April 5, 1896, Scarborough and Selman quarreled in an El Paso alley; Scarborough put four bullets in Selman, who died later on the operating table. Scarborough was tried for murder; he was acquitted but was forced to resign as U.S. deputy marshal.

For a while, Scarborough bought and sold livestock around Fort Davis, Texas, before moving to Deming, New Mexico, where he resumed his old activities as a stock detective and deputy sheriff. In early April 1900, in pursuit with two companions of cattle rustlers near San Simon, Arizona, he took a bullet in the leg and could no longer ride. His associates rode to San Simon for a wagon and transported him to Lordsburg, New Mexico. It had no doctor. They waited for a train, then took him to Deming, New Mexico, where he died on the operating table, primarily from loss of blood. His death came four years to the day after John Selman died on the operating table in El Paso. George Scarborough is buried in Deming.

See also: HARDIN, JOHN WESLEY; MILTON, JEFFERSON DAVIS; MROSE, HELEN BEULAH; MROSE, MARTIN; SCARBOROUGH, GEORGE EDGAR JR.; SELMAN, JOHN HENRY

SCARBOROUGH, George Edgar, Jr. (1879–1945)

Few men could rightfully be allowed bragging rights as the son of an indisputably renowned southwestern lawman, but George Edgar Scarborough Jr. was an exception. By the time he was 18, Ed was riding with posses made up of his father, Jeff Milton, and Frank McMahan. As a detective for the Grant County Cattleman's Association, based out of Deming, New

Mexico Territory, the elder Scarborough seemed pleased that his son Ed was following in the law enforcement tradition.

His father was slain in 1900. Twenty-year-old Ed remained in the law enforcement harness, holding a dual commission as a deputy sheriff in addition to being an assistant to Frank McMahan, his father's successor as cattle-range detective. Meanwhile, George Stevenson and James Brooks had escaped from the Grant County jail at Silver City, New Mexico; over in Arizona, robbers Burt Alvord, Billy Stiles, and Bravo Juan Yoes had broken out of the Cochise County jail. The country was now awash in fugitives, rustlers, and other ne'er-do-wells.

Ed had already trailed and captured one suspected outlaw (Jerome Adams) and lodged him in the Grant County jail. Shortly thereafter, someone murdered Deputy Sheriff W. D. "Keechi" Johnson. A coroner's jury determined that Ralph and Roy Jenks (brothers) and Henry Reinhart were responsible for Johnson's death, although one of the suspects, Ralph Jenks, who had been Johnson's prisoner, swore the deputy had been ambushed by unknown assailants. From Silver City a posse composed of Sheriff James K. Blair, Don McMahan, J. Marvin Hunter, and Ed Scarborough left for the upper Gila River to investigate. At the mining town of Mogollon the lawmen arrested Roy Jenks and Rinehart, but in the vicinity of Duck Creek Jenks tried to grab Ed Scarborough's shotgun. Ed jerked his six-shooter and shot him three times—twice in the chest, once in the head. Later at Silver City, as a common legal maneuver by friends of the lawman, Scarborough was arrested. The case was presented to the grand jury, which absolved the lawman of any fault in the shooting.

Despite the legalities, some citizens questioned the operational abilities of Scarborough. A Grant County sheriff even removed Scarborough's deputy commission when some cattle association members became disgruntled at what they considered to be Ed Scarborough's high-handed arrest techniques. Nevertheless, the evidence was not of sufficient standard to assure conviction in court. Also, not everyone was a detractor, and eventually Ed was elected constable and reappointed deputy sheriff.

Ed arrested Tod Carver (T. C. Hillard), wanted in Arizona Territory for killing Frank LeSueur and Augustus Gibbons. Scarborough delivered Carver to Arizona authorities, who in return released Carver to Utah lawmen for murders committed there. As many suspected, Carver was one of those responsible for Ed's father's death, although he was never charged with the crime.

With his good name somewhat restored, Ed Scarborough entered the Arizona Rangers when that unit formed in 1901. Of the appointment one newsman wrote, "Scarborough was brought up in the saddle and is an excellent marksman. He doesn't know what fear is." Well, he may not have known fear, but an overbearing attitude and general disorderliness caused Ed's dismissal from the Arizona Rangers after just nine months.

At Deming, New Mexico, Ed was arrested for the unauthorized carrying of a revolver, but the charges were dropped. In August 1904 he was arrested for a Deming robbery, but after numerous delaying tactics the charges were dismissed. Five years later he fled to California after being charged with horse theft in New Mexico.

Ed returned to Arizona in 1915 and worked for the Wagon Rod Ranch in Cochise County. However, Scarborough had serious difficulty with rancher John Clinton over where to graze the cattle, so on June 18, 1915, Ed shot Clinton four times in the chest. Scarborough fled but was later captured, tried, and convicted of murder in the second degree. Ed Scarborough entered the Arizona State Prison in May of 1916. A year later, accompanied by two other inmates, Ed escaped and this time successfully hid in Mexico. He was never recaptured.

See also: ARIZONA RANGERS; SCARBOROUGH, GEORGE ADOLPHUS

SCOTT, William (a.k.a. Bill Scott) (1854–1913)

William "Bill" Scott was born at the edge of the East Texas piney woods in Walker County. His family moved to Dallas sometime prior to 1870. Although there are conflicting reports as to just how he was employed for his first few years of adulthood, clearly by the time he was 24, Bill Scott had opted for the life of a career lawman.

After a bit of law enforcement experience as a deputy sheriff at Dallas, Scott and an associate, E. W. "Jack" Smith, volunteered to trap the infamous Sam Bass, all for a healthy slice of a reward offered by the Union Pacific Railroad. Assuming an undercover role and developing a relationship with a gang member's brother, Scott infiltrated the outlaw organization and furnished crucial intelligence to the Texas Rangers.

On May 1, 1878, he was put on the payroll as a private in June Peak's Company B. Later, after testifying before the grand jury, he was transferred to George W. Arrington's Company C. While he was not present at Round Rock when the furious shootout occurred that ended the Sam Bass saga, for his invaluable role in the overall investigation Bill Scott received a share of the reward.

After varying assignments with the Texas Rangers, always advancing through the ranks, Bill Scott became a captain on May 1, 1886, eight years to the day after becoming a ranger. Just a few months later, on November 9, Scott led a six-man detail in Brown County after fence-cutting horse thieves. Refusing to surrender, the outlaws opened fire. They injured none of the rangers, but two of the lawbreakers were later found dead, and two others were found dying by the fence line. One of the deceased outlaws was none other than Constable Buck Harlow, shot in the chest just below the badge he had tarnished.

While leading Company F rangers on a patrol in Sabine County on March 31, 1887, outlaws ambushed the party, killing Pvt. J. H. Moore. Capt. Bill Scott was shot through the lungs, Sgt. J. A. Brooks had three fingers shot off, and Pvt. J. H. Rogers suffered a wound to his arm and side. As for the outlaws, desperado Bill Connor lay dead, his brother seriously wounded.

On April 30, 1888, Captain Scott relinquished his Texas Ranger commission and turned his attention to railroad contracting in Mexico. During one incident, Bill Scott was attacked by a dozen Mexicans, who gave the ex-ranger several stab wounds. With sheer grit and determination, he drove off his attackers. After that he settled in San Antonio, where on November 12, 1913, he died from a fall.

See also: BASS, SAM; TEXAS RANGERS

SCULL, Sally (a.k.a. Sarah Jane Newman) (1817–?)

Sarah Jane Newman, alias Sally Scull, is legendary in Texas. She apparently arrived in what became the state of Texas with the Stephen F. Austin colony and married Jessie Robinson on October 13, 1833. The couple had two children and were divorced on March 6, 1843. Less than two weeks later, Sally married George H. Scull, and the pair eventually had two children, Nancy and Alfred. Although she outlived George, Sally forever kept his surname.

On October 17, 1852, Sally married John Doyle, who soon afterwards dropped out of sight. Some stories had it that she shot him and dumped his body in Kinney's Tank near Corpus Christi. Sally then married Isiah Watkins in 1855 but divorced him less than three years later. After Watkins, she married a much younger man, Christopher Horsdorff.

From her husbands, she inherited two ranches. She gave up skirts, spoke excellent Spanish, and could curse in both Spanish and English. She could be a tough boss. Sally often carried a coiled whip as well as a revolver, in the process retaining a crew of rugged Mexican cowboys who drove horses back and forth across the border. A European visitor described her as "a North American amazon, a perfect female desperado. She can handle a revolver and a Bowie Knife, appears at dances well armed, and has shot several men at merry-makings." During the Civil War she ran cotton from East Texas to the port of Bagdad, Mexico, where English ships took it on board for later processing for the Confederacy.

Rumor had it that her last husband, Christopher Dorsdorff, had her murdered either in 1866 or 1876, her body being buried in a shallow grave near Agua Dulce (Sweet Water) Creek. There are stories of one of her hands grasping up through the dirt. A Texas state historical marker a few miles south of Goliad on alternate Highway 77 to Refugio explains the legend and history of Sally Scull.

SCURLOCK, Josiah Gordon (a.k.a. Doc Scurlock) (1849–1929)

Doc Scurlock, who likely studied medicine in New Orleans, was born in Talapoosa, Alabama, and was the most educated desperado involved in the Lincoln County War. He went to Mexico at the age of 20, spent maybe a year there, and then returned to ride for New Mexico's John Chisum in 1871.

As a good cattleman, he did not believe in rustling, so for a year or so after 1875 he helped decorate trees with the bodies of men who had attempted to steal cattle and had been caught. Scurlock and several others removed Jesús Largo from Sheriff Saturnino Baca's custody and lynched him near Lincoln on July 18, 1876. On September 2, Scurlock also (unintentionally) shot and killed Mike Harkins during a confrontation in a Lincoln carpenter shop. Scurlock was a member of the party that killed Morris Bernstein, the Mescalero Indian agency clerk.

Doc Scurlock assumed leadership of the McSween fighting men during New Mexico's Lincoln County War; his name, however, never emerged as a household word. By late 1879, Scurlock began shifting away from his boisterous past. He had survived the fighting, although he did not mature as the most handsome of the Regulators—he had several missing teeth, the result of someone's bullets entering the front of his face and exiting without striking the backbone. A little disfigurement did not stop him from marrying 16-year-old Antonia Miguela Herrera. They had 10 children. The Scurlocks moved to Eastland, Texas, in 1919, where he farmed, wrote poetry, and joined the Theosophical Society. He died in Eastland, reportedly of a heart attack, on July 25, 1929. Scurlock never discussed his turbulent life and career.

See also: BILLY THE KID; LINCOLN COUNTY WAR

SELMAN, John Henry (1839–1896)

John Henry Selman was born in Madison County, Arkansas, the sixth child. In 1858, the Selmans moved to Grayson County, Texas, and two years later John joined the 22nd Regiment of Texas Cavalry, stationed at Fort Washita, Choctaw Nation, Indian Territory (Oklahoma). In April 1863, he deserted. By now his father seems to have died. John packed up his mother, brothers, and sisters and moved west to Fort Davis, near Albany, Texas (a community now extinct and not to be confused with the present Fort Davis). Here he ranched, farmed, and fought Indians. He also enlisted in the Stephens County company of the Texas State Troops. The 1870 census showed him working as a laborer in Colfax County, New Mexico, and as married with two children, John and William. Two years after that, he was ranching near Fort Griffin, Texas. He had also joined a group of vigilantes known as the OLM, meaning "Old Law Mob." Folks later called it the Tin Hat Brigade. For whatever reason, Selman killed a man named Haulph in Fort Griffin.

Selman also became a deputy to Shackelford County sheriff John Larn. As a deputy, Selman killed a man named Shorty Collins. Meanwhile, the cattle herds of Larn as well as Selman unaccountably grew, causing suspicion and unease among their neighbors. Hides from their pens, with odd and blotched brands, turned up in the Clear Fork River. Selman and Larn claimed that the hides had been thrown into the river to frame them. On June 22, 1878, a group of men arrested Larn and took him to the Fort Griffin jail, where nine rifles executed him while he stood inside a cell.

Selman, having gotten word of Larn's arrest, slipped away, showing up in Lincoln County, New Mexico, by the end of the month. There he and his brother Tom—known as Tom Cat—organized a gang known as Selman's Scouts. They raided the George Coe ranch on the Hondo River. Selman killed a man named Little Hart during a dispute over leadership. The gang committed murders and rapes. In November 1879, when New Mexico governor Lew Wallace issued an amnesty proclamation, it included about everybody except John Selman and his scouts. The gang at that point broke up, John heading for the (present) Fort Davis, Texas, where he came down with a full-blown case of smallpox. He survived, but it seriously pitted his face. The Texas Rangers arrested him and returned him to Albany, Texas, where cattle-theft warrants were still outstanding. However, no one pressed charges. Meanwhile, John's brother Tom had recently been apprehended and lynched by the OLM somewhere near or in Albany. By now, John's wife had died, so he married a Hispanic girl and disappeared with her and his two boys into Mexico. By April 1888, his second wife had died, so John and the two boys moved to El Paso, Texas. There on August 23, 1893, the 57-year-old Selman married 16-year-old Romula Granadine.

On April 5, 1894, Bass Outlaw, a former Texas Ranger dismissed for drunkenness but now a U.S. deputy marshal, came to El Paso. He and John Selman visited Tillie Howard's sporting house, where Bass fired a revolver shot in the bathroom. Tillie rushed into the backyard blowing her police whistle, while Bass pursued her and tried to take it away. Texas Ranger Joe McKidrict attempted to break up the conflict, but Bass shot him in the back and then in the head. At that moment Constable John Selman reached the back porch and jumped off. He and Bass fired at each other. Selman's bullet struck Bass over the heart, while Outlaw's bullet whistled past Selman's head. However, the gunpowder burned Selman's eyes, and he staggered back, screaming "I can't see. I can't see!" At that instant, Outlaw fired again, the bullet striking Selman above the right knee, severing an artery.

Selman stumbled off to bleed and be patched up. However, from that time on he could not see well,

Gunman and El Paso constable John Selman (R. N. Mullin Collection)

especially at night, and he walked with a limp, as well as a cane.

At about this same time, noted gunslinger John Wesley Hardin came to town, hung out his law shingle on El Paso Street, and agreed to represent New Mexico cattle rustler Martin Mrose, who was hiding in Ciudad Juarez, Mexico. Hardin also coveted Helen Beulah Mrose, the wife of Martin, and since this presented problems, Hardin encouraged his client Martin to cross the Rio Grande on the night of June 21, 1895. To guarantee Martin's safety, Hardin had arranged for U.S. Deputy Marshal George Scarborough to protect Martin and lead him across the railroad bridge shortly after 9 P.M. However, on the north side, former El Paso police chief and now U.S. Deputy Marshal Jeff Milton and Texas Ranger Tom McMahan met Mrose and the three of them shot Mrose to death. John Selman was also likely involved in that murder, since he claimed afterward that Hardin had promised to pay him for his part in the Mrose killing but never had.

Meanwhile, John Selman Jr. had become an El Paso police officer. He arrested Beulah Mrose one night and charged her with carrying a revolver and with being drunk and disorderly. She paid a $50 fine.

The arrest and fine upset John Wesley Hardin, and he reportedly threatened John Selman Jr. Old John Selman, as he was generally called to distinguish him from his son, Young John Selman, now took up the cause. He and Hardin argued on San Antonio Street during the afternoon of August 19, 1895. Hardin said he didn't have a gun.

That evening at somewhere around 10 or 11 o'clock, Hardin wandered down to the Acme Saloon at the northwest corner of San Antonio and Utah Streets. He passed Selman sitting on a barrel near the doorway, walked inside to the far end of the bar, later moved back closer to the door, rolled some dice, then said to a nearby grocer, "Brown, you have four sixes to beat."

At that instant Constable John Selman stepped through the door, fired four quick shots, and Hardin was history. The first bullet hit Hardin in the back of the head. Selman was tried for murder. On February 12, 1896, the jury announced itself hung, 10 to 2 for acquittal.

At this point things started to go wrong. On April 2, 1896, 21-year-old police officer John Selman Jr., and the 15-year-old daughter of the soon-to-be Mexican consul in El Paso decided to elope and get married in Ciudad Juarez. When they could not locate a priest, they retired to a hotel for the night. When the girl's mother learned of events, she grabbed the Juarez chief of police, and they searched every hotel until they found the love bugs. The girl went home; young John went to the Mexican prison in Juarez.

Four days later, on April 6, Old John, worried about his son and drinking too much, left the upstairs room of the Wigwam Saloon, took a stairway down into an alley, and encountered U.S. Deputy Marshal George Scarborough. Selman asked for Scarborough's help in getting his son out of the Mexican jail. Scarborough refused. One word led to another, and Scarborough put four bullets into Old John Selman, who died that afternoon on the operating table at Sister's Hospital (Hôtel Dieu). John Selman is buried in El Paso's Concordia Cemetery.

As for John Selman Jr., he broke out of the Juarez prison on May 7 and made his way across the Rio Grande into El Paso. Young John never saw his El Paso sweetheart again, as her mother immediately sent her to Mexico City. John subsequently joined the army and was wounded in the Philippines. In 1937, at the age of 67, he was playing cards one evening with friends in Rockdale, Texas. He suddenly stood straight up, shouted, "O Lord, I don't want to die!" and fell dead across the card table.

See also: HARDIN, JOHN WESLEY; LARN, JOHN; MROSE, HELEN BEULAH; MROSE, MARTIN; OUTLAW, BASS

SEVERNS, Harry (a.k.a. Harry Tracy) (1875–1902)

Wisconsin is the state that Harry Tracy called home, although New York State and Missouri are also possibilities. For a while in his youth he worked as a logger and a railroader before burglarizing a house and going to the Utah State Penitentiary on July 11, 1897. He escaped three months later, on October 8, and put in appearances at Brown's Hole and the Hole-in-the-Wall in the Wyoming, Colorado, and Utah area, although he probably met only obscure members of the Wild Bunch.

In Aspen, Colorado, he went to jail for killing Brown's Hole rancher Valentine Hoy. He again escaped, drifting to Portland, Oregon, this time with David Merrill, an escaped convict. Both were arrested in February 1899, charged with robbery, and sent to the Oregon penitentiary in March 1899.

On June 9, 1902, both men escaped, killing three guards in the process and working their way into Washington State, where Tracy killed Merrill for reasons known for sure only by the two men. Tracy later said the two had drunkenly fought a duel, agreeing to step off 10 paces, turn, and fire. Tracy stepped off eight.

Near Woodinville, Washington, two posses converged near a railroad stop named Wayne Station. One of them, with newspaper reporters Karl Anderson and Louie Sefrit along, stumbled upon Tracy. However, in the brief gunfight, Tracy killed policeman Charles Raymond and wounded Anderson. Moments later he killed Chief Deputy John Williams.

Tracy now lurched toward Seattle, entering a farmhouse near the outskirts and forcing a Mrs. Van Horn not only to prepare him a meal but wash his clothes. She managed to tip off a grocery boy concerning her visitor, and the youngster informed Sheriff Ed Cudihee, who gathered a posse and surrounded the Seattle house. An hour or two later, Tracy left the house with two men in front as shields. When the posse screamed for him to surrender, Tracy turned his rifle their way, killed two, and fled. He slept that night in a cemetery, then twisted and turned for weeks as he worked his way out of the state. Farmers here and there noted his presence, but the fugitive always slipped eastward before the law could organize.

On August 5, 1902, a five-man posse from Creston, Washington, converged on a barn where Tracy had been holding a family hostage after helping them repair the building. Tracy saw the lawmen coming, grabbed his rifle, and fled—not fast enough, because a bullet shattered his leg below the right knee, severing an artery as it passed through. From there he crawled into a wheat field, taking another bullet in the right thigh. He now shot himself in the head. One of the greatest manhunts in Western history had finally ended.

The body was removed the next morning and transported to Davenport, Washington, where viewers whacked off bits of hair and pieces of clothing. From there the authorities transferred it to the prison graveyard of the Oregon State Penitentiary at Salem.

See also: BROWN'S PARK; HOLE-IN-THE-WALL; WILD BUNCH

SHARP, John S. (1853?–?)

Little is known about the origins, or in fact the ending, of John S. "Jim" Sharp, and possibly it really doesn't matter much. What is known about a smidgen of time in his middle years will suffice to take measure of his character, or lack of it. He stood about five foot three inches, and every inch was, by most accounts, bad to the bone. Most people suspected he came from Texas, but regardless, by his 30th birthday he had ambled into southeast Arizona Territory and had struck up something of a friendship with Curly Bill Brocius.

On August 26, 1881, at Charleston, Arizona, Francisco Lara was exiting his adobe home when Sharp happened to ride by. Perhaps the men exchanged words, or maybe Sharp was feeling particularly mean. At any rate, he pulled his revolver and shot Lara dead. A posse, of course, went in pursuit, and within a few days the lawmen had Sharp tucked in the Cochise County jail at Tombstone. Sharp, of course, did not stay long. On October 24,

two days before the Gunfight at the OK Corral, Sharp, accompanied by a cattle-stealing prisoner named Milt Hicks, and another thief named Charles "Yank" Thompson overpowered their jailer, Charlie Mason, and escaped. A posse composed of Sheriff John Behan, Deputy Billy Breakenridge, Buckskin Frank Leslie, and the Earp brothers, Wyatt, Virgil, and Morgan, chased the men but came up empty.

Sharp should have left the territory but didn't. Instead he acquired a partner named Bill Davies, and the two of them robbed a Contention, Arizona, saloonkeeper on September 7, 1882. This time Sheriff Behan probably took John Sharp into custody. A judge sentenced Sharp to 10 years in the Territorial Prison at Yuma, but even so the term proved only temporary. On January 26, 1883, Sharp broke out of prison and disappeared.

See also: BEHAN, JOHN; EARP, WYATT BERRY STAPP; EARP, VIRGIL; EARP, MORGAN; YUMA TERRITORIAL PRISON

SHARPS Rifle

The Sharps "Old Reliable" was a high-caliber, single-shot cartridge rifle, the most famous of its kind. Christian Sharp developed it. His rifles operated by throwing forward the trigger guard and sliding a block downward, uncovering the breech. Returning the trigger guard to its place closed the action. Cartridges supplanted the percussion cap after the Civil War. Most rifles were .45 caliber with 30-inch barrels, the weapons weighing between nine and 12 pounds. The Sharps would fire rapidly, making it a handy weapon when anticipating scraps with Indians or outlaws.

SHEARS, George (?–1864)

George Shears may or may not have been born in Montana, but he got there as quickly as he could. As it is, we know more about his death than his life, expect that he must have spent most of his life in outlawry. He rode with Henry Plummer, but only until the winter of 1864, when the vigilantes captured him. He reportedly cooperated with his captors, telling everything he knew, but they still made him climb to the top of a ladder, a rope having been tied around the top rung, the opposite end around his neck. While the vigilantes held the ladder upright, Shears reached the top, turned, and reportedly said, "Gentlemen, I'm not used to this. Shall I jump off or slide off? The vigilantes advised him to jump. He said goodbye, and leaped out into space, dying almost instantaneously when the slack went taut. "Shall I jump off or slide off?" from that moment on became a humorous and often-repeated vigilante expression.

See also: PLUMMER, WILLIAM HENRY

SHEDD, Warren H. (1829–1904)

Born in New York, Warren H. Shedd meandered through several states before purchasing the San Augustine Ranch in 1881, on the eastern slope of the Organ Mountains in New Mexico. Due to its geographical location on the west side of the immense Tularosa Basin, and because of a dependable water source, the ranch became a required stop for travelers. It thus became both famous and infamous.

With true entrepreneurial spirit, Shedd developed the ranch into a significant, although at times questionable, operation. Eventually, it contained a store, hotel, and restaurant, and quite naturally a saloon and whorehouse. However, what many uninitiated strangers didn't see was the undercurrent of criminality that made Shedd's ranch a focus for dubious characters, and from time to time the scene of wicked violence.

Warren Shedd was on good speaking terms with nearly all the notables of the Lincoln County War, including Jesse Evans, Jim McDaniels, Tom Hill, Alexander McSween, John Tunstall, Jimmy Dolan, Dick Brewer, and most of the other players, as well as numerous territorial politicians and prominent personalities.

Quite naturally, where liquor flowed as freely as refreshing spring water, tempers sometimes collided, such as when Chris Logan killed his tormentor; when Fred Bascom shot a fellow gambler out of the saddle; when Al Carver killed a guy named Cardwell; or when the horse-stealing Mes brothers were gunned down by a group calling itself a posse. Shedd, with considerable skill, would slyly wink and look the other way when outlaws or fugitives required commissary or a hiding place. A bill of sale for livestock transactions wasn't necessary. Business flourished. Warren Shedd had all the nefarious commerce on the west side of the Tularosa Basin pretty well locked down.

In 1882, Shedd sold much of his real-estate interests to Benjamin Davies, a highly respected livestock breeder (president of the Dona Ana County Stock Association), and began devoting his efforts to minimum enterprises, which never proved successful. For a man who had once been such a dominant figure in an untamed land, pictures of the past faded with times as did Shedd. Warren Shedd died on May 19, 1904, in the care of relatives at Elgin, Illinois. The ranch ended up in the hands of another southwestern powerhouse, William Webb Cox.

See also: COX, WILLIAM WEBB; EVANS, JESSE J.; GARRETT, PATRICK FLOYD JARVIS

SHERIFFS

Only a few sheriffs of the Old West would have fit the popular image of the straight-shooting law enforcer standing in the middle of the street and blowing away the bad guys. Sheriffs were politicians who went before the voters every two years, and whereas many were deadly with a gun, most depended upon their deputies for day-to-day law enforcement. However, since a sheriff was generally better known among the voters than his deputies and had the ultimate responsibility, he would be the one to raise posses, take charge, and lead them.

In addition to considerable paperwork, his duties consisted primarily of keeping the peace. In this respect he and his deputies chased bank, train, and stage robbers; forced rowdies out of saloons; locked up drunks and local troublemakers; ordered unwanted individuals out of town; and resolved domestic disputes. The sheriff hanged the convicted or delivered them to prison, collected taxes, enforced quarantines, shot stray dogs when they became too much of a nuisance, organized fire brigades, kept order in the courtroom, and cleaned the jail. When he found a few minutes for reflection, he glanced at the calendar and decided it was time to start shaking hands with voters again. For all this he usually received a small monthly stipend, as well as mileage fees and rewards.

SHIBELL, Charles Alexander (1841–1908)

Unlike many of his contemporaries, Charles Alexander Shibell received a rather extensive college education in Iowa before he crossed the plains to California. As a bright, ambitious 21 year old, Shibell signed on with Col. James H. Carleton's California Column (Union) as a teamster and walked onto the Arizona stage in 1862.

Shibell, a partisan Democrat, served from 1867 to 1869 as an inspector of customs at El Paso. He then returned to the Tucson area, ranched, prospected, and worked as a deputy under Sheriff William Sanders Oury of Pima County.

By at least one account Shibell was a participant in the infamous Camp Grant Massacre. During his long tenure in Arizona, Charley was from time to time involved in skirmishes with raiding Apache. During 1865 alone, Indians raided his ranch three times, although rare indeed was the early Arizona settler who was not occasionally confronted by Indian depredations.

Charles Shibell in 1876 became sheriff of Pima County, its 12,000,000 acres containing a scattered population of 3,000. However, he had been in office but a few days before he had to drop his administrative duties (as tax assessor and collector) and arrest a dangerous murderer, Thomas Kerr. From then on, burdened by paperwork and the colossal size of the county, there was little time for routine patrol or preventive law enforcement. In Tucson, there was paperwork to complete, a jail to maintain, arrests to be made, subpoenas to be served, and an occasional pursuit of escaping prisoners.

Naturally as the Arizona Territory "opened up," the sheriff's headaches increased. To the south and southeast of Tucson lay the Mexican border, an almost unbelievably isolated area, perfect for smuggling cattle, horses, and other contraband back and forth across the international boundary. The vacuum filled with disputable characters. As new towns sprang up, they too overflowed, the riffraff meandering from one boomtown to the next. Stagecoach robberies seemed epidemic.

William W. Brazelton in particular grabbed Shibell's attention. On the night of August 19, 1878, Shibell and his deputies staked out a site where Brazelton expected food and ammunition. During the ensuing shootout, or murder, as some claim, the career of the noted desperado came to an abrupt end. Regardless of how it was done, the Arizona populace cheered, and Shibell was handily reelected sheriff in 1878.

East of Tucson, as Tombstone began to flourish and Republican Party politics started taking hold, Shibell sensed a challenge to his Democratic administration. He gave Wyatt Earp (a Republican) an opportunity to become a deputy, but he terminated the commission when Earp publicly supported Shibell's political rival, Bob Paul.

In the hotly contested election of 1880, Shibell was defeated by Paul, although the decision was argued before the Arizona Supreme Court. After his defeat, Shibell operated the Palace Hotel in Tucson. When Democrats regained control of the Pima County sheriff's office, Charles Shibell became the number-two man (undersheriff) in Eugene O. Shaw's administration.

In one stirring adventure, Shibell and U.S. Marshal William Kidder Meade, accompanied by deputies, rode in pursuit of suspects who had robbed a Southern Pacific train at Stein's Pass, New Mexico, on February 22, 1888. The lawmen followed the trail deep into Mexico, where they belatedly reported their mission. The Mexican authorities jailed them for illegally entering the country. After two weeks, the embarrassed possemen were released without their horses and shooting irons, and returned home, absent any prisoners.

At 48 years of age, Shibell changed careers, successfully campaigning for the office of county recorder, a position to which he continually won reelection until his death from natural causes on October 21, 1908.

See also: BRAZELTON, WILLIAM; EARP, WYATT BERRY STAPP; MEADE, WILLIAM KIDDER

SHINN, George (?–?)

George Shinn was obscure at both ends of his life. He appeared from out of nowhere and ultimately vanished the same way. In the end he wasn't as successful as he was awkwardly dangerous in his chosen occupation as a desperado. He and four other men attempted to rob the Central Pacific out of Colfax, California, on September 1, 1881. They managed to derail the train, but when no one on board cooperated by opening their wallets, the outlaws panicked and vanished, taking nothing but bad tempers with them. Within 10 days lawmen had rounded up the luckless robbers; George Shinn was marched off to the San Quentin Prison at San Rafael, California. At the end of three years he requested a pardon. He had a good record, and numerous influential names supported him, but the governor refused the request.

Shinn and another inmate, Charles Dorsey, a stage robber locked up for killing a passenger, now teamed up. On December 1, 1887, they took advantage of pouring rain and, without any challenges, drove a horse-drawn cart through the prison gates and disappeared. They made it to Sacramento, then moved south and east through Arizona, New Mexico, and Texas, all the while engaging in a series of holdups before arriving in Chicago, where both men were arrested by Wells Fargo and Pinkerton agents. The bandits readily confessed, the media subsequently dubbing them "the most daring desperados of the Pacific Coast." Upon being returned to Oakland, California, the lawmen and outlaws were greeted by overwhelming crowds. Even a brass band showed up and played.

Dorsey now returned to San Quentin, while Shinn went to Folsom Prison, where the authorities released him in 1899. After that he dropped from sight, and all efforts to trace him have come to naught.

SHORT, Luke (1854–1893)

Luke Short was born in Mississippi, but within a year or two his folks had moved to East Texas to work on a farm. At a very young age he hired out as a cowboy, working the cattle trails between Texas and Kansas, in the process noting that whiskey peddlers and gamblers lived much more clean, relaxed, and pleasant lives than wranglers did.

In later years, Luke would be described as a fastidious dresser, a man with a small, even frail body that supported a somewhat oversized head. He stood about five feet six inches in height and weighed about 125 pounds. A thick, drooping mustache partially obscured a clean-shaven face. Thinning brown hair sometimes hung wistfully over bright blue eyes.

By 1876, Short joined whiskey peddlers 100 or so miles north of Sidney, Nebraska, their clients primarily being Sioux Indians. Stories exist—but evidence does not—that he was frequently arrested by U.S. soldiers and charged with selling whiskey to Indians.

From October 6 to 8, 1878, during a Cheyenne uprising, Short was hired out as a dispatch rider and civilian scout at $10 a day to ride from Ogallala, Nebraska, to the roving headquarters of Maj. Thomas T. Thornburgh. After that he drifted over to Leadville, Colorado, where he allegedly killed a man named Brown during a gambling dispute. He moved next to Dodge City, Kansas, and from there to Tombstone, Arizona, where he became a house dealer in the Oriental Saloon. Here he killed Charlie Storms, a well-known gambler, during an argument over a card game. Short shot Storms three times.

Luke Short: sometimes a gunfighter, always a gambler and a dandy (Author's Collection)

After being given a hearing and released, Short returned to Dodge City and worked as a house dealer in the Long Branch Saloon. He also became a central figure in the so-called Dodge City War. It all started with the mayoral election of Larry Deger and his reform ticket. Once in office his administration passed two ordinances, one prohibiting brothels and the second making bordello employees, in the eyes of the law, equivalent to individuals having no visible means of support—in other words, subject to arrest as vagrants.

Under the law, the Long Branch Saloon became a brothel, and some of its female entertainers were arrested. The city also arrested Luke for shooting at policeman Lewis Hartman. A judge subsequently ordered Luke to leave town. Several officers escorted him to the train. Other gamblers got the same treatment.

Short went to Kansas City but made plans for returning to Dodge. He wrote all his friends and associates. He petitioned Governor George Glick for state action. Newspapers picked up the story, and what had previously been a controversy now became the Dodge City War. The word went out that Luke Short was returning to Dodge with an army of gunfighters. The governor alerted National Guard companies. They and groups of peace officers met the train, but it had no Short and no gunfighters on it.

Blizzards of telegrams crisscrossed the state. Then, on June 5, Luke Short, Wyatt Earp, Charlie Bassett, Frank McLane, and Bat Masterson stepped off the train at Dodge. On June 6, city officials wired Governor Glick about this endangerment to law and order. The city asked for militia, and the governor sent Gen. Thomas Moonlight. He mediated the dispute. The mayor settled down, and Luke Short gathered a group of gunmen and had their photo taken together. Historians have dubbed it "Luke Short and his Dodge City Peace Commission."

In November 1883, Luke Short and his partner sold the Long Branch Saloon and went to Fort Worth. In August 1884, Short sued Dodge City for $15,000. The matter was settled out of court.

In February 1887, a Fort Worth gunman and former city marshal, Timothy Isaiah Courtright, better known as "Longhaired" Jim Courtright, now owned his own detective agency. He primarily provided "protection" to his clients, and he approached Short about protection money. Short refused, one word led to another, and both men reached for weapons. Courtright proved the faster, but his weapon caught in his own watch chain. Luke Short simply began pulling the trigger. One bullet shattered Courtright's revolver cylinder and blew off his right thumb. Another struck Courtright in the heart. Still another buried itself in the right shoulder, as two final shots thundered into the wall. Courtright died quickly. It took only a little longer for Luke Short to get out of jail.

Following the gunfight with Jim Courtright, Luke Short practically went into retirement. His last shooting occurred on December 23, 1890, in a gambling dispute. Charles Wright, with a shotgun, blew off part of Luke's left thumb and buried the other pellets in his left leg. Luke wounded his opponent, who promptly fled.

Luke visited Geuda Springs, Kansas, in August 1893 for treatment of dropsy but died there of the disease on September 8. He is buried in the Oakwood Cemetery at Fort Worth.

See also: COURTRIGHT, TIMOTHY ISAIAH; DODGE CITY, KANSAS; DODGE CITY WAR; EARP, WYATT BERRY STAPP; MASTERSON, WILLIAM BARCLAY

SHOTGUN (a.k.a. Double-barreled Shotgun, Scattergun)

This weapon never got much play in Western movies, but it remained a favorite weapon of Western lawmen, stagecoach drivers, and (sometimes) saloon owners. It had a certain effectiveness in crowd control and even one-on-one situations. At short range a gunman need not be a good shot in order to be persuasive. Shotguns have always been relatively inexpensive, and at short range they do not require pinpoint accuracy. This in itself adds to their popularity, particularly for home defense.

SIRINGO, Charles Angelo (1855–1928)

Charles Siringo epitomized the cowboy detective. He was born in Matagorda County, Texas, and grew up as a cowboy. His experiences while driving cattle on the Chisholm Trail became fodder for an autobiography entitled *Fifteen Years on the Hurricane Deck of a Spanish Pony.*

Charles A. Siringo (Robert G. McCubbin Collection)

In 1886, he joined the Pinkerton National Detective Agency, and working out of the Chicago office he spent the next 20 years trailing criminals around the West. He sought the Wild Bunch at the Hole-in-the-Wall, infiltrated a labor union in Utah, and on occasion acted as bodyguard. His *Lone Star Cowboy,* published in 1919, received a favorable audience; his *History of Billy the Kid,* published in 1920, was obviously not written to set the record straight but to cash in on a growing Billy the Kid biography market.

Siringo later bitterly criticized the Pinkerton Agency for filing injunctions stopping him from publishing *Two Evil Isms,* an expose of what he knew about the firm. His *Riata and Spurs,* published in 1927, did include some agency details. It was his best book. He died in Hollywood, California.

See also: COGHLAN, PATRICK; PINKERTON NATIONAL DETECTIVE AGENCY

SIX-SHOOTER

Most lawmen, gunfighters, cowboys, desperadoes, etc., carried what in the 20th and 21st centuries were commonly called six-shooters, revolvers, pistols, handguns. In the old Wild West, "pistols" seems to have been the favorite descriptive name. Of course, there was also a salon, muff, parlor, or saloon pistol, a reference to any light, small-caliber weapon frequently carried by a lady.

A difference between these six-shooters is that some were single-action and some were double-action. A single-action revolver, or six-shooter pistol, required only that the trigger be pulled. A double-action required that the weapon be cocked—in other words, that the hammer be pulled back before the weapon could be fired. Those who carried double-action weapons generally cocked the weapon with the thumb as they pulled it from the holster, belt, or pocket, and thus had it ready to fire practically as soon as it cleared the leather. As a general rule also, while the weapons were known as six-shooters, meaning a bullet in all six chambers of the cylinder, the hammer usually rode on an empty chamber, in order to prevent misfires, such as shooting oneself in the leg.

Some lawmen were known for the caliber of weapon they carried. Wild Bill Hickok, for instance, favored the .36 Navy Colt. Other individuals used the .44 Army. Billy the Kid liked the .44-40. Dallas Stoudenmire preferred the Smith & Wesson .44.

Pinkerton agents and policemen generally favored small, easily concealed revolvers, such as a Smith & Wesson .38 Fifth Model, hammerless revolver. Heck Thomas liked the Colt New Navy Model 1892 .38-caliber revolver. In short, the weapons preferred by outlaws, lawmen, and gunfighters were as varied as their own personalities.

SLADE, Joseph Alfred (a.k.a. Jack Slade) (1824–1864)

Jack Slade, as he preferred to be called, was born in Carlyle, Illinois, but left home in the 1840s. He saw action during the Mexican War, in 1858 working as a Colorado line foreman for the Central Overland California and Pike's Peak Express Company. Slade was a drinking fool, a working fool, and a fighting fool, and he could do any of the three with equal vigor and joy. However, he also had romance in his blood, and during this period the short, roly-poly, sometimes schizophrenic Slade married a pretty young lass known only as Virginia.

No sooner had Slade taken on the Overland Mail job, however, than word came down that over in Colorado a French Canadian named Jules Reni had been stealing company horses. Reni might have even worked for the company; the facts are not clear. But whether the theft was in-house or not, Slade rode over to investigate.

The two men met in the street, and Slade realized quickly that perhaps he should have stayed in the main office. Reni started shooting, his first two bullets knocking Slade down. Three more bullets struck the writhing man. Reni then emptied a shotgun into his victim, altogether firing roughly 13 slugs into Slade. After Reni turned and left, several bystanders, including company employees, carried the blood-soaked Slade off to a bunkhouse.

Reni expected Slade to die, and when he didn't, Reni apparently hung around the area for an opportunity to do a more thorough and workmanlike job of killing him. Instead, the advantages now fell to Slade. In 1859, several cowboys caught Reni watching the Slade ranch near Cold Springs, Colorado. Slade ordered them to bind Reni to a fence post. Then, swigging deeply from a whiskey flask, Slade methodically pulled his six-shooter and commenced shooting Reni in the arms and legs. After tiring of the game, he jammed his six-shooter into Reni's mouth and fired. Then pulling out his knife, he cut off both of Reni's ears. For the remainder of his life he used one of them as a watch fob.

Slade now left (or was forced out of) his Overland Mail position. He and Virginia drifted to Fort Halleck, Wyoming, where Jack in 1862 nearly killed an unnamed civilian. Now, with an arrest warrant dogging him, he and his wife moved on to Montana, ranching and farming near Virginia City—which was not named for his wife, as has been claimed. Jack killed no one there, but his drunken, rowdy behavior caused uproars wherever he went. The vigilantes at first warned him, then banned him from even entering the town, but all that was a waste of good air.

One evening as the drunken Slade shot and swaggered his way through the community, vigilantes grabbed him by the arms and dragged him toward the cross-bar of a corral gate. At this point, Jack Slade began pleading for his life, begging in such a pathetic matter that a few of the vigilantes forced a brief reconsideration—giving Jack sufficient time to send someone for his wife.

But it was too late. As they put the rope around his neck on March 10, 1864, he cried, "My God! My God! Oh, my poor wife! Must I die like this?" And he died like that.

His wife, Virginia, arrived an hour later, found his body lying in the street, and decided she would take it back to Illinois for burial. From somewhere she acquired a casket largely made of tin and filled it with alcohol, the fluid her husband loved so well. Four months later, the body reached Salt Lake City, where it had become so odorous that it went no farther. On July 20, 1864, Jack Slade was interred in the local Mormon cemetery. As for his wife, Virginia, she sold the ranch, moved, remarried, and divorced. Then she vanished.

As an aside, the author and humorist Mark Twain claimed to have met Jack Slade somewhere out West in a saloon during 1861. Twain described the gunman as "so friendly and so gentle spoken that I warmed to him in spite of his awful history."

SLAUGHTER, John Horton (1841–1922)

One of Arizona's most famous sheriffs and cattlemen, John Slaughter was born in Sabine Parrish, Louisiana, served in the Confederate army, joined the Texas Rangers, and by the 1870s had his own cattle ranch in Frio County, Texas. He was short, about five foot six inches, stocky, and always wore expen-

John H. Slaughter (Robert G. McCubbin Collection)

sive clothes, including a vest. He married in 1871. He and the wife moved to Arizona, where she died a few years later. Meanwhile, John drove cattle back and forth across the Mexican border, and although he got away with it—and always claimed to have done it legally—disturbing questions arose.

Although Slaughter had likely killed Apache and perhaps Mexicans in defense of his herds, he shot his first recorded man, Barney Gallagher, near Fort Sumner, New Mexico, in the fall of 1876. Barney was supposed to have been, and probably was, a rustler.

On March 11, 1879, New Mexico governor Lew Wallace had Slaughter arrested on cattle-theft charges. After being released, the 37-year-old Slaughter married the 18-year-old Viola Howell in May and moved to Charleston, 10 miles southwest of Tombstone, Arizona. There he had a brief encounter with the Clanton family, called them thieves, and ordered them off his land. They left. Then in 1886, John Slaughter ran for sheriff of Cochise County and won, serving from 1877 to 1890. His motto: Shoot first—then yell, "Throw up your hands!"

It wasn't long before Slaughter killed cattle rustlers Guadalupe Robles and Nieves Derom. Several others fell before his flaming guns, or those of his deputies. When John stepped down as sheriff the slayings didn't stop. Slaughter killed a man named Childers and his unknown friend. He also tracked a gambler and horse thief named Arthur "Pegleg" Finney and killed him, on September 20, 1898.

On February 16, 1922, John Slaughter himself died in bed, with his boots off.

SMALL, Charles (1862?–1893)

Speculation would lead to inference that Charles Small was a Texas product, since for several years Charley lived as a notorious character in West Texas, New Mexico, and below the border. Small reportedly found employment as a cowboy for the San Vincente Company on the Pipe Line Ranch, but by September 1887 Charley was being sought for questioning regarding a train robbery near Pantano, Arizona. At Deming, New Mexico, private detective John Gilmo tried to arrest Small, but Charley jerked his six-shooter and might have killed him had not deputy Dan Tucker intervened. Small readily (and wisely) submitted to arrest. An investigation, however, turned up no evidence against Small, so Tucker freed him.

Back on the train, Southern Pacific Railroad detective Fred Burke tried to rearrest Small. Charley snapped that "he was tired of being arrested, and did not propose to surrender, but that if the detective wanted him very bad he could telegraph the sheriff to make the arrest when the train arrived at Silver City." So Burke and Small made the trip to Silver City, where Burke dropped the matter, the local newspaper noting, "These detectives are fast becoming the laughing stock of the entire country. They have made seven or eight arrests, and have in every instance turned their men loose. Such action is unbecoming of Pinkerton's men, and is calculated to make a strong feeling against them. They should have some evidence before making an arrest, or give the job up and go home."

Small could not stay out of trouble, however, and within a brief time was reportedly involved in the robbery of the Mexican Central at Mapula, Chihuahua. One of Small's confederates, "Doc" Hines, later confessed to the crime, although the Mexican and Texas governments haggled for so long that Charley Small vanished and no one noticed.

Small continued his borderland career, on one occasion becoming a hired gun for trans-Pecos ranchers, seemingly in constant battle with Mexican outlaws. On July 11, 1893, near Del Rio, Charley Small was arrested for smuggling, but he was soon out on bond and back at Langtry, where customs inspector F. A. Cunningham suspected him of leading a gang of rustlers. A short time later on July 22, Small, with a seemingly diminished capacity for common sense, picked a fight with Texas Rangers Sgt D. L. Musgrave and Tom Lewis. The rest of the story is summed up in Musgrave's report to headquarters: "This morning we were fired on by Chas Small a noted desperate character and he was killed by me."

See also: GILMO, JOHN W.; TUCKER, DAVID

SMITH, James L. (1838–1914)

This Smith was born in Maryland, served in the Union army, and after the war became chief of detectives for the metropolitan police in New Orleans. Following the Battle of Liberty Square in 1875, however, Smith went to work for the Union Pacific and wound up in Cheyenne, Wyoming, helping to organize an Indian police force on the Pine Ridge Reservation. From there he trailed rustlers and other outlaws back and forth, in the process—as one rancher—reported it, killing enough people "to have a small but respectable-sized graveyard." He trailed the Doc Middleton gang to Sidney, Nebraska, killing Joe Smith and Charley Reed.

Smith captured Cornelius "Lame Johnny" Donohue, who had been raiding Sioux herds, and bundled him on a stage bound for Rapid City. Unfortunately, somewhere along the route, someone lynched "Lame Johnny."

On March 10, 1880, a large amount of gold on a Union Pacific train at Sidney, Nebraska, disappeared. Someone had cut a hole in the floor and carried off the bars. Smith suspected Sheriff Cornelius M. McCarty, who controlled not only the local political establishment but the criminal underworld as well. Smith decided to investigate. McCarty owned the Capital Saloon, so Smith wasn't all that welcome when he stepped inside. Bartender Patrick Walters and Smith immediately argued about the honesty of railroad police, and as one word led to another, both pulled guns. Walters went down with a bullet in the stomach. Smith was tried for attempted murder but was acquitted.

On New Year's Eve 1880, Smith decided to test his luck again. He and Dennis Flannigan, alias Douglas Black, had a long history of mutual threats, but after a few drinks they made amends, at least until they visited Smith's room at a local hotel, where Smith shot Flannigan three times. He died quickly, but Smith was again acquitted. A year later, in 1881, Smith became head of the Indian police at the Apache Mescalero Reservation, near today's Ruidoso in southern New Mexico. Three years later, Smith was hired away from the Mescalero by Tom Sturgis of the Wyoming Stock Growers Association. One of his detectives had been murdered in Nebraska, and Sturgis wanted Smith to investigate the crime.

As crimes go, this one was solved relatively easily. The slayer was Johnny Smith, a brother-in-law of the murdered man; James Smith trailed John Smith to near Nogales, Mexico, where he learned that another man had already shot and killed him. Smith thereafter turned his attention to the pursuit of Harry Longabaugh for theft, trailing him to Billings, Montana, where Smith and Eph Davis made the arrest. Longabaugh spent a year and a half in Sundance, Wyoming, and left there with a name eventually to become famous—the Sundance Kid.

While there is some suggestion that Smith thereafter pursued members of the Wild Bunch, he himself was soon arrested on bootlegging and gambling charges in Boulder, Colorado. He went to jail, and in 1914, while cleaning his cell, he drank a mixture of water and lye—and died moments later. He is buried in the Riverside Cemetery at Denver, Colorado.

See also: MIDDLETON, DOC; SUNDANCE KID

SMITH, James W. (a.k.a. Six Shooter Bill; John Henry Hankins) (1856–1882)

This desperado was likely born in Texas, where in 1878 he was suspected of murder in Cook County. Bat Masterson later arrested him in Dodge City, Kansas, and charged him with horse theft. He next showed up in Las Vegas and Deming, New Mexico, before drifting over to Tombstone, Arizona. In 1881, some San Simon ranchers caught him stealing cattle, but he escaped to Mimbres, New Mexico, where after becoming something of a vice king, he was hustled off to Benson, Arizona. In Laredo, Texas, he killed the chief of police, then fled to Cibolo, Texas. There, this traveling man quarreled with two cowboys, and one of them shot him dead.

See also: MASTERSON, WILLIAM BARCLAY

SMITH, Tom (a.k.a. Bear River Tom Smith) (1830?–1870)

No one can prove where and when Smith was born, but most historians suspect the city of New York, a few insisting that he worked there as a city policeman. By the end of the Civil War, he had found employment in Wyoming and Colorado as a construction supervisor for the Union Pacific Railroad. In Bear River, Wyoming, where Smith would get his nickname, hard feelings broke out between the townspeople and the railroad workers, the upshot being that Smith shot a man and then during a riot managed to lock townspeople—whom he referred to as "vigilantes"—in a store. From this moment on, Tom Smith became Bear River Tom Smith. He also became city marshal of several railroad towns before becoming chief of the Abilene, Kansas, police force in June 1870. He made it a point practically never to wear a gun when enforcing the law.

Bear River Tom Smith (Author's Collection)

However, it wasn't but five months later when—relaxing that rule—he shoved a revolver in his pocket as he went out to arrest Andrew McConnell, who had shot and killed his neighbor. Smith and Deputy J. H. McDonald rode the 10 miles out to McConnell's dugout, where the accused and a friend, Moses Miles, waited. McConnell immediately shot Smith in the chest, and Smith returned the fire, wounding his adversary. Meanwhile, Miles, although wounded, had driven off McDonald. Miles and McConnell then wrestled Smith to the ground. While he lay there, Miles picked up an ax and practically severed Smith's head from his body.

SMITH & Wesson

Smith & Wesson in 1869 manufactured the Model No. 3 .44-caliber single-action American, the first "real" cartridge revolver. This led to the Schofield .45 and the .44-caliber Russian model. The Schofield had a seven-inch instead of the usual eight-inch barrel, its top latch making it easy to break the gun open for loading and unloading. The gun was well balanced, and it shot and functioned as well as the Peacemaker at 25 to 50 yards.

SMITH & Wesson Schofield

The Schofield began its life as an 1875 single-action .45 caliber revolver. While its rounds did not carry quite the punch of the .45 Army Colt, it saw more use. The cartridges were easily ejected or dumped, rather than poked out. However, the Schofield, while more accurate than the Peacemaker, was also a more expensive weapon, perhaps because it was so finely crafted.

SMUGGLERS Trail

Old timers often referred to this path as the Sonora Trail, or sometimes just as "the Trail," but it essentially wound south from Tombstone, Arizona, through McNeal and the Coronado National Forrest, the Peloncillos Mountains, the Animas Valley, past Cloverdale and into Sonora, Mexico. Across this trail flowed all kinds of contraband between the United States and Mexico, in both directions. Stolen cattle and horses, of course, were the primary products, but gold and ore shipments attracted consider-

able attention too. This rather secluded path had no real terminal, and it was intersected by numerous side trails. It opened in the late 1860s or 1870s, reached its greatest activity during the late 1870s and 1880s, and most likely did not go completely out of business as a smuggling route until sometime during the early 1900s.

SOILED Doves

The term "soiled doves" is more of a Victorian term than a Westernism, but newspaper editors in the old West loved it. Furthermore, it is impossible to understand prostitution in the Wild West if one does not understand Western society in general, which, for the purpose of this statement, was divided into two kinds—married and unmarried. Most professional and business people were married. The vast majority of men, however, were loose, free, and single: cowboys, miners, mule skinners, soldiers, laborers, gamblers, roughnecks, drifters, outlaws, lawmen, and so forth. It also followed that they were generally young, had little education, lived from payday to payday or job to job, and being far from home, were little subject to the civilizing restraints of church, family, or friends.

Prostitutes originated from all over the country, and around the world. They had sometimes been kicked out by family or husbands. Their names changed as often as their underclothes, and by the time they had been around for a few years, they had generally lost their looks as well as their manners and soft language.

Most towns licensed the girls as well as the districts or houses in which they worked. The fees ran $5 a month and up. A police officer usually collected. The money paid by these unfortunate women generally supported the police force as well as other city departments.

Prostitutes rarely left the districts where they lived and worked unless they were leaving town. Doctors visited the districts in order to treat the girls; the girls did not go to the offices to see the doctors. On one occasion in El Paso, Texas, during a hot July day, three girls thought they were just as good as anyone else and invaded the municipal pool. The "decent" citizens immediately bailed out in horror and called the police. The police tried to coax the girls out, but they refused, forcing the officers to wade in after them. A judge fined the girls $10 each and gave each one three days in jail. A local newspaper applauded this judicial decisiveness.

Brothel areas were frequently referred to as "red light districts," because trainmen, getting ready to leave town, hung their red, glowing lanterns on brothel doors or placed them on window insets so supervisors could find them. The upper-class brothel areas—frequently having two-story houses with nice furniture and better-dressed girls—became "reservations," meaning districts set aside by known street boundaries. The structures were usually called "parlor houses," because when the men entered, the madams hustled out to look them over; if they passed inspection, meaning "looked like they had money in their pockets," she would shout, "Company in the parlor, girls!" The girls would then trot out, parade the wares, and the deals would be made.

Stepping down a notch were less ornate brothels. These usually attracted middle-class clients. The businesses were not quite as expensive, and the girls were not quite as well dressed, but the situation worked.

Last, or at the bottom of the list, were the "cribs," strings of single rooms along a street, usually referred to as "the line." It consisted of a Dutch door with a prostitute leaning over and soliciting passersby. A single bed, a chair, a wash basin, and a bottle of carbolic acid usually constituted the furniture. An oil cloth draped on the foot of the bed ensured that muddy boots did not destroy the luster of the top cover. The cribs catered to assembly-line sex, the fees usually being in coins rather than paper.

Prostitutes in the American West numbered in the thousands, ranging in age from what looked like 10 years to what looked like 1,000. They seldom used their correct names, and some had forgotten what they were. Pregnancies happened all the time, and abortions were common, although risky. Children grew up in brothels, the madams and girls usually going out of their way to protect and guide the youngsters. Romanticized books and movies to the contrary, prostitute beatings—sometimes by the client but more often by pimps and madams—happened with regularity. By middle age, a prostitute had frequently lost the use of one eye, had gone through miscarriages and abortions, had survived at least one venereal disease, had failed at suicide (usually by drug overdose), had blacked out due to too much whiskey or the wrong medication, and bore an assortment of knife wounds, burns, bruises, missing teeth, and broken bones. Very few ever changed their ways or occupations, and almost none married well or retired in financial security. To view photos of soiled doves is to view the West as Tragedy.

See also: CALAMITY JANE; CYPRIAN; HELL'S HALF-ACRE

SONTAG, John (1860–1893)

John Sontag was born in Minnesota, his father died four years later, and he adopted the name Sontag from his stepfather. He left home in 1878 and became a brakeman with the Southern Pacific in California. An accident in 1887 either caused his discharge or left him unable to work; he thereafter never said a kind word about railroads.

While Sontag convalesced and brooded, he met a fellow brooder named Christopher Evans. They agreed that railroads needed to repay a lot of grief. Their train robberies started almost at once, with minor hits at Cape Horn Mills and later at Pixley, two men being slain during the latter caper. In 1890, Sontag's brother George joined the duo, and a couple more trains went down.

On August 3, 1892, the Sontag boys and Chris Evans hit a train just west of Fresno, a robbery leading to the capture of George Sontag, who went to Folsom Prison after apparently confessing and naming names. His information led investigators to the doorstep of John Sontag and Chris Evans, where a shootout left Deputy Sheriff Oscar Beaver dead. A month later the Southern Pacific and Wells Fargo firms posted a $10,000 reward for John Sontag and Chris Evans. The two outlaws fled to the nearby mountains, where Sontag and Evans ambushed a posse, killing Vic Wilson and Andy McGinnes. For his part, Sontag took a bullet in his arm, painful but not serious.

Due to telegraph communications, Sontag and Evans now became two of the most famous fugitives in the country, though neither abandoned their mountain hideout. However, with trackers all over the area it was just a matter of time, and on June 11, 1893, time ran out. A posse ambushed the two fugitives near a site called Stone Corral, where lawmen shot them to pieces. A posse took them into custody the next morning, a photographer photographing Sontag lying despondent and near death in a pile of hay, straw, and manure.

After being taken to the Fresno County jail, Evans recovered quickly, though he lost an arm and an eye. As for John Sontag, an arm and shoulder had practically been shot away, causing tetanus and peritonitis to set in. His jaws locked, and soup had to be "piped" in by way of a broken tooth. Even so, he bit his tongue in half before dying on July 3, 1893. He was buried in Fresno's Catholic Cavalry Cemetery.

SPENCE, Pete (1852–1914)

The desperado Lark Ferguson, who was born in Louisiana, by 1874 was serving in the Texas Ranger Frontier Battalion of Capt. Warren Wallace Ferguson. He was a second lieutenant in what became known as "the Nueces and Rio Grande Company." It operated around Corpus Christi during the early 1870s. He killed a Mexican cowboy sometime around July 4, 1874, then killed another the following month. These two killings were likely the reasons why he left the rangers. On August 1, 1875, he was in trouble again, a grand jury handing down an indictment for horse theft. Then, on August 24, 1876, he participated in the Seeligson Bank robbery in Goliad. By the mid and beyond 1870s, Live Oak and Maverick Counties of Texas wanted him for murder. Lark Ferguson therefore changed his name to Peter Spence and moved his operations to Arizona. By 1878, he had been arrested for murder in Pima County. A jury voted to acquit, and Pete moved to Tombstone, where he and gunman/feudist Frank Stilwell spent their time carousing in saloons and allegedly robbing stagecoaches. Both were arrested in Bisbee but were later released, in the process becoming part of the Cowboy gang, whose leaders were the Clanton boys. This made them bitter enemies of the Earp brothers, although both Spence and Stillwell were in jail and missed the famous street fight of October 26, 1881.

When Virgil Earp was assassinated on December 28, Pete Spence and Frank Stillwell were identified as two of several possible culprits. The same happened on March 18, 1882, when Morgan Earp went down. This time the remaining Earps and friends went after the two men, although Spence turned himself in to Tombstone authorities and was placed in protective custody. As for Stillwell, the Earp party caught him messing around the train cars in the Southern Pacific railroad yards in Tucson and shot him to death.

Spence at this time opted for a lower profile, becoming a deputy sheriff in Grant County, New Mexico, where a newspaper in July 1886 referred to him as "one of the best peace officers in the West." A week later he beat to death a man named Rodney O'Hara. Then, during a saloon fight at Morenci, Arizona, he killed "Curley" Martinez, a young Mexican cowboy. The *Tempe News* of April 15, 1893, opened an editorial by shouting, "Pete Spence kills another Mexican in cold blood. THAT MAKES FIVE." This slaying earned Pete five years in the Yuma penitentiary, but he was released in November 1894 after serving 15 months.

He thereafter wandered around Arizona and in August 1901 was treated like a returning hero in Tombstone. He even married Phin Clanton's widow on April 2, 1910, Phin being a brother of the Clanton boys slain at the OK Corral.

Spence died of pneumonia in 1914 and was buried in an unmarked grave in the Pioneer Cemetery at Globe, Arizona.

See also: GUNFIGHT AT THE OK CORRAL; EARP, VIRGIL; EARP, BERRY STAPP WYATT

SPILLMAN, C. W. (1837–1862)

On August 21, 1862, C. W. Spillman, William Arnett, and B. F. Jermagin rode into Gold Creek, Montana, with six good horses and nothing to show how and why they had them. Four days later, two additional men rode into town, claiming they were trailing horse thieves, specifically the three men mentioned. Arnett tried to make a fight of it and was shot dead. Spillman and Jermagin surrendered. Jermagin turned out to be a local cowboy who had had the bad luck to have ridden along with the other two. He was turned loose, and that left only Spillman to be tried.

The vigilantes listened to his courtroom confession and waited patiently as he apologized and wrote a letter to his father asking for forgiveness. Then they quietly hanged him at 2:22 in the afternoon, the first death in the Montana vigilante movement.

See also: VIGILANCE COMMITTEES

STANDIFER, Bill (1860?–1902)

Bill Standifer was born in cattle country at Lampasas, Texas. He not only grew up in cattle country but died in cattle country. Bill Standifer was a cattleman—an indisputably tough-as-cowhide kind of cattleman.

By 1879, Bill Standifer was cowboying for Ike Mullins ranch in Tom Green County, not far from San Angelo. During the spring roundup a dispute broke out between young Standifer and an older and more worldly John Mahan, a rancher from Gonzales County. Facing a Winchester in the hands of a Mahan supporter, Standifer accepted a horsewhipping. Several weeks later, Bill Standifer hunted up Mahan, who was still with the roundup, but by this time in Runnels County. Sensing the seriousness of Standifer's intent, Mahan snapped a quick shot, the bullet zinging past the young cowboy's head. Standifer's bullet, however, broke Mahan's wrist. Mahan whirled his horse and fled but did not get far, because Standifer killed both horse and Mahan. Standifer then headed south to the Big Bend area of Fort Davis, where while partying at a saloon he shot and wounded two black troopers. This time the Texas Rangers caught and delivered him to Coleman, Texas, for trial regarding the Mahan killing. The 12 jurors called it self-defense. The black soldiers didn't die, but they also didn't own any cows. So their case was dismissed!

In the Panhandle, Standifer reportedly killed a rustler near Estacado; whether it was actually true or not, the scattered populace thought enough of his gunfighting reputation to elect him Crosby County sheriff in 1880. After the post office at Dockums was robbed, Sheriff Standifer and Deputy Charlie Quillen tracked the outlaws west into New Mexico. Two days later, with the two rogues in custody, the quartet started home. At a squatter's dugout, where they stopped for the night, the two desperadoes wrenched away Quillen's rifle and shot the deputy in the chest. Standifer, who had been standing outside, rushed to subdue the prisoners. Quillen survived his wound. However, once everybody reached Dickens County, Standifer discovered that he did not have the post office robbers at all but instead fugitives wanted for two murders and six robberies.

After this stint as sheriff, Bill Standifer hired out as a "protection man," meaning a range detective, for the Spur Ranch. Pink Higgins, another Lampasas lad hired by the Spur, joined him.

The ranch, although huge, wasn't big enough for both of them, however, not two men with legitimate man-killing reputations and old grievances. On October 1, 1902, the two Spur employees dueled with rifles at 62 paces. When the smoke cleared, only Pink Higgins was still standing. Higgins then telephoned the local sheriff, reporting that he thought he had killed Bill Standifer. N. N. Rodgers, a seasoned lawman himself, replied, "If you are not sure you better go back and finish the job."

See also: HORRELL-HIGGINS FEUD

STARR, Henry (1873–1921)

Henry Starr, an outlaw, as well as three-eighths Cherokee Indian, stood tall, at six foot seven. Born near Fort Gibson in Indian Territory (Oklahoma), he attended the Cherokee Mission School and worked as a cowhand, but he was jailed and fined in 1891 for selling whiskey to Indians. Following that, he was arrested and jailed for stealing a suitcase; then he went big time and graduated to stealing horses. In 1892, he and his gang held up the Missouri Pacific and then killed deputy U.S. Marshal Floyd Wilson when Wilson attempted to arrest the gang. The outlaws slung Wilson over the saddle and slapped his horse into Fort Smith. The gang, enlarged now due to publicity, subsequently robbed three banks, a passenger train, and a railroad depot, all in less than three months.

Starr now decided to relax, but he was captured in Colorado and transported to Fort Smith, where Judge Isaac Parker sentenced him to hang. The accused responded by screaming, "Don't try to stare me down. I've looked many a better man than you in the eye. Save your wind for your next victim. If I am a monster, you are a fiend, for I have only put one man to death, while you have slaughtered many with your jawbone."

Starr certainly sounded bold, but somewhere along the way he decided that the date of his execution was not a good day to die, so he commenced a string of appeals that finally brought his case back to court, where he was assessed 15 years in the federal prison at Columbus, Ohio.

Before he could be taken to Columbus, in June 1875, Cherokee Bill attempted to escape from the Fort Smith jail. Gunfire erupted across the prison, the break ending only when Henry Starr talked Chero-

Henry Starr (Robert G. McCubbin Collection)

kee Bill into surrendering. That act earned Starr a pardon from President Theodore Roosevelt in January 1903.

However, he had no sooner stepped out of one prison than Colorado authorities arrested him for a previous robbery and sentenced him from seven to 25 years in the Canon City Penitentiary. Starr was paroled in 1915.

As soon as Starr hit the streets, he and whatever remained of his old gang struck two banks at Stoud, Oklahoma, on March 17. However, as he fled, a 17-year-old boy put a bullet in his leg, and Starr was back in prison. This time he received a sentence of 25 years in an Oklahoma penitentiary, although he served only four. The state paroled him in 1919, and he moved from prison to starring in a movie about how crime does not pay. But even then he had not learned his lesson. In 1920, he robbed two banks, one in Chandler and one in Davenport, Oklahoma. On February 18, 1921, he hit the People's National

Bank in Harrison, Arkansas. But Harrison, Arkansas, would be his last holdup. He entered the bank wearing a suit, demanded cash, and was shot with a rifle. He died of his wound four days later, on February 22.

STARR, Myra Maybelle (a.k.a. Belle Starr) (1848–1888)

Belle Starr was born Myra Maybelle Shirley on February 5, 1848, in Carthage, Missouri, the daughter of John Shirley, a farmer and hotel owner. The family educated her. She became a competent pianist and well read. Her brother Bud—a guerrilla fighter—was slain in the Civil War. Her discouraged father moved the family to near Dallas, Texas, following the war, and there she met Jim Reed, who also had been a guerrilla fighter. They married on November 1, 1866, and promptly returned to Missouri. In September 1866, she gave birth to a daughter, who became Rosie Lee, although Belle called her Pearl.

In Missouri, Jim Reed tended to go wild. He rustled cattle and sold whiskey. Rumors arose regarding dead men on his backtrail, so the family moved to California, where a son, James Edwin Reed, was born. Meanwhile, Reed continued to rob and kill, going on forays into Texas and Arkansas. Belle went home to her parents. In the meantime, Reed held up a Texas stage, fled to Oklahoma, then twisted back to near Paris, Texas, where he was slain by a posse on August 6, 1874.

As a widow, Belle came on difficult financial times, so she drifted into Indian Territory (Oklahoma), where she married Sam Starr, a part–Cherokee Indian and the son of Tom Starr, a renegade outlaw. The Starrs lived at Younger's Bend, a rendezvous point for some of the worst class of outlaws. Belle and Sam were arrested for horse theft; Judge Isaac Parker at Fort Smith, Arkansas, sentenced both to one year in the House of Corrections at Detroit. After nine months, the authorities released them. They returned to Younger's Bend, where a son, Eddie, was born, and where Sam returned to his old trade of horse stealing, while she had her photo taken with Blue Duck, a convicted murderer. The photo shows a woman who looked twice her 38 years.

In the meantime, Belle persuaded her husband to surrender, but while awaiting trial, he and Tom West shot each other to death at a dance. Belle had once again become a widow. Fearing she would lose her property, she married another Cherokee, Jim July, who was 15 years her junior. In the meantime, her son, Eddie, became a horse thief. Pearl became a prostitute.

It was too late for Belle Starr to turn her life around. On February 2, 1888, someone blasted her out of the saddle with a shotgun. A neighbor, Edgar Watson, was acquitted, and no one else ever went to trial. Pearl arranged the funeral.

See also: PARKER, JUDGE ISAAC

ST. LEON, Ernest (a.k.a. Diamond Dick)
(1859?–1898)

Although he is usually mentioned, albeit briefly, in general histories of the Texas Rangers, Ernest St. Leon and his exploits tower well above most of the other gunmen who grabbed the 20th century spotlight. On the southwestern border he was a genuine force.

Of French extraction, St. Leon was born in Canada but at an early age migrated with his parents to San Antonio, Texas, where as a young man he chose to become an attorney, studying for the bar exam. He gave that up, the record indicating that St. Leon, with a certain wanderlust and a desire for adventure, enlisted in the U.S. cavalry and served a stint in Wyoming.

Returning to the Lone Star State, on September 1, 1890, Ernest St. Leon enlisted in the Texas Rangers at Brewster County in the Big Bend area. He was definitely not a "dandy," but because of his obviously advanced level of education, and since he always sported a large diamond stickpin, his fellow lawmen nicknamed him "Diamond Dick."

Four months later the rangers summarily discharged St. Leon. By some accounts the problem was imbibing to many liquid refreshments, and by others it was misappropriating ranger supplies, some said to feed his family. At any rate he promptly found

Belle Starr (Robert G. McCubbin Collection)

233

employment in the silver mines at Shafter, Texas, the mines in those days being the constant target of Mexican smugglers who would steal ore by the packtrain load and then scoot south and sell it across the border.

Ranger sergeant John Hughes decided to stop the thefts, and since Hughes believed St. Leon had a fluent grasp of Spanish and was in fact honest and trustworthy, Hughes concocted a plan that included Diamond Dick. It began with the Texas mine owner pretending to discharge St. Leon because he had a Mexican wife, an act not raising any suspicions due to already considerable racial tensions at the Shafter mine area. St. Leon now operated in an undercover capacity. Pretending to be thoroughly incensed at mine management, he infiltrated the group of thieves responsible for the major ore thefts. Learning of a large planned midnight theft, St. Leon alerted Hughes.

Accompanied by Ranger private Lon Oden, Hughes set a trap along the intended route of the outlaws. The three Mexican suspects, accompanied by undercover agent Diamond Dick, all appeared at a prearranged location. Upon their refusal to submit to arrest, a furious six-man gun battle erupted, and the three ore smugglers were killed. In order to maintain a measure of investigative integrity and not compromise the clandestine role played by St. Leon, the news releases noted that four bandits had been killed in the blistering exchange, one of them Diamond Dick.

St. Leon and his wife now secretly departed for Mexico, where he found employment with the Mexican Central Railroad. On one occasion he shot and killed two train robbers. Meanwhile, on June 30, 1893, Texas Ranger captain Frank Jones was killed in a gunfight with Mexican bandits at Pirate Island, in the lower El Paso Valley. John Hughes replaced the respected Jones as the new company commander, and Hughes again turned to Ernest "Diamond Dick" St. Leon, assigning him another undercover identity. Hughes dispatched St. Leon to the south side of the Rio Grande, his job to avenge Frank Jones's death. There could be no official reports from Mexico, but Diamond Dick's mission was a success. Someone killed Antonio and Pedro Olguin, the two gang leaders responsible for Captain Jones's death.

St. Leon then reenlisted in the Texas Rangers on September 1, 1893. One day, Captain Hughes commented to St. Leon about the striking hand-tooled saddle, with silver adornments, that he used. St. Leon

quickly dismounted, loosened the latigo, slid the rigging from the horse's back, and laid the saddle at Hughes's feet, a gift from a generous and indisputably appreciative St. Leon.

St. Leon temporarily left the ranger service in 1894 but reenlisted again on October 1, 1897. At Socorro, Texas, on August 20, 1898, deputizing Dr. Breaux, a civilian, he attempted to arrest three drunken cowboys for creating a disturbance. The arrest went smoothly, but for unexplained reasons Diamond Dick not only turned the trio loose but accompanied them with the doctor to a saloon, where all five began drinking.

For whatever reason, the three cowboys then pulled their guns and shot Dr. Breaux dead on the spot. They then began shooting St. Leon. Seriously wounded, he was removed to the ranger encampment at Ysleta, where he lingered for nine days, succumbing on August 29 to his wounds. The identity of the shooters remains a mystery.

Ernest St. Leon is buried in El Paso's Concordia Cemetery.

See also: HUGHES, JOHN REYNOLDS; JONES, FRANK; TEXAS RANGERS

STOUDENMIRE, Dallas (1845–1882)

Dallas Stoudenmire stood at least six foot two, was born in Aberfoil, Alabama, and although underage joined the Confederate army in 1862. After his discharge, he wandered off to Columbus, Texas, allegedly killed a man or two, served a stint in the Texas Rangers, and then with his brother-in-law, Samuel M. "Doc" Cummings, rode west to Socorro, New Mexico. From there Stoudenmire and Cummings moseyed down to El Paso, Texas, where Dallas became city marshal on April 11, 1881.

Stoudenmire carried two six-shooters, one in each hip pocket. One had the standard barrel length. The other was a "belly gun," meaning its short barrel made it suitable for close-in fighting—for ramming into an opponent's belly and pulling the trigger.

On April 14, with Stoudenmire on the job three days, the bodies of two Mexican *vaqueros* were brought by buckboard into El Paso. They had been slain while searching for stolen cattle in the Rio Grande *bosque* (thickets) near Anthony, New Mexico. An inquest followed, held in a couple of adobe rooms near the head of El Paso Street. With the testimony finished, El Paso city marshal Dallas

Stoudenmire left first, strolling across the street to the Globe Restaurant. Gus Krempkau, the English/Spanish translator, left a few minutes later, followed by the accused slayers—former city marshal George Campbell and his sidekick, New Mexico rancher and rustler Johnny Hale.

Once outside, Campbell called out to Krempkau, accusing him of making slanted translations. The two men cursed and argued briefly, then Campbell turned to get on his horse. At this moment, Johnny Hale, who had seated himself with a whiskey bottle in a nearby adobe window, shouted, "I'll take care of this for you, George." With that he shot Gus Krempkau down.

From across the street, Dallas Stoudenmire left the restaurant on the run, at the same time pulling his long-barreled, very accurate six-shooter. When perhaps 30 yards from Johnny Hale, he aimed, fired, and killed an innocent bystander. Undeterred, he recocked, aimed, and fired again. This time Johnny Hale dropped dead. At this point George Campbell, aghast at the three quick deaths, began screaming, "This is not my fight." The big marshal put a bullet in him too, and now four dead men lay in the street in practically as many seconds.

On the following Sunday, April 17, with the marshal not yet on the job for a week, he and Doc Cummings were walking north on El Paso Street when yet another former city marshal, Bill Johnson, attempted to kill him with a double-barreled shotgun. He missed. Stoudenmire and Cummings altogether put nine bullets in Bill Johnson, and he died sprawled across a stack of bricks being used to build the State National Bank.

The Manning brothers, Frank, James, and Doc, owners and proprietors of the Manning Saloon on El Paso Street, as well as the Coliseum Saloon and Variety Theater farther south on El Paso Street, now started their own feud with Stoudenmire and Cummings. On February 14, 1882, James Manning shot Doc Cummings inside the barroom of the Coliseum Saloon. Cummings stumbled out onto the dust of El Paso Street, gave a loud groan, and died.

Stoudenmire, who was out of town that week getting married in Columbus, Texas, returned to find his brother-in-law dead. He and the Mannings therefore began threatening each other. The newspapers printed horror stories regarding a possible bloodletting in El Paso. According to the newspapers, some residents—not wishing to be caught in a possible cross fire—had already moved to other localities.

Two of El Paso City Marshal Dallas Stoudenmire's personal revolvers (Navy Colts .36-caliber percussion models 1851) (Author's Collection)

Meanwhile, Stoudenmire, anxious to show he hadn't lost his edge, started placing targets in the streets representing the Four Dead Individuals in Five Seconds. After crowds had gathered, Stoudenmire drunkenly blew holes in the targets for the benefit of those who had missed his memorable display of marksmanship the first time around.

Still, cooler heads prevailed. Interested parties brought the Manning brothers and Stoudenmire together, and everyone agreed to a peace treaty. Here is how the *El Paso Daily Herald*, of April 16, 1882, worded it:

We the undersigned parties having this day settled all differences and unfriendly feelings existing between us, hereby agree that we will hereafter meet and pass each other on friendly terms, and that bygones shall be bygones, and that we shall never allude in the future to any past animosities that have existed between us.

Witness	Signed
R. E. Campbell	Dallas Stoudenmire
J. F. Harrison	J. Manning
E. V. Hogan	G. F. Manning
J. P. Hague	Frank Manning

Signing a peace treaty, however, might have made the citizens and politicians feel better, but it failed to ease the smouldering animosities. Stoudenmire sometimes drank so heavily that he would slide off the bar stool, sprawl across on the wooden floor, and loudly snore. No one dared awaken him.

Something had to be done, so the mayor and city council gathered for a special meeting on the evening of May 27. They invited Dallas Stoudenmire to explain why he should not be dismissed as city marshal. The marshal walked in twirling a six-shooter on his finger, and spoke only one sentence: "I can straddle every God damned alderman in this room." Then he turned around and left. In the silence that followed, one of the aldermen turned to the mayor and the others and said, "I don't know about you folks, but I'm not voting to dismiss him."

But even Stoudenmire realized it was over. The mayor and aldermen had met on Friday. By Monday, the marshal had sobered and decided to do the right thing. He wrote out his own resignation. On the following day, the federal government appointed him to the position of U.S. deputy marshal, with headquarters in El Paso. Stoudenmire's former deputy and ex–Texas Ranger James B. Gillett became city marshal.

In early September, U.S. Deputy Marshal Dallas Stoudenmire, with a wad of fugitive warrants folded in his shirt pocket, took the train to Deming, New Mexico. He returned to El Paso around 10 o'clock that night. A conductor poured him off the train. He then wandered down to the Manning Saloon, walked in and looked around, then stumbled down to "the line," a row of brothels, where he spent the night.

Upon arising the next morning, one of the first things he heard was that the Manning brothers were looking for him—and planned to kill him. "Why do they want to kill me?" mumbled Stoudenmire. "Because you were looking for them in their saloon last night," came the answer. Stoudenmire responded that a mistake had been made. He had not been looking for the Mannings but for other wanted individuals.

Well, a mistake in judgment had obviously been made; all day long emissaries hustled back and forth between the Mannings and Stoudenmire. As a result, the disputants agreed to meet that afternoon in the Manning Saloon and sign another peace treaty.

Stoudenmire walked in and found James and Doc Manning playing pool. "Where's Frank?" he asked. Jim glanced around, said "I'll go find him," and left.

Doc and Dallas now bellied up to the bar and ordered drinks. Stoudenmire, who already had had too many, began mumbling that too many people around town were telling lies. The little doctor snapped, "Stoudenmire, you are the liar." The two men now reached for their guns, the little doctor evidently already having his hand in his coat pocket. His first shot hit the marshal in the shoulder, and Stoudenmire's weapon clunked to the floor. The doctor cocked and fired again, this time the bullet striking the marshal squarely in the shirt pocket, where it buried itself in that folded wad of wanted notices. Nevertheless, the impact knocked Stoudenmire backward through the bat-wing doors and out onto El Paso Street.

The doctor followed him outside, intending to kill him, but by this time Stoudenmire had his other weapon in hand. He fired, and the bullet struck the doctor in the arm, the doctor's weapon spinning into the dirt. Stoudenmire, now in severe pain and breathing heavily, bent over and struggled to recock his six-

El Paso City Marshal Dallas Stoudenmire in 1881 (Western History Collection, University of Oklahoma)

shooter between his knees. Doc Manning, however, ran up and wrapped both arms around the marshal. The two men reeled against the wall, the doctor hanging on to stay alive, the marshal struggling to shake him loose and kill him.

By this time, James Manning, who had gone to look for Frank and had heard shooting back at the saloon, came on the run and found the two men wrestling, twisting, and turning, bouncing off the Manning Saloon's outside wall. Frank reached into his pocket, pulled out his own six-shooter, cocked it, aimed at Stoudenmire's bobbing and weaving head, jerked the trigger, fired, missed, and shattered a barber pole. Frank cocked it again, aimed once more, and fired. This time the bullet struck Stoudenmire behind the right ear; the former marshal collapsed in the dirt with a screaming Doc Manning on top of him.

The county seat, Ysleta, tried the Mannings for murder and acquitted them. Within two years they were gone from El Paso. Frank died in the Arizona Home for the Insane. Doc practiced medicine in Scottsdale, Arizona, and died there. James wandered the West for many years. He died in Los Angeles and is buried in Forest Lawn.

As for Dallas Stoudenmire, the El Paso Masonic Society bought him a $15 suit and shipped him to Columbus, Texas, for burial.

See also: GILLETT, JAMES BUCHANAN

SUNDANCE Kid

See LONGABAUGH, HARRY

SUTTON-TAYLOR Feud

This, the longest and bloodiest feud in Texas history, took its name from the two leading warring families—the Suttons and the Taylors. The feud had its roots in the Civil War, the trouble starting in DeWitt County, which was about halfway between San Antonio and the Gulf Coast. Here shotguns, six-shooters, lynch ropes, and graves were common solutions to complex social and racial problems.

William Sutton was born in 1846, and although he fought for the Confederacy, he supported the Union occupation of Texas. He represented the Suttons in the Sutton-Taylor feud, although he had powerful ranching allies, such as James W. Cox and Joseph Tumlinson. He also had support from Union general Joe Reynolds, the military commander of Texas. Reynolds

selected the mean-spirited Jack Helm as a leader of "the Regulators," a group of special officers hired primarily to enforce the Sutton point of view.

Jack Helm later wrote that he had "been summoned by military authorities to arrest desperados in Texas known as the Taylor Party, "party" being a colloquialism for gang, group, or faction. Helms described them as about 40 in number, and by newspaper count his own righteous "party" had already killed around 21 persons in two months.

Two leaders of the Taylor party, Hays and Doboy Taylor, plus some of their friends and kinfolk, killed a black sergeant in a saloon at Mason, Texas, during 1867. Fort Mason's Major Thompson subsequently tried to arrest the Taylors and was shot dead, allegedly by Doboy Taylor.

In 1868, the 22-year-old Billy Sutton, as a deputy sheriff in a Helm posse, caught up with several accused Taylor outlaws, and during a running gun battle the posse killed Charlie Taylor. In late August 1869, Helm and his Regulators approached the Creed Taylor Ranch, where a brief gun battle occurred, Hays Taylor being the only one slain. Doboy was wounded but escaped, not being killed until December 1871, when he was shot to death during a personal quarrel having nothing to do with the feud. A state of terror now existed in the Texas counties of San Patricio, Bee, DeWitt, Goliad, and Wilson.

On July 1, 1870, Texas organized its state police, with Helm as one of four captains. During the following month, his detachment arrested Henry and Will Kelley of the Taylor faction and shot them to death on August 26 in the nearby woods. In October, with charges of brutality and embezzlement buzzing about his head, Helm was dismissed from the state police. Bill Sutton now moved up in the police leadership.

Late one evening during the summer of 1872, Sutton and several loyalists lured Pitkin Taylor out of his home by ringing a cowbell. Taylor assumed his cattle had gotten into his cornfield and went to investigate. Several rifles cracked, and Pitkin died a short time later.

Jim Taylor and friends now went after Willie Sutton and on April 1, 1873, ambushed and wounded him in a Cuero, Texas, saloon. A month later, on May 15, the Taylors caught some of the Sutton party, specifically James W. Cox and W. S. "Jake" Christman, between Helena and Yorktown, Texas. Suddenly a cloud of black smoke engulfed the Regulators, Cox, in particular. Cox died with 19 buckshot in his body and a slashed throat. Someone had really disliked him.

In July or August of the same year, 1873, James Taylor and John Wesley Hardin caught up with Jack Helm in a little town called Albuquerque, Texas (the town no longer exists). They blasted Helm with buckshot and six-gun bullets and rode quietly on their way.

On the following day a large party of Taylors placed the Joe Tumlinson home near Yorktown under siege. Within hours, however, the sheriff arrived and talked both parties into signing a peace treaty, even though the peace lasted only until December 30, 1873, when someone shot and killed a Taylor man named Wiley Pridgen. An engaged group of Taylors now pinned the Suttons down in Cuero, the siege being lifted only when Joe Tumlinson rode in with a large group of Suttons.

The feud now wound down, with few folks left to kill besides the leaders. Bill Sutton made plans to go by steamer from Indianola, Texas, across the Gulf and overland to Kansas, where some of his cattle were currently being driven. On March 11, 1874, he, his pregnant wife Laura, and a cattleman friend and employee, Gabriel Slaughter, walked up the gangplank at about two o'clock in the afternoon. However, as Sutton approached the ticket booth, James and Bill Taylor started shooting, then scrambled away amid a scene of blood, gore, two dead men, and a screaming widow.

As for James Taylor, on May 25, 1874, he and John Wesley Hardin murdered Brown County deputy sheriff Charles Webb on the streets of Comanche, Texas. That killing would eventually cost Hardin nearly 16 years in the Texas State Prison. As for Taylor, his life was much shorter. He and two friends, Mace Arnold and A. R. Hendricks, died during a running gunfight with peace officers at Clinton, Texas, on December 27, 1875.

This left only Capt. Joe Tumlinson, the final leader of the Sutton faction. With his wars behind him, it was time to go. He became ill, got religion, was baptized, and died in bed many years later.

Bill Taylor, the other assassin of Sutton, was caught and jailed on a ship in Indianola, Texas, but swam free on September 15, 1875, when a hurricane destroyed Indianola forever. His freedom was only momentary, however. He was captured and went on trial in Texana, Texas, in May of 1878. A jury acquitted him of the Sutton slaying, and within a couple of years he had dropped from sight. The bloody Sutton-Taylor feud had finally meandered and stumbled to a close.

See also: HARDIN, JOHN WESLEY

SWING a Wide Loop

To "swing wide loop" meant to catch everything, even things that do not belong to you. The expression especially applied to someone rounding up livestock who did not care how many of his neighbor's cattle might also be included.

TAGGART, Frank (1858–1884)

Originally from Iowa, the youthful cowboy Frank Taggart drifted, when not yet out of his twenties, through parts of Utah and Arizona before temporarily alighting along the Gila River in western New Mexico. Partnering with black cowboy George Washington Cleveland, Mitch Lee, and Christopher "Kit" Joy, Taggart assisted in robbing the Southern Pacific train near Gage Station, west of Deming, on November 24, 1883. Because the robbers killed the train engineer, Theopolis C. Webster, such notables as railroad detective Len Harris, Wells Fargo detective James B. Hume, ex–Grant County sheriff Harvey Whitehill, and for a while, Deming's dangerous deputy, Dan Tucker, were all involved in the pursuit.

Taggart, who had "a large mouth which in conversation is always wreathed in smiles," was probably not smiling when he was finally arrested near St. Johns, Arizona. Placed in jail in Silver City, Taggart and his accomplices (along with others) broke out of confinement on March 10, 1884, stealing firearms and horses. A running gun battle erupted between outlaws and posse members. Taggart was severely wounded and was captured. A local newspaperman reported, "It was here determined without a dissenting voice that Mitch Lee and Frank Taggart should, by request, attend a neck-tie party." Sensing the end was indeed near, Taggart admitted he was guilty of robbing the train but accused Mitch Lee of murdering Webster.

One newspaper man reported that "Taggart died hard of strangulation—a throat disease that is becoming extremely common among their ilk in this section."

See also: CLEVELAND, GEORGE WASHINGTON; JOY, CHRISTOPHER; LEE, A. MITCHELL; TUCKER, DAVID; WHITEHILL, HARVEY HOWARD

TASCOSA Shootout (a.k.a. the Big Fight)

Tascosa, Texas, located in the Texas Panhandle, by any standard did not amount to much in terms of size. It still doesn't. It is remembered today primarily because of a shootout that occurred on March 21, 1886, a shootout having its roots in a cowboy strike during the spring of 1883.

The big outfits in a sense brought the strike on themselves. Until recently the big outfits had allowed cowboys to own a few horses and run a few head of livestock, which wasn't all that big a deal, since the ranchers themselves not only operated on public land but had been taken over by large corporations and foreign owners. So in the spring of 1883, the cowboys, who had usually been paid around $35 a month, gathered together, selected a natural leader, and wrote the following proclamation:

We the undersigned cowboys of Canadian River do by these present agree to bind ourselves into the following obligations, viz:

First: that we will not work for less than $50 per mo and we farther more agree no one shall work for less than $50 per mo. after 31st of Mch.

Second: Good cooks shall also receive $50 per mo.

Third: Any one running an outfit shall not work for less than $75 per mo.

Any one violating the above obligations shall suffer the consequences. Those not having funds to pay board after March 31 will be provided for 30 days at Tascosa.

Twenty-four cowboys signed it, and as of that moment, they were all on strike. Within a few weeks, the number of cowboys joining the association rose to roughly 200.

Some of the big ranchers immediately fired their employees. Others raised their salaries $5 a month or tried to bargain individually with employees. The LS Ranch offered Tom Harris, the cowboy leader, a large jump in salary if he would stay on and identify others who should be offered more money, although not as much as asked. Harris refused, saying, "No, I'll stay with the boys." He was immediately fired.

As it turned out, the strike lasted barely 30 days. The cowboys quickly ran out of money, primarily because they blew what they had in the saloons and brothels of Tascosa. Furthermore, Tom Harris mysteriously died. With Harris gone, the strike collapsed for lack of strong leadership. What replaced him was civil disorder.

Most cowboys reacted bitterly against the big ranchers, and the big ranchers retaliated by blacklisting them, meaning the cowboys could not find work at any rate of pay. Some of the cowboys then began homesteading on government land, often stealing cattle from the owners and either changing the brand or, in the case of mavericks (unbranded cattle), sticking their own brands on calves even though everyone knew who they belonged to. The practice became known as "mavericking."

The big ranchers (often referred to by cowboys as the "Syndicate") now retained Pat Garrett, the famed slayer of Billy the Kid. Garrett put together a group of gunmen he called "rangers," not to be confused with the Texas Rangers. Cowboys usually referred to them as "Pat Garrett–LS Ranch Rangers," meaning private lawmen hired and paid by the LS Ranch, and supervised and led by Pat Garrett.

Garrett managed to get three edicts against the small ranchers. One, they could not wear firearms. Two, small-time cattlemen and owners could not participate in the big, yearly roundup on the open range where unbranded cattle were divided. Third, Garrett got a court decree whereby brands of beginning ranchers had no validity in law.

What made a confusing situation even more confusing was that some of the small ranches had refused to support the cowboys, and some of the larger ranchers believed a settlement should be worked out with the smaller ranchers. Garrett's LS Rangers now added a third dimension, a controversial force from outside. As the entire Panhandle began forming factions, Garrett realized he was in a lose-lose situation. In disgust, he disbanded his rangers and rode off to other adventures.

The former rangers now became cowboys and gunmen. Four of them—Fred Chilton, Frank Valley, Ed King, and John Lang—rode into Tascosa on the evening of March 20, 1886. They expected to attend a Mexican *baile*, and at about two in the morning they headed for the Equity Bar, near the end of Main Street. Ed King dismounted, intending to put his arms around Sally Emory, then walk toward her dwelling. But he never made it. A local cowboy named Lem Woodruff shot him dead.

Woodruff took refuge in a saloon along with his friends—Louis ("the Animal") Bousman, Tom and Charles Emory, and the Catfish Kid. There may have been others. As they plotted, the other LS men returned—Chilton, Valley, and Lang—all three of whom commenced firing into the saloon. Two men were wounded, and four men died in "the Big Fight." Those killed were LS men Frank Valley, Ed King, Fred Chilton, plus a bystander named Jesse Sheets—who still in his bedclothes, happened to step outside his home just as the guns started banging. Charles Emory and Lem Woodruff were wounded. Both recovered.

After daylight arrived, four coffins were fashioned from barn siding and lined. The funeral procession included almost everybody, friends and enemies, and was nearly two miles long. The accused slayers—Bousman, Woodruff, Lang, Emory, and the Catfish Kid—went on trial for murder. A jury acquitted all four.

See also: EMORY, THOMAS; GARRETT, PATRICK FLOYD JARVIS

TAYLOR, Elizabeth (?–?)

This lynching victim, born in Wales as Elizabeth Jones, came to the United States, where in 1869 she married James H. Taylor. They farmed and ranched in Clay County, Nebraska. Her husband gave her three children, but he died, some believe of poisoning, on May 27, 1882. Her father and a hired man also mysteriously disappeared. Elizabeth constantly argued and fought with her neighbors, their disputes being about cattle; most of her neighbors believed that she and her twin brother, Thomas, controlled an organized gang of cattle rustlers. One of her sons shot a neighbor during a livestock dispute.

On the night of March 15, 1885, approximately 50 vigilantes, some masked and some not, came calling on the household, removing Elizabeth and her twin brother Thomas and perhaps others, to a bridge over the Blue River, where all were lynched. They are buried in the Spring Ranche Cemetery.

TETTENBORN, William Rogers (a.k.a. Russian Bill) (1850–1881)

Reportedly the progeny of Russian nobility, William Rogers "Russian Bill" Tettenborn ended up by whatever mysterious route, some believe through San Francisco, in the Southwest. According to Bill himself, he received a bullet wound in the leg in Fort Worth and was stabbed in the shoulder while in Denver. These reports may or may not have merit, in view of Bill's "vaporing braggadocio." Another account said "he had a fierce blond mustache and blond hair which hung to his shoulders; he carried a six-gun at each hip and a long knife in his boot, and was always telling how tough he was."

By June 1880, 30-year-old "Russian Bill" had taken up residence at Shakespeare, a rowdy mining camp in southwestern New Mexico and home to a whole cadre of soon to be well-known misfits, robbers, renegades, and rustlers. Yet, despite commentary to the contrary, a passel of honest folks lived there too. Most of the time Bill fit in with the former, although his nefarious reputation was somewhat offset by the fact that for a time he was a legitimate miner, in fact a mining recorder for the Stonewall District.

But there can be little doubt that "Russian Bill" willingly—and sometimes gloriously—strutted the town's single street, a member in reasonably good standing with Shakespeare's uncouth, unvarnished, wild, and woolly crowd.

Russian Bill, however, miscalculated on one occasion. He stole a horse and headed east, straight into the arms of Dan Tucker, the Grant County deputy

stationed at Deming, New Mexico. Tucker returned the horse and thief to Shakespeare. There the authorities locked Tettenborn in a room with his sometime buddy Sandy King. The citizens of Shakespeare decided to take matters into their own hands. King and Bill were led from prison by a party of 70 men and hanged.

In the absence of a gallows or even a tree, the pair were hanged from a cross beam in the Grant Hotel dining room. A stranger passing through by stage who asked why the fellows had been lynched was reportedly told that "one was a horse thief and the other was a damned nuisance."

Russian Bill's mother later inquired of the postmaster and sheriff why she no longer received letters from her admittedly wayward son. Someone wrote back, sadly advising that her boy had passed away from throat trouble.

See also: KING, SANDY; TUCKER, DAVID

TEXAS Rangers

"It is easy to see a graveyard in the muzzle of a ranger's gun," said an unknown Texas outlaw in 1874. He obviously knew whereof he spoke.

For 150 years, the Texas Rangers have been praised as saviors and occasionally denounced as murderers. Many Hispanics despised them; state legislators were often suspicious of them; but the average citizen venerated them. Texas Rangers and the Alamo are the most cherished, enduring traditions of Texas, and yet few people know when, why, or how they originated, or how they achieved their heroic status. They remain the oldest statewide law enforcement body on the North American continent.

During the mid-1820s, when it was still joined to Mexico, the soil of Texas ran red with the blood of Texan, Mexican, and Comanche warriors. Obviously, the settlers could not farm and fight too, and just as obviously, Mexico could not provide adequate protection. So in an effort to hold the line, a Texas leader named Stephen F. Austin coaxed the Mexican government into retaining 10 volunteers to "range" over wide areas so as to note the whereabouts of the Indians. From this description later arose the Texas Rangers as we think of them today. In 1835, 25 men formed one ranging company, a group of young and single civilians.

During its republic years from 1836 to 1845, Texas could ill afford a standing army. Yet, the new

Texas Rangers in camp somewhere in the Big Bend country of Texas in the early 1880s (Division of Manuscripts, Library, University of Oklahoma)

nation desperately needed protection from its Comanche and Mexican predators. The solution was to enlist well-mounted fighting men. Sometimes they were called "gunmen," occasionally "spies," and frequently "mounted riflemen." But most settlers referred to them as "rangers."

From 1836 into the mid-1840s, the rangers survived primarily because they worked more cheaply than military units, although in 1846 they became part of U.S. general Zachary Taylor's army as it rumbled south across the Rio Grande and into Mexico. The rangers at this time took on a distinct international reputation for hard, vicious, relentless fighting.

Following the Mexican War, U.S. troops patrolled the border, and the rangers sank into relative obscurity. During the Civil War the rangers again achieved prominence, increasing their numbers and occupying former army posts. Terry's Texas Rangers, officially known as the Eighth Texas Cavalry of the Confederate States of America, fought in some of the most dramatic engagements of the conflict. Following the surrender of Texas to federal armies, the U.S. military abolished the ranger forces.

Lawlessness became so rampant during the 1870s that Governor F. J. Davis created the state police, a universally hated organization, although probably more effective than most historians have acknowledged. It never numbered over 200 men, and 40% were black. However, in 1873, the state police was abolished because of political infighting, racial controversy and hatred, and statewide distrust.

In its place, Governor Richard Coke in 1874 created two organizations of Texas Rangers: the Frontier Battalion and the Special Forces. These units numbered between 20 and 30 men each. The men furnished their own equipment, including horses and weapons, dressed as they pleased, enlisted for from three to six months, elected their own officers, and drew $1.25 a day "to range and guard the frontier."

Maj. John B. Jones commanded the Frontier Battalion. It concentrated on Indians as well as outlaws. The battalion, among other things, broke up the Horrell-Higgins feud and discouraged a similar dispute in Kimble County. It killed the notorious train robber Sam Bass and organized a special group of rangers to stop the El Paso Salt War. When Major Jones died in 1881, a variety of individuals took his place: notably C. L. Nevill at Fort Davis, George W. Arrington in the Panhandle, and Capt. George W. Baylor at Ysleta in West Texas.

Leander McNelly, a former divinity student, handled the Special Forces, and it focused on Texas desperadoes and Mexican bandits. Whether these fugitives came in dead or alive didn't seem to matter. The Texas legislature assigned the Special Forces Company to the restoration of law and order. Obviously, the rangers needed good leadership as well as efficient weapons. With the death of McNelly in 1877, Lee Hall and John Armstrong took command.

Out of the Texas Rangers arose some of the most dogged individuals Texas has ever produced: Ben McCulloch, Sam Walker, Big Foot Wallace, and John Coffee Hays. Their characteristic weapon came from an obscure inventor named Samuel Colt. He put together the .34-caliber, five-shot, repeating revolver. The gun was awkward, even dangerous for the user (it had no trigger guard), and its caliber was small, but it could be fired several times without reloading. Two revolvers per person meant 10 rounds per man without reloading. Texas ordered several hundred revolvers. Upon approaching Indian enemies the rangers would fire a single round—then wait for the charge. The carnage could be terrible.

By the 1880s, the Special Forces and the Frontier Battalion had started to fade away as separate, distinct units, becoming just "Texas Rangers." On January 29, 1881, Baylor's group fought the last Indian battle in Texas, killing 10 or 12 Apache in West Texas near Sierra Blanca. The Special Force existed until 1881, the Frontier Battalion, until 1901.

By the turn of the century the frontier had vanished, and the rangers seemed destined to do likewise. They numbered 24 men in 1900, and it seemed that they might be vanishing along with the red man and the buffalo. However, in July 1901, Governor Joe Sayers revived them, organizing four companies of 20 men each into "a ranger force sufficient for the purpose of protecting the frontier against marauding and thieving parties, and the suppression of lawlessness and crime throughout the state."

Throughout the early 1900s the rangers protected court proceedings, cowed mobs, and trailed outlaws. Nevertheless, some of their luster faded when successive governors used them for political

Engraving of the Texas Rangers fighting Indians (Institute of Texian Cultures, San Antonio)

purposes, especially as strike breakers. When a new law in 1919 established ranger strengths, duties, and pay, several legislators accused the force of drunkenness, murder, and torture. To be rangers, one report stated, applicants had to have a reputation "of killers and insolvency, . . . and they usually have both." By the 1930s, the rangers were thoroughly politicized. The badge could be purchased by just about anybody. Furthermore, they had been downgraded substantially to "state rangers," their task during World War I being to guard the Rio Grande border with Mexico. They were withdrawn in late March 1919.

Yet better times were coming. During that same decade the rangers were placed under the Texas Department of Public Safety.

A ranger's duties today are simply to assist state and local law enforcement when asked. The sheriff of any county always remains the chief law enforcement officer. A ranger must have at least eight years of law enforcement experience, two of which must have been served in the Department of Public Safety.

While there are no uniforms, there are certain specifics—a ranger must wear boots and a conservative western-cut suit. A western hat is "practically mandatory." A ranger badge is always pinned to the shirt and in plain sight. Incidentally, the ranger badge is still stamped from the Mexican cinco (5) peso coin, of 1947–48 vintage.

See also: ARMSTRONG, JOHN BARCLAY; ARRINGTON, GEORGE WASHINGTON; ATEN, IRA; BASS, SAM; EL PASO SALT WAR; GILLETT, JAMES BUCHANAN; HALL, JESSE LEIGH; HAYS, JOHN COFFEE; HORRELL-HIGGINS FEUD; JONES, JOHN B.; MCNELLY, LEANDER H.; NEVILLE, CHARLES

THOMAS, Henry Andrew (a.k.a. Heck Thomas) (1816–1870)

This famous southwestern lawman was born in Georgia, and by his 18th birthday had become an Atlanta policeman. He moved to Texas, worked as an expressman, operated a Fort Worth private detective agency, then made the jump to Arkansas, where he worked as a lawman for federal judge Isaac

Texas Rangers in El Paso, 1896 (Author's Collection)

Parker. During this period he, Chris Madsen, and Bill Tilghman became known as the "Three Guardsmen," remaining friends until their deaths. Thomas was something of a dandy in terms of his everyday dress, but he chose dangerous individuals to pursue. He helped chase down the Jennings crowd, as well as the noted outlaw Bill Doolin, although his exact role in Doolin's death is debatable.

Later in life he served as a U.S. deputy marshal for Oklahoma and was a chief of police at Lawton, Oklahoma. He died of Bright's disease in Lawton on August 15, 1912.

See also: DOOLIN, WILLIAM M.; MADSEN, CHRISTIAN; PARKER, JUDGE ISAAC; TILGHMAN, WILLIAM MATTHEW JR.; WEST, RICHARD

THOMPSON, Ben (1842–1884)

The gunman Ben Thompson was born on November 11, 1842, at Knottingly in West Riding, Yorkshire, England. His father reportedly served as an officer in the Royal Navy. In 1851, his parents migrated to the United States and settled in Austin, where Ben worked as a printer. In 1858, he wounded a Negro youth and was arrested, fined $100, and sentenced to 60 days in jail. Governor Hardin Runnels ordered him released after a brief period. Two years later he allegedly killed a man in a knife fight in a darkened room in New Orleans. However, the evidence documenting this event is not overwhelming.

Back in Austin, Ben joined the Confederate army on June 12, 1861, serving primarily in Col. John R. Ford's Second Regiment of Texas Mounted Rifles at Camp Carrizitas. He reenlisted as a sergeant on June 20, 1862, but was soon reduced to private, his escapades having become legendary, including stories that he had killed men in private quarrels. Only one instance—the slaying of John Coombs—can be verified, although military and civilian records are incomplete. Like most other Texas soldiers, Thompson became a prisoner of war for three months in 1865. After the war, Thompson married Catherine Moore of Travis County. She gave birth to a daughter as well as a son, Benjamin Jr.

Following the Civil War Thompson became a foreign mercenary in the army of Maximilian in Mexico. When the Juarez rifles executed Maximilian, however, Ben hustled back to Texas. He lived in Austin until September 2, 1868, when a family dispute caused him to shoot and wound his wife's

Heck Thomas (Robert G. McCubbin Collection)

brother, James Moore. That drew a sentence of four years in the state penitentiary at Huntsville. U.S. President Grant pardoned him in 1870.

The hustling Thompson, now a full-fledged gambler and gunman, formed a verbal partnership with gambler Phil Coe to open the Bull's Head Saloon in Abilene, Kansas. A year later in 1871, City Marshal Wild Bill Hickok shot Coe dead. Ben was in Kansas City at the time, and he quickly learned that because no partnership agreement existed on paper, he owned nothing. Meanwhile, he and his wife suffered a carriage accident that cost her an arm. By 1872, the family was back in Austin.

On August 15, 1873, Ben, his brother Billy, and a few friends were in Ellsworth, Kansas, where the brothers gambled in Joe Brennan's Saloon. Tempers flared, and Billy Thompson fired a shotgun into the unarmed Sheriff Chauncey Whitney. Ben then held

Ben Thompson (Robert G. McCubbin Collection)

Back in Austin in 1879, Thompson campaigned for city marshal but was defeated. However, the winner did not serve his full term, and in December 1880 Thompson ran again and won. In spite of the fact that Thompson seldom spent a sober day on the job, he was reelected a year later.

In July 1882, Thompson took his son and daughter to San Antonio, but instead of enjoying himself with family he resurrected an old feud with Jack Harris, owner of a variety theater. Although Thompson had been posted (barred) from entering, he insisted on forcing his way in—and that led to a confrontation. A shootout began, and Ben killed Harris with a revolver shot that pierced his lung. A jury acquitted Thompson on January 20, 1883.

Ben was back in San Antonio on March 11, 1884, arriving with John King Fisher, a gunman and deputy sheriff of Uvalde County. Among other adventures, the two men entered a variety theater and took seats in the balcony. At about 11 P.M., Fisher and Thompson began arguing with the management and staff, a confrontation that ended with a fusillade of bullets. Thompson was shot dead, hit by nine bullets. Fisher received 13. A jury ruled the deaths justifiable. Ben Thompson is buried at Oakwood Cemetery in Austin.

See also: COE, PHILIP HOUSTON; FISHER, JOHN KING; HICKOK, JAMES BUTLER; THOMPSON, WILLIAM.

everybody off until Billy made his escape. Whitney died three days later.

Ben returned to Austin where, on Christmas night 1886, the Capital Variety Theater ejected James Burdett, a friend of Thompson's. Burdett stormed back in, and Thompson took his part. In the fighting that followed, Ben Thompson shot the owner, Mark Wilson, four times, killing him. Bartender Charles Matthews fired a rifle at Thompson, the bullet nicking Thompson's hip. Ben retaliated by shooting the bartender through the mouth (he survived). The state tried Ben Thompson for murder, but he was acquitted.

In March 1879, the Santa Fe Railroad retained Bat Masterson to hire an army of gunfighters and prevent the Denver & Rio Grande Railroad from gaining first access to the Royal Gorge, a huge gap sometimes dubbed the Grand Canyon of the Colorado Mountains, where the Arkansas River cut through. However, Ben Thompson sold out to the Denver and Rio Grande Railroad for figures estimated between $3,000 and $5,000.

THOMPSON, William (a.k.a. Billy Thompson)
(1845?–1897)

This younger brother of Ben Thompson was born in Knottingly, England, and in 1851 came to the United States, where the family settled in Austin, Texas. Along with his brother Ben, Billy joined the Second Regiment of Texas Mounted Rifles and saw some action in Louisiana, but primarily guarded the Mexican border. In March 1868, during an Austin bordello rendezvous, he shot and killed Lance Sgt. William Burke, chief clerk in the U.S. Adjutant General's Office. Billy fled to Indian Territory (Oklahoma) for a brief period, then rode into Rockport, Texas, a month or two later and killed 18-year-old Remus Smith.

Billy and brother Ben Thompson then moved to the Grand Central Hotel in Ellsworth, Kansas, in 1872–73. For a while, Billy—who was about six feet, dark complexioned, and had brown hair and gray eyes—lived with Emma Williams until she switched her affections to Wild Bill Hickok. Molly Brennan also shared Billy's pillow on occasion. Since her husband Joe owned a saloon, the Thompson brothers made it their gambling hangout. On June 10, 1873, City Marshal Edward O. Hogue arrested Billy Thompson for firing a weapon while intoxicated. Billy paid a $15 fine. Two weeks later on June 30, city policeman John ("Happy Jack") Morco arrested Billy for carrying a six-shooter, being intoxicated, and assaulting Happy Jack.

July passed without incident, but on August 15, 1873, Ben Thompson and several Texas gamblers, John Sterling among them, were gambling in Brennan's Saloon. Apparently, Thompson and Sterling gambled in cahoots with each other and settled up after the games. In this instance, Sterling not only refused to share but slapped the unarmed Thompson's face. Happy Jack Morco drew his pistol and forced Thompson away from Sterling.

Thompson found his brother, Billy, almost too drunk to hold the shotgun, so he took it away, told him to go to his room and sober up, handed the gun to someone else, and walked into the main street, screaming for the Texans to come out and fight. By now, Sheriff Chauncey B. Whitney and former policeman Jack deLong had reached the scene and had talked Ben Thompson into going back inside the saloon and sobering up.

Meanwhile, Billy Thompson had recovered his shotgun and rejoined his brother and the sheriff inside the Brennan Saloon. At this moment, a commotion started that lured Ben outside, followed by Whitney, followed by Billy. Unfortunately, the drunken Billy stumbled near the door, and in doing so fired a shotgun blast into Chauncey B. Whitney from behind, instantly killing him. Ben screamed, "For God's sake, Billy, you have shot our best friend!"

Billy escaped, perhaps to Nebraska. Three years later, on September 26, 1876, the Texas Rangers took him into custody near Austin and extradited him to Kansas. A jury acquitted him of murder. Billy next turned up in Buena Vista, Colorado, where he reportedly served a brief stint as town marshal before appearing in June 1880 at Ogallala, Nebraska. There he and saloon owner William Tucker argued over a prostitute; on June 21, Billy ambushed Tucker, shooting him in the left hand as Tucker served drinks from behind the bar. Tucker rushed outside with a shotgun and peppered Thompson from the rear. With the town now ready to lynch Billy, Bat Masterson

slipped him out of town on a train. He escaped to Dodge City and from there to El Paso, Texas, where he briefly became something of a confidence man. The Texas Rangers arrested him, and Deputy Sheriff Frank Manning, a long-time friend of Billy's, took him under guard to Austin, where he was turned loose on his own recognizance. Billy disappeared.

On May 7, 1883, Texas governor John Ireland offered a reward of $200 for Billy Thompson, as the state still wanted to try him on the 15-year-old charge of murdering Remus Smith. Well, Thompson did go to trial; he was found not guilty on December 11. He next put in a San Antonio appearance and was in the city when Ben Thompson and John King Fisher were shot to death in the Vaudeville Theater on March 11, 1884.

Billy Thompson now all but dropped out of sight, dying at the age of 52, reportedly of a stomach abscess, in Houston on September 6, 1897. His burial took place in Bastrop, Texas.

See also: MASTERSON, WILLIAM BARCLAY; MORCO, JOHN; TEXAS RANGERS; THOMPSON, BEN

THOMPSON, William J. (a.k.a. Big Bill Thompson) (1857–1906)

This little-known lawman, stockman, and cowboy took his nickname, "Big Bill," from the fact that he stood six feet four inches tall and weighed 280 pounds. He was born in Bethny, Missouri; his family owned huge ranches in northern New Mexico and southern Colorado. Apparently, Big Bill eventually had enough of being a cowboy, so he moved to Durango, Colorado, was appointed undersheriff of La Plata County, and in 1896 was elected Durango's first town marshal. In January 1896, he shot it out with two robbers and buried one. In 1904, he became sheriff of La Plata County, while his friend Jesse Stansel became town marshal.

The Colorado legislature in 1905 passed laws forbidding gambling, prostitution, and open bars on Sunday until midnight. Thompson announced he would enforce the law; Jesse Stansel said the businesses would remain open.

On Sunday, January 8, 1906, an hour or so before midnight, Sheriff Thompson ordered the El Moro Gambling Hall to close. Stansel said it would remain open. The two lawmen argued, then took their dispute to the street, where they began firing at each other. With blood all over the place, they gave up shooting and started clubbing each other with their six-shooters. Finally Thompson gasped and fell, muttering, "Stansel, you have killed me."

Thompson had taken five bullets, any one of which might have killed him. He had fired only twice, Stansel taking one bullet in the lungs, and an innocent bystander the other. The bystander died. So did Thompson. He is buried in the Animas City Cemetery.

Stansel was tried for murder and acquitted. He subsequently resigned as town marshal and moved to El Paso, Texas. As for Durango itself, the saloons, gambling halls, and brothels continued their wide-open operation.

THURMOND, Frank (1840–1908)

Born on November 21, 1840, in Jackson County, Georgia, gambler Frank Thurman, at the age of 21 years, signed on as a private in the Confederate army. He saw considerable action.

After the war, joined by his brothers who followed at various times, Frank migrated to Texas, settling at San Antonio. By the mid- to late 1860s, Frank had opened the University Club, one of the hottest gambling spots in the Alamo City. Although he was raised as a stereotypical southern gentleman, someone who knew Frank commented that "he wasn't the kind of a guy you could cry in front of," implying that Frank was all business, all the time. Frank Thurmond never gave ground to anyone.

During a dispute over a gambling game, Frank Thurmond pulled his knife and killed a man. By now he had become a cunning professional gambler, wise enough to leave town, and by the mid-1870s he was a frequent presence in North Texas at such communities as Dennison, and further west at Fort Griffin, better known as "The Flat."

Somewhere along the route, probably at The Flat, Frank met Lottie Deno. The chronology is murky at best. The most interesting story concerning the pair is that Frank lost considerable money to "Doc" Holliday. At that point, Lottie stepped in and took control of the game, beating the little dentist out of everything but his southern accent.

At any rate, Frank and Lottie ended up in New Mexico during 1879, making their home in various communities before finally moving to Deming in 1882. It was in New Mexico that the "Gambling Queen of Hearts" openly adopted the name Charlotte Thurmond and later legally married Frank.

Meanwhile, Frank Thurmond was not unaccustomed to barroom violence. His presence at several Silver City shootouts is probable, for he gave testimony at one hearing regarding a shooting affray in which four lawmen were involved, one of them being the victim, the others the defendants. Then again, at Deming, during a heated dispute, Frank killed Dan Baxter with a Bowie knife. He came clear on a self-defense plea. On another occasion, Frank received a gunshot wound but recovered.

Still later, at Deming, in a disagreement over the ability of a bank to manage his money, Frank forced a bank teller to fork over cash. The criminal case was ultimately dismissed.

In the end, however, Frank Thurmond and Lottie became respected New Mexico residents, cattle people, and mining speculators. Frank eventually became a vice president of the Deming National Bank, a firm he had allegedly once robbed. Throughout the community, and indeed the whole Southwest, Frank Thurmond became known for his word and for staunchly standing by his friends. He passed away as a result of throat cancer at Deming on June 4, 1908. Lottie died at Deming, 26 years later, on February 9, 1934.

See also: DENO, CHARLOTTE; FORT GRIFFIN, TEXAS, VIGILANTES; HOLLIDAY, JOHN HENRY

TILGHMAN, William Matthew Jr. (1854–1924)

This famous southwestern lawman was one of the "Three Guardsmen," along with marshals Heck Thomas and Chris Madsen. Born at Fort Dodge, Iowa, he farmed and worked as a sutler; by 1872 he had become a buffalo hunter. Later in life he claimed to have killed several desperadoes in Oklahoma Territory with dynamite during 1874. A year later he became a Dodge City deputy, and in 1886 a city marshal. In Guthrie, Oklahoma, he became a U.S. deputy marshal, helping capture Annie McDougal (Cattle Annie) and Jennie Metcalf (Little Britches). In 1888, he shot and killed a childhood friend, Ed Prather.

Tilghman participated in the Oklahoma land rush, afterward becoming a city marshal of Perry, Oklahoma, sheriff of Lincoln County, and chief of police in Oklahoma City. In 1896, he captured the wanted outlaw William Doolin in a bathhouse at Eureka Springs.

Later in life and nearing retirement, he produced a silent film called *The Passing of the Oklahoma Out-*

William H. (Bill) Tilghman (Robert G. McCubbin Collection)

laws, something of a self-promotion. In 1924, the story goes, Oklahoma governor Martin E. Trapp asked Tilghman to police and bring order to the oil-boom town of Cromwell. Another story has it that Tilghman went to Cromwell to collect graft for the governor. There Tilghman was shot and killed by a Prohibition agent named Wiley Lynn—whom, some stories indicate, Tilghman was trying to shake down. Anyway, a jury agreed with Lynn that the shooting had been self-defense. Lynn himself later resigned as a federal agent, started drinking even more than usual, and died in a 1932 shootout at Madill, Oklahoma. An innocent bystander, Rody Watkins, was slain in the crossfire.

In the late 1900s, the Three Guardsmen came under intense historical reevaluation, many researchers believing that the exploits of these three men had been more self-promotional than factual.

See also: DOOLIN, WILLIAM M.; MADSEN, CHRISTIAN; THOMAS, HENRY ANDREW; WEST, RICHARD

TOMBSTONE, Arizona (a.k.a. the Town Too Tough to Die)

Southern Arizona has always been well known for its mining. In 1877, Edward L. Schieffelin discovered substantial silver outcroppings in the San Pedro Valley 75 miles southeast of Tucson. The Tombstone Mining District originated because of this strike, and because folks had been telling Schieffelin for months that the only thing he would find in this godforsaken wasteland would be his tombstone. The territory of Arizona thus created the county of Cochise. By 1881 the mining town of Tombstone, with an approximate population of 10,000, had become the county seat. Tombstone drew economic strength from the mines, the military, the cattle industry, and the Mexican border. The Tombstone Epitaph became its newspaper. Churches sprouted. So did the saloons and gambling halls. Desperadoes with names like John Ringo, Doc Holliday, William Brocius, Luke Short, Pete Spence, and Frank Leslie rode the dusty streets like lords. Lawmen with names like Wyatt, Virgil, and Morgan Earp fought Cowboys with last names like Clanton and McLaury, their famous feud ending abruptly during the even more famous shootout known as the Gunfight at the OK Corral.

By the early 1890s, water began creeping into underground mining shafts; the mines started closing, and folks began drifting away. By 1911, all production had stopped, and by 1929 the county seat had left Tombstone and shifted to Bisbee.

Following the Great Depression, Tombstone began reinventing itself as "the town too tough to die." Museums and dining establishments reopened. A few hotels moved in. The main street, the OK Corral, and the nearby Yuma Territorial Prison became tourist attractions. The local graveyard became Boot Hill, a site where the lucky and unlucky, the good, the bad, and the very bad, became the objects of thousands of tourist visits and questions each week. Thus the town too tough to die lives on.

See also: EARP, MORGAN; EARP, WYATT BERRY STAPP; EARP, VIRGIL; HOLLIDAY, JOHN HENRY; GUNFIGHT AT THE OK CORRAL

TOM, Simpson Hugh (1839–1915)

Simpson Hugh Tom was born three years after the battle at the Alamo. The youngster from Washington County, Texas, signed on at the age of 16 (1855)

with Capt. James H. Callahan's company of Texas Rangers. On one bold mission the rangers chased Lipan Apache into Mexico.

On October 2, 1855, the rangers, accompanied by a civilian force looking for a fight, crossed the Rio Grande near Eagle Pass. The next day, in a pitched battle, the invading force lost four men and suffered seven wounded but drove a group of Indians and Mexicans south. After that battle, the rangers recrossed the Rio Grande by way of the Mexican town of Piedras Negras, setting fire to the village before finding safety on the Texas side. For the sacking of Piedras Negras, Captain Callahan was dismissed from the Texas Rangers. Just what role S. H. Tom played is speculative, but he was there, although admittedly at a young and inexperienced age.

During the Civil War, S. H. Tom served as a company captain in Col. J. C. McCord's Frontier Regiment. After the conflict, Tom ranched in Wilson and Atascosa Counties, eventually establishing a 20,000-acre spread.

During the fall of 1878, at the Frank Mitchell ranch, Captain Tom caught up with Mexican drovers and requested a bill of sale for horses in their possession. The bandits opened fire, and Tom killed two.

On February 13, 1915, Capt. Simpson Hugh Tom, at age 75, died. He was remembered as one of south Texas's most honored citizens.

TOWN Marshal

City councils, usually at the persuasion of their mayors, hired town marshals to be what would eventually become known as the chief of police. In the so-called Wild West, the jobs primarily went to proven gunmen like Wild Bill Hickok and Wyatt Earp. These men were hired to keep the peace within the municipal limits; they retained assistant marshals to do much of the legwork. A marshal served at the pleasure of the mayor and city council, was usually reimbursed for his expenses, and drew a small stipend as well as a percentage of fines and fees. His duties could range from facing up to outlaw gangs, raising posses, collecting taxes and fines, corraling drunks, arresting— and sometimes protecting— crooked gamblers, getting bucket brigades started for fires, and chasing naked bathers out of small streams and rivers.

See also: EARP, MORGAN; EARP, VIRGIL, EARP WYATT BERRY STAPP; HICKOK, JAMES BUTLER; STOUDENMIRE, DALLAS.

TUCKER, David (a.k.a. Dan Tucker) (1849?–1892?)

Little is known regarding the beginnings of Tucker's life, other than that he told an 1880 census enumerator that he was 31 years of age and had been born in Canada. Several reports indicate he grew up in Indiana and later moved over to Colorado. According to rumors, he killed a black man in Colorado and fled to New Mexico, where he operated Lea's Station on the Jornada del Muerto before finally alighting at Silver City and pinning on a Grant County deputy sheriff's badge in 1877.

Numerous press clippings document Tucker's wide-ranging law enforcement activities in Grant County. None, however, make derogatory comments, which is somewhat unusual for a time when partisan politics played such a significant role in any sheriff's or marshal's administration. An example referred to a disturbance in a Silver City barroom: Atanacio Bencomo created a ruckus, and when Tucker attempted to arrest him, he fought first and fled second. The local newspaper reported the suspect "died from being struck by a ball from a pistol held in the hands of Deputy Sheriff Daniel Tucker."

On another occasion, a black soldier, Tom Robinson, refused to obey Tucker's command. He too was shot, but only in the arm. Shortly thereafter another suspect lunged at the deputy with a knife before fleeing in a thunderstorm. Tucker dropped him in the dark with a two-handed pistol shot at a distance of 85 steps.

During late 1877, El Paso County sheriff Charles Kerber put out an urgent call for volunteers to augment his inadequate forces during what was becoming known as the "El Paso Salt War." Tucker responded with a mercenary New Mexico contingent that has often been described as "hard faced and battle scarred." While these forces were successful in getting the situation under Anglo control, they were particularly brutal, in some cases criminal. There is no evidence Dan Tucker personally participated in the rapes, murders, and general pillaging, but he did little to intercede. After the "war" petered out, Tucker returned to Silver City.

In addition to deputy sheriff duties, Dan Tucker became the first town marshal of Silver City, and it wasn't too long before the local editor declared, "Marshal Tucker has put a stop to the discharge of firearms upon our streets." Evidently, Juan García didn't read the paper, or maybe he was just new in town. He resisted arrest, and this time the newspaper mentioned that Tucker had been "charged with killing a man who resisted arrest, had a hearing in front of Justice Givens. . . . It was a case of justifiable homicide."

When Deming, in southern Grant County, burst on the scene as a bustling but wild and woolly railroad boomtown, Dan Tucker arrived to keep the peace. He ran off such reprobates as "Six-Shooter" and "Three-Shooter" Smith; by one press account, he arrested 26 lawless individuals in just three days. Such notables as "Big Ed" Burns, a notorious con man who worked the railroad towns looking for suckers, would frequently ride straight through Deming, not getting off the train until it was well east or west of Tucker's jurisdiction.

On an undisclosed mission in Arizona, an unknown assailant seriously wounded Tucker. However, Tucker recovered and returned to his own bailiwick. In another instance, Tucker gunned down the riotous Charley Hugo. When "Russian Bill" Tettenborn fled Shakespeare, it was Dan Tucker who laid the steel bracelets around his wrists and returned him to the mining camp. As for Jack Bond, he rode his horse onto the verandah at the Deming Depot, and Dan Tucker shotgunned him out of the saddle. Later, after the infamous "Bisbee Massacre," it was Dan Tucker who arrested York Kelly, one of the suspects. Kelly was returned to Arizona and hanged.

After a stagecoach firm began operations between Silver City and Deming, Dan Tucker supplemented his sheriff's salary by riding as a Wells Fargo shotgun rider, his mere presence on the coach a preventative measure in itself. One old-timer wrote, "He was just a nice man, quiet, didn't bother anybody, but don't bother him!"

It is generally believed that Wyatt Earp and his cohorts didn't want "to bother him" either. During their flight to avoid murder prosecutions in Arizona, the fugitives chose to bypass Deming and Dan Tucker.

One who did bother him, at least for a split second, was fellow deputy sheriff James Burns. At Silver City one August (1882) night, Burns became boisterously drunk and disruptive, occasionally pulling out his six-shooter and flourishing it wildly. The new city marshal, G. W. Moore, and a part-time deputy sheriff, Billy McClellan attempted to arrest Burns at the Centennial Saloon. Tucker, already in the barroom, added his expertise. When it was over, Burns lay

dead on the floor. The three lawmen were arrested, and Moore and McClellan were found not guilty. Tucker's case was dismissed.

During his only known press interview, Dan Tucker confessed to a local newspaperman that "he had been obliged to kill eight men in this county [Grant] besides several in Lincoln and Dona Ana counties." Dan Tucker was badly wounded at Deming, during an 1884 brothel shooting, but not seriously enough to keep him from accepting an appointment as a U.S. deputy marshal in October of 1885.

In the fall of 1888, Tucker left New Mexico for California. He returned in 1892 for a visit, the local press noting, "During the early days in Grant county, when it was in the transition state, when the rustlers and bad men were giving way to the peaceable citizens, Dan Tucker and his shot gun were two of the greatest civilizers in the county. Dan had a way of killing the bad man and then reading him the warrant."

After the visit, Tucker returned to California, where several who knew him in New Mexico reported that he later died of natural causes in the county hospital at San Bernardino.

See also: BURNS, JAMES; EL PASO SALT WAR; TETTENBORN, WILLIAM ROGERS

TURKEY Creek Canyon, Battle of

On the night of July 11, 1899, train robbers often known as the "Wild Bunch" stopped and robbed Train No. 1 of the Colorado and Southern Railroad at Twin Mountain, near Folsom in Union County, New Mexico. Desperadoes Sam Ketchum, Elza Lay, Will Carver, and "Red" Weaver blew open the safe and wrecked the express car. Before leaving, they paused to eat peaches and pears, washing them down with whiskey.

The robbery alerted practically every lawman in the Southwest. Union County sheriff Saturino Pinard called together a posse of four men. Wells Fargo special agent John Thacker quickly arrived from San Francisco. The U.S. marshal for New Mexico, Creighton M. Foraker, put together a posse. Finally, William Henry Reno, special agent for the Colorado and Southern Railroad, organized a posse of 16 men and transported them to Folsom by special train.

The posses picked up the outlaw trail and followed it for nearly 20 miles before a driving rain

Elza Lay (Robert G. McCubbin Collection)

forced them to return to Folsom. At this point, most of the men from Colorado went home, but they had no sooner left than the others received information that Lay, Ketchum, and Carver were in Turkey Creek Canyon. So on the morning of July 16, an eight-man posse composed of U.S. Marshal Wilson Elliott, Sheriff Edward Farr, James Morgan, William Reno, Deputy Sheriffs F. H. Smith and Henry Love of Colfax County, and Perfecto Cordoba (or Cordova) and Santiago Serna (or Silva) all rode toward Turkey Creek Canyon. Serna dropped out along the way.

At about a quarter to five in the evening of July 16, the posse emerged from a patch of scrub oak, Elliott motioning for everyone to dismount. At a distance of about 250 yards, he had seen smoke curling skyward. Reno, Farr, and Smith moved off to the left, the others to the right.

Suddenly a disheveled Elza Lay walked into view. Farr, Elliott, and Reno fired, hitting Lay in the shoulder and knocking him to the ground.

Four outlaw horses stood near the fallen Lay, and Elliott shot one of them. The battle now became general, Sam Ketchum grabbing his rifle and firing at Farr. Elliott fired several times at Carver as Carver scurried hatless through the brush and up the slope to a rocky knoll, where he took a stand, firing now at Reno, Smith, and Farr who were at least 200 yards across the canyon.

Farr and Smith both jumped behind a pine tree not large enough to cover one of them, let alone two. Carver then shot Smith, his bullet passing through the fleshy part of Smith's left leg, knocking him down and putting him out of the fight.

Meanwhile, the wounded Lay crawled back to camp, found his rifle as well as some cover, and, he claimed later, fainted for about 10 minutes. All the while Ketchum kept firing at Cordoba and then at Farr, both of whom were about 150 yards distant. This caused Elliott, Love, and Cordoba to all start firing at Ketchum, Elliott's bullet finally breaking Ketchum's left arm just below the shoulder. Ketchum was now out of the fight.

Meanwhile, Lay revived and resumed shooting at Farr, who was standing behind a small pine. Lay aimed at the center of the tree and fired; the bullet went through the trunk and through Farr's chest. Far fell dead across Smith's body. Lay then fainted again and took no further part in the battle.

Carver, because of his position, now controlled the battlefield. He pinned down Reno who, at Smith's request, jumped up and left for Folsom to get help. As for Carver, he continued shooting, sending a bullet and fragments of a knife in his pocket into Love's thigh. The wound would eventually kill Love. Meanwhile, Elliott and the others waited for darkness and then abandoned the canyon.

The outlaws propped Ketchum up on his horse, and with Lay on one side and Carver on the other, they slowly rode away. The battle of Turkey Creek Canyon was over.

See also: CARVER, WILLIAM RICHARD; KETCHUM, SAMUEL W.; LAY, WILLIAM ELLSWORTH; WILD BUNCH

TURNOW, John (a.k.a. Wild Man) (?–?)
This wild man turned outlaw grew up in the forests of the Olympic Peninsula of western Washington, specifically along the Wynooche River in Gray Harbor County. Evidently a lot of people knew him, perhaps pitied him, but also feared him. A man with few if any

friends, he stood about six feet five and weighed around 250 pounds. He reportedly broke jail in 1909, spent time in the Oregon insane asylum, and broke out of there too. Then he returned to his peninsula woods.

In 1910, he killed two men for unknown reasons, leaving their bodies in the forest. By March 1911, his hideout had been pinpointed along the Satsop River near Oxbow. Sheriff Colin McKenzie and Deputy A. V. Elmer went in after him, and within a couple weeks their bodies turned up too. The state now placed a $5,000 reward on Turnow's head.

In April 1912, the manhunt ended when Deputy Sheriff Giles Quimbly and loggers Charles Lathrop and Louis Blair took deep breaths, loaded their rifles, and went in after him. During the resultant gunfight, Turnow killed both loggers. Deputy Quimbly ducked behind some brush, hugged the ground, waited until he got a look at his man, and emptied his rifle. Then he raced for civilization, returning later with a larger posse. They found Turnow lying on his back, dead, still clutching his rifle, his ragged beard and ragged clothes soaked with blood.

UNDERWOOD, Henry (1846–?)

This desperado was born in Indiana, served in the Union army, moved to Kansas, and by 1871 had reached Denton County, Texas, where he rode with the Sam Bass gang. He allegedly shot a couple of men in Texas; later he was indicted, but not prosecuted, for burning a church. On Christmas Day the Denton, Texas, authorities arrested him on a Kearney, Nebraska, charge that he had participated with Bass in a railroad holdup. Underwood escaped from jail, however, and returned to Texas, rejoining the Sam Bass gang in late March 1878. On April 10, he participated in a Sam Bass train robbery near Dallas, but he was wounded in the arm during a skirmish with lawmen near Denton on June 9. Four days later he participated in the Salt Creek fight with lawmen, and afterward simply rode away. Some legends say he moved to Kansas, to Illinois, and to Mexico. Whatever and wherever, he vanished from sight.

See also: BASS, SAM; TEXAS RANGERS

VÁSQUEZ, Tiburcio (1835–1875)

Tiburcio was probably born in Montgomery County, California, where he became a legendary social bandit, an outlaw coming of age after the Mexican War, a man blaming Americans for his troubles, accusing them of coveting Hispanic women and detesting Mexican men. He requested and received his mother's blessing to become an outlaw. Beginning in 1856, he rustled cattle and horses primarily to satisfy his own lusts for women and gambling. He spent time in and out of San Quentin, led a murderous raid on Tres Pintos, California, and was finally arrested in 1874 when he seduced one of his friends' wives, and the friend betrayed him to the authorities. He was executed at Los Angeles in March 1875.

VENARD, Stephen (1823–1891)

Steve Venard, like so many of his contemporaries, headed toward the setting sun, seeking his fortune in the California mining camps during the early 1850s. Although he failed to fill his pot with tons of gold, he never considered returning to Lebanon, Ohio. At Nevada City, Steve engaged in mercantile and freighting enterprises, eventually accepting a position as town marshal in 1864, a part-time job but one to his liking.

California was awash in stagecoach robberies during this period, and Nevada City was not an exception. On May 15, 1866, just a few miles from town,

Tiburcio Vásquez (Robert G. McCubbin Collection)

three highwaymen forced a Wells Fargo & Co. coach to a caterwauling halt, then leaving with $8,000 in gold dust. The pursuing posse, of which Venard was a member, didn't know it at the time, but the bandits were Robert Finn, George Moore, and George Shanks. Cutting for sign (looking for clues), Venard became separated from his fellow possemen, but he doggedly stuck to the trail. With Steve's fearless reputation for bravery, and his widely known marksmanship with his repeating Henry carbine, other posse members were not overly concerned. Single-handedly, Steve Venard caught up with the outlaws; after an ensuing battle, three robbers lay sprawled dead in the dirt.

Three years later (1869), Steve Venard, by now holding a deputy sheriff's commission, arrested David "Little Jakey" Jacobs, a charter member of a notorious gang working the area. After that, Steve Venard joined Wells Fargo, first as a guard and then as a detective. He worked his cases often in conjunction with the company's chief of detectives, James B. Hume. Never marrying, Venard devoted his life to the pursuit of outlaws. He died of kidney failure on May 20, 1891, at Nevada City, California.

See also: HUME, JAMES B; WELLS FARGO

VERMILLION, Jack (a.k.a. Texas Jack) (?–?)

Vermillion was one of those wandering desperadoes who seem to have been everywhere, but not much is known about his life. During the 1870s, Vermillion focused his activities in Kansas; by 1878 he had reached Leadville, Colorado. In Las Vegas, New Mexico, he teamed up with, or at least tagged along with, Doc Holliday and the Earps. He and the Earps reached Tombstone, Arizona, around 1880. He left Tombstone with the Earps a year or two later. He participated during the Earp murders of Frank Stillwell and Florentino Cruz. Not long after that he became a confidence man in Denver, but by 1889 he

was in Guthrie, Oklahoma. Following that he dropped from sight.

See also: EARP, WYATT BERRY STAPP; HOLLIDAY, JOHN HENRY; TOMBSTONE, ARIZONA

VIGILANCE Committees (a.k.a. Vigilantes)

At certain times and at certain places in the American West, especially in mining towns, isolated areas where for a variety of reasons the law had not arrived or was ineffective, some sort of discipline had to arise. In the absence of suitable jails or paid, responsible lawmen, without courts and court officials, vigilance committees arose to suppress violent crime. In these instances justice might not have always been served, but the community reaction to crime was quick, sudden, and to the point.

Vigilantes operated in practically every western state, although they seem to have been the most active in California, Montana, Nevada, and to a lesser extent, New Mexico and Texas. The vigilantes ordinarily held a prior, brief court (meeting) of their own, most of their subsequent actions being by consensus. In California, these gatherings were generally called "miners courts" and could involve anywhere from a half-dozen to 100 or so men. After hearing the evidence, usually verbal, the group decided on punishments, usually from among four and five possibilities: nothing, warnings, banishment, the lash, or execution. While death could be by rifle fire, it generally came by hanging. Most hangings were from trees, but telegraph poles, ladders, windmills, rafters, and even doorknobs served the purpose.

California and Montana seem to have had the most active vigilantes. California was unique in that its vigilante movement, which began in the mining camps, soon overflowed into more populated areas and larger towns, such as San Francisco.

See also: FORT GRIFFIN, TEXAS, VIGILANTES; PLUMMER, WILLIAM HENRY; SAN FRANCISCO VIGILANTES

WAGNER, John (a.k.a. Dutch John) (?–1864)

This German-born outlaw with a heavy accent joined the Henry Plummer gang in Montana and was, by some accounts, "a murderer and a highwayman for years." In late 1863, he and others bungled an attempt to rob a train of wagons and pack animals bound from Montana to Salt Lake City. A man named Neil Howie captured Wagner and handed him over to the vigilantes in Bannack. Wagner wrote his mother saying his execution would be just. He is buried in Bannack.

See also: VIGILANCE COMMITTEES

WALKER Colt

Samuel Hamilton Walker, a noted Texas Ranger, was born in Maryland but fought in Alabama's Creek Indian campaign. He took part in the so-called Adrian Woll invasion and the Somervell and Mier expeditions against Mexico. In 1844, he joined John Hays's company of Texas Rangers, later fighting in practically every major battle of the Mexican War, including the battle of Monterrey in September 1846. At this point, Walker went to Washington, D.C., as a recruiter, and while in this position he visited Samuel Colt and suggested changes to the Colt revolver. Out of their discussions arose a four-pound dragoon pistol of .44 caliber with a nine-inch barrel. It had a stationary, or rigid, trigger, plus trigger guard. The inscription on the right side said "U.S.

1847." This was the first Colt six-shooter, a weapon to become famous as the "Walker Colt." It possessed additional firepower, was easier to load, and was much more sturdy than previous models.

Walker returned to the Mexican War, where he primarily battled guerrillas operating in the countryside. He was killed in action on October 9, 1847, and was buried at Hacienda Tamaris, Mexico. His remains were moved to San Antonio in 1948.

See also: COLT REVOLVER; HAYS, JOHN COFFEE; TEXAS RANGERS

WALTERS, William (a.k.a. Bronco Bill) (1860–1921)

Bronco Bill was probably born in Austin and worked as a New Mexico/Texas cowboy until 1877. He apparently participated in the Horrell-Higgins feud, but by 1888 he had been arrested in Separ, New Mexico, for horse theft. He broke out of the Silver City, New Mexico, jail on April 20, 1892. During the next few years he attempted a few botched robberies and broke out of the Socorro, New Mexico, jail. In 1896, he attempted to hold up the Atlantic & Pacific passenger train west of Albuquerque, and one of his comrades was killed. He later tried to rob stagecoaches, and since that wasn't particularly successful, he switched back to trains in an abortive holdup near Stein's Pass, New Mexico, on December 9, 1897. The following March 29 he hit a train near Grants,

New Mexico, following that on May 24 with another train strike near Belen. There he reportedly walked away with $20,000. Within a brief time, several lawmen ambushed Walters and his companions; although the outlaws turned things around and killed three of the officers. On July 29, 1898, Walters and one of his gang members, Kid Johnson, were severely wounded by lawmen Jeff Milton and George Scarborough. Walters was indicted for three killings and went immediately to the Santa Fe Penitentiary. On April 16, 1911, he escaped, but he was caught, returned, and (incredibly) pardoned by the governor on April 17, 1917. Following that, he went to work as a cowboy on the Diamond A Ranch near Hachita, New Mexico, dying three years later when he fell off a windmill. William Walters had bad luck practically all his life. The only successful thing he seems to have done was break out of jail.

See also: HORRELL-HIGGINS FEUD; MILTON, JEFFERSON DAVIS

WARE, Richard Clayton (1851–1902)

Nineteen-year-old R. C. "Dick" Ware migrated with his parents from Floyd County, Georgia, to the Lone Star State in 1870. Settling at Dallas the family prospered, but after six years something still seemed to be missing in Ware's life. He enlisted in the Texas Rangers on April 1, 1876.

During his ranger years Ware saw exhilarating service, but one event propelled him onto the historical stage more than any other. Ware and his rangers were dispatched to Round Rock, Texas, in July 1878. Their mission was to remain incognito, and, if they found their intelligence accurate, to capture or kill the notorious Sam Bass and his gang before or when it attempted to rob the Williamson County Bank.

With lawmen spread out in discreet locations throughout the town, Ware opted to take advantage of an unusual surveillance site. He climbed into Henry Burkhardt's barber chair and was glancing out the window while being shaved when the outlaws nonchalantly rode into town, dismounted, and entered a store.

Noticing that the new arrivals were carrying arms, Maurice B. Moore, an out-of-town deputy assisting the rangers, and Williamson County deputy and ex-ranger Ahijah W. "High" Grimes entered the store behind the trio. The outlaws recognized their danger

and drew their six-shooters, firing a hailstorm of bullets into the lawmen. Grimes died instantly. Before he wilted to the floor, a seriously wounded Moore shot two fingers off Bass's right hand. Amid the noise, blue smoke from black powder, and utter confusion, the murderers fled to the street. Ware, upon hearing the gunfire, with lather still on his face, jumped from the barber chair, rushed outside, recognized what was happening, and engaged the outlaws in battle. Other rangers as well as citizens opened fire.

The battle continued. A bullet punched through Sam Bass's kidney. Deliberately and with precision Dick Ware sighted in on Seaborn Barnes's left ear and dropped him dead on the spot.

Somehow Bass and Frank Jackson escaped from the lawmen's withering fusillade. Outside Round Rock, the critically wounded Sam Bass dismounted and awaited the posse's arrival. Jackson continued in flight while the dying Bass was discovered and brought into town. At five minutes to four the afternoon of July 21, 1878, the 27-year-old Sam Bass expired.

"Dick" Ware usually is credited with firing the shot that led to Bass's demise. However, an inquest determined that Ware had dealt the death shot to Barnes; ranger George Harold had killed Bass.

Ware subsequently became the first elected sheriff of Mitchell County; he consequently tendered his resignation to the Texas Rangers on February 1, 1881. The county reelected him for five more cycles, and Ware participated in numerous adventures. On one occasion, he assisted his fellow brother of the badge, George Scarborough, sheriff of neighboring Jones County, in a search for and ultimate capture of desperadoes A. B. "Add" Cannon and Joe Brown. On another occasion in 1889, Ware, who was temporarily filling in as postmaster of the newly formed Crosby County, was robbed at gunpoint by George Spencer and John Harvey. Ware gave chase, captured the holdup men, and ultimately sent them to the state prison at Huntsville.

After Ware's fifth term as Mitchell County sheriff, President Grover Cleveland on April 25, 1893, appointed him as the U.S. marshal for the Western District of Texas. He retained that position until political changes forced his resignation in January of 1898.

Although he received criticism regarding the appointment of deputies Bass Outlaw and George Scarborough, who were under indictment for murder, "Dick" Ware was well respected throughout

Texas and was remembered for his commitment to law and order. He died in Fort Worth of heart trouble on June 25, 1902.

See also: BASS, SAM; CANNON, A. B.; GRIMES, ALBERT CALVIN; HAROLD, GEORGE; OUTLAW, BASS; TEXAS RANGERS

WATSON, Ellen (a.k.a. Ella Watson, Cattle Kate) (1861–1889)

Ellen Watson likely was born near Ontario, Canada, but her family later migrated to Lebanon, Kansas, where she married a farmer named William Pickell. They later divorced, and Kate, as she was now generally known, began drifting about, by most accounts living as a prostitute, waitress, housekeeper, cook, whatever it took to stay alive.

Sometime during the mid- to late 1880s, she showed up in Sweetwater Valley, Wyoming, where she teamed up with James Averell, a saloon keeper and homesteader. The couple might also have married, although if so, both seem to have retained separate, although side-by-side, ranches, which they stocked with stolen steers from nearby large outfits. One story has it that the voluptuous Watson swapped sex for cattle; if so, her bed must have been constantly warm.

Whatever, the big ranchers charged her and Averell with cattle theft, and Averell retaliated with letters to the editor, all bitterly attacking the Wyoming stockmen. Meanwhile, Averell and Cattle Kate, as she was becoming known, seemed to have plenty of money and lots of livestock until their good fortune came to a violent end on July 20, 1889, when neighboring ranchers rounded up both Kate and James Averell, loaded them into a buckboard, drove them to the banks of the Sweetwater River, and lynched them from nearby cottonwood trees. By some accounts their hands were not tied; if so, they slowly strangled while desperately trying to free themselves.

See also: CANTON, FRANK; JOHNSON COUNTY WAR

WEBB, John Joshua (1847–1882?)

This lawman/desperado seems to have been born in Keokuk County, Iowa, and to have worked as a hunter and teamster for surveyors before drifting into other occupations by the time he reached Dodge City, Kansas, in 1877. There he served as an occasional policeman as well as a sometime posse member for Bat Masterson. He rode with lawmen during a futile pursuit of the outlaw Sam Bass.

By 1880, he had drifted south and west to Las Vegas, New Mexico, where he became a special officer as well as city marshal in early 1880. While wearing the badge, he attempted to hold up a business house and killed Michael Kelliher during the botched robbery. A jury thought he ought to hang for that, but Governor Lew Wallace commuted the sentence to life. In the meantime gunman David Rudabaugh killed a jailer during an unsuccessful attempt to free Webb.

Webb and Rudabaugh were now in the same San Miguel County jail; they and two others, on September 19, 1881, attempted to break out. Guards thwarted the escape, in the process killing an unidentified prisoner. On December 3, Webb, Rudabaugh, and five others did escape. Rudabaugh was likely slain later in Chihuahua City, Mexico, during a drunken cantina fight. Webb disappeared, one report saying he died at Winslow, Arizona, of smallpox.

See also: BASS, SAM; MASTERSON, WILLIAM BARCLAY; MASTERSON, JAMES; RUDABAUGH, DAVID

WELLS Fargo

In March 1852, a group of expressmen, among them Henry Wells and William George Fargo, organized a company to deliver mail, packages, and paper from the East to San Francisco. From there the shipments would be distributed to California mining camps. The business became so successful that Wells Fargo also entered banking, dropping off packages at the mining camps, purchasing gold dust for $15 an ounce, and later selling it to the U.S. Mint for $18.

Since stagecoaches carried money as well as prosperous passengers, in addition to the driver, they also carried shotgun guards. The firm also utilized an extensive system of investigators and gunmen, people who operated on their own as well as in cooperation with local, state, and federal authorities. While the number of robberies, attempted robberies, and killings has never been tabulated, over a period between the late 1850s and early 1900s the numbers ran into the dozens. Without Wells Fargo, the West would not have been nearly as wild.

By 1864, Wells Fargo & Co. (as it was known then), which already had financial interests in the Overland Mail Company, had plunged deep into purchasing stage lines throughout California and

Nevada. It even operated a successful Pony Express route for faster, if more limited, service. By 1866, practically every successful overland distributor in the West had united under the name of Wells, Fargo & Co. Then in 1901, the company kept the same name, but under different management moved its headquarters to New York. In the process it merged with other firms such as the American Railway Express Company. Today Wells Fargo is a giant factor in American growth and history, although it is frequently remembered in terms of banks, stagecoaches, stagecoach robberies, and thrilling days of yesteryear.

WELLS, Samuel (a.k.a. Charlie Pitts) (?–1876)

This Independence, Missouri–born desperado joined the James gang, participating in the July 7, 1876, train robbery at Otterville, Missouri. Fresh from that he rode with the James-Younger bunch to Northfield, Minnesota, and participated in the First National Bank robbery of September 7.

Along with the others, he retreated south through and across the Minnesota rivers and forests, sticking with the Youngers when the two groups split up. A posse trapped the Youngers, however, and Charlie Pitts died during the gunfight. One of the possemen cut off his ear. The body was sent to St. Paul, arriving in such a foul condition that the flesh had to be removed from the bones. Dr. Henry F. Hoyt kept the skeleton in his Chicago office for many years.

See also: JAMES BROTHERS; NORTHFIELD RAID; YOUNGER BROTHERS

WEST, Richard (a.k.a. Little Dick) (1865–1898)

This Texas-born outlaw worked as a cowboy until 1892, when he met Bill Doolin, an Oklahoma outlaw whom West helped rob Missouri's Southwest City Bank on May 10, 1894. That wasn't the luckiest thing he ever did, as he suffered severe wounds while killing one man and wounding another, the dead man being a Missouri state senator, J. C. Seaborn.

On April 3, 1885, Little Dick helped Doolin rob a train at Dover, Oklahoma, after which West dropped out of sight for 12 years until reappearing in Tecumseh, Oklahoma, as the organizer and head of the Jennings gang. But from here on, Little Dick's life was just one financial disaster after another; he continuously hit Oklahoma trains, but nothing happened. A

successful robbery against the Rock Island on October 1, 1897, hardly brought in sufficient funds to feed the outlaws' horses. It was time for Richard West to go, and the law caught up with him near Guthrie, where a posse led by Heck Thomas and Bill Tilghman shot him to death.

See also: DOOLIN, WILLIAM M.; TILGHMAN, WILLIAM MATHEW, JR.; THOMAS, HENRY ANDREW

WHEELER, Benjamin F. (a.k.a. Ben Burton; Ben Roberston) (1854–1884)

This desperado/lawman grew up in Rockdale, Milam County, Texas. He left Texas in 1878 after a shooting that left another man wounded, then moved on to Caldwell, Kansas, where be became City Marshal Henry Brown's assistant marshal.

Not long afterward, he and Brown and others held up a bank in Medicine Lodge, Kansas, where Wheeler killed the cashier, George Geppert. The commotion aroused the town, the residents shooting Brown to death and capturing Wheeler and two others. All were promptly lynched.

See also: BROWN, HENRY

WHEELER, Frank S. (?–1932)

The early history of this Arizona lawman is obscure. He was born in Hazelhurst, Mississippi. By 1880, the family had migrated to Texas, settling at Vernon in Wilbarger County. Frank spent much of his youth as a cowboy and in 1900 moved to Arizona, where he joined the Arizona Rangers on September 10, 1902. He was a tall man, about six feet three inches, and as quiet as he was thin. Only one man ever stayed with the Arizona Rangers longer than Frank Wheeler.

The Arizona Rangers were organized along the same lines as the Texas Rangers and in many respects were as much like a military organization as a police one. Wheeler worked primarily in Graman, Cochise, and Pima Counties, with the majority of his investigations centering around Yuma. In 1905, he married Lenora Rieff. They would have 10 children.

Many years earlier Kerrick had killed a sheepherder in California and got 20 years in San Quentin but was pardoned. In late June 1907, Wheeler and Yuma County deputy sheriff John Cameron trailed two horse thieves, James Kerrick and Lee Bentley, for five burning days toward the Mexican border. The lawmen tracked them down on June 30 at a water seep known as Sheep Dung Tanks in the western end of Pima County. Early in the morning, after the lawmen called on the two men to surrender, a gunfight erupted, and the two outlaws died.

Later at an inquest, Ranger Frank Wheeler made the following statement:

When we were sure they were dead we put them on their own horses and rode twenty-five miles with them to the Ten Mile Wells, ten miles from Ajo, Arizona. We sent word to Sentinel to wire Pima County for a coroner. A coroner refused to come, and a wire was sent to Silver Bell for the justice of the peace, and he refused to come. So it was all day Sunday and until 2 o'clock Monday when Sheriff Pacheco [of Maricopa County] arrived, before we buried the men. We did not dare leave them on top of the ground any longer, on account of the heat, so I made boxes for them, and lowered them into the ground. Even when Pacheco got there the bodies were decomposed beyond recognition.

Wheeler also noted that no rewards had been offered for the two outlaws.

After the rangers disbanded in 1909, Wheeler became a full-time Yuma County deputy sheriff, a part-time guard at the territorial prison, and a night watchman for the Laguna Dam project. Meanwhile, Wheeler and his wife permitted two girls to live in a tent in their yard while attending school. For whatever reason, the arrangement went sour, for the girls' father and his brother-in-law, Frank Butts, attempted to remove the girls and their property. A fight subsequently started between Wheeler and the father and then between Wheeler and both men. A few days later Wheeler and Butts collided again at the Barrelhouse Saloon. This time Wheeler shot Butts; he almost died. Wheeler was fined and released.

Within the next year or so, Wheeler developed bronchial asthma, and his health steadily deteriorated. He died of heart failure on December 20, 1932.

See also: ARIZONA RANGERS; WHEELER, HARRY

WHEELER, Harry (1875–1925)

This lawman, who may or may not have been related to Arizona Ranger Frank Wheeler, was born in Jacksonville, Florida, the son of a career army officer. In 1897, he joined the U.S. Army, served in the cavalry in South Dakota as well as in Arizona Territory, and

might have made a career of it except that a horse kicked him in the stomach on October 9, 1901. He took his discharge, then joined the Arizona Rangers as a private in July 1903. Three months later he made sergeant, and on the night of October 30, 1904, at about 11:30 P.M. in the Palace Saloon in Tucson, he tasted blood.

Harry Wheeler interrupted a gambling game robbery, and he and outlaw Joseph Bostwick exchanged shots, Wheeler's being the more effective. Bostwick died of a chest wound, and Wheeler went on to other assignments. In July 1906, the Arizona Rangers promoted him to lieutenant.

Not too many months after that, James A. Tracy married an already much-married woman. He left her when he found out, but distance and feelings were two different things; Tracy became aggravated when she married someone else. The brooding Tracy tracked down the two in Benson, Arizona, and threatened to kill them. Fortunately, Harry Wheeler happened to be around. His attempted arrest ended in an exchange of gunfire. Tracy shot Wheeler twice, and Wheeler shot Tracy four times. Tracy died.

Soon afterward, Capt. Thomas Rynning resigned from the Arizona Rangers, and Lt. Harry Wheeler accepted promotion to his position. Wheeler became an exceptional leader and administrator, working in particular with Arizona lawmen like Cochise County deputy sheriff George Humm, the two of them going after George Arnett, a horse thief. At about 3 A.M. on the night of May 5, 1908, the officers stumbled onto Arnett in the dark. Both sides exchanged shots from horseback, and early the next morning, following the horses' trail, they found Arnett dead alongside the road.

The Territory of Arizona dissolved its ranger force in 1909, at which time Wheeler became a deputy sheriff of Cochise County. In January 1911, he became sheriff.

In 1917, the very patriotic Wheeler joined the army to fight in World War I, but he was found physically unfit and discharged that same year. He subsequently went back to work as sheriff of Cochise County, at the same time becoming very offended by the IWW, the International Workers of the World. It seems that the union had picked this particular time to call a strike, which meant that the United States during this period of war would suffer a reduction in copper production. Wheeler resolved the strike by rounding up dozens of strikers, most of them at gunpoint, loading them on a train, and shipping them into the middle of the Arizona–New Mexico desert, where they were turned loose to fend for themselves. The event—known as the Bisbee Deportations—created national headlines.

With the deportation controversy raging about his ears, Wheeler joined the Arizona 308th Cavalry, took officer training at Fort Myers, Virginia, and by July 1918 was in Brest, France. But he was ordered back to Arizona to face charges of "kidnapping and unlawful arrests" with regard to the Bisbee Deportations. Eventually, all charges were dropped, and Wheeler became a police officer in Douglas, Arizona. He resigned in 1920 and thereafter worked his ranch and participated in numerous charitable fund-raising activities. He died in Douglas, Arizona, of pneumonia on December 15, 1925.

See also: ARIZONA RANGERS; RYNNING, THOMAS H.

WHITE, George E. (1831–1902)

Cattle king George E. White was born in Lewis County in what is now West Virginia, but in 1849 he found himself in California with thousands of other Gold Rush dreamers. He opened a ferry service across the Sacramento River. Then, for whatever reason, he migrated to Missouri. By 1854, however, he had returned to California, settling in the beautiful Round Valley of the Sacramento River. Within three years (1857) he owned 5,000 acres in Yolla Bolly country and operated a ranching empire with 700 head of cattle. From that time on, digging for gold was behind him—gold was on the hoof. To make sure he hung onto it, White staffed and protected his empire largely with desperadoes who killed intruders on the spot. This did not keep him out of court, of course, but he did enjoy trials and their legal formalities.

A physician once described White as a "tall, handsome man, uneducated, a person who spelled Cat with a K," but he "had a retinue of retainers who were as loyal to him as Highlanders to their Chief." White established a small town called Covelo, where he owned most of the buildings and many of the businesses. His murderous foreman, John David Wathen, better known as "Wylackie John," occasionally shot people at White's request and did his best to run off several of White's wives when the boss tired of them. Squatters and people who for one reason or another had aroused White's anger turned up

either missing or dead. White usually confiscated their property, while Wylackie John burned the house and sometimes buried the bodies. Most had been shot; some had been poisoned. White got away with this primarily because he lived and operated in a remote, mountainous region.

White went through wives in a hurry, usually accusing them of infidelity, and the courts went along with him. Some of the women countersued, charging that he and Wylackie John planned to kill them.

The only woman White really trusted was a San Francisco spiritualist who went by the name of Mrs. Whitney. But even she did not foresee that Wylackie John would pull a gun on a friend. However, John was too slow, and the "friend" killed him.

White replaced Wylackie John with a cattleman named Alfred "Jack" Littlefield, who had a fondness for other people's horses. Jack beat a horse-theft charge in open court, but a few months later, in September 1894, someone shot him in the back. He survived that only to be lynched, then cut down and tied to a tree, evidently by some of White's men. John had not only a broken neck from the rope but three bullets in him.

Although the court trial went on for years, and White was suspected as a co-conspirator, he never went before a jury. In fact, throughout his life, others had done his killing. He had been in danger only once, when he accidentally shot himself in the leg. He died later of stomach cancer and was buried on his own property in a huge, heavy, metal casket. The newspapers mentioned that even as he died, his last wife was in the process of suing him for divorce and demanding a lot of money. The *San Francisco Examiner* recalled that "in the early days he had many quarrels with neighboring cattle men, and those who ventured too close to Round Valley never got away again, although no one was ever found who would tell what happened. In this way several men met sudden death."

WHITEHILL, Harvey Howard (1837–1906)

Harvey Howard Whitehill is most often mentioned as the first lawman to arrest Billy the Kid, doing so at Silver City, New Mexico Territory, when the future badman was a mere child.

Whitehill was born at Bellfontaine, Ohio, on September 2, 1837. By the time he was 21 years old he was already a seasoned miner in Colorado, having prospected at such sites as Cherry Creek, Leadville, and Russell Gulch. A staunch Democrat, Harvey Whitehill served as sergeant-at-arms in the first Colorado territorial legislature. At the outbreak of the Civil War, Whitehill joined the Union army, spent most of his military career in New Mexico, and was discharged on December 19, 1865. In 1870, after a five-year stint prospecting around Elizabethtown, New Mexico, Harvey migrated to the area that would become Silver City. His son Wayne was born in that community.

As one of the founding fathers of Silver City, Whitehill was appointed county coroner. When the incumbent sheriff, Charles McIntosh, disappeared into Mexico, Harvey assumed that position. It was while sheriff that Whitehill arrested "the Kid," ostensibly to teach the youngster a rehabilitative lesson. Billy failed to get the message.

Sheriff Whitehill led many Apache patrols, fought in numerous skirmishes, and was generally considered a brave and courageous man. Although commonly characterized as the sterling example of an unarmed lawman who talked brigands into the jailhouse, that description was somewhat belied by the fact that one day while at the courthouse, he bumped into the corner of a table and the revolver in his pocket discharged. The bullet struck a bystander.

Naturally, Whitehill had responsibility for a host of administrative duties, but on the criminal side, he successfully presided over one double hanging, plus several single ones. He performed admirably in developing solid leads, properly identifying the suspects, and arresting those involved in the Gage train robbery (the first in the territory), in which train engineer Webster was murdered. A major portion of the much-sought-after reward went to Whitehill.

Whitehill defeated Pat Garrett for a seat in the territorial legislature at Santa Fe, and after that campaigned for and was elected Grant County sheriff. He also had extensive ranch holdings on the Mimbres River. After the loss of his first wife, Harriet, Harvey remarried and settled at Deming, where he continued to oversee his cattle operations and real-estate holdings until his death from natural causes on September 9, 1906. Had he not incarcerated or even met Billy the Kid, his life would still qualify as a rich one.

See also: BILLY THE KID; CLEVELAND, GEORGE WASHINGTON; GARRETT, PATRICK FLOYD JARVIS

WILD Bunch

Most outlaw gangs in the Old West were loosely knit groups of men whose membership, relationship, leadership, personalities, and numbers varied across months and years. However, only one of these groups had the name Wild Bunch. The initial Wild Bunch participants seem to have been Robert Leroy Parker, better known historically as Butch Cassidy; Harry Longabaugh, better known as the Sundance Kid; Ben Kilpatrick, better known as the Tall Texan; Harvey Logan, better known as Kid Curry; William Ellsworth Lay, better known as Elza Lay; and Flatnose George Curry. Other well-known stalwarts included Matt Warner, Tom McCarty, and Will Carver. Around 1889 or 1890, these men collectively formed the nucleus of a gang known as the Wild Bunch (a newspaper—it is unclear which—coined the name). As outlaw groups go, this one was more cohesive than most, although at best it never numbered over 30, and a majority of these drifted in and out. There does not seem to have been any clearly defined leader, although outlaws such as Butch Cassidy, the Sundance Kid, and the Tall Texan made most of the headlines and tended to be the spokesmen. Harvey Logan (Kid Curry) was the most homicidal.

The gang operated out of localities with such interesting names as Hole-in-the-Wall, located in Wyoming's Bighorn Mountains, Robbers Roost in Utah, and Brown's Park in Colorado. After Butch Cassidy and the Sundance Kid fled to South America sometime around early 1902, the Wild Bunch essentially ceased to exist.

See also: BROWN'S PARK; CARVER, WILLIAM RICHARD; CASSIDY, BUTCH; CURRY, GEORGE SUTHERLAND; HOLE-IN-THE-WALL; KILPATRICK, BEN; LAY, WILLIAM ELLSWORTH; LOGAN, HARVEY; ROBBERS ROOST; SUNDANCE KID; TURKEY CREEK CANYON, BATTLE OF

WILLIAMS, Andrew Jackson (1847–1887)

Andrew Jackson Williams—usually called A. J. Williams—was born in Conway County, Arkansas, his father Curtis being a first cousin of Abraham Lincoln through Lincoln's mother's side of the family. The family moved to Eastland County, Texas, during the early 1870s. There, local ranchers accused him of rustling. By the 1880s, the Texas authorities led by Jones County sheriff George Scarborough had chased him into Chaves and Eddy

Counties of New Mexico. There they captured and returned him to Texas. Although acquitted on all charges, Williams tried to escape from jail as well as bribe the sheriff. So Scarborough pressed additional charges. On October 3, 1887, Williams spotted George Scarborough and his brother Will in the Road-to-Ruin Saloon in Haskell, Texas. Williams, bent on assassination, slipped into the saloon with a shotgun, but the lawmen had been warned. The Scarborough boys killed him. Subsequently charged with murder, both were found not guilty and released. George Scarborough was defeated in his bid for reelection as sheriff.

WILLIAMS, Charles (1861–1880)

Originally from Ohio, this 25-year-old made a name for himself at Shakespeare, New Mexico. By some accounts Williams was a cattle rustler working his way through Texas. But regardless of his vocation, or lack of one, "Charley" Williams spent most of his time sucking down drinks in saloons.

On June 1, 1880, Charley stepped out of the Roxy Jay Saloon and noticed a resident taking a nap. The consumptive F. W. Mollitor had not the slightest idea his end was near. When Williams's "eyes fell upon the prostrate man lying on the bench, he drew his own pistol, turned it toward him and fired. Not a word had passed between them." Townsmen quickly arrested Charley and sent him to Grant County sheriff Harvey Whitehill at Silver City.

Williams arrived at Silver City, was placed in jail, and was later released on a $1,000 bond. However, he argued with a man named Crittenden over a mining claim. In this case, Crittenden, the mine owner, took a page from the Williams book. He leveled his rifle at Charley and shot him dead. The case against Williams for murdering Mollitor was closed with a simple notation in the county jail book, "Died by wound before trial—July 23, 1880." As for Crittenden, he vanished into Mexico.

See also: WHITEHILL, HARVEY HOWARD

WILLIE Boy (1881–1909)

Willie Boy probably had a "real" name, but if so it wasn't recorded. His father was probably a Paiute Indian, his mother a Chemehuevi. By 1900, he was living in Victorville, California, and working as a farm laborer. He was arrested there in 1905, charged

with drunkenness and disturbing the peace. A judge sentenced him to two weeks in the San Bernardino County jail.

Wille Boy had previously tried to marry Nita Bonaface, but her father, "Old Mike," refused to bless even the possibility of marriage. Willie then either eloped with her or kidnapped her, but Mike Bonaface and his family tracked them down and at rifle point took his daughter back. But Willie would prevail. The Bonaface family worked for the Marshal Gillman Ranch near Banning, where the workers usually camped on the property. On the night of September 26, 1909, Willie Boy slipped into the Gillman house, removed a .30–30 Winchester rifle, walked out to the sleeping Bonaface family, and shot Mike through the left eye. He took Nita with him as he fled, leaving the Bonaface family so terrified that they did not report the slaying until late the next day. The greatest manhunt in the history of southern California now began.

Although Willie Boy knew the country, he was on foot and pulling along a terrified girl. As for the posses, they were usually mounted, automobiles being of no use in that rugged, roadless country. Nevertheless, the posses did not know where to search, although they suspected that Willie was heading for Mexico. So ranchers were notified, travelers were warned, and small settlements mobilized. As the net tightened, Willie felt the pressure and realized the girl was slowing him down. She likely was not as affectionate as he had hoped, and knowing that the two of them could never outrun their pursuers, he shot her in the back, leaving the body where it lay. A posse found her remains on September 30.

Willie continued east toward Twentynine Palms, California, and the Colorado River. On October 6, 1909, several posse members cut Willie's trail on Bullion Mountain, but while the lawmen discussed strategy, Willie commenced shooting with that same stolen Winchester, killing four of the posse's five horses and wounding Deputy Sheriff Charles Reche in the hip. Reche spent the rest of the day lying in the hot sun, since nobody could get to him.

Willie, always short of ammunition, saved his last round for himself, sticking his big toe against the trigger and shooting himself in the chest. The posse—hearing the shot—did not attach any significance to it. The lawmen assumed it to be a stray round.

On October 15, still another posse discovered the body of Willie Boy, shot through the chest, dead by his own hand. The body was so badly decomposed that posse members cremated it. Since then several books and articles have been published, as well as a movie, entitled *Tell Them Willie Boy Is Here*. As a result of this publicity, Willie Boy, instead of being an outlaw and murderer, has become something of a social hero and legend.

WILSON, Vernon Coke (1855–1892)

By 1876, Vernon Coke Wilson, a nephew of Texas governor Richard Coke, had made it from Virginia to Texas. Enlisting in the Texas Rangers on September 23, Vernon Wilson eventually served under the noted lawman Capt. Neal Coldwell.

Somewhat unusually, especially for a daring Texas Ranger, Vernon Wilson seemed rather inept with firearms and in the handling of livestock. But had "B movies" been around at that time, Vernon would have been a natural, for he was noted for his excellent guitar playing and pleasant singing voice.

Vernon Coke Wilson's claim to fame as a Texas Ranger comes not from an audacious shootout but for a message-carrying mission. Holding the rank of a ranger corporal, Wilson was at Austin, the state capital, performing administrative tasks when speeding events overtook months of systematic plodding. Learning of at least a viable chance to intercept Sam Bass and his gang at Round Rock, Maj. John B. Jones confronted two perplexing problems: there were neither rangers nor a telegraph near Round Rock. Wilson therefore saddled his gray horse and rode 65 miles to Lampasas by dawn, arriving in time to catch the stagecoach. Undaunted but exhausted, Wilson took the stage from Lampasas to San Saba, a 50-mile trip. Upon reaching town, he located a stable, rented a horse, and finally reached the ranger camp, some three miles distant, where he gave his message to Ranger lieutenant N. O. Reynolds. The lawmen gathered their arms and ammunition, saddled their horses, loaded a wagon, and departed for Round Rock. Wilson hopped into the back of the jostling wagon and went to sleep.

Oddly, Wilson never participated in the Sam Bass gang shootouts on July 21, 1878. Nevertheless, in recognition of his outstanding effort and the exhausting ride, Major Jones awarded Vernon the rifle belonging to Sam Bass, a well-deserved trophy.

Wilson then moved on to become chief of mounted inspectors for Arizona and New Mexico Territories in 1885. Later, he traded that job for a position of special officer for the Southern Pacific Railroad, stationed in California.

On September 13, 1892, during a blistering battle with train robbers John Sontag and Chris Evans at Sampson's Flats, California (near the western edge of the Sequoia National Forest), Vernon Coke Wilson died in a hail of bullets when the outlaws emerged from a cabin. Other lawmen avenged his death. Sontag was later killed outright; Evans, although severely wounded, survived and was imprisoned.

See also: BASS, SAM; JONES, JOHN B. SONTAG, JOHN

WILSON, William (a.k.a. Billy; David L. Anderson) (1861–1911)

This desperado/lawman was born in Trumbell County, Ohio, moved to Texas, and from there went to Lincoln County, New Mexico. He owned a livery stable, and on the side he counterfeited money. After being exposed, Billy transferred to the Pecos River region, where he joined up with outlaws, including Billy the Kid. He was captured by Sheriff Pat Garrett and his posse during the Christmas 1880 standoff at Stinking Springs, not too far from Fort Sumner, New Mexico. The territory charged Wilson with counterfeiting money, and a Santa Fe court assessed 25 years. Wilson escaped, however, and moved to Texas, where he married and, on August 1, 1891, was appointed a mounted inspector for the U.S. Customs Service. New Mexico governor William T. Thornton, a former attorney for Wilson, now filed a plea for a presidential pardon. Two men who wrote letters in Wilson's behalf were former Lincoln County sheriff Pat Garrett, now U.S. Customs collector in El Paso, Texas, and James J. Dolan, formerly of the Lincoln County War house of Murphy. That was a generous and forgiving act on Dolan's part, since he had once been the recipient of one of Wilson's phony $100 bills.

Wilson received his pardon on July 24, 1896, and went on to become sheriff of Terrell County, Texas. He was killed by a drunken cowboy and buried in Bracketville, Texas.

See also: BILLY THE KID; GARRETT, PATRICK FLOYD JARVIS, LINCOLN COUNTY WAR

WILSON, William (?–1875)

By most accounts William Wilson was a paid assassin. This supposed Texan rode into Lincoln, New Mexico, and on August 2, 1875, shot and killed Robert Casey, a Texas cattleman who had criticized the Murphy-Dolan organization, a faction deeply involved in New Mexico's forthcoming Lincoln County War.

Wilson thus became the first person legally hanged in Lincoln County. As he stood on the trapdoor, he reportedly started to confess but also to accuse Lawrence Murphy of paying him to kill Robert Casey. But as Wilson started to speak, Murphy kicked the trapdoor release, and Wilson plummeted through. He seemed to die almost instantly, so the body was removed and placed in a coffin.

Later, as everybody sat around eating their lunches, a woman began screaming, saying she had seen Wilson breathing. Two factions now began arguing. One claimed that he had already been hanged, so he should be revived and released. The Murphy faction screamed otherwise. Its members placed a rope around his neck, jerked him back to the crossbar, and kept him hanging there until everyone was absolutely certain he was dead.

See also: LINCOLN COUNTY WAR

WINCHESTER

Winchester is one of those weapons with a romantic name, but the .44-40 center-fire weapon, with its all-steel action, was useful as well as popular. Furthermore, the gun held 14 rounds with one in the chamber. Its heft and feel made it suitable for short- as well as long-range shooting. Its most popular calibers were .44-40, .38-40, and .32-20. The weapon was as reliable as it was indestructible.

WOODMAN, May (1856–?)

Less than two years after the infamous Tombstone shootout between the Earps and the Cowboys, another hell-to-pop yarn was born on Allen Street in front of the Oriental Saloon. In February 1883, an unidentified person placed a notice in the *Tombstone Epitaph* reporting that Bill Kinsman intended to marry May Woodman. An angry Kinsman then took out a notice of his own, publicly declaring he was not then or ever going to tie the matrimonial knot with Miss May Woodman. To a rough crowd of sporting men and miners it had all been a joke. But to May Woodman, it was humiliation. On February 23, 1883, the 27-year-old May Woodman, .38-caliber revolver in hand, walked up to William Kinsman and shot him dead. Upon realizing that she had indeed killed him, May jubilantly jumped about, glad he was dead. The pair had been cohabiting.

In May 1883, May was convicted of manslaughter and sentenced to five years in the territorial prison, but while languishing in the Cochise County jail awaiting her transfer, she attempted suicide by overdosing on morphine. The renowned Dr. George Goodfellow managed to save her life. Later, while still in the county jail, May suffered a miscarriage. By that time public sympathy had switched from the victim to the shooter, but May went to prison anyway.

Among allegations that while in custody May Woodman had once again became pregnant, a number of prominent citizens signed petitions requesting her release. Acting Governor H. M. Van Arman, seeking to rid himself and the territory of any further death and bad humor, offered May Woodman a deal. He would release her if "she would immediately go beyond the limits of this Territory and continue to reside without the limits of the Territory of Arizona." May accepted the conditional pardon on March 15, 1884. She walked out of prison, caught a westbound train for California, and dropped from sight.

WORTHINGTON, Peter (a.k.a. Jack Gordon) (1825?–1864)

Peter Worthington is generally thought to have been born in Maryland or Virginia. At the age of 17, he killed a man and fled west, probably to El Paso del Norte, present-day Ciudad Juarez, Chihuahua, Mexico, across the Rio Grande from El Paso, Texas. Here in late 1846, during the Mexican War, Worthington signed on with Col. Alexander Doniphan and his Missouri Volunteers, then invaded Chihuahua. By some accounts, Gordon later lived with the Mescalero Apache of southern New Mexico and rode with them during raids on white settlements. In 1849, he acted as a guide for both the army and the rangers against the Indians. Around 1850, he left for California.

For the next few years, Jack Gordon was rumored to be traveling with lawmen in search of rewards, or being chased by lawmen who sought him on charges ranging from horse theft to highway robbery and murder. To his way of thinking, Gordon sometimes had to kill in order to acquire a certain horse, and once he had done so, there was no reason for qualms about emptying the pockets of unlucky victims. After all, they had no further use for gold.

In April 1858, a trader identified only as "the Dutchman" killed his partner, an equally obscure individual known only as Harris, rumored to be carrying $4,000 on a pack mule. Gordon then tracked down and killed the Dutchman, but according to reports found no money on him.

Gordon had obviously come into funds, however. Some of it he spent in opening his own hog-raising business, then in a partnership with a rugged Pole called "Old Cap," but formally referred to as George Groupie. Of course, both partners accused the other of less than honest acts and intentions, and the partnership broke up with Old Cap threatening to kill Gordon.

In late December 1864, the two men met on the street at Tailholt, California. Groupie fired first, his shotgun pellets striking his opponent in the belly. Gordon sank immediately to his knees, muttering, "I'm killed." Bystanders carried him to the nearby store of Levi Mitchell, where Gordon, seeing Groupie approaching, squeezed off a revolver shot. Down went Old Cap.

As it turned out, Old Cap survived, but Jack Gordon did not live through the night. He was buried behind Mitchell's store. The state did not prosecute George Groupie.

YARBERRY, Milton J. (a.k.a. John Armstrong) (1849–1883)

Although he was born at Walnut Ridge, Arkansas, as John Armstrong, somewhere along the line John changed himself into Milton J. Yarberry. Under that assumed name, he checked out of this world and into the next.

Reportedly, when still in his twenties John Armstrong murdered a man in Sharp County, Arkansas, or so thought the sheriff, who posted a $200 reward. Armstrong escaped the charge only to be implicated in another killing at Helena, Arkansas. From there he remained "on the dodge" and continued his ill-conceived career choices. Reportedly, John Armstrong teamed up with "Mysterious" Dave Mather and Dave Rudabaugh, creating a rustling gang that operated between Fort Smith, Arkansas, and Texarkana, Texas. Rumor held the trio responsible for the death of a prominent cattleman, killed when a robbery went bad. Regardless of his guilt or innocence, Armstrong was under the impression that the law was closing in on him, and he killed a man walking behind him one day, thinking he was a detective. He was mistaken—it was "an inoffensive traveler." Little difference did it matter to John, however; he scooted over to Decatur, Texas, and assumed the new name of "Johnson."

At Decatur he operated a saloon and pool hall, at least for a time (1876–77), before once again fleeing the law, leaving another body lying face down in the dirt. By other accounts the outlaw even pulled a short stint as a Texas Ranger. Regardless, it can be documented that by 1879, John Armstrong, now known as Milton J. Yarberry, was in East Las Vegas, New Mexico Territory, as a member of the Dodge City gang.

With associates such as Hyman G. Neil, a.k.a. "Hoodoo Brown," Tom Pickett, Joe Carson, "Big Jim" Dunagan, William (Bill) Goodlet, John Henry "Doc" Holliday, and others, there is little doubt about how Milton J. Yarberry was earning his living.

Surprisingly, Yarberry became the Albuquerque chief of police, but by 1881 he was entangled in another controversy. He and lawman Harry Brown, the son of a prominent Tennessee family, were vying for the affections of a young, attractive divorcée, Sadie Preston. On March 27, 1881, in front of an Albuquerque eatery, Milton Yarberry shot—and kept shooting—Harry Brown. Brown died on the spot. Pleading self-defense at the trial, Milton J. Yarberry walked free.

Three months later, on June 18, Charles D. Campbell died from three bullets fired from Yarberry's six-shooter. Yarberry surrendered to the sheriff and this time was taken to Santa Fe and locked in the jail. At trial the following year, Yarberry again proffered self-defense as his motive. This time the jury paid no attention. It sentenced Yarberry to death,

Yarberry promptly broke jail but was almost as promptly recaptured. On February 9, 1882, the authorities escorted Milton Yarberry to Albuquerque and hanged him that afternoon at about three o'clock.

See also: MATHER, DAVE; RUDABAUGH, DAVID

YOUNG, WILLIAM (a.k.a. Apache Bill)
(1844–1935?)

Bill Young's story is unique, not so much for thrilling exploits as a law enforcement officer as for the fact that he survived to maturity and beyond. For whatever reason, in 1852, when he was but eight years old, Bill Young left his birthplace, Philadelphia, Pennsylvania, and started down the Santa Fe Trail, and from there went on into Arizona. One evening, camped with a wagon train on the San Pedro River, Bill played and wandered. About 100 yards from the wagon train's protective environment, he was snatched up, placed onto the back of an Apache's horse, and spirited away.

In the Chiracahua Mountains of southeastern Arizona, the Apache raiders turned Bill over to the women. There he stayed, working and learning the Apache tongue and becoming Indianized.

By age 10, young Bill was accompanying Apache fighting men on raids, holding the horses while the serious work took place. Four years later, he was an active participant on a raid into Mexico. It was there that life changed again for the war-painted, pale-faced teenager. Mexican soldiers captured Bill thinking he was an Indian; he escaped death only because someone pointed out his light-colored hair and blue eyes. The Mexican forces turned Bill over to military authorities at Fort Buchanan. Although Bill by now had forgotten his real name, Maj. Richard Ewell put the clues together and notified Bill's parents.

During the Civil War, Bill Young enlisted under his mother's maiden name. Eventually mustered out, he next signed on as an Apache scout and interpreter due to his understanding of the Indian language and his exuberant spirit of adventure. Finding his way to New Mexico in 1870, Young left military service and ambled about Tularosa, eventually alighting at Silver City. It was at Silver City that Young, commonly known as "Apache Bill," served as a deputy sheriff for Harvey Whitehill and later for his successor, Andrew Laird. Always reticent about his particular personal exploits, Apache Bill chased outlaws and desperadoes along the Mexican border for years before moving to California, where he died in an Old Soldier's Home sometime around 1935.

YOUNGER Brothers

The four Younger brothers (altogether there were 14 children) were born at Lee's Summit, Missouri: Cole (1844–1916); James (1848–1902); John (1851–74); and Robert (1853–99). They grew up as farmers, but when Kansas Jayhawkers raided the farm and killed their father, they became Confederate guerrillas. Cole and Jim were with William Clarke Quantrill on August 21, 1863, when he pillaged and burned Lawrence, Kansas. Cole even went so far as to disguise himself as an old woman; sticking his horse's reins in his teeth, he shot down a couple of Union soldiers as he galloped past on his way out of Independence, Missouri. Of these two brothers, Jim stayed with Quantrill throughout the Civil War. Cole may have split off and joined other groups.

Following the Civil War, the four Youngers and Frank and Jesse James teamed up and unleashed a long string of train and bank robberies, using their training from their years as guerrilla warriors. On

Bob Younger shortly before his death (Author's Collection)

Cole Younger in later life (Author's Collection)

Jim Younger in later life (Author's Collection)

March 16, 1874, John and Jim Younger shot it out with police officers and Pinkerton agents, Jim taking a bullet in the thigh. John shot agent Louis Lull, who in turn put a bullet through John's throat. They both died.

On September 7, 1876, eight horsemen—Cole, Jim, and Bob Younger; Charlie Pitts; William Chadwell; Frank and Jesse James; and Clell Miller—decided to rob the Northfield, Minnesota, bank. Jesse, Bob Younger, and Charlie Pitts stepped inside and ordered cashier Joseph L. Heywood to open the safe. He refused, and the outlaws slit his throat. A teller attempted to escape and was wounded. A Swedish boy scurried outside, and the robbers shot him down.

The gunfire attracted everyone in town who owned a weapon. Clell Miller and William Chadwell were slain by enraged citizens, and Bob and Cole Younger were seriously wounded. The pursuit continued across the countryside. Charlie Pitts went down two weeks later during one of the most intensive manhunts in Minnesota. Bob, Jim, and Cole Younger surrendered. Jesse and Frank James escaped.

All three Youngers pleaded guilty to murder charges and entered the state prison at Stillwell. In 1889, Bob died of tuberculosis. Jim and Cole were released in 1899 but had to remain in Minnesota. Jim tried to settle down and get married, but when the young lady refused his overtures, he committed suicide. Cole sold insurance and tombstones and in 1903 returned to Missouri, where he and Frank James briefly operated a Wild West show. Cole Younger died at Lee's Summit, Missouri, in 1916.

See also: ANDERSON, WILLIAM C.; JAMES BROTHERS; PINKERTON NATIONAL DETECTIVE AGENCY; QUANTRILL, WILLIAM CLARKE; WELLS, SAMUEL

YUMA Territorial Prison

In 1875, the Arizona legislature approved the construction of a territorial prison near Yuma. In April 1876, the territory laid the cornerstone, and three months later seven prisoners were escorted into the enclosure. Within 10 years, the facility had electricity, a blower to circulate air, and even a library. An adobe wall averaging six feet thick and 16 to 18 feet high surrounded the building; its foundation rested on solid rock. Over 3,000 men and women, most of them desperate murderers, served time here, walking around in striped suits, their heads shaved. They came from 21 different countries, including Anglos, Indians, blacks, Chinese, and Mexicans. A gunman named Buckskin Frank Leslie was probably the most famous. Photographs survive of them all.

It is a popular myth that no one ever escaped from the prison; in fact, at least 26 fled the walls and were never recaptured. The largest single jailbreak occurred in October 1877, when seven Mexican prisoners captured the superintendent, Thomas Gates, and walked him through the sally port. It ended with four dead prisoners, and Superintendent Gates stabbed so many times that although he survived, he soon retired.

The prison closed due to overcrowding on September 15, 1909. Thereafter, Yuma High School sometimes conducted classes inside the old prison. The Veterans of Foreign Wars frequently met there. The superintendent's home briefly became a hospital. Gene Autry, John Wayne, and other actors made films there during the 1930s and 1940s.

See also: LESLIE, NASHVILLE FRANKLIN

Bibliography

Adams, Ramon F. *A Fitting Death for Billy the Kid.* Norman: University of Oklahoma Press, 1960.

———. *Six-Guns and Saddle Leather.* Norman: University of Oklahoma Press, 1954.

Adams, Verdon R. *Tom White: The Life of a Lawman.* El Paso: Texas Western Press, 1972.

Alexander, Bob. *Dangerous Dan Tucker: New Mexico's Deadly Lawman.* Silver City, N.M.: High Lonesome Books, 2001.

Anaya, Paco. *I Buried Billy.* College Station: Tex.: Early West, 1991.

Anderson, John Q., ed. *Tales of Frontier Texas (1830–1860).* Dallas: Southern Methodist University Press, 1966.

Askins, Col. Charles. *Texans, Guns & History.* New York: Winchester Press, 1970.

Bailey, Lynn R. *A Tenderfoot in Tombstone: The Private Journal of George Whitwell Parsons: The Turbulent Years: 1880–82.* Tucson, Ariz.: Westernlore Press, 1996.

———. *The Devil Has Foreclosed: The Private Journal of George Whitwell Parsons: 1882–87.* Tucson, Ariz.: Westernlore Press, 1997.

Ball, Larry D. *Desert Lawmen: The High Sheriffs of New Mexico and Arizona.* Albuquerque: University of New Mexico Press, 1992.

———. *Elfego Baca in Life and Legend.* El Paso: Texas Western Press, 1992.

———. *The United States Marshals of New Mexico and Arizona Territories, 1846–1912.* Albuquerque: University of New Mexico Press, 1978.

Bartholomew, Ed. *Black Jack Ketchum: Last of the Holdup Kings.* Houston, Tex.: Frontier Press, 1955.

———. *Kill or Be Killed.* Houston, Tex.: Frontier Press, 1953.

Baylor, George Wythe (edited with an introduction by Jerry D. Thompson). *Into the Far Country: True Tales of the Old Southwest.* El Paso: Texas Western Press, 1996.

Bell, Bob Boze. *Outlaws & Gunfighters of the Wild West.* Phoenix, Ariz.: Bose, 1999.

Bennett, Joseph E. *Six Guns and Masons.* Highland Springs, Va.: Anchor Communications, 1991.

Boddington, Craig, ed. *America: The Men and Their Guns That Made Her Great.* Los Angeles: Petersen Publishing, 1981.

Boessenecker, John. *Gold Dust & Gunsmoke: Tales of Gold Rush Outlaws, Gunfighters, Lawmen, and Vigilantes.* New York: Wiley, 1999.

———. *Against the Vigilantes: The Recollections of Dutch Charley Duane.* Norman: University of Oklahoma Press, 1999.

———. *Lawman: The Life and Times of Harry Morse, 1835–1912.* Norman: University of Oklahoma Press, 1998.

———. *The Grey Fox: The True Story of Bill Miner, Last of the Old Time Bandits.* Norman: University of Oklahoma Press, 1992.

———. *Badge and Buckshot: Lawlessness in Old California.* Norman: University of Oklahoma Press, 1988.

Boethel, Paul C. *Sand in Your Craw.* Austin, Tex.: Vonboeckmann-Jones, 1959.

Brant, Marley. *Outlaws: The Illustrated History of the James-Younger Gang*. Montgomery, Ala.: Elliott and Clark, 1997.

Brown, Richard Maxwell. *No Duty to Retreat: Violence and Values in American History and Society*. Norman: University of Oklahoma Press, 1994.

Bryan, Howard. *Incredible Elfego Baca: Good Man, Bad Man of the Old West*. Santa Fe, N.M.: Clear Light, 1993.

———. *Wildest of the Wild West: True Tales of a Frontier Town on the Santa Fe Trail*. Santa Fe, N.M.: Clear Light, 1988.

Bullis, Don. *New Mexico's Finest: Police Officers Killed in the Line of Duty, 1847–1999*. Santa Fe: New Mexico Department of Public Safety, 2000.

Burows, Jack. *John Ringo: The Gunfighter Who Never Was*. Tucson: University of Arizona Press, 1987.

Burrows, William E. *Vigilante!* New York: Harcourt, Brace, Jovanovich, 1976.

Calhoun, Frederick S. *The Lawmen: United States Marshals and Their Deputies, 1789– 1989*. Washington, D.C.: Smithsonian Institution Press, 2000.

Carmony, Neil, ed. *Whiskey, Six-Guns and Red Light Ladies: George Hand's Saloon Diary, Tucson, 1875–1878*. Silver City, N.M.: High Lonesome Books, 1994.

Carranco, Lynwood, and Estle Beard. *Genocide and Vendetta: The Round Valley Wars of Northern California*. Norman: University of Oklahoma Press, 1981.

Chrisman, Harry E. *The Ladder of Rivers: The Story of I.P. (Print) Olive*. Denver: Sage Books, 1962.

Cline, Don. *Antrim & Billy*. College Station, Tex.: Creative, 1990.

Coe, George. *Frontier Fighter*. Albuquerque: University of New Mexico Press, 1934.

Cox, Mike. *Texas Ranger Tales*. Plano, Tex.: Republic of Texas Press, 1997.

Cox, William R. *Luke Short and His Era: A Biography of One of the Old West's Most Famous Gamblers*. New York: Doubleday, 1961.

Cramer, T. Dudley. *The Pecos Ranchers in the Lincoln County War*. Orinda, Calif.: Branding Iron Press, 1996.

Crutchfield, James A., Bill O'Neal, and Dale L. Walker. *Legends of the Wild West*. Lincolnwood, Ill.: Publications International, 1995.

Cunningham, Eugene. *Triggernometry: A Gallery of Gunfighters*. New York: Press of the Pioneers, 1934.

Davis, John L. *The Texas Rangers: Their First 150 Years*. San Antonio, Tex.: Institute of Texan Cultures, 1975.

DeArment, Robert K. *George Scarborough: The Life and Death of a Lawman on the Closing Frontier*. Norman: University of Oklahoma Press, 1992.

———. *Knights of the Green Cloth: The Saga of the Frontier Gamblers*. Norman: University of Oklahoma Press, 1982.

———. *Bat Masterson: The Man and the Legend*. Norman: University of Oklahoma Press, 1979.

DeMattos, Jack. *The Earp Decision*. College Station, Tex.: Creative, 1989.

———. *Masterson and Roosevelt*. College Station, Tex.: Creative, 1984.

Douglas, C. L. *Famous Texas Feuds*. Austin, Tex.: State House Press, 1988.

Drago, Harry Sinclair. *The Legend Makers: Tales of the Old-Time Peace Officers and Desperadoes of the Frontier*. New York: Dodd, Mead, 1975.

———. *Road Agents and Train Robbers: Half a Century of Western Banditry*. New York: Dodd, Mead, 1973.

Dugan, Mark. *Bandit Years: A Gathering of Wolves*. Santa Fe, N.M.: Sunstone Press, 1987.

Dykes, Jeff C. *Law on a Wild Frontier: Four Sheriffs of Lincoln County*. Washington, D.C.: Potomac Corral of the Westerners, 1969.

Earle, James H. *The Capture of Billy the Kid*. College Station, Tex.: Creative, 1988.

Edwards, Harold L. *Goodbye to Billy the Kid*. College Station, Tex.: Early West, 1995.

Egloff, Fred R. *El Paso Lawman: G.W. Campbell*. College Station, Tex.: Creative, 1982.

Emmett, Chris. *Shanghai Pierce: A Fair Likeness*. Norman: University of Oklahoma Press, 1953.

Ernst, Donna B. *Sundance: My Uncle*. College Station, Tex.: Creative, 1992.

Erwin, Richard E. *The Truth about Wyatt Earp*. Carpinteria, Calif.: O.K. Press, 1992.

Etulain, Richard W. and Glenda Riley, eds. *With Badges & Bullets: Lawmen & Outlaws in the Old West*. Golden, Colo.: Fulcrum Press, 1999.

Faulk, Odie B. *Tombstone: Myth and Reality*. New York: Oxford University Press, 1972.

Fisher, O.C., and J.C. Dykes. *King Fisher: His Life and Times*. Norman: University of Oklahoma Press, 1966.

Flanagan, Mike. *The Old West: Day by Day.* New York: Facts On File, 1995.

Freeman, G. D. *Midnight and Noonday: Or the Incidental History of Southern Kansas and the Indian Territory, 1871–1890.* Norman: University of Oklahoma Press, 1984.

Fulton, Maurice Garland. *History of the Lincoln County War.* Tucson: University of Arizona Press, 1968.

Garrett, Pat F. *The Authentic Life of Billy, the Kid* (an annotated edition with notes and commentary by Frederick Nolan). Norman: University of Oklahoma Press, 2000.

Gatto, Steve. *The Real Wyatt Earp: A Documentary Biography.* Silver City, N.M.: High Lonesome Books, 2000.

Gibson, A. M. *The Life and Death of Colonel Albert Jennings Fountain.* Norman: University of Oklahoma Press, 1986.

Gillett, James B. *Fugitives from Justice: The Notebook of Texas Ranger James B. Gillett.* (introduction by Michael D. Morrison). Austin, Tex.: State House Press, 1997.

———. *Six Years with the Texas Rangers: 1875 to 1881.* Chicago: R. R. Donnelly and Sons, 1943.

Gilliland, Maude T., comp. *Wilson County Texas Rangers: 1837–1977.* N. P.: privately published, 1977.

Gober, James R., and B. Byron Price, eds. *Cowboy Justice: Tale of a Texas Lawman.* Lubbock: Texas Tech University Press, 1997.

Greer, James Kimmins. *Texas Ranger: Jack Hays in the Frontier Southwest.* College Station: Texas A&M University Press, 1993.

Gulick, Bill. *Outlaws of the Pacific Northwest.* Caldwell, Idaho: Caxton Press, 2000.

Haley, J. Evetts. *Jeff Milton: A Good Man with a Gun.* Norman: University of Oklahoma Press, 1948.

Hardin, John Wesley. *The Life of John Wesley Hardin as Written by Himself.* Norman: University of Oklahoma Press, 1961.

Harkey, Dee. *Mean as Hell.* Albuquerque: University of New Mexico Press, 1948.

Harrison, Fred. *Hell Holes and Hangings.* Claredon, Tex.: Claredon Press: 1968.

Harvey, Clara Toombs. *Not So Wild: The Old West.* Denver: Golden Bell Press, 1961.

Hatley, Allen G. *Texas Constables: A Frontier Heritage.* Lubbock: Texas Tech University Press, 1999.

Henderson, Harry McCorry. *Colonel Jack Hays: Texas Ranger.* San Antonio, Tex.: Naylor, 1954.

Hertzog, Peter. *A Directory of New Mexico Desperados.* Santa Fe, N. M.: Press of the Territorian, 1965.

Hickey, Michael M. *The Death of Warren Baxter Earp: A Closer Look.* Honolulu: Talei, 2000.

Hollon, E. Eugene. *Frontier Violence: Another Look.* New York: Oxford University Press, 1974.

Horan, James D., and Paul Sann. *Pictorial History of the Wild West.* New York: Crown, 1954.

Hornung, Chuck. *The Thin Gray Line: The New Mexico Mounted Police.* Fort Worth, Tex.: Western Heritage Press, 1971.

Jacobsen, Joel. *Such Men as Billy the Kid: The Lincoln County War Reconsidered.* Lincoln: University of Nebraska Press, 1994.

James, Bill C. *Buck Chadborn: Border Lawman.* Wolfe City, Tex.: Henington, 1995.

———. *Sheriff A. J. Royal.* N.P.: Privately published, 1984.

———. *Jim Miller: The Untold Story of a Texas Lawman.* Carrollton, Tex.: Privately published, 1982.

Jenkins, John H., and H. Gordon Frost. *I'm Frank Hamer: The Life of a Texas Police Officer.* Austin, Tex.: Pemberton Press, 1968.

Jensen, Ann. *Texas Ranger Diary & Scrapbook.* Dallas: Kaleidograph Press, 1936.

Johnson, David. *John Ringo.* Stillwater, Okla.: Barbed Wire Press, 1996.

Jordan, Philip D. *Frontier Law and Order.* Lincoln: University of Nebraska Press, 1970.

Keating, Bern. *The Flamboyant Mr. Colt and His Deadly Six-Shooter.* New York: Doubleday, 1978.

Keith, Elmer. *Sixguns by Keith.* New York: Bonanza Books, n.d.

Keleher, William A. *Violence in Lincoln County: 1869–1881.* Albuquerque: University of New Mexico Press, 1957.

Kilgore, D. E. *A Ranger Legacy: 150 Years of Service of Texas.* Austin, Tex.: Madrona Press, 1973.

Klasner, Lily. *My Girlhood among Outlaws.* Tucson: University of Arizona Press, 1972.

Leibson, Art. *Sam Dreben: The Fighting Jew.* Tucson, Ariz.: Westernlore Press, 1996.

McCright, Grady E. *Jesse Evans: Lincoln County Badman.* College Station, Tex.: Early West, 1983.

McKanna, Clare V. *Homicide, Race, and Justice in the American West, 1880–1920.* Tucson: University of Arizona Press, 1997.

McGivern, Ed. *Book of Fast and Fancy Revolver Shooting.* Chicago: Follett, 1975.

McGrath, Roger D. *Gunfighters, Highwaymen & Vigilantes.* Berkeley: University of California Press, 1984.

Marohn, Richard C. *The Last Gunfighter: John Wesley Hardin.* College Station, Tex.: Creative, 1995.

Martin, Cy. *Whiskey and Wild Women: An Amusing Account of the Saloons and Bawds of the Old West.* New York: Hart, 1974.

Martin, Douglas D. *Tombstone Epitaph.* Albuquerque: University of New Mexico Press, 1951.

Martin, Jack. *Border Boss: Captain John R. Hughes—Texas Ranger.* San Antonio, Tex.: Naylor, 1952.

Metz, Leon C. *John Wesley Hardin: Dark Angel of Texas.* El Paso; Tex.: Mangan Books, 1996.

———. *Dallas Stoudenmire: El Paso Marshal.* Norman: University of Oklahoma Press, 1993.

———. *John Selman: Gunfighter.* Norman: University of Oklahoma Press, 1992.

———. *Pat Garrett: The Story of a Western Lawman.* Norman: University of Oklahoma Press, 1974.

Miller, Joseph, ed. *The Arizona Rangers.* New York: Hastings House, 1972.

Miller, Nyle H. and Joseph W. Snell. *Great Gunfighters of the Kansas Cowtowns, 1867–1886.* Lincoln: University of Nebraska Press, 1963.

Miller, Rick. *Sam Bass & Gang.* Austin, Tex.: State House Press, 1999.

———. *Bloody Bill Longley.* Wolfe City, Tex.: Henington, 1996.

Nolan, Frederick. *The West of Billy the Kid.* Norman: University of Oklahoma Press, 1998.

———. *The Lincoln County War: A Documentary History.* Norman: University of Oklahoma Press, 1992.

Oden, Alonzo. *Texas Ranger Diary and Scrap Book.* Edited by Ann Jensen. Dallas: Kaleidograph Press, 1936.

O'Neal, Bill. *Clay Allison: Portrait of a Shootist.* Seagraves, Tex.: Pioneer Book, 1983.

———. *Henry Brown: The Outlaw Marshal.* College Station, Tex.: Early Press, 1980.

———. *Encyclopedia of Western Gunfighters.* Norman: University of Oklahoma Press, 1979.

O'Neil, James B. *They Die but Once: The Story of a Tejano.* New York: Knight, 1935.

Owen, Gordon R. *Two Alberts: Fountain and Fall.* Las Cruces, N.M.: Yucca Tree Press, 1996.

Paine, Albert Bigelow. *Captain Bill McDonald: Texas Ranger.* New York: J. J. Little and Ives, 1909.

Parsons, Chuck. *Bowen and Hardin.* College Station, Tex.: Creative Publishing, 1991.

———. *Captain C. B. McKinney: Law in South Texas.* Wolfe City, Tex.: Henington Publishing, 1993.

———. *The Capture of John Wesley Hardin.* College Station, Tex.: Creative Publishing, 1978.

———. *James Madison Brown: Texas Sheriff, Texas Turfman.* Wolfe City, Tex.: Henington Publishing, 1993.

———. *Phil Coe: Texas Gambler.* Wolfe City, Tex.: Henington Publishing, 1984.

———. *Pidge: A Texas Ranger from Virginia.* Wolfe City, Tex.: Henington Publishing, 1985.

Parsons, Chuck, and Marianne E. Hall Little. *Captain L. H. McNelly, Texas Ranger: The Life and Times of a Fighting Man.* Austin, Tex.: State House Press, 2001.

Patterson, Richard. *Butch Cassidy: A Biography.* Norman: University of Nebraska Press, 1998.

———. *Historical Atlas of the Old West.* Boulder, Colo.: Johnson Books, 1985.

———. *Historical Atlas of the Outlaw West.* Boulder, Colo.: Johnson Books, 1985.

Peters, James Stephen. *Mace Bowman: Texas Feudist, Western Lawman.* Yorktown, Tex.: Hartmann Heritage, 1996.

Pierce, Dale. *West Coast Characters.* Phoenix, Ariz.: Golden West, 1991.

Prassel, Frank Richard. *The Western Peace Officer: A Legacy of Law and Order.* Norman: University of Oklahoma Press, 1972.

Preece, Harold. *Lone Star Man: Ira Aten, Last of the Old Texas Rangers.* New York: Hastings House, 1960.

Price, Paxton P. *Pioneers of the Mesilla Valley, 1823–1912.* Las Cruces, N.M.: Yucca Tree Press, 1995.

Rash, Philip J. *Desperados of Arizona Territory.* Laramie, Wyo.: NOLA, 1999.

———. *Gunsmoke in Lincoln County.* Laramie, Wyo.: NOLA, 1997.

———. *Trailing Billy the Kid.* NOLA, 1995.

Rattenbury, Richard C. *Packing Iron: Gunleather of the Frontier West.* Millwood, N.Y.: Zon International, 1993.

Raymond, Dora Neill. *Captain Lee Hall of Texas.* Norman: University of Oklahoma Press, 1940.

Reese, John Walter. *Flaming Feuds of Colorado County.* Salado, Tex.: Anson Jones Press, 1962.

Rickards, Colin. *Mysterious Dave Mather.* Santa Fe, N.M.: Press of the Territorian, 1968.

———. *Bowler Hats and Stetsons.* London: Ronald Whiting and Wheaton, 1966.

Robinson, Charles M. *The Men Who Wore the Star: The Story of the Texas Rangers.* New York: Random House, 2000.

Rosa, Joseph G. *Jack McCall, Assassin: An Updated Account of His Yankton Trial, Plea for Mercy, and Execution.* Great Britain: English Westerners Society, 1999.

———. *Wild Bill Hickok: The Man and His Myth.* Norman: University of Oklahoma Press, 1996.

———. *Age of the Gunfighter: Men and Weapons on the Frontier 1840–1900.* Norman: University of Oklahoma Press, 1993.

———. *The Gunfighter: Man or Myth?* Norman: University of Oklahoma Press, 1969.

Rosa, Joseph G., and Robin May. *Gun Law: A Study of Violence in the Old West.* Chicago: Contemporary Books, 1977.

Rose, Cynthia. *Lottie Deno: Gambling Queen of Hearts.* Santa Fe, N.M.: Clear Light, 1994.

Rynning, Thomas H. (As told to Al Cohn and Joe Chisholm). *Gun Notches.* New York: Frederick A. Stokes, 1931.

Samora, Julian, Joe Bernal, and Albert Pena. *Gunpowder Justice: A Reassessment of the Texas Rangers.* Notre Dame, Ind.: University of Notre Dame, 1979.

Samuelson, Nancy B. *Shoot from the Lip: Legends and Lies of the Three Guardsmen of Oklahoma, and U.S. Marshal Nix.* Dexter, Mich.: Thompson Shore, 1998.

———. *The Dalton Gang Story: Lawmen to Outlaws.* Dexter, Mich.: Thompson Shore, 1992.

Schmitt, Jo Ann. *Fighting Editors.* San Antonio, Tex.: Nayor, 1958.

Schoenberger, Dale T. *The Gunfighters.* Caldwell, Idaho: Caxton, 1971.

Secrest, William B. *Lawmen & Desperados: A Compendium of Noted, Early California Peace Officers, Badmen and Outlaws: 1850–1900.* Spokane, Wash.: Arthur H. Clark, 1994.

Selcer, Richard F. *Hell's Half Acre.* Fort Worth: Texas Christian University Press, 1991.

Serven, James E., ed. *The Collecting of Guns.* New York: Bonanza Books, Crown, n.d.

Shirley, Glenn. *Guardian of the Law: The Life and Times of William Matthew Tilgeman.* Austin, Tex.: Eakin Press, 1988.

———. *West of Hell's Fringe: Crime, Criminals, and the Federal Peace Officer in Oklahoma Territory, 1889–1907.* Norman: University of Oklahoma Press, 1978.

———. *Shotgun for Hire.* Norman: University of Oklahoma Press, 1970.

Shirley, Glenn, ed. *The Life of Texas Jack: Eight Years a Criminal: 41 Years Trusting in God.* Quanah, Tex.: Nortex Press, 1973.

Simmons, Marc. *When Six-Guns Ruled: Outlaw Tales of the Southwest.* Santa Fe, N.M.: Ancient City Press, 1990.

———. *Ranchers, Ramblers and Renegades: True Tales of Territorial New Mexico.* Santa Fe, N.M.: Ancient City Press, 1984.

———. *Six-Gun and Silver Star.* Albuquerque: University of New Mexico Press, 1955.

Sims, Judge Orland L. *Gun Toters I Have Known.* Austin, Tex.: Encino Press, 1967.

Sinise, Jerry. *George Washington Arrington: Civil War Spy, Texas Ranger, Sheriff and Rancher.* Burnet, Tex.: Eakin Press, 1979.

———. *Pink Higgins: The Reluctant Gunfighter.* Quanah, Tex.: Nortex Press, 1973.

Sitton, Thad. *The Texas Sheriff: Lord of the County Line.* Norman: University of Oklahoma Press, 2000.

Skiles, Jack. *Judge Roy Bean Country.* Lubbock: Texas Tech University Press, 1996.

Sonnichsen, C. L. *Pass of the North.* El Paso: Texas Western Press, 1968.

———. *Tularosa: Last of the Frontier West.* New York: Devin-Adair, 1963.

———. *I'll Die Before I'll Run: The Story of the Great Texas Feuds.* New York: Devin-Adair, 1962.

———. *Ten Texas Feuds.* Albuquerque: University of New Mexico Press, 1957.

———. *Billy King's Tombstone: The Private Life of an Arizona Boom Town.* Caldwell, Idaho: Caxton, 1942.

Stamps, Roy, and Jo Ann Stamps, trans. and comps. *The Letters of John Wesley Hardin.* Austin, Tex.: Eakin Press, 2001.

Steele, Phillip W. *Outlaws and Gunfighters of the Old West.* Springdale, Ark.: Heritage, 1991.

———. *Jesse and Frank James: The Family History.* Gretna, La.: Pelican, 1887.

Stephens, Robert W. *Mannen Clements: Texas Gunfighter.* N.P.: Privately Published, 1996.

———. *Texas Rangers: Indian War Pensions.* Quanah, Tex.: Nortex Press, 1975.

———. *Texas Ranger Sketches.* Dallas: Privately Published, 1972.

———. *Walter Durbin: Texas Ranger and Sheriff.* Claredon, Tex.: Claredon Press, 1970.

———. *Lone Wolf: The Story of Texas Ranger Captain M.T. Gonzaullas.* Dallas: Taylor, n.d.

Sterling, William Warren. *Trails and Trials of a Texas Ranger.* Norman: University of Oklahoma Press, 1959.

Sutton, Robert C. *The Sutton-Taylor Feud.* Quanah, Tex.: Nortex Press, 1974.

Tanner, Karen Holliday. *Doc Holliday: A Family Portrait.* Norman: University of Oklahoma Press, 1998.

Tefertiller, Casey. *Wyatt Earp: The Life behind the Legend.* New York: Wiley, 1997.

Tise, Sammy. *Texas County Sheriffs.* Albuquerque, N.M.: Oakwood, 1989.

Toepperwein, Herman. *Showdown: Western Gunfighters in Moments of Truth.* Austin, Tex.: Madrona Press, 1974.

Trachtman, Paul. *The Gunfighters.* Alexandria, Va.: Time-Life Books, 1974.

Trafzer, Cliff, and Steve George. *Prison Centennial, 1876–1976.* Yuma, Ariz.: Rio Colorado Press, 1976.

Traywick, Ben. *That Wicked Little Gringo: The Story of John Slaughter.* Tombstone, Ariz.: Red Marie's Bookstore, 2001.

———. *Wyatt Earp's Thirteen Dead Men.* Tombstone, Ariz.: Red Marie's Bookstore, 1998.

———. *Frail Prisoners in Yuma Territorial Prison.* Tombstone, Ariz.: Red Marie's Bookstore, 1997.

———. *The Clantons of Tombstone.* Tombstone, Ariz.: Red Marie's Bookstore, 1996.

———. *John Henry: The Doc Holliday Story.* Tombstone, Ariz.: Red Marie's Bookstore, 1996.

———. *Historical Documents and Photographs of Tombstone.* Tombstone, Ariz.: Red Marie's Bookstore, 1994.

———. *The Chronicles of Tombstone.* Tombstone, Ariz.: Red Marie's Bookstore, 1990.

———. *John Peters Ringo: Mythical Gunfighter.* Tombstone, Ariz.: Red Marie's Bookstore, 1987.

———. *Marshal of Tombstone: Virgil Walter Earp.* Tombstone, Ariz.: Red Marie's Book Store, 1985.

———. *John Henry Holliday: Tombstone's Deadliest Gun.* Tombstone, Ariz.: Red Marie's Bookstore, 1984.

———. *A Town Called Tombstone.* Tombstone, Ariz.: Red Marie's Bookstore, 1982.

Turner, Alford E., ed. *The O.K. Corral Inquest.* College Station, Tex.: Early West, 1981.

Tuska, Jon. *Billy the Kid: A Bio-Bibliography.* Westport, Conn.: Greenwood Press, 1983.

Utley, Robert M. *Lone Star Justice: The First Century of the Texas Rangers.* Oxford: Oxford University Press, 2002.

———. *High Noon in Lincoln: Violence on the Western Frontier.* Albuquerque: University of New Mexico Press, 1987.

———. *Four Fighters in Lincoln County.* Albuquerque: University of New Mexico Press, 1986.

Virgines, George E. *Western Legends and Lore.* Wauwatosa, Wis.: Leather Stocking Books, 1984.

Walker, Donald R. *Penology for Profit: A History of the Texas Prison System, 1867–1912.* College Station: Texas A&M University Press, 1988.

Walton, M. W. *Life and Adventures of Ben Thompson.* Austin, Tex.: Steck, 1956.

Waters, Frank. *The Earp Brothers of Tombstone: The Story of Mrs. Virgil Earp.* Lincoln: University of Nebraska Press, 1960.

Watts, Peter. *A Dictionary of the Old West.* New York: Knopf, 1977.

Webb, Walter Prescott. *The Texas Rangers: A Century of Frontier Defense.* New York: Houghton Mifflin, 1935.

Weddle, Jerry. *Antrim Is My Stepfather's Name: The Boyhood of Billy the Kid.* Tucson: Arizona Historical Society, 1993.

Wellman, Paul I. *A Dynasty of Western Outlaws.* New York: Doubleday, 1961.

White, Owen. *Lead and Likker.* New York: Minton, Balch, 1932.

Wilson, John P. *Merchants, Guns & Money: The Story of Lincoln County and Its Wars.* Albuquerque: Museum of New Mexico Press, 1987.

Addendum

Readers seeking further information regarding western violence are advised that practically every western state, county, and community has historical societies, most of them scholarly, groups that publish information on a regularly scheduled basis about events and personalities relating to their regions' or states' historical past.

At least two national monthly magazines, sold on newsstands as well as by subscription, are *Western Publications,* out of Cave Creek, Arizona; and *Wild West Magazine,* operating out of Leesburg, Virginia. Both magazines, while not scholarly, publish some of the best in diverse western history.

Numerous Westerner International organizations (called "Westerner Corrals") also exist around the country. Several publish exceptional historical journals on a regular basis. Examples are the Chicago, Denver, and Los Angeles corrals.

Finally, there are two national associations that regularly publish scholarly "gunfighter" material. They are NOLA (National Association of Outlaws and Lawmen) and WOLA (World Association of Outlaws and Lawmen.) Both are based in the United States, and membership is encouraged.

Index

Boldface page numbers denote major treatment of a topic. Those in *italics* denote illustrations.

A

Abilene x, **1**, 41, 48, 117, 187, 208, 227, 245
abolitionists 90
Abraham, David **1–2**
Acme Saloon 109, 177, 218
Adams, Arch 56
Adams, J. H. 58
Adams, Jerome 214
Adamson, Carl 94
Adobe Saloon 194
Agnew, Pat 126, 192
Ah Bang 179
Ah Foy 83
Alamo Saloon 1, 117
Alberding, Sophie 198
alcalde 2
Alcatraz 8
Allen, Billy 120
Allen, Hugh 101
Allen, James **2**
Allen, Joe *161*
Allen, Tom 32
Allison, Bill 67
Allison, John 4
Allison, Martha 5
Allison, Robert A. **3–4**. *See also* Allison, Robert Clay
Allison, Robert Clay xi, 3–4, 54–55
Allison, William Davis "Dave" **4–5**, 98, 157
Alonzo, Harry. *See* Longabaugh, Harry; Sundance Kid
Alvarez, Francisco 62
Alverson, Leonard 10
Alvord, Albert Wright "Burt" **5–6**, 214
Alvord/Stiles gang 69
American Railway Express Company 260
Amityville Sanitarium 56
Anadarko Indians 106

Anderson, Billy 34
Anderson, David L. **265**
Anderson, George. *See* Miner, William "Bill"
Anderson, Hugh 103
Anderson, Josephine 6
Anderson, Karl 218
Anderson, William C. "Bloody Bill" **6**, 132, 172, 200
Anderson, William W. "Plug Hat" 192
Angel, Frank Warner **6–7**, 193
Angel, Paula 7
Angus, Red 135
Antrim, Catherine 21, 22
Antrim, Henry **21–24**. *See also* Billy the Kid
Antrim, Joseph "Joe" 22
Antrim, Kid **21–24**. *See also* Billy the Kid
Antrim, William Henry Harrison 7, 21, 22
Apache. *See also* Mescalero
    at Fort Sumner 86
    Free and 88–89
    Horn on 121
    on Horrell 123
    Hunt and 128
    Kinney on 144
    Lincoln County War and 154
    on McComas family 179
    McDaniels and 163
    Perry and 194
    Rynning on 210
    on Shibell 221
    Texas Rangers and 18, 95, 99, 136, 180, 225, 243, 250, 266
    Whitehill on 263
    Worthington with 99, 266
    Young and 269
Apache Kid **7–8**, 120, 121, 206
Apodaca, Maximo 48
Applegate, Bill 111
Arcade Saloon 29
Arizona Home for the Insane 237
Arizona National Guard 148

Arizona Pioneers Home 123
Arizona Rangers 4–5, **8–9**, 141, 148, 176, 181, 210, 215, 260–261
Arizona Sentinel 112, 176
Arizona Territorial Prison 20, 26, 83, 112, 176, 197, 215. *See also* Yuma Territorial Prison
Arkansas Jack. *See* Greathouse, James "Whiskey Jim"
Arkansas Tom 102, 168
Armijo, Geronimo 12
Armstrong, John. *See* Yarberry, Milton J.
Armstrong, John Barclay **9**, 243
Army, U.S.
    Baker on 14
    Baylor in 17
    Coghlan in 48
    Colt .45 used by 193
    Diehl and 202
    Hays and 113
    Hickok in 115
    Horn in 121
    King in 168
    Kinney in 143–144
    on Lee-Peacock feud 151, 152
    Leslie in 153
    Longley in 159
    Madsen in 165
    on McNelly 165
    Meade on 171
    Miner in 174
    O'Neill in 188
    Peel in 32
    on Quantrill 200
    Rynning in 210
    Selman in 216
    Selman Jr. in 218
    Short and 222
    St. Leon in 233
    Texas Rangers in 242, 250, 266
    Wheeler in 261
Arnett, George 261
Arnett, William B. 32, 230
Arnold, Mace 238

Arrington, George Washington "Cap" **9–10**, 215, 242
Askew, Joe 87
Atchison, Topeka & Santa Fe Railroad 64, 102, 150, 169
Aten, Ira **10**, 125
Atkins, David "Dave" **10–11**
Atkinson, John 77
Atlanta Penitentiary 141
Atlantic & Pacific Railroad 192, 257
Austin, Charles 119
Austin, Stephen F. 215, 241
Austin Statesman 147
Authentic Life of Billy the Kid..., The (Garrett) 93
Avant, Jessie Lefettie "Fate" 182
Averill, James 259
Axtell, Samuel B. 4, 156
Aztec Land and Cattle Company 196. *See also* Hash Knife Ranch

B

Baca, Abram **12**
Baca, Antonio 12
Baca, Cipriano 182
Baca, Elfego **12–13**
Baca, Enofrio 12, 95
Baca, Saturnino **13–14**, 216
Baca brothers 95
Bacon, Henry 112
badlands, badlander **14**, 62
Badlands National Park 14
badman **14**
bad medicine **14**
Bailey, William 102–103
Baker, Cullen Montgomery **14**, 159
Baker, Frank 22, 155, 176
Baker, Sam 126
Baker, Theodore 15
Bald Knobbers **15–16**
Baldoc, John 151
Baldwin, Lucius 60
Banks (cattle thief) 187
Barber, John Tolliver 201
Barefoot, Clem 203
Barela, Manuel 107
Barela, Ysabel 144
Barker, Kid 105
Barnes, John (rancher) 89, 110
Barnes, Johnny (outlaw) 101
Barnes, Seaborn 17, 110, 258
Barnett, Frisky 32
Barnett, J. Graham "Bush" **16**
Barnum, P. T. 85

Barrelhouse Saloon 261
Barrett, Thomas 90, 91
Barron, Dan 55
Barrymore, Maurice 56
Bascom, Fred 220
Bass, Lon 194
Bass, Sam xii, 9, 10, 14, **16–17**, 100, 110, 136, 180, 215, 242, 254, 258, 259, 265
Bassett, Bud 148
Bassett, Charles E. "Charlie" 65, 223
Bates, Eolin 194
Baylor, George Wythe **17–18**, 26, 135, 136, 180, 242, 243
Baylor, Helen 95
Baylor, John Robert 18, 77, 95
Baylor, John Walker 17
Baylor, William 102–103
Baylor University 17
Beal, John 182
Beard, E. T. "Red" 160
Beard, Mose 207
Beaver, Oscar 229
Beck, H. "Ole" 142
Beckham, Joe 156
Beckwith, Bob 156
Beehan, John xi
Behan, Albert Price 19
Behan, John Harris "Johnny" **18–20**, 29, 72, 83, 103, 104, 113, 114, 123, 153, 164, 180, 219
Bell, James W. **20–21**, 24, 186
Bell, Tom 118
Belle Fourche robbery 40, 158, 185
Bencomo, Atanacio 250
Bender, John **21**
Bender, John Jr. 21
Bender, Kate 21
Ben Dowell's Saloon 86, 99
Bennett, C. 2
Bennett, H. A. 194
Bennett, Mary 160
Bentley, Lee 260–261
Bernstein, Morris 216
Berry, George A. 70
Berry, James (merchant) 15, 16
Berry, Jim (outlaw) 16, 17
Beslinga, Donanciano 89
"Big Fight, the" **239–240**
"Big Nose" Kate **122–123**
Big Tree 122
Billy Owen's Saloon 72

Billy the Kid ix, x, xii, **21–24**
   as badman 14, 48, 63, 125
   Bowdre and 27
   on Brady 144
   Brown and 30
   capture of 20
   Chapman and 43
   in El Paso Salt War 144
   Evans and 79
   at Fort Sumner 85
   Garrett on xi, 54, 75, 78–79, 86, 92, 93, 198
   as gunfighter 81, 105, 201, 224
   Leyba and 154
   Lincoln County War and 155, 156, 170
   Moore on 74
   on Morton 176
   mother of 201
   on Olinger 186
   Pickett and 195
   Rudabaugh and 209
   stepfather of 7
   Whitehill on 262, 263
   Wilson and 265
Bingham, George 80
Birchfield, Walter 157
Bisbee Deportations 262
Bisbee Massacre **25**, 251
Bisbee stage robbery 72, 153
Bishop, Tom 183
bite the dust **25**
Black, Douglas 227
Black, Samuel 34
Black Bart **25–26**, 127
Black Book, the **202**
Blackfoot Reservation 157
Black Hills gold rush 183
Black Jack Ketchum gang 39, **139**, 141, 149
Blair, James K. 214
Blair, John **25**
Blair, Louis 253
Blake, "Tulsa Jack" 101, 102
Bland, Billy 55, 147
Blaylock, Celia Ann "Mattie" **25**, 71, 72
Blazer's Mill, gunfight at 30, 155
Blevins, Andy 196, 197
Blevins, Charles 197
Blevins, Hamilton 197
Blevins, Mark 196, 197, 208
Blount, Jack 171

Blue Duck 232
Blue Mountain Gang 162
Bobbitt, Gus 173
Bode, Frederick 70, 73
Boer War 11
Boessenecker, John 212
Boise Federal Penitentiary 97
Boles, Charles E. **25–26**, 127
Bolton, Martha 84
Bonaface, Nita 264
Bonaface, "Old Mike" 264
Bond, Jim "Jack" **26**, 251
Bonney, William H. **21–24**, 92. *See also* Billy the Kid
Book, the (The Ranger's Bible) **202**
Boomers 44
Boot, Joe **26**, 111, 112
Boot Hill **26–27**, 104, 116–117, 249
Borajo (priest) 88
Border Boss **125–126**
border draw **27**
border roll **208**
border shift **27**
Boren, Bill 151–152
Boren, Henry 151, 152
Boren, Isham 152
Born, Dutch Henry 124
Borrajo, Antonio 76
Bosque Gang 126
Boss Saloon 189
Bostwick, Joseph 261
Boucher, Arthur **101**
bounty hunter **27**
Bourke, John P. 19
Bousman, Louis "The Animal" 75, 78, 240
Bowdre, Charles "Charlie" 23–24, **27**, 75, 79, 86, 93, 155
Bowdre, Manuela 75
Bowe, Thomas "Tom" **27–28**
Bowen, Bill 124
Bowen, Jane 109
Bowen, Tom 54
Bowman, Mason T. "Mace" 3
Boxer Rebellion 20
Boyce, Rube 67
braceros 33
Bradley, Benjamin 108
Bradly, John 205
Bradshaw, Mollie 153
Brady, William 13, 21, 22, 24, 30, 43, 144, 155, 170, 176
Brassell, James W. 53
Brassell, Philip 53

Brazel, Wayne 54, 94, 173
Brazelton, William "Bill" Whitney **28**, 221
Breakenridge, William M. "Uncle Billy" **28–29**, 101, 219
Breaux, Dr. 234
Brennan, Joe 245, 247
Brennan, Molly 168, 169, 247
Brennan's Saloon 176, 247
Brewer, Dick 23, 30, 155, 220
Briscoe, Joe 92
Bristol, Warren 95
Broadwell, Dick 60, 61
Brocius, William "Curly Bill" **29–30**, 53, 71, 72, 73–74, 101, 164, 202, 219, 249
Bronough, William 174
Brooks, J. A. 215
Brooks, James 214
Brooks, S. S. 30
Brooks, Travis C. 206
Brown, Bob 69
Brown, Charles 176
Brown, George 198
Brown, Harry 268
Brown, Henry Newton 30, 155, 260
Brown, Hoodoo 2, 38, 64–65, 268
Brown, James Madison **30–31**
Brown, Joe 37, 258
Brown, Maud 98
Brown, Neal 167
Brown, Neil 65
Brown, Richard Maxwell xi
Brown's Hole, Brown's Park **31**, 40, 45, 121, 149, 162, 218, 263
Bruce, A. D. 52
Brunter (suspect captured by Reeves) 205
Bryant, Charles "Black Face Charlie" **31**, 60
Bryant, Elijah S. "Lige" 39
Bryant, Sy (Ci) 114
Buckboard Days (Alberding) 198
Bucket of Blood Saloon 190, 197
bucking the tiger **81**
Buckley, William 61. *See also* Three Fingered Jack
Buffalo Bill, Wild West Show 36, 63, 117, 207
Buffalo Curly **162**
buffaloed **31–32**
Bull, John Edwin **32**
Bullion, Ed 10

Bullion, Laura 39, 141–142
Bull's Head Saloon 1, 48, 245
Burdett, James 246
Burdett, Robert Lee **33**
Burke, Clinton 36
Burke, Fred 226
Burke, William 246
Burkhardt, Henry 258
Burleson, Peter 54
Burlington Railroad 196
Burns, Edward "Big Ed" **33**, 251
Burns, James D. **33–34**, 96, 251
Burns, Tom **34**
Burns, Walter Noble ix, x
Burton, Ben **260**
Burwell, B. B. *161*
buscadero **34–35**
bushwhackers, bushwhacked 6, **35**, 134, 146
Butcher Knife Bill 87
Butler, Lieutenant 29
Butler, Polly 115
Butterfield Overland Stage Company 90
Butts, Frank 261
Byler, Jake 39
Byler, Viana 39
Bymes, Edward "Big Ed" **33**

C

Cahill, Frank "Windy" 22, 79
Cahill, Robert "Bob" 204
Calamity Jane 36, 62, 63, 117
Caldwell 41, 45
Cale, James E. 87
California Column 85–86
California Jim 107
California Rangers 160, 178
Callahan, James H. 250
Cameron, John 260
Campbell, Charles D. 268
Campbell, George 235
Campbell, William "Billy" 43, 79
Campbell & Hatch's Billiard Parlor 70, 73
Camp Cooper Ranch 147
Camp Grant Massacre 221
Camp Roberts 9
Canadian River Cattle Association 198
Cananea Consolidated Copper Company 5, 210
Cannary, Martha Jane 36, 117. *See also* Calamity Jane

Cannary, Robert 36
Cannon, A. B. "Add" **37**, 258
Canon, J. Y. 82
Canon City Penitentiary 131, 232
Cantley, Charles L. 37
Canton, Frank M. **37–38**, 96, 97, 122, 135, 182
cap-and-ball gun **38**
Capital Saloon 226
Capital Variety Theater 246
Cardenas, Manuel 4
Cardis, Louis 76, 77
Carleton, James H. 86, 220
Carlyle, James "Jim" 20, 21, 100, 209
Carnes, Herff A. **38**
Carrasco, Florencio 186
Carson, Joe **38–39**, 64, 169, 195, 268
Carson, Kit 86, 196
Carter, Harvey 126
Carver, Al 220
Carver, Dave 10
Carver, Tod 214, 215
Carver, William Richard "Will" 10, **39–40**, 41, 139, 141, 159, 251, 252, 263
Casey, Mike 154
Casey, Robert 266
Cash, Edward "Ed" **40**
Cassidy, Butch xii, 10, 39, **40–41**, 45, 63, 118, 141, 148, 149, 157, 158, 159, 162, 172, 195, 263
Cassidy, Mike 40
Castillo, Juan 62
Castillo, Julio 52
Castle Gate coal mine 172
Catfish Kid 240
Catron, Thomas B. 154, 199
"Cattle Kate" **259**
"Cattle King of the Pecos" 163
cattleman 53
cattle rustling **41**, 53, 71, 85
cattle town **41**. *See also* cow towns
Centennial Saloon 33, 34, 96, 251
Central Overland California and Pike's Peak Express Company 224, 225
Central Pacific Railroad 162, 221
Chacón, Augustino 176–177
Chadborn, Daniel Joseph "Buck" **41–42**, 207
Chadwell, William **42**, 270
Chambers, Lon 74, 75, 78

Champion, Nate 122, 135, 158
Chandler, John 101
Chapman, George 96
Chapman, Huston Ingraham 23, **42–43**, 79
chaps 83
Charlie (Indian) 70
Chase's Gambling Hall 32
Chatto 89
Chávez, Carlos 37, 47, 51, 52
Chávez, Juana 13
Chávez y Chávez, José **43**
Chelson, Tom. *See* Hill, Thomas "Tom"
Cheney, Bill 207
Cheney, John 166
Chenowth, Howard **43–44**, 141
Cherokee 44, 50, 79, 98, 126
Cherokee Bill 51, **98**, 231–232
Cherokee Strip **44**, 60, 181
Chew, Sid 209
Cheyenne 222
Chicago, Kid. *See* Sundance Kid
Chickasaw Enterprise 205
Childes, William 87
Chilton, Fred 240
Chinese immigrants 20, 94
Chisholm Trail x, 1, 41, **45**, 64, 223
Chisum, John 30, 79, 154, 163, 216
Choctaw 125, 216
Christian, Bob 121
Christian, William T. "Black Jack" **44–45**, 121, 139, 179
Christiansen, Christina 162
Christiansen, Willard Erastus 45, 162. *See also* Warner, Matt
Christman, W. S. "Jake" 237
Church Hill Battle 205
Cimarron News and Press 4
Ciudad Juarez 77, 99, 109, 145, 150, 174, 177, 178, 201, 204, 214, 218, 245, 266
Civil War
    Allison in 3
    Anderson in 172
    Antrim during 7
    Arrington during 9
    Baker in 14
    Baylor in 18
    Boles in 25
    bushwhacking during 35
    California Column in 85–86
    Clantons in 46
    Coe in 47

Coomer during 51
Courtright in 52
Dake in 58
Duffield during 68
Earp in 70
Fort Fillmore in 53
Fountain in 86
Gainesville hangings and 90
Harold in 110
Hickok during xii, 115
James brothers in 131
Jayhawkers during 134
Jones in 136
Kansas during 1
Lane in 146
lawlessness after x
Lowe in 160
Mathews in 169
McCord in 250
Miller in 172
Notch-Cutters and 183
Sanders in 211
Scull during 216
Shirley in 232
Sutton-Taylor feud during 237
Texas Rangers during 242, 250
Whitehill in 263
Younger brothers during 269
Young in 269
Claiborne, William Floyd "Billy the Kid" **45–46**, 153
Clanton, Alonzo 46
Clanton, Esther Ann 46
Clanton, John Wesley 46
Clanton, Joseph Isaac "Ike" 19, 45, 46, 47, 53, 71, 72, 73, 103–104
Clanton, Mary Elsie 46
Clanton, Newman Haynes "Old Man" **46–47**
Clanton, Phineas Fay "Phin" 46, 47, 230
Clanton, William Harrison "Billy" 46, 70, 71, 72, 73, 103–104
Clanton family 45, 71, 101, 153, 225, 230, 249
Clark, Jack 28
Clark, John 166
Clark, Tom 75
Clarke, Gaylord Judd 86
Clements, Gip 109
Clements, Mannen 77
Cleveland, George Washington 37, **47**, 51, 52, 96, 137, 150, 239
Cleveland, Grover 170, 171, 258

Clifford, Frank 74

Clifton, Dan "Dynamite Dick" 66, 101, 102

Clifton House 3

Clinton, John 215

Close and Patterson's Saloon 39

Club Saloon 159

Clum, John 104

Coast Flyer 41

Cochise 86

Cody, William Frederick. *See* Buffalo Bill, Wild West Show

Coe, Frank 23, 79

Coe, George 155, 217

Coe, Philip Houston "Phil" xii, **47–48**, 108, 117, 245

Cofelt, Matt 151

Coffeyville Bank robbery 60–61

Coghlan, Patrick **48–49**

Coke, Richard 136, 165, 166, 242, 265

Colbert, Chuck 3, 4

Coldwell, Neal 50, 265

Coleman, E. B. 45

Colfax County War 199

Coliseum Saloon 235

College of Washington and Lee 79

Collier, John 44

Collins, Ben 173

Collins, Joel 16–17

Collins, Shorty 216

Collins Gang 16–17

Colorado Penitentiary 68

Colorado & Southern Railroad 139, 251

Colt, Samuel 49, 243, 257

Colt revolver **49**, 81, 105, **180**, **193**, 224, 228, 257

Comanche 18, 49, 92, 100, 113, 124, 125, 136, 168, 206, 241, 242

Comanche Club 63

Comancheros **49**

Commercial Detective Agency 52

Comstock, Henry Griswold 146

Comstock Bandit. *See* Harris, Jack

Coney Island Saloon 94

Confederacy Conscription Act 90

Confederate army 165, 187, 200, 225, 234, 237, 245, 246, 248

Congress, U.S. 58, 192

Conklin, A. M. 12, 95

Connelly, Charles 61

Connor, Bill 215

Conscript Law 90

constable **49**

Contention City **49–50**

Cook, Anthony 168

Cook, James (desperado) 98

Cook, Jim (scout) 128

Cook, Thalis Tucker 50

Cook, William Tuttle "Bill" **50–51**, 98

Cooley, Scott 166, 207

Coolly, Joe 189

Coombs, John 245

Coomer, Daniel "Dan" **51–52**

Coomer, Jesse 51

Cooney, Dave 179

Coop, Jim 172

Cooper, Andy 196, 197

Cooper, Charles 3, 4

Cooper, Gary 81, 118

Cooper, Robert 97

Copeland, John 155, 156

Copper Queen Mine 114

Cordoba, Perfecto 252

Cornett, Brackett 201

Cougar, Charles 109

Coughlin, Patrick 52, 198

Courtright, "Longhaired Jim" 27, **52–53**, 223. *See also* Courtright, Timothy Isaiah

Courtright, Timothy Isaiah 52–53, 115, 223. *See also* Courtright, "Longhaired Jim"

Cowboy Camp Meetings 95

Cowboy Detective, The (Siringo) 196

Cowboy gang 29, **53**, 103, 207, 230, 249, 266

cowboys x–xi, **53**, 71, 239–240

cow towns 41, 45, 64, 75, 102–103, 211. *See also specific cow towns*

Cox, James W. "Captain Jim" 53, 237–238

Cox, Melissa 53

Cox, Perry 181

Cox, William Webb "W. W." **53–54**, 93, 94, 181, 220

Coyote Jack 164

Crabtree, William "Bill" **54**

Craig, Henry 85

Crane, "Slim Jim" 101

Cravens, James 205

cribs 229

Criminal Reminiscences and Detective Sketches (Pinkerton) 196

Crittenden, Thomas H. 85

Crittenden (mine owner) 264

Crocker, Dud 209

Crockett, David "Davy" **54–55**

Crompton, Zack 111

Crook, George 36, 89, 96, 121

cross draw 27

Crow, James H. 187

Cruger, William R. "Bill" **55–56**, 147

Cruz, Florentino 73, 135, 164, 256

Cudihee, Ed 219

Cullen, Ed 10, 139

Cullom, Virgil 87

Cummings, George M. 123

Cummings, Samuel M. "Doc" 234

Cummins, Nellie 56

Cunningham, F. A. 226

Cureton, Jack J. 54

Curley, Sam 153

Curly, Red **143**

curly wolf **56**

Currie, Andrew 56

Currie, James **56**

Curry, George (New Mexico governor) 43, 151

Curry, George Sutherland "Flat Nose" 40, **56–57**, 157, 158, 263

Curry, Kid 40, **157–158**, 263. *See also* Logan, Harvey

Custer County Livestock Association 187

Customs Service, U.S. 38, 42, 69, 79, 94, 101, 153, 174, 221, 226, 265

Cutler, Abraham 199

cutting for sign 256

cyprian 57

D

Daggs brothers 196

Daily Nugget 122

Daisy Dean silver mine 120

Dake, Crawley P. **58–59**, 71

Dallas Herald 85

Dalton, Adeline 59

Dalton, Bob 59, **60–61**

Dalton, Emmett **59**, 60, 61

Dalton, Frank 59

Dalton, Grattan "Grat" **59**, 60, 61

Dalton, Lewis 59

Dalton, Mason Frakes "Bill" **59–60**, 61

Dalton, William Marion "Bill" 101, 102, 168

Dalton Gang 31, 63, 66, 156, 165, 181, 195

Daly, John **61**
Daniels, Ben 167
Daniels, William A. "Billy" 25, 114
Dart, Isom 121
Dash (army sergeant) 64
Davidson, George 2
Davies, Benjamin 220
Davies, Bill 219
Davis, "Big Jack" 127
Davis, Eph 227
Davis, F. J. 242
Davis, George 2
Davis, Jack 16–17
Davis, Jeff 179
Davis, John **175–176**
Davis, Lillie 39
Dawes, N. E. 52
Day, Barney 99
deadfall 62
Dead Man's Hand 117
Deadwood **62**, 117, 153, 157, 162, 183
Deadwood Dick 63
Dean, James 62
Dean, T. J. 99
Deane, William 57
DeArment, Robert "Bob" 63, 97, 129
Deger, Lawrence E. "Larry" 65, 66, 166–167, 222
Delaney, William 25, 114
Del Norte stage 174
deLong, Jack 247
Deming hangings 62
Denny, H. M. 176
Deno, Charlotte "Lottie" 33, **63**, 97, 248
Denson, John 207
Denton Mare, the 16
Denver & Rio Grande Railroad 246
Denver Post 191–192
Denver Times 162
Derby & Day 2
Derom, Nieves 226
Derringer, Henry, Jr. 63
Derringer pistol **63**
DeSpain, Wesley 107
desperado 63. *See also specific desperadoes*
DeTell, Hugh 127
Dexter Saloon 74
Diamond-A Cattle Company 43–44
Diamond Dick 185, **233–234**
Dickson, James 91

Diehl, Pony 164, **202. See also** Ray, Charles T. "Pony Deal"
die with their boots on **63**
dime novels **63**, 105, 117
Diplomacy on Tour (play) 56
Dixon, Billy 151, 152
Dixon, Bob 151, 152
Dixon, Charles "Charlie" 151, 152
Dixon, John Hugh "Irish Jack" 54, 151, 152
Dixon, Simpson **63–64**, 151
Dixson, Simp. *See* Dixon, Simpson
Dobrzinsky, Abraham **1–2**
Dodge, Fred 40, 159
Dodge City **64**
    as cow town x, 41
    Deger in 166–167
    Earps in 64, 65, 66, 71, 73, 74
    Holliday in 64, 119
    Hurricane Bill in 166
    Mastersons in 166–167, 168, 169, 227
    Mather in 169
    Olive in 188
    Rudabaugh in 209
    Short in 222, 223
    Thompson in 247
    Tilghman in 248
    Webb in 259
Dodge City gang 2, 38, **64–65**, 107, 268
Dodge City Peace Commission 65, 66, 223
Dodge City War **65–66**, 169, 222–223
Dodge House 64
Dog Canyon Ranch 151
Dolan, James "Jimmy" 43, 154–155, 194, 220, 265
Dominguez, L. 92
Dona Ana County Stock Association 220
Doniphan, Alexander 99, 266
Donohue, Cornelius "Lame Johnny" 226
Donovan, Arthur 102
Doolin, William M. "Bill" 60, 61, **66**, 101, 102, 168, 181, 245, 248, 260
Doolin Gang 156, 165, 181
Dooner, Pierson 68
Dorsey, Charles 221–222
Dorsey, John 39
Double Dobie gang 25

Dow, Les 138
Dowd, Daniel "Big Dan" 25, 114
Doyle, John 216
Draggoo, Rozilla 70
Draper, Jim 97
drift tax 75
drummer 37, 87
Duane, Charles P. "Dutch Charley" **66–67**
Dublin, Dell 67
Dublin, Jimmy 67
Dublin, Richard "Dick" **67**, 94–95
Dublin, Role 67
Dudley, Nathan 43
duel, dueling xi–xii, **67**
Duffield, Frank 129
Duffield, Milton B. **67–68**
Dugi, Giovanni 107
Dulaney, Arthur 102
Dull Ranch 106
Dunagan, "Big Jim" 268
Dunbar, Levi 94
Dunham, Bill 142
Dunlap, John **68–69**. *See also* Three Fingered Jack
Dunn, Bill 122
Dunn brothers 102, 181
Durbin, Walter 101
Durst, Mollie 9
"Dutchman, the" 267

E

Eaker, J. P. 20
Earhart, Bill 207
Earp, James 72
Earp, Joe 173
Earp, Louisa 70
Earp, Morgan **70**, 71, 72, 73, 103–104, 119, 120, 164, 219, 230, 249
Earp, Virgil xi, xii, 19, 33, 46, 47, 58, 59, 64, **70–71**, 72, 73, 82, 103–104, 119, 120, 123, 164, 180, 219, 230, 249
Earp, Warren 73
Earp, Wyatt Berry Stapp xi, xii, **71–74**, 82, 250
    Behan and 18, 19
    Blaylock and 25
    on Brocius 29, 30
    Burns and 33
    on Cahill 204
    Clanton and 46, 47
    Dake and 58, 59

in Dodge City 64, 65, 66
in East Las Vegas 64
in El Paso 77
on faro 81
in gunfight at the OK Corral
    103–104
as gunfighter 105
Holliday and 119, 120
Johnson and 135
Leslie and 153
McMaster and 164
on Sharp 219
Shibell and 221
Short and 223
in Tombstone 70, 207, 249
on Tucker 251
Earp brothers 29, 71, 83, 123, 153,
    230, 256. *See also specific Earp
    brothers*
East, James Henry "Jim" 74–75, 78
Eckstein, Sam 33
Eddy, Charles B. 177
Eddy-Bissell Cattle Company 177
Edmunds Act 171
Egan, Armstrong 16
Egan, Thomas J. "Dad" 16
Eiverson, Chris 160
Elder, "Big Nose" Kate 50, 71, 119,
    120, 122–123
Elephant Butte Dam 126
Elkins, Stephen B. 199
Elks 54
Elliott, Wilson 252
Ellis, Charles 77
Ellsworth x, 41, 45, **75**
Elmer, A. V. 253
El Moro Gambling Hall 247
El Paso 77
El Paso Daily Herald 18, 235
El Paso Lone Star 143
El Paso Masonic Society 237
El Paso Morning Times 92
El Paso Salt War 75–77, 79, 86, 88,
    136, 144, 163, 242, 250
Emory, Charles 240
Emory, Sally 240
Emory, Thomas "Poker Tom" 75,
    78–79, 240
English, J. W. 168
Enríquez, Juan 83
Equity Bar 240
Espalin, José 93, 94, 181
Estes, Dave 207

Evans, Christopher "Chris" 34, 229,
    230, 265
Evans, Jesse J. 43, **79–80**, 144, 155,
    163, 194, 220
Evans, Joseph W. 58
Everett, Robert 2
Ewell, Richard 269
Ewing, Thomas Jr. 6
Exchange Saloon (El Paso) 144
Exchange Saloon (Montana) 32

F

Faber, Charles 4
Fall, Albert B. 13, 151
Fargo, William George 259
faro **81**
Farr, Edward J. 139, 149, 252
Fashion Saloon 154
fast draw **81–82**
Feely, J. H. **82**
Feliz, Rosa 178
Fellows, Dick 127
fence-cutting wars **82–83**, 106, 125,
    134
Ferguson, James 126
Ferguson, Lark. *See* Spence, Peter
    "Pete"
Ferguson, Sandy **143**
Ferguson, Warren Wallace 230
Fernandez, Juan 118
feuds **83**. *See also specific feuds*
Fielder, James S. 37
*Fifteen Years on the Hurricane Deck
    of a Spanish Pony* (Siringo) 223
filibusters 94
Fimbres, Manuela **83**
Findlay, Cornelius 58
Finley, Jim 87, 100
Finn, Robert 256
Finney, Arthur "Pegleg" 226
    First Fast Draw, The (L'Amour)
    14
Fisher, John King 9, **83–84**, 246,
    247
Fisher, Kate 122–123
Fitzgerald, Mike 135
Fitzsimmons, "Ruddy Bob" 74
Five-Day Battle 30, 163, 170, 194
Flake's Bulletin 152
Flannigan, Dennis 227
Flat, the 55, 85, 97, 248
Flatt, George 172
Fleming, J. W. 95
Fletcher, Quirino 79

Flores, Antonio 192, 193
Floyd, Hank 115
Fly, C. S. 69
Flynn, James 73, 207
Fly's Photography Studio 71, 104,
    123
Folsom Prison 34, 88, 222, 229
Foraker, Creighton M. 251
Ford, Charles "Charlie" **84–85**
Ford, J. C. 88
Ford, John R. 245
Ford, Robert "Bob" **84–85**, 133,
    138
Fore, Frank 173
Fornoff, Fred 182
Forrest, Nathan B. 3, 151
Forrester, William 209
Forsythe, Joe 203
Fort Bayard 51, 188
Fort Bliss 77
Fort Buchanan 269
Fort Concho 98, 146
Fort D. A. Russell 122
Fort Davis 79, 216, 217, 231, 242
Fort Dodge 64, 248
Fort Elliott 168
Fort Fetterman 191
Fort Gibson 98, 231
Fort Grant 148
Fort Griffin 55, 63, 85, 92, 97, 100,
    115, 119, 122, 146, 147, 166, 198,
    216, 217, 248
Fort Gunnybags 212
Fort Halleck 225
Fort Huachuca 148
Fort Lancaster 142
Fort Mason 67, 237
Fort McKavett 67
Fort McKinney 135
Fort McPherson 144
Fort Meade 130
Fort Richardson 122
Fort Scott 146
Fort Selden 79, 144
Fort Sill 115
Fort Smith 98, 126, 165, 192, 205,
    231, 232, 268
Fort Stanton 77, 79, 154, 156, 186,
    198
Fort Stockton 42, 143, 207
Fort Sumner 75, 79, **85–86**, 92, 93,
    154, 195, 198, 209, 225, 265
Fort Terrett 142
Fort Washita 216

Fort Worth 173, 223, 241, 244, 259
Fort Worth & Denver Railroad 126
Foster, Johnny 148
Foster, Martha 14
Foster, Will 122
Fountain, Albert Jennings 13, 43, 48, 53, 76, **86–87**, 93, 126, 144, 151, 192, 195, 199
Fountain, Henry 13, 43, 53, 87, 93, 151
Fowler, Bud 16
Fowler, Joel A. 87, 100
Fox (associate of Bull) 32
Franklin (Arizona governor) 153
Franks, George W. "News" **39–40**
Frazer, Bud 173, 206
Frazier, Sam **87–88**
Fream, Dave 187
Fredericks, William 88
Free, Mickey **88–89**
Free Academy of New York 6
Freedmen's Bureau 14
Freeze, John Doe 70
Freis, John Doe 70
Fremont, John C. 19
French, Albert 86, 87
French, Jim 155
French's Saloon 154
Frescas, Alaris 52
Fritz, Emil 154
Fronteriza Mining Company 185
Frontier Times Magazine 10
Frost, Henry 134
Frye Cattle Company 5, 157
"Fugitives from Justice" list. *See List of Fugitives from Justice*
Fullerton, John F. 182
Fullerton's Rangers 182
Fulton, R. H. 172
Fusselman, Charles 89, 110, 125, 126, 192

G
Gaines, Louis 188
Gainesville hangings **90–91**
Gaither, Charles 94
Gallagher, Barney 225
Galveston, Battle of 165
Galveston Daily 18
gambling 1, 41, 65, 115, 247, 248. *See also* faro
"Gambling Queen of Hearts." *See* Deno, Charlotte "Lottie"

Gannon, Charles 5, **156–157**. *See also* Loftis, Hillary U. "Hill"
García, Juan 250–251
García, Taurino 62
García, Three Fingered Jack 61, 68–69, 147–148, 160, 178
Gard, George 34
Garibaldi, Giuseppe 77
Garlick, William Henry **91–92**
Garner, John Nance 93
Garrett, Elizabeth 92
Garrett, John 92
Garrett, Patrick Floyd Jarvis "Pat" 82, **92–94**
    on Billy the Kid ix, x, xi, 20, 23, 24, 75, 78–79, 86, 156, 186, 195
    on Bowdre 27
    Brazel and 173
    Cox and 54
    in El Paso 77
    Emory and 79
    on Fountain 126
    on Lee 151
    Leyba and 154
    on Newman 181
    on O'Folliard 50
    on Parra 192
    Poe and 198
    on Rudabaugh 209
    Syndicate and 240
    Whitehill and 263
    on Wilson 265
Garrett, Poe 94
Gates, Thomas 113, 206, 271
Gatlin, Bill 75
Gauss, Gottifried 24
Gem Saloon 63, 123, 124, 204
George, Frederick **52**
George Washington University 133
Georgia State Prison 175
Geppert, George 30, 260
Geronimo 121, 210
Gerry, Melville 192
Gibbons, Augustus 214
Gibson, Dave 154
Gibson, L. E. 134
Gibson, Volney 134
Giddings Tribune 160
Gillespie, John 101
Gillett, Helen Baylor 135
Gillett, James Buchanan "Jim" 12, 54, 67, 77, **94–95**, 135, 180, 202, 236

Gillett, James S. 94
Gilliland, Fine 50
Gilliland, James "Jim" 87, 93, 151
Gilliland, John 196
Gillman, Marshal 264
Gilmo, John W. 33, **95–96**, 226
Gilmore, John W. 95–96
Gilson, William C. "Bill" 97
Givens, Justice 251
Glazner, William C. 37
Gleason, Harvey **96–97**
Glick, George 222
Globe-Phoenix stage 111, 112
Glover, Mike 104
Gobles, Reese 111
Golden, Johnny 63, **97**
Gold Rush, California 105, 152, 160, 164, 178, 212, 255, 262
Goldsby, Crawford 51, **98**. *See also* Cherokee Bill
Gonzáles, Danacio 52
Good, Isham J. 98
Good, James 116
Good, John 98
Good, Milton Paul "Milt" 5, **98–99**, 157
Good, Sam 101
Good, Walter 98
Goodbread, Joseph 205
Goodfellow, George 70, 114, 128, 266
Goodlet, William "Bill" 268
Goodlet & Robert's Saloon 2
Goodnight, Charles 3
Goodnight-Loving Trail x, 3, 41, 146
Gordon, Jack **99**, 266–267
Gordon, James 116
Gorras Blancas, Las 43
Graham, Billy 196, 197
Graham, John 196, 197
Graham, Tom 196, 197
Granadine, Romula 217
Grand Lake shootout **99–100**
Grant, Joe 23
Grant, Ulysses S. 192, 199, 245
Grant County Cattleman's Association 214
Graves, Mit 175
Graves, William "Whiskey Bill" **100**
Greathouse, James "Whiskey Jim" 20, 87, **100**
Greathouse Ranch 209
Great Northern Railroad 41, 141, 158, 159

Great Train Robbery, The (film) 34
Greene, William Cornell 5, 210
Greer brothers 32
Grey, Zane 197
Griego, Francisco "Pancho" 4
Griffin, Alexander 164
Griffith, Frank S. 148
"Grim Chieftain" 146
Grimes, A. W. "Caige" 17. *See also* Grimes, Ahijah W. "High"
Grimes, Ahijah W. "High" 100, 258. *See also* Grimes, A. W. "Caige"
Grimes, Albert Calvin "Al" **100–101**
Groesbeck (sheriff) 54
Grounds, William A. "Billy the Kid" 29, **101**, 128
Groupie, George "Old Cap" 267
Groupie, Samuel 99
Guadarrama, Juan 92
Guadarrama, Mariana 92
Guadarrama, Sabino 92
gunfighter **105**
gunman **105**
gunslinger **105**
Gutiérrez, Apolonaria 23, 92
Gylam, Jacob C. 123

H

Hadley, Charley **149**
Hale, Johnny 235
Hall, Jesse Leigh. See Hall, Lee
Hall, Lee 9, 53, 74, 75, 78, 84, 106, **106**, 165, 243
Hall (ex-Regulator) 205
Halsell, Harry 203
Halsell, Oscar 203
Hamilton, Bill 127
Hamilton, Bob 127
Hamilton, Charlie 118
Hammett, Dashiell 196
Hammit, O. J. 82
Hancock, Louis 207
Hand, Dora 138
hangings **62, 90–91, 106–107**, 212, 256. *See also* lynching
Hankins, John Henry **107, 227**
Hanly, Pat 203
hardcase **107**
Hardin, Elizabeth 108
Hardin, James 108
Hardin, Jane 109
Hardin, Joe 109
Hardin, John Wesley ix, xi, xii, 63, 101, **108–110**

on Abilene 1
Armstrong on 9
as badman 14, 81, 105, 201
Coe and 48
Dixon and 63, 64
in El Paso 77
Gillett on 94
on Helm 238
Hickok and 117
Mrose and 150, 174, 177, 178, 201, 214, 217, 218
Ringo and 207
road agent spin used by 208
Selman and 218
on Webb 238
Hardin, Tom 10, 11
Harding, Warren G. 13
Harkins, Mike 216
Harlan, J. J. "Off Wheeler" 33
Harley, E. A. 101
Harlow, Buck 215
Haro, Francisco 150
Harold, George 17, **110**, 258
Harper, Bettie 94
Harper's Magazine 117
Harrington, "Alkali Jim" 174
Harrington, Frank 139–140
Harris, Andy 165
Harris, Jack 63, 84, **110–111**, 246
Harris, Len 96, 239
Harris, Tom 240
Harris, William H. 65
Harrison, Charlie 154
Hart, Charlie 200
Hart, Dick 171
Hart, Edward "Little" **111**
Hart, Pearl 26, **111–112**
Hart, William S. 34
Hartlee, B. F. "Frank" **112–113**
Hartman, Lewis 222
Harvey, John 258
Harvey, Walter M. 95
Hash Knife Ranch 142, 176, 196, 197
Haskay-Bay-Nay-Ntay. *See* Apache Kid
Haskins, Joe 111
Hatch Saloon 164
Hawken rifle 196
Hawkins, Joe 209
Hayes, Rutherford B. 58
Haynes Saloon 188
Haynor, Ham. *See* Rayner, Hamilton
Hays, Bill 146, 147

Hays, Coffee Jack. *See* Hays, John Coffee
Hays, John Coffee xi, **113–114**, 147, 243, 257
Haywood, Ralph 5, 157
Hazelton, Tim 67
Hazen, Joe 157
Hearne, William B. 13
Heath, John A. **114**
Heaven's Gate (film) 135
Heffington, Isaac 184
Heffron, Gus 54, 55
Helen's Defeat 205–206
Helldorado: Bringing the Law to the Mesquite (Breakenridge) 29
Hell's Half-acre **114–115**
Helm, Jack 108, 237, 238
Henderson, Frank 203
Henderson, William "Bill" **115**, 147
Hendricks, A. R. 238
Hendrickson, Andrew 45
Henry, James **163**
Henry, Tom 38–39
Henry gang 169
Herndon, Albert G. 17
Herold, George 89
Herrera, Antonia Miguela 216
Herrera, Antonio 7
Herrera, Fred 69
Herrera, Manuela 27
Heywood, Joseph L. 270
Hickok, James Butler "Wild Bill" xi, 82, **115–117**, 250
    in Abilene 1
    Calamity Jane and 36
    Coe and 47, 48, 245
    in Deadwood 62
    in dime novels 63
    as gunfighter xii, 81, 105, 201, 224
    Hardin and 108–109, 208
    McCall on 162
    Williams and 247
Hickok, William Alonzo 115
Hicks, James 45, 121
Hicks, Milt 219
Higgins, John Calhoun Pinckney "Pink" **117–118**, 123, 124, 231
High Fives gang 179
High Noon (film) 64, **118**
Hill, Frank 186
Hill, Joe 101
Hill, Thomas "Tom" 79, 155, 194, 220

Hill, Will 92
Hillard, T. C. 214
Hindman, George 22, 30, 155, 170
History of Billy the Kid (Siringo) 224
Hite, Wood 84–85
Hixon, John 102, 182
Hodges, Thomas J. "Tom" **118**
Hogan, Ben 32
Hogan, Ed 112
Hogg, James 122
Hogue, Edward O. 247
Holbrook, Joseph 55
Hole-in-the-Wall 31, 40, **118**, 125,
    152, 157, 218, 224, 263
Holliday, Henry 118
Holliday, John 118
Holliday, John Henry "Doc" xi,
    118–120
    Behan on 19
    "Big Nose" Kate and 50, 71,
        119, 120, 122–123
    Clanton and 46
    in Dodge City 64, 119
    in East Las Vegas 64
    Elder and 50
    McMaster and 164
    at OK Corral gunfight 70
    Thurmond and 248
    in Tombstone 71, 73, 103–104,
        119, 122, 123, 207, 249
    Vermillion and 256
    Wells Fargo stage holdup and 72
    Yarberry and 268
Holliday, Mary Jane Beckett 175
Holmes, Joseph T. 68
Holmes, William A. "Hunkydory"
    120–121, 206
Holshousen, Madge 108
holsters 34–35
Holt, John 54
Holzhey, Joe 104
Hoodoo War **166**
Hoover's Saloon 167
Horn, Tom 35, 45, **121**, 152, 153,
    195
Horner, Joe **37–38**, 122. *See also*
    Canton, Frank M.
Horony, Mary Katherine **122–123**.
    See also Elder, "Big Nose" Kate
Horrell, Benjamin F. "Ben" **123, 124**
Horrell, Elizabeth 123
Horrell, James Martin "Mart" 54,
    111, 117, **123, 124**
Horrell, John W. **123, 124**

Horrell, Merritt 117, **123, 124**
Horrell, Samuel (father of Samuel L.)
    123
Horrell, Samuel L. "Sam" 117, 123,
    124
Horrell, Thomas L. "Tom" 54, 111,
    123, 124
Horrell, William C. **123–124**
Horrell brothers **123–124**
    Horrell-Higgins feud 54, 94,
        123, **124**, 136, 242, 257
Horsdorff, Christopher 216
    horse theft **124–125**
Horton, Alexander 206
Hos-cal-te 121
House, Reid 16
House, the 30, 154, 155
House, Thomas Jefferson 38–39
House of Representatives, U.S. 146
Houston, Louis 126
Houston, Sam 94, 206
Houston & Texas Central Railroad
    17
Howard, Charles 76, 77
Howard, James "Tex" 25, 114
Howard, John J. 123
Howard, Thomas "Tom" 84, 132.
    See also James, Jesse
Howard, Tillie 186, 189, 217
Howard, Zee "Josie" 84
Howell, Viola 225
Howie, Neil 257
Howlett, Richard "Dick" 28
Hoy, George 72
Hoy, Valentine 218
Hoyt, Henry F. 260
Hubbard, Early 123
Huckert, George 129
Hudson, Richard 28
Huerta, Victoriano 77
Hueston, Tom 102, 168
Hughes, Ben **126–127**
Hughes, Henry 125
Hughes, James (father of Jim) 126
Hughes, James "Jim" **126–127**
Hughes, Jimmy 101
Hughes, John Reynolds 4, 10, 38,
    50, 91, 92, 95, **125–126**, 173, 185,
    186, 234
Hughes, Louis Cameron 96
Hughes, Will 125
Hugo, Charley 251
Hume, James B. "Jim" 26, **127**, 239,
    256
Humm, George 261

Hunt, Callie May 39
Hunt, Hugh 128
Hunt, Zwingle Richard "Zwing" 29,
    101, **128**
Hunter, Charles 175
Hunter, J. Marvin 214
Hunt's Canyon 128
Hurricane Minnie 166

I

Idaho State Penitentiary 172
Ike, Jim 100
I'll Die Before I'll Run (Sonnichsen)
    151
Imperial Valley Irrigation System 149
Indians. *See also specific Indian tribes*
    bad medicine of 14
    Behan on 19
    Brown on 30
    Cooper and 196
    as horse thieves 124
    LeFors and 152
    liquor sold to 148
    Packer and 191
    Reeves on 205
    Riley and 207
    Sharps rifle and 219
    Smith and 226, 227
    Starr and 231
    Texas Rangers and 136, 142,
        242, 243, 266
    in Yuma Territorial Prison 271
Indian wars 94, 95, 113, 117, 121,
    153, 180, 190, 210, 216, 257
Ingalls, gunfight at **101–102**
Innocents 197
Interior Department, U.S. 13
Ireland, John 247
Irwin, "Rustling Bob" 111
Isaacs, George 10
Italian Jim 61. *See also* Three
    Fingered Jack
Ivers, Alice **129–130**
Ives, George 130, 198
IWW (International Workers of the
    World) 261–262

J

Jack Harris's Vaudeville Saloon 63
Jackson, Charles 205
Jackson, Francis M. "Frank" 17,
    110, 258
Jackson, J. C. 51
Jackson, Teton **95–96**, 122
Jacobs, David "Little Jakey" 256

Jacobs, William 197
Jacomo, Carlos 154
jails **131**
James, Bob 134
James, Frank **131–133**, 183, 200, 269, 270
James, Jesse xii, 6, 14, 42, 60, 84, 85, **131–133**, 138, 183, 196, 200, 269, 270
James, Jesse Edward (son of outlaw) 84, 133
James, Mary 84
James, Zeralda "Zee" 132, 133
James brothers **131–133**, 134, 195. *See also* James, Frank; James, Jesse
James gang 42, 63, 172, 182–183, 260. *See also* James, Frank; James, Jesse
James-Younger Wild West Show 133
Jamison, James 15
Jarrott, James 173
Jaybird-Woodpecker War 10, **133–134**
Jayhawkers 90, 91, **134**, 146, 200, 269
Jefferies, William Robert 55
Jenkins, James **107**
Jenkins, Sam 57, 157
Jenks, Ralph 214
Jenks, Roy 214
Jennings, "Albert" 177
Jennings, Helen. *See* Mrose, Helen Beulah
Jennings, Steve 177
Jennings gang 245, 260
Jennison, Charles R. "Doc" 134, 146
Jermagin, B. F. 32, 230
Jerry Scott's Saloon 124
J. J. Dolan & Co. 169
Jockey Club 63
John Kinney gang 18, 29, 202. *See also* Kinney, John
Johnson, Annie Frazer 42
Johnson, Arkansas 17
Johnson, Bill 235
Johnson, Dick 151, 152
Johnson, Edwin W. **134–135**
Johnson, Jack. *See* Johnson, John "Turkey Creek"
Johnson, John. *See* Yarberry, Milton J.
Johnson, John "Turkey Creek" 73, **135**
Johnson, Kid 258
Johnson, Nita 42

Johnson, R. S. 207
Johnson, Tom 171
Johnson, W. D. "Keechi" 214
Johnson, William 61
Johnson (cattle rustler) 51
Johnson County War 37, **135**, 157, 158, 185
Johnston, Albert Sidney 18
Johnston, A. V. E. 6
Jones, Buck 34
Jones, Elizabeth 240–241
Jones, Frank. *See* Sundance Kid
Jones, Frank (Texas Ranger) 126, **135–136**, 145, 188, 234
Jones, John B. 77, 124, **136**, 166, 242, 265
Jones, Stanton 174
Jones Commercial College 206
Joy, Christopher "Kit" 37, 47, 51, 52, 96, **136–137**, 150, 239
Juarez. *See* Ciudad Juarez
July, Jim 233
Junction City Union 1
Justice, A. L. 204
Justice, John 28
Justice Department, U.S. 6–7, 38, 58

K

Kahn, Henry 119
Kansas City (Kansas) x, 41
Kansas Pacific Railroad 75
Kay, Jim 100
Kealy, James H. 71
Kearney, Kent 93
Keating, Paul 95
Kelley, Henry 237
Kelley, James H. "Dog" 65, 138, 166, 167
Kelley, Lawson 187
Kelley, Neut 121
Kelley, Will 237
Kelliher, Michael 2, 64, 65, 259
Kelly, Charles 45
Kelly, Daniel York "Yorkie" 25, 114, 251
Kelly, Ed **138**, 182
Kelly, Nigger Jim 138, 187
Kelly, York. *See* Kelly, Daniel York "Yorkie"
Kelso, Mariah 46
Kemp, David Leon "Dave" xi, **138**, 194
Kemp, Leon 138
Kemp & Lyell's Silver King Saloon 138

Kendall, Thomas 149
Kenedy, James W. **138–139**, 187
Kenedy, Mifflin 138
Kennedy, Charles 55
Kennedy, Mart 44
Kennedy (cofounder of King Ranch) 74
Kennedy (lieutenant colonel) 68
Kennedy (murderous rancher) 3
Kerber, Charles 250
Kerr, Thomas 221
Kerrick, James 260–261
Ketchum, Ami 187, 188
Ketchum, Jack 12
Ketchum, Samuel W. "Sam" 39, **139**, 149, 251, 252
Ketchum, Tom "Black Jack" 10, 39, **139–141**
Kidder, Jeff P. **141**
Kilburn, William Harvey "W. H." 44, **141**
Kile, John 116, 117
Killeen, May 153
Killeen, Mike 70, 153
Kilpatrick, Benjamin Arnold "Ben" 39, 41, **141–142**, 159, 263
Kilpatrick, George 39, 40
Kimball, Richard 164
Kimbell, Russel G. "Rush" **142–143**
King, Ed 240
King, Luther 143
King, Melvin 168–169
King, Sandy 101, **143**, 241
King, William 5
King (cofounder of King Ranch) 74
King of the Rustlers 144
King Ranch 44, 74
Kinney, John 18, **143–145**, 163, 164
Kinney, Nathaniel N. "Nate" 15–16
Kinsley Graphic 209
Kinsman, William "Bill" 266
Kiowa 136
Kirchner, Carl **145**
Kirtland, Richard 127
Kosterlitzky, Emilio 210
Kramer, Stanley 118
Krempkau, Gus 235
Ku Klux Klan 63, 117
Kyle, E. **98–99**

L

labor movement 195, 196, 210, 224, 239–240, 244, 261–262
Lady Gay Saloon 167
Lafferr, Joseph N. 47, 52, 137

Laird, Andrew B. 37, 269
Lake, Frank 182
Lake, Jacob 105
Lambert, Fred 182
Lambert's Saloon 4
L'Amour, Louis 14
Landusky, Pike 157
Lane (cattle thief) 187
Lane, James Henry 134, **146**
Lane's Brigade 146
Lang, John 240
Lankford, Ace 67
Lantier, Ike 117
Lara, Francisco 219
Lara, Rupert 48
Largo, Jesús 13, 216
Larn, John M. 55, 85, **146–147**,
     206, 216–217
Las Quevas War 9
Last Chance Hill 61
Las Vegas Gazette 107
Las Vegas Optic 107
Lathrop, Charles 253
Laustenneau, W. H. "Jack"
     147–148. *See also* Three Fingered
     Jack
law and order **148**
Lawrence, Andrew "Long Green" 74
Lay, William Ellsworth "Elza" xi,
     40, 45, 139, **148–149**, 172, 251,
     252, 263
Lazure, Charley **149**
Leatherwood, Robert "Bob" 28, 69
Leavenworth Penitentiary 209
Ledbetter, A. G. 95
Lee, A. Mitchell "Mitch" 37, 47, 51,
     52, 96, 137, **149–150**, 239
Lee, Beauregard **150**, 177
Lee, Bob 151
Lee, Harper 95
Lee, James 150
Lee, Oliver Milton 53, 87, 93, 98,
     150–151
Lee, Susan 150
Lee-Peacock feud **151–152**
Lees, Isaiah Wrigles **152**
LeFors, Joe 121, **152–153**
Leonard, Billy 101
LeRoy, Kitty **153**
Leslie, Bucksin Frank. *See* Leslie,
     Nashville Franklin
Leslie, Nashville Franklin 45–46,
     153, 219, 249, 271
LeSueur, Frank 214
Levagood, Alice 30

Leverton, John 10
Levy, James H. "Jim" **154**
Lewis, Albert 6
Lewis, Callie 109
Lewis, Elmer "Kid" 156
Lewis, Jake 98
Lewis, Tom 226
Leyba, Marino **154**
Liberty Square, Battle of 226
Liddil, Dick 84–85
*Life of John Wesley Hardin as
     Written by Himself, The* (Hardin)
     109
Lincoln, Abraham 195, 263
Lincoln, Fredia. *See* Bullion, Laura
Lincoln County War **154–156**
     Angel and 193
     Baca in 13
     Billy the Kid in 22, 23, 79
     Brown in 30
     Chávez in 43
     constables in 49
     Evans in 79
     Garrett during 93
     Hart in 111
     Kinney in 144
     Mathews in 169–170
     McDaniels in 163
     McSween in 13, 23, 49, 144,
          154, 155, 156, 163, 170, 194,
          220
     Murphy-Dolan organization in
          266
     Perry in 194
     Scott in 176
     Scurlock in 216
     Shedd and 220
     Tunstall in 7, 154, 155, 170,
          194, 220
Linn, Charles "Buck" 204
List of Fugitives from Justice 108,
     202. *See also* Ranger's Bible
"Little Arkansas" 108
Littlefield, Alfred "Jack" 262
Littlefield, George 30, 78, 79
Little Hart 217
Loftis, Hillary U. "Hill" 5, 98–99,
     156–157
Logan, Chris 220
Logan, Harvey 40, 41, 56, 57, 141,
     157–158, 159, 263
Logan, John "Johnny" 56, 57, 157,
     158
Logan, Lonie 56, 57, 157, **158**
Lohman, Martin 94

Lonergan, Jeremiah 116
Lone Star Cowboy (Siringo) 224
Lone Star Saloon 167
Long, Crockett 161
Long, Jack. *See* Long, John
Long, Jim 20–21
Long, John 155, 170
Longabaugh, Harry 40, 41, 125,
     158–159, 227, 263. *See also*
     Sundance Kid
Long Branch Saloon 64, 65, 222,
     223
Long Hollow Ranch 125
Longley, William Preston "Bill" 30,
     159–160
Long Necked Charley **149**
López, José 52
López, Red 77
Los Pinos (Indian) Agency 191
Louis XIV 81
Love, Dick 38
Love, Harry **160**, 178
Love, Henry 139, 252
Love, Thomas D. 51
Loving, Oliver 3
Lowe, Anthony 39
Lowe, "Rowdy Joe" **160**
LS Ranch 74, 75, 240
Lull, Louis 270
Lyell, Ed 194
lynching 160–161, 180, 198, 211.
     See also hangings
Lynn, Wiley **161**, 249
Lyons, Jack 38
Lyons, James G. 67

M

MacKenzie, Ranald S. 100
Mackey, Tom. *See* Holliday, John
     Henry "Doc"
MacMahan, Tom 217
Madero, Francisco 77
     Madsen, Christian "Chris" 66,
          102, **165**, 182, 245, 248
Maes, Patricio 43
Magruder, John B. 18
Mahan, John 231
Mahony (deputy sheriff) 33
Mail, U.S. 6, 37
Maish, Fred 68
Majors (Pony Express agent) 115
Majors, Alexander 115
Maledon, George **165**
"Man Burner." *See* Olive, Isom
     Prentice "Print"

Manning, Frank 235, 237, 247
Manning, G. F. "Doc" 235, 236, 237
Manning, James "Jim" 235, 236, 237
Manning Saloon 235, 236, 237
Marco, Banjeck 120
Marcus, Josephine Sarah "Josie" 19, 25, 72, 74
Marlow, Alf 134
Marlow, Charles 134
Marlow, George 134
Marlow, Llwellyn 134
marshals, town 250
marshals, U.S. 82, 148
    Armstrong, John Barclay 9
    on bounty hunting 27
    Bryant and 60
    Cantley, Charles 37
    Canton, Frank 38
    Dake, Crawley P. 58, 59, 71, 73
    Duffield, Milton B. 68
    Elliott, Wilson 252
    Foraker, Creighton M. 251
    Gard, George 34
    Gleason on 96
    on Hughes brothers 126
    Madsen, Chris 165
    Meade, William Kidder 170–171, 221
    Moore, G. W. 33–34
    Nix, Evett 102, 182
    Pratt, John 199
    Scarborough, George 112
    Ware, Richard C. "Dick" 37, 189, 258
Martin, Carl 43–44
Martin, Charles "Charlie" 165–166
Martin, H. 163
Martín, Juan 123
Martin, Juan Miguel 7
Martin, Pablita 7
Martin, Robert "Dutch" 29
Martin, William A. "Hurricane Bill" 166
Martínez, Atanacio 155
Martinez, "Curley" 230
Martínez, Mickey 88–89
Martínez (Mexican lieutenant) 171
Marysville-Downieville stage 127
Mason, Barney 75, 78
Mason, Charlie 219
Mason County War 166, 207
Masons 10, 54
Masterson, Ben 65
Masterson, Edward John "Ed" 64, 65, 166–167, 168, 169

Masterson, James "Jim" 64, 65, 71–72, 102, 166, 167–168, 182
Masterson, James (killer of Johnson) 61
Masterson, Thomas 166
Masterson, William Barclay "Bat" 64, 65, 166, 167, 168–169, 209, 223, 227, 246, 247, 259
Masterson brothers xi. See also specific Masterson brothers
Mather, Cotton 169
Mather, David "Mysterious Dave" 38, 64, 77, 169, 268
Mathews, Jacob Basil "Billy" 22, 43, 155, 169–170, 194
Matthews, Charles 246
Matthews, Joseph Beck 147
Matthews, Mary 147
Matthews (doctor) 70
maverick, mavericking 170, 240
Maverick, Samuel A. 170
Maximilian 9, 48, 245
Maxwell, Lucien 86
Maxwell, Pete 24, 86, 93
Maxwell Land Grant Company 199
Mayes, Elijah 17
Mayfield, John 9, 50–51
Maynard, Ken 34
McBride, Charles 115
McBride, John 77
McCaffry (district attorney) 68
McCall, John "Jack" 117, 162
McCanles, David C. 116
McCanles, William Monroe 116
McCarthy, Charles 12
McCarty, Bill 162
McCarty, Catherine 21–22
McCarty, Cornelius M. 226
McCarty, Fred 162
McCarty, George 162
McCarty, Henry x, 21–24, 43, 92. See also Billy the Kid
McCarty, John Thomas "Tom" 40, 45, 158, 162–163, 263
McClellan, William "Billy" 33, 34, 96, 251
McCluskie, Arthur 103
McCluskie, Mike 102, 103
McCollum, Ike 127
McComas, Charles "Charley" 179
McComas, H. C. 179
McComas, Mrs. H. C. 179
McConnell, Andrew 228
McCool, Lon 38, 122
McCord, J. C. 250

McCowan, Mahlon 177
McCrea, Mike 199
McCulloch, Ben 113, 243
McCulloch, Henry 113, 200
McCullough, Clay 4
McCullough, Dora 4
McCullough, John 55
McCullough, Patsy 4
McCully, Edward "Ed" 163
McCully, Thomas "Jackson" 163
McDaniels, James "Jim" 163–164, 194, 220
McDonald, J. H. 228
McDonald, W. H. 187
McDonald, William C. 62, 182
McDougal, "Cattle Annie" 248
McDowell, John 61. See also Three Fingered Jack
McEhanie, Bill 60
McGee, Thomas 10
McGinnes, Andy 229
McGinnis, William 148–149
McGurk, Mary 166
McIntosh, Charles 263
McKenzie, Colin 253
McKeown, Hugh 30
McKidrict, Joe 217
McKimie, Robert "Little Reddy" 16
McKinney, Thomas C. "Kip" 24
McKinney (sheriff) 101
McLane, M. Frank 65, 223
McLaury, Frank 71, 72, 73, 101, 103–104, 120, 249
McLaury, Robert 45, 46, 53, 249
McLaury, Thomas "Tom" 19, 45, 46, 53, 71, 72, 73, 101, 103–104, 120, 249
McMahan, Don 214
McMahan, Frank 109, 174, 177, 178, 214
McMahan, Mary 213
McMaster(s), Sherman W. 73, 164, 202
McMurtry, James 164
McMurtry, William 164–165
McNab, Frank 155, 156
McNeal, Alex G. 104
McNelly, Leander H. 9, 106, 165, 243
McNew, William "Bill" 87, 93, 151
McSween, Alexander 13, 14, 23, 30, 43, 49, 111, 144, 154, 155, 156, 163, 170, 194, 216, 220
McSween, Susan 23, 43, 79

Meade, William Kidder **170–171,** 221

Meagher, John 171–172

Meagher, Michael **171–172**

Meeks, Henry "Bub" 40, **172**

Merchant, Edward 205

Meriwether, David 196

Merrill, David 218

Mes brothers 79, 163, 220

Mescalero 163, 216, 227, 266. *See also* Apache

Mesilla Valley Independent 87

Metcalf, Jennie "Little Britches" 248

Mexican Central Railroad 226, 234

Mexican Revolution 13, 77, 91, 145

Mexican War 49, 59, 71, 99, 113, 118, 146, 160, 224, 242, 257, 266

Middleton, Doc **207,** 226

Middleton, Eugene 8, 121, 206

Middleton, Harry 208

Middleton, John 155

Middleton Ranch 197

Miles, Billy 15, 16

Miles, Jim 16

Miles, Moses 228

Miles, Nelson 8, 168

Millar (doctor) 70

Miller, Charles D. 62

Miller, Clell 132, **172,** 183, 270

Miller, "Deacon Jim." *See* Miller, James Brown "Killin' Jim"

Miller, James Brown "Killin' Jim" 77, 94, *161,* **172–173,** 206, 207

Miller, Jesse 179

Miller, Jim (Arizona gunman) 206

Miller, Jim Buck 123, 124

Millican, L. R. 82

Mills, Alexander H. 123

Mills, John Gillis 99, 100

Milton, David 45

Milton, George 183

Milton, Jefferson Davis "Jeff" 5, 69, 77, 109, **173–174,** 177, 178, 214, 217, 258

Miner, William "Bill" **174–175**

Minnesota State Prison 132

Missouri Pacific Railroad 201, 231

Mitchell, Belle 175

Mitchell, Frank 118, 123, 124, 250

Mitchell, Levi 267

Mitchell, Luther 187, 188

Mitchell, Mary Jane 175–176

Mitchell, Maude 175

Mitchell, Nelson "Cooney" 175

Mitchell, William "Bill" **175–176**

Mix, Tom 34

Moderators **205–206**

Molliter, F. W. 264

Molvenon, William 197

Monterrey, Battle of 257

Montgomery, James 134

Montoya, Joaquin 154

Moonlight, Thomas 158, 223

Moor, D. Z. 149

Moore, Catherine 245

Moore, C. R. 91, 92

Moore, Eugenia 60

Moore, George (desperado) 256

Moore, G. W. (lawman) 33–34, 96, 251

Moore, James 245

Moore, J. H. 215

Moore, J. L. 62

Moore, Maurice B. 17, 258

Moore, Sam 10

Moore, W. C. "Outlaw Bill" 74

Moorman, Charles 205

Moorman, Helen Daggett 206

Morales, Jesús 107

Morco, John "Happy Jack" **176,** 247

Morehead, James 2

Moreno, Alberto 176

Moreno, María **176**

Morgan, Georgia 114

Morgan, James 252

Mormon Kid 45

Mormons 171

Morning Telegraph 169

Morris, Harvie 23

Morris, John C. 204

Morris Detective Agency 34

Morse, Harry 26

Mortimer, C. E. 77

Morton, William Scott "Buck" 22, 155, **176,** 194

Mossman, Burton C. "Burt" 8, **176–177,** 210

Moyer, Bill 154

Mrose, Helen Beulah 109, 110, 150, 174, **177,** 201, 214, 217, 218

Mrose, Martin 109, 150, 174, **177–178,** 201, 214, 217

Mullen, William 2

Mullins, Ike 231

Mulrey, John 116

Murphy, House of 22, 49, 111, 176, 194, 265

Murphy, Jim 17

Murphy, John 154

Murphy, Lawrence G. 30, 154, 155, 266

Murphy (Arizona governor) 83

Murphy-Dolan organization 111, 176, 194, 266

Murray, Elmore 44, 141

Murray, John 2

Murray, Rod 187

Murrieta, Joaquin 99, 160, **178**

Muse, Herbert E. "H. E." **178–179**

Musgrave, D. L. 226

Musgrave, George **179**

Myres (lieutenant) 55

N

Nakedhead, James 126

Nance, Dow 151

National Guard 223

Navajos 86

Navy Colt **180,** 224

Neagle, Dave 154, **180**

Neal, Forrest 87

Neal, "Pony" 87

necktie party **180**

Neil, Belle 32

Neill, Hyman G. 2, 38, 64–65, 268

Nelson, Earl 209

Nemitz, David 28

Nesmith, George 48

nesters 173

Neutrality Act 38

Nevada State Penitentiary 127, 162

Nevill, Charles L. **180,** 242

Newcomb, George "Bitter Creek" 60, 66, 101, 102, 168, **180–181**

Newman, Norman 93, **181**

Newman, Sarah Jane **215–216**

New Mexico Mounted Police **181–182**

New Mexico Penitentiary 15, 126

New Mexico State Tax Commission 198

New Mexico Territorial Militia 167

New Military Institute 198

New Monthly Magazine 115

Newton x, 41, 45, **102–103**

Nickel, Kels 121

Nickel, William "Willie" 121, 152

Nix, Evett Dumas 102, **182**

Nixon, Mrs. Tom 169

Nixon, Tom 16–17, 169

No. 10 Saloon 117, 162

No Duty to Retreat (Brown) xi

Nolan, Nicholas 100

Nolly, Albert 25

Northfield Raid **182–183**
Northwest Mounted Police 175
Norton, Charlie 168
Norwood, Ed 75
Notch-Cutters **183–184**
Nueces and Rio Grande Company
    230
Nueces Strip 106, 165
Nunn, Pat 43–44, 141
Nutt, Cal 187
Nuttall and Mann's No. 10 Saloon
    117
Nye, John A. **183**
Nymyer, A. B. 194

O

Occidental Saloon 19, 103
Ochoa, Lola 5, 6
O'Day, Tom 158, **185**
Oden, Alonzo Van "Lon" **185–186**,
    189, 234
O'Folliard, Tom 23, 27, 50, 75, 79,
    86, 93
O'Hara, Rodney 230
OK Corral, gunfight at the 19, 46,
    47, 71, 72, **103–104**, 120, 123,
    207, 230, 249
O'Kelley, Edward Capeheart 85
Oklahoma State Penitentiary 126
Old Law Mob (OLM) 147
Old San Simon Gang 149
Olguin, Antonio 234
Olguin, Pedro 234
Olinger, John Wallace 186
Olinger, Robert "Bob" 21, 24, **186**
Olive, Bob 187
Olive, Ira 187
Olive, Isom Prentice "Print" 138,
    183, **187–188**
Olive, James 187
Olive, Julia 187
Olive, Thomas Jefferson "Jay" 183,
    187
OLM (Old Law Mob) 216
Olney, Joe 101
Olympic Dance Hall 4
O'Neill, William Owen "Bucky"
    188, 209
Oregon State Penitentiary 218, 219
Oriental Saloon 45, 71, 153, 222,
    266
O'Rourke, John 202
Orozco, Pascual 5, 38, 77, 91
Orr, Thomas 14
Orrick, John C. Jr. 9–10

Osage Nation 59, 125
Osage Trail 21
Osborn, Thomas A. 21
Osborne Hill gunfight 164
Otero, Celestino 13
Otero, Miguel 13, 43
O'Tool, Oscar "Barney" **188**
Oury, William Sanders 221
Outlaw, Baz "Bass" 125, 186,
    188–189, 217, 258
Outlaw Trail (Kelly) 45
Overland Mail Company 111, 121,
    259
Owens, George 69
Owens, Jake 111
Owens, Lewis 69
Owens, Perry **189–190**, 197
Owens, William 31

P

Packer, Alferd **191–192**
packing iron **192**
Paddy Welche Saloon 116
Paine, John 208
Palace Saloon 261
Papago 171
Paramore, Green 208
Parham, Young 12
Parker, Fleming **192**
Parker, George 179
Parker, Isaac C. "Hanging Judge"
    50, 59, 98, 126, 165, **192**, 199,
    204–205, 231, 232, 244–245
Parker, Quanah 125, 168
Parker, Robert Leroy. *See* Cassidy,
    Butch
parlor houses 229
Parra, Geronimo 89, 110, 125, 126,
    192–193
Parrott, George "Big Nose" **193**
Parsons, George 46
Pascoe, B. F. 206
Pascoe, William H. 88
Pasos, Ysidoro 89, 110
*Passing of the Oklahoma Outlaws,
    The* (film) 248–249
Paul, Bob 171, 221
Payne, E. W. 30
Peabody Mine 1
Peacemaker **193**, 228
Peacock, A. J. 65, 167
Peacock, Lewis 151
Peak, June 215
"Pecos Bob." *See* Olinger, Robert
    "Bob"

Pecos Valley Town Company 194
Peel, Langford 32
Peel, Martin R. 29, 101
Peg-Leg robberies 67
Pennsylvania College of Dental
    Surgery 119
peonage laws 199
Peppin, George 22, 155, 156, 170
Peppin's posse 111
Pérez, Mariana 86
Perkins, Jack 94
Perkins, Richard 127
Perrine, George 70, 153
Perry, C. C. 51
Perry, Forrest 105
Perry, Matthew C. 189–190
Perry, Samuel R. "Sam" **193–194**
Perry Tuttle's Dance Hall 103
Peterson, Len 26
Petty, Mary 14
Phenix **194**
Philpot, Eli "Bud" 29, 122, 143
Phoenix Herald 188
Pickell, William 259
Pickett, Thomas "Tom" 75, **195**,
    268
Piedras Negras, sacking of 250
Pierce, Cad 75
Pierce, Charley 60, 66, 101, 102,
    181
Pinard, Saturino 251
Pine Ridge Reservation 226
Pinkerton, Allan 195, 196
Pinkerton, William 152
Pinkerton National Detective Agency
    xii, 13, 40, 121, 132, 158, 159,
    195–196, 222, 224, 226, 270
Pioneer stage 110–111
Pipes, Samuel J. 17
Pirate Island 135, 145
Pitts, Charlie 132, 183, 260, 270
Place, Etta 40, 41, 159, 208
Place, Harry. *See* Sundance Kid
Plains rifle **196**
Pleasant Valley Coal Company 149
Pleasant Valley War 83, 190,
    196–197, 206, 208
Plummer, Rachael 49
Plummer, William Henry 100, 130,
    197–198, 203, 219, 257
Plummer gang 130, 183, 203. *See
    also* Plummer, William Henry
Poe, H. H. 50
Poe, John William 24, 48, **198**
Pointer, John **198–199**

Poker Alice 129–130
Polk, Cal 74, 78
Pond, Arthur 174
Pond Mining Company 61
Pony Express 260
Poole, Tom Bell 127
Poplar Grove, gunfight at **104–105**
Porter, Benjamin C. 56
Porter, Charles 154
Porter, Fannie 39
Potter, Jim 142, 143
Potter, John 142, 143
Potter, Mack 67
Potts, Bill 16–17
Powell, Sylvester 172
Powers, Bill 60, 61
Powers, John N. "Jap" 10, 139
Powers, Tom 94
Prather, Ed 248
Pratt, John **199**
Preston, Sadie 268
Price, Anthony "One Arm" **199**
Pridgen, Wiley 238
prisons **131**. *See also specific prisons*
Progressive movement 147
Prohibition 33, 42, 161, 249
prostitution 1, 57, 62, 65, 114–115,
    228–229, 247, 248
Pruitt family 173
Punteney, Walt 158
Putman, Bob 182
Putman, Jim 50

Q

Quantrill, Caroline Clarke 200
Quantrill, William Clarke 6,
    131–132, 134, **200**, 269
Queen, Samuel Dawson "Kep"
    200–201
Queen, Victor "Vic" **201**
Queen Saloon 45
quick-draw artist **201**, 213
quick on the trigger **201**
Quillen, Charlie 231
Quimbly, Giles 253

R

Raine, William Macleod 29
Ranch, Tom 74
Ranch Saloon 194
Randall, "Big" Bill 39
Rangel, José 62
Ranger's Bible 108, 156, **202**
Rankin, James 193
Ransom's Saloon 102

Rash, Madison 121
Raton Range 3
Rattlesnake Dick **149**
Ray, Charles T. "Pony Deal" 101,
    163, **202**. *See also* Diehl, Pony
Ray, Ned **203**
Ray, Nick 135
Raymond, Charles 218
Rayner, Hamilton **203**
Rayner, Kenneth 203
Rayner, William R. "Bill" 203, **204**
Raynor, Bill. *See* Rayner, William R.
    "Bill"
Raynor, Ham. *See* Rayner, Hamilton
Reche, Charles 264
Reconstruction 108, 146, 151
Red Front Saloon 103
red light districts 229
Redman, William 99, 100
Red Sash Gang 157, 158
Reed, Charlie 55, 147, 226
Reed, Henry **181**
Reed, James Edwin 232
Reed, Jim 232
Reed, Rosie Lee "Pearl" 232, 233
Reeves, Bass 82, **204–205**
Reeves, George 204–205
Reformers 65
Regulators 14, 23, 30, 43, 155–156,
    176, **205–206**, 216, 237
Reinhardt, Ben 163
Reinhart, Henry 214
Renetería, Eusebio 62
Reni, Jules 224–225
Rennick, "Cowboy Bob" 204
Reno, Louisa 187
Reno, William Henry 251, 252
"reservations" 229
revolvers
    Colt **49**, 81, 105, **180**, **193**,
        224, 228, 243, **257**
    Derringer **63**
    fanning **81**
    Schofield 81, 228
Reynolds, George 206
Reynolds, Glenn 120–121, **206**
Reynolds, Gussie 206
Reynolds, Joe 237
Reynolds, N. O. 54, 67, 265
Rhodes, John 197
Rhodius, Charles 151
"Rhymin' Ranger" *See* Oden, Alonzo
    Van "Lon"
Riata and Spurs (Siringo) 224
Rice, Bud 51

Richmond, Battle of 134
Rieff, Lenora 260
rifles 6, 35, 193, 196, 219, 266
Riggs, Annie 207
Riggs, Barney 42, 113, **206–207**
Riley, James "Jim" 103
Riley, James M. **207**
Rinehart, Isaiah 55
Ringgold, John 166, **207–208**. *See
    also* Ringo, John Peters
Ringo, John Peters xi, xii, 45, 46,
    53, 73, 101, 120, 153, 166, 202,
    207–208, 249
Ringo, Mary 207
Rivers, Art 125
road agent spin 117, **208**
Road-to-Ruin Saloon 264
Robbers Roost 40, 162, **208**, 263
Roberson, Bob 75
Roberson, Horace L. 5, 98, 157
Roberston, Ben 260
Roberts, Andrew L. "Buckshot" 23,
    30, 155
Roberts, Anna 25, 114
Roberts, Dan W. 20, 142
Roberts, James Franklin "Jim"
    208–209
Roberts, Judd 10
Roberts, Oran N. 18
Robinson, Jessie 215
Robinson, Tom 250
Robles, Guadalupe 226
Robson, Frank 69
Rock Creek Massacre 115
Rodgers, N. N. 231
Rodríguez, José 62, 152
Rodríguez, Perfecto 44, 141
Roering, Peter 29
Rogers, Dick 167
Rogers, Isaac 98
Rogers, J. H. 215
Rogers, John H. 156
Rogers, William H. 127
Roland, Joseph F. 127
Romero, Benigno 107
Romero, Desiderio 2
Roosevelt, Theodore "Teddy" 94,
    165, 232
Rosa, Joseph 115, 117
Rose, Al 206
Rose, Frank 13
Roseman, H. E. 104
Ross, Lawrence 134
Ross, Tom 5, **156–157**. *See also*
    Loftis, Hillary U. "Hill"

Ross, William 66
Roswell Masonic Lodge 198
Rough Riders 165, 188, 210
Rowdy Kate 160
Roxy Jay Saloon 264
Royer (sheriff) 99, 100
Rucker, Oliver 32
Rudabaugh, David "Dave" 75, **209**, 259, 268
Ruddle, Allen 160, 178
Rugg, George 127
Rule, Richard 113
Runnels, Hardin 245
running iron **209–210**
Rurales, Mexican 210
Rusher, Bob 182
Rusk, Thomas 113
Russell, Charles T. 149
Russell, Henry "Baldy" **175–176**
Russell, Scott 92
Russell, William Henry 115
Russell (Pony Express agent) 115
Russell's Canyon 128
Rustlers Trail 46
Ryadam, Ellen 70
Ryan, Jerry 206
Ryan, Thomas 154
Rynning, Thomas H. 4–5, 8, 141, 195, **210**, 261

S

Sacramento Union 86
Saga of Billy the Kid, The (Burns) ix
Salome 179
saloons 1, **211**, 212. *See also specific saloons*
salt 75–77, 86
Sam Bass gang 136, 195. *See also* Bass, Sam
Sam Eckstein's Saloon 33
Sample, Owen W. "Red" 25, 114
Samuel, Archie 132, 196
Samuel, Reuben 131
Samuel, Zeralda 132
San Carlos Reservation 7, 8
Sánchez, Juan 62
Sanders, Wilbur Fiske **211**
Sandoval, Gabriel 43
Sandoval, Pablita 7
Sandy Bob stage 127
San Francisco Chronicle 34
San Francisco Examiner 262
San Francisco Vigilance Committee 17–18

San Quentin Penitentiary 26, 34, 60, 163, 174, 192, 197, 203, 221, 222, 255, 260
Santa Fe Railroad 121, 177, 246
Santa Fe Ring 154, 199
Santa Fe Territorial Penitentiary 62, 149, 192, 202, 258
Santa Fe Trail 19, 269
San Vicente Company 226
Satanta 122
Sayers, Joe 243
scabbard **213**
Scarborough, George Adolphus 37, 39, 77, 109, 157, 174, 177, 178, **213–214**, 217, 218, 258, 263, 264
Scarborough, George Edgar, Jr. 112, 213, **214–215**
Scarborough, Will 264
scattergun **223**
Schieffelin, Edward L. 249
Schofield revolver 81, **228**
Schunderberger, John "Dutchy" 64
Schwartz, John **191–192**
Scott, William "Bill" **215**
Scotten, Ed 203
Scull, Alfred 215
Scull, George H. 215
Scull, Nancy 215
Scull, Sally **215–216**
Scurlock, Josiah Gordon "Doc" 27, 155, 156, **216**
Seaborn, J. C. 260
Seaman, Carey 60
Sears, Jim 61. *See also* Three Fingered Jack
Second Texas Mounted Rifles 18
Secret Service, U.S. 21
Sefrit, Louie 218
Segura, Melquiades 22
Seiber, Al 120
Selman, John Henry ix, 77, 109, 110, 111, 147, 174, 177, 178, 186, 189, 214, **216–218**
Selman, John, Jr. 216, 218
Selman, "Tom Cat" 111, 217
Selman, William 216
Seminole Whiskey Trail 205
Semi-Weekly News 18
Serna, Santiago 252
Seven Rivers men 155–156
Severns, Harry **218–219**
Shadley, Lafe 102, 168
Shamblin, J. M. 134
Shane (film) 135
Shanks, George 256

Sharkey, Tom 74
Sharp, Christian 219
Sharp, John S. "Jim" **219**
Sharps rifle **219**
Shaw, Bob 167
Shaw, Eugene O. 221
Shaw, M. F. 171
Shears, George **219–220**
Shedd, Warren H. **220**
Shedd Ranch murders 79, 163, 220
Sheehan, Larry 171
Sheeks, David 16
Sheets, Jesse 240
sheriffs **220**
Shibell, Charles Alexander "Charley" 28, 72, 171, **220–221**
Shiloh, Battle of 18
Shingle & Locke Saloon 154
Shinn, George **221–222**
Shirley, Bud 232
Shirley, John 232
Shirley, Myra Maybelle. *See* Starr, Myra Maybelle
shootist 105
Short, Edward 31
Short, Luke 27, 52–53, 65–66, 115, **222–223**, 249
Shoshone 97
shotgun **223**
Shriners 10
Shroyer, Lou 159
Sieber, Al 7, 8, 89, 121
Sieker, Lamar P. 10
Silva, Jesús 43
Silva, Santiago 252
Silver City Rangers 164
Silver City Saloon 28
Silver King Saloon 145, 194
Simmons, Frank 89
Simon, Paul 62
Sinclair, Walter 127
Sioux 96, 222, 226
Sippy, Ben 71
Siringo, Charles Angelo "Charlie" 48, 74, 75, 79, 159, 195–196, **223–224**
Sitting Bull 210
six-shooter **224**
"Six Shooter Jim" 153
Skaggs, John 17
"skins, death of the" 187
Slade, Joseph Alfred "Jack" **224–225**
Slade, Virginia 224, 225
Slaughter, Gabriel 238

Slaughter, John Horton 5, 45,
     225–226
Slaughter, John (stage driver) 16
Slaughter's Kid **180–181**
slaves, slavery 14, 90–91, 131, 134,
     146, 200
Sloter, Charles 108
Small, Charles "Charley" 96, **226**
Smalley, Jim 108
Smith, "Bear River Tom" **227–228**
Smith, Billy 142
Smith, Charley 107
Smith, E. W. "Jack" 215
Smith, Erastus "Deaf" 113
Smith, F. H. 252
Smith, Frank 205
Smith, James L. **226–227**
Smith, James W. "Six-Shooter Bill"
     107, 227, 251
Smith, Joe 226
Smith, John "Johnny" 227
Smith, Peg-Leg 124
Smith, "Rackety" 137
Smith, Remus 246, 247
Smith, Sam 155
Smith, "Three-Shooter" 251
Smith, Tom 25
Smith, Will (lawman) 171
Smith, William (desperado) 30
Smith & Wesson **228**
Smugglers Trail **228**
Sociedad de Bandidos, La 43
Socorro Sun News 12, 95
soiled doves **228–229**
"Sombrero Jack" 22
Sonnichsen, C. L. 77, 151
Sonora Trail 228
Sontag, George 229
Sontag, John 34, **229–230**, 265
"Sooner" wagon 102
Southern Express 175
Southern Pacific Railroad 10, 20, 47,
     59, 96, 137, 139, 150, 158, 171,
     174, 221, 226, 229, 230, 239, 265
Spanish-American War 20, 106, 121,
     164, 188, 210
Sparks, Sam 30–31
Sparrow, Joe 188
Speakes, Bob 111
Speed, Dick 102, 168
Speers, George 172
Spence, Peter "Pete" 70, 72, 73, **230**,
     249
Spencer, Charles 37, 47, 51, 52

Spencer, George 258
Spicer, Wells 45, 73, 104, 119
Spiers, John 4
Spillman, C. W. 32, **230**
Spotswood, Tom 17
Spy of the Rebellion, The (Pinkerton)
     196
St. Leon, Ernest "Diamond Dick"
     185, **233–234**
St. Louis Express 84
St. Mary's Convent 36
Stagg, Thomas 52
Standifer, William "Bill" 118, **231**
Stanley, Bill 201
Stansel, Jesse 247–248
Starr, Belle **232–233**
Starr, Eddie 232, 233
Starr, Henry **231–232**
Starr, Myra Maybelle **232–233**
Starr, Sam 232
Starr, Tom 232
Staunton, Dick 45
Staunton, Isaac 45
Sterling, John 247
Stevenson, Frank 26
Stevenson, George 214
Stewart, Cicero 149
Stewart, Frank 75
Stiles, William "Billy" **42**, 132, 214
Stilwell, Frank 70, 72, 73, 120, 135,
     164, 230, 256
Stinson Ranch 196
Stone, Luke 67
Storms, Charlie 222
Story, Tom 205
Stoudenmire, Dallas ix, 77, 95, 224,
     234–237
Stowell, Belle 153
Strawhun, Samuel O. 116
Sturgis, Tom 227
Styles, Bill 183
Sullivan, Alvira "Allie" 70–71
"Sullivan of Tucson." *See* Ah Foy
Sundance Kid 39, 40, 41, 125, 141,
     158–159, 208, 227, 263
Sunset Flyer 142
Supreme Court, U.S. 8, 140
Sutherland, Bill **162**
Sutherland, Urilla 71
Sutton, Laura 238
Sutton, William "Billy" 237, 238
Sutton-Taylor feud 53, 83, 106, 109,
     165, **237–238**
Swafford, Frank 125

Swan Land and Cattle Company 121
Swartz, John 40, 159
Swilling, Jack 58
swing a wide loop **238**
Sydnor, Sallie 18
Syndicate, the 240

T

Tafolla, Carlos 8
Taft, William 182
Taggart, Frank 37, 47, 51, 52, 96,
     137, 150, **239**
Tall Texan **141–142**, 263. *See also*
     Kilpatrick, Benjamin Arnold "Ben"
Tascosa Shootout 78, 79, **239–240**
Taylor, Bill 238
Taylor, Charlie 237
Taylor, Creed 237
Taylor, Doboy 237
Taylor, Elizabeth **240–241**
Taylor, Frank 15
Taylor, George L. 15
Taylor, Hays 237
Taylor, James H. 240–241
Taylor, James "Jim" 237, 238
Taylor, Pitkin 237
Taylor, Thomas 241
Taylor, Tubal 15
Taylor, Zachary 160, 242
Tays, John B. 29, 77
Tbalt, Nicholas 130
Tell Them Willie Boy Is Here (film)
     265
Tempe News 230
Terrell, Zeke 117
Terry, David Smith 18
Terry, Kyle 134
Tettenborn, William Rogers "Russian
     Bill" 101, 143, **241**, 251
Tewksbury, Edwin "Ed" 196, 197
Tewksbury, Frank 196
Tewksbury, James "Jim" 196, 197
Tewksbury, John 196, 197
Tewksbury-Graham feud 208
Texas and Southwestern Cattle
     Raisers Association 98, 157
Texas Bitulithic 20
Texas Department of Public Safety
     244
Texas Dick 167
Texas Express 60
Texas fever 64
Texas Flyer 139
Texas News 151

Texas & Pacific Railroad 17, 56, 126

Texas Penitentiary xi, 5, 10, 29, 80, 92, 99, 109, 122, 157, 176, 238, 245, 258

Texas Rangers xii, 148, **241–244**

Allison, William Davis 4

Arizona Rangers and 8

Armstrong, John 9, 243

Arrington, George W. 9–10, 215, 242

Aten, Ira 10, 125

on Atkins 11

on Baca 12

Barnett, Bush 16

Baylor, George Wythe 18, 135, 180, 242, 243

Baylor, John R. 95

Bell, James W. 20

Bingham, George 80

Bond, Jim 26

on bounty hunting 27

on Brocius 29

Brooks, J. A. 215

Burdett, Robert Lee 33

Callahan, James H. 250

Cantley, Charles 37

Carnes, Herff A. 38

on cattle theft 41

Coldwell, Neal 50, 265

on Collins gang 17

Colt revolver used by 49

Cook, Thalis Tucker 50

Cooley, Scott 207

Coolly, Joe 189

Cureton, Jack J. 54

on Dublin 67

Durbin, Walter 101

in El Paso Salt War 77, 144

on fence cutting 83

Ferguson, Lark 230

Ferguson, Warren Wallace 230

Frazier, Sam 87–88

Fusselman, Charles 89, 110, 192

Garrett and 93

Gillett, James 12, 54, 67, 94, 135, 180, 202, 236

on Good 98

Grimes, Ahijah W. "High" 258

Grimes, Albert Calvin 100–101

Hall, Lee 9, 53, 84, 106, 165, 243

on Hardin 109

Harold, George 17, 110, 258

Hays, John Coffee 113–114, 243, 257

on Higgins clan 118, 124

Horner, Joe 122

on Horrell brothers 124

Hughes, John R. 10, 38, 50, 91, 125–126, 173, 185, 186, 234

on Hughes brothers 126

on Hurricane Bill 166

Jaybird-Woodpecker War and 134

Jones, Frank 126, 135–136, 188, 234

Jones, John B. 77, 136, 166, 242, 265

Kimbell, Russell G. 142–143

Kirchner, Carl 145

Linn, Charles "Buck" 204

on Loftis 156

in Mason County War 166

McCulloch, Ben 243

McKidrict, Joe 217

McMahan, Frank 109, 174, 177, 178, 214

McMahan, Tom 217

McMaster, Sherman W. 164

McNelly, Leander 84, 165, 243

Milton, Jeff 174

Moore, J. H. 215

Musgrave, D. L. 226

Nevill, Charles L. 180, 242

New Mexico Mounted Police and 181

Oden, Alonzo Van 185–186, 189, 234

Outlaw, Bass 125, 126, 186, 188–189, 217

Peak, June 215

Pickett, Tom 195

Putman, Jim 50

on Queen 201

Ranger's Bible and 202

Reynolds, N. O. 54, 265

Roberts, Dan 20, 142

Rogers, John H. 156, 215

Russell, Scott 92

Scott, Bill 215

Scotten, Ed 203

on Selman 217

Slaughter, John 225

Spence, Pete 230

St. Leon, Ernest 233, 234

on Standifer 231

Stoudenmire, Dallas 234

Tays, John B. 29, 77

on Thompson, Billy 247

Tom, S. H. 249–250

Walker, Sam 49, 243, 257

Wallace, Big Foot 113, 243

Ware, Dick 17, 67, 110, 258

White, J. C. 38

Wilson, Vernon Coke 265

Wright, Milam 38

Yarberry, Milton 268

Thacker, John 34, 251

Thatcher, Agnes Lake 117

Theatre Comique 119

Theosophical Society 216

Thirty Years a Detective (Pinkerton) 196

Thomas, George 159

Thomas, Henry Andrew "Heck" 66, 102, 182, 224, **244–245**, 248, 260

Thompkins, Carlotta (Charlotte) J. 97

Thompson, Ben 47, 48, 84, 176, 207, **245–246**, 247

Thompson, Benjamin Jr. 245, 246

Thompson, Billy 75, 176

Thompson, Charles "Yank" 219

Thompson, H. A. "Hi" 102

Thompson, William "Billy" 245, **246–247**

Thompson, William J. "Big Bill" **247–248**

Thompson (major) 237

Thornburgh, Thomas T. 222

Thorne, T. H. **149**

Thornton, Oliver C. 39

Thornton, William T. 265

Three Fingered Jack 61, **68–69**, **147–148**, 160, 178

Three Guardsmen 161, 165, 245, 248, 249. *See also specific Three Guardsmen*

Thurman, Charlotte 63, 248

Thurman, Frank 63

Thurmond, Charlotte 248

Thurmond, Frank 33, 96, **248**

Tidball, Zan L. 59

Tilghman, William Matthew Jr. "Bill" 66, 102, 161, 165, 167, 245, **248–249**, 260

Timberlake, James 85

Tin Hat Brigade 115, 147, 216

Tisdale, John 37

Tivoli Gambling House 13

Tolbert, Chuck 3
Tolby, F. J. 4, 199
Tom, Charles 156
Tom, Simpson Hugh **249–250**
Tombstone 72, **249**
    Boot Hill Cemetery at 47
    Cowboys in 266
    Diehl in 202
    Earps in 58, 59, 70, 71, 72,
       103, 207, 221, 249, 256, 266
    gunfight at the OK Corral in
       103–104
    Heath in 114
    Holliday in 71, 73, 103–104,
       119, 122, 123, 207, 249
    Horn in 153
    Hunt in 128
    Johnson in 135
    Leslie in 153
    Masterson in 169
    McMaster in 164
    Meade in 171
    Neagle in 180
    Oriental Saloon in 46
    Ringo in 207
    Sharp in 219
    Shibell in 221
    Short in 222
    Smith in 227
    Smugglers Trail from 228
    Spence in 230
    Vermillion in 256
    White in 71
Tombstone Birdcage Theater 153
Tombstone Epitaph 29, 73, 249, 266
Tombstone Mill and Mining
  Company 29, 101
Tombstone Nugget 29
Tompkins, Carlotta J. 63
To the Last Man (Grey) 197
Townsend, Jim 115
Townsend (cowhand) 12
Tracy, Harry 31, **218–219**
Tracy, James A. 261
Trapp, Martin E. 249
Travis Rifles 9
Traywick, Ben 27
Treasury, U.S. 203
Tres Jacales 135
Trousdale, David A. 142
Truitt, Isaac "Little Ike" 175
Truitt, James 175
Truitt, Sam 175
Tubbs, W. G. 129

Tucker, "Dangerous Dan" 26, 33,
    34, 47, 51, 96, 107, 114, 143, 149,
    188, 199, 226, 239, 241, **250–251**
Tucker, David. *See* Tucker,
    "Dangerous Dan"
Tucker, William 247
Tumlinson, Joseph "Joe" 237, 238
Tunstall, John 6–7, 22, 23, 43, 79,
    154, 155, 170, 176, 194, 220
Turkey Creek Canyon, Battle of 139,
    149, **251–252**
Turner, Marion 111
Turner, Turk 187
Turner, Will 44
Turnow, John "Wild Man" **252–253**
Tutt, David "Dave" xii, 116
Tuttle, Perry 103
Twain, Mark 225
Twelve Years in a Texas Prison
    (Good) 5
Two Brothers Saloon 194
Two Evil Isms (Siringo) 224
Tyler, Jesse M. "Jack" 57, 157

U

Underwood, Henry 16, 17, **254**
Union army 165, 191, 226, 237,
    254, 263
Union League 90, 151
Union Pacific Railroad 1, 17, 32, 40,
    141, 159, 215, 226, 227
United States v. Captain Jack 8
United Verde Copper Company 209
University Club (San Antonio) 63,
    248
University of Michigan 172
Unruh, Frank 15
Unruh, Kate 15
Updegraff, Al 65, 167
Upson, Ash 93
Utah Penitentiary 45, 218

V

Valley, Frank 240
Van Arman, H. M. 266
Vasquez, Auguste Park 196
Vásquez, Tiburcio **255**
Vaudeville Variety Theater 84, 246,
    247
Vaughn, James Theodore "Dorrie"
    54, 124
Vedder, John 197
Vega, Cruz 4
Venard, Stephen "Steve" **255–256**

Vermillion, "Texas Jack" **256**
Victorio 18, 95, 180
vigilantes
    in California 66, 163, 198, **212,**
       213, **256**
    in Montana 100, 130, 203, 211,
       219–220, 225, 230, **256**, 257
    in Nebraska 241
    necktie party of 180
    in Nevada 61
    in New Mexico 95, 111, **256**
    in Texas **85**, 106, 109, 115,
       124, 147, 183–184, 206, 216,
       256
    in Wyoming 166, 193
Villa, Pancho 42, 62, 77
Vincent, Henry 193

W

Waco Bill 68
Waddell, William B. 115
Waddell (cattle thief) 187
Waddell (Pony Express Agent) 115
Waggoner, Dan 156
Wagner, "Dutch John" **257**
Wagner, Jack 167
Waite, Fred 155
Wakefield, James 200
Walker, Alf 167
Walker, Samuel Hamilton "Sam" 49,
    113, 243, 257
Walker Colt 49, 81, **257**
Wall, William 45
Wallace, Big Foot 113, 243
Wallace, Jim 29
Wallace, Lew 23, 24, 43, 217, 225,
    259
Wallace (ranch hand) 34
Walla Walla Prison 105
Walters, Emma 169
Walters, Patrick 226
Walters, William "Bronco Bill"
    257–258
Ward, Jerome 114
Warde, Frederick 56
Warde-Barrymore Combination 56
Ward's Dance Hall 28
Ware, Richard Clayton "Dick" 17,
    37, 67, 110, 189, **258–259**
Warne, Kate 195
Warner, David 123
Warner, Frank 163
Warner, Matt 40, 45, 158, 162, 263
War of 1812 190

Warren Wagon Train Massacre 122
Waterson, Nellie 85
Wathen, John David "Wylackie John" 262
Watkins, Isiah 216
Watkins, Rody 249
Watson, Edgar 233
Watson, Ella. *See* Watson, Ellen
Watson, Ellen **259**
Weaver, "Red" 251
Webb, Charles 94, 109, 238
Webb, Jim 205
Webb, John Joshua 2, 64–65, 209, **259**
Webber, Edward P. 99
Webster, Alonzo B. 65
Webster, Charles 91, 92
Webster, Theopolis C. 47, 239, 263
Weidman, Bessie 106
Weightman, George "Red Buck" 66, 101, 156
Weiler, Mathilde 186
Wells, Henry 259
Wells, Samuel 183, **260**. *See also* Pitts, Charlie
Wells Fargo **259–260**
    Black Bart and 26
    Cleveland and 47
    on Cullen 139
    Dake and 59
    on Dorsey 222
    Earp at 70, 72
    on Evans 229
    Holliday and 72, 122
    Hume at 127, 239
    McMaster at 164
    Milton at 69, 174
    Miner and 174
    on Shinn 222
    on Sontag 229
    Thacker at 34, 251
    Tombstone-to-Benson stage 119
    Tucker at 251
    Venard at 256
Wesley, John (desperado) 30
Wesley, John (founder of Methodism) 108
Wessen, Henry H. 31
West, James 169
West, Jessie *161*
West, Richard "Little Dick" 66, **260**
West, Tom 232
Western Trail 41
Wham, Joseph 171

Wharton, John Austin 18
Wheeler, Benjamin F. "Ben" 30, **260**
Wheeler, Frank (cowboy) 194
Wheeler, Frank S. (Arizona Ranger) **260–261**
Wheeler, Harry 8–9, **261–262**
Wheller, Henry M. 42
White, Ephraim 127
White, Fred 29, 71, 72, 202
White, George E. **262**
White, J. C. 38
White Elephant 52
Whitehill, Harriet 263
Whitehill, Harvey Howard 22, 28, 47, 51, 95, 96, 107, 137, 149, 178, 188, 199, 239, **262–263**, 264, 269
Whitehill, Wayne 199, 263
White House Saloon 37
White Mountain Apaches 7
White Oaks posse 20
Whitley, William "Bill" 201
Whitney, Chauncey B. 75, 176, 245, 246, 247
Whitney, Mrs. 262
Whorf, W. G. 171
Wichita Falls State Hospital 11
Wichita x, 41, 45
Widdowfield, Robert 193
Wigwam Saloon 177, 218
Wilburn, Aaron 111
Wilburn, Frank 111
Wild Bunch xii, 14, 40–41, **263**. *See also specific Wild Bunch members*
    at Brown's Park 31, 40, 45, 149, 162, 218, 263
    Carver in 39
    Cassidy in 195
    Curry in 57
    Dalton brothers in 59
    in Deadwood 62
    at Hell's Half-acre 115
    at Hole-in-the-Wall 40, 118, 125, 157, 218, 224, 263
    as horse thieves 125
    Ketchum and 139
    Kilpatrick in 141
    Lay in 149
    Logans in 57, 157
    Meeks in 172
    O'Day in 185
    at Robbers Roost 40, 162, 208, 263
    Siringo on 224
    Smith on 227

    Sundance Kid in 158–159
    Tracy and 218
    at Turkey Creek Canyon 251–252
    Warner in 45, 162
Wild West Show, Buffalo Bill's 36, 117, 207
Wilkerson, Annie 122
Williams, Andrew Jackson "A. J." 213, **263–264**
Williams, Benjamin F. 86–87
Williams, Bill 207
Williams, Bob 75, 78
Williams, Charles. *See* O'Tool, Oscar "Barney"
Williams, Charles "Charley" **264**
Williams, Curtis 263
Williams, Emma 246–247
Williams, Helen. *See* Mrose, Helen Beulah
Williams, Jesse 179
Williams, Jim 67
Williams, John **50–51**, 218
Williams, Mike 48, 117
Williams, O. W. 20
Williams, Thomas "Tom" 123, 124
Williamson, Tim 166
Willie Boy **264–265**
Wilson, Floyd 231
Wilson, John B. "Squire" 23, 49, 155
Wilson, Mark 246
Wilson, Steve 37
Wilson, Vernon Coke **265**
Wilson, Vic 229
Wilson, William "Billy" 75, **265**
Wilson, William (justice of the peace) 12
Wilson, William (paid assassin) 13, **266**
Winchester rifle 193, **266**
Winn, Ed 97
Winters, Jim 157
Witty, George 34
Wolf of the Washita. *See* Allison, Robert A.
Wood, Burl R. 62
Wood, Leonard 210
Woodman, May **266**
Woodpeckers 133–134
Woodruff, Lem 240
Woods, James 37
Woods, Tom 141
Wool Growers Association 152

Wooten, Ben 176
World War I 77, 182, 244, 261–262
Worley, John 166
Worthington, Peter **99, 266–267**
Wren, Bill 124
Wright, Charles 223
Wright, Milam 38
Wright, Tom **5–6**
Wyoming Land and Cattle Company
    152
Wyoming State Penitentiary 40, 185
Wyoming Stock Growers Association
    37, 135, 227

X
XIT Ranch 30, 78

Y
Yaqui Indians 62
Yarberry, Milton J. **268–269**

Yeager, Erastus 198
Yoas, "Bravo Juan" 69
Yoast, John 207
Yoes, Bravo Juan 214
Young, Jack 101
Young, William "Apache Bill" **269**
Young, William C. 91
Younger, Augusta 207
Younger, Bob 132, 183
Younger, Coleman "Cole" 132, 133,
    183, 200, 207, 269, 270
Younger, James "Jim" 132, 183,
    269, 270
Younger, John 269, 270
Younger, Robert "Bob" 269, 270
Younger brothers 59, 134, 138,
    182–183, 260, **269–270**
"Young Seven Up" 108. *See also*
    Hardin, John Wesley

Yuma Territorial Prison **270–271.**
    See also Arizona Territorial Prison
    Alvord/Stiles gang in 6, 69
    Apache Kid in 8, 120
    employees of 171, 210, 261
    Gilmore in 96
    Heath in 114
    Leslie in 153
    Moreno in 176
    O'Neill and 188
    Riggs in 206
    Sharp in 219
    Spence in 230
    Three Fingered Jack in 148
    as tourist attraction 249

Z
Zaff, Victoria H. 19